WITHDRAWN

OPEN
SECRET

MARC CHAGALL,

"Moses Breaking the Tablets of the Law"

OPEN SECRET

Postmessianic Messianism and the Mystical Revision of

MENAḤEM MENDEL SCHNEERSON

ELLIOT R. WOLFSON

COLUMBIA UNIVERSITY PRESS
New York

COLUMBIA UNIVERSITY PRESS
Publishers Since 1893
New York Chichester, West Sussex
Copyright © 2009 Columbia University Press
All rights reserved

Library of Congress Cataloging-in-Publication Data
Wolfson, Elliot R.
Open secret : postmessianic messianism and the mystical revision of
Menaḥem Mendel Schneerson / Elliot R. Wolfson.
p. cm.
Includes bibliographical references and index.
ISBN 978-0-231-14630-2 (cloth : alk. paper)
1. Schneerson, Menaḥem Mendel, 1902–1994—Teachings. 2. Habad.
3. Habad—History. 4. Mysticism—Judaism. I. Title.

BM755.S288W64 2009
296.8'3322—dc22

2009009363

Casebound editions of Columbia University Press
books are printed on permanent and durable acid-free paper.

Printed in the United States of America
c 10 9 8 7 6 5 4

References to Internet Web sites (URLs) were accurate
at the time of writing. Neither the author nor Columbia University Press
is responsible for Web sites that may have expired or changed
since the book was prepared.

BM
755
.S288
W64
2009

FOR BOB DYLAN

the man in the long black coat

The ultimate perfection of the days of Messiah
is the aspect of birth, the revelation of the divine light
within the depth of a person's heart.

—SHNEUR ZALMAN OF LIADI, *TORAH OR*, 55B

Emancipate yourselves from mental slavery,
None but ourselves can free our minds.

—BOB MARLEY, *REDEMPTION SONG*

CONTENTS

PREFACE

On a cold and rainy Saturday night in November 1972, several weeks before my sixteenth birthday, I and a few friends made a pilgrimage to 770 Eastern Parkway in the Crown Heights section of Brooklyn, New York, the world headquarters of the Ḥabad-Lubavitch movement. Having grown up in an orthodox community made up predominantly of East European Jewish refugees, I was well aware of the phenomenon of Ḥasidism, and especially Ḥabad, which had already established itself as a major force as purveyors of orthodox Judaism in America and beyond to other parts of the Diaspora and within the boundaries of the modern state of Israel. Especially memorable is the fact that my sixth-grade Talmud teacher was a Lubavitcher, and he was wont to transmit the teachings of his Rebbe, Menaḥem Mendel Schneerson, on special occasions; he would even, from time to time, begin the daily lesson with a *niggun* (the ḥasidic term for a wordless melody) in an effort to inspire the class, an approach that was by no means typical in the decidedly antiḥasidic (or, in the conventional vernacular, mitnagdic) yeshiva that I attended. Additionally, it was not uncommon for Lubavitch emissaries to visit the synagogue where I prayed on Sabbaths and holidays, translating the message of the Rebbe for a wider audience. In spite of this more than casual acquaintance with Ḥabad, nothing had prepared me for the first visit to its spiritual and physical epicenter.

Many memories of childhood and adolescence have already dimmed, but the memory of that night remains starkly vivid. I felt as if I returned to a place at once strangely familiar and familiarly strange. I recall that one of the Lubavitchers with whom we met asked each of us about our Hebrew birthdays. When I told him that I was born on Friday, 19 Kislev, but, since I was born after sunset, technically my date of birth was 20 Kislev, his eyes opened wide. He inquired if I knew the significance of those dates. I told him that I did not, and he then explained to me that 19 Kislev is the most special day on the Ḥabad calendar, known as the New Year of Ḥasidism and as the Festival of Redemption, as it commemorates the release of Shneur Zalman of Liadi, the Alter Rebbe, from Russian prison in 1798. He also explained that because every holiday (at least in the Diaspora) is celebrated on two days, 20 Kislev was treated as an extension of the nineteenth, and that this doubling was even more significant when the nineteenth fell on Friday and the twentieth on Sabbath, the day that proleptically portends the future-to-come. Finally, he said, "Pay attention, this day bears your destiny."

Through the years, I have studied the teachings of the Ḥabad-Lubavitch masters as part of my intellectual diet and, at various times and in various places, I have also maintained something of a personal connection to the movement, but it was not until July 2005 that I began to understand the conversation I had on that November night thirty-seven years ago. After the death of my father on May 19 of that year (10 Iyyar 5765), I decided to accept the invitation of Avrum Ehrlich to participate in the First International Summer Program in Jewish Studies at Shandong University in Jinan, China. Of the books that I brought with me to China, there were several volumes of the Lubavitcher Rebbe's talks and discourses, as I needed to begin to prepare a lecture I was scheduled to give at the conference sponsored by the Skirball Department of Hebrew and Judaic Studies, New York University, "Reaching for the Infinite: The Lubavitcher Rebbe—Life, Teachings and Impact," November 6–8, 2005. The topic assigned to me was the Rebbe's kabbalah. As it happens, a key text that informed my thinking was a discourse that I read when I visited the Ḥabad House in Beijing on the Sabbath of July 26. It seemed to me especially fitting that this would be the case, that the opening of the path would come into view on the Asian continent. Early on, I made a decision to pursue the academic study of Jewish mysticism rather than specializing in either Hinduism or Buddhism, though I have continued through the years to seek points of affinity between these disparate spiritual orbits. In this book, too, that effort is clearly on display. At a crucial juncture in the second chapter on the nature of what I have called apophatic embodiment, I invoke parallels with the Mahāyāna doctrine of emptiness. Beyond that specific example, the interpretation of Ḥabad philosophy that I offer here is colored by my dabbling in Buddhist texts, including the presentation of the messianic ideal as attaining—through negation—the consciousness that extends beyond consciousness, crossing beyond the river to the shore of nondiscrimination, the shore where there is no more need to speak of the shore.

The decision several months after the conference to write a monograph on the religious philosophy of Menaḥem Mendel Schneerson took me by surprise, as the trajectory of my work seemed to be moving in a different direction. Quite frankly, after having written extensively on Jewish mysticism, I expected to be writing a broader philosophical book on some aspect of the phenomenology of mystical experience, instead of delving yet again into one tradition, let alone one figure as representative of that tradition. But somehow I was compelled to stay the course, and the more I studied Schneerson's writings, the more enmeshed I became in the vast and intricate web of Ḥabad material, the more I began to feel resonances of my life's work on the history of kabbalah. It soon became clear to me that, in this book, I would not only be retelling my own intellectual portrait of Jewish esotericism from a different angle but I would also find confirmation of my hermeneutic belief that by digging into the soil of a specific cultural matrix one may uncover roots that lead to others. It is my hope, though by now not my expectation, that the readership of this book will not be limited to Jewish scholars or even to scholars of Judaica. In line with Rosenzweig's assessment of *The Star of Redemption*, I am willing to describe this work as a "Jewish book," if it is understood that this locution does not imply that it deals exclusively with "Jewish things," but rather that it enfolds and exceeds the principle that the particular, in all of its unpredictability, sheds light on a universal that must repeatedly articulate its universality from the vantage point of the particular. And, as Rosenzweig expressed his own aspiration, if others will be responsive to the "Jewish words," they have the potential of renewing the world.

As I proceeded with the onerous task of sifting through thousands of pages, I began to ponder the words spoken to me many years ago by the young and enthusiastic Lubavitcher. Now, it seemed, I finally had a response to the question I had been asked many times in the past, "What got you interested in Jewish mysticism?" The answer, I have come to realize, is contained in what I was told that night in Brooklyn, "this day bears your destiny!" I have long since departed from orthodoxy, but, by working intensively on the Ḥabad material, I have reclaimed something of my own destiny, ostensibly determined by the indeterminate hour of my birth. In the language of the well-known maxim attributed to R. Aqiva, "Everything is foreseen but permission is still given"—that I could have chosen otherwise is beyond doubt, but then, it would not have been my choosing. The terms of my own liberation, the possibility of becoming less of the more I need to be less, are to be met by taking hold of that paradox.

Working on the Rebbe has proven a burdensome undertaking. This is so for a variety of reasons, but mostly due to the sheer wealth of material generated by the recording of virtually every word he offered publically and the numerous letters he either dictated or wrote in the course of four decades. In such a huge corpus, repetition is inevitable. The duplication of themes across several decades presents a distinctive problem. Prima facie, it would seem that this would make things easier: once crucial motifs have been identified, many redundant passages could be ignored. In reality, however, each recurrence is unique, and, indeed, it is precisely in the iteration that novelty is to be sought. The homiletical genius of the Rebbe, a quality familiar in diverse masters, consisted of his ability to meet the moment always, to offer a genuine replication, an utterance both derivative and innovative. The reverberation, therefore, cannot simply be passed over.

Beyond these considerations, the difficulty is compounded by the intertextuality of his thought, the many layers of biblical, rabbinic, and mystical traditions. Again, this is not so exceptional, but when one adds to this the fact that Schneerson's teachings echo the vast corpus of the six Ḥabad-Lubavitch masters who preceded him, one can appreciate that it is not possible to write about him without taking all of them into account. In spite of the great demand imposed by this interconnectivity, I set as a challenge for myself to write a book on the seventh Rebbe that would demonstrate effectively his indebtedness to the others; in my view, the only faithful and responsible way to present his thinking is by traversing this curvature of temporal linearity: to get to the seventh, one must know the first, but the first cannot be known except through the seventh. It should be clear, however, that neither I nor the publisher, Columbia University Press, would have found it feasible or desirable to cite all the relevant texts to substantiate the main points of my argument. Accordingly, my methodology has been to make a judicious selection of citations, offering the reader enough textual evidence to support my explanations, but not so much that he or she would be overwhelmed. I trust that I have made my choices sensibly and that I have argued my case convincingly.

27 April 2008

EIGHTH DAY OF PASSOVER

NOTE ON THE TRANSLITERATION

I have followed two systems of transliteration in this book, one for Hebrew and the other for Yiddish. However, in instances where Hebrew words appeared in passages that I was translating directly from a Yiddish text, I rendered them in accord with the standard transliteration of Yiddish.

OPEN
SECRET

INTRODUCTION
Behind the Veil Unveiled

Truth did not come into the world naked,
but it came in types and images.
The world will not receive truth in any other way.

—*GOSPEL OF PHILIP*

IN THE CATEGORY OF INTRIGUING CHARISMATIC religious leaders of the twentieth-century, we can surely count Menaḥem Mendel Schneerson (1902–1994), the seventh master of the Ḥasidic dynasty known as Ḥabad-Lubavitch. The second half of the hyphenated term is the Yiddish version of Lyubavichi, the town in Russia where the headquarters of the movement were established by Dov Baer Schneersohn, the Mitteler Rebbe (1773–1827); the first half is an acronym for *ḥokhmah*, *binah*, and *da'at*, "wisdom," "understanding," and "knowledge," a reference to the three upper aspects of the ten kabbalistically enumerated divine emanations[1] and their corresponding psychological faculties, *nefesh*, *ruaḥ*, and *neshamah*, the triadic nature of intellect (*sekhel*).[2] The peregrinations of the Rebbe, as Schneerson is honorifically called by his followers, tell the tale of an East European Jew of Ḥasidic royalty who was raised in the traditional environs of Russia and Latvia and then sojourned in Berlin and Paris, where he studied philosophy, mathematics, and engineering in universities and thus began to experience something of West European culture before making his way to America in 1941, eventually assuming leadership of the sect in 1951 after the death of his predecessor and father-in-law, Yosef Yiṣḥaq Schneersohn (1880–1950), the Friediker Rebbe. Menaḥem Mendel can be viewed, therefore, as a genuine bridge between the proverbial old and new worlds; a paragon of ultraorthodoxy in a secular society committed ideologically and constitutionally to the separation of church and state, a tenet that he undermined to some extent by his own belief that America is distinguished from all other modern nations by its placing trust in God at the center of its national consciousness; a critic of American secularism and materialism, even as he appreciated that the socioeconomic advantages afforded the Jews imparted to this diasporic experience a distinctive role in the drama of world redemption; a man passionately devoted to articulating a mystical rationalism for a post-Holocaust generation marked by the fascination with science and technology, and yet a staunch defender of creationism, a relentless opponent of evolution, who questioned the very validity of scientific methodology, albeit at times on scientific grounds;[3] a radical messianic visionary, who promoted a conservative political agenda both in the United States and in Israel; a lover of all Jews but an inflexible opponent of the Conservative and Reform movements;[4] a relatively reclusive contemplative, who expended an inordinate amount of time and energy building a movement whose tentacles would reach virtually every corner of the civilized world where a Jew might be found. In Schneerson, we find an instantiation of the primary precept that animates the religious philosophy he devotedly transmitted and subversively transformed, the *coincidentia oppositorum*, in the locution of Nicholas of Cusa, or the *aḥdut hashaweh*, the "equanimous one," in the indigenous kabbalistic terminology,[5] which is rendered more typically in Ḥabad discourse by the expressions *hashwa'ah* and *hishtawwut*.[6] Existentially embodying this metaphysical principle, Schneerson displayed the capacity to combine contradictory sensibilities in one subject—in the precise phraseology of the Ḥabad lexicon, *leḥabber shenei hafakhim be-nose eḥad*[7]—and hence he occupied the position of the middle between extremes, at times astutely camouflaging views that might be reckoned heterodox by the canons of ultraorthodoxy.

Ḥabad is perhaps best known as the movement that promulgated its fundamentalist ideology by aggressively promoting ritual observance amongst Jews, a campaign that was buttressed in the last decades of the twentieth century by an acute apocalyptic sensibility that even led many of the Lubavitchers (assigned the name *meshichistim*) to identify the seventh Rebbe as the long-awaited redeemer.

The messianic controversy surrounding Ḥabad, chiefly centered on the question as to whether Schneerson himself accepted this identification, has commanded much attention in the public eye. This is reflected as well in the scholarly arena where most of the current work has been focused on this topic. There is a sharp division amongst scholars, some arguing for an active messianism,[8] bolstered by the belief in the Rebbe's resurrection, which, according to one detractor, has rendered Ḥabad a sect outside the fold of traditional Judaism,[9] and others maintaining a more attenuated perspective,[10] even though the latter (as the thousands of Lubavitchers who adhere to the antimessianic bias of the central leadership of the movement, the Aggudat Ḥasidei Ḥabad) would have a hard time denying that Schneerson (following the lead of his predecessor)[11] explicitly identified his era as the terminus of the *iqvota di-meshiḥa*, the "footsteps of the Messiah," the rabbinic idiom that marks the period right before the onset of the redemption.[12] This generation is an impoverished one, lacking comprehension of divinity, but this detriment is also its benefit, since the state of depravity facilitates the meekness necessary to accept the yoke of heaven, which conceived mystically entails the sacrifice of self (*mesirat nefesh*) and the eradication of egocentricity (*biṭṭul ha-yesh*).[13] The depth of Schneerson's apocalyptic determination can be seen as well in his applying to his historical moment (from the start to the end of his leadership) the rabbinic statement regarding the redemption,[14] "all the calculated times have come to an end, and the matter is dependent on repentance."[15] The mode of service appropriate to Jews living in the generation before the end is the worship of repentance (*avodat ha-teshuvah*), for "by means of repentance they will be immediately redeemed[16] in the true and perfect redemption through our righteous Messiah, verily soon [*be-qarov mammash*]."[17] In this matter, the seventh Rebbe carried forward the messianic program of the sixth Rebbe, famously encoded in the slogan that he publicized in 1941 and 1942, stirred by the persecution of Jews that led to his escape from Europe to America, where he established a new home, *le'altar li-ge'ullah*, "forthwith to redemption," or in the more expanded version, *le'altar li-teshuvah le'alṭar li-ge'ullah*, "forthwith to repentance, forthwith to redemption," which he would sometimes even use to end his personal letters.[18] On occasion, as early as 1952 and as late as 1991, Schneerson spoke more urgently of his generation as the "footsteps of the footsteps of the Messiah" (*iqvota de-iqvota di-meshiḥa*),[19] which is to say, the end of the end, the moment that is before the beginning of what is to come after the end.

The intensity of his messianic zeal and the centrality it played in his worldview cannot be denied. As scholars have duly noted, above all else, the effort expended in disseminating the mysteries of the tradition indiscriminately to every Jew bespeaks the seventh Rebbe's eschatological ardor. What has not been sufficiently appreciated, however, is the extent to which the language of messianism may have been a facet of Schneerson's esoteric dissimulation, the ultimate secreting of the secrecy, the bestowal of a secret so open that it is presumed that there is no secret. This third option is what shall be explored in this book. Let me be clear by stating that I am not ascribing to Schneerson a progressive political orientation that, in any way, advocated a break with rabbinic normativity. It would be intellectually dishonest to deny or even to diminish the conformist tendencies that informed the seventh Rebbe's approach in the social realm. And yet the religious philosophy that may be elicited from the body of his thought is not only conceptually sophisticated but daringly innovative. For scholars of esoteric traditions, in particular, there may be some wisdom to be gleaned from the example of Schneerson and the other Ḥabad masters—a radical theopoetics is not necessarily incompatible with a conservative politics. This is not to say that the latter is an inevitable consequence of the former; on the contrary, a case can be definitely made that forward-thinking thought can engender a left-wing politics. Nevertheless, as the example of Ḥabad illustrates, the opposite may also be true.

Some of the details or conclusions proffered by Shaul Shimon Deutsch in what has been judged by Lubavitchers to be a controversial biography of the formative years of Schneerson may be disputed, but his title *Larger Than Life* speaks volumes and points to the unique challenge that confronts the researcher who sets out to study this figure using the canons of critical scholarship.[20] The fact that Schneerson is referred to reverentially as the Rebbe long after his death suggests that it is not only the extreme messianic wing of the movement that regards his presence as still potent and inspiring. Significantly, he is not identified as the "previous Rebbe," a denomination that is customarily used to designate the sixth Rebbe. One might contend that he is not referred to in this way because there is no heir that would render this adjective meaningful. But this is no explanation;

the fact that no successor has been appointed is precisely the point that needs to be scrutinized; this has only reinforced the belief amongst some of the ḥasidim that the Rebbe continues to function as the rebbe. This is not simply a hypothetical conjecture; the argument can be supported empirically, by observing practices and pondering statements of belief that are predicated on the assumption that Schneerson is even more vibrantly alive after his physical death, which is interpreted docetically as an apparent withdrawal rather than an actual termination. This sentiment is enhanced by technological means (particularly videotape)[21] that have preserved the facade of immediacy through the audio and visual memory of the seventh Rebbe.[22]

Consider the following two illustrations: the ritual of individuals opening the published version of Schneerson's responsa, known as the *Iggerot Qodesh* (The sacred letters), so that they may receive an answer to a query, and the placing of a written request for his intervention on his grave.[23] *Magic* is the first word that comes to mind, and indeed these are acts that correspond to what scholars have been prone to classify as magical. What one calls it, however, is irrelevant. The doing of these rituals—not to mention even more extreme "sensory practices of embodiment" performed by the fanatical *meshichistim* at 770 Eastern Parkway in Brooklyn, designated as the House of Messiah (*beit mashiaḥ*), which are aimed at making the absent Rebbe present[24]—is what is meaningful, as they portend the faith that Schneerson is still, perhaps even more, efficacious in influencing events in this world, and hence his physical death can be seen as merely apparent. Precisely what the seventh Rebbe said about his father-in-law's passing in a talk on 8 Adar I 5710 (February 25, 1950) came to be applied to him:

> The single difference for us is that in the past someone could think that when he came to the Rebbe he could tell him things that he wanted to tell, and to hide things that he wanted to hide from the Rebbe, but now it is clear to all that the Rebbe also knows the things that are concealed within us, for in the past the Rebbe was garbed in a physical body, which is not so now, since he is above the limitations of the physical body, wholly in a state of spirituality. Moreover, inasmuch as "the righteous man who dies is found in all of the worlds more than when he is alive"[25] . . . it is certain that the Rebbe governs the world in its entirety . . . as it was until now,

> and, on the contrary, "with greater rank and with greater strength" (Gen 49:3). And just as until now every one of us maintained that the Rebbe would lead us to greet our righteous Messiah, so it must be maintained now as well.[26]

The death of the sixth Rebbe actually augmented his efficacy, since he was not restricted anymore by a corporeal body and therefore he could accomplish greater providential feats, including returning to the world to lead the Jewish people to welcome the Messiah.[27] The physical demise of the sixth Rebbe is merely a test of faith, the concealment of truth, which is part and parcel of the "birth pangs" that precede the coming of the savior. The intent of the test is to empower the ḥasidim "to push away and to destroy the concealment and withdrawal, so that the truth will be revealed."[28] At work here is an eschatological appropriation of the rabbinic principle for divine governance and the meting out of justice, *middah keneged middah*, literally, "measure for measure," the ethical-theological equivalent to the third of Newton's laws of motion, to every action there is an equal and opposite reaction: by believing in the postmortem influence of the sixth Rebbe, which requires one to perceive the footprints of the invisible in the field of the visible, the concealment as concealment is disclosed, the visible is rendered invisible in the truth unmasked as the mask of truth. That Schneerson never fluctuated from this conviction can be demonstrated on the basis of a plethora of passages. Suffice it here to cite the following statement offered in his advancing years on 20 Shevaṭ 5752 (January 25, 1992): "The ascent and elevation of the leader of our generation are revealed more on the day of his death,[29] as is known, for then all of his actions, his teaching, and the work he did all the days of his life ascend, and this is revealed below, to the point that 'he brings deliverance throughout the land' (Ps 74:12)."[30]

The righteous status of the holy man renders his extinction mere illusion, as he is more alive in death than in life, no longer constrained by the spatial and temporal constrictions of corporeality; indeed, the "eternality" (*niṣḥiyyut*) attributed to the soul after its separation from the body is itself a mode of temporality, the "flux of time [*hemshekh ha-zeman*] that exceeds measurement and boundary."[31] It is no exaggeration to say that the vast majority of Lubavitchers presently believe that what Schneerson said about the sixth Rebbe pertains to him, that is, he continues to affect the physical and spiritual matters of people's lives, particularly with respect to the activity of bringing the redemption, and some even believe that he will rise from the grave to lead the Jewish people into the messianic era. This may strike the ear as discordant or blasphemous, but the underlying assumption can be described accurately as a hyperliteral reading of the rabbinic dictum that the wicked are called "dead" even in their lives, whereas the righteous are called "living" even in their deaths.[32] To understand the particular way this belief is inflected in Ḥabad thinking, it is important to recall the passage in the letter of consolation by the Alter Rebbe, Shneur Zalman of Liadi (1745–1812), over the death of Menaḥem Mendel of Vitebsk,[33] printed as the twenty-seventh section of *Iggeret ha-Qodesh*, the fourth part of the standard editions of the *Tanya*, the foundational treatise of the movement, the "Written Torah of Ḥasidism":[34] "And this is what is written in the holy *Zohar*, that the righteous one, who has passed away, is found in all the world more than in his life . . . this is with respect to the worship of God, in heavenly matters, and with respect to mundane matters, it says explicitly in the holy *Zohar*, that the righteous protect the world, more in their deaths than in their lives, and if not for the prayer of the righteous in that world, the world would not exist even for a moment."[35]

Relying on the authority of the zoharic text,[36] Shneur Zalman takes seriously the claim that the righteous person is accorded greater efficacy and providential sway over the physical world after the death of the body.[37] Even more pertinent is a passage from *Tiqqunei Zohar*,[38] which is paraphrased at the end of this section from *Tanya*, according to which the aura of Moses extends to the six hundred thousand souls that make up the body politic of Israel.[39] The typological parallel between the first and the final redeemer, a theme notably pronounced in the strata of zoharic literature known as *Ra'aya Meheimna* and *Tiqqunim*, had a profound impact on later generations of kabbalists, including the luminaries of the sixteenth-century Safedian revival, theologians of seventeenth-century Sabbatianism, and Ḥasidic masters of the eighteenth, nineteenth, and twentieth centuries.[40] The case of Ḥabad, and even more specifically its last Rebbe, is not eccentric in this regard, but this does not minimize the crucial importance of this motif in their overall outlook.[41] In the first instance, the dispersion of Moses in every generation (*itpashṭuta de-moshe be-khol dara we-dara*) signifies the capability of every Jew to expand his or her consciousness (*da'at*) to the point of being assimilated within the divine and to draw down the infinite light into the world.[42] However, the righteous sages, the "eyes of the congregation" (*einei ha-edah*) and the "leaders of the generation" (*nesi'ei ha-dor*), incarnate this archetype in an exceptionally distinctive fashion—indeed, Moses, the "first leader" (*nasi ha-ri'shon*), serves as the paradigm for the Ḥabad-Lubavitch masters[43]—as they are rooted in the aspect of *Keter*, the simple will of the Infinite, and, as a result, they have the ability to arouse the transcendental aspect of the soul (*yeḥidah*), in virtue of which one is incorporated into the One (*yaḥid*).[44]

The sixth Rebbe deduced from this principle that Israel ben Eliezer (1698–1760), the Ba'al Shem Ṭov, "master of a good name," generally abbreviated as the Beshṭ, should be considered the "Moses of Ḥasidism" and Shneur Zalman of Liadi, the "Moses of Ḥabad."[45] As he expressed the matter in a letter dated 29 Tishrei 5704 (October 28, 1943):

> Our teacher, the Beshṭ, his soul is in Eden, is the aspect and gradation of Moses, the first of the leaders of Israel [*ro'sh nesi'ei yisra'el*] in the course of all the generations until the luminous time of the disclosure of our righteous Messiah, verily soon. . . . The dispersion of Moses in each and every generation, in each generation until the coming of our righteous Messiah, is the dispersion of the power of our teacher, the Beshṭ, his soul is in Eden, and the disclosure in each generation is the revelation of the supernal light more strongly, and this is in accord with the manner of the order of the elevations, from elevation after elevation, of the holy soul of our teacher, the Beshṭ, his soul is in Eden, for when he was in this world, there was a disclosure of the aspects of *nefesh*, *ruaḥ*, and *neshamah*, and after his departure from this world, in the secret of "Greater are the righteous [in death than in life]," and the revelations in the disciples of his disciples and in the last generations are revelations that are revealed through the gradations of *ḥayyah* and *yeḥidah* of the soul of our teacher, the Beshṭ, his soul is in Eden.[46]

Through the intermediary of the Beshṭ, each master of Ḥabad is an avatar of Moses, which, as Schneerson emphasized, does not mean that the particular Rebbe is simply a spark of Moses, but rather that he is the "totality" of his being (*der gantser moshe*), indeed, the "very same" person (*der zelber moshe*), albeit reincarnated in a different body.[47] The messianic conceit implied here is made explicit by Schneerson, "the interiority of Moses is the interiority of the Messiah."[48] The sixth Rebbe was thus identified explicitly by his son-in-law as the "leader of our generation" (*nasi dorenu*), the "Moses of our generation" (*moshe she-be-dorenu*),[49] and as the metempsychosis of the Besht.[50] Just as Moses embodied the divine essence in his being, since he served as the means by which the Jews could be conjoined to the presence (expressed in Deut 5:5 through the image of his standing between God and the Israelites), so, too, the Rebbe of Ḥabad is described both as the personification of godliness and as the intercessor through whom members of the community can receive the teaching of the Besht, the inner light of the Torah, so that they may cleave to the Infinite.[51] The Friediker Rebbe, in particular, is described as the "one who revealed the secrets of Torah in our generation, and by means of his teaching we are all bound to the Tree of Life, which is the interiority of the Torah, and through it there is attachment and communion with the living God."[52]

Applying the zoharic locution in a similar fashion to his father-in-law,[53] Schneerson was convinced that, just as the effect of Moses is dispersed through and augmented over time, so the influence exuded by the sixth Rebbe had grown more powerful after his death in spite of, or because of, the fact that his presence was not empirically apparent to the coarse senses.[54] It should come as no surprise, therefore, that he believed that the leadership of Yosef Yiṣḥaq would even continue in full force after the future redemption,[55] an idea sustained by the view that the supremacy of the leadership (*nesi'ut*) of Moses, through whom the Torah was revealed, will be maintained vis-à-vis the Messiah, and thus all the leaders will preserve their potency, expressly the sixth Rebbe, who has an unrivaled affinity to Moses, since he is the leader of the last generation, the generation of the Messiah, which, in Lurianic terms,[56] is the return (*gilgul*) of the first generation that wandered through the desert.[57] A related, but somewhat different, view is expressed by Yosef Yiṣḥaq in discussing the anniversary of the death (*yahrzeit*) of his father, Shalom Dovber Schneersohn (1860–1920), the RaShaB: the shepherd does not abandon his flock,[58] a locution that likely was meant to bring to mind Moses, who is dubbed the "faithful shepherd" (*ro'eh ne'eman*, *ra'aya meheimna*) based on the scriptural description of his vocation (Exod 3:1).[59] The seventh Rebbe extended this characterization to his predecessor: "By means of this we can understand that the dispersion of Moses in each and every generation relates to my saintly teacher and father-in-law, Admor,[60] for he will be with us when we go to greet the face of our righteous Messiah, as the faithful shepherd does not desert his flock."[61] This idea is corroborated as well by the additional principle that "just as God places his essence in the Torah, similarly, the righteous, who innovate with respect to the Torah by their efforts in the study of Torah with all the strength of their souls to the point of self-sacrifice, enter their essences into the Torah. Therefore, when we study and toil in the teaching of the righteous one . . . we receive all the powers that are extended through him."[62] The study of the teaching of the Friediker Rebbe is labeled by Schneerson (on the basis of a zoharic passage[63] as well as a tradition of the Beshṭ transmitted by Menaḥem Naḥum of Chernobyl[64]) as the gesture of "spiritual prostration" (*hishtaṭḥut be-ruḥaniyyut*), as it provides the means to be connected to him, which is equivalent to the physical act of lying prostrate on the grave.[65]

Schneerson's belief that the sixth Rebbe was the "master of redemption" (*ba'al ha-ge'ullah*)[66] persisted his whole life, a faith that fueled his own messianic fervor and possible posturing, as I have already intimated and shall elaborate. This conviction was commensurate with the salvific duty entrusted by Schneerson to the seventh generation, the generation positioned in the liminal space between epochs, the "last generation of the exile and the first generation of the redemption."[67] The significance of seven in Judaism is obvious and hardly merits elaboration, but two textual sources, one scriptural and the other talmudic, are worthy of note, as they underscore, in particular, the eschatological import of this number. The first is the verse "When you acquire a Hebrew slave, he shall serve six years; in the seventh year he shall go free, without payment" (Exod 21:2), and the second is the dictum transmitted in the name of R. Qaṭina, "Six thousand years shall the world exist and one [thousand] shall it be desolate, as it is written 'And the Lord alone will be exalted in that day' (Isa 2:11)."[68] The messianic responsibility that Schneerson attributed to himself and to his generation was undoubtedly inspired by these texts.[69] In the discourse from 10 Shevaṭ 5711 (January 17, 1951), the first *yahrzeit* of the death of the sixth Rebbe, a talk that is considered within Ḥabad to be the inaugural address of the seventh Rebbe, Schneerson laid the apocalyptic foundation for his own teaching and practice. As was his wont through the duration of his leadership, on this day, Schneerson would explicate a section from Yosef Yiṣḥaq's own discourse from 10 Shevaṭ 5710 (January 28, 1950), a treatise released in advance to be studied as a commemoration of the death of his grandmother, but, as it transpired, this was the day of his own passing.[70] In the beginning of that discourse, known as *Ba'ti le-Ganni*, based on the opening words from Song of Songs 5:1, or as the *Ma'amar ha-Hillula*, reference is made to the rabbinic tradition[71] that from Abraham to Moses there were seven righteous men, whose task it was to draw down the divine presence (*Shekhinah*) into the physical world after its having been driven away by the sins of seven generations from Adam to the Egyptians in the time of Abraham.[72] Commenting on this, Schneerson remarked:

> In the language of the rabbis, blessed be their memory,[73] all things sevenfold are cherished, though not everything cherished is sevenfold. It is clear from this that the essence of the gradation is that it is the seventh, and since it is the seventh it is cherished by us. . . . And thus my saintly teacher and father-in-law, Admor (when he first came to America), explained that also in the matter of the privileging of the sevenfold the advantage of the first is discerned . . . and he explained the level of the first, who was Abraham our father, on account of his worship, which was the worship of self-sacrifice. . . . So great was the level of his worship and self-sacrifice that the reason Moses merited that the Torah be given through him was that the sevenfold is privileged, and he was the seventh in relation to the first. . . . And this is the esteem of the seventh, that it draws down the *Shekhinah* and, more than this, it draws down the essence of the *Shekhinah* and, more than this, it draws down to the lower beings. And this is what is demanded from each of us in the seventh generation . . . for we find ourselves in the footsteps of the Messiah, at the end of the footsteps [*be-siyyuma de-iqvota*], and the work is to complete the drawing down of the *Shekhinah*, and not only the *Shekhinah* but the essence of the *Shekhinah* and specifically in the lower beings. . . . This is the very preciousness of the seventh generation, for several powers were given and revealed on our account. And, by means of the service in this manner, the essence of the *Shekhinah* will be drawn

> below into this corporeal and material world, and it will be on a higher level than before the transgression.[74]

The importance of the occasion when this sermon was delivered cannot be overstated, for while Schneerson had given talks to Lubavitch ḥasidim prior to this one, there is no doubt that this performance marked his coming of age. One must be struck not only by the brilliance of Schneerson's homiletical skill on display at this auspicious occasion but also by the sagacity exhibited through what was judiciously left unspoken. Indeed, it is by attending to the unsaid in what was spoken that we can really hear what he wanted to say. Taking over as the seventh master, Schneerson personalizes the message of his predecessor without explicitly making his own person the issue, a self-effacing modesty that endured until the end of his life. The seven righteous men responsible for drawing the divine presence back into the material realm (Abraham, Isaac, Jacob, Levi, Qehat, Amram, and Moses) correspond to the seven masters of the Ḥabad-Lubavitch dynasty from Shneur Zalman to Menaḥem Mendel. Using this calculus, the seventh Rebbe corresponds symbolically to Moses. Insofar as Moses was declared the humblest of all human beings (Num 12:3), he can be viewed as the actualization of the character trait of self-sacrifice associated with Abraham, whence one may adduce the principle that the seventh is like the first.[75] This does not contradict the point I made above regarding Schneerson's identification of the sixth Rebbe as the "Moses of the generation," since he accepted the view that each master embodies the spirit of Moses and, moreover, he thought of himself as nothing but the extension of his predecessor. The moment that this talk was delivered, accordingly, was delineated not only as the period right before the coming of the Messiah but even more emphatically as the terminus of that period. Just as Moses had the mandate to reveal the Torah in the world—thereby fusing the natural and the supranatural—so, too, Schneerson assumed the duty of completing the work of redemption begun by the sixth Rebbe, who is, for this reason, compared to Moses,[76] by making the world a habitation for the divine, that is, of immaterializing the material by materializing the immaterial. It is surely reasonable to wonder if, already at this early date, Schneerson had the sense that he was the end of the line, that for messianic reasons there could be no one to succeed him, that the work of redemption had to be completed by his efforts, a possibility that has even led to the speculation that he deliberately adopted an ascetic lifestyle in relation to his wife to ensure that there would be no offspring.[77]

Prima facie, one might suppose that since we are dealing with a contemporary personality, in contrast to studying an individual from the distant past, the scholar should be able to separate the wheat of historical fact from the chaff of pious embellishment. The judiciousness of this expectation notwithstanding, it seems that chronological proximity does not alleviate the methodological problem. If we are honest, we must admit that any attempt to speak of the seventh Rebbe will be fraught with the danger of providing a hermeneutical lens that is too narrow to view the many facets of the phenomenon at hand. I do not mean that it is impossible to apply the standards of historical criticism to study Schneerson's life and thought. It is feasible, and indeed imperative, and the analyses to be found in this book will uphold the highest canons of scholarship in which I have been trained. The issue, rather, is that it does not seem tenable to sever the realistic from the fictional in a clear-cut way, as the latter is what engenders the former, although it may be commonly assumed by scholars that the opposite is true. Every academic endeavor to converse about the Rebbe, whether the approach is textual-philological or anthropological-sociological, is willy-nilly circumscribed within this narratological framework.

The concern I am raising becomes more transparent when we mull over the question of sources and the respective levels of reliability and legitimacy accorded them. Needless to say, the material available to the scholar will vary in accord with one's methodological discipline. The social scientist will rely less on the texts ascribed to the Rebbe and will seek to assess his life by examining ethnographic evidence, including interviews and/or surveys with members of the community who have lived the experience of Ḥabad. The more conventional text scholar, by contrast, will investigate the Rebbe's letters and discourses to determine the contours of his worldview. While there is obviously a noteworthy difference between these approaches, a dilemma is shared nonetheless. To state the matter openly, though not as nuanced as I would like, it is not apparent to me that any methodology can presume to divest the Rebbe of his garb as rebbe, so that the person of Menaḥem Mendel Schneerson will come into clear view. Lest there be any misunderstanding, let me state unequivocally that I do not deny that there are more and less reliable sources, nor am I suggesting that it is impossible to ascertain any historical information about the Rebbe's life outside of his persona as the movement's leader. Of course, this is possible, as other scholars have already demonstrated. What I am arguing, however, is that the very notion of a Ḥasidic rebbe must be understood as a composite figure, a corporate entity, if you will, a man whose identity is configured by his followers and perhaps also by his opponents. In this respect, I am aligning myself with a postmodern conception, indebted to Foucault, which deems identity a matter of genealogical fabrication rather than genetic factuality. The imaginative flourishes are no less vital to understanding identity construction than are the data retrievable through rational and quantitative means of exploration, to wit, the anatomical, psychological, and sociological assumptions.

When it comes to the life of the seventh Rebbe, the analytic tool of cultural anthropology is itself somewhat compromised. Interviews or surveys conducted with Lubavitchers reveal the extent to which hagiographic representation is the norm and not the exception, and, even if the target audience is individuals who were in and then left the movement, the hagiography, though it may assume a negative valence, still prevails in shaping opinions about the Rebbe and Ḥabad. From this vantage point, misrepresentation is an intrinsic part of the official history of the movement, a fact, I hasten to add, that applies to Ḥasidism from its so-called origins, as the biographical sketches of the Beshṭ can never be completely separated from the legendary accounts of his life and death.[78] The very best attempts to reconstruct the history of the Beshṭ prove the point. This is incontestably the case with respect to the seventh Rebbe. As Jan Feldman put it, "the tendency to romanticize the Rebbe can be maddening for a researcher who expects modern individuals to be aware when they are inflating the good and ignoring the bad, thereby creating a superhuman hero who can do no wrong. Moreover, what outsiders regard as the stuff of legend and lore is likely to be regarded as unassailable truth by many community members."[79] I would go a step further and argue that even the more sober attempts to treat the Rebbe or the movement in scientifically verifiable terms cannot free themselves entirely from the grip of hagiography. Simply put, without that there would be no framework within which to study the life of Menaḥem Mendel Schneerson, and this is as true for the scholar as it is for the partisan. Attempts to penetrate through the shroud of hagiography are futile, if it is presumed that one can remove that shroud entirely to observe some naked historical truth. The only truth that may be observed is truth garbed in the appearance of truth.

Even the textual sources themselves do not help us out of this labyrinth of figurative dissembling.[80] To be sure, the letters dictated, written, or paraphrased on the basis of the words spoken by Schneerson,[81] the few texts we know he compiled himself, such as the commentary on the Passover Haggadah, marginal glosses on the transcriptions of his own discourses (*siḥot*), and the divinely inspired homilies (*ma'amarim*) or those of previous masters, and the notebooks and diary fragments written in his own hand, published respectively as *Reshimot* and *Reshimat ha-Yoman*, are various kinds of literature that should be accorded high priority as documents to be utilized in the search to ascertain his opinions. However, the issue of transcription is more convoluted and uncertain. Assuredly, the individuals in charge of publishing this material, the *ma'arekhet oṣar ha-ḥasidim*, have religiously upheld the need to inform the reader about the Rebbe's various levels of involvement with textual production by making the distinction between a text that has been edited (*mugah*) and one that has not (*bilti mugah*). I am not confident, however, that these classifications will prove to be sufficient for one who undertakes a historical reconstruction that would stand the test of the most circumspect scrutiny. We are still beholden to a translation from the linguistic matrix of Yiddish to Hebrew and to the transition from the medium of oral communication to written. Appeal to other media, such as audio or video tapes, alleviates the problem to some degree but not completely, since many of the discourses were given on Sabbaths or holidays when there could be no electronic recording.

As it happens, Schneerson addressed the quandary facing the scholar in the introduction to the collection of discourses by the fifth Rebbe, the RaShaB, that was published under his auspices:

> In several of these transcriptions [*reshimot*], we could not clarify who wrote the transcription or, as it is referred to by the ḥasidim, "putting down the précis of the discourse" [*meniaḥ ha-hanaḥah shel ha-siḥah*], and hence it is impossible to know

> how exact it is. But pay attention to this, that the ones who wrote all these transcriptions were amongst the faithful who were extraordinary [*ḥasidim watiqim*] for whom every word and remark of their Rebbe was holy to them. There is no question that they tried with all their capability to guard the language of the master, not to add to it or to detract from it, though it is possible that due to the length of the discourse and the like, the transcriber may have erred with respect to some words, and particularly in the place that he wrote in Hebrew and the discourses were spoken in Yiddish . . . but in general the matters are certainly exact.[82]

These words can be applied legitimately to the Rebbe himself—our knowledge of his teaching is greatly due to the outstanding disciples who transcribed his words, but there shall always remain a gap between written texts and oral recitation in the event that access to the latter is only through the former.[83]

In this book, I will explore some of the main contours of Schneerson's thought, with particular emphasis on the manner in which he used secrecy to dissimulate the dissimulation and thereby (re)cover truths uncovered. To walk this path inevitably leads to the need to lay bare Schneerson's messianic agenda, which is intricately tied to his understanding of the breaking of the seal of esotericism in the dissemination of Ḥasidic wisdom. As the primary focus of this monograph is the seventh Rebbe, a brief remark concerning his indebtedness to previous Lubavitch masters is in order here. This debt is palpable through the intricate threads of his thinking in which are interwoven the many texts composed by his predecessors.[84] In the oral and written expositions promulgated in his name, Schneerson embodied, as it were, the paradoxical essence of Ḥasidism, as he himself delineated it in the *Qunṭres Inyanah shel Torat ha-Ḥasidut,* a discourse delivered on 19 Kislev 5726 (December 13, 1965), the "festival of redemption" (*ḥag ha-ge'ullah*)[85] or the day of celebration (*hillula*) observed by Lubavitchers as the Rosh ha-Shanah of Ḥasidism and the "holiday of holidays" (*ḥag ha-ḥaggim*),[86] as it commemorates both the anniversary of the passing of Dov Baer, the Maggid of Międzyrzecz, in 1772, and the release of the one considered in Ḥabad hagiography to be his most cherished pupil,[87] Shneur Zalman of Liadi, from imprisonment in 1798. On the one hand, the "substance" of Ḥasidism is described as an "essential point abstracted from particular matters" (*nequddah aṣmit ha-mufsheṭet me-inyanim peraṭim*), but, on the other hand, inasmuch as it is the essential point, all the manifold aspects are found in and branch out from it. In a related but slightly different terminological register, it can be said that Schneerson comported the kabbalistic mystery of *ṣimṣum*, the condensation of the infinite light to a point, the indivisible unit that comprehends everything in its seemingly endless divisibility. In a manner curiously similar to the account of individuation offered by Jung,[88] we can aver that the seventh Rebbe is reduced to a drop of water, but one that contains all of the ocean, or to a grain of sand through which one can behold the world in its entirety. Just as Jung equates the "inner experience of individuation" with what the mystics name "the experience of God"—the "smallest power" confronting the "greatest power," the "smallest space" containing the "infinite"—so we can think of Schneerson becoming an "in-dividual," that is, a "separate, indivisible unity or 'whole,'"[89] the individuated point that comprises the totality of what is, the jot that bears the essence of the Infinite (*aṣmut ein sof*), according to Ḥabad nomenclature, the *yod* that is the first letter of the name YHWH, the alphabetic cipher that semiotically represents the ten *sefirot*, the manifest hiddenness of the hidden manifestation. Metaphorically speaking, in relation to the six masters that preceded him, the seventh Rebbe—in an act of utmost humility—makes himself into such a point, his words echoing the voices that came before him, especially the sixth Rebbe, Yosef Yiṣḥaq, father of his wife Ḥaya Mushqa.[90] All seven masters of Ḥabad-Lubavitch are bound together in such a way that in each one the sum of all the others is to be found, and hence it is not appropriate to differentiate between one Rebbe and another; however, there is an element of sequential propinquity, which makes the preceding master in the chain the one with the most influence on his successor.[91] Indeed, it is evident that the seventh Rebbe unwaveringly understood his vocation as completing the directive of his predecessor,[92] to whom he continually referred as the "leader of the generation" (*nasi ha-dor*), even after his somatic demise, a locution that had clear messianic implications, as the term *nasi* is the technical appellation affixed to Moses, the first redeemer (*go'el ri'shon*) and the paradigm for the final redeemer (*go'el aḥaron*).[93] Thus, for example, in the talk delivered on 19 Kislev 5711 (November 28, 1950), several months after the death of the sixth Rebbe, the not yet coronated seventh Rebbe said, "The essence is that the

Rebbe himself should come quickly in our day, the soul in body, and take us out of exile, the physical exile and the spiritual exile, to the redemption."[94] In the inaugural discourse *Ba'ti le-Ganni*, on the first *yahrzeit* of Yosef Yiṣḥaq's passing, Schneerson repeated his conviction:

> And my saintly teacher and father-in-law, Admor, "who bore our sickness, and who endured our suffering" (Isa 53:4), "but he was wounded because of our sins, crushed because of our iniquities" (Isa 53:5), just as he saw our torment, he should come swiftly in our days to redeem his flock from the spiritual exile and from the physical exile together . . . and, moreover, he should conjoin and bind us to the substance and essence of the Infinite, blessed be he. And this is the inner intent of the descent and concatenation of the worlds, and the matter of the transgression and its rectification, and the matter of the death [*silluqan*] of the righteous, for by this means the glory of the blessed holy One ascends [*istalaq*]. When he leads us out of exile "with an exalted hand,"[95] "and all of Israel will have light in their dwellings" (Exod 10:23), and "Then Moses and the Israelites will sing [this song to the Lord]" (Exod 15:1), "The Lord will reign forever and ever" (Exod 15:18) . . . and they conclude "And the Lord shall be king [over all the earth; in that day] the Lord shall be one and his name shall be one" (Zech 14:9). All this comes about on account of the death of the righteous, which is harder than the destruction of the Temple, and since we have been through all these things, now the matter depends only on us—the seventh generation. And we should merit to see the Rebbe here below, in a body, beneath the ten handbreadths, and he should redeem us.[96]

There is no ambiguity in these words: Yosef Yiṣḥaq is portrayed as the suffering servant, and the redemption is facilitated by his leaving the world,[97] based on the principle that the death of a righteous man is a disappearance only in appearance, for, in truth, it is a higher mode of manifestation, indeed, the disclosure of the light is so forceful that it occasions the escalation of the divine glory. The term *histallequt*, accordingly, is used to refer to this death, but it does not denote an ascent to some domain above the mundane, but rather the aspect of exaltation (*romemut*) that may apply to one who remains below in the terrestrial realm.[98] However, the seventh Rebbe also expected the sixth Rebbe to return physically in order to complete the deliverance of the Jewish people, and, consequently, it is reasonable to assert that he considered him to be the Messiah.

A gripping affirmation along these lines is found in the conclusion of a talk presented a few weeks later, on 27 Shevaṭ 5711 (February 3, 1951):

> And the verse continues, "he shall serve six years, and in the seventh he shall go free" (Exod 21:2), by means of the completion of the work now in the six thousand years of the world,[99] for even though it is a limited time, all the work will be completed within it, and then "the earth will be filled with knowledge of the Lord" (Isa 11:9). . . . By means of this work, through which the deceit [*sheqer*] and knot [*qesher*] of the world are transformed into the boards of the Tabernacle [*qarshei ha-mishkan*],[100] the Moses of our generation, who is my saintly teacher and father-in-law, Admor, binds their *yeḥidah* with the aspect of his *yeḥidah* . . . and by means of this "in the seventh he shall go free," that is, the disclosure of the future, through the agency of Moses, the first redeemer and the last redeemer, he should redeem us quickly in our days and swiftly from the last, bitter exile in which the darkness is compounded.[101]

Schneerson did not vacillate from this belief, referring recurringly to his father-in-law until the very end of his days as the "leader of our generation," the "sole emissary of our generation" (*der eyntsiger sholiach dorenu*), and the "sole Messiah of our generation" (*der eyntsiger moshiach dorenu*).[102] It should be noted that there are statements that suggest that Schneerson distinguished the Friediker Rebbe and the Messiah, but there is little doubt that, even in those contexts, he ascribed an active messianic role to his predecessor. Very often, this role is linked to his release from Soviet prison on 12–13 Tammuz 5687 (July 12–13, 1927). It will be recalled that Yosef Yiṣḥaq himself dramatized this delivery from incarceration as a sign of the liberation of the Jewish people more broadly.[103] Following suit, Schneerson portrayed this day as the "foundation of the endurance and existence of all matters of Judaism for all the days after it, to this day, and to the end of all the generations. . . . The essence of the service of my saintly teacher and father-in-law, Admor, leader of our generation, was to draw near and to accelerate the redemption, as he proclaimed and publicized . . .

forthwith to repentance, forthwith to redemption [*le'altar li-teshuvah le'altar li-ge'ullah*]."[104]

The messianic enthusiasm of the seventh Rebbe, which was there from the start of his assuming the mantle of leadership, though surely intensifying in the course of time, has to be seen in this light, as he fancied himself the leader of the seventh generation, the generation that was meant (even if against its will) to fulfill the redemptive mission first set by Yosef Yiṣḥaq, but that, in some sense, goes back to Shneur Zalman, and through him to the Beshṭ.[105] If Schneerson attributed a messianic status to his predecessor and imagined he was nothing but his extension, it seems incontrovertible to conclude that he harbored messianic pretensions of his own. To cite one illustration from the talk delivered to the international conference of Lubavitch emissaries on 25 Ḥeshvan 5752 (November 2, 1991):

> The complete and true redemption must be immediately and without delay [*tekhef u-mi-yad*] through the agency of our righteous Messiah, the emissary [of whom it was said] "the one you will send as your agent" (Exod 4:13), my saintly teacher and father-in-law, Admor, the leader of our generation, and this is extended to the one who has filled his place [*memalle meqomo*] after him,[106] for he [the sixth Rebbe] has filled the place of his father, Admor, his soul in heaven [the fifth Rebbe],[107] as it has been said several times in relation to the seven branches of the candelabrum and the seven guests [invited to the *sukkah* on the festival of Tabernacles].[108]

In the continuation, Schneerson emphasizes that the name of his predecessor was Yosef. Given the allusion to the seven Ḥabad-Lubavitch masters, we can assume that the intent is that the sixth Rebbe symbolically corresponds to *Yesod*, and the seventh Rebbe to *Malkhut*, respectively the sixth and seventh emanations when the sefirotic pleroma is divided into the upper three and the lower seven.[109]

It is of interest to recall in this connection another comment from the *Quntres Inyanah shel Torat ha-Ḥasidut:*

> The *sefirah* of *Malkhut* is the aspect of divinity that is appropriate to the world, and thus the coordinates of space and time issue from her (and are appropriate to her). The *sefirah* of *Yesod* is the aspect of divinity that is above the classification that is

> appropriate to this world, for in all of the attributes that are above the *sefirah* of *Malkhut* the coordinates of space and time are not appropriate . . . and the matter of the unification [*yiḥud*] of *Malkhut* with *Yesod* is the disclosure of the light of the Infinite, which is above the worlds, in the aspect of divinity that is garbed in the world. . . . The aspect of *Malkhut* itself is united with the *sefirah* of *Yesod* until they become one matter—"the king that lives eternally" [*melekh ḥai we-qayyam*].[110]

The conjunction of *Yesod* and *Malkhut* constitutes the lower unity (*yiḥuda tata'ah*) that is marked by the manifestation of the light of the Infinite, which transcends the spatiotemporal boundaries of the physical cosmos.[111] This unity, which makes possible the existence of a reality seemingly independent of God, is to be fully revealed epistemically and ontically only in the days of Messiah. I shall return to this theme in Schneerson's teaching, with special reference to the (re)construction of gender implied thereby, but the main point to underline at this juncture is that the relationship of the ninth and tenth emanations can be applied to the rapport between Yosef Yiṣḥaq and Menaḥem Mendel: just as *Malkhut* completes the efflux that she receives from *Yesod*, so the vitality and legitimacy of the seventh Rebbe are derived from the clout of the sixth Rebbe.[112] From this vantage point, it is possible to view the life of Schneerson as a form of self-effacement, which rendered him feminine in relation to his predecessor, a point immortalized in the fact that he is buried to the left of his father-in-law. As I have already noted, however, the seventh master cannot be severed from the first, who comprises the whole lineage in his being. Taking this into account, it must be borne in mind that the claims I will make in this study for Schneerson's ideas should not be construed as if I were avowing them to be uniquely his own; on the contrary, he is better viewed as a repository, a vessel overflowing with the gnosis he received from the six masters who preceded him.

To state the matter even more ardently, the issue of novelty is not my concern, as I do not think it is a manifestly relevant or helpful hermeneutical lens through which to speculate on the contribution of the seventh Rebbe to the history of Jewish thought. This is not to deny that twists and turns on the path he walked are reflective of the variegated factors that informed his existential reality, particularly in twentieth-century America where he assumed the role of leader and oversaw the expansion of a Ḥasidic dynasty into an international movement of remarkable reach and persuasion. To mention one example, which will be discussed in greater detail in chapter 6, Schneerson even cast his messianic vision in terms of the American commitment to secure the inalienable right of every human being to be free, a principle that he invoked especially in the struggle to allow Jews to leave the oppression of the former Soviet Union.[113] Many other themes could be adduced to illustrate the manner in which living in a postwar liberal democracy shaped the seventh Rebbe's oratory and ideology. Notwithstanding the legitimacy of this allegation, and the prudence of always taking historical context into consideration, I would insist that the complex patterns of Schneerson's worldview need to be evaluated with a different conception of temporality in mind, a notion of time that calls into question the model of aligning events chronoscopically in a sequence stretched between before and after. The roots of this alternative sense of time run deep in the rabbinic *imaginaire*; indeed, one might even say the midrashic temperament is captured in the saying "There is no before or after in Scripture" (*ein muqdam u-me'uḥar ba-torah*), a dictum that philosophically implies that what comes after may be before what comes before, it was after.[114] The nexus established between hermeneutic reversibility and temporal diremption is enhanced in the medieval kabbalistic teaching according to which God and Torah are explicitly identified. Consequently, the line separating divinity and textuality is significantly narrowed. The lack of any chronological order in the sefirotic pleroma—in the language of *Sefer Yeṣirah*, which is frequently cited by kabbalists, "their end is fixed in their beginning and their beginning in their end like a flame bound to the coal"[115]—is the ontological underpinning of the inability to impose a linear template onto the scriptural narrative. The following passage from the anthology of kabbalistic secrets *Shoshan Sodot*, a work likely available to Ḥabad masters,[116] can be considered a succinct formulation of this prevalent view: "If you comprehend the secret of their saying, may their memory be blessed, that there is no before or after in the Torah, you can comprehend the secret that the *sefirot* are comprised within one another like a flame bound to the coal, and there is no before or after here, for in any side of which you take hold, there the flame will be found."[117]

In this vein, the hermeneutic at play in Schneerson's thinking—and it should come as no surprise from what I have already written that I do not allege exceptionality in this regard—champions a temporal configuration that is circular in its linearity and linear in its circularity.[118] What is brought forth each moment is a renewal of what has been, albeit always from a different vantage point. As Schneerson put it himself in one context, reflecting on the novel interpretations of Torah offered by Jews through the generations:

> From the standpoint of the supremacy of the status of Israel (who are engraved in his thought, blessed be he)[119] their novelties also become a portion of the Torah as it is in the thought (wisdom) of the blessed holy One, that is, these novelties issue from Israel, but they are in his thought (wisdom), blessed be he, even before they are brought about anew by Israel, since the past and the future are one in relation to him, blessed be he . . . but in his thought, blessed be he (prior to their having been produced by Israel), they are in the gradation that is above time (the past and future are one) and hence they are in the ultimate concealment, the concealment that is not in existence [*he'lem she-eino bi-meṣi'ut*], and when they are generated by Israel they come into existence.[120]

New interpretations of Torah that come to light in the course of history preexisted in the infinite thought or wisdom of the divine, the supernal Torah that emanates from the essence (*aṣmut*), the "ultimate concealment" (*takhlit ha-he'lem*), to which not even the quality of being can be attributed, the "essential hiddenness" (*he'lem ha-aṣmi*) that "is above every gradation and disclosure,"[121] the transcendence that transcends the triadic division of time, the eternal present wherein past and future are indistinguishable as it is perpetually becoming what it has always never been. To speak of novel explanations, therefore, is to discern that what is new is new precisely because it is old, that what is disclosed in the guise of the unprecedented is a concealment of the erstwhile. I do not think it inappropriate to apply this conception of time and hermeneutics to the seventh Rebbe himself. Accordingly, there is no attempt here to constrict the presentation of the material diachronically, nor a pretense to the claim of originality, unless the latter is understood as the reiteration of truth already spoken as something yet to be spoken. Innovation consists precisely in this repetition.[122]

I would thus respectfully take issue with the observation of Rachel Elior that the continuity of Ḥabad's existence as a social phenomenon "raises a mistaken expectation regarding the possibility of revealing the unalloyed spiritual continuum, as it were, underlying the movement's extended history. This expectation is related to the common assumption that it is possible retrospectively to learn the historical origin of Ḥabad and its spiritual background during its early stages, by moving backwards from the study of its present manifestations and contemporary reality."[123] This assumption, Elior goes on to say, "cannot satisfy the standards of historical criticism. A basic postulate of historical and philological research maintains that a system of ideas that remains active over a long time, confronting transitory situations and varieties of cultural reality, will not maintain its primary form of existence without being marked by the changes that have taken place in external reality."[124] I do not agree with Elior's contention that it is problematic to adopt a "retrospective study," whereby one draws conclusions about "earlier ideas and social manifestations of a historical phenomenon from its later stages," just as I do not think it is accurate to reverse this argument. That is to say, I think it is perfectly plausible to draw inferences about the later stages from the earlier and about the earlier stages from the later. In a phenomenon like Ḥabad Ḥasidism, the continuities of thought are as impressive as the discontinuities that would be explained by historical change, a possibility explicitly rejected by Elior as well: "Moreover, it must be stated clearly that just as the social, spiritual, or communal significance of Ḥabad today sheds little light on its origins in the late eighteenth century, similarly one ought not seek the meaning of its current guise in the doctrines of the first generations."[125] In my estimation, the study of Ḥabad requires a hermeneutic based on a notion of time at odds with the linear conception undergirding this comment. The critical scholar, no less than the pious adept, must be attuned to the sense of time at play in Ḥabad speculation, and only then can one appreciate that the meaning of the first master's teaching is to be sought in the seventh, even as the meaning of the seventh master's teaching is to be sought in the first. From this ideational stance, cause and effect are completely reversible, and hence one can legitimately move through the present from past to future or from future to past.

Let me conclude the introduction by noting that when we attempt to gauge the life and impact of the seventh Rebbe, we are indeed reaching for the Infinite; there is always a surplus that we cannot know and about which we cannot speak.

To work on Schneerson is humbling—in the diction of Ḥabad, an act of *mesirat nefesh*—as it is necessary to let go of the egological quest for factual truth and yield to the phantasmagoric weight of the narratological scheme. In this gesture of yielding, one comes to discern that a portrait of the Rebbe cannot be painted in isolation from the disciples who give shape to his comportment in the guise of disseminating the Ḥasidic doctrines through textual transmission or in the guise of carrying out the mission to spread orthodox practice in the social sphere; the Rebbe and his ḥasidim are bound in a circle of dialectical reciprocity such that the identity of one is constructed and construed in light of the other. Whether a scholar approaches Menaḥem Mendel Schneerson from a philological or an ethnographic perspective, there is no manner of beholding him that is not beholding through a garment. To paraphrase a well-known Sufi sentiment, the presumption that one can see without a veil is the greatest of veils.

But, one might ask, is this not contradicted by the fact that the seventh Rebbe emphasized, following the masters who came before him, that the messianic era will be marked by a vision of the essence of the light of the Infinite (*aṣmut or ein sof*) without any garment (*beli levush*).[126] In the final section of chapter 2, I will engage this matter in more detail, but suffice it to say that it is viable to take this at face value and to envision the eschatological goal as a seeing divested of any intermediary, an idea linked exegetically to the verse "Your master will no longer be covered and your eyes will see your master" (Isa 30:20).[127] Consider, for example, the formulation of the sixth Rebbe: "It is impossible for there to be a disclosure of the intellect without the garment of thought, and thus, when the light of the intellect is disclosed, letters are produced, but above there can be a disclosure of light without any garment."[128] The phenomenological question that beckons to be asked, however, concerns the nature of what is disclosed in this disclosure of light without any garment. Can such disclosure be anything but occlusion? I think it is closer to the spiritual marrow of Ḥabad, as it were, to surmise that the seeing without a garment consists of coming to see that there is nothing ultimately to see but the garment that there can be a seeing without any garment. The very notion of removing all garments, in other words, is the ultimate garment, and, consequently, what is seen of the light without any garment is the very garment through which the light is (un)seen. The soteriological promise of a gnosis that consists of the disclosure of the essence (*gilluy ha-aṣmut*)[129] does not betoken the revelation of an entity subject to representational replication, but rather the event of unconcealment in which the manifest ceases to be hidden in its manifestation. In the epochal metamorphosis of the eschaton, the concealment, as such, is unconcealed, the withdrawal itself withdrawn, and hence the nature of being will not be thought of as what abides as concealed in its unconcealment but as what transpires in the concealing of the concealment.[130]

Let us consider the following words of Yiṣḥaq Aizaq ha-Levi Epstein, the dedicated devotee of Dov Baer:

> Thus you are one but not in number,[131] and you are not signified by any letter or sign, and you have no acknowledged name at all, and what is given the designation divinity [*elohut*] is entirely from the perspective of the worlds, for in order to create worlds or to govern worlds, the light of the Infinite was constricted [*nitṣamṣem or ha-ein sof*] so that there would be a deity of the world [*lihyot elohei olam*], but the light of the Infinite does not change, God forbid, but rather its disclosure in the worlds is through the constriction of the name *divinity* [*be-ṣimṣum de-shem elohut*], for the worlds are from the language and matter of concealment [*he'lem*], that is, the concealment of the unity and simplicity of the light of the Infinite [*he'lem aḥdut u-peshiṭut or ha-ein sof*], and in order for there to be any disclosure through the concealment [*lihyot eizeh gilluy tokh ha-he'lem*], the concealment must remain in its being [*ha-he'lem yish'ar be-qiyyumo*]."[132]

The full assonance of the wordplay *ha-olam* and *he'lem* will be rendered more overtly in subsequent chapters; here we can note that it conveys that theistic language is appropriate only if we think of the infinite reality (beyond mathematic computation and linguistic demarcation) vis-à-vis the world, but the world can be said to reveal the divine to the extent that the latter remains concealed therein. As Epstein put it elsewhere, in the days of the week, which figuratively symbolize the fragmented time of history, "the divine light is intentionally hidden and concealed," so that there might be the semblance of an autonomous nature, but on the Sabbath, which symbolizes the atemporal time of redemption, one can comprehend the light in its essence, and the differentiated beings are revealed to be, in truth, aspects of the Infinite, which yields the paradox that "in relation to the Infinite, concealment is also disclosure, as disclosure is infinite" (*legabbei ha-ein sof ha-he'lem hi gam ken gilluy de-gilluy hu ein sof*).[133] To be exposed, the Infinite must be camouflaged, to be forthcoming, it must be withheld. Envisioning the essence in Ḥabad tradition may be cast as apprehending the "absolute nonbeing of the event,"[134] which "results from an excess of one, an ultra-one,"[135] the oneness beyond the distinction of one and many. The unicity consigned to the end is a visual attunement to the void of all being, the void of all things fully void, the breach of unity by which the unity of the breach (dis)appears in and through the cleft of consciousness. In this temporal crevice and spatial hiatus, the symbolic is imagined as real, the real as symbolic. I trust the excursions of this book will help others to lift many veils, but I am ever mindful that, with every veil lifted, another will be unfurled. To apprehend this truth, I submit, is the key to unlocking the open secret of the seventh Rebbe's postmessianic messianism.

I

CONCEALING THE CONCEALMENT
The Politics of the Esoteric

There is no purpose to truth but to know that it is the truth.

—MAIMONIDES, *PERUSH HA-MISHNAYOT*, SANHEDRIN 10:1

As with any truth-statement, truth is undeclarable; so it is called a truth-statement.

—*THE DIAMOND SŪTRA*

Pointing the Way Metatextually

TO STATE THE OBVIOUS AT THE OUTSET: INSOFAR AS Ḥabad is an actual movement, a social scientific methodology would seem to be especially suitable to studying the seventh Rebbe. Not only is there no need in this case to rely exclusively on a philological-textual analysis, but one could raise serious questions about the legitimacy of adopting such an approach. In my judgment, however, there is still much to be gained from an investigation of this sort. As a scholar who has been intrigued by and written repeatedly on the phenomenon of secrecy, it does not appear to me credible to engage this matter without delving carefully into Schneerson's teachings. I have already acknowledged the limitations of this interpretive stratagem. For the most part, these teachings have been communicated in transcriptions and translations made by a small and highly deft circle of scribes. Schneerson did have a hand in this process, often reading and correcting secondary versions of his talks and discourses, but this is not so for a considerable percentage of the extant literary corpus. This proviso notwithstanding, the texts are a vital path to lead back from the written to the oral. It is from the standpoint of the chiasm between textuality and aurality that we must consider the matter of Schneerson's esotericism.

I am not oblivious to the fact that thousands of individuals affiliated with Lubavitch have no knowledge of or interest in the intricacies of the esoteric doctrines strewn about their Rebbe's sermons, discourses, and epistles. The fact remains, nonetheless, that these doctrines were the bone and breath of his being. There is no conceptual ground to distinguish in Schneerson's mind between social reality and its imaginal counterpart. On the contrary, given the impact on his way of thinking of the traditional kabbalistic perception of the physical world as a mirror image of the sefirotic pleroma, which, in turn, is a mirror image of the Infinite that is beyond image, why should one assume that for him mundane matters could be understood without their symbolic double? Why should one entertain the possibility that he would have affirmed a notion of facticity stripped of the sheath of metaphoricization? Under the influence of the modern discipline of anthropology, there has been a tendency on the part of some scholars of religion to distinguish elite and popular forms of pious devotion. It is surely reasonable to think of the social phenomenon of Ḥabad in these terms, but, from the standpoint of the seventh Rebbe, this is a pointless distinction. What one might consider popular religion—exemplified by the activities of members of his sect—is infused in his mind, his rhetoric, and his actions with mystical significance. Indeed, the performative effectiveness of his teaching was the ability to create a meditational space with his spoken words—even if they were not understood by the majority of his audience—and to relate the most convoluted kabbalistic matters to the basic acts and beliefs that define Jewish orthopraxy. In Schneerson's worldview, the meaning of events that transpire in history is to be ascertained through the prism of theosophic symbolism.[1] Therefore, I think it relevant to begin my analysis with a reflection on the seventh Rebbe's kabbalah and the place his thinking occupies in the history of Jewish esotericism.

Intellectual Mysticism and the Ḥabad Tradition

In considering this question, it should be borne in mind that one of the ways that the Ḥabad-Lubavitch dynasty distinguished itself is the use its teachers have made of the technical terminology and symbols of Lurianic kabbalah. This influence is attested already in the *Tanya* of Shneur Zalman as well as in his other works. As Naftali Loewenthal surmised, the selective employment of Lurianic concepts by Shneur Zalman was an attempt "to make the teachings of the Maggid and the Baal Shem Tov rationally meaningful to a Hasidic following which was composed of scholarly men who, in the main, made no claim to pneumatic attainment."[2] This strategy prevailed as a cornerstone of Lubavitch philosophy and continued to evolve into more and more levels of complexity through the generations.

As it happens, Loewenthal's schematization parallels Schneerson's own understanding of the distinctive contribution of Ḥabad. Thus, for example, in a discourse from 21 Kislev 5714 (November 28, 1953), he offered a brief survey of the history of Jewish esotericism and the increased tendency to reveal secrets since the time of Isaac Luria in the sixteenth century. The novelty of Shneur Zalman is described as his having "revealed the interiority of the Torah in the teaching of Ḥasidism through a manner that is comprehended by the human intellect . . . to all of Israel, without the limitation of conditions."[3] In a second passage, the overall purpose of *Tanya* is linked to the power "to cut and to destroy the shell that prevents the study of the interiority of the Torah."[4] Needless to say, this theme was reiterated countless times by Schneerson. For instance, in a speech delivered on 21 Kislev 5750 (December 19, 1989), he commented that the title "leader of Israel" (*nasi be-yisra'el*) was assigned to Shneur Zalman to signify that he "comprised all the people of the generation of which he was the leader—men, women, and children." Moreover, the day that commemorates his release from prison is called the festival of redemption (*ḥag ha-ge'ullah*), for "the content of the matter of the liberation of the Admor ha-Zaqen on the nineteenth of Kislev applies to each and every one in Israel, as the Admor ha-Zaqen himself explained after his liberation that the teaching of Ḥasidism does not belong only to those who were called in that period 'the pious' (*ḥasidim*), but to all of Israel."[5] The impulse to publicize secrets is closely tied to the view that the uniqueness of the Alter Rebbe consisted of his ability to cause others to repent, to augment the number of returnees (*ba'alei teshuvah*).[6] The dissemination of the mysteries of Torah is viewed from this vantage point as a yearning to bring estranged Jews back to the fold. On account of this desire, Shneur Zalman was given the title "master of redemption" (*ba'al ha-ge'ullah*).[7] The locution (applied as well by the seventh Rebbe to his predecessor)[8] is meant to underscore that Ḥabad was to carry out the apocalyptic mission to completion, a mission there from the inception of the movement, a mission that rests on the belief that undoing the seal of esotericism is allied to this propitious moment after the appearance of the Beshṭ and his heralding the messianic epoch, an era in which the secrets are revealed, culminating in the promise that the essence of godliness will be seen without any garment.

Applying this understanding beyond the specific contribution of Ḥabad, Schneerson offered a similar explanation of Ḥasidism more generally in the *Qunṭres Inyanah shel Torat ha-Ḥasidut*:

> The innovation of the teaching of Ḥasidism is that each and every person, even if one does not have an elevated soul [*neshamah gevohah*] and one has not purified oneself, can comprehend divinity, for by means of the fact that the teaching of Ḥasidism explains the matters of the esoteric portion [*ḥeleq ha-sod*] of the Torah and brings them in proximity to the intellect through examples and similes from the potencies and properties of the soul—"from my flesh I shall behold God" (Job 19:26)—the possibility is granted to each and every person to apprehend this portion of the Torah as well, and not only through the intellect in one's divine soul but also through the intellect in one's rational soul, and even through the intellect in one's animal soul.[9]

Whatever differences one may detect in the manifold teachings of the successive leaders of the Ḥabad-Lubavitch dynasty, a common thread that ties them together is the quest to disseminate mystical knowledge within an intellectualist framework, thereby forging a synthesis of the ecstatic and the scientific, the mystical and the philosophical. I will explore this topic in greater detail in chapter 2, but suffice it here to repeat that the cerebral encasing of the kabbalistic core of Ḥabad teaching is a feature that endures through the generations of Lubavitch masters. The Friediker Rebbe's description of the Alter Rebbe's *Liqquṭei Torah*, an anthology of discourses on parts of the Pentateuch, can serve as a testimonial to the unique contribution of the movement as a whole: "In this book of books . . . of Ḥabad Ḥasidism, the true content of the orientation of our master the Ba'al Shem Ṭov with respect to two principles, the knowledge of the Creator and the love of Israel, is elucidated in a philosophical explanation."[10]

The letters and writings penned by Menaḥem Mendel, as well as other documents based on his oral presentations, share this outlook. I offer the following passage from the talk on 1 Nisan 5725 (April 3, 1965) as illustrative of the point:

> The intent and purpose of creation is that there will be in the world a disclosure of the light of the Infinite that is above any relationship to the worlds, and this disclosure is (in the main) through study and the diffusion of the interiority of the Torah, for the interiority of the Torah from its own vantage point is above disclosure (the concealment of the Torah), and by means of the study of the interiority of the Torah through understanding and comprehension, and particularly by means of its diffusion outward . . . we draw forth the light that is above any relationship to the worlds, until the point that the essence of the light that is above disclosure will be disclosed in the world.[11]

Many of the themes compacted in this citation will be unpacked in this chapter and the one following. Here I simply underscore the locution "study of the interiority of the Torah through understanding and comprehension" (*limmud di-fenimiyyut ha-torah be-havanah we-hassagah*); even though the ultimate objective of esoteric learning is not to cultivate rational comprehension but to foster the obliteration of self,[12] the modality of study involves the power of reason, and thus the term *intellectual mysticism* seems to me a fitting expression to characterize the orientation of the seventh Rebbe. Indeed, as will become more apparent in the continuation of our analysis, the (allegedly) unlimited distribution of the secrets of the interiority of the Torah, which are identified with the theosophic structures of the world of emanation (*olam ha-aṣilut*), through the channel of the intellect in the corporeal world is the special responsibility associated with the generation of the footsteps of the Messiah, and, we may suppose, with the particular role that Schneerson assumed for himself.

Esotericism and the Impulse to Communicate Secrets

Given the preponderance of textual evidence, it would be both practically impossible and methodologically imprudent to delineate all the relevant ideas and terms in the texts ascribed to Schneerson that are culled from Luria and his disciples, not to mention other kabbalistic sources such as the *Zohar* in its disparate literary components. I limit the focus of this chapter to a particular topic that is crucial in ascertaining the seventh Rebbe's relationship to kabbalah, the emphasis on esotericism. As I have argued in several previous studies, the view of secrecy promoted by kabbalists—and in this matter the fault line does not fall, in my opinion, along the reigning typological distinction between theosophic and ecstatic kabbalah—relates to the inability to communicate the secret, which is not to be explained primarily in terms of the unworthiness of a particular recipient but is rather associated with the inherent ineffability of the truth that must be kept secret. This is not to suggest that kabbalists have not also embraced the rhetoric of esotericism based on the presumption that secrets must be withheld from those not fit to receive them, an orientation hinted at in classical rabbinic thought and developed more systemically by medieval philosophical exegetes, especially Maimonides. The esoteric hermeneutic in many kabbalistic sources does indeed resonate with this elitist political posture, but it goes beyond it, inasmuch as the very disclosure of the secret demands concealment. Utterance of the mystery in a linguistic garb, whether oral or written, is possible because of the inherent impossibility of its being uttered. It follows that even for the adept, who demonstrates unequivocally that he deserves to be a recipient of the esoteric tradition, there is something of the secret that remains hidden in the act of its transmission.[13]

With respect to Ḥasidism, the issue of secrecy presents a unique problem. The matter was stated soundly, though somewhat pedantically, by Buber: "And just because 'the simple man' is so important, there cannot be any esoteric Hasidism, in contrast to the Kabbalah, so long as the movement retains its original strength and purity. There is no shutting up of the mysteries; everything is fundamentally open to all, and everything is again and again repeated so simply and concretely that each true believer can grasp it."[14] In the specific case of Ḥabad, if we are to presume, as I think we should, that its impetus initially was to communicate the infinite, in Loewenthal's locution, what role should be accorded kabbalistic esotericism? Here it is apposite to recall that a number of Ḥasidic masters had leveled criticism against Shneur Zalman on the grounds that he divested Lurianic kabbalah of its esoteric character by clothing it in an intellectual manner that rendered the arcane and allusive symbolism more accessible.[15] To some extent, the condemnation is exaggerated, but it also harbors a measure of truth. The ethos of the movement doubtless has been to distribute the recondite theosophic doctrines and contemplative practices of the kabbalah to a wider audience, a task that was perceived to be mandated by the Besht̩'s own report in the letter (known in Ḥasidic lore as the "Holy Epistle," *Iggeret ha-Qodesh*, or as the "Letter Concerning the Ascent of the Soul," *Iggeret Aliyyat ha-Neshamah*) that was written circa 1752 and sent to his brother-in-law Gershon of Kuṭov, but first published in 1781 in Korets as an appendix to Jacob Joseph of Polonnoye's *Ben Porat Yosef*.[16] In the critical passage of the document, the Messiah assures the Besht̩ that redemption will come when his teachings were publicized and revealed in the world and his wellsprings were spread outward, *yafuṣu ma'yenotekha ḥuṣah* (Prov 5:16).[17] Proponents of Ḥabad-Lubavitch have assumed that, of all the Ḥasidic sects, they have carried out this mandate most faithfully. From this standpoint, the tenor of this group from its inception may be judged messianic in nature.

The textual evidence is overwhelming, and here I will mention only a few telling illustrations, the first from the sixth Rebbe and the others from the seventh. In a talk delivered to the gathering of the Aggudat Ḥasidei Ḥabad on 19 Elul 5701 (September 10, 1941), Yosef Yiṣḥaq observed that people who do not know anything about Ḥasidism in general or about Ḥabad Ḥasidism in particular commonly make the error of assuming that kabbalah and Ḥasidism are "one entity expressed in different forms." In an effort to correct this miscalculation, he explained that the former is the study of esoteric matters by a limited group of people, the elect (*yeḥidei segullah*) of a given generation, whereas the latter is about publicizing these secrets to afford every Jew the opportunity of being incorporated into the essence. The Besht̩ provides the model: just as a builder first lays the foundation of the edifice, so he concentrated on teaching children the esoteric truths in a manner that they could apprehend. Like the kabbalah, Ḥasidism is a "deep religious philosophy" that proffers a "comprehensive explanation" of sublime matters, such as the existence of the Creator and the creation of the world, but it is also a way of life that "ignites in the heart of a person a burning flame at the time of the fulfillment of the commandments." The teaching of Ḥabad is the ideal, insofar as it comprises these two purportedly contradictory characteristics, "cold understanding," on the one hand, and "passionate feeling," on the other.[18] The clash, however, is only superficial, for a more profound grasp of the matter sheds light on the fact that the basis for the latter is in the former and that the fruition of the former is in the latter. To accomplish these two objectives, therefore, it was incumbent on the Alter Rebbe, and, in his wake, the other Lubavitch masters, to spread the secrets more widely.

In a letter from 10 Kislev 5711 (November 19, 1950) addressed to Lubavitchers all over the world, several months before assuming his reign as the seventh Rebbe, Schneerson invoked a letter written on the same day in 5710 (December 1, 1949) by the sixth Rebbe, in which he stressed the need for the study of Ḥasidism to extend to every Jew rather than being limited to a small percentage of the population.[19] This message is related, moreover, to the teaching of the Besht to the effect that the wellsprings have to overflow outward as "a preparation and vessel for the coming of the Messiah."[20] Schneerson notes that the key phrase "Your wellsprings will spread outward" (*yafuṣu ma'yenotekha ḥuṣah*) implies three conditions: a. *yafuṣu*—"will spread"—denotes that it is obligatory to broadcast the Ḥasidic doctrines publicly to every place where Torah is studied; b. *ma'yenotekha*—"your wellsprings"—indicates that the teaching must both flow ceaselessly from the source and trickle out drop by drop without concern for quantity; c. *ḥuṣah*—"outward"—suggests that the teaching must be ubiquitous and not confined to the synagogue or to the academy, nor should it be limited to a select group, since it belongs to the totality of the Jewish people.[21] Here in a nutshell is the agenda that Schneerson set for himself based on his belief that the need to diffuse the secrets was augmented in the time of his predecessor, the leader of the generation, given the proximity to the messianic coming. As he put it in a letter from 1 Sivan 5711 (June 5, 1951),

> Now is the time of the footsteps of the Messiah, the footsteps of the footsteps, and in accord with the proclamation of my saintly teacher and father-in-law, Admor, which he said and repeated several times, all that remains to be purified are trifling

> matters, and it is received as well that the vessel for bringing the coming of the Messiah is the dissemination of the wellsprings outward. . . . By means of engagement with the Torah, and especially the light that is in the Torah, which is the teaching of Ḥasidism, the darkness will be transformed into light.[22]

The purpose of the overflow of the wellsprings is the transformation of darkness into light (*ithapkha ḥashokha li-nehora*), however, the increase in the emanation of light is commensurate to the amplification of darkness.[23] Just as the darkness is greatest right before the dawn, the need to propagate secrets is proportionate to the intensification of their concealment. Paradoxically, then, the dark itself is proof of the imminence of redemption,[24] and the more one thinks about the darkness, the more one will think about the light.[25]

Every Jew can and must be engaged in the study of the interiority of the Torah, its secret content, for by so doing, one can comprehend the light of the root of one's soul and thereby bring about the enlightenment that is the messianic era. Since the function of the Messiah is to reveal the mysteries, the instrument appropriate to bring the Messiah is the study of those mysteries.[26] In a letter from 30 Av 5714 (August 29, 1954), Schneerson refers to both Ḥayyim Viṭal and the Gaon of Vilna to substantiate the point that the length of exile is prolonged by the privation of the study of the interiority of the Torah and thus in the seventh generation, the time of the footsteps of the Messiah, it is especially necessary to augment this dimension.[27] In a talk marking the seventh anniversary of the death of his father-in-law, 10 Shevaṭ 5717 (January 12, 1957), Schneerson remarked,

> Thus it is clear that whoever believes in the Beshṭ, and in the words that the Beshṭ heard from the King Messiah, is obligated to believe also that now there are the wellsprings of the Beshṭ, and there is now the matter of the dissemination of the wellsprings—hence he should believe that he may arrive on any day [*ma'amin be-khol yom she-yavo*],[28] verily will the Messiah come [*ot ot kumt moshiach*]. . . . And, consequently, this is clear proof that the holy task of disseminating the wellsprings of the Beshṭ and the leaders after him, so that they shall also spread outward, is incumbent upon each of us, for the coming of the Messiah in actuality here below is dependent on this.[29]

To cite one final example from the talk on 27 Tishrei 5719 (October 11, 1958): "On behalf of the matter of 'Your wellsprings will spread outward,' our rabbis and leaders would dispatch emissaries to different places in order to disseminate the wellsprings of the teaching of Ḥasidism, as it was in each and every generation. And in the last generations—since the Messiah must come immediately [*ot ot darf shoyn moshiach kumen*], and his arrival is dependent on the spreading of the wellsprings outward—this is with an increased distance and magnitude."[30] On occasion Schneerson cited the following zoharic passage, which lends credence to the Ḥabad interpretation of the aforementioned Beshtian epistle: "In the sixth hundredth year of the sixth [millennium],[31] the gates of wisdom above and the fountains of wisdom below will open, and the world will be prepared to enter the seventh, just as a man prepares on the sixth day, as the sun is about to set, to enter the Sabbath . . . and the sign for this is 'In the six hundredth year of Noah's life . . . all the fountains of the great deep burst apart [and the floodgates of the sky broke open]' (Gen 7:11)."[32] In Schneerson's mind, this text confirms the view that the messianic era will be marked by the widespread study of the "wisdom above" (*ḥokhmata le'eila*), the interiority of the wisdom of Torah (*ḥokhmat ha-torah*), together with the proliferation of the "wisdom below" (*ḥokhmata letatta*), the sciences of the world (*ḥokhmot ha-olam*). Whatever criticisms Schneerson leveled against some of the scientific commonplaces in his day, this text demonstrates that he basically follows Maimonides by affirming the value of natural sciences in the pursuit of metaphysical truth. Schneerson, moreover, assumes a homologous relation between the wisdom of Torah above and the sciences of the world below. The Torah of the Messiah, accordingly, will reveal the unity of the divine in the world (*vos iz megalleh achduso shel ha-kadosh barukh hu in velt*), so that "the world itself will be worthy to be a vessel for the unity of the Lord" (*az velt gufa vert a keli tsu achdus ha-shem*).[33] But if his mandate was indeed this unconditional and maximal disclosure of secrets, in what way is esotericism still viable? Needless to say, a discussion of the role of secrecy in Ḥabad cannot be isolated from the larger question of the place accorded this matter in Ḥasidism more generally.[34] In this chapter, however, I necessarily limit my attention to this topic in the religious philosophy promulgated by or in the name of the seventh Rebbe, itself not a small undertaking.

The text that will serve as the springboard for my reflections appears in an unedited discourse of Schneerson for the second day of Shavuot, 7 Sivan 5713 (May 21, 1953). The comments of Schneerson are inspired by the talmudic passage,[35] according to which Judah and Ḥezeqiah, the sons of R. Ḥiyya, were sitting at a table with Rabbi and, after having consumed a significant amount of "strong wine," remarked as follows: "The son of David cannot appear until the two ruling houses in Israel will have come to an end, the Exilarchate in Babylon and the Patriarchate in Palestine." In response to their words, Rabbi exclaimed: "You throw thorns in my eyes, my children!" But R. Ḥiyya comforted his master by reminding him that the numerical value of *yayin* is seventy, which is the numerology of the word *sod* as well. The matter is captured in the proverbial statement, "When wine goes in, the secret comes out," *nikhnas yayin yaṣa sod*, the rabbinic analogue to the Latin epigram *in vino veritas*. Extrapolating from the numerical equivalence of *yayin* and *sod*, Schneerson concluded that wine signifies the disclosure of the concealed. Applying this idea to the aforementioned talmudic passage, the words "son of David" are interpreted figuratively as the "disclosure of the secret that is in the soul," and the word "until" (*ad*) is decoded as a reference to—I assume it should be vocalized as *ed*, that is, the word gives witness to—the "secret that is in the secret" (*sod she-be-sod*), and this is the "essence of the soul" (*eṣem ha-neshamah*).[36] The theme is repeated in a second passage close to the conclusion of this discourse: "The matter of wine is secret, that is, the disclosure of the secret and of the secret within the secret, for this is the essence of the soul that is rooted in the essence."[37] Both the "secret" and the "secret that is in the secret" relate to the ontological status of the soul, but the latter, in particular, underscores that the soul is embedded in the essence of divinity, which is to say, the soul is consubstantial with God. This enrootedness makes possible the unity that is characteristic of the messianic era. Insofar as that time promises discernment of the essence without intermediary, it is reasonable to conclude that the *secret within the secret* is the dimension of Torah most relevant to the epoch of redemption.[38] But what can we say of that secret enfolded in the secret, the unconcealment of what has been concealed in the showing that is the concealment of concealment?

Here it is relevant to note that in some contexts the seventh Rebbe, following the lead of previous Ḥabad masters, invokes a threefold rather than a twofold distinction. Thus, for instance, in a private talk given to the students of Tomkhei Temimim connected to the festival of Ḥanukah 5714 (1953), he noted that the Torah can be compared to water or bread, wine, and oil, which correspond respectively to the exoteric (*galya*), the mysteries (*razin*), and the mysteries of the mysteries (*razin de-razin*), identified further as the "teaching of Ḥasidism."[39] In a discourse delivered years later on 15 Shevaṭ 5744 (January 19, 1984),[40] the day celebrated rabbinically as the new year of the trees, Schneerson again evoked the same threefold distinction, but in that context he cites as his source a discussion in Dov Baer's *Imrei Binah*,[41] where bread symbolically denotes the external sense (*nigleh*), wine, the secret (*sod*, *raz*) or wonder (*pele*) that can be revealed—the disclosure of the essence (*gilluy ha-aṣmut*)—and oil, the concealed secret (*sod satum*), the mystery of mysteries (*raza de-razin*), the esoteric dimension that can never be exposed. The first kind of secret, which is identified further as the "reasons and secrets of the commandments" (*ṭa'amei we-sodot ha-miṣwot*) is to be disclosed in the messianic era, in contrast to the second kind of secret, also called by the zoharic expressions the "hidden wisdom" (*ḥokhma'ah setima'ah*)[42] of *Arikh Anpin*,[43] the "concealed of all the concealed" (*setima de-khol setimin*),[44] or the "head-that-is-not-known" (*reisha de-lo ityeda*),[45] which forever remains shrouded.

Although Schneerson refers to the passage from Dov Baer, his view is actually closer to the account of the threefold distinction found in a discourse of Yosef Yiṣḥaq from 2 Nisan 5689 (April 12, 1929). With a slightly varied emphasis, the sixth Rebbe described the most abstruse layer of meaning, the *razin de-razin*, which is symbolized by oil, as the "hidden wisdom and the matter of mindfulness that is in the soul, to know and to discern the Infinite, which is not known at all by knowledge or comprehension, but rather by the repose of the soul . . . the conjunction of the essence of the soul to the essence of the Infinite, blessed be he."[46] It is noteworthy that the seventh Rebbe accepts the modification of his predecessor in challenging the contention of Dov Baer that there are secrets inherently beyond disclosure. On the contrary, the innermost element of secrecy entails the expansion of consciousness, designated by the technical term *da'at*, which I rendered as "mindfulness," to the point that the soul is bound to the Infinite, a prolepsis of the messianic future. The wine, therefore, figuratively represents the ideal of contemplation (*hitbonenut*) by means of which the concealment is concealed and the essence disclosed in the force of divinity above nature wrapped in the guise that is nature.[47] When it is revealed that there is nothing left to conceal, there is nothing more to reveal, and hence there is no more need to distinguish visible and invisible, external and internal, holy and profane.

In the mind of Schneerson,[48] this is the underlying intent of the talmudic dictum that one must get so inebriated on Purim that it is no longer possible to discern the difference between "cursed is Haman" and "blessed is Mordecai."[49] Just as the consumption of wine on the physical plane brings about the nullification of the senses (*biṭṭul ha-ḥushim*), so, in the spiritual plane, the disclosure of secrets can lead to a state of conjunction (*devequt*) that culminates in the abrogation of one's being (*biṭṭul meṣi'ut*) and the expiration of the soul (*kelot ha-nefesh*).[50] Attentive to the existential danger that might result from an excessive desire to be incorporated in the Infinite, a state that is associated exegetically with Nadab and Abihu, the sons of Aaron who died because "they drew too close to the presence of the Lord" (Lev 16:1),[51] Schneerson emphasized that the highest pietistic ideal accords with the rabbinic description of Aqiva's experience of Pardes, the orchard of speculation, "he entered intact and he exited intact,"[52] that is, one must return to the world, to participate in the reintegration of the souls in their embodiment, to worship in such a manner that one creates a habitation for the divine in the terrestrial realm (*asiyyat dirah lo yitbarakh ba-taḥtonim*).[53] When translated sociologically, the uncovering and distribution of secrets, the ostensible breaking of the code of esotericism, undergirds the mission of Ḥabad, based, as we have seen, on the locution of Proverbs 5:16 paraphrased in the rejoinder of the Messiah to the Beshṭ as reported in the latter's letter to Gershon of Kuṭov, to spread the wellsprings outward (*hafaṣat ha-ma'yanot ḥuṣah*) and to scatter the tenets and practices of Judaism in every corner of the civilized world.[54] The extent to which the conventional kabbalistic hermeneutic of secrecy is supposedly subverted can be gauged from Schneerson's assertion that the custom of the Ḥabad masters was to disseminate knowledge without considering the position or status of the potential recipient and without any preconceived conditions, so that the inner light would be circulated in a manner that would reach every Jew indiscriminately.[55] In this matter as well there is an eschatological overtone, as a distinctive mark of the Messiah is related to his humility and self-negation, character traits that allowed him to teach Torah even to "simple men" (*anashim peshuṭim*).[56] Relying on the observation of his father-in-law,[57] Schneerson distinguished between the "teaching of Ḥasidism in general" and the "teaching of Ḥabad Ḥasidism," for, while the Beshṭ explained that every Jew had the capacity to worship God, it was the Alter Rebbe who explained the mechanics of that worship.[58] As I noted earlier, in the discourse of 21 Kislev 5714 (November 28, 1953), Schneerson, basing himself on earlier sources, including a comment from Shneur Zalman's *Iggeret ha-Qodesh*,[59] gives a historical account of the gradual breaking of kabbalistic esotericism with regard to the study of the interiority of the Torah (*limmud penimiyyut ha-torah*), which began with Isaac Luria, continued with the Beshṭ, and was intensified with the promulgation of matters pertaining to Ḥasidism from the first to the sixth master of Ḥabad.[60] In Schneerson's discourse *Ba'ti le-Ganni* on 10 Shevaṭ 5730 (January 17, 1970), he repeated (as he frequently did through the years) the injunction to reveal the "supernal treasure" (*oṣar ha-elyon*) so that there would be a "dispersion of the wellsprings of the interiority of the Torah outward" (*hafaṣat ha-ma'yanot di-fenimiyyut ha-torah ḥuṣah*).[61] The practical enterprise of propagation, which heralds the aspect of the eternal redemption that is beyond spatial and temporal demarcation,[62] is sustained by the contemplative attainment of spiritual extermination (*biṭṭul ha-yesh*).

In a discourse delivered on Shabbat Ḥanukah, 25 Kislev 5743 (December 11, 1982),[63] Schneerson similarly utilized the distinction between wine and oil to mark the difference between the mysteries of Scripture (*razei de-torah*) and the mysteries of mysteries (*razin de-razin*). In that context, however, the matter is somewhat more complicated, as he tried to synchronize discrete and seemingly conflictual traditions—on the one hand, the view that water is higher than wine, the former correlated symbolically with *Ḥokhmah* and the latter with *Binah*, and, on the other hand, the view that water corresponds to the exoteric meaning and wine to the esoteric. The apparent difficulty is resolved by appeal to the principle that what is highest descends to what is lowest (*de-khol ha-gavoha be-yoter yored lemaṭah yoter*). From one angle, wine is superior to water, as it is by nature connected to the aspect of concealment, but, from another angle, water is superior to wine, as it derives from a source that is even more elevated. What is important to emphasize is the interpretation of the talmudic dictum "When wine goes in, the secret comes out" that Schneerson offered on this occasion: as wine is produced by bringing it out from the grapes in which it was concealed and covered, so through an interpretive endeavor the exegete can bring forth the disclosure of the secret from concealment within the literal body of the text. This applies to the two aspects of the esoteric, the more accessible and the more obscure, the former symbolized by wine and the latter by oil. Just as wine is derived more easily from grapes than oil from olives, so the effort required eliciting the mysteries from the Torah is not as great as what is necessary to adduce the mysteries of mysteries. The mysteries consist of the aspect of "concealment that is proximate to disclosure" (*he'lem ha-qarov le-gilluy*), whereas the mysteries of mysteries are the aspect of "concealment that is not proximate to disclosure" (*he'lem she-eino qarov le-gilluy*).[64] The crucial point is that, ostensibly, Schneerson did not accept the opinion that there are secrets that can never be revealed. To be sure, he still maintains that oil is different from wine, insofar as it is above the aspect of disclosure even after it has been pressed out of the olives—a point that is substantiated by the empirical fact that it is customary to drink the latter but not the former.[65] Nonetheless, the seventh Rebbe plainly affirmed the possibility of exposing the innermost secrets, albeit through an augmented exertion. At least, this is what appears to be the case, what the overt intent of his words conveys:

> From generation to generation, as the darkness is augmented, and consequently, the lassitude increases, we are in greater need of the teaching of Ḥasidism. Therefore, from generation to generation, our masters revealed and publicized more and more of the teaching of Ḥasidism—whether by disseminating Ḥasidism with amplified understanding and comprehension or by the matter of publicizing, for they broadcast this more so that it could reach all the Jews. Therefore, it is understood how enormous is the obligation and how grand is the privilege of each and every person to spread the wellsprings of the teaching of Ḥasidism and the ways of Ḥasidism outwards, for in our generation, when the darkness expands more and more, there is a greater necessity to attain this.[66]

The duty to transmit esoteric wisdom even justifies the use of languages other than Hebrew.[67] There is no challenge to the venerable view that Hebrew is singularly the "sacred language" (*leshon ha-qodesh*), but, for the sake of imparting the wisdom, it is permissible to avail oneself of other languages. The model is the sixth Rebbe, who in the effort to reveal the inwardness of Torah would converse in Hebrew as well as Yiddish, the official exilic language (*golus shprakh*), a custom that was already sanctioned, according to Shneur Zalman, by the Beshṭ.[68] Even more noteworthy is Schneerson's insistence that the vehicle of expression need not be limited to these two languages, but it may also include other diasporic languages, such as English and French, so that the "matters of the inwardness of Torah will reach all Jewry." In this very matter of linguistic investiture, we can discern a crucial aspect of the interplay of concealment and disclosure:

> Even though one draws and brings down in a manner that everyone will be able to understand, on account of which there is a need for a matter of covering and encasing, it is nonetheless a golden overlay,[69] that is, although there is a dispersal with respect to simple matters, this also relates to more lofty matters—all the matters of the teaching of Ḥasidism: not only the revealed [*galya*] that is in Ḥasidism, that is, the contextual [*peshaṭ*], figurative [*remez*], and homiletical [*derush*] that is in Ḥasidism, but also the secret [*sod*] that is in Ḥasidism, the secret within the secret [*sod she-be-sod*], that is, the kabbalistic matters passed on in the teaching of Ḥasidism but not explained—these, too, can be transmitted in other languages, and not only in the sacred language and in Yiddish.[70]

Applying the familiar kabbalistic notion of four levels of meaning in Scripture—*peshaṭ*, *remez*, *derash*, and *sod*, signified by the acrostic *pardes*[71]—to the teaching of Ḥasidism,[72] Schneerson speaks of the "secret within the secret," which he further identifies as the kabbalistic matters that have not yet been openly explicated. To accommodate the need to divulge more and more of the kabbalistic wisdom, so that the disclosure of the essence necessary to bring the Messiah will be realized,[73] it is acceptable to deploy languages other than Hebrew and Yiddish. This would seem to lead inevitably to the conclusion that nothing substantive of the esoteric remains in the seventh Rebbe's pedagogical campaign—it is obligatory to explain the most inscrutable matters in such a way that the simplest of Jews can fathom them.[74] However, before we concede the point, it would be prudent to delve more deeply into the contours of the secret within the secret.

Concealing the Concealment: Contemplation and Intention of the Heart

The nexus of secrecy and the soul is illumined further and much more expansively in another discourse of Schneerson that was delivered on Simḥat Torah, 23 Tishrei 5714 (October 2, 1953). In the context of discussing different expressions of joy during the festivals of Sukkot, Shemini Aṣeret, and Simḥat Torah, Schneerson expounded the virtue of wine as the means that exposes the secret that is concealed in both the human and divine realms:

> You should understand initially the matter of happiness as it is written "[But the vine replied,] 'Have I stopped yielding my new wine, which gladdens God and men'" (Judges 9:13), for wine brings one to happiness as this is the matter of the disclosure of the concealment [*gilluy ha-he'lem*], for just as in corporeality [*gashmiyyut*] wine at first is gathered in its grapes and by means of threshing it comes forth from concealment to disclosure, similarly the function of wine in spirituality [*ruḥaniyyut*] is to disclose the hidden. This is the matter of "When wine goes in, the secret comes out," that is, the function of wine is like the substance of wine . . . at first it is hidden and afterwards it goes forth from concealment to disclosure. Therefore, its function is to disclose the inwardness in the soul that is hidden. And this is the reason why much wine reddens the face, for wine discloses the inner vitality that is concealed, and the hidden blood is revealed in the face. And the matter in this is that in everything there is an interior [*penimiyyut*] and an exterior [*ḥiṣoniyyut*], the interior is that which receives the life-force and efflux from its source and the exterior is the overflow to what is other. This matter is found in all of the four types [of being], the inanimate, the vegetative, the animal, and the rational . . . and, especially in the case of Israel, there is an interior and an exterior, the interior is the divine soul that is conjoined to divinity [*nefesh ha-elohit devuqah ba-elohut*] in the image of the man upon the throne,[75] and the exterior is that which sustains the body. Thus, in the case of Israel, there is also corporeal vitality from the divine soul [*ḥiyyut*

> *ha-guf hu mi-nefesh ha-elohit*], but the interior is concealed, and what is revealed is only the aspect of the exterior that sustains the body. And this is the matter of the wine that discloses the interior, for when wine enters, the secret comes out, that is, the wine reveals the interior of the soul that is conjoined to divinity.[76]

Utilizing a distinction well attested in kabbalistic sources, which has its roots in rabbinic and medieval philosophic texts, all of reality is schematized in terms of the inner and outer binary. All forms of existence—the inanimate, vegetative, animal, and rational—display this twofold comportment, but Schneerson is particularly interested, as we might expect, in the application of this structure to the rational or human being, identified more specifically as Israel. In consonance with the viewpoint affirmed by the author of *Tanya*, and reaffirmed, as far as I can tell, by every other master in the Lubavitch lineage, there is a qualitative difference between the soul of the Jew and the soul of all other ethnicities: the latter possess an animal soul (*nefesh ha-bahamit*), which derives from the aspect of the shell, the demonic other side (*siṭra aḥara*), which is located in the left chamber of the heart, whereas the former is endowed with the divine soul (*nefesh ha-elohit*), the spark that emanates from the light of the Infinite and is located in the brain as well as in the right chamber of the heart.[77] In Schneerson's comments, there is an echo of another idea found in *Tanya* and repeated in other Ḥabad sources: the animal soul of Israel draws its sustenance from the divine soul.[78] The latter is revealed by the former, and, hence, the mystical meaning of the rabbinic dictum "When wine enters the secret comes forth" is that just as in the matter of wine that which is hidden in the grape is revealed, so in the matter of the soul of each Jew the divine spark that is hidden in the body is revealed. The secret of the secret entails discernment that in its most inwardness the soul is conjoined to divinity, which is to say, the soul is consubstantial with God, an insight that significantly closes the ontic gap separating human and divine, a gap typically assumed to be a basic consequence of the monotheistic principle as it has evolved in the course of Jewish history.

In the continuation of the discourse another level of the esotericism is revealed when it is noted that wine alludes to the divine attribute *Binah*, which is connected with the form of worship that is the "matter of contemplation [*inyan ha-*

hitbonenut] through which is disclosed the interiority of the soul that is conjoined to divinity."[79] A distinction is made between two kinds of contemplation: the first is related to the discernment that "all the matters of the world are divine" (*kol inyenei olam hu elohut*) or that "the purpose of the entire world is only the divine" (*takhlit kol ha-olam hu raq elohut*), but there is a superior form that is attained by one who detects that the "essence of the vitality of the world is only from the divine [*she-eṣem ḥiyyut ha-olam hu raq me-elohut*], for the divine potency engenders and sustains the world in every moment and hence all the vitality of the world is only the divine [*ḥiyyut ha-olam hu raq elohut*]." The contemplation that the purpose of the world is divine provides the impetus to live a life of nomian piety centered on the commandments of the Torah, whereas the contemplation that the essence of the vitality of the world is divine arouses a "running back to divinity" (*raṣo le-elohut*), which is expressed through the inculcation of the love and fear of God. Schneerson is quick to point out that the second level of contemplation also relates to fulfillment of the commandments, an idea that is supported by an explicit citation of a passage from *Tanya* where love is depicted as the root of all the 248 positive commandments and fear the root of the 365 negative commandments,[80] a taxonomic classification that can be traced back to thirteenth-century kabbalistic treatises.

The forms of contemplation are aligned with two philosophical approaches with respect to the question of the relationship of God to the world. The former and less theologically dangerous orientation, which corresponds to what is usually called by historians of religion *panentheism*, considers the one reality to be unified in and yet distinct from all matters of the world, and hence everything in the chain of becoming is part of the evolving whole that is the divine source, and the latter is the far more challenging view—what is referred to as *acosmism*[81]—that there is no independent ontic status to the world, that God is the only substance in reality and thus the world in all of its multiplicity and differentiation is negated, since it is but a manifestation of the divine essence. Schneerson (drawing from the vast array of sources available that articulate the intricacies of Ḥabad thought) adds a third level of nondualist discernment, the level that corresponds to the inner secret, the secret of the secret, which transcends both the affirmation of the underlying unity of God in all things implied in the panentheistic mysticism of the first form of contemplation and the paradoxical identity of God and world implied in the acosmic mysticism associated with the second form of contemplation. Insofar as contemplation is a form of apprehending the divine through the forces that are hidden, it follows that when the latter are in a state of limitation (*hagbalah*), contemplation is restricted to the divinity that is present in the procession of being that emanates from the Infinite, or, according to the precise locution of the text, the "order of concatenation" (*seder ha-hishtalshelut*),[82] but when the form of contemplative worship is above the revealed forces, then one attains the state of the "intention of the heart" (*re'uta de-libba*), "contemplation of the mystery of divinity that transcends the order of concatenation." If we are to speak of comprehension connected to this intention of the heart, then it is comprehension of what one does not comprehend, the *via negativa* (*hassagat ha-shelilah*), a well-known motif in medieval philosophic and kabbalistic sources.[83] By apprehending that one cannot apprehend, one comes to experience—the Hebrew used to render what was presumably the original Yiddish is *nirgash*, a term that denotes the intimacy of a sensory feeling—the mystery of divinity (*hafla'at ha-elohut*) and "through this one comes to the intention of the heart, and this is the matter of when wine enters the secret comes out, that is, by means of contemplation in the mystery of divinity, the interiority of the soul is revealed, and this is the matter of the conjunction of the intention of the heart."[84]

In this part of the discourse, the listener/reader is introduced to the esoteric dimension of the nexus between the secret and interiority of the soul. The concealed nature of the latter is revealed through contemplation of the wonder that transcends the ontic chain. The intrinsic correlation of secrecy and the incomprehensible confirms what in my estimation is a feature that has been shared by the different schools of Jewish esotericism that flourished in the middle ages: to express the matter in contemporary philosophical terms, the secret is what cannot be reified, the essence that cannot be essentialized, a movement toward transcendence envisioned as the invisible and declaimed as the ineffable, a transcendence transcended by the transcending of transcendence.[85] Beyond the panentheistic and acosmic insights associated with the two levels of contemplation is the apophatic awareness of the divine enigma, the transcendence that is designated as the conjunction of the intention of the heart (*devequt di-reu'ta de-libba*), a knowing that consists of the unknowing by which the Jewish soul attains the state of being bound to the essence (*hitqashsherut aṣmit*).[86] But how does one know that one does not know? In another unedited discourse from Shabbat Sheqalim, 25 Adar I 5711 (March 3, 1951), Schneerson appropriated the formulation of Shalom Dovber in his own discourse on Shabbat Sheqalim, 29 Adar I 5679 (March 1, 1919), and distinguished two types of the intention of the heart. The critical passage from the RaShaB reads:

> It is known that there are two types of intention of the heart, for there is an intention of the heart that comes about through contemplation, for even though the will is the essential will [*raṣon aṣmi*], the arousal of the will [*hit'orerut ha-raṣon*] nonetheless is by means of contemplation of the light of the Infinite that is above the order of concatenation. . . . And there is an intention of the heart that is in the essence of the soul that does not [come about] through contemplation at all, but it is in the essence of the soul that is conjoined to the essence of the point of the heart [*nequddat ha-lev*].[87]

Repeating these words almost verbatim, Schneerson affirms that "there is the aspect of the intention of the heart that comes about through contemplation, for even though it is beyond comprehension, it nonetheless emerges from contemplation, and there is an aspect of the intention of the heart that does not come about through contemplation but it is in the essence of the soul that is attached to the essence of the point of the heart."[88] The aspect of soul of which he speaks was not thought to be shared universally by all human beings, but it is described rather as the "point of Judaism [*nequddat ha-yahadut*] that is in each and every one from Israel, which is bound to the essence."[89] The utilization of the image of the dot to characterize the soul that is unique to the Jew is meant to underscore a spatial delimitation that is nevertheless beyond spatialization and delimitation, as punctiformity cannot be expressed protractedly even if we presume the point to be the beginning of all extensionality. The "Jewish point," *nequddat ha-yahadut*,[90] which renders the Yiddish *dos pintele yid*, is to be construed ontologically and semiotically, that is, it is the marker—the *yid* no doubt must be also read as *yod*, the punctiform letter that is the beginning of both the name YHWH and the word *yehudi*—of the divine aspect of the soul (*nefesh elohit*) that surpasses the horizon of reason, and it also signifies the conjunction of the Jew to the light of *Ein Sof*, a monopsychic state that summons the eradication of ontic difference, *biṭṭul ha-yesh*, a blurring of the boundary between finite and infinite.[91]

The full intent of what is implied here can only be gainsaid by proper philological attunement to the key expression *re'uta de-libba*, an idiom derived from several zoharic passages,[92] two of which are most important for understanding the Ḥabad usage: in one instance, the "intention of the heart" is described as the internal state of mental concentration that is connected with "worship of the soul" (*ovada de-nafsha*), which is contrasted with "worship of the body" (*ovada de-gufa*), also identified as "ritual worship" (*ovada de-miṣwah*).[93] The second instance is an explanation of the traditional liturgical gesture of saying the words "O Lord, open my lips," *adonai sefatai tiftaḥ* (Ps 51:17), prior to the Amidah prayer: "Here is the purpose of the intention of the heart, to elevate the will from below to above until the Infinite [*lesalqa re'uta mi-tatta le'eila ad ein sof*]."[94]

The expression is appropriated by Ḥabad masters to demarcate the highest level of consciousness that transcends thought, intellect, and even the will.[95] To cite a few examples: in a passage from *Torah Or*, the anthology of Shneur Zalman's discourses on Genesis, Exodus, and Esther committed to writing by his brother, Judah Leib of Yanovitch, and compiled by his grandson, Menaḥem Mendel Schneersohn (1789–1866), commonly referred to as the Ṣemaḥ Ṣedeq,[96] *re'uta de-libba* is described as the "disclosure of the light of the Infinite in the extinction of the will in relation to the will of the blessed One" (*gilluy or ein sof be-viṭṭul ha-raṣon le-raṣon yitbarakh*),[97] that is, the complete nullification of the finite will in the infinite will of the Absolute, a state of affairs that he characterizes in *Tanya* (and elsewhere) as the supreme form of love that ensues from the immeasurable greatness of the essence.[98] Expanding this theme in a homily included in *Liqquṭei Torah*, Shneur Zalman writes:

> The aspect of the interiority of the heart [*penimiyyut ha-lev*] is the intention of the heart [*re'uta de-libba*] and the mysteries of the heart [*ta'alumot ha-lev*] that are way beyond reason and knowledge apprehended and comprehended through the agency of the comprehension of the soul and its intellection, and it is the aspect of divinity [*beḥinat elohut*] in the soul that is revealed in the aspect of *yeḥidah* . . . and

> this illumination is from the aspect of that which surrounds all worlds [*sovev kol almin*] . . . that is, he, blessed be he, is alone as before the world was created, and he is not in the category of worlds at all, and the aspect of the concatenation is not relevant to him at all. . . . And there is the root of the point of the interiority of the heart [*shoresh nequddat penimiyyut ha-lev*], inasmuch as the love of the Lord is above the aspect of reason and knowledge in the aspect of the intention of the heart.[99]

In the formulation of his son, Dov Baer, *re'uta de-libba* signifies the act of spiritual martyrdom (*mesirat nefesh*), the annihilation of the individual in the "point of the simple will" (*nequddat ha-raṣon ha-pashuṭ*), that is, the will that does not allow for any differentiation or individuation, the will through which the essence and substance of the incomprehensible is realized in the quietistic experience of self-abnegation.[100]

Schneerson's use of the term draws upon this rich philological and conceptual background—and, needless to say, there are many other relevant texts that I could have cited. The crucial point for our purposes is the use he makes of this complex of themes to articulate the nature of the secret. For him the secret is not merely a cognitive or epistemological term, that which we cannot know or that which we must conceal from others, nor is it simply an ontological term, the designation of the mystery of being that is indecipherable by the human mind; it is rather what I will call a meontological concept that at once affirms the transcendence of God and affords the mechanism by which that transcendence is transcended. The secret of the secret, or what is sometimes designated on the basis of the zoharic locution the "concealed of all the concealed" (*setima de-khol setimin*),[101] alludes to the limitless beyond all quantitative delimitation, the facet of *Keter*, in some contexts identified graphically as the skull (*gulgolet*), which comprises the light of the Infinite that is above the theistic aspect of God designated by the technical language for divine transcendence "encompassing all worlds" (*sovev kol almin*), which is set in contrast to the phrase that denotes divine immanence "filling all worlds" (*memalle kol almin*).[102] Even though the boundless cannot be constricted within any of the four worlds that make up the different planes of reality, it is compressed in all its vastness within the point of the heart, the essence of the soul conjoined to and completely eradicated within the light of the Infinite through the act of self-sacrifice (*mesirat nefesh*) that is above the intellect.[103] In the final analysis, as Shneur Zalman had already taught, messianic deliverance comes about through love of God, the "worship of the heart," which issues from the "aspect of the point of the inwardness of the heart." Insofar as the essence lodged within the "depth of the heart" (*umqa de-libba*) is "beyond the aspect of knowledge" (*lema'lah mi-beḥinat ha-da'at*), it follows that the Messiah, who symbolically represents the "disclosure of the aspect of that universal inner point" (*gilluy beḥinat nequddah penimit ha-kelalit*), comes when one is unaware, literally, "when knowledge is removed" (*be-hessaḥ ha-da'at*).[104] Explicating this matter, Schneerson remarked,

> It is necessary to know that we stand on the boundary of the land of Israel, and through one's power and one's capability, in one moment and in one second, one can enter the land of Israel in the true and complete redemption—by means of revealing the point of the inwardness of the heart . . . for this is the matter of the redemption and the coming of the particular Messiah in each and every Jew . . . and, consequently, when one reveals the point of the inwardness of one's heart, and all of the Jews do as well, then the general redemption in the coming of the Messiah will be realized in actuality.[105]

Secrecy, Circumcision, and the Meontological Overcoming of Nature

In a discourse delivered on 16 Kislev 5729 (December 7, 1968), the threefold distinction that I have elicited from the earlier source is reiterated. In that context, the focus is on three gradations of love, which correspond to different types of worship: the first gradation is the love that proceeds from "contemplation of the greatness of the Lord that is manifest in the existence of created beings" and the second and more elevated gradation is the love that proceeds from "contemplation of the mystery of the light of the Infinite." Neither of these forms of love apprehends the essence of the divine, since both fall under the category of comprehension (*hassagah*), even though the latter is not a matter of positive knowledge (*yedi'at ha-ḥiyyuv*) but a matter of negative knowledge (*yedi'at ha-shelilah*).

That which thought cannot grasp is comprehended by the intention of the heart, the third level of love that transcends the love ensuing from contemplation, the "essential will that is above reason and knowledge" (*rașon așmi she-lema'lah mi-ța'am wa-da'at*).[106] The intention of the heart is illustrated by the image of the love of the father for a son, an "essential love" that does not come by way of contemplation, a love that is an "essential bond from the side of the essence of the soul."[107] This level of love is beyond the panentheistic and acosmic perspectives, which are associated with the two forms of contemplation; indeed one who has attained this state (though neither the word *one* nor *state* is particularly helpful or appropriate to describe this form of love, which is the love of God with all one's might according to the formulation of Deut 6:5) moves beyond the world itself as the inexhaustible and ineffable will in its inessentiality—the essence whose essence it is to resist being essentialized—is completely removed from the chain of becoming. Often Schneerson expressed this point by utilizing a time-honored play on words, especially cherished by Ḥabad thinkers, the world (*ha-olam*) is a place of concealment (*he'lem*),[108] for the divinity is hidden within the cloak of corporeality. I shall delve more deeply into this topic in the following chapter, but let me here note one passage wherein a contrast is drawn between the two months in which the new year is celebrated, the first month of Nisan and the seventh month of Tishrei, the former, which is the aspect of mercy (*ḥesed*), "instructs about the disclosure of the name YHWH," whereas the latter, which is the attribute of *Malkhut* constructed from the aspect of strength (*gevurah*), indicates that "the light is in concealment" (*ha-or hu be-he'lem*). *Malkhut*, therefore, is the "aspect of concealment" (*beḥinat ha-he'lem*) that is manifest in contingent beings.[109] One who can see beneath the veil discerns the light, which is "beyond nature" and "above the worlds,"[110] in the varied material forms of the cosmos, but the light is rendered visible through the veil precisely because it is veiled therein—in the zoharic formulation cited repeatedly by Ḥabad thinkers, "and everything before Him is considered as naught" (*we-kholla qameih ke-lo ḥashivin*).[111] In its true substance, the light is the "essential hiddenness" (*he'lem ha-așmi*),[112] the hiddenness that is the essence that betrays no essence as it is the unity beyond differentiation and, therefore, beyond unity, a concealment that can be revealed only to the extent that it is concealed.

Drawing on a symbolic notion found in much older sources, including his predecessors in the Lubavitch dynasty, Schneerson aligns the ontological structure with the number seven and the meontological surplus with the number eight. The mathematical correlation supplies the context to articulate the matter of secrecy as it relates specifically to circumcision, which is linked to mystery and is to be performed on the eighth day. The critical passage is the beginning of the discourse delivered on Shabbat Teshuvah, 8 Tishrei 5723 (October 6, 1962), an appropriate setting given the thematic connection established (already by the Alter Rebbe[113]) between circumcision of the flesh, removing the foreskin of the heart (Deut 10:16), and repentance:

> "No man shall be in the Tent of Meeting when [Aaron] goes in to make expiation in the Shrine" (Lev 16:17). In the Yerushalmi it is [stated] even those about whom it is written "the image of their face was the image of a human" (Ezek 1:10).[114] The Ṣemaḥ Ṣedeq explained in his discourse, which begins "This," that the disclosure that comes forth when the high priest entered the Holy of Holies is the disclosure of that which is above the concatenation. As it is [written] in the midrash[115] on the verse "Through this Aaron shall enter [into the Shrine]" (Lev 16:3), by means of what merit did Aaron enter into the Holy of Holies? The merit of circumcision accompanied him, and circumcision was given on the eighth, for the eighth is above the concatenation. And as it is [written] in the midrash[116] on the verse "The secret of the Lord is with those who fear him" (Ps 25:14). What is the "secret of the Lord"? Circumcision. The disclosures of the concatenation are from the revealed aspect [*galya*] of the blessed holy One, but the disclosure that ensues on account of circumcision is from the concealed aspect [*satim*] of the blessed holy One, and therefore it is called the "secret of the Lord" [*sod yhwh*], for the secret is what is hidden and concealed [*de-sod hu mah she-hu satum we-ne'lam*]. When the high priest entered the Holy of Holies, the disclosure of the secret of the Lord came forth. Hence, even those about whom it is written "the image of their face was the image of a human" were not there, for with respect to this disclosure there is no place for created beings, not even for the angels whose face is that of a human.[117]

The nexus of circumcision and secrecy is an archaic motif enunciated in classical rabbinic literature and expanded considerably in medieval kabbalah. In line with the older sources, augmented by a vast array of Ḥabad texts, Schneerson utilizes this cluster of themes to articulate the inherently duplicitous (in the two-fold sense of doubling and dissimulating) dialectic of esotericism: the disclosure that is induced by the cut of circumcision is from the aspect of the concealment of God, which is the secret of the Tetragrammaton,[118] for the secret must be revealed as hidden if it is the secret that is hidden as revealed. The point is conveyed by Schneerson's comment that when the high priest entered the Holy of Holies the disclosure of the secret of the Tetragrammaton takes place, a disclosure of what is not manifest or expressed, that is, the disclosure of the concealment that is perforce a concealment of the disclosure.

The nature of the esoteric is clarified further by the link that is forged between mystery and the number eight, which signifies both spatial and temporal transcendence. The command to perform circumcision on the eighth day, therefore, is explained theurgically as the means to facilitate the disclosure of the "foundation of the primordial anthropos" (*yesod de-adam qadmon*), the source of the rectification (*shoresh ha-tiqqun*) within the light of the Infinite,[119] which is mythically identified as Hadar, the eighth of the Edomite kings delineated in Gen 36:31–39,[120] the only one whose death is not mentioned and whose spouse, Meheṭabel, is specified. This gradation, moreover, alludes symbolically to the messianic harp, which consists of eight strings,[121] and thus the revelation prompted by this rite anticipates the fusion of the concealed and the revealed that will be fully realized in the future.[122] I shall return to this amalgam of images in the conclusion of the book, but what is critical to emphasize at this juncture is that circumcision is the vehicle through which the Jew (it behooves me to note, parenthetically, that apologetic excuses notwithstanding, the Jewish male is obviously privileged, even if one protests that symbolically the act is feminizing, not in the sense of a castration but in the exposure of the crown that anticipates the superior status of the female to be attained in the eschaton) is bound to the essence that transcends the natural order of space and time. From that vantage point, circumcision supersedes even the most sacred of divine names, since it is equated with Torah, and Torah represents the condensation of the limitless light into delimited form. As Shneur Zalman expressed it, "Circumcision is above the name YHWH . . . and above the aspect of Torah, which lowers itself below. . . . And thus the rabbis, blessed be their memory, said 'Great is circumcision, for thirteen covenants were decreed in relation to it.'[123] . . . In order for there to be the disclosure and emanation of the aspect of circumcision . . . it is by means of the thirteen attributes of mercy, which are above wisdom and intellect, and therefore it is above the aspect of the name YHWH, and above the aspect of Torah."[124] Hence, by means of circumcision, which is related to the eighth day, the high priest was able to enter the Holy of Holies on Yom Kippur wherein he performed eight sprinklings (*hazzayot*) of the sacrificial blood, one above and seven below.[125] The one above symbolizes the "disclosure of the unity that is unified with the essence" (*gilluy ha-yeḥidah she-hi meyuḥedet im ha-aṣmut*), and the seven below the "disclosure of the unity that emanates in the revealed forces, the concatenation that is in man" (*gilluy ha-yeḥidah yumshakh be-khoḥot ha-gilluyim hishtalshelut she-ba-adam*).[126] The import of the number eight and Yom Kippur is underscored by the fact that it is the eighth day after Rosh ha-Shanah, the last of the ten days of repentance (*aseret yemei teshuvah*). The number eight is also linked to and sheds light on the phenomenon of repentance, an idea buttressed by the citation of two talmudic dicta, repentance brings healing to the world[127] and healing is fixed on the eighth day.[128] Just as the number eight represents that which is above nature, the meta-physical, so repentance, and especially the repentance associated with Yom Kippur, is a matter that exceeds the parameter of the physical universe. The mystical efficacy of penitence is expressed in the fact that by repenting one can atone for transgressive acts that are punishable by the strict letter of the law. Contrition results in forgiveness, which has the power to turn one thing into its opposite, to transform demerits into merits, and thus it must be rooted in a divine gradation that is beyond the binary of guilt and innocence, that is, above the polarity of good and evil that is integral to the revealed aspect (*nigleh*) of the Torah and the commandments. By contrast, the concealed aspect (*nistar*) discloses the hypernomian,[129] an elocution that is a precise rendering of a phrase used by Schneerson to label the superior form of piety, *lema'lah mi-torah u-miṣwot*.[130] In chapter 4, I shall delve into the matter of hypernomianism and the transvaluation of the law in Schneerson's conception of the messianic Torah. Suffice it here to underscore that the lower form of worship, which is dependent on and reinforces the dichotomous structure of traditional ritual behavior or the exoteric (*nigleh*), facilitates the subjugation (*itkafya*) of evil to good, but the higher form of worship, which is identified as the intention of the heart and corresponds to the esoteric (*nistar*),[131] entails the transubstantiation (*ithapkha*) of evil into good. This is the clandestine import of the tradition (attributed to R. Eleazar) that all of the holidays with the exception of Purim would be abrogated in the messianic era.[132] Purim alone will be celebrated in the future, for this holiday signifies on the spiritual plane the transformation of one thing into its antinomy, the hypernomian ideal encapsulated in the scriptural motto *we-nahafokh hu*, "and the opposite happened" (Esther 9:1).[133]

The consummate expression of the conflation of opposites is the dictum (transmitted in the name of Reish Laqish) that repentance has the power to transpose blameworthy acts (*zedonot*) into meritorious acts (*zekhuyyot*),[134] a transposition that is associated with Yom Kippur, the day of atonement, when transgressions of the contrite are wiped away, as repentance (when it is done from the standpoint of the love of God, *teshuvah me-ahavah*) has the capacity to "transform evil entirely to the good in actuality" (*ha-ra nehpakh legamrei lihyot ṭov mammash*).[135] This point is enhanced, additionally, by the idea suggested in a passage from *Tiqqunei Zohar* that the expression *yom kippurim* should be decoded as *yom ke-purim*, "a day like Purim."[136] That Yom Kippur will be rendered analogous to Purim implies that the latter is superior to the former. Both days demand self-sacrifice (*mesirat nefesh*), a form of worship (*avodah*) that is above reason and knowledge, but, in the case of Yom Kippur, this is carried out through ascetic renunciation, whereas, in the case of Purim, it is realized through sensual indulgence.[137] The excessive joviality is a ceremonial enactment of the philosophical principle of the coincidence of opposites, as Purim inhabits the place within the divine economy where the spiritual and material converge in the sameness of their divergence. Translated ethnically, if the distinction between Jew and non-Jew (typologized respectively by Mordecai and Haman) is no longer operative, the claim to Israel's chosenness is seriously compromised.[138] Subversively interpreting a dictum attributed to R. Joshua ben Qorḥah, "From the day that Moses died, no prophet arose and innovated a commandment for Israel except for the commandment of Purim, but the redemption of Egypt is celebrated in seven days and the redemption of Mordecai and Esther is celebrated for only one day,"[139] Schneerson remarked that Purim will be observed "in all times and in all periods without distinctions, since it is derived from the aspect of 'one day' [*yom eḥad*], which is the matter of the unity [*aḥdut*] above."[140] The redemption associated with Purim, consequently, is rendered superior to the exodus from Egypt, as the festival that commemorates the latter is celebrated over a seven-day period, which symbolizes the division of worldly time, whereas the former is celebrated on one day, a temporal signpost for the timeless time, the time before time, that is, the nonserial time that precedes the chronological splintering of time into past, present, and future.

Purim ritually embodies the utopian principle of the "departure from measurement and boundary" (*yeṣi'ah mi-medidah we-hagbalah*),[141] as its spiritual basis is the hypernomian gesture of "self-sacrifice from the perspective of the essence of the soul that is entirely above knowledge."[142] A cardinal feature of Ḥasidism is to emphasize that all acts of pious devotion require joy, and this is especially so with regard to holidays according to the scriptural mandate (Deut 16:11, 14), but Purim is distinguished by the commandment to be exceptionally cheerful, to celebrate with an exultation that is "above measurement, boundary, and the human intellect," a jubilation that is "from the perspective of the essence of the soul, which is above reason and knowledge."[143] In this regard, Purim proleptically enacts the final redemption, the messianic moment marked by the carnivalesque undermining of the binaries necessary to the nomian axiology.[144] In nondifferentiated unity, guilt is registered as innocence. Typical of Ḥabad, the profound mystical truth is instantiated in the seemingly trivial custom (already mentioned above) to drink wine on Purim to the point that it is no longer possible to discern the difference between "blessed is Mordecai" and "cursed is Haman." Precisely on account of the overcoming of binary opposition does Purim qualify as the quintessential ritual parody of the lawful liberation from law, the ascendancy of the material/feminine over the spiritual/masculine, themes to be discussed in greater detail in the ensuing chapters. Schneerson draws the appropriate consequences of the hypernomian basis and purpose of this festival:

> Even though the matter of Purim is above measurement and boundary, it extends below to matters of eating and drinking, "days of feasting and merrymaking, and an occasion for sending gifts" (Esther 9:22), "one must eat meat and drink wine"[145] . . . for through this is expressed the superiority of Purim vis-à-vis Yom ha-Kippurim,

that is, Purim is the pattern of the future-to-come. And from this we can also understand what is related to the gesture of Purim during the whole year—for the matters above measurement and boundary extend below to the extreme, literally, to the matters of eating and drinking.[146]

Torah as Primordial Parable: Deferral and Retracing Literal Metaphoricity

Prima facie, it would seem that the seventh Rebbe's kabbalah is predicated on a dramatic debunking of esotericism, as he was committed to a categorical dissemination of the secrets of tradition in the hope of preparing the way for the messianic end-time, which will be marked by the complete disclosure of all that has been hidden, the breaking of the final seal of mystery in the concealment of the concealment. And yet, given the conception of Torah affirmed by the Ḥabad masters, it is not possible to speak of a total dissolution of the code of secrecy. Something of the secret must persist if it is maintained that the core text, the textual incarnation of the divine light, reveals by concealing that which is revealed, so that it conceals by revealing that which is concealed. The tone was already set in a passage from Shneur Zalman's *Liqquṭei Amarim*, the first section of *Tanya*: "As it says in the *Zohar*,[147] 'the Torah and the blessed holy One are entirely one,' that is, the Torah is the wisdom and will of the blessed holy One, and the blessed holy One is unified in his glory and in his essence, for he is the knower, the knowledge, [and the known], as we wrote above in the name of the Rambam.[148] But the blessed holy One is called Infinite, 'his greatness cannot be fathomed' (Ps 145:3) and 'thought cannot grasp him at all.'"[149] The final assertion is paired with the identification of Torah and God, a belief that has been endorsed axiomatically by kabbalists since the thirteenth century, though there is solid textual evidence that it is indeed much older. In kabbalistic lore, as I have already briefly noted, the equation of God and Torah is corollary to two further identifications, God and the name, on one hand, and the name and Torah, on the other. What is crucial for our purposes is Shneur Zalman's utilization of this equation to distinguish between the aspect of the divine essence that is garbed in the Torah and the aspect that is not garbed; the apophatic utterance, "thought cannot grasp him at all" (*leit maḥashavah tefisa beih kelal*), drawn from a discourse on the nature of God placed in the mouth of Elijah in the introduction to *Tiqqunei Zohar*,[150] applies only to the latter, for when the essence is garbed in the Torah, it can be comprehended. Indeed, this act of enclothing (*hitlabbeshut*), epitomized in the zoharic sentiment that God and Torah are one, is the kabbalistic way of articulating the theopoetic mystery of incarnation, the paradox of the delimitation of the limitless, the ideational underpinning of the halakhic basis for the mystical ideal of *devequt*, communion with and conjunction to the divine through implementation of the commandments.[151]

Shneur Zalman alludes to this secret in a passage from *Sha'ar ha-Yiḥud we-ha-Emunah*, published as the second part of *Tanya*, "the source of vitality [*meqor ha-ḥiyyut*] is the spirit of the mouth of the blessed holy One, which is garbed in the ten sayings that are in the Torah."[152] Based on much older sources, the ten sayings of the Torah are correlated with the ten *sefirot*, which collectively make up the name (YHWH) by which the nameless is declaimed. The statement that the spirit (*ruaḥ*) is garbed in the ten sayings of the Torah is another way of expressing the idea that the light is configured in the ten emanations of the Godhead. Elsewhere in the writings that preserve Shneur Zalman's teaching, the Torah is portrayed as the vessel through which the "light of the intellect" (*or ha-sekhel*) is revealed, in which the "letters of thought" (*otiyyot ha-maḥashavah*), that is, the letters prior to any oral or written gesticulation, assume form through the "permutation of the letters of the word" (*ṣerufei otiyyot ha-dibbur*).[153] The ultimate source of the letters is the "supernal word" (*dibbur elyon*), spoken as written and written as spoken, through which the infinite light is first manifest.[154] Commenting on the provocative opening to the *Zohar*, "In the beginning of the will of the King, he engraved the engravings in the supernal luster,"[155] Shneur Zalman remarked that "the source of the letters is in *Keter* and the letters themselves in *Ḥokhmah*, that is, the disclosure of everything . . . and thus it is in all the worlds and in all the gradations up to the highest of gradations, for each and every thing is called by the aspect of letters, and there is an aspect of the letters of the Infinite [*beḥinat otiyyot ein sof*] as well, and they are also called the disclosure of the Infinite [*ha-gilluy shel ha-ein sof*]. Therefore, it is necessary for the letters to elevate the intellect and by means of them the intellect will change."[156]

All of reality can be viewed from this hyperlinguistic orientation—the substance of everything, from the highest to the lowest manifestation of the one essence, consists of the permutation of the letters, which articulate and thereby incarnate the word or wisdom of the divine, which is, when cosmically cast, the light of the intellectual overflow.[157] The letters, consequently, are grist for the mill of contemplation, that is, the elevation and transformation of intellect comes by way of meditating on the letters, the veils that reveal the light by concealing the light. This is the intent of the reference to "letters of the Infinite." How could letters demarcate the Infinite? It is not enough, philosophically speaking, to locate the letters in the "terminus" and "lowest gradation" of the light of the Infinite.[158] First, it is not clear that we can assign meaning to speaking of an end and nadir within the light of the Infinite, the light that is presumed to be above distinction and partition. Second, even if we conjectured that we could account for this reasonably, we are still left with a thought pattern that behooves us to affix a point of crossing the periphery, a point that is positioned between the infinite and the finite, a point that escapes our ability to know or to name, the transcendent signifier, which is perforce without sign, other than perhaps as the sign that eludes signification.[159] The conception of letters in the Infinite, the distinguishing marks of the indistinguishable, brings the mind to the brink of just such a paradox.

Influenced by the version of Lurianic kabbalah advanced by Israel Sarug and mediated through the *Emeq ha-Melekh* of Naftali Bachrach, Shneur Zalman remarked that the letters are the trace (*reshimu*) that is left behind in the space (*ḥalal*) after the removal (*histallequt*) of the light. The trace marks both the absence and presence of that of which it is a trace—even if that is nothing but a trace—and hence the letters are compared to a garment that simultaneously reveals and conceals the essential hiddenness.[160] How else could the hiddenness, which is deemed essential, be revealed except as concealed? It is in this sense that we can attempt to take hold of the notion of letters within the Infinite—the trace of light envisioned from the light of the trace. According to the striking formulation of Dov Baer, the mystery consists of knowing the "aspect of the letters of the primordial Torah [*otiyyot ha-torah ha-qedumah*] that is in the essence of the Infinite in actuality [*be-aṣmut ein sof mammash*]."[161] Elaborating this theme in a second context, he identifies the "supernal brain that is before the curtain that divides" (*moaḥ ila'ah she-lifnei ha-parsa ha-mafsiq*)[162] as the "aspect of the holy Torah that at first was actually comprised in his essence, blessed be he," the "light that illumines the essence of the Infinite, blessed be he," the "light of the essence of Torah," which is arrayed in a garment (*nitlabbesh bi-levush*) that is called the "primordial parable" (*meshal ha-qadmoni*).[163] Before the curtain[164] was formed—a mythopoeic way to account philosophically for the division within the indivisible that is the effect of the primary withdrawal (*ṣimṣum ha-ri'shon*)—the light of the Torah was incorporated in the essence of the Infinite (*aṣmut ein sof*) or the light of the Infinite (*or ein sof*), the indivisible will (*raṣon pashuṭ*) that is the source of life (*meqor ḥayyim*) of all that comes to be in the chain of becoming.[165]

Ḥabad cosmology builds on the platform of the Lurianic interpretation of the beginning as the contraction of the infinite origin that begets the space (*ḥalal*) devoid of itself, the vacuum that comes to be as what must have already been within the plenum, as the plenum, by definition, cannot not be but all-comprehensive, and hence it must comprehend in the nothingness of its being even the being of its nothingness. In the beginning, the light of the essence (*or ha-aṣmut*) is garbed in a garment that is the primordial parable of the Torah, the mantle of the name through which the nameless is revealed to the degree that it is concealed.[166] I note, in passing, that a likely source for Dov Baer's image is the comment of the eleventh-century exegete, Solomon ben Isaac (Rashi), to the expression *meshal ha-qadmoni* in 1 Samuel 24:14: "The primordial parable of the world is the Torah, which is the parable of the blessed holy One." But more to the point than Rashi's interpretation of the scriptural expression is its adaptation by Shneur Zalman:

> The Torah is also garbed in letters, for the source of the letters of the Torah is above the aspect of the Torah. The Torah comes forth from *Ḥokhmah*, and the source of the letters is above in the aspect of *Keter* . . . and the Torah is called the "primordial parable" [*meshal ha-qadmoni*] . . . for the matter of the parable is to analogize what is rendered parabolic in a manner that it will be understood from the parable [*inyan ha-mashal hu lehamshil et ha-nimshal be-ofen she-yuvan mi-tokh ha-mashal*]. The parable is thus another matter that is not the substance of what is rendered parabolic [*ha-mashal hu inyan aḥer she-eino mahut ha-nimshal*], but what is rendered parabolic is understood from it since it is comparable to it in some respect. And this

> is what is written "and through the prophets I was imaged' [*u-ve-yad ha-nevi'im adammeh*] (Hos 12:11). And the sages, blessed be their memory, compared the prophetic vision [*mar'eh ha-nevu'ah*] to a speculum [*aspaqlaryah*], for just as when one sees in a speculum it appears actually so in the likeness of the form, its semblance and its image, but it is not actually the body of the form itself. . . . Thus every comprehension of the prophets of the divinity, blessed be he, is naught but the aspect of likeness and image, and just like a parable whence is understood what is rendered parabolic. With respect to divinity, however, it says "no man shall see me and live" (Exod 33:20).[167]

The Torah displays the twofold structure of the parable, an outer shell revealing an inner core, albeit by concealing it. Rooted in older kabbalistic doctrine, Shneur Zalman inscribes the hermeneutical paradigm in an incarnational theology. The image of the "primordial parable," *meshal ha-qadmoni*, conveys the idea that the Torah is the parable of the "primal One of the world" (*qadmono shel olam*), identified further as the "light of the Infinite, blessed be he, in itself," the single and distinctive One (*eḥad u-meyuḥad*) signified by the essential name YHWH, the One "that was, is, and will be concurrently, above place and above time" (*hayah howeh we-yihyeh ke-eḥad lema'lah min ha-maqom u-lema'lah min ha-zeman*).[168] In order for there to be something other than nothing, a "life-force for the worlds" (*ḥiyyut le-olamot*), the illumination that springs from the Infinite breaks into the binary of an "encompassing light" (*or maqqif*) that "surrounds all worlds" (*sovev kol almin*) and an "inner light" (*or penimi*) that "fills all worlds" (*memalle kol almin*).[169] The equation of God and Torah, the cornerstone of what I have elsewhere called "textual embodiment" and "poetic incarnation,"[170] is depicted in these parabolic terms to indicate that the Torah both remains other to the light it incarnates and serves as the medium through which that light is refracted in the limbs of the name, the letters of the Hebrew alphabet, which materialize differently on each of the worlds or planes of reality. As the parable of the primordial One, who cannot be represented, the Torah is the image of the imageless and thus preserves the sense of difference it attempts to bridge. It is, we might say, the pretext, the showing that conceals in the very manner that it reveals. The mythopoeic axiom that God and Torah are identical—so central to the kabbalistic imaginary—presupposes that disparate matters are juxtaposed in the (dis)semblance of the name incarnate. In that respect, the Torah as primordial parable points to the inherent metaphoricity of language, the convergence of the literal and the figurative.[171] The insight was voiced by Shmuel Schneersohn (1834–1882), the fourth Lubavitcher Rebbe:

> The matter of the garment is that the Torah is called the "primordial parable," for it is the parable to comprehend the aspect of the primal One of the world. The matter is that in order to apprehend an unfathomable conception, it is arrayed in a parable, for, even though the parable garbs and hides the conception, by means of the parable we understand the idea and without the parable we could not understand it at all. In this way, we can understand the matter of the Torah as the parable for the primal One of the world, which is within it, and by means of it the comprehension of divinity can be comprehended.[172]

Reiterating this view, the seventh Rebbe taught in the discourse *Ba'ti le-Ganni*, on 10 Shevaṭ 5726 (January 31, 1966), "Therefore the Torah is called 'parable' because it is like this conception that is concealed from its own perspective and it can be revealed only in a concealed manner."[173] The Torah is the primordial parable as it reveals the innately concealed essence of the primal One by concealing it, for, had it not been concealed, it could not have been revealed as the essence that is concealed. Schneerson avows the duplicity of esotericism that has informed the kabbalistic hermeneutic from early on, the belief that the exposure of the secret, if it is the secret that is exposed, must itself be secretive, and hence the replication of secrecy is guaranteed, even when—indeed, especially when—the secret is fully exposed, and, consequently, the concealment as such is concealed.[174]

Let us recall the distinction that Schneerson made in a talk from the last day of Passover, 22 Nisan 5712 (April 17, 1952), between two kinds of miracle: "miracles that are above nature" (such as the turning of water into blood or the splitting of the Red Sea) and "miracles that are cloaked in the ways of nature." This distinction is, in part, based on the taxonomy of the "hidden miracle" that can be traced to Naḥmanides: complementing open miracles, there are miracles that occur in nature and thus occlude their miraculous nature.[175] Schneerson insists on a further distinction, miracles garbed in natural phenomena but discerned as miracles (such as those of Purim and Ḥanukah) and miracles so deeply masked in the garments of nature that they are not even discerned as miracles. The source of the miracles garbed entirely in nature is higher than the source of the miracles that are beyond nature; the former embraces the paradox of the infinite light being disclosed in the finite, whereas the latter entails a disclosure that obliterates the finite; the miracles garbed in nature in such a manner that their miraculous character is not detected arise from the highest place within the Godhead, the utmost singularity of the divine, which we can determine only in its indeterminacy (based on the description of God in Ps 136:4 as the one "who alone works great marvels" *le'oseh nifla'ot gedolot levaddo*).[176] From this we may adduce the principle that the profoundest mystery is the mystery that is not acclaimed as a mystery, the occlusion that occludes itself by seeming to have nothing to occlude. This crucial hermeneutical point has not been appreciated by scholars who have written on the seventh Rebbe's commitment to the proliferation of secrets as part of his apocalyptic campaign to reveal the new Torah.[177] While I do not deny that Schneerson understood the messianic mission of Ḥasidism in general, and of Ḥabad in particular, to render the esoteric lore more exoteric, I maintain that something of the secret reverberates in the divulsion of the secret. Put simply, there can be no lifting of a final veil, no defrocking of truth to an ultimate nudity, for in the eventuality of such an absolute exposure, there would truly be nothing to expose. Put even more simply, the most secretive of secrets is the open secret, the secret that is so fully disclosed that it appears not to be a secret. This, I presume, is the intent of the comment that the parabolic nature of the Torah requires that its concealed meaning always be revealed in a concealed manner.

To cite Shneur Zalman again:

> The first source and root of the Torah is the aspect of Wisdom . . . and it is called "primordial parable," for even though the light of the Infinite, blessed be he, is exalted and elevated manifold levels without end or limit above Wisdom . . . nevertheless within it dwells and is attired the light of the Infinite, blessed be he, for he and his wisdom are verily one. Therefore it is called the "primordial parable," just as a parable is a garment in relation to what is rendered parabolic and by means of

> which we can grasp it and comprehend it, so is Wisdom the garment for the Infinite, blessed be he . . . and through it and by means of it we can reach the Infinite, blessed be he.[178]

It is this paradox that Shneur Zalman had in mind when he asserted that even the Torah of the pleroma of divine emanation (*torah de-aṣilut*),[179] about which it is said that "he and his lives are one" (*de-ihu we-ḥayohi ḥad*),[180] is still to be conceived as a parable in relation to the "supernal emanator."[181] Moreover, insofar as the Torah is rooted and unified in this light, the incomposite will of the inessential, it is possible to elicit the cosmological implications of this symbolism.[182] Externally, it may seem as if there is a reality outside of God, but, internally, the (ir)reality turns out to be merely apparent. The realm of differentiated being—the order of concatenation—is nothing but the one light of wisdom compacted in the twenty-two letters of the Torah, which are branches of the tree whose trunk is the Tetragrammaton. All that comes to be in the chain of becoming is an instantiation of this parabolic dissimulation, the image of the hidden essence that appears to be apparent in the image of the apparent world that appears to be the hidden essence. As we shall see in the next chapter, for the seven masters, corporeality is to be measured from this textological perspective.

2

A/VOIDING PLACE
Apophatic Embodiment

In Bodhi there is no tree,
Nor a mirror bright,
From the beginning not a thing is,
Where can the dust alight?
—Hui-neng

In this chapter, I shall consider the nature of the material world and embodiment in Schneerson's teaching. The proper determination of this topic is critical to an assessment of his messianic vision, for, as we have already seen, the latter is troped as the disclosure of the essence in the physical plane. Ostensibly, it would seem that such a disclosure entails an assault on the esoteric proclivity to resist the indiscriminate dissemination of secrets. And yet the vision is a fulfillment of the promise in the letter of the Beshṭ that the Messiah will appear in the terrestrial realm when the wellsprings of wisdom are opened and overflow outward. Other scholars have paid attention to both these critical topics, but none, to the best of my knowledge, have focused on their congruence.

To highlight the novelty of my approach, let us recall Rachel Elior's claim that the creation of a "messianic mythology that reshaped history and promised immediate redemption" on the part of Yosef Yiṣḥaq Schneersohn "was the result of a transformation in the very heart of Habad mystical theosophy. Messianic theodicy, or the apocalyptic justification and rationalization of God's apparent helplessness and *impotence* in light of the Holocaust—replaced mystical acosmistic theosophy of the *omnipotence* of God that had prevailed continuously in Habad since the end of the eighteenth century."[1] I do not deny that the eschatological hope was greatly intensified in the sixth Rebbe and that this was triggered by the crisis facing the Jewish people in the Second World War. Furthermore, as I already clarified in the introduction, the messianic enthusiasm of the seventh Rebbe is a continuation of the temperament of his father-in-law. However, I think it is mistaken to assume that the "apocalyptic perception of history" is a revolutionary transformation of the "mystical acosmism" of Ḥabad. On the contrary, from the inception, the cosmological and apocalyptic are intertwined branches that cannot be severed.[2] Ḥabad messianism, which reached a climactic pitch in Schneerson, is a form of enlightened consciousness—a soterial recasting of the biblical mandate to know the name—that entails an illumination in space and time from the infinity that is beyond space and time and in virtue of which the spatial and temporal coordinates of the world are nullified in their affirmation and thus affirmed in their nullification. In the course of this chapter, the theoretical issues that underlie this statement will be discussed and properly contextualized, but suffice it here to emphasize that the messianic ideal of Ḥabad, even in the heightened version proffered by the last two masters, centers about the (un)veiling of the (im)materiality that I shall call the *apophatic body*,[3] in lieu of the more familiar term *acosmism* that has been utilized to characterize Ḥabad cosmology.

Before turning to the primary material, a word about this neologism is in order, as it might strike the ear as a fusion of words that do not sit together so easily. What, after all, is it to speak of a body about which nothing can be spoken? From both a commonsense and more erudite perspective, it would seem that body, however we are to conceive it, presents itself with a gravitas that makes it hard, if not impossible, to depict it apophatically. How would we take hold of such a body, how would such a body take hold of us? In considering the matter more circumspectly, however, one comes to appreciate that not only is there no contradiction in lumping these terms together, but it is precisely their juxtaposition that opens a path for us to contemplate embodiment. In speaking of body, the body spoken is no longer the lived body of which one has (un)spoken. The body, one might say, is precisely what cannot be spoken but as the no-longer-spoken-once-spoken, an apophatic body, spoken in its unspokenness. The texture, the touch, of what we confront and what confronts us in our materiality, however we are to construe the latter, resists the reduction of the corporeal to the linguistic. We face being, and name it, but, in so naming, we discern the opposition of that which we face, the discreteness and distinctiveness of what must remain other to consciousness as it is part of consciousness as the other just as consciousness is part of it as other. One may be critical of thinking consciousness in terms of the structure of intentionality, the for-itself and for-the-other, but there seems to be no way around the taint of the mirror image. Language, on this score, is not a bridge that connects mind and matter, a communication of the linguistic being of things, in Benjamin's telling formulation;[4] it is, rather, an open enclosure—a circumscription—that reveals the twofold inflection of the apophatic body. To mull over a matter so ponderous in its immateriality, one would be wise to calibrate one's thinking in accord with contemporary quantum physics, as a mundane orientation is not amenable to rendering the stuff of being most abstract at the basest level of concreteness and most concrete at the highest level of abstraction.

Intellect Beyond Intellect:
Faith, **Via Negativa,** *and Visionary Gnosis*

The philosophical piety promulgated by the proponents of Ḥabad eschews any conflict between mysticism and reason,[5] though it is also the case that the two are not identical. We do well to speak here of intersection rather than equation. Commenting on the relationship of scholasticism and mysticism in medieval Christian philosophy, Heidegger wrote, "Philosophy as a rationalistic structure, detached from life, is *powerless*; mysticism as irrational experience is *aimless*."[6] In spite of important historical differences, it would not be erroneous to think of Ḥabad in these terms: the rational and the mystical are complementary, but they are not indistinguishable; the order supplied by the one must be completed by the vitality furnished by the other. In the final analysis, Lubavitch masters have uniformly endorsed an epistemological agnosticism, acknowledging the innate inability of the human mind to ascertain knowledge of the divine essence, but they nonetheless viewed reason as the means to attain the gnosis that Shneur Zalman described as the "conjunction of thought and intellect" (*devequt ha-maḥashavah wa-sekhel*),[7] a transrational state of intellectual enlightenment or illumination,[8] which is also identified as faith (*emunah*).[9]

Here it is pertinent to recall that Shneur Zalman and his fraternity were criticized by other Ḥasidic masters, led by Abraham of Kalisk in 1797, for emphasizing the role of intellect as a vehicle of contemplation instead of affirming as the pietistic ideal a pure and simple faith that is not only beyond but also antithetical to reason.[10] The matter was, as one might expect, more complex than the polemical condemnations would suggest, for according to Shneur Zalman, and those who followed and elaborated his teaching, the highest level that one can attain in worship relates to the attribute of faith that does indeed exceed the limit of intellect and language.[11] The following statement from *Torah Or* can be considered illustrative: "To comprehend the matter of blessings . . . all of Israel believe . . . that which the philosophic sages and scientists tire of understanding by their intellects, for faith is above comprehension and the intellect [*lema'lah min ha-hassagah we-ha-sekhel*], even above the comprehension that is in the root of the divine soul that is in Israel . . . for thought cannot grasp it [*leit maḥashavah tefisa beih*]."[12] The recommended way to attain this faith is through prayer, as faith is connected intrinsically to blessing, the efflux of light that overflows from the fountain of life, the essence of the Infinite, beyond the comprehension of the "natural intellect of the animal soul" (*sekhel ha-ṭiv'i de-nefesh ha-bahamit*) and even beyond the "wisdom, understanding, and knowledge of the divine soul" (*ḥokhmah binah da'at de-nefesh ha-elohit*),[13] which is unique to the Jewish people.[14] The mystical import of the liturgical gesture of blessings, established by the men of the great assembly, was

> to draw down the disclosure of this faith [*lehamshikh gilluy emunah zo*], so that the being of the light of the Infinite, blessed be he, will be blessed and will issue forth in the disclosure below. The order of concatenation, the drawing forth of the disclosure, from the first was so that the Lord would be our God [*lihyot yhwh elohenu*], the disclosure of the light of the Infinite, blessed be he, in the souls of Israel [*gilluy or ein sof barukh hu bi-neshamot yisra'el*], to be "our God" actually in the aspect of annihilation [*lihyot elohenu mammash bi-veḥinat biṭṭul*], for they are from the interiority of the worlds [*penimiyyut ha-olamot*].[15]

We can detect in this passage the interweaving of the theosophical, cosmological, and anthropological threads that inform the warp and woof of the way of contemplation (*hitbonenut*) in the speculative core of Ḥabad: faith denotes 1. the divine light that transcends intellect, 2. the emanation of that light in all that exists, and 3. the form of worship by which the Jewish soul (particularly the pneumatic aspect *yeḥidah*, which is thought to be unique to the Jew) attains mystical gnosis of the light and is annihilated/incorporated therein. What is customarily referred to in Western metaphysics as the chain of being is designated in Ḥabad (based on earlier kabbalistic sources) as the "order of concatenation" (*seder ha-hishtalshelut*),[16] which shows itself as the "drawing forth of the disclosure" (*hamshakhat ha-gilluy*). Philological precision is warranted here, as it sheds light on the spot where the ontological and phenomenological collude—the truth of being (*mahut*) is the being of truth, the truth of the essence (*aṣmut*) is the essence of truth,[17] determined from the vantage point of what appears, the manifestation of the essential light (*or ha-aṣmi*) that must remain hidden and thus can be revealed only through the drape of darkness,[18] the "aspect of the concealment of the essence that is above the aspect of light" (*beḥinat he'lem ha-aṣmut she-lema'lah mi-beḥinat or*),[19] the "supernal dark" (*ḥoshekh elyon*) whence there was a disclosure of the light of the Infinite (*gilluy or ein sof*),[20] the "supernal light" (*or elyon*) too luminous to be revealed as light but through a veil of light,[21] just as the splendor of the sun becomes visible only as it is refracted through layers of the atmosphere. In a noteworthy passage from *Torah Or*, Shneur Zalman refers to the "Infinite in itself" as the "aspect of the luminescence that is the source of the light and from which the light emanates" (*beḥinat ha-ma'or she-hu meqor ha-or u-mimmenu nimshakh ha-or*).[22] In other Ḥabad sources, the distinction between the concealed essence and the manifest light is made even more sharply. The discussion in one of the treatises of Shalom Dovber is demonstrative of the point. On the one hand, insofar as light by nature entails disclosure (*gilluy*) and the essence is too hidden (*he'lem*) to be included in the category of disclosure (*be-geder ha-gilluy*), it is reasonable to presume that the aspect of light is "like something added to the essence" (*kemo davar nosaf al ha-eṣem*). On the other hand, it is not apposite to speak of the light as something supplemental, since it is the "disclosure of the essence" (*gilluy ha-eṣem*) and not some "other substance" (*mahut aḥer*).[23] Grappling with this philosophical quandary, the seventh Rebbe astutely observed that the "light that is comprised in the essence is not in the category of disclosure, for all that is comprised in the essence is like the essence," whence it follows that "the light as it is comprised in the luminescence is not in the aspect of the existence of light at all [*ha-or kemo she-hu kalul be-ha-ma'or eino bi-veḥinat meṣi'ut or kelal*], since it is not in the category of disclosure, but it is only in the aspect of possibility [*we-hu raq bi-veḥinat yekholet*]."[24]

I will return to this insight regarding the depiction of the light comprised in the essence whose actuality it is to be pure possibility, but at this point what needs to be underscored is that ritual performance in general, and the act of blessing in particular, has the effect of drawing this possibility, the light that is contained in the essence, from concealment to disclosure,[25] albeit a disclosure that perforce is a concealment, as the concealment that is disclosed cannot be disclosed but through being concealed, the paradox that holds the key to understanding the incarnational dimension of Ḥabad.[26] According to Shneur Zalman, the liturgical act, epitomized in the formulaic *barukh hu*, "blessed be he," empowers one "to draw down from that which is above place to the aspect of place [*lehamshikh min lema'lah min ha-maqom li-veḥinat maqom*] . . . to draw down from that which is above time to the aspect of time [*lehamshikh min lema'lah min ha-zeman li-veḥinat zeman*]."[27] Stripping away the corporeal to become a vessel of light and drawing down the effluence of light into the corporeal are two ways to view the self-same phenomenon. To quote Shneur Zalman again, "In truth, the one is dependent on the other, for by means of the annihilation one causes the emanation [*al yedei ha-biṭṭul gorem ha-hamshakhah*]."[28]

The principle is elucidated by the gestural example of the prostration during the standing prayer of the eighteen benedictions (*shemoneh esreh*), specifically when the worshipper utters "blessed are you, O Lord." The prostration corresponds to the aspect of annihilation (*biṭṭul*), also described in the image of the feminine waters (*mayyin nuqvin*), the impetus to stimulate, and the liturgical utterance to the aspect of emanation (*hamshakhah*), troped as well in the image of the masculine waters (*mayyin dukhrin*), the capacity to overflow. One can arrange these matters sequentially, so that the drawing down is posed as consequent to the stripping away, as the citation from Shneur Zalman suggests, but it is also possible to reverse the causal order and to pose the stripping away as consequent to the drawing down.[29] Be that as it may, the basic monotheistic precept of Judaism is transposed in Ḥabad into the quietistic ideal of abnegation (*biṭṭul*) or sacrifice of self (*mesirat nefesh*),[30] referred to in various other ways as well, including debasement (*shiflut*), submission (*hakhna'ah*), great love (*ahavah rabbah*), and desire of the heart (*re'uta de-libba*). To believe in one God is to be conjoined to, indeed incorporated within,[31] the will (*raṣon*) or supernal holiness (*qodesh ha-elyon*) that is "ontically extinguished in the light of the Infinite" (*ha-baṭel bi-meṣi'ut be-or ein sof*). Just as the natural inclination of the flame is to rise and to be integrated in its source, the elemental fire, so the impulse (*ḥefeṣ*) of the human soul—represented paradigmatically by the Jew—the aspect of wisdom (*ḥokhmah*) in which there is the light of the Infinite (*or ein sof*), "yearns in its nature to separate and go out from the body, to cleave to its root and source in the Lord . . . so that it will be nothing and naught [*ayin wa-efes*] and its existence will be entirely eradicated there [*titbaṭṭel sham bi-meṣi'ut legamrei*], and nothing will remain of its first substance and essence."[32]

Many passages could be adduced to illumine further the aspect of wisdom in the divine soul (*nefesh elohit*) that is "above knowledge and intellect" (*lema'lah mi-da'at wa-sekhel*),[33] but I will mention only one other particularly poignant discourse from 1805 delivered on the Sabbath known in the rabbinic calendar as *shabbat naḥamu*, literally, the "Sabbath of comfort," that is, the Sabbath that always follows the Ninth of Av, the fast day that commemorates the destruction of both Jerusalem Temples, on which Isaiah 40 is read as the prophetic section, a chapter that begins with God's call to comfort the people of Israel. Shneur Zalman's exposition is framed as a meditation on the verse "Know this day, and consider in your hearts that the Lord is God in heaven above and in earth below, there is no other" (Deut 4:39), a verse from the Torah section that is always read liturgically on that very Sabbath. Reflecting on the scriptural command to know that the Lord (YHWH) is God (Elohim)—the mystical intent of which alludes to what kabbalists have long referred to as the mystery of the androgyne (*sod du-parṣufim*), the coupling of mercy to the right and judgment to the left, the sacred union of male and female, the potency to bestow and the capacity to receive[34]—Shneur Zalman distinguishes between knowledge (*da'at*) and faith (*emunah*): the former entails discernment of the immanence of the divine light (*or elohi*) in the world, the enclothing of soul in body (*hitlabbeshut nefesh be-guf*), signified by the technical expression *memalle kol almin*, "filling all worlds," and the latter the transcendent dimension of that light, marked linguistically as *sovev kol almin*, "encompassing all worlds."[35] One apprehends the immanence of God through an intellectual vision (*re'iyyah sikhlit*), which shares something of the tangibility of the physical sense of sight (*re'iyyah ḥushit*),[36] but the transcendence of divinity, the light that is "above the aspect of being attired in the worlds" (*lema'lah mi-beḥinat hitlabbeshut be-olamot*), is known through contemplation (*hitbonenut*) that is "beyond the intellect" (*lema'lah min ha-sekhel*),[37] an apophatic contemplation, we can rightly say, since what is contemplated is what we cannot contemplate, not an incomprehensible something but the limit of all possible comprehension, that which thought cannot grasp at all, *leit maḥashavah tefisa beih kelal*, to use the zoharic dictum employed by Shneur Zalman and repeated often in Ḥabad sources.[38] I discussed this particular affirmation of apophasis in the previous chapter and I will return to it further on, but for now the crucial point is to appreciate the distinction that is upheld between knowledge and faith. Only through the latter does one ascend to the hidden Wisdom (*ḥokhmah setima'ah*), the

> supernal will [*rașon ha-elyon*] that is above knowledge, which in the human soul is the aspect of *yeḥidah*, the aspect of abnegation [*beḥinat biṭṭul*] in relation to him, blessed be he, above knowledge and comprehensible understanding . . . the incomposite will [*rașon pashuṭ*] that is without any comprehensible reason or intellect, which extends from the aspect of the supernal Crown [*keter elyon*] that has already been purified [*nitbarer kevar*], that is, this aspect is only in holiness, the aspect of nullification with respect to the light of the Infinite, blessed be he.[39]

One could dedicate a whole chapter, perhaps an entire treatise, to unpacking all that is implied in this text and to do justice to all the sources upon which it is based. Of necessity, however, I must exercise self-restraint, and hence I will only signpost the points that are most germane to the analysis of apophatic embodiment. First, the transcendent, the dimension of the Godhead that is not subject to representation, whether mental or physical, corresponds pneumatically to *yeḥidah*, the aspect of the soul that is beyond individuation, the essential and simple will above reason and the intellect,[40] and in virtue of which the line separating divine and human may be crossed in contemplation, which results in the disclosure of divinity (*gilluy elohut*) to the soul in a state of ecstasy (*hitpa'alut*).[41] What is implied in Shneur Zalman's words is made more explicit in the formulation of his son Dov Baer: "This is the aspect of *yeḥidah* that is in the soul whose root is in the aspect of the essence [*beḥinat ha-aṣmut*]. Therefore, it has an aspect of essential nullification [*biṭṭul aṣmi*] that is above *Ḥokhmah*."[42] Second, the attainment of this unity beyond apprehension—technically speaking, the language of attainment is problematic as there is nothing to attain (t)here but nothing that is not (un)attainable, and yet we have no choice but to utilize the term metaphorically to specify this quest to reach, both upwardly and inwardly, the place above place and the time above time[43]—comes about through ceremonial observance, which is ground ultimately in faith rather than knowledge. Indeed, even the minimal halakhic routine should and can be endowed with this mystical valence predicated on the consubstantiality of God and the Jewish soul. As Shneur Zalman put it, "the worship of the Lord in the human soul is the aspect of the disclosure of the light of the Infinite in the aspect of *yeḥidah* in the divine soul, which is far above the aspect of any comprehension and understanding."[44]

The commandments are the means by which one achieves a state of conjunction (*devequt*), a merging of the human and divine wills, the abnegation of self and its integration into the unified One (*yaḥid meyuḥad*), which results in drawing down the indivisible, infinite light into the veneer of a finite world of differentiation.[45] The ritual directives can serve this role as they are, kabbalistically imagined, limbs of the body of the Torah, a notion of corporeality that is not inconsequential to understanding the apophatic embodiment we are seeking to articulate in these reflections.[46] The matter will be explored in detail in the following chapter, but let me here note that a rudimentary axiom of the kabbalistic worldview is the belief that the Torah is the linguistic body, the body made of the twenty-two Hebrew letters, which are sealed in the name YHWH.[47] In Ḥabad thinking, the name is identified, moreover, as the "aspect of the light of the Infinite that is in its essence . . . which is the aspect of the disclosure, that is, what can be revealed and disseminated like the ray of the sun from the sun."[48] Insofar as the Torah is the name, we can say that the "essence of the Torah is unified in its essence . . . in the interiority of the light of the Infinite."[49] Through the agency of the Torah, therefore, one can serve as a conduit for the emplacement of the light that exceeds all limitations in the world of delimitation, to transfigure materiality immaterially, or, in the rabbinic locution,[50] which is often evoked by the Ḥabad-Lubavitch masters, to make a habitation for the divine below (*dirah ba-taḥtonim*).[51] To cite Shneur Zalman again, "The fulfillment of the commandments is verily from his essence, blessed be he . . . he gave of his essence to us, as it were, so that we could verily draw down his essence, blessed be he."[52] In his introductory discourse on 10 Shevaṭ 5711 (January 17, 1951), to which I have already made reference, Schneerson commented on this fundamental paradox of Ḥabad cosmology, the *mysterium coniunctionis* of the Infinite being incarnate in the finite, the (non)being beyond nature materializing within the non(being) of nature, "The ultimate purpose of creation and the concatenation of the worlds is that the blessed holy One desired that he would have a habitation in the lower beings. . . . By means of the worship within it, by means of the subjugation and transformation [*itkafya we-ithapkha*], the essence is revealed, and for its sake there was the creation and concatenation of the worlds."[53]

This idea provides the ontological basis for moral action—in line with the older kabbalistic tradition, Ḥabad thinking does not separate ontology and ethics[54]—as the good is determined on the grounds that the very possibility of there being something rather than nothing is due to the paradoxical identity of transcendence and immanence.[55] But perhaps we should speak of meontological in place of ontological, as the basis for the ethical demand to be nothing is the nihility that is the ultimate void of being. In the formulation of the Mitteler Rebbe, the essence of the soul's self-sacrifice consists of "the nullification and integration into the aspect of the nothing of the Infinite itself in an essential nullification [*ha-biṭṭul we-hitkallelut bi-veḥinat ayin de-ein sof aṣmo be-viṭṭul aṣmi*] . . . and not merely the aspect of the nullification of something to nothing [*beḥinat biṭṭul ha-yesh le-ayin*]."[56] Implicit here are the two forms of annihilation distinguished by Ḥabad masters, the "nullification of existence" (*biṭṭul bi-meṣi'ut*) and the "nullification of something" (*biṭṭul ha-yesh*), which correspond to the "essential nothing" (*ha-ayin ha-aṣmi*) and the "nothing of the something" (*ayin shel ha-yesh*), that is, the nothing that is not in relation to anything but to its own nothingness, the nothing that is not even and therefore more than nothing, and the nothing that is nothing only in relation to something other that comes forth from the nothing, though that other itself can be nothing other than nothing, the more that is less than the less that is more.[57] The nullification of existence, which is also marked semantically as the "essential nullification" (*biṭṭul aṣmi*), that is, the nullification of essence, completely obliterates all differentiation in the divine nothing (*biṭṭul ha-yesh le-ayin ha-elohi be-takhlit*). The semblance of individuality is undone, as the one assimilated into the essential nothing, the true worshipper of God (*oved yhwh be-emet*), has no sense of self at all (*eino margish et aṣmo kelal*).[58] Elsewhere Dov Baer describes what we might call the dissolution of the egocentric consciousness: "This is the aspect of the actual nothing [*ayin mammash*] and this is the aspect of humiliation and modesty [*ha-shiflut we-ha-anawah*], which is called the essential annihilation [*biṭṭul aṣmi*], for his soul is essentially like dust in relation to everything."[59] Moses, who is described scripturally as the humblest of all human beings (Num 12:3), represents the archetypal realization of this ideal: "From the perspective of his being conjoined to the essence, the nullification of his self was through an intense integration to the point that he did not feel his self at all [*mi-ṣad hitdabbequto el ha-eṣem hayah biṭṭul ha-yesh shelo be-hitkallelut aṣum ad she-lo hayah margish ha-yesh shelo kelal*]."[60] Pneumatically, emulating Moses, who is in the aspect of the supernal knowledge (*da'at elyon*),[61] one can become the actual nothing through effacement of self. Casting the ecstatic experience theosophically, it can be said that the one who attains nondual mindfulness embodies the "aspect of the supernal perimeter [*ha-maqqif elyon*] that comprises all the opposites in one union [*ha-kolel kol hafakhim be-ḥibbur eḥad*], for it encompasses from every side in an equanimity without a linear division at all [*be-hashwwa'ah aḥat beli hitḥallequt qawwin kelal*]. Before him the darkness and light are equal, everything is considered as equal, and he renders equal the small and the big, all things are esteemed as one in the aspect of nullification before him."[62] The spiritual awakening is dependent on the prophetic potential to be realized in the "essential nothing of the interiority of *Keter*," the infinite will wherein opposites coincide, and thereby mimic the capacity "to transform darkness to light" (*le'ithapkha ḥashokha li-nehora*), an aptitude that derives from "the most supernal power, the aspect of encompassing all worlds [*sovev kol almin*], which is the light of the Infinite [*or ein sof*] that is in the [world of] emanation in the aspect of the general perimeter [*maqqif kelali*] that surrounds the four worlds of emanation [*aṣilut*], creation [*beri'ah*], formation [*yeṣirah*], and doing [*asiyyah*], and there it says 'darkness is not dark for you' and before him 'darkness is as light' (Ps 139:11), in actual equanimity [*be-shaweh mammash*], as in the well-known example of the rotating circle in which there is no up or down."[63]

Needless to say, this principle is repeated frequently in Ḥabad literature in general and in the discourses of the seventh Rebbe in particular. As a representative illustration, I will cite from Schneerson's discourse delivered on 7 Sivan 5717 (June 6, 1957), the second day of Pentecost:

> The integration [*hitkallelut*] of the two opposites is by means of the disclosure of the supreme light that is above the two of them. And this is [the meaning of] what is written "Who built his chambers in heaven and founded his vault on earth" (Amos 9:6), for heaven [*shamayim*] is [a combination of] fire [*esh*] and water [*mayim*], and this is the aspect of mercy [*ḥesed*] and strength [*gevurah*], and the one "who built his chambers in heaven" refers to the construction of heaven from the supernal aspect, and this is the matter of the emanation of *Keter* upon *Ze'eir Anpin*, for by means of this precisely is [the claim] "founded his vault on earth" accomplished, that is, by means of the aspect of "his chambers," which is the emanation of *Keter*, the integration of the attributes is achieved. Even though the aspect of *Ze'eir Anpin* from itself has an aspect of *Keter* . . . by means of the integration the more supernal aspect emanates, and this is the aspect of the interiority of *Keter*.[64]

The coincidence of opposites is the mystery that is referred to as the "supernal wonder" (*pele ha-elyon*),[65] or what we may call the *mystery of mysteries*, as it is the mystery that encapsulates the paradoxical characteristic of all mystery, although essential to the nature of mystery is an indeterminacy that renders its imprint constantly different, *a genuine repetition that erupts from an originary transformation*, to appropriate the language of Heidegger,[66] always having already been the retrieval of what is yet to come. To avail myself of another Heideggerian turn of phrase, the integration of opposites is not "the coalescence and obliteration of distinctions," but rather "the belonging together of what is foreign" (*Zusammengehören des Fremden*).[67] The supreme expression of this belonging together—the conundrum that is the origin, the *pele* that is the *alef*—is the manifestation of the infinite light beyond nature in the timespace continuum of material nature, the mystery of incarnation that is the secret of the garment.[68] The unmasking of this secret—the absurdity of the measurable world serving as the abode for the immeasurable essence—consists precisely of an aporetic withholding, a not-wanting-to-be-transparent, lest the lucidity obscure the concealing of the concealment that uncovers the nonbeing of being in the recovery of the being of nonbeing.[69]

I will translate one relevant citation from Shalom Dovber, not because of the uniqueness of his words, but because of their coherent clarity, a trait that earned him the appellation "the Rambam of the teaching of Ḥasidism":[70]

> It is known that the purpose of creation and the generation of the worlds, and the purpose of the intention of the descent of the soul to the body, is to draw down the disclosure of the light of the Infinite in the worlds by means of the Torah and commandments, and this is the matter of the unity of the light of the Infinite that encompasses all worlds in that which fills all worlds [*yiḥud or ein sof ha-sovev kol almin bi-memalle kol almin*] . . . for this is the matter of drawing down the disclosure of the essence of the light of the Infinite, as this is the purpose of the intent in the production of the worlds and the descent of the soul in accord with the dictum that the holy One, blessed be, desires to have a habitation in the lower beings.[71]

The unity of the transcendent and the immanent is beyond the range of the lower knowledge (*da'at taḥton*), which relates to our propensity to differentiate opposites—*zeh le'ummat zeh*, "one vis-à-vis the other"[72]—and hence it rests on a binarian logic, a depiction evidently inspired by the scriptural image of the Tree of Knowledge of Good and Evil.[73] From that dipolar vantage point, spirit is set in opposition to matter, even though all our efforts must be to unify the two. By contrast, faith

> reaches that matter that the eye of the intellect [*ein ha-sekhel*] cannot comprehend at all, as it is said, "no thought can grasp you at all," the meaning of "you" is your being and your essence in actuality; the thought of the vision of wisdom cannot

> grasp it at all, but only the power of faith through which one actually believes in his being and in his essence. Even though one does not see with the eye of the intellect or with the vision of the eye, the might of faith is so strong that it is as if one actually saw with one's eyes his being and his essence, which no thought can grasp.[74]

Faith is thus a nondual gnosis, the higher knowledge that exceeds the dyadic structure of ratiocination, a vision of the "the simple will [*rașon pashuț*] that is above reason and knowledge and above the aspect of the lights being garbed in vessels,"[75] the "aspect of the essence of the light of the Infinite,"[76] wherein light and darkness are made equal (*shaweh u-mashweh or we-ḥoshekh*),[77] the "single equanimous light" (*or eḥat shaweh*),[78] the light that is the surplus of light,[79] the unique One (*yaḥid*) entirely beyond division and therefore both more and less than the enumerated one (*eḥad*),[80] the holiness that has "already been purified," that is, the holiness purged of all unholiness and hence beyond being holy. Faith, therefore, provides access to that which the seventh Rebbe dubbed as the "without boundary that is above being without boundary" (*beli gevul she-lemaʿlah mi-beli gevul*),[81] or, in the language of his namesake, Menaḥem Mendel, the third Rebbe, "the light of the Infinite in relation to which the wisdom of emanation and human wisdom are actually indistinguishable."[82] Based on the older kabbalistic principle of *aḥdut ha-shaweh*, the "equanimous one,"[83] in Ḥabad the term *hashwa'ah*, "equanimity" or "indifference," is applied "to the essence of the light of the Infinite" (*așmut or ein sof*), the luminosity that is "beyond the perimeter of the concatenation,"[84] as it transcends both the light that "encompasses all worlds" (*sovev kol almin*) and the "illumination that is garbed in the world . . . in the aspect of that which fills all worlds" (*memalle kol almin*).[85] As was his custom, Schneerson expressed the complex philosophical issue straightforwardly: "his essence, blessed be he, is simple in absolute simplicity [*pashuț be-takhlit ha-peshițut*] and it is devoid of all forms [*mushlal mi-kol ha-șiyyurim*], and it is not fitting that there be anything opposing him."[86] The traditional theological notion of divine omnipotence, and the corollary idea that nothing is impossible before God, is understood precisely in terms of the capacity of opposites to be combined in the power of the Infinite.[87] The way to access that essence in which opposites are indistinguishable is through faith, the aspect of worship that exceeds comprehension; the former corresponds to the transcendent dimension (*maqqif*) and the latter to the immanent (*penimi*). Of all the nations the Jews have been entrusted with the privilege and possibility of attaining the former. Indeed, from the example of Moses, we discern the wisdom of apophasis: "the more that one comprehends, the comprehension itself necessitates additionally that there are matters above the intellect, to the point of the saying that the end of knowledge is not to know."[88] The "discernment of the essence" (*hakkarat ha-eṣem*) constitutes the "end of knowledge, which is that they do not know you, and this matter, too, is portrayed by Moses our master, for he is from the aspect of 'I pulled him out of the water' (Exod 2:10), above the aspect of disclosure and concealment."[89]

Here we both note an important affinity and mark a significant discrepancy between the leaders of Ḥabad, beginning with Shneur Zalman, and the medieval sage Maimonides, who patently functioned as their spiritual mentor.[90] Just as the *via negativa* embraced by Maimonides served to augment rather than to abolish physical and metaphysical inquiry of a scientific nature[91]—the former designated as *ma'aseh bere'shit*, the "account of creation," and the latter as *ma'aseh merkavah*, the "account of the chariot"—so the perspective expounded by Ḥabad encourages the exercise of intellect to plumb the depths of the universe and to probe the unfathomable mystery of God. Shneur Zalman set the tone by insisting that the acquisition of knowledge of the *seder hishtalshelut*—the technical term for the standard four worlds of kabbalistic ontology—is the "great commandment" (*miṣwah rabbah*) proclaimed in the verse "Know this day, and consider in your hearts that the Lord is God in heaven above and in earth below, there is no other" (Deut 4:39). By attaining such knowledge one acquires a "perfect heart" (*lev shalem*) and ascertains that the comprehension of existence entails divesting it of corporeality (*hassagat ha-meṣi'ut hu lehafshiṭ mi-gashmiyyut*).[92] To apprehend reality, one must strip it of its materiality, a reversal of the process of creation of something from nothing (*beri'ah yesh me-ayin*), "the annihilation of something into nothing" (*ha-biṭṭul yesh le-ayin*),[93] to the point that "corporeality is eradicated into nothing in the extreme" (*ha-gashmiyyut baṭel le-ayin be-takhlit*).[94] As Shneur Zalman put it elsewhere, "The aspect of the nullification of something [*beḥinat biṭṭul ha-yesh*] is the opposite of the root of the matter of the break [*shevirah*],[95] which was for the sake of the disclosure of the light precisely in the aspect of something [*hitgallut ha-or li-veḥinat yesh dawqa*]." Yet, it is this inverse mirroring that facilitates the causal connection between the "nullification of something into nothing" (*biṭṭul ha-yesh le-ayin*) and the "drawing of nothing into something" (*hamshakhat ayin le-yesh*).[96] Only when one sees from the vantage point of this double extinction—the nothing becoming something that is nothing—does one comprehend the far-reaching monopsychic (as opposed to the conventional monotheistic) meaning of the verse from Deuteronomy proclaiming that apart from God there is no other, that is, appearances notwithstanding, there appears to be no being (*mahut*) but the "actual nothing" (*ayin mammash*) that everything is apparently.[97] In the essence of this void, the substance of all discriminate beings, including the personal God of biblical and rabbinic Judaism, is rendered insubstantial. Not to advance to this stage is to allow theism to elide into idolatry.

From Something Nothing Between Nothing and Something

The paradoxical nature of Ḥabad cosmology leads to the assertion that "it is impossible for something to come to be from something,"[98] an explicit rejection of the well-known philosophical maxim *ex nihil, nihil fit*, "from nothing, nothing comes," since the source of all that exists is the "aspect of the true nothing of the essence of the light of the Infinite in actuality" (*beḥinat ayin ha-amitti de-aṣmut or ein sof mammash*).[99] With regard to this *true nothing*, Ḥabad plainly deviates from Maimonides, for while the latter also identified ultimate human felicity as a state of conjunction whereby the intellect rids itself of its bodily encasement and is united with the Active Intellect, the last of the incorporeal intellects that emanate from God, he did not offer a cosmology that would deprive the world of its material investiture. For Maimonides, there is no logical principle that would allow for the dialectic inversion of being into nothing, and even his commitment to the dogma of *creatio ex nihilo* is suspect; by the logic of *ex nihil, nihil fit*, the presumed traditional doctrine of *yesh me-ayin*, the creation of something from nothing, is a marvel beyond the intellect of created beings,[100] but it still falls short of the absurdity implied in the oxymoronic identification of something (*yesh*) and nothing (*ayin*). I will not enter into a discussion of the earlier sources that influenced Ḥabad, though I hasten to add that these sources, which go as far back as the thirteenth century, are not irrelevant, and a more extended treatment of this topic would demonstrate the importance of the motif to the kabbalistic sensibility more generally. I will emphasize that, for Ḥabad, it is this paradox that undergirds the mystical duty of purifying the

> materiality of the world and its density [*ḥomriyyut ha-olam we-gassuto*] . . . so that it will not be in the aspect of something and a separate thing in and of itself [*beḥinat yesh we-davar nifrad bifnei aṣmo*], but rather everything will be comprised in the aspect of nothing [*ha-kol yukhlal bi-veḥinat ayin*], for the purpose of the creation of the worlds from nothing to something [*takhlit beri'at ha-olamot me-ayin le-yesh*] is to transform the aspect of something into the aspect of nothing [*le'ahafakha mi-beḥinat yesh li-beḥinat ayin*], and then "the Lord shall be my God" [*we-hayah yhwh li le'lohim*] (Gen 28:21), for "God" [*elohim*] is the concealment and withdrawal [*ha-he'lem we-ha-ṣimṣum*], so that there will be worlds created from nothing to something [*lihyot ha-olamot nivra'im me-ayin le-yesh*], and the "Lord" [*yhwh*] is the aspect of the interiority of the light of the Infinite, blessed be he, that sustains and brings into being.[101]

The secret pronounced in this text is expressive of the *coincidentia oppositorum* applied to the primary ontological binary: *creatio ex nihilo* is construed in a mystical vein, as we can speak of the drawing out of something from nothing only to the extent that we comprehend that everything amounts to and is integrated in this nothing, a matter that is not simply a cognitive insight but a way of seeing that alters reality, a specularity that divests the universe of its gross physicality, restoring the multiplicity of all being to the indistinct and indifferent one that comprehends everything in the nothingness of its (not) being every nothing. The paradox is expressed as well in terms of the traditional unification of the divine names YHWH and Elohim, which correspond respectively to the attributes of mercy and judgment. In Ḥabad symbolism, YHWH names the essence that is above nature (*lema'lah min ha-ṭeva*) and Elohim its appearance in nature (*ṭeva*).[102] Shneur Zalman already expressed the matter in *Sha'ar ha-Yiḥud we-ha-Emunah* as an exegesis of the verse "For the Lord God is sun and shield" (Ps 84:12): just as the sun has a buffer that makes it possible for created beings to endure its light, so the name Elohim "protects" the name YHWH, that is, the name Elohim, the veil of nature, makes apparent the essential name YHWH, which signifies that the essence brings everything into being from nothing (*mehawweh et ha-kol me-ayin le-yesh*).[103]

> Thus the name Elohim is the name of the attribute of strength and contraction [*middat ha-gevurah we-ha-ṣimṣum*], and therefore it is also numerically *ha-ṭeva* because it conceals the light above that generates and sustains the world, and it appears as if the world stands and is governed in the way of nature. The name Elohim is a shield and sheath for the name YHWH, to conceal the light and vitality that emanates from the name YHWH, so that it will bring forth from nothing to something, and it will not be revealed to created beings, which result in their being decimated in existence [*yevaṭṭelu bi-meṣi'ut*].[104]

Commenting on this seminal text, the seventh Rebbe wrote, "the coming-into-being of the world [*hithawwaut ha-olam*] is from the name YHWH . . . but if the coming-into-being of the world were only from the name YHWH, the world would be annihilated in existence [*baṭel bi-meṣi'ut*]. Therefore, the actual coming-into-being was by means of the name Elohim."[105] The harnessing of the names, therefore, alludes to the "matter of the garbing" (*inyan ha-hitlabbeshut*), the paradox that the concealed light of the Infinite is revealed in the garment that is the world through which it is concealed, for had it not been concealed, the beings of the world would be utterly eradicated (*beṭṭelim be-takhlit*) like the ray of sunlight that is completely obliterated by the radiance of the sun.[106] The matter of the array can also be comported in the image of the light being enclosed in the vessels.

> The explanation for the unification of the lights and the vessels is from the perspective of their root in the names YHWH and Elohim, for YHWH is the source of the lights and the name Elohim is the source of the vessels, as it is written, "For the Lord God is sun and shield" (Ps 84:12), for the shield has two functions—first, it conceals the light of the sun, and second, through concealing the essence of the light, it reveals the light below, and thus it is with respect to the names YHWH and Elohim, for the name Elohim conceals the light of YHWH and reveals it in the vessels.[107]

The conjunction of YHWH and Elohim bespeaks the mystery of incarnation (*hitgashshemut*), the amalgamation of the antinomies of materiality and spirituality (*hafakhim de-gashmiyyut we-ruḥaniyyut*),[108] which is sometimes referred to as the "inscrutable power to act" (*koaḥ mafli la'asot*),[109] since the spiritual beyond space and time is combined with the corporeal that is bound by space and time, and, as a consequence, the "aspect of the light that is above the aspect of being garbed in the vessels will enter the vessels, and, moreover, it will extend to the corporeality, and then the corporeal will be in a different manner."[110] Again, we note the confluence of the ontological and the phenomenological—to be is to appear, to be seen, though what is seen is the unseen, the invisible of the visible, the limitless light delimited in the constriction of the vessels, the concealment (*he'lem*) that makes possible the manifestation (*gilluy*) of transcendence, that which encompasses all worlds (*sovev kol almin*) and shines without boundary (*beli gevul*) through its occlusion in the aspect of immanence, that which fills all worlds (*memalle kol almin*) and shines through the measure of contraction (*ṣimṣum*).[111] This is the intent of Shneur Zalman's well-known assertion that it is erroneous to interpret the Lurianic doctrine of *ṣimṣum* literally (*kfshuṭo*); this is not to deny the withdrawal as such, but rather to highlight that there is nothing but withdrawal, every manifestation of the ipseity of the Infinite is a concealment, since there is no reality but the inherently hidden essence that becomes more occluded in its being disclosed.[112] The one who apprehends the collusion of these opposites in the identity of their opposition will discern the immateriality of the material, an acosmic naturalism that is conceptually quite far from the naturalist cosmology accepted by Maimonides.[113]

In spite of this obvious difference, Shneur Zalman adopts an elementary tenet of the Maimonidean approach, maintaining—against his critics—that one could not worship God wholeheartedly unless one first attained knowledge of divinity, an idea linked exegetically to the advice David offered Solomon "know the God of your father, and serve him with perfect heart and eager soul" (1 Chronicles 28:9). On the one hand, love of God is "beyond the limit of comprehension and thought cannot grasp it at all," but, on the other hand, the only way to achieve this level is for one "to accustom one's intellect and one's understanding to comprehend the supernal intelligibles that are abstracted from corporeality. . . . By faith alone one's soul is not actualized . . . for there is no entry into the interiority of the heart, so that the heart will be aroused, except by knowledge, as it says, 'know the God of your father, and serve him with perfect heart.'"[114]

Apart from the matter of influence, it is plausible to say that Ḥabad has been informed by a distinctive way of reading Maimonides. Rather than viewing him as an advocate of a rationalism that stands in opposition to mystical devotion, Ḥabad masters look upon the "great eagle" of medieval Jewish society as articulating a "rational religion" that is at the same time a "philosophic mysticism"[115] in terms that well apply to their own kabbalistically inspired cogitations. Consider, for example, Shneur Zalman's depiction of the divine soul "that comprehends and contemplates constantly and apprehends the light of the Infinite, blessed be he, and it has no other comprehension."[116] This wisdom is further characterized as the "supernal knowledge" (*da'at elyon*) in relation to the "lower knowledge" (*da'at taḥton*), the human intellect that is aligned with the animal soul and that apprehends the corporeality of the world. The ultimate felicity consists of joining these two forms of knowledge, the knowledge of a unity beyond differentiation and the knowledge of a unity predicated on the pairing of what has been torn asunder, a conjunction that is presented in the explicitly heteroerotic terms of the Song of Songs. Bracketing the importance of the erotic symbolism, the conjoining of the two kinds of knowledge indicates that contemplation of the Infinite that is above nature is contrasted with, but also set in homology to, the apprehension of nature. Here we come upon the iteration of a familiar esoteric trope, the way through the veil is through the veil.

The point is epitomized in a passage in the Ṣemaḥ Ṣedeq's *Derekh Miṣwotekha*.[117] The "Greek wisdom" (*ḥokhmah yewanit*) of philosophy and the "divine wisdom" (*ḥokhmah ha-elohit*) of kabbalah are contrasted on the grounds that the former is a mode of comprehension (*hassagah*) that always has as its object a discrete comprehensible form (*ṣiyyur ha-mussag*), whereas the latter is an "intellectual vision" (*re'iyyat ha-sekhel*) in which there is a "disclosure of the Infinite" (*gilluy ein sof*), and hence it is symbolized by the letter *yod*, the subtle point (*nequddah daqqah*) that comprises in its infinitesimality the totality of all that was, is, and shall be—a compresence of the three tenses of time in the timeless time, which is the mystical connotation of the Tetragrammaton, the one true being that is both outside and within the order of concatenation[118]—an excess of totality that exceeds even the totality of excess. The wisdom of the divine tradition (*ḥokhmat ha-qabbalah ha-*

elohit), which is the prophetic legacy distinct to the Jewish people, is an intellectual vision (*re'iyyat ha-sekhel*), but one that is nonetheless characterized as belief (*emunah*), a faith that surpasses, even if it does not contradict, discursive reason. We are told, therefore, that the true tradition is "to believe in the Lord and in his commandments, for he fully transcends the aspect of wisdom and comprehension, and thought cannot grasp him at all, even the supernal wisdom. When the Lord wishes it for the community or for an individual, he makes known through prophecy, which is above the intellect, the disclosure of his divinity, blessed be he, and the goal of the wisdom is the belief in the interiority of the Torah and in its secrets, and this was the miracle of Ḥanukah with divine wisdom prevailing over Greek wisdom, which is philosophy."[119] As the conclusion of the passage makes clear, the inner intent of the festival of Ḥanukah is the overpowering of kabbalah over philosophy, divine wisdom over Greek wisdom, faith over reason. The teleology of the traditional wisdom is to believe in the interiority of the Torah and its secrets, a belief that imparts gnosis about the divinity, but a gnosis that transcends knowledge, an apophatic ideal that is expressed in the aforementioned zoharic language, *leit maḥashavah tefisa beih kelal*.[120] The zenith of the contemplative ascent is to discern the intrinsic inability of the mind to fathom the divine, and yet this mystical state of learned ignorance, to know that one cannot know, is described as the "aspect of the illumination of wisdom" (*beḥinat he'arat ha-ḥokhmah*), which is described further as the "gaze of the intellect that is above comprehension" (*seqirat ha-sekhel she-lema'lah min ha-hassagah*)[121]—above comprehension, but a gaze of intellect nonetheless.

This is the position affirmed by the seventh Rebbe as well. Numerous texts could be cited in support of this claim, but suffice it here to mention his words in a letter from 21 Shevaṭ 5716 (February 3, 1956) that both "simple faith" (*emunah peshuṭah*)[122] and "inquiry and knowledge" (*ḥaqirah wa-da'at*) are necessary on the path of devotion. He adds that it is not only that "there is no contradiction between the two, but, on the contrary, the one completes the other."[123] The ultimate rationale for pious worship is faith, but, as Schneerson is quick to point out, quoting Maimonides from the beginning of his code of Jewish law, as well as the corresponding passage from the zoharic stratum known as *Piqqudin*, the "foundation of foundations and the pillar of wisdoms" is to acquire knowledge of God.[124]

In the tradition of medieval Jewish philosophers, epitomized by Maimonides, Ḥabad masters affirm that it is a religious obligation to strive for this knowledge,[125] even as they concede that it surpasses intellect and understanding.[126]

To apprehend the essence that is beyond reason, therefore, one must rely on faith. From neither the Maimonidean nor the Ḥabad perspectives, however, is this blind faith or faith that is opposed to reason; it is, rather, a suprarational faith, a faith that reaches the "intellect hidden from every idea,"[127] the "intellect-that-is-above-intellect" (*sekhel mi-lema'lah min ha-sekhel*), in the felicitous formulation of Dov Baer,[128] or, in the language of the Ṣemaḥ Ṣedeq, the "supernal knowledge" that "is garbed in the souls of Israel in a discernment without any comprehensible knowledge,"[129] the disclosure of which promotes the awareness that "everything is considered as if it were actually not" (*kolla ke-lo ḥashiv mammash*)."[130] Accordingly, there is no conflict between the unremitting demand to know and the inescapable inability to know. In pursuing the supernal knowledge that is above wisdom and understanding, one comes to know that one does not know, and to not know that one does not know is truly not to know. The degree to which the orientation of Maimonides is synchronized with Ḥabad on this issue is exemplified in another passage from Dov Baer wherein the philosophic characterization of divine knowledge as the indivisible unity of knower, knowing, and known[131] is presented as an exact parallel to the mystical insight that there is nothing outside of God (*ein ḥuṣ mimmenu*). To say that there is nothing outside of God means not only that God comprehends all that is, but that there is no being independent of God, a truth that can be discerned only from its opposite, that is, from the fact that the (non)being of God is veiled in the guise of that which seems independent, a mystery that the mind cannot contemplate and the mouth cannot articulate.[132]

Light Beyond Light: Acosmic Naturalism and Apophatic Panentheism

It has been well noted that the doctrines and practices of Ḥabad are deeply indebted to previous kabbalistic teaching, especially to the complex theosophic system cultivated by Isaac Luria and his disciples in the sixteenth and seventeenth centuries.[133] Of the many Lurianic ideas that have informed Ḥabad thought, one whose influence surely cannot be underestimated is the topos of the shattering of the vessels (also referred to as the death of the primordial kings of Edom) in *olam ha-tohu*, the world of chaos that preceded the dissemination of the light in structured form, and the consequent dispersion of these shards to which are attached sparks of light. Just as Luria and the transmitters of his teaching had emphasized, exponents of Lubavitch lore—in line with other Ḥasidic masters who trace their way of thinking to the Beshṭ—have repeatedly stressed that all of reality is infused with divine light, and that the telos of human existence, which is fulfilled most perfectly in the rituals of the Jewish people, is to liberate these holy sparks from their encasement in the demonic shells of the material word (a process that is referred to technically as *berur*) and to restore them to the light of the Infinite whence they emerged, the One in which opposites can no longer be differentiated but as opposites that are differentiated in virtue of being (in)different.[134]

From Shneur Zalman to Menaḥem Mendel, Ḥabad masters (inspired by the orientation of the Maggid of Międzyrzecz) have interpreted the kabbalistic cosmology, which provides the ideational underpinning of the ethical pietism and messianic activism,[135] in a manner that on the face of it hovers conceptually between pantheism and panentheism, that is, the belief that God is synonymous with nature and the belief that God is the One that is inseparable from and yet not quite identical with nature, that all being is in God but God is not identical with all being.[136] It would appear, however, that neither panentheism nor pantheism as such is adequate to render the Ḥabad perspective, as both the transcendental and immanental aspects, *sovev kol almin* and *memalle kol almin*, are characterizations that are notionally and semantically meaningful only in relation to the world, but the light of the Infinite in and of itself, a transcendence that transcends the distinction between transcendence and immanence, is "not in the category of worlds at all," and therefore it is beyond the ontic splitting into the encompassing light and the inner light.[137] How, then, do we understand the passages that seem to affirm that the world and God are indistinguishable? Would these not clash with the insistence that divinity in its essence is above nature? We might propose that there is no discord, as those passages are not speaking about the unique One (*yaḥid*, *eyntsik*) "unified in the essence" (*meyuḥad be-eṣem*) but of the one (*eḥad*, *eyner*) that is characterized by a "division of particulars" (*hitḥallequt peraṭim*), the multiplicity of beings that constitute the "world of differentiation" (*alma di-feruda*).[138] From another perspective, however, this response is not satisfactory, for even if we grant that the divine essence is not circumscribable within the dual frame of the light-that-is-transcendent and the light-that-is-immanent, we would insist nonetheless that it cannot be completely removed therefrom. Indeed, the vocation of the Jew in giving witness to the oneness of the Creator underscores the point. The key expression in the declaration of faith "Hear, O Israel, the Lord our God, the Lord is one" (Deut 6:4) is "the Lord our God," *yhwh elohenu*, the two names that respectively denote that which is above nature (*lema'lah me-ha-ṭeva*) and nature (*ha-ṭeva*).[139] In professing that "the Lord is our God," the worshipper gives verbal assent to and thereby participates in the puzzle of incarnation, the commingling of the metaphysical and physical. The liturgical confession, therefore, is the axial event that provides habitation for the light that exceeds the boundaries of time and place in the world that is bounded by time and place.[140] In the words of Shneur Zalman:

> The name YHWH instructs that he is above time, for he was, is, and will be in one moment . . . and he is also above place for he brings about constantly the entire aspect of place from above to below and in the four sides. Even though he, blessed be he, is above place and time, he is nonetheless found below in place and time, that is, he is unified in the attribute of his kingship [*mityaḥed be-middat malkhuto*] whence place and time emanate and come to be, and this is the lower unity [*yiḥuda tata'ah*] . . . that is, his essence and substance, blessed be he, which is called the Infinite, blessed be he, verily fills the whole earth in time and place . . . everything is filled uniformly from the light of the Infinite, blessed be he . . . for everything is in the aspect of place that is ontically nullified in the light of the Infinite, blessed be he [*ha-baṭel bi-meṣi'ut be-or ein sof barukh hu*], which is garbed in it by means of the attribute of his kingship that is unified in him, blessed be he. The attribute of his kingship is the attribute of constriction and concealment [*middat ha-ṣimṣum we-hahester*], which conceals the light of the Infinite, blessed be he, so that time and place will not be obliterated entirely from their existence.[141]

Material space can contain the immaterial beyond spatial delimitation, a possibility actualized in the Temple, which is imagined archetypically as the place above place.[142] By proclaiming the oneness of God, worshippers theurgically "draw down the disclosure of the light of the Infinite that is above the aspect of place, so that it will be revealed in the aspect of place and the place will be annihilated [*yitgalleh bi-veḥinat maqom lihyot ha-maqom baṭel*], and this is 'the Lord is one.'"[143] In his inimitable style, the seventh Rebbe captures the paradox pithily, "the disclosure that is above place, which shines in place, was from the perspective of place itself [*ha-gilluy di-lema'lah me-ha-maqom she-he'ir ba-maqom hayah mi-ṣad ha-maqom aṣmo*]."[144] Elaborating in another context on what I called above (following Heidegger) the belonging together of the foreign, Schneerson put it as follows:

> The joining of nature with what is above nature is by means of the disclosure of the essence that is beyond both of them. . . . And this is also the reason why there must be a joining of the two matters of nature and what is above nature, for the root of each one of these matters is in the light of the Infinite, and by means of the joining of these two matters is the drawing down of the essence, that is, through this there is the possibility (from the perspective of the world as well) that by means of worship there will be in the world the drawing down of the disclosure of the essence, and through this the intention of the creation of the world (nature) will be perfected, for the blessed holy One desires that he will have a habitation in the beings below.[145]

The possibility of experiencing God's presence in nature (Elohim) is dependent on dialectically discerning the dimension of divinity that is absent from nature (YHWH). To appropriate the fecund neologism of Catherine Keller,[146] we can say that Ḥabad cosmology espouses an *apophatic panentheism*: the One is affirmed in everything to the extent that everything is negated in relation to the One, but the One is negated in relation to everything to the extent that everything is affirmed in the One. "Negated" is a careful rendering of *biṭṭul*, the technical terminology of Ḥabad's contemplative praxis, which we can translate into the contemporary jargon of *denegation*. By *denegate* I mean to eradicate, to uproot by clutching the root, or to efface, as effacing is always also a facing of what cannot be faced. The double gesture of the One denegated in relation to the totality of all things and the totality of all things denegated in relation to the One, issues from the void of the Infinite, the chasm in which everything is nothing in virtue of being everything, and nothing is everything in virtue of being nothing. To speak of God's (non)being is an apophatic dictum, and therefore unutterable, as it rests on presuming the capacity for the other in that which has no other, a capacity that kabbalists assign to the withholding that expands, the riddle of *ṣimṣum*, the concealment within the actual nothing that bears the potential to become every other nothing in actuality, the supernal Wisdom, *ḥokhmah*, which is decoded as *koaḥ mah*, the potential of what-is-to-become.[147] I note further that the word *mah*, which denotes the indeterminacy of this potentiality, is numerically equivalent to forty-five (*mem he* = 40 + 5), which is the same numerology as the letters of the Tetragrammaton when spelled out in full (*yw"d h"a wa"w h"a* = 10 + 6 + 4 + 5 + 1 + 6 + 1 + 6 + 5 + 1) and the word *adam* (*alef dalet mem* = 1 + 4 + 40). The linguistic and mathematical convergences (derived from much older kabbalistic sources) are meant to communicate that the light of consciousness, the divine life-force (*ḥiyyut elohi*) manifestly hidden in all that appears to be in the chain of becoming,[148] assumes the imaginal form of the human, the embodiment of the name YHWH, which is the Torah. In the space between the really apparent and the apparently real, the potential actuality of nothing and the actual potentiality of something, are identified in the opposition of their identity. We might say, therefore, that God is in the world exclusively to the extent that the world is in God inclusively, but the world is in God inclusively as what is other in relation to God, just as God is in the world exclusively as what is other in relation to the world. Apophatic panentheism, accordingly, presumes a reciprocal transcendence whereby God and world abide in the difference of their belonging-together, indeed they belong together precisely in virtue of their difference.[149] Rehearsing an exegesis of *el olam*, the title by which Abraham addressed God (Gen 21:33), which can be traced to Shneur Zalman,[150] Shmuel, more commonly referred to as the Rebbe MaHaRaSh, enunciates the fundamental cosmological insight of Ḥabad: "The souls of Israel join the world to the divinity, so that the world will not be a separate being and entity unto itself, but rather the world will be nullified vis-à-vis the divinity, as it is written 'and Abraham invoked there the name of the Lord, the everlasting God' [*el olam*], and not the 'God of the world' [*el ha-olam*], for the world and the divine are all one [*she-olam we'lohim ha-kol eḥad*], since the world is actually nullified vis-à-vis the divinity [*lefi she-olam baṭel mammash le-elohut*]."[151] On the one hand, God and world are proclaimed to be identical, but, on the other hand, they are presumed to be different, otherwise there would be no need for the Jew to conjoin them. There is no contradiction, however, as the identity of the difference depends on the difference of identity. As Shmuel's son, Shalom Dovber, put it,

> It says *el olam* and not *ha-olam*, that is, the world is not a separate entity but the divinity, just as the substance of the fruit is the light (or substance) of the power of the plant that is materialized, and analogously, the vessels are the very light whence the vessels are made, which is the trace [*roshem*][152] . . . but this is like the light that is materialized . . . for all the created entities are the light and splendor that emanate from the divine potency that overflows on them and brings them into being, for the divine illumination itself materializes and becomes the aspect of the existence of something, and this is *el olam*, the world is the divinity in actuality [*she-ha-olam hu elohut mammash*].[153]

Reiterating this theme, Menaḥem Mendel emphasized that the message of Abraham, and by extension the mystical import of Judaism, is the realization that "the reality of the world is divinity" (*meṣi'ut ha-olam hu elohut*).[154] Tellingly, he included a similar observation in his inaugural address from 10 Shevaṭ 5711 (January 17, 1951): "It is not *el ha-olam*, that is, the divinity as an entity unto itself and the world as an entity unto itself, but rather the divinity rules over and governs the world, for the world and divinity are entirely one [*she-olam wa-elohut hu kolla ḥad*]."[155] Instead of using the construct *el ha-olam*, "God of the world," which would suggest that the divine and the cosmic are separate, the two terms are placed in apposition, *el olam*, which can be decoded as the God who is the world. In the void of radical denegation, there is no opposition—not even the opposition of no opposition—and hence alterity persists in the interlude between the one and the other, the hiatus wherein one is perpetually becoming, and therefore never is, the other. Here we mark the temporal implications of the miracle of creation (*ḥiddush*) as an apophatic incarnation, the constant renewal (*hitḥaddeshut*) of something from nothing to produce the generation (*hithawwut*) of something that is nothing, the same other that returns always as what has never been but as already other to the same.[156]

The negativity that doubly binds God and world yields what we may also call *acosmic naturalism*. The adjective *acosmic* connotes that there is no world that is not enfolded in the essence that is the light of the Infinite, whereas the noun *naturalism* indicates that there is no unfolding without the enfolded, no manifestation but in the occlusion that is the world, an idea, as we will see, buttressed by the wordplay *ha-olam* and *he'lem*, "the world" and "concealment." The calling into question of the independent status of beings vis-à-vis the one true being, which is central to Ḥabad cosmological thinking, has to be seen from within the spectrum of this seemingly contradictory elocution. For example, in the *Tanya*, we read that

> all of the created entities in relation to him are actually annihilated in existence [*beṭelim eṣlo bi-meṣi'ut mammash*] like the annihilation of the letters of speech and thought in their source and their root, the substance of the soul and its essence . . . a physical example of this is from the matter of the annihilation of the splendor and light of the sun in its source that is the body of the sphere of the sun that is in the sky . . . for there it is annihilated in existence in its source and it is as if it is not in existence at all. And thus verily by way of analogy is the annihilation of the existence of world and its fullness vis-à-vis its source, which is the light of the Infinite, blessed be he.[157]

Just as the letters, whether spoken or contemplated, are obliterated in the soul that is beyond language, and just as the rays that reach the earth are extinguished in the sun in heaven, so all things in the created universe are nullified in the light that is the essence of the Infinite.

To cite another illustration from Shneur Zalman. The exegetical subtext of this passage is the description of the Torah based on the portrayal of Wisdom in Proverbs 8:30 as "toying" (*mesaḥeqet*) before God: "The matter is that the aspect of playfulness [*seḥoq*] is the aspect of the eradication of something into nothing [*biṭṭul ha-yesh le-ayin*], as it is written 'God played a joke on me' [*ṣeḥoq asah li elohim*] (Gen 21:6), that is, the name *elohim* conceals and hides the light of the Infinite, blessed be he, so that the world will appear as a substance and as a separate being [*lihyot nir'eh ha-olam le-yesh we-davar nifrad*], and its existence would not be annihilated [*she-lo yibaṭṭel bi-meṣi'ut*] like the splendor of the sun in the sun."[158] The toying around metaphorically denotes the negation of opposites, the crossing of boundaries, the nullification of something into nothing (*biṭṭul ha-yesh le-ayin*), a reversal of the process of creation of something from nothing (*yesh me-ayin*). The mystical nuance of this traditional notion is alluded to in the reading of Sarah's comment upon giving birth to Isaac, *ṣeḥoq asah li elohim*, "God played a joke on me." The name *elohim*, which signifies the attribute of judgment, conceals the light of the Infinite so that in the staging of creation the world dissimulates as an independent reality. The cosmic prank, so to speak, is the garbing of YHWH, the light of the Infinite, in Elohim, the veil of nature.[159] The contemplative's ability to turn that around in the act of *biṭṭul*, to see through the veil, is a mode of participating in this divine trick, referred to as well as the play of *sha'ashu'im*. Through the act of self-sacrifice brought about by the all-consuming love one has for God, the individual causes the descent of the "supernal delight" (*ta'anug elyon*)—the power of the boundless will through which the divine essence wills what it wills without internal desire or external compulsion[160]—to be garbed in the Torah, an act that is also troped, on the basis of earlier kabbalistic sources,[161] as God's bemusing himself in his own essence (*sha'ashu'a she-be-aṣmuto*). The pietistic gesture is communicated in the verse "I took delight in your Torah," *ani toratkha shi'asha'ti* (Ps 119:70): one augments the semiotic and erotic sport of *sha'ashu'a* by means of *ani*, the "I," which consists of the same letters as *ayin*, "nothing," that is, "the aspect of the abnegation of substance [*biṭṭul ha-yesh*] as one makes *ayin* from *ani*, and thus even in the study of the Torah, there is no aspect of substance but the abnegation of substance."[162] The charade of an independent reality is fully disclosed in the messianic era when all sense of alterity is dispelled, a point made rhetorically by the promise that even the demonic other will be subjugated (*itkafya siṭra aḥara*) and the dark will be transformed into light (*ithapkha ḥashokha li-nehora*).[163] The terms *itkafya* and *ithapkha* in the Ḥabad lexicon signify two modes of unification, the former the sublimation of one thing by its opposite, the latter the transmutation of one thing into its opposite.[164] The two are causally aligned, as evil must be sublimated before it is transmuted into the good, but the transmutation of evil into good is unmistakably the superior mode.[165] In the end, as in the beginning, indeed in the origin before the beginning,[166] darkness will itself become an aspect of the light, for the two cannot be distinguished in the essence of the Infinite.

Echoing this theme, the seventh Rebbe commented in the sermon on the essence of Ḥasidism, which was delivered on 19 Kislev 5726 (December 13, 1965):

> Also with respect to the aspect of the Torah that is united with his blessed essence, it is said, "toying before him" (Prov 8:30), the bemusement (and joy) that is above comes by way of the purification [*berur*] and rectification [*tiqqun*] of the darkness—the darkness transmuted into light. And this is "toying before him": precisely through the aspect of the darkness being transmuted into light—"toying"—which is in the Torah, its interiority is expressed as it is united with the interiority of the light of the Infinite, blessed be he—"before him."[167]

The full intent of the motif can be culled from a discourse delivered by Schneerson in the previous decade, on 28 Tammuz 5713 (July 11, 1953):

> As it says, "God joked with me," for it is precisely on account of the fact that the matter of the nullification [*inyan ha-biṭṭul*] is realized with respect to the entities that come from the name Elohim, which are in the aspect of something [*yesh*], the nullification of something to nothing [*biṭṭul ha-yesh le-ayin*], that the matter of the joke [*ṣeḥoq*] and pleasure [*ta'anug*] comes to be above, and similarly it is written, "and Leviathan that you created to toy with" (Ps 104:26), for Leviathan is from the language of joining [*ḥibbur*][168] . . . and the matter of joining applies specifically when there are two things separate from each other. This matter is particularly in the work related to the nullification of something [*ha-avodah de-viṭṭul ha-yesh*], for something and nothing are two things that are separate from one another, and even so the nullification of something to nothing is realized [*po'alim biṭṭul ha-yesh le-ayin*], and by means of this especially the matter of the joke comes to be.[169]

The playfulness of the divine is expressed in the dissembling of a world that appears to be independent of God, which is the esoteric meaning of the traditional dogma of *creatio ex nihilo* (*beri'ah yesh me-ayin*). We can participate in the showing of the nonapparent by turning the apparent something into the actual nothing. The essence of worship is to reach the state of *ithapkha*, of transforming something into nothing, but this cannot be achieved without having realized the *itkafya*, the subjugation of something by nothing. Schneerson communicates this idea as well in terms of the distinction between two kinds of knowledge, which we have already encountered. Whereas the supernal knowledge is considered above as something but below as nothing, the lower knowledge is considered below as something but above as nothing. The contrast between the two kinds of knowledge occasions a corresponding difference in two forms of denegation. The lower knowledge brings about nullification of something (*biṭṭul ha-yesh*), the supernal knowledge nullification of existence (*biṭṭul bi-meṣi'ut*).[170] The former is an illustration of *itkafya*, the subduing of one thing by its opposite, the latter an example of *ithapkha*, the transmutation of one thing into its opposite. In this state of annihilation, it is no longer meaningful to speak of permanence or transience, something or nothing, existence or nonexistence; hence there is no need for grouping one with the other. Beyond effacing the creation of something from nothing by transforming the something into nothing, the nothing itself is negated, the annihilation annihilated.

As I noted above, the more effective nomenclature to capture the acosmic naturalism of Ḥabad in all its subtleties and ramifications is the supposedly incongruous *apophatic panentheism*. This term implies that the world is not thought to be an illusion vis-à-vis the hidden essence as much as it is conceived to be a veil through which the illusion can be apprehended and thereby unveiled for the illusion it appears to be, an unveiling in which the hidden essentiality is (un)veiled. Nature, accordingly, is not denied real existence, as if it was the "veil of Maya,"[171] but rather it is the veil that reveals the unveiling of the veil. The one who acquires this gnosis perceives that the world is suffused with divine reality, that there is, paraphrasing the zoharic locution favored by many Ḥasidic masters, no place devoid of the divine.[172] It follows that enlightened consciousness, which is a prolepsis of redemption, consists not in thinking that spirituality can overcome materiality, that the infinite essence is a noumenal negation of the phenomenal,[173] but in the realization that the distinction between the two collapses in the identity of their difference. As Schneerson put it, "spirituality and materiality are on a par."[174] A simple and pithy utterance—*ruḥaniyyut we-gashmiyyut shawin*—three words that challenge the binary that has prevailed in Western culture through the ages, evident at times in Ḥabad literature itself. To speak of the parity between spirit and matter, however, is not to reduce one term to the other. On the contrary, the Ḥabad viewpoint seeks to avoid monism of either an idealist or a materialist nature.[175] The issue, rather, is the parabolic replication according to which the spiritual is specularized through the prism of the corporeal, and the corporeal through the prism of the spiritual. Herein is the alchemical basis for the ontic potential of a God that is really apparent and of a world that is apparently real. Thus Shneur Zalman remarked that the "supernal mystery" (*seter elyon*) that dons the light of the Infinite is called *Arikh Anpin*, literally, the "long face," to indicate that "it can extend below as well . . . for before him, blessed be he, spirituality and materiality are equal [*ki qameih yitbarakh shaweh u-mashweh ruḥaniyyut we-gashmiyyut*], and thus the disclosure will be below in the lower unity as it is in the upper unity."[176] With respect to the Infinite, there is no distinction between spiritual and material, as the two are, philosophically speaking, indifferent, *shaweh u-mashweh ruḥaniyyut we-gashmiyyut*.[177] The transcendence that is above nature (*lema'lah min ha-ṭeva*) is always immanent in nature (*ha-ṭeva*) as what is beyond the natural, mathematically depicted by the number eight and semiotically by the letter *ḥeit*, a symbolic complex that gathers round itself a kaleidoscope of images and themes strewn about the landscape of Ḥabad, based on much older kabbalistic lore. The crucial point that may be elicited from these dense and convoluted texts is that God and world are identified in their mutual difference, the one that is in but still other to the other, the "wholly other" that embraces in its wholeness the possibility of being other to, and therefore both more and less than, the whole. Ḥabad masters have long understood that sameness must be construed as neither identical with nor different from difference. To contemplate that God and world are the same is to apprehend the parabolic truth par excellence, a truth that affirms the identity of what is identified as different. The dual mirroring is such that world appears as the image of God and God as the image of world, an apparent truth, the truth of what appears to be true, a truth that is called in kabbalistic and Ḥasidic vernacular variously as *levush*, *malbush*, or *hitlabbeshut*, the secret of the garment that alludes to the incarnational understanding of the Torah as the primordial parable (*meshal ha-qadmoni*), the mark of (dis)similitude where truth appears in the image of truth, as I discussed at length in the last section of the previous chapter.

The discerning of this truth is not the consequence of the return of all things to the essence, a "theosophic cosmology" based on the mystical ideal of *apokastasis*,[178] but rather it comes about through the indifferent essence being drawn into and hence garbed within the world of differentiation. The point is made incisively in Schneerson's description of the messianic realization of the materialization of the divine light in the physical domain: "the truth of the matter of a habitation for him, blessed be he, in the lower beings is that there shall also be a disclosure that is above the emanation [*amittat ha-inyan de-dirah lo yitbarakh ba-taḥtonim hu she-yihyeh gam ha-gilluy she-lema'lah me-aṣilut*]."[179] Could the paradox of an acosmic naturalism—the visible as specter of the invisible—cut deeper against itself? To be messianically attuned is to perceive that the revelation of godliness in the cosmos is the highest disclosure, indeed the showing of the unshowing, the essence without form or figure.[180] The façade of worldhood—or what is called nature (*ṭeva*), which includes the physical and the metaphysical—provides the ontic condition that makes possible the epistemic awareness that all that exists is naught but a veil by which the infinite light beyond nature (*or ein sof lema'lah min ha-ṭeva*) is manifest by being hidden. When viewed from this angle, the phenomenal world can be considered theophanic, it reveals the divine, but it can do so only by concealing it, since what it reveals is the concealed.[181] Translating this conception into a semiotic register, the "aspect of exaltation, the infinite essence" (*beḥinat ha-romemut aṣmut de-ein sof*),[182] is symbolized by *alef*,[183] the silent letter that is the fount of the other letters, which, according to an archaic kabbalistic belief, are comprised within and emerge like branches from the root word, the name YHWH, the mystical essence of Torah, gestured concomitantly as phonic image and graphic sound—a point that problematizes the privileging of either the visual or auditory in kabbalistic symbolism.[184] As I have long maintained, the distinction between logocentric and grammatological is not an adequate speculum through which to glance on this material. Reality—the essence that is hidden as the hidden essence—is this *alef*, the embryo of all that is, was, and shall be impressed in this letter, the mute resonance of the vacuum that is the plenum, the murmuring vibration of the nothing that is everything. Orthographically, as kabbalists were wont to point out already in the second half of the thirteenth century, the *alef* can be decomposed into three markings, a *yod* above, a *yod* below, and the *waw* in the middle, the numerical value of which is twenty-six (10 + 10 + 6), which is also the sum of the letters YHWH (10 + 5 + 6 + 5), the name that signifies the compresence of the three modes of time. The *alef*, therefore, is the *pele*, the enigma that is the Tetragram, the stuff that philosophers call being.

In some measure, the terms *apophatic panentheism* and *acosmic naturalism* map on to the philological distinction used by Ḥabad masters between the "upper unity," in which the world is effaced vis-à-vis the One, and the "lower unity," in which the One is effaced vis-à-vis the world.[185] Despite the significance of this distinction, the dialectical drift of Ḥabad thought should give one pause from applying it too sharply—"lower" and "higher" are themselves subject to the same undoing: what is attained through the lower is always already compacted in the higher, which is always already evolving in the lower. The depth of the paradox is exposed when the veil of being is lifted to reveal the being of the veil that is recurrently (re)veiled in the (un)veiling of the veil. Messianic consciousness, which is at all times a matter of the future attainable in the present as the past-that-is-perpetually-yet-to-come-as-what-has-already-been, turns on becoming aware that the real divergence between divine and cosmic is merely apparent, and the apparent divergence real. The theological presumption of either God or world independent of one another comes under suspicion with the proper attunement or vision to the nature of nature when considered from the perspective of the essence (*aṣmut*), the "divine light that shines above nature" (*or ha-elohi me'ir lema'lah min ha-ṭeva*), as the second Rebbe put it,[186] or, in the language of the seventh Rebbe, the "light that is higher than being garbed in the world" (*or vos iz hecher fun hislabshus in velt*), the "light that is beyond the concatenation" (*ha-or she-lema'lah me-hishtalshelut*).[187] Surely, this unknowable and unnameable essence, the "aspect of the essential nothing that is the nothing of the concealment of the essence" (*beḥinat ha-ayin ha-aṣmi she-hi ayin shel he'lem ha-aṣmut*),[188] cannot be essentialized as it points—allusively rather than indexically—to the one reality (*meṣi'ut*) or substance (*mahut*) to which neither being nor nonbeing may be attributed in the absence of the other. For something to be, it must be nothing.

The (in)essentiality is thus characterized as the "essential concealment that is not in existence at all as it is also concealed to itself" (*he'lem ha-aṣmi she-eino bi-meṣi'ut kelal we-hu he'lem gam le-aṣmo*),[189] a concealment-of-essence that is the essence of concealment, an essence that is (in)essentially concealed, the *aṣmut* that is *he'lem*. Insofar as the essence is defined as an essential concealment, the revelation of that essence must of necessity be a revelation of nothing, that is, a revelation in which what is revealed is the concealment and hence a revelation that is, in essence, a concealment.

The matter of this immateriality is made explicit in the description proffered by Dov Baer of the "essential and hylic concealment" (*he'lem ha-aṣmi we-hiyyuli*), the "source of the coming-to-be of the disclosure of light," the aspect of the Infinite that "does not yet fall under the category of concealment and disclosure."[190] By using the adjective *hylic* to describe the hidden essence, Dov Baer is echoing the age-old assumption that matter in its essential materiality lacks any definitive characteristic of its own, comprising instead the potential of every being that is to come to be, the *koaḥ mah*, according to the kabbalistic gloss on the term *ḥokhmah*, the wisdom of God, which was appropriated as well by the Ḥasidic masters.[191] More specific to the vocabulary of Ḥabad thought, hylic matter is deployed as a symbol to depict the concealed aspect of Wisdom (*ḥokhmah setima'ah*) that is within *Keter*, the abyss (*tohu*) that is the matrix of the four elements in potentiality and not in actuality, according to Shneur Zalman,[192] or the "aspect of the essential hiddenness of the Infinite" (*beḥinat ha-he'lem ha-aṣmi de-ein sof*), as the RaShaB put it,[193] the amorphous mass—weightless and without dimensions—that conserves all possible forms in its formlessness. This essential inessentiality, or the inessential essentiality, is depicted as well by other figurative tropes, including the elemental fire (*esh ha-yesodi*) that comes forth when the stone is struck, the ether (*awir*) that is the "concealment of light in its essential source" (*he'lem ha-or bi-meqoro ha-aṣmi*),[194] the potential for luminosity that is prior to the "first withdrawal" (*ha-ṣimṣum ha-ri'shon*), and the consequent disclosure of the concealment,[195] the mystery of the hidden darkness that is before the showing of light, the substance (*mahut*) that is comprehended only apophatically (*hassagah zo derekh shelilah*) by way of comprehending that there can be no comprehension but that there is no comprehension (*hassagat ha-shelilah*).[196] The ultimate reality, which cannot be conceptualized or named, is the "light of the incomposite and essential grace of the light of the Infinite,"[197] the essence that is portrayed either as a darkened light or as the luminal darkness that precedes the fissure into light and dark.

One might have logically expected that antecedent to this splintering, we should not speak of either light or dark, as neither term would be meaningful in the elimination of its correlate. Alternatively expressed, to speak of the identity of opposites in the essence would be as limiting as speaking of their nonidentity; to contemplate what is beyond duality, we must ponder the suspension of all opposition, even the opposition of opposites that have been rendered (non)identical in their opposition. The essence, accordingly, is neither light nor dark because it is both light and dark, albeit not identically or differently, indeed beyond the identity of identity and difference. Ḥabad's perspective on the essence would correspond, on this account, to Schelling's notion of the "absolute indifference" of the being or essence (*Wesen*) that precedes all ground and is thus referred to as the "original ground," the *Ungrund*, literally, the *nonground*.[198] For comparative purposes, it is worthwhile citing one passage in full:

> We have, then, one being [*Ein Wesen*] for all oppositions, an absolute identity of light and darkness, good and evil. . . . There must be a being before all ground and before all that exists, thus generally before any duality. . . . Since it precedes all opposites, these cannot be distinguishable in it nor can they be present in any way. Therefore, it cannot be described as the identity of opposites; it can only be described as the absolute *indifference* [*Indifferenz*] of both. . . . Indifference is not a product of opposites, nor are they implicitly contained in it, but rather indifference is its own being separate from all opposition, a being against which all opposites ruin themselves, that is nothing else than their very not-Being [*Nichtsein*] and that, for this reason, also has no predicate, except as the very lacking of a predicate, without it being on that account a nothingness or non-thing.[199]

The essence spoken of by the Ḥabad masters can be described as the indifference predicated with respect to the nonground that precedes any ground, an indifference that precludes the possibility of attributing the two basic principles—referred to by a number of binary pairs, real and ideal, darkness and light, good and evil—as opposites, for to do so would be to ascribe difference to the indifferent. It is not even sufficient to say that the nonground is both concomitantly, to speak of this one being (*ein Wesen*) as undifferentiated. What is tenable is to attribute the opposites to the nonground as nonopposites. From the disjunction of their nonbeing (*Nichtsein*), neither one nor the other, emerges the conjunction of both one and the other.[200]

In Ḥabad thought, the nature of the one true reality is delineated in terms that are very close to Schelling's depiction of the nonground. Thus, for example, Shneur Zalman remarked that in the essence of the light of the Infinite, "darkness and light are equal before him in one equanimity" (*shawin qameih be-hashwa'ah aḥat*). With respect to this indifference, the scriptural assertion that the "light is superior to darkness" (Eccles 2:13) cannot be upheld, for "the light and darkness are identified before him in the aspect of nullification in one equanimity" (*mishtawwim qameih ha-or we-ha-ḥoshekh bi-veḥinat ha-biṭṭul be-hashwa'ah aḥat*).[201] And yet many passages from Shneur Zalman, and the other Lubavitch masters, attest that they continued a path that stretches back a considerable distance, according to which the Infinite, though indiscriminate and hence beyond demarcation, is nevertheless characterized by one of the binary terms to the exclusion of its contrary. We even find, as I have documented at length elsewhere, that the highest aspect of the divine is depicted as a world of pure masculinity, a world wherein the feminine is implanted in the masculine as the capacity for difference, but a difference that appears nonetheless to be absorbed in the identity of the same.[202] Lest there be any misunderstanding, let me state unequivocally that I do not think that there is an indigenous logic that would impose this onto kabbalistic doctrine, but, in my reading of the sources, I have observed, time and again, that the exclusively male kabbalists identified the masculine, and more specifically the phallic, potency as the root of gender dimorphism, an assumption that is expressed in sundry ways, but perhaps most poignantly in the interpretation of circumcision as the ritual that symbolically enacts the mystery of the divine androgyne.[203] From this assumption there follows the further one that both genders are circumscribed in a closed circle of nondifferentiation—to be contrasted with an open circle of indifference—much like the serpent eating its tail, according to the archaic mythological image. A critical and influential formulation of this ideal is the zoharic description of the uppermost configuration of the Godhead, "There is no left in the concealed Ancient One, for everything is right,"[204] a dictum that is summoned in Ḥabad literature.[205] We may conclude, therefore, that the ideal of *hashwa'ah*, the equalization of opposites, did not entail historically or textually (though logically it may have) an indifference that transcends difference indifferently, but rather a coincidence whereby one of the opposing terms is entwined in the other.[206] When kabbalists speak of a reality where there is no left, they mean that everything is right, and not that there is neither left nor right.[207] This may be difficult for us to digest, as we presume that binary pairs, such as right and left, are correlative terms, therefore the meaning (let alone presumed existence) of one is dependent on the other. The difficulty aside, this is precisely what the traditional kabbalistic outlook demands of the interpreter. Similarly, in Ḥabad contemplation, the essence, as we have seen, is depicted as either light or dark, indeed as the supraluminous effulgence in which light and dark are no longer distinguishable, but the light is still privileged, as even when the essence is described as being neither light nor dark what is intended is that the light comprises the darkness or that the darkness is indistinguishable from the light. The highest aspect of the Godhead and its corresponding element in the soul, *yeḥidah*, are routinely depicted as an incomposite light without division (*or pashuṭ beli hitḥallequt*),[208] but it is light nonetheless. Consider the pronouncement of the RaShaB concerning the "light of the Infinite without any withdrawal or concealment at all" (*or ein sof beli shum ṣimṣum we-he'lem kelal*), which is characterized further as the "aspect of the light that shines for itself" (*beḥinat or ha-me'ir le-aṣmo*)."[209] Note as well that the two types of unification distinguished in Ḥabad thought, *itkafya* and *ithapkha*, both presume that one term of the binary prevails over the other—the dark is either subjugated by or transfigured into the light.

Ha-Olam He'lem: Worldhood and Withdrawing the Withdrawal

A key to comprehending this apophatic ontology is a wordplay used on numerous occasions by the Ḥabad masters that links two expressions consisting of the same consonants, *ha-olam*, "the world," and *he'lem*, "concealment." In the previous chapter, we already referred to this verbal play, but it is necessary to examine it here in greater detail. Although many passages could be cited to illustrate the point, I will commence the discussion with a concise formulation offered by the sixth Rebbe in a discourse from the night of Simḥat Torah, 23 Tishrei 5691 (October 14, 1930):

> World [*olam*] is the language of concealment [*he'lem*], for the root of the concealment [*shoresh ha-he'lem*] is from the first withdrawal [*ṣimṣum ha-ri'shon*], as the intent of the withdrawal is for the sake of the disclosure [*ha-gilluy*] . . . and, if the matter of the withdrawals in the order of the concatenation [*ha-ṣimṣumim de-seder hishtalshelut*] is the diminution of light for the sake of disclosure, how much more so with regard to the first withdrawal, whose matter is the removal of the light entirely, is it clear that its intention is for the sake of disclosure![210]

In the sixth Rebbe's comment, one can detect the two principal ways that the juxtaposition of the words *olam* and *he'lem* can be interpreted, both of them esoteric, to be sure, but the former overtly so, and the latter more clandestinely, portending the duplicity of the secret, the secret doubling itself, the secret of the secret, the secret secreted as secret.

In the first instance, the supposition that the world can be viewed from the vantage point of concealment suggests that the ontic chain (*seder hishtalshelut*) can reveal the hidden light only by hiding it, for, if it were not hidden, how could it be revealed as the light that is hidden? All reality that proceeds from the essence—in Lurianic terms, from the primordial anthropos (*adam qadmon*) to the physical world of doing (*olam asiyyah*)—can be viewed as the progressive concealment and disclosure of the light, indeed, a concealment that is a disclosure in virtue of being a concealment. The spatiotemporal universe is a place of darkness, but a darkness that makes the light visible, the darkness where the light of God is manifestly concealed. As the seventh Rebbe put it, "the concealment and hiddenness in the world is from the perspective of the essence of the existence of the world [*der helem ve-hester vos in velt iz mi-tsad ir etsem metsius fun velt*]" and "for this reason it is called *olam* . . . which is from the expression *he'lem*."[211] The word *ṭeva*, "nature," designates the

> divine vitality [*ḥiyyut ha-elohi*] that sustains the created beings, and it is the divine force [*koaḥ elohi*] that brings about the created beings from nothing to something. . . .

> For the matter of nature [*inyan ha-ṭeva*] that is in it is also from the expression "submersion" [*ṭevi'ah*], since the being [*hithawwut*] is in the manner of withdrawal and concealment [*be-ofen de-he'lem we-hester*], as the potency that brings into being is concealed and hidden in the created entities. . . . The reason for this is that the divine vitality is garbed in the created entities by means of the garments that conceal . . . but the divine force that brings the created entities into being is distinct from the created entities and is not garbed in them.[212]

The dialectic exploited in Ḥabad sources is a central facet of kabbalistic ontology from the Middle Ages, but it was given bolder formulation and unprecedented emphasis by sixteenth-century kabbalists who assiduously asserted that concealment is disclosure, and disclosure concealment (*ha-gilluy hu ha-he'lem we-ha-he'lem hu ha-gilluy*).[213] The cosmos appears as a reality separate from and independent of God, but the one who sees with the eyes of faith knows that this is mere appearance, as the garments of nature (*levushei ha-ṭeva*) are the "concealment and withdrawal" (*ha-he'lem we-ha-hester*) of the divine.[214] "The world, which is under time and space, is as naught and nothing [*ke-ayin wa-efes*], and it is annihilated in the light of the Infinite, blessed be he, which is above the concatenation, for it is not in the category of time and space."[215] The world (*ha-olam*), therefore, is essentially a form of concealment (*he'lem*)—it conceals the light so that it may be revealed, as there can be no extension without withholding, no showing without hiding, no presence without absence.[216] With respect to divinity, however, as Shneur Zalman already expressed it in *Tanya*, the concealment conceals its concealment, since we cannot speak of withdrawal in the infinite plenum, and hence "before him all is considered as actually naught [*qameih kolla ke-lo ḥashiv mammash*]."[217] The last statement, which is derived from a zoharic passage,[218] is reiterated unrelentingly in Ḥabad literature as a slogan to impart what is often referred to as the acosmic ideal of the disbanding of the being of everything when viewed in relation to the Infinite. In a manner reminiscent of the paradoxical language of a Zen koan, Shneur Zalman spoke of the Infinite, the incomprehensible essence that transcends the cosmological distinction between transcendence (*sovev kol almin*) and immanence (*memalle kol almin*), as "that before which it is actually considered as not actually [*qameih mammash ke-lo mammash ḥashivu*], and it is as if there were no worlds there at all."[219] The concealment of which we speak, therefore, the concealment before the withdrawal of the light, is a correlative term; its meaning can only be evaluated from the perspective of an impulse for the one to be related to another, an impulse that is ultimately inexplicable, as it implies some degree of otherness within the essence that contains all things and hence in relation to which there can be no other. The incomprehensibility of this belief notwithstanding, the kabbalistic wisdom that "the disclosure of the light of the Infinite is for the sake of the worlds"[220] rests on the supposition that the potential for alterity is the aspect of concealment concealed in the concealment of the concealed essence, an essence whose inclusivity includes the excluded, even as its exclusivity excludes the inclusive. This capacity for otherness, the possibility of the divine donning the dress of the various worlds, is linked to the attribute of judgment, the quality of constriction that facilitates the emanation of light, the attribute of kingship (*middat malkhut*) or, more specifically, the "kingship of the Infinite" (*malkhut de-ein sof*),[221] the "kingship-that-is-within-the-kingship" (*malkhut she-be-malkhut*),[222] the "capacity for exaltedness" (*koaḥ ha-hitnasse'ut*) that is not possible "without the other" (*beli zulat*).[223] As Schneerson put it in a discourse delivered on 24 Nisan 5712 (April 19, 1952):

> The yoke of the kingdom of heaven [*ol malkhut shamayim*][224] is in the aspect of the essence that is also above that which encompasses all worlds. It has been explained elsewhere that in the light of the Infinite before the withdrawal there is also an aspect of the kingship of the kingship of the Infinite [*she-gam be-or ein sof she-lifnei ha-ṣimṣum yesh beḥinat malkhut de-malkhut de-ein sof*], as the withdrawal was in this gradation. . . . Hence, in the aspect of the kingship of the Infinite prior to the withdrawal [*bi-veḥinat ha-malkhut de-ein sof lifnei ha-ṣimṣum*], there is the matter of kingship [*yeshno inyan malkhut*].[225]

In line with a phallocentric system of signification, the potential for otherness is engendered as feminine, but, in some respects, Ḥabad thought (reaching a climax in the seventh Rebbe) resists the dominant patriarchal structure, and the delineation of the female as the site of alterity problematizes the hegemony of the masculine; femininity is essentialized as the aspect of the essence that is the possibility (*yekholet*) of all that is to become, the essence, therefore, whose essence it is to withstand essentializing. The inessential is linked, moreover, to the name that is "the radiance [*ha-ziw*] contained in the luminescence [*kalul ba-ma'or*] before the world was created, which is merely the matter of what is in the potentiality of the holy luminescence [*inyan mah she-yesh bi-yekholet ha-ma'or*] of the blessed holy One, to illumine from him an illumination when he desires to radiate."[226] To state the matter in slightly different terms, the feminine is the matrix of materiality, the infinite potentiality for finitude that continuously gives shape to the creative actuality of the one true substance, the necessary contingency that is, ipso facto, necessarily contingent. It is in this sense that the feminine dimension within the Infinite, *malkhut de-malkhut de-ein sof*, is the concealment (*he'lem*) that makes possible the existential-ontological conditions of the world (*ha-olam*). Commenting in another homily on the midrashic dictum that prior to the world God and his name were alone,[227] Schneerson remarked that the "name" contained in the Infinite (*ha-shem ha-kalul be-ein sof*) is "the aspect of delimitation in that which has no limit [*beḥinah shel hagbalah be-tokh mah she-ein lo gevul*], the root for there being a world, for there being the aspect of the other in relation to the Infinite that upholds everything [*shoresh lihyot olam lihyot beḥinah zulat legabbei ein sof ha-nose et ha-kol*]."[228] Inasmuch as the essence is the substratum of all things that are to become, it can have no authentic other, but, precisely because this is so, the potentiality for disclosure vis-à-vis the other (*gilluy el ha-zulat*) must itself be concealed in the concealment as the dimension of difference lodged in the heart of the indifferent, the aspect of the name embedded in the unnameable, the feminine capacity for limitation and boundary expressed in the concealed world (*alma de-itkasya*), which consists of the realm of emanation, and the revealed world (*alma de-itgalya*), which comprises the realms of creation, formation, and doing, the quaternity of traditional kabbalistic cosmology.[229]

He'lem ha-Olam: Meontological Disclosing

There is, however, a second and deeper interpretation of the juxtaposition of *ha-olam* and *he'lem*, and one that, in my opinion, may even go beyond the labels *acosmic naturalism* and *apophatic panentheism,* indeed perhaps beyond any and every imaginable terminological register. As the sixth Rebbe put it, in contrast to all other attributes wherein concealment is connected to disclosure (*he'lem ha-shayyakh el ha-gilluy*), in the case of *Malkhut*, the "concealment is more interior" (*he'lem penimi yoter*), that is, the hiddenness associated with the feminine is not some latent power (*koaḥ ne'lam*) that will be revealed in a particular disclosure, which is consequently antecedent to the concealment, but the power of latency as such (*ha-koaḥ kemo she-hu be-he'lem*), the concealment within the concealed essence that ontologically precedes disclosure (*qodem ha-gilluy*).[230] The juxtaposing of the terms *ha-olam* and *he'lem* intimates that what is concealed in the disclosure of world is not the divine light that is concealed but the concealment of that light, that is, the concealment of the concealment that is only further concealed in its disclosure. Worldhood partakes essentially of this (in)essentiality, a meontology that issues from the insight that "prior to the world having been created all of the gradations were annihilated and unified in the light of the Infinite in an absolute unity without any aspect of the existence of something."[231] The tangibility of the world is determined, therefore, from the standpoint of this annihilation, something-that-is-nothing, the reality of illusion, in contrast to nothing-that-is-something, the illusion of reality. To deny that would be to conceal the concealment in such a way that the concealment would not be concealed. One of the most blatant articulations of this extremely subtle point is made by Aaron Halevi Horowitz of Staroselye, a disciple of Shneur Zalman:

> The essence of the unity and of the faith is that apart from him there is nothing at all [*she-ein zulato kelal*], and he is simple in utter simplicity [*pashuṭ be-takhlit ha-peshiṭut*] and equanimous in the utmost equanimity [*shaweh be-takhlit ha-hashwwa'ah*] on account of which all the beings that exist in the world are all created from privation to actual being in a new being from nothing to something [*meḥuddashim me-he'der el hawayah mammash be-hawayah ḥadashah me-ayin le-yesh*], that is, their existence should not be described as a concealment of concealment [*he'lem de-he'lem*].[232] Therefore all the worlds and existents were previously in the aspect of nothing [*beḥinat ayin*].[233]

There is only one reality, the one that is incomposite and indifferent, the-nothing-that-contains-everything-annihilated-in-the-nothing-that-is-everything. As Aaron Halevi put it elsewhere, "one must nullify the body from the perspective of the contemplation and faith in his divinity, blessed be he, that he is the root and source of all the worlds, and the physical worlds do not attain any substance in relation to him."[234] The "him" in relation to which the worlds are nothing is itself nothing. The double bind of this nothingness is the meontological truth one must come (not) to know.

To comprehend the Ḥabad perspective, I have found it beneficial to adopt a form of logic akin to what in the Mahāyāna tradition is referred to as *madhyamaka*, the middle way, a logic that, in the locution I have availed myself of in previous studies, posits the identity of opposites in the opposition of their identity.[235] Translated in a more technical vein, the logic to which I refer is based on the tetralemmic scheme: S is P; ~P; both P and ~P; neither P nor ~P.[236] The middle of the four-cornered logic, which some scholars consider to be the core of Buddhist philosophy, should not be conceived of as a meridian point situated equidistantly between extremes, the venerated golden mean between excess and privation in the Western philosophical tradition, but as the indeterminate space that contains both and neither of the extremes, the absent presence that is present as absent, the lull between affirmation and negation, identity and nonidentity, the void that cannot be avoided. In this middle excluded by the logic of the excluded middle, purportedly contradictory properties are attributed and not attributed to the (non)substance at the same time and in the same relation, whence it follows that the propositions (A · ~A) and ~(A · ~A) converge in the point of their divergence.

It goes without saying that I am mindful of the methodological difficulties that this kind of comparative analysis entails. Without obfuscating the semantic and conceptual discrepancies that divide these two cultural environments, I would argue that there is philosophic merit in applying the Mādhyamika presentation of emptiness (*śūnyatā*) and dependent origination (*pratītyasamutpāda*) as a heuristic tool to analyze the cosmological and metaphysical teachings of Ḥabad.[237] The most important insight is already imparted by the Centrist school's founder, the Indian sage Nāgārjuna (c. 150–250), known honorifically as the second Buddha: emptiness itself must be empty. The claim that all phenomena do not exist inherently ensnares the mind in a self-subverting paradox: it asserts a truth that is true only if it is false, but it is false only if it is true, in a manner analogous to the contention "Everything I say is false"—if this statement is true, it must be false, but if it is false, it must be true.[238] Epistemologically, the doctrine of emptiness entails the discernment that the ultimate truth is that there is no ultimate truth, that the essential reality is that there is no essential reality, that nature is inherently devoid of an inherent nature.[239] The paradox is vividly disclosed in the following passage from Nāgārjuna's *Mūlamadhyamakakārikā*, considered a foundational text of the Mādhyamika tradition:

> *Whatever is the essence of the Tathāgata,*
> *That is the essence of the world.*
> *The Tathāgata has no essence.*
> *The world is without essence (22:16).*[240]

If we substitute the term *Ein Sof* for Tathāgata, we would have a perfectly apt formulation of what I have called the meontological perspective of Ḥabad: the essence of the world is the essence of *Ein Sof*, but the latter has no essence, and hence the former is without essence. Most astoundingly, Ḥabad speculation on the essence—the nothing that everything is in virtue of the everything that nothing will not be—bears an especially striking affinity to the logic of the middle explicated in the *Mountain Doctrine*, a treatise by Döl-bo-ba (1292–1361), considered to be the founder of the Jo-nang-ba sect of Tibetan Buddhism. I could have chosen from a vast array of sources, but, for the purposes of this analysis, I will cite one passage to illustrate what I take to be an astonishing conceptual affinity between the two contemplative paths. The text I will consider is initiated as a reflection on the characterization of emptiness in the *Differentiation of the Middle and the Extremes* (*Madhyāntavibhāga*) by Maitreya, the Buddha's regent: "The non-existence of the entities of duality / And the nature of non-entities is the character of emptiness."[241] Expounding this wisdom, Döl-bo-ba probes more profoundly into the contrast between ultimate emptiness and self-emptiness:

> Mere self-emptiness does not fulfill its role. Why? It is because that which is the ultimate emptiness not only clears away the extreme of non-existence—"not exis-

> tent and not non-existent"—but self-emptiness does not clear away the extreme of non-existence. Concerning this, whereas conventional phenomena do not at all exist in the mode of subsistence, the extreme of existence is the superimposition that they do. Whereas the partless, omnipresent pristine wisdom of the element of attributes always abides pervading all, the extreme of non-existence is the deprecation that it does not exist and is not established and is empty of its own entity. That which is the middle devoid of those extremes is the basis devoid of all extremes such as existence and non-existence, superimposition, and deprecation, permanence and annihilation, and so forth, due to which it is the final great middle. It is non-material emptiness, emptiness far from an annihilatory emptiness, great emptiness that is the ultimate pristine wisdom . . . for the character of the emptiness that is the final mode of subsistence, the mere emptiness of non-entities is not sufficient. Rather, the emptiness that is the [ultimate] nature of non-entities [that is, emptiness that is the ultimate nature opposite from non-entities] is required.[242]

The closest philological analogue to the Mādhyamika concept of "emptiness" in the Ḥabad lexicon appears to be the term *efes*. I cannot here properly engage the multivalency of this term, but let me state that it is applied by Ḥabad masters to the Infinite (*ein sof*), since, as Shneur Zalman put it, paraphrasing previous kabbalistic sources,[243] there "is no comprehension with respect to it" (*ki ein bo shum tefisah*),[244] and thus it is the "negation of thought" (*afisat ha-ra'yon*).[245] The word *efes* is often paired with *tohu*, the "abyss,"[246] as it is the voidness that is the "essence of the Infinite," the aspect of light whose "existence is nullification" (*meṣi'uto hu ha-biṭṭul*),[247] that is, for it to be, it must be not. And yet, the nothing of being-not is to be distinguished from the nothing of not-being; the former is marked linguistically by *efes* and the latter by *ayin*. The conceptual distinction can be expressed in terms of two aspects of denegation, *biṭṭul ha-yesh*, the nullification of disparate beings, and *biṭṭul ha-ayin*, the nullification of nullification. It seems to me legitimate to think of *efes* as the semantic and conceptual equivalent to the emptiness that Döl-bo-ba described as the final mode of subsistence, the emptiness that is consummately empty and therefore empty even of the emptiness of which it is fully empty, the emptiness that is neither empty nor nonempty,[248] neither existent nor nonexistent, neither different nor the same,[249] the middle devoid of the middle, the ultimate lacking the ultimate.[250] The goal of the mystical path, one might say, is to be zeroed, to dematerialize into the "consummate nil" (*efes gamur*),[251] the insubstantiality of what is to become, the nonentity that neither is nor is not because it both is and is not. Consider the formulation of the third Lubavitcher Rebbe: "In relation to the divine vitality [*ḥiyyut elohut*] that sustains us, we are eradicated from existence [*beṭelim mi-meṣi'ut*], and in the aspect of the actual naught [*efes mammash*], like the ray of the sun when it is in the body of the sphere of the sun . . . there is no more existence at all apart from his existence, blessed be he, and this is the complete unity [*ha-yiḥud ha-gamur*]."[252] The description here, as the Ṣemaḥ Ṣedeq explicitly states in another passage,[253] is necessarily limited, as the example of the sunlight in relation to the body of the sun is still too dualistic to capture the utter extermination that pertains to one who has become the "actual naught," annihilated to the point of being nothing beyond the point of being nothing. Explicating the statement of the Ṣemaḥ Ṣedeq that "*efes* is a greater annihilation [*biṭṭul yoter*] than *ayin*,"[254] his son Shmuel commented that "*ayin* has the letters of *ani*, which is the aspect of something [*beḥinat yesh*], and it is only annihilated in the aspect of nothing [*raq she-hu baṭel bi-veḥinat ayin*], which is not so with *efes*, the aspect of the absolute annihilation [*beḥinat biṭṭul mi-kol we-khol*], for there is no existence of anything there."[255]

Döl-bo-ba's contrast of ultimate emptiness and self-emptiness corresponds to the distinction between *biṭṭul bi-meṣi'ut* and *biṭṭul ha-yesh*. The denegation associated with the former clears away the extreme of existence and the extreme of nonexistence, whereas the denegation of the latter clears away the extreme of existence but not the extreme of nonexistence. To occupy the space of the middle, the verbal and logical correlate to what is conceived meontologically as the void, one must pass beyond the *ayin* of *biṭṭul ha-yesh*, the nothing of the nullification of existence, to the *efes* of *biṭṭul bi-meṣi'ut* , the naught of the nullification in existence, the "actual integration" (*hitkallelut mammash*), which entails the annihilation of both existence and nonexistence, as "there is no existence at all but only essence" (*she-lo yesh shum meṣi'ut kelal raq ha-aṣmut*).[256] The second nullification, therefore, yields the not-nothing, the positivity of the double negative, a voiding of the distinction between being and not-being in an absolutely relative way. When the truth that the essence is neither existent nor nonexistent—in the infinite power, *yesh* and *ayin*, something and nothing, "are identical with no distinction at all" (*shawwin beli hevdel kelal*)[257]—is coupled with the traditional notion of creation of something from nothing, we are faced with another insurmountable paradox. The annihilation of all beings in the nothing makes possible the bringing forth of each discrete being as something from nothing, and yet, insofar as all beings persist in that nothing, to the extent that they are annihilated therein, every innovation cannot but be a renewal of that annihilation. If one were to disavow either of these claims, one would be guilty of concealing the concealment that is the world.

The objective, then, is not to negate the negation, to discard the veil of nature, but to see through it and thereby discover that there is no seeing without a veil. Again, Nāgārjuna's account of the tetralemmic wisdom regarding the possibility of knowing the emptiness of Tathāgata may be helpful to understand Ḥabad thinking about the essence that is unthinkable, even as the unthinkable essence:

> *"Empty" should not be asserted.*
> *"Nonempty" should not be asserted.*
> *Neither both nor neither should be asserted.*
> *They are only used nominally (22:11).*[258]

From the ultimate standpoint, the perspective of the emptiness that is neither empty nor nonempty, the everyday world is nonexistent. The enlightened one knows, however, that this nonexistence does not imply a negation of the existence of the phenomenal world, but a reassessment of its existence, a shift from presuming that there are independent substances to perceiving the relativity and codependency of all that comes to be in the chain of becoming.[259] The gnosis of awakening consists of discerning that the true nature of things (*tattva*) is emptiness (*śūnyatā*), a truth that is identical to or compatible with the cosmological principle of dependent origination (*pratītyasamutpāda*).[260] In the disclosure of this disclosure, one perceives the world recovered in the formless void, whence everything comes to be in the nothingness of its being. The capacity to negate all beings in the emptiness of their being is thus to affirm them in the being of their emptiness, to realize the absence of their presence through the presence of their absence. The point is epitomized in the first chapter of *The Discrimination Between the Middle and the Extremes* (*Madhyānta-vighāga*), a crucial text for the mind-only (*vijñapti-mātra*) Buddhist school: "Because of existence, non-existence and again existence . . . everything is said in the Mahāyāna to be neither void (*śūnya*) nor non-void. This is the middle path (*madhyamā pratipad*)."[261]

The belief in the duality of subject and object as discriminate substances, what is called "false ideation" (*abhūta-parikalpa*), gives rise to existence, which in turn yields its opposite, the introspection that instructs the mind in the existence of non-existence. As a consequence, existence and nonexistence are no longer thought of as antinomies—even the distinction between mind only and external objects is overcome, as the perception of the former yields the nonperception of the latter, whence the nonperception of the former is apperceived[262]—and hence everything is said to be neither empty nor nonempty. Analogously, in Ḥabad philosophy the essence functions as the substratum underlying the plethora of phenomena that constitute the world, but in this substratum all things subsist in the being of their nothingness to the degree that they are nullified in the nothingness of their being. The substratum, in other words, is not an independently existing thing with discernible properties that can be pigeonholed and named; it is a linguistic sign by which we organize the phenomenal events that constitute our experience of the world. The conceptualizing mind is always at risk of essentializing the essence, of clinging to the void as though it were something to which to cling, but this is to misapprehend the nature of the essence that transcends all empirical determinations and thought constructions and therefore cannot be reified as an innately existing entity. If we are to speak of substance, it is the substance (*mahut*) that is the abyss (*tehom*), the substance that is nothing.[263] In this ground, which is the absence of ground, abiding and nonabiding are one and the same.

Messianic Disrobing: Seeing the Garment of No Garment

One might protest that there is ample textual evidence that Ḥabad masters do speak of a full disclosure of the essence (*gilluy ha-aṣmut*) without any apparel (*beli levush*),[264] a depiction that is called upon especially to characterize the messianic era. Following earlier sources, this vision is derived exegetically from a number of key apocalyptically charged verses, such as "Your master will no longer be covered and your eyes will see your master" (Isa 30:20), "The glory of the Lord shall appear, and all flesh, as one, shall behold that the mouth of the Lord has spoken" (Isa 40:5), "For every eye shall behold the Lord when he returns to Zion" (Isa 52:8).[265] Would the vision here envisaged not suggest an immediate seeing of the light, a beholding of the naked truth? If we entertain this prospect as real, would it not pose a challenge to the ultimate nothingness that the nothing ultimately is claimed to be? Ḥabad masters speak of a full disclosure of the essence, but, at the same time, they assert that the essence is not something—not even nothing—with which to be reckoned. In exposing the essence without cover, there is no truth there to be uncovered.[266]

To give a sense of the kabbalistic legacy upon which Ḥabad masters would be drawing, I mention here one passage from Abraham Azulai's *Ḥesed le-Avraham*, a treatise composed in the early part of the seventeenth century:

> The divisions of the worlds are emanation [*aṣilut*], creation [*beri'ah*], formation [*yeṣirah*], and doing [*asiyyah*]. The world of emanation [*olam ha-aṣilut*] receives the light of the Infinite [*or ha-ein sof*] verily without any veil [*masakh*] or garment [*levush*], like the soul that extends to the whole body, and all the ten *sefirot* are a garment in relation to it, and it is their soul. This is not the case in the rest of the worlds, which draw their light by means of a veil and a garment like the matter of the garment in relation to the body and the body in relation to the soul.[267]

Azulai tries to contrast the first of the four worlds with the other three by noting that it receives the light of the Infinite without any intermediary. At the same time, however, he describes the ten *sefirot*, which constitute the substance of the world of emanation, as a garment in relation to that light. Imagining the *sefirot* cannot but be from the vantage point of the garment; they are a veil that unveils in veiling the unveiling of the veil. Azulai's text verbalizes the principle of (dis)semblance that has been espoused by numerous kabbalists through the generations: there is no way to see the light but through a simulacrum; the concealed can only be revealed through being concealed in what is revealed. Neither adept nor scholar, I submit, can escape from this hermeneutic circle. In the poignant language of a critical zoharic passage, the secrets encoded in the text of the Torah are seen from within the garment (*mi-go levusha*), not by removing it, that is, the mystical sense, which corresponds to the divine light, is apprehended through the literal; the mystery of the spirit is envisioned through the mantle of the letter.[268] The following passage from the RaShaB attests to the place that this ideal occupies in Ḥabad thought:

> The intellect is the vitality of the letters, and the light of the intellect is garbed in each and every letter from these permutations . . . thus there is the matter of the letters [*ḥomer ha-otiyyot*], which is equal in all of them, and the image of the matter [*ṣiyyur ha-ḥomer*], and the form of the intellect [*ṣurat ha-sekhel*] that is in them. The image of the matter, which is the external form [*ha-ṣurah hiṣoniyyut*], is in accord with the pattern of the internal form [*ha-ṣurah penimiyyut*], for the letters are formed exactly in this fashion, so that they can be vessels for the light . . . for the light of the Torah . . . is revealed precisely in these letters, and precisely in this image.[269]

The internal, intelligible form corresponds to the light, but there is no way to perceive the latter except through the external, material form of the letters in which it is cloaked. As will grow increasingly apparent, the eschatological ideal of visualizing the essence without mediation is consistent with and preserves this axiom of kabbalistic esotericism.

One of the critical passages that informed the presentation of this ideal is from the first part of the *Tanya*, which is worthy to cite in full:

> The purpose of the concatenation of the worlds and their descent from gradation to gradation is not for the sake of the supernal worlds . . . but the purpose is for this lower world, for thus it arose in his will, blessed be he, that there would be spiritual serenity before him when the other side is subjugated and darkness is transformed into light [*kad itkayfa siṭra aḥara we-ithappekh ḥashokha li-nehora*], so that the light of God, the Infinite, blessed be he, shall shine in the place of darkness and the other side of this world entirely with a greater lift and with a greater strength, and "light is superior to darkness" (Eccles 2:13), compared to its illumination in the supernal worlds, for it shines there by means of garments [*levushim*] and the concealment of the face [*hester*

> *panim*] that cover and hide the light of the Infinite, blessed be he, so that they will not be nullified in existence. And thus the blessed holy One gave the Torah to Israel, which is called "strength" and "power," and as the saying of the rabbis, blessed be their memory,[270] that the blessed holy One empowers the righteous to receive their reward in the future-to-come, so that they will not actually be nullified in existence, in the light of the Lord that will be revealed in the future without any outfit, as it is written, "Your master will no longer be covered [that is, he will not be hidden from you through a wing or a garment] and your eyes will see your master" (Isa 30:20), and it is written, "For every eye shall behold [the Lord when he returns to Zion]" (Isa 52:8).[271]

A contrast is drawn between the present and the future. In the former, even with respect to the supernal worlds, the light of the Infinite can be manifest only through the garment, a state of occlusion referred to by the technical term *hester panim*, literally, the "concealment of the face."[272] The latter is characterized as the illumination of that light without any accoutrement, a direct vision of the divine, which is presented as the purpose of creation. The state is reached when the other side is subjugated and the darkness is transformed into light, an allusion to the two phases of enlightenment discussed above, the conquering of evil (*itkafya*) and the consequent transmutation of it into its opposite (*ithapkha*).

The point is expanded in a second passage from the *Tanya*:

> The purpose of all the withdrawals [*ṣimṣumim*] is to create the corporeal human body [*guf ha-adam ha-ḥomri*], to subdue the other side, so that the "light is superior to darkness" (Eccles 2:13), as one raises the divine and vital soul, and its garments and all the faculties of the body to the Lord exclusively. . . . "The glory of the Lord shall appear, and all flesh, as one, shall behold" (Isa 40:5), for this is the purpose of the concatenation of all the worlds, so that the glory of the Lord "will fill all the earth" (Isa 6:3), precisely in the aspect of disclosure, to transform darkness to light and bitterness to sweetness. . . . And this is the purpose of the intent of man in his worship, to draw down the light of the Infinite, blessed be he.[273]

The seeing of God without regalia, then, comes about when one subdues the other side, when the shell is shattered, the evil inclination slaughtered, so that the dark can be transformed into light. The task of the Jew in the present is to draw the light of the essence into the world, but in the future that light will be revealed below as it is above, and the cosmos itself will be exposed as the epiphany of the invisible, the mask that unmasks the (un)masking of the mask.[274] The vision, accordingly, is through the flesh, an actual perception, as opposed to an idealization or conceptualization,[275] beholding the limitless essence indwelling within the limits of nature. In this awakened mindfulness, opposites converge in their diverging convergence, and the veil of nature no longer hides the face of the veil in the veiling of the face—one discerns in discarding the veil that the face is the veil, that YHWH is Elohim.

The status of the messianic vision is illumined by the symbolic depiction of the exodus from Egypt as "an exit from limitations and boundaries" (*ha-yeṣi'ah me-ha-meṣarim u-gevulim*) occasioned by "the disclosure of the essence of the Infinite."[276] As Shneur Zalman expresses it in one context, "in the days of the Messiah, the illumination will be from the aspect of the naught [*beḥinat efes*] that is above the aspect of the nothing [*beḥinat ayin*]."[277] To go out unreservedly from all limitation and boundary is to enter this void, the no-thing that is more nothing than the nothing. I surmise, moreover, that the seeing of the void must be interpreted esoterically, yielding the ultimate secret, which is the open secret, the secret that hides itself in the ruse that there is no secret. Seeing without a garment, in other words, consists of coming to see that there is nothing to see but the garment that one can see without any garment. "The purification," writes Shneur Zalman,

> is not complete until the future, and as long as there is a portion of evil in the good, there cannot be a revelation below of the aspect of the supernal savor [*ṭa'am*] and delight [*oneg*] hidden in the commandments, for the shell conceals. . . . However, in the future, when the portion of evil will be completely purified from the good, then it is written, "Your master will no longer be covered and your eyes will see [your master]" (Isa 30:20), that is, the aspect of the hidden wisdom [*ḥokhmah setima'ah*] of *Arikh Anpin* will be revealed . . . but now it resides surreptitiously [*shokhen be-he'lem*] by means of the garments of the ritual action [*levushin de-ma'aseh ha-miṣwot*].[278]

In the exilic state, ritual actions are the garments through which the hidden wisdom is "garbed in the will furtively" (*melubbash be-raṣon be-he'lem*), but in the future the concealed light (*or ha-ganuz*) will be disclosed through a direct vision, a comprehension of the hidden wisdom, which is linked to the rabbinic category of the reasons for the commandments (*ṭa'amei miṣwot*).[279]

In the fourth chapter, we will return to this distinction between the commandments and their rationales, but here it is important to underscore that the vision of the end is enunciated as an actual seeing of the essence of the light of the Infinite—the supernal delight (*oneg elyon*)[280]—without any raiment or obstruction. But what is seen? As Dov Baer expressed it in one of his miscellaneous reflections on this matter, the ultimate vision is a contemplation (*hitbonenut*) of the "actual essence that transcends the entire concatenation of that which encompasses and that which fills," that is, comprehension of the essence beyond the ontological binary of transcendence and immanence. The one who has this vision, the possibility of which he assigns uniquely to Israel, is in an expanded state of consciousness (*moḥin de-gadlut*), which can also be described (echoing an older rabbinic eschatological trope) as deriving sustenance directly from the essence of the light of the Infinite.[281] Yet the locus of that vision remains the world—"as it is above in actuality in its essence, it will be revealed to them below."[282] When this is taken into account, even the disclosure without a covering turns out to be another form of covering; redemption, one might say, is this mode of re/covery, an uncovering of the (un)covering, and hence the "vision of the substance of the essence" (*re'iyyah be-mahut ha-aṣmut*) is expressly a revelation of the light of the Infinite, the power of YHWH, in the corporeal body (*guf ha-gashmi*).[283] There is no question that the gnosis of the essence is thought to be on a par with physical vision, even though, as Dov Baer's son and successor, Shmuel, rightly put it, "the essence of the purpose of creation is that there will be a disclosure of divinity that is not by means of the concatenation,"[284] that is, the object of the visual contemplation is the essence that is outside the ontic parameters of worldhood manifest within those very parameters. Schneerson, in consonance with the masters who preceded him, made this point repetitively. To take a typical example: "Therefore he is called King Messiah [*melekh ha-mashiaḥ*], for the teaching of the Messiah will be in the aspect of vision [*re'iyyah*], which is the aspect of the perimeter [*maqqif*], but this perimeter extends also to the interiority [*penimiyyut*] . . . the matter of vision will be actualized for all of Israel. . . . All this will be in the future redemption . . . for then there will be a sensory vision [*re'iyyah ḥushit*], as it written 'and all flesh, as one, shall behold that the mouth of the Lord has spoken' (Isa 40:5) . . . so that there will be a disclosure of the essence [*hitgallut ha-aṣmut*] below."[285] To see nature from the vantage point of this emptiness is the vision of the essence that is the goal of the path.

An especially lucid articulation of the messianic vision that typifies Ḥabad thinking is offered by Shalom Dovber:

> And this is the matter of "Jacob, my servant" (Isa 41:8), that is, the aspect of one who worships God [*oved elohim*] (Mal 3:18), to rectify the concealment of the name Elohim, so that there will be a disclosure of the name YHWH. But [the name] "Israel" is on account of "for you have striven with Elohim" (Gen 32:29), he prevailed and ruled over the name Elohim, that is, the name Elohim does not hide and conceal, and this is the aspect of the disclosure of YHWH without any concealment at all. Jacob also draws forth the disclosure of the name YHWH by means of the worship in the name Elohim, to rectify the concealment, and by means of this specifically the disclosure of the name YHWH is drawn forth . . . for after the purification [*berur*] and rectification [*tiqqun*], he knew YHWH from the very withdrawals and concealments. . . . This is through the concealment of the name Elohim, that is, when it is garbed in the world [*olam*] and the reality of existence [*meṣi'ut ha-yesh*] that comes to be from the name Elohim, and through them and by means of them he knows YHWH, for the disclosure of the name YHWH will shine for him. . . . Even so, since the knowledge is through the concealment of the name Elohim, this is not an actual disclosure of YHWH as it is. . . . And it is known that the root of the being of existence [*shoresh hithawwut ha-yesh*] and the root of all the concealments [*shoresh kol ha-ha'alamot*] are from the aspect of the essential concealment of the Infinite [*beḥinat he'lem ha-aṣmi de-ein sof*], for this is, in truth, the disclosure of the supernal light without measure . . . and the truth of the disclosure that will be in the future is that the concealment itself will illumine [*amittit ha-gilluy she-yihyeh le'atid she-ha-he'lem be-aṣmo ya'ir*]. . . . The truth of this disclosure will be when the purifications are complete, but in this manner it shines even now for the elevated souls,

> who have reached the level of "May you see your world in your lifetime."[286] . . . And, just as from the perspective of the name YHWH itself the coming to be of the world was not possible, similarly, after it has come to be, in relation to the name YHWH, it is completely nullified and it does not conceal at all. . . . And it is in this way in time and in place, when there is an illumination in them from the aspect that is above time and place, then time and place are nullified [*we-al derekh zeh hu bi-zeman u-maqom ke-she-me'ir bahem he'arah mi-beḥinat she-lema'lah mi-zeman u-maqom az ha-zeman u-maqom beṭelim*].[287]

That eschatological ideal centers about the revelation of the name YHWH, the essence of the Infinite, but there are two phases, which correspond to the names Jacob and Israel. The former signifies the disclosure of the name YHWH through the intermediary of Elohim, the garb of the material cosmos, and the latter, the disclosure without any garment. The world, accordingly, is the concealment by which the concealment is revealed by being concealed. The utopian future, by contrast, is a revelation of that concealment to the point that the world that is the concealment of that concealment no longer conceals what was revealed in being concealed, but reveals what was concealed in being revealed. *The truth of the disclosure that will be in the future is that the concealment itself will illumine*—what will be revealed is the concealment, but the concealment can only be revealed if it is concealed, and this is precisely the crux of the messianic promise of the disclosure of the name without any concealment. The vision in the future will be a "tangible seeing of the substance" (*re'iyyat mahut mammash*), which is a direct perception of the eye (*re'iyyat ayin*) rather than an intellectual vision (*re'iyyah de-ein ha-sekhel*), but, unlike the prophetic vision (with the exception of Moses[288]) that is mediated through the image refracted in the prism of *Malkhut*, attested in the verse "And through the prophets I was imaged," *u-ve-yad ha-nevi'im adammeh* (Hos 12:11), the final vision is a seeing of "the concealment of the essence of the light of the Infinite in actuality" (*ha-he'lem de-aṣmut or ein sof mammash*) without any similitude.[289] The atemporal and aspatial quality of this phenomenon is enhanced by the claim that already in the present sublime souls—the Beshṭ is singled out as an example—are capable of the prophetic vision that exceeds the boundaries of space and time. If we are justified to speak of an apocalyptic idea of history in the sixth and seventh masters of Ḥabad-Lubavitch, it needs to be comprehended from the vantage point of the "worship of the souls of the aspect of Israel, which is not to rectify the aspect of the concealment [*letaqqen beḥinat ha-he'lem*], but to be in the aspect of the nullification of existence in the aspect of conjunction to the light of the Infinite [*lihyot bi-veḥinat biṭṭul bi-meṣi'ut bi-veḥinat devequt be-or ein sof*] and to draw down the aspect of the disclosure of the light of the Infinite from above to below."[290] The final goal, therefore, does not entail the eradication of the physical world in the nothingness of the Infinite, but the transfiguration of the spatiotemporal reality such that it no longer delimits or conceals the essence beyond space and time. The seventh Rebbe thus emphasized that Moses was commanded to "make planks for the Tabernacle" (Exod 26:15), "for this is the work of altering the permutation of the deceit of the world [*lahafokh et ha-ṣeruf de-sheqer ha-olam*]: from the permutation of the letters *sheqer* [deceit] one can make *qeresh* [board], which is the matter of the darkness changing into light [*ithapkha ḥashokha li-nehora*]."[291] Similarly, the task for every Jew is to prepare nature to be a habitation for the supernatural, "to make planks for the Tabernacle from the deceit of the world,"[292] so that the disclosure of the divine will not be through the shell of "withdrawals, concealments, and garments above," but rather in the manner of "the truth of the Lord that will endure forever" (Ps 117:2).[293] The scriptural tropes of the glory of God appearing (Isa 40:5) and the master no longer being hidden (Isa 30:20) allude to this manifestation without concealment, which is to say, the manifestation of the concealment, the unveiling of the veil through the veil of unveiling.

Further support for my interpretation may be elicited from the attempt on the part of Ḥabad masters to link the Messiah to the state of mindfulness designated as *afisat ha-ra'yon*, the negation of thought, the (un)knowing of the "naught that is a greater abnegation than the nothing" (*efes hu biṭṭul yoter me-ayin*), for it is "more than nothing" (*mer eyder nisht*).[294] This more-than-nothing—more nothing than nothing—is the essence voided of its essentiality, the indistinct beyond the distinction of being indistinct, the abyss before there was a before, before which there might be an after, the indifferent in which identity of difference and difference of identity are indistinguishable. From the vantage point of the lower form of denegation, *biṭṭul ha-yesh*, the spatiotemporal world is annihilated in the light of the Infinite that is outside of space and time,[295] but from the vantage point of the higher form of denegation, *biṭṭul ha-ayin*, the world of particularity is reconfigured as an expression of the void that is empty of being empty. In my judgment, the esoteric dimension of Ḥabad, which is only amplified by the revelation of secrets, relates to a contemplative understanding of the traditional geopolitical messianic ideal along these lines. To be redeemed is to attain the highest level of nullification in *efes*, the *biṭṭul bi-meṣi'ut*, which ensues from the mind negating the negation of negation by being incorporated into the nothing-that-is-more-than-less-than-nothing. One of the key ways that this is expressed is as an interpretation of the passage from the morning prayers in the Sabbath liturgy, *efes biltekha go'alenu limot ha-mashiaḥ*, "There is naught but you, our redeemer in the days of the Messiah." Exoterically, the expression *efes biltekha* conveys the monotheistic belief that there is no divinity other than God, but, esoterically, it alludes to the meontological truth that even God is annihilated in the naught (*efes*) that is more than nothing (*ayin*), as nothing is still too much of a something to be naught. To drive this point home, the words *efes biltekha* are contrasted with the phrase that immediately precedes them, *we-ein zulatekha*, "there is none other than you." Shalom Dovber compared the avowal "there is none other than you" to the "nullification of the vessels" (*biṭṭul ha-kelim*), since it implies that "there is an existence, but it is annihilated" (*she-yesh meṣi'ut ella she-baṭel*), and the assertion "there is naught but you" to the "nullification of the light" (*biṭṭul ha-or*), which suggests "that there is no other existence at all" (*she-ein meṣi'ut zulat kelal*).[296] Elaborating on this distinction, Yosef Yiṣḥaq commented, insofar as the light that issues from the essence (*ha-or ha-nimshakh min ha-aṣmut*) is the "aspect of the nothing itself" (*beḥinat ayin aṣmo*) and the "nothing is nullification" (*ayin hu biṭṭul*), it follows that the nullification of the light (*biṭṭul ha-or*) involves three aspects, the "nullification of the privation of the orientation of place" (*biṭṭul de-he'der tefisat maqom*), the "nullification of there is none other than you" (*biṭṭul de-ein zulatekha*), and the "nullification of there is naught but him" (*biṭṭul de-efes bil'ado*). The disclosure in the future-to-come relates specifically to the third aspect, as there will be the "discernment of the comprehension of the nullification of there is naught but you" (*hakkarah be-ha-hassagah de-ha-biṭṭul de-efes biltekha*), that is, the principle of nullification (*efes biltekha*) will itself be nullified. The exilic condition, in contrast to the messianic state, is characterized by two kinds of deceit, one that covers the truth (*sheqer mekhasseh al ha-emet*) and the other that dissembles as truth (*sheqer nidmeh la-emet*). The concealment of exile, which is of the latter type, signifies the ultimate deception, the ontological posturing of there being something other than nothing. It is this (dis)simulation that prevents us from perceiving that God is "our redeemer constantly" (*go'alenu tamid*); in the future, however, the nullification itself will be nullified, as there will be no more pretense of there being existence outside the essence that will need to be nullified, and, as a consequence, the truth that there is no truth to unearth (since there is no more deceit to disguise) will be seen without any obstruction.[297] The soteriological secret harbored by the Ḥabad masters (a secret that, ironically, still seems to be hidden from those who think they have revealed the secret) is encapsulated in the discernment that the futurity of apocalyptic anticipation—waiting for the Messiah to appear—is not a matter of chronological time at all, but a mental state whereby and wherein one realizes that what is to come intermittently is already present perpetually.[298]

Let us recall here a letter written on 27 Nisan 5712 (April 22, 1952) in which Schneerson stated explicitly that he accepted the opinion of his father-in-law regarding the imminent coming of the Messiah, who is described as "standing behind the wall, awaiting the termination of the clarifications and purifications of each and every one of us through minor adjustments."[299] Positioning the redeemer behind the wall (an image derived from the description of the beloved in Song of Songs 2:9 as inflected in the midrashic application of the image to the Messiah)[300] is to suggest that he is already here, and what needs to be done to secure his appearance is to dismantle the wall. Indeed, in a talk delivered on 19 Kislev 5699 (December 12, 1938), the sixth Rebbe stated explicitly that "the Messiah is already near, he is behind the wall" (*az moshiach iz shoyn korev er iz ahintern vant*); hence all that is necessary is a "good sense of hearing and a sense of sight so that one will hear his voice and see" (*gutn chush ha-shemiah un a chush ha-reiyah iz shomea kolo ve-roeh*).[301] Messianic expectation, on this score, is to be fulfilled by bringing to light what is currently occluded, rendering manifest the presence presently absent in its absent presence by learning to hear and to see. It is fair to say that Schneerson understood his mission precisely in these terms. In the talk on Simḥat Torah, 23 Tishrei 5712 (October 23, 1951), he glossed the aforecited words of his predecessor as "the reality is that he is 'standing behind our wall,' and he should come immediately" (*ot ot halt er bay kumen*).[302] Several years later, in a talk from 26 Nisan 5716 (April 7, 1956), Schneerson repeated that "we are found in the generation of the Messiah—and as his honorable holiness, my teacher and father-in-law, Admor said a number of times that now is the time of 'There he stands behind the wall' (Song of Songs 2:9) . . . for the Messiah will come immediately in actuality" (*bald mammash ot ot kumt bald moshiach*).[303] Toward the end of his life, already frail and doubtlessly sensing his mortality acutely, he expressed the matter with augmented exigency. Thus, for example, in a talk delivered on 23 Av 5751 (August 3, 1991), Schneerson observed that the practice of scrutinizing one's soul (*ḥeshbon ha-nefesh*) during Elul, the month preceding the ten days of repentance from Rosh ha-Shanah to Yom Kippur, is a matter that, halakhically conceived, is dependent on time (*inyan she-ha-zeman gerama*), and hence it instructs us that the "true and complete redemption" (*ha-ge'ullah ha-amittit we-ha-sheleimah*) is concurrently a present reality and a future eventuality. It is, therefore, necessary "to be engaged all the time in thought and speech concerning the redemption and to seek to bind all the matters of this time with the redemption, and the labor of the children of Israel is to accelerate the redemption." The conflation of the two temporal modalities is conveyed by the Jew liturgically proclaiming, "I will wait for him on any day that he arrives," even as "all the signs" (*kol ha-simanim*) point to the fact that the messianic promise has been fulfilled, attested by the rabbinic rendering of the verse "There he comes" (Song of Songs 2:8) as an indication that the Messiah has come previously.[304] If we think of these two dicta from the perspective of a linear temporality, they would appear to be contradictory, for, if the latter is true, and the Messiah has come, the former seems false, as there is no truth to claim that one is waiting for the arrival of what has arrived, but, if the former is true, and the sentiment of awaiting the Messiah's arrival is sincere, the latter is false, as it cannot be true to say that the Messiah has arrived when one is genuinely anticipating his arrival. If, however, these dicta are examined from an alternate temporal perspective, what I have called the linear circle or the circular line, then they would not be contradictory at all. In the return of what has always been what is yet-to-come, it is precisely the absent presence of the Messiah that imparts meaning to the pending advent of his present absence.

As I have argued, Ḥabad masters connect this temporal insight to the contemplative ideal of *biṭṭul*, the obliteration of all particularity, including the particularity of the obliteration of particularity. In the annihilation of annihilation, the difference between time and eternity collapses, not, however, through the demolition of the world, the sublation of finitude, and the annulment of time in the face of a timeless infinity,[305] but through an opening that allows one to see the world as the manifestation of the essence that is concealed, a revealing of the veil as veil. The seeing of the veil through the veil is expressed in the rabbinic language of the divine presence making its habitation below. "In the days of the Messiah," wrote Shneur Zalman, "there will be 'naught but you' [*efes biltekha*], that is, the perfection of the Messiah . . . for in those days there will be a disclosure of divinity [*hitgallut elohut*] in this corporeal world [*ha-olam ha-gashmi*], 'and the earth will be filled with the knowledge of the Lord' (Isa. 11:9). . . . In the days of the Messiah, there will be a disclosure of divinity in this lower world and there will be naught but him [*efes bil'ado*], the naught that is higher than nothing [*efes gavoha me-ayin*], and he will not ascend to be higher, since the essence of his dwelling will be in the lower beings."[306] The paradoxical import of this idea is brought into sharper relief by the Ṣemaḥ Ṣedeq: "In the days of the Messiah there will be a disclosure of the aspect of the naught [*gilluy beḥinat efes*], and thus the material reality will not conceal [*ha-yesh ha-gashmi lo yastir*], two opposites [will cohere] in one subject."[307] How can there be a disclosure of the naught? What is revealed when what is revealed is the absolute nothing that is even more nothing than nothing? The messianic ideal instantiates the paramount meontological *coincidentia oppositorum*, the "aspect of the essence of the Infinite that is entirely above the aspect of manifestation [*beḥinat aṣmiyyut ha-ein sof she-lema'lah mi-beḥinat gilluy legamrei*]" is manifest in the multiple forms of the spatiotemporal world.[308] The material reality will no longer conceal, because the garment itself will be exposed as a garment and, consequently, the world of phenomena will not be considered a distinct substance that hides the revelation of divinity (*lo yihyeh ha-yesh davar nivdal we-lo yihyeh mastir le-gilluy elohuto*).[309] Playing with the same complex of ideas, the seventh Rebbe remarked that in messianic times the aspect of the negation of thought (*afisat ha-ra'yon*) would be revealed and "then the material reality will not conceal at all" (*ha-yesh ha-gashmi lo yastir kelal*), an idea anchored textually in the prophetic prediction "The glory of the Lord shall appear, and all flesh, as one, shall behold that the mouth of the Lord has spoken" (Isa 40:5).[310] In the exilic circumstance, nature is a veil that conceals the light of the essence so that it may be revealed, but in the messianic state of mind the veil is unveiled and the veiled is finally unveiled as the veiled.

The "ultimate concealment" (*takhlit ha-he'lem*), remarked Schneerson, is "the concealment that is not in existence" (*he'lem she-eino bi-meṣi'ut*)[311]—in the ultimate concealment even concealment must be concealed. Messianic perspicacity is linked precisely to this doubling of concealment in the disclosure of the world abiding always in the passing of its passing. Redemption is thus described as the time when the "concealment that is above revelation" (*he'lem she-lema'lah mi-gilluy*) will be revealed below "in actuality" (*be-fo'al mammash*).[312] But how is the revelation of a concealment that is above revelation to be revealed? The response offered by Schneerson, which intensifies the paradox, relates to the compresence of the three dimensions of temporality connected to the advent of the Messiah. Insofar as the time of redemption is hidden and concealed, it relates to the future, but the expectation of the redemption demands that one believe that it can occur at any moment, which transforms that future into the present, albeit a present that is always becoming past, as the time of redemption must always be a matter of futurity. "The explanation of this—according to what was said that matters of redemption are from a level that is above the categories of concealment and disclosure, for by means of this the union of concealment and disclosure comes to be. An illustration of this relates to the time of redemption—it is above the dimensions of time, for by means of this the union of future with present and past comes to be, for the future redemption is from the moment of the present until the moment of the past."[313] The concurrence of the three temporal modes in the messianic juncture, which, needless to say, betokens an imitation of the mystery of the Tetragrammaton, provides a path to comprehending the revelation of the concealment that is beyond revelation.

What, then, is revealed? Let us consider carefully another sketch of the messianic revelation offered by the seventh Rebbe:

> The disclosure of the essence [*gilluy ha-aṣmut*] will be especially in the future . . . for there will be a disclosure of the essence above the name YHWH and above YHWH himself. Before the world was created he and his name alone were,[314] that is, YHWH himself and the name YHWH, and in the name itself there are two aspects, the disclosure for itself and the disclosure as it is appropriate for the worlds. However, in the future there will be a disclosure of the essence that is above the aspect of "his name" and also above the aspect of "he." Hence, this disclosure will be equal for everyone, for even though then there will also be division of gradations, this will be from the perspective of the comprehension of the aspect of the name YHWH, but in the knowledge of the essence that is above YHWH they will all be identical. . . . For the matter of knowledge here is not to be explained from the language of cognition and comprehension, but it is the matter of knowing and union, the union of the soul with the essence.[315]

The ultimate revelation is the disclosure of the essence, which is even beyond the disclosure of the name. This disclosure is a form of knowledge (*yedi'ah*) that is not a cognitive state but a gnosis that entails the "union of the soul with the essence and substance of the Infinite, blessed be he" (*hitqashsherut ha-neshamah be-aṣmut u-mahut ein sof barukh hu*),[316] a nondual consciousness wherein all difference is overcome. Yet, as the above passage makes clear, the sense of difference will be retained in the messianic future—which is already in the present because it has always been in the past—"there will also be a division of gradations" from the perspective of the name YHWH. Significantly, as we have seen, the name is linked symbolically to the aspect of the feminine demarcated within the Infinite, *malkhut de-ein sof*, as she personifies the potential for limit in that which has no limit, positioned as the midpoint of the void that renders opposites identical in their opposition. Preserving and overturning a primitive hierarchical bias, the hylic character of the feminine is valorized as the locus of the concealment (*he'lem*) that is the world (*ha-olam*), the apophatic body that is present in the absence of its absence. The diasporic claim that the Jewish people will be dispersed to the "end of the entire world" (*ad sof kol ha-olam*) is applied esoterically to "the nullification (*sof*) of the concealment and hiddenness (*olam*), for an end and a conclusion to all the concealment and hiddenness comes to be, as the point of this matter is that by means of the descent of Israel in exile they come to the elevation that is in the redemption."[317] This play of projecting/withholding—what is withheld is the projection that is the world projected as withholding—persists even in the eschaton, and thus the full disclosure of the essence in which all distinctions are eradicated cannot be severed from the disclosure of the name in which the distinctions are preserved.

I conclude this chapter with the elaboration of this theme in Schneerson's discussion of the festival of Tabernacles delivered on 13 Tishrei 5738 (September 25, 1977), the anniversary of the passing of the fourth Rebbe in 1882. Building on the rabbinic teaching that it is appropriate for "everyone in Israel to dwell in one booth,"[318] Schneerson asserted that the mystical intent of the halakhic demand to inhabit "one booth" (*sukkah aḥat*) is that one might attain "the one aspect [*beḥinah aḥat*] that is entirely above even the category of the matter of number . . . the essence of God, may he be blessed. For the intent of [the word] *one* [*aḥat*] is [the aspect of soul] *yeḥidah* . . . and the name *yeḥidah* is on account of the fact that it receives from the unique One [*yaḥid*], and, similarly, this is the aspect of the one booth whose matter is that of *yeḥidah*."[319] The material booth symbolically embodies the notion of the immaterial unity that exceeds all division (*hitḥallequt*), a unity that is beyond the arithmetical demarcation of the number one and that corresponds pneumatically to the aspect of *yeḥidah*. The disclosure of this unity, the "drawing down of the essence openly" (*hamshakhat ha-aṣmut be-gilluy*) to be fully revealed in the messianic age when the master is not covered (Isa 30:20) and the glory will be seen by all flesh (Isa 40:5), is through the agency of the edifice constructed below in the corporeal world; indeed, the booth signifies the physical structure that shelters the metaphysical transcendence.[320] The doctrine of incarnation, which is the basis of Ḥabad cosmology and also serves as the foundation for its pietistic ideal of mystical quietism, the suffering of the nonbeing of the world through the eradication of its being, rests on affirming that it is only through the garment that one can see without any garment, that seeing without a garment means seeing that we cannot see but through a garment. With this paradox in hand, we can proceed to explore the allegedly positive status accorded the body in the seventh Rebbe's conception of the future.

3

SEMIOTIC TRANSUBSTANTIATION OF THE SOMATIC

Charnelle est encore la parole d'au-delà,

où la chair n'est plus.

—EDMOND JABÈS, *AELY*

Elevation of the Corporeal and the Naturalization of the Supranatural

One of the striking features of spiritual practices promoted in the second half of the twentieth century and continuing into the twenty-first century is the emphasis placed on reclaiming the body for a new vision of fulfillment and healing. An obvious example that comes to mind, by no means the only one of relevance, is the phenomenon of Esalen. Typical of this turn is the comment of Nicholas Gagarin, "What the people at Esalen have got, in the simplest terms, is the body. For 15,000 years civilization has repressed the body. Now, suddenly, it is coming awake."[1] Although the statement is somewhat exaggerated, we can speak of a *somatic utopianism* indicative of new age spiritualities that characteristically sanction bodily centered techniques such as yoga, tantra, meditation, massage, and even some forms of the martial arts in an effort to integrate consciousness and the physical.[2] Reversing the traditional privileging of spirit over matter, there has evolved a deep sense of the inherent embodiment of consciousness—a trend well attested in a number of scholarly disciplines including philosophy, religious studies, feminist criticism, cultural anthropology, and evolutionary psychology[3]—and the consequent need to perfect the mind through attending to the welfare of the body. It should come as no surprise that popular works on kabbalah reflect a similar emphasis on an embodied spirituality.[4] What is surprising, however, is that a version of this paradigm shift is operative in the thought of the seventh Rebbe of Ḥabad-Lubavitch, though, as we shall see, the matter is too complex to ascribe to him a simple and unequivocal affirmation of the material body.

An interesting formulation of the centrality of the corporeal was offered by Schneerson on 23 Ḥeshvan 5721 (November 13, 1960) in an interview with a reporter from the newspaper *Davar* who asked if there were any similarities between Jews in America returning to Judaism and revolutionary movements like the "beatniks." In his response, Schneerson remarked that the key difference between Judaism, on one hand, and Christianity and Islam, on the other, lies in the fact that the former ascribes positive value to this world whereas the latter seek ways to flee from it.[5] Leaving aside the woefully obvious weakness of this characterization of the other religions of Abraham, it is telling that, according to Schneerson, the distinctive feature of Judaism lies in its positive attitude to the world. One could argue justifiably that he articulated a rather conventional view, but this should not blind us to the fact that something distinctive is at work in the seventh Rebbe's presentation, especially as it relates to his vision of the eschaton. In a text written when Schneerson was a young man in Paris and preserved in his own hand, he already anticipated the inversion that was to become so central to his later thinking:

> The greatness of the level of the children of Israel is that they are found in this corporeal world parallel to the level of the angels. Thus we have found that in the future-to-come the soul [*neshamah*] will be sustained from the body, and this highlights the level of the corporeal body [*ha-guf ha-gashmi*] in relation to the soul. And this is . . . [the import of] "many miracles" [*nissei nissim*] (the matter of the name Yoḥanan)[6] precisely, for it is not enough that the corporeal world [*ha-olam ha-gashmi*] will be elevated to be equal to the spiritual [*ruḥani*]—and this [is the meaning of] "miracle" [*nes*] from the word "elevation" [*haramah*]—but it will be above it.[7]

It is not sufficient to imagine the eschaton as a leveling out of the difference between body and soul, but it must be seen as the moment when the former is elevated to a higher status than the latter. In the continuation of this diary entry, Schneerson accounts for this reversal by noting (on the basis of a correlation attested in older aggadic and kabbalistic sources) that just as the ten commandments are holy, so too are the ten sayings by means of which the world was created. The distinction between the words of creation and the words of revelation is that the former deal with the manifest (*gilluy*) and the latter with the hidden (*he'lem*). As a consequence of human transgression, however, the holiness of the world has been concealed—a point driven home by the now familiar play on words between *ha-olam* and *he'lem*.[8] In the future the matter will be rectified, and the spiritual essence of the corporeal will be manifest as the corporeal essence of the spiritual, an idea that Schneerson expressed as well in his personal notebooks in terms of the belief that the land of Israel, which is holy, will spread forth in all lands, and then "it will be revealed to every eye that the whole of the world in its entirety, which was created by means of the ten sayings, is holy."[9] If the land of Israel spreads forth so that it is everywhere, then there is no more distinction between it and other lands and, consequently, no more distinction between holy and unholy.[10] Here it is pertinent to recall another passage from the notebook in which Schneerson recorded a comment of the third Rebbe, the Ṣemaḥ Ṣedeq: "And you know that the land of Israel is the disclosure of divinity [*gilluy elohut*] by means of involvement with the Torah and worship of the heart."[11] Clearly, the implication of this remark is that the very notion of the land must be expanded beyond a strict cartographical demarcation. This is not to suggest that the seventh Rebbe denied the special status attributed traditionally to the land of Israel.[12] His affirming a religious Zionist ideology, even insinuating himself in the affairs of the modern state of Israel, weighing in on several critical issues including the important question of whether or not the chief rabbinate should recognize nonorthodox conversion as legitimate—a religious issue that has had significant political implications for Israeli citizens—indicates otherwise. Nevertheless, the aforementioned remark intimates that, in its mystical sense, or what Ḥabad masters would refer to as the interiority of the Torah, the land of Israel cannot be limited to a particular physical space; rather, it signifies the revelation of the divine through Torah study and prayer, an experience that presumably can take place in any location.

Explicating the statement in the traditional Passover Haggadah, "Now here but next year in the land of Israel, now as servants but next year as free men," the Friediker Rebbe commented, "It can be inferred that it is possible to be in the land of Israel—the intent is those who feel the sanctity of the land—and even so to be in the aspect of slaves. 'Free men'—the intent is when the light of the Torah shines."[13] Rendering the liturgical decree figuratively, the contrast between being in the Diaspora this year and in the land of Israel next year is not primarily geographical in nature, and hence, reading against the text, there is not a one-to-one correlation between the Diaspora and being enslaved, on the one hand, and the land of Israel and being free, on the other hand. To be in the land refers to those "who feel the sanctity of the land," which may be experienced outside the physical boundaries of the land, just as it is possible to be in servitude inside those boundaries.[14] Drawing out the implications of his father-in-law's dictum, Schneerson explained: "Even in the land of Israel it is possible to be in the situation and the condition of 'slaves,' and furthermore, the exile in the land of Israel through the wicked of Israel is much worse than the exile outside the land through the wicked of the nations of the world."[15] Liberation is, first and foremost, to be enlightened by the light of the Torah, a state of distended consciousness that defies spatial delimitation.

The extreme right-wing political tendency of Lubavitch, illustrated in the official uncompromising resistance to returning any of the captured territories to the Palestinians, has commanded much attention. There is no attempt on my part to defy or to defend this position, but it is also necessary to take seriously that the seventh Rebbe, in consort with a stance taken by his predecessors, affirmed a diasporic conception that unhinges the very notion of the land from a narrow topology. In a comment made toward the end of his life, Schneerson insisted that the task for the "last generation of the exile and the first generation of the redemption" was

> to make the land of the other nations into the land of Israel, even in the lowest place . . . for by elevating the lowest place, all the other places of the land of the other nations are elevated. And this matter is accomplished through the "house of our master" . . . for the light comes forth from it to the whole world, to make of the world in

> its entirety the land of Israel. This is the matter of "in the future, the land of Israel will spread to all the lands," and "in the future, Jerusalem will spread forth in all of the land of Israel," for all of the synagogues and houses of study in all of the world will be joined to the Temple in the true and perfect redemption by our righteous Messiah, the leader of the generation, for he is the Messiah of the generation.[16]

The unique status accorded the land of Israel, and especially Jerusalem, are affirmed in this passage, but, at the same time, they are undermined to some extent by the messianic mission to transform the entire world into the land of Israel. These words are not to be taken as merely hyperbolic. The very essence of the notion of holiness promulgated by Ḥabad depends on breaking down the boundaries between Israel and the Diaspora. The center of this undertaking shifted from the Temple in Jerusalem to the "small sanctuary" (*miqdash me'aṭ*) at 770 Eastern Parkway in Brooklyn, New York, which is designated the "house of our master" (*beit rabbenu*), that is, the sixth Rebbe, also identified as the "redeemer of Israel." From that location, the teachings of Ḥasidism spread forth throughout the world, thereby sacralizing every civilized space. Schneerson supports his explication by noting that the numerical value of *beit rabbenu* is 770, the same value as the expression *paraṣta*, which is derived from the verse "you shall spread out to the east and to the west, to the north and to the south" (Gen 28:14). The numerological equivalences indicate that the light has disseminated from this location until the point that "all the dimensions of the world are elevated to the gradation of the land of Israel." The "bursting of the boundary" (*periṣat gader*) is linked to the Messiah, concerning whom it says, "What a breach you have made for yourself," *paraṣta alekha pareṣ* (Gen 38:29), whence it follows that the site established by Yosef Yiṣḥaq as the world headquarters of the Lubavitch movement is "the very place of the future Temple" (*maqom ha-miqdash gufeih di-le-atid*).[17]

What is crucial for the analysis of this chapter is the recognition that the expanded sense of the land is related directly to appreciating the eschatological elevation of the corporeal over the spiritual. The body is the locus of the ideal vision, and therefore it would be accurate to speak of this enhanced mental state as *thinking in the flesh*, but it is a transfigured flesh, a body extricated from bodily constriction. "In the future-to-come, there will be the disclosure of divinity in the entire world," so that when people "look upon the reality of created beings, they will see only the source of their vitality."[18] The status of the material when viewed through this messianic prism—the prism that is the prism of the prism—is a form of embodiment by which the body becomes a veil to unveil the veiling of the veil, a body absent to itself in the presence of the manifest structures of (dis)appearance in the world,[19] the revealed concealment of the concealed revelation. Neither corporeality nor spirituality is avowed as such, but rather a hybrid phenomenon that overcomes the binary of the idealist and the materialist perspectives, "corporeality-within-spirituality" (*gashmiyyut she-be-ruḥaniyyut*), which is concurrently "spirituality-within-corporeality" (*ruḥaniyyut she-be-gashmiyyut*).[20] On this score, "true spirituality" requires that the physical becomes a "vessel and dwelling" for that which is "above the way of nature."[21] "The reason for creation in general and that of the creation of humanity in particular and their purpose," wrote Schneerson in the summer of 1945, "is on account of the blessed holy One, who desires a habitation especially in the lower entities, that is, the lower entities . . . of the material being will be in the aspect of nullification, for by means of this the divine light of the Infinite, blessed be he, will dwell upon and be revealed within them. This nullification is the purpose and foundation of the Torah and the commandments . . . which are given below in material things, as the soul that is garbed specifically in the corporeal body, so that being can be transformed into nothing and it will become a vessel for divinity."[22]

In the final analysis, the body that is lionized as positive is an immaterial materiality, a materiality determined from the standpoint of the divine essence, the one veritable reality before which everything is naught. From the naturalistic angle, every empirical being is imagined to be real and what transcends sense experience is castigated as nothing, but from the divine angle, the opposite of what we sensorily apprehend is true, for what we imagine as nothing is the one true something, and all that is below is considered vis-à-vis this reality as if it were not—in the zoharic idiom paraphrased frequently by Ḥabad masters,[23] *kolla qameih ke-lo ḥashivin*—the actual nothing that is nothing actually. As we have seen in chapter 2, this nondual insight is the deeper import of the monotheistic faith of Judaism. In one of his better-known discourses from 5629 (1869), which deals with the fundamental obligation of the Jew to unify the divine, Shmuel Schneersohn expressed this metaphysical axiom in terms of the consonants of the word *eḥad*, "one," the last word in the proclamation of God's unity (Deut 6:4): the *alef* is the Infinite, the *ḥeit*, whose numerical value is eight, alludes to the seven heavens and the earth, and the *dalet*, whose numerical value is four, alludes to the four spirits of the world, that is, the four cardinal points, east, west, north, and south. In uttering the word *eḥad*, therefore, one intends that "even though the seven heavens, the earth, and the four spirits were created, they are nonetheless absolutely nullified [*beṭelim be-takhlit*] vis-à-vis the aspect of the *alef*, which is the aspect of the Infinite [*ein sof*], the master of the world [*alufo shel olam*]."[24]

Let us recall the conclusion we reached in the previous chapter: the cosmos (*olam*) is the concealment (*he'lem*) in a twofold sense—it conceals the light it reveals and it reveals the light it conceals. The (non)being of the material, therefore, does not imply a negation of appearance in the face of an immaterial reality, but rather recognition of the appearance of negation as the veil of the real immateriality. Ḥabad messianism is ultimately about the cultivation of the state of mindfulness that transforms the something into the nothing whence the something came (not) to be. As Yosef Yiṣḥaq remarked at the end of a discourse from 27 Adar II 5700 (April 6, 1940), a discourse of special significance, as it was delivered on *Shabbat ha-Ḥodesh*, the Sabbath immediately preceding the beginning of Nisan, the month in which the festival of Passover is celebrated, just several weeks after his return to settle in New York on March 19, thus capturing a renewed sense of enthusiasm related to the anticipation of liberation fostered by celebration of this holiday in a new land with its promise of freedom: "Therefore Nisan is the month of redemption, and this is [the import of] 'This month shall mark for you the beginning of the months' (Exod 12:2), for Nisan is the time of redemption and the first of all the months of the year . . . and this month will also be in the months of the year, which are garments of the nature of this world, as this is the month of redemption, which is above nature, that is, in nature the divinity that is not garbed in nature will be felt as well [*she-gam ba-ṭeva yihyeh nirgash ha-elohut ha-bilti mitlabbesh ba-ṭeva*]."[25] Redemption consists of attaining this level of cognitive acuity, whereby nature becomes the arena within which the supranatural is suffered empirically. Derrida once wrote, "There is no nature, only effects of nature: denaturation or naturalization. Nature, the meaning of nature, is reconstituted after the fact on the basis of a simulacrum . . . that it is thought to cause."[26] The particular simulacrum that interests Derrida, and on the basis of which the likeness of nature is imagined, is literature—a reversal of the more conventional understanding of mimesis, since here appeal is made to the belief that life imitates fiction—but we can take the liberty to appropriate his words and apply them in the case of Ḥabad to the essence hidden in the manifestation of the hiddenness of its manifestation. The universe is constellated on the basis of this imaginal body—apparently inapparent as long as our conception is clouded by the distinction between appearance and nonappearance—in the likeness of the guise of that which is perceived only in the guise of the likeness, the garbing of what is beyond nature in the specter of nature.

Numerous texts could be cited to demonstrate that this was the view of the seventh Rebbe as well. For instance, in a letter from 27 Elul 5717 (September 23, 1957), he wrote,

> The distinguishing mark of the month of Elul is "[On your behalf my heart says,] 'Seek my face,' I seek your face, O Lord" (Ps 27:8), a time when a person searches for his interiority, and the way to this is to consider not only the divinity that is disclosed through his actions and his providence in the world but also "your face, O Lord" [*panekha yhwh*], the interiority above [*ha-penimiyyut shel ma'lah*], for the world and its fullness is considered as naught before him [*ke-lo ḥashiv qameih*], and by means of this the interiority that is in the world is also revealed, for in relation to him the world and its fullness, as they are grasped in the exteriority [*be-hiṣoniyyut*], are also not considered, and precisely there is the world that is entirely good and beautiful [*olam she-kullo ṭov we-yofi*],[27] and only by means of this do we find respite of the soul [*menuḥat ha-nefesh*], not the respite of the soul of the people of India, by contrast, which is cessation and termination [*hefseq wi-shevitah*], but the respite to which the people of Israel aspire is an ascent "from strength to strength"[28] [*aliyyah me-ḥayil el ḥayil*], to the perfection of the good and the beautiful [*ha-sheleimut ha-ṭov we-ha-yofi*].[29]

The contrast that Schneerson draws between the respite of the soul affirmed by the people of India, which entails the cessation and termination of life, a likely allusion to the concept of nirvāna that is central to both Hinduism and Buddhism, and the respite of the soul affirmed by the people of Israel, which entails the progressive ascent to the world of pure goodness and beauty, is patently oversimplified, but it is of interest that at this relatively early date he must have had a premonition about the allure of Eastern forms of spirituality for secular and disenfranchised Jews craving a modicum of religious ardor in what might have felt like the putrefied environment of traditional Jewish practice. Be that as it may, what is most important for this analysis is Schneerson's assertion that the way that leads one to discover one's own sense of interiority is to consider the divine not merely from the perspective of what is overtly revealed in God's providential presence in the natural world, but from the perspective of the interiority of what is above, marked scripturally as the face of YHWH, that is, the essence of the light of the Infinite, in relation to which the corporeal world in all of its particularity is reduced to nothing.[30] The positive valence accorded the body in Schneerson's messianic worldview is to be contemplated from this meontological perspective—the material is dematerialized to the point that bodiliness is conceived of as nothing but the incarnation of the letters of the Hebrew alphabet comprised in the ineffable name. The carnality of the world is tied to the flesh of the word through which the void acquires a presence in the absence of the void.

Corporeal Worship: Reclaiming the Material (Im)materiality

To comprehend the embodied sense of disembodiment—in contrast to a disembodied sense of embodiment—tendered by Schneerson, it is necessary to consider the implications of what I have called the acosmic naturalism or apophatic panentheism of Ḥabad cosmology. Yoel Kahn, one of the men who were delegated with the responsibility to reiterate and to write down the oral discourses of the seventh Rebbe, cogently observed, "The divine truth is that there is nothing outside of the blessed holy One—'there is none beside him' (Deut 4:35). . . . This is the 'knowledge of the blessed holy One,' but in the sensible world there is a reverse discernment. The world is a 'world of deceit' [*alma de-shiqra*],[31] and the deceit that is in it is not only that people in the world lie, but that the essence of the appearance of the world as an autonomous reality is a deceit."[32] Kahn goes on to say that through observance of the commandments and study of the Torah, especially the inner meaning of the text, the Jewish people are granted the capacity to discover that "all of existence is for the sake of Israel and the Torah, and they can even cause this discernment to penetrate into the world itself, and thus peace is achieved in the world—for even the world that appears as a reality separate from God senses that the truth is that 'there is none beside him.'"[33] Bracketing the obvious ethnocentric slant of this statement,[34] which is consistent with the view expressed in a plethora of Ḥabad sources, it is of interest that the notion that the Torah is the intermediary that makes peace between God and the world is interpreted acosmically, that is, the peace amounts to the awareness that there is no independent existence outside of the divine, an awareness that is presented as unique to the Torah perspective and therefore realized most perfectly by the Jews who are bound by the law in a distinctive way. Such an orientation would seemingly lead to world denial, to flight from the spatiotemporal realm, a radical denegation, *biṭṭul bi-meṣi'ut*, "nullification of existence," as opposed to *biṭṭul ha-yesh*, "nullification of something." Yet, as Kahn argues, invoking the teaching of the Beshṭ, the goal for the Jew is not to destroy the physical through abstinence, but to turn the body into an instrument to serve God, to become a vessel through which the transcendent light is manifest in the world, a pietistic ideal that is known as *avodah be-gashmiyyut*, "worship through corporeality,"[35] or, according to Schneerson's turn of phrase, *avodah be-guf we-im ha-guf*, "worship in the body and with the body."[36]

As many have discussed this principle, I will not dwell on it here, but I will note that the "corporeality" in this expression is not to be understood as the material flesh that is subject to generation and corruption, but, in accord with a notion of the corporeal attested in much older kabbalistic sources, as the hyperliteral body, the body that is letter. To serve God corporeally, therefore, means to elevate the physical body by transmuting it into this other kind of body. The fiat of divine creation is the word, which is to say, the stuff of creation consists of this word, the Torah, the name, the twenty-two Hebrew letters. And, since God and his word are one, of creation it may be said that there is no place devoid of the divine.[37] The Ḥasidic notion, contrary to some popular and even scholarly portrayals, is not about the veneration of carnality or a complete rejection of asceticism.[38] I would contend that the ideal of corporeal worship, the charge to sanctify the world by transforming darkness into light, is a modification and domestication of ascetic renunciation.[39] That this is a valid interpretation for Ḥabad may be illustrated from the following comment of Shneur Zalman: "The foundation and root of the entire Torah is to elevate and to raise up the soul over the body grade by grade until the source and root of all the worlds, and also to draw down the light of the Infinite, blessed be he, into the community of Israel."[40] Reiterating the point in another context, Shneur Zalman remarked: "Therefore the Torah was given to Israel because the Torah is called 'strength,' since it gives power and strength to the divine soul to overpower the materiality of the body and of the animal soul and their coarseness [*lehitgabber al ḥomriyyut ha-guf we-nefesh ha-bahamit we-gassutan*], to go out 'from confinement' (Isa 42:7)."[41]

In the embodied person of each Jew, a battle rages between the divine and animal souls, as both seek to gain control over the body.[42] The very purpose of the descent of the soul to this world and its being garbed in the body is to rectify this struggle by separating the good from the evil of the impure shells.[43] The crude animality conceals the light of the divine soul, but because the Torah is rooted in the highest recesses of the divine, it bears the light that empowers it "to break the materiality of the animal soul" (*lishbor et ḥomriyyut nefesh ha-bahamit*) and thereby "bind the soul that is in the body to the light of the Infinite."[44] The state of exile is interpreted pneumatically as a condition of the soul being submerged in corporeal desire; the messianic era, by contrast, is marked by the purification of the somatic, which makes possible the fleshly manifestation of the divine glory in a sensual, physical vision (*re'iyyah gashmit ḥushit*)—the shattering of the shell of materiality is precisely what facilitates the visual apprehension of godliness in material nature.[45] The body as such is the deceit that covers the truth, but everything physical has a spark of good, and hence the task is purification (*berur*), separating the core and its husk, to reveal the truth of the deceit as deceitfully true and therefore truly deceitful, to uncover the covering. Admittedly, in Ḥabad terminology, the way to demolish the corporeal is through the corporeal, that is, to transform the base material, which is linked to the animal soul and is often depicted as that which imprisons the divine soul,[46] into the material that is spiritual, the body infused with the light of the essence that is embodied in the garment of the Torah.

The directive, therefore, is for one to bring about the "disclosure of the light of the Infinite, blessed be he, on one's soul to the point that even the vitality of the body, the animal soul, and all of their faculties are transformed and 'restored to the Lord' (Ps 22:28), and the darkness is converted into light."[47] To attain "actual integration in the light of the Infinite, blessed be he" (*hitkallelut be-or ein sof barukh hu mammash*),[48] which is an alternate way of expressing the drawing down of that light on the soul, obviously necessitates overcoming the limitations of the body. The twofold task, as Dov Baer remarked, is connected to the names Israel and Jacob. The former denotes the ascent of the soul "in the aspect of the essence of the simple will, the hidden thought from the concealed of the concealed," and the latter the descent of the soul "in a body and physical matter, so that there will be verily the nullification of autonomous reality."[49] Just as the beginning of the sefirotic gradations is fixed in their end, so the two aspects of soul are fully integrated. Indeed, precisely because the essence is rooted in the corporeal can there be a revelation of the inner light that is, by means of ritual observance, beyond the corporeal. As Shalom Dovber put it, interpreting the words "Out of the depths I call you, O Lord" (Ps 130:1), the Jew is obligated "to draw down the aspect of the depth and the interiority of the Torah of the Lord and the commandments of the Lord from the aspect of the interiority and essence of the light of the Infinite, blessed be he, so that it will illumine the interiority of our souls . . . to banish from us every evil and despicable trait of the natural dispositions."[50]

Much has been made of the change in orientation on the part of the seventh Rebbe with respect to the status of the body in relation to the soul, but a careful examination of his comments illustrates that he continues the view expressed by his predecessors, beginning with the Alter Rebbe. This view does not unequivocally extol corporeality in the manner of some contemporary spiritual paths; on the contrary, seeking physical pleasure, including the pursuit of monetary wealth, is deemed a form of idolatry.[51] Israel's angelic vocation calls for cultivating a contemplative state of ecstasy by divesting the divine soul of carnal desires, and thus the Jewish people are called the "ranks of the Lord," *ṣiv'ot yhwh* (Exod 12:41)—a title allotted to them precisely as they departed from Egypt—for they are empowered to "conquer the world" by waging a war against the boorish instincts of the animal soul through sacrifice of self.[52] The ideal for all Jews, and not just for the righteous, is set in the verse "For I am poor and needy, and my heart is pierced within me" (Ps 109:22):

> One's heart must be emptied of all matters of the world, as only then can it become a vessel for the blessings of the Lord. . . . And this is the meaning of "my heart is pierced within me," for it is an empty vessel, and when it is an empty vessel, then the heart is a vessel for the comprehension of the brain, and the comprehension of one's brain will act upon the heart. . . . Thus, apropos of the disclosure of the Torah and the commandments in this world, which is the aspect of the essence, it can be understood that immersion in desires confounds the disclosure, for when one is submerged in desires, then one cannot be an instrument for the disclosure of the light.[53]

Schneerson's teaching prescribes a transformation of the sensual body into what I have called the linguistic body, the body that is constituted by the letters of the Torah, which are comprised in the Tetragrammaton. Thus, for instance, in a letter from 18 Adar 5716 (March 1, 1956), responding to a question about the appropriateness of seeking the counsel of a medical doctor, Schneerson wrote:

> The saying of the rabbis, blessed be their memory, that the 248 positive commandments correspond to the 248 limbs and the 365 negative commandments to the 365 veins, is known[54]—for the matter and the health of the physical body [*guf ha-gashmi*] of the Jewish man [*ish ha-yisra'eli*] in general are dependent on his spiritual body [*gufo ha-ruḥani*], that is, on his stature and condition in the fulfillment of the positive commandments and the observance of the negative commandments, but since we are found in this world, through the will of the Creator of the world we were created in the lowest level, that is, in the corporeal form [*ṣurah gashmit*], and his providence in the externality [*hanhagato be-ḥiṣoniyyut*] appears to fleshly eyes as if it were natural [*ṭiv'it*], and hence with respect to several matters and issues there must be a holding on to nature.[55]

Following a long-standing kabbalistic reworking of the earlier rabbinic conception, Schneerson offers a hyperliteral understanding of the correlation of the body of the Jewish male and the Torah. The well-being of the physical body is dependent on this spiritual body. In the final analysis, the former is merely the corporeal form by which the latter is apprehended, just as divine providence that is above nature—the intellectual efflux of light—appears in the guise of nature. In a letter written on 10 Kislev 5724 (November 17, 1963) dedicated to the theme of the festival of redemption on the nineteenth of the same month, Schneerson remarked that the soul (*neshamah*), which is described as both standing in its image before God and hewn from beneath the throne of glory, is "entirely spiritual" such that "from its own perspective it has no relationship at all to physical and corporeal matters, and how much more so to matters of desire, which are aroused and come to be only from the side of the body and the animal soul."[56] In spite of this vast chasm that separates soul and body, God

> wants the soul, which is in actuality "a portion of the divine from above,"[57] to descend below and to be garbed in a corporeal and material body, to be bound and unified to it through the duration of several decades. That is to say, during those several decades the soul will be in a condition that is in total opposition to its essential nature. And all of this—in order to fulfill the mission of the Creator, to purify the body [*lezakkekh et ha-guf*] and to illumine matters of this physical world that apply to the human in the light of the Infinite [*be-or ein sof*], to make them a temple and a tabernacle for his blessed presence [*shekhinato yitbarakh*].

Based on the Ḥasidic principle of "descent for the sake of ascent" (*yeridah ṣorekh aliyyah*), the soul's plummet "from the sublime pinnacle to the deep pit"[58] facilitates the "greater elevation" that comes about by "fulfilling the will of the Creator," thereby implementing the edict "in all your ways know him" (Prov 3:6).[59] The afflictions that the soul suffers in its corporeal embodiment are rendered negligible in light of this aim; indeed, it is only in the "deep pit" of the material world that the soul can "reach the height of its gradation," which is "even above the level of the angels."[60] We may conclude, therefore, that while the worship of God is to be carried out through the body and not by extreme forms of abstemiousness,[61] the ideal—even for the simplest of Jews—is not an unqualified exaltation of the corporeal but rather an ascent to the superior level of the spiritual and a distancing from physical matters. This is the inner meaning of the sacrificial rite: by means of the sacrifice the animal soul is transformed into an "offering to the Lord" (*qorban la-yhwh*), that is, bestiality is transmuted into holiness, and one thereby "reaches the essence of the light of the Infinite, which is above any connection to the worlds."[62] In this regard, *sheḥiṭah*, the ritual slaughter of animals, also epitomizes the path of piety, as it is an action that likewise elevates the animal soul to the point that it is "negated and incorporated into the divine soul, which is called *adam*, *eddammeh le-elyon* (Isa 14:14)."[63] Through the presumed philological connection between the word *adam* and the expression *eddammeh le-elyon*, "I will be likened to the most high"—an exegetical ploy that occurs in earlier kabbalistic sources[64] and is repeated numerous times in the discourses and writings of the seventh Rebbe as well as the other Ḥabad masters—in conjunction with the rabbinic idea, greatly expanded by kabbalists,[65] that the term *adam* applies most ideally to the Jewish people,[66] an essential homology is established between the Jew and the divine. As Schneerson insists in another context, the purpose of the creation of the human being is for the sake of "spiritual worship" (*avodah ruḥanit*), but this goal is achieved when one does not desire physical matters, and the body becomes an "empty vessel" (*keli reiqan*) to hold the "corporeal influence" (*hashpa'ah ha-gashmit*). In such a case, it is legitimate to speak of the materiality (*gashmiyyut*) being identical with the spirituality (*ruḥaniyyut*), for the physicality of the material has been substantially transformed.[67] Although the matter is cast again in terms of the goal of humanity in general, it is evident that this relates most accurately to the Jew. To be sure, Schneerson (in consonance with the philosophical approach adopted by Maimonides) identifies the essence of human existence with the faculty of speech (*medabber*), but even in such contexts it is clear that speech in its truest sense, and hence the true human, is more constricted to the Jew, the lower human (*adam ha-taḥton*), who is capable of assimilation (*hitkallelut*) in the supernal human (*adam ha-elyon*).[68] This is the esoteric implication of the scriptural depiction of Israel as "one nation on the earth," *goy eḥad ba-areṣ* (2 Sam 7:23; 1 Chron 17:21), that is, the unity of the Jews is related to their unique calling to serve God by drawing the divine light into the earthly domain.[69]

As I have emphasized repeatedly, Schneerson's approach is based on the teachings of the six Ḥabad masters who preceded him. Especially relevant is Shneur

Zalman's insistence that, even when one is enwrapped in liturgical worship, love of God is realized necessarily through and with the body.[70] More specifically, two kinds of worship are distinguished: the first is the form of ecstasy (*hitpa'alut*), which is designated the "great love" (*ahavah rabbah*), that is so intense (*aṣumah*) the heart cannot contain it and hence the soul yearns to leave the body; the second is a form of ecstasy that can be contained by the vessel of the heart, and its primary objective is to draw down the divine efflux from above into the material world.[71] Worship, therefore, consists of two phases, the self-annihilation that results from the conjunction (*devequt*) of the soul in the light of the Infinite and the drawing down of that light through the fulfillment of Torah and ritual commandments to sustain the material world.[72] From a chronological perspective, the latter is consequent to the former, as Shneur Zalman himself put the matter, "It is precisely the nullification of something into nothing that causes the drawing down of nothing into something" (*u-viṭṭul ha-yesh le-ayin dawqa gorem hamshakhat ayin le-yesh*).[73] However, from the perspective of the incorporation of all things in the infinite essence,[74] and the corollary principle of the *coincidentia oppositorum*, the two must be viewed as expressions of a single phenomenon.[75] In metaphoric terms, the dual movement of worship may be depicted as the ascent and descent (*aliyyah wi-yeridah*) of the angels on the ladder envisaged by Jacob in his dream at Bethel (Gen 28:12) or as the running to and fro (*raṣo wa-shov*) of the creatures seen by Ezekiel in his vision of the chariot by the Chebar Canal in Babylonia (Ezek 1:14). The going up must be followed by coming down, the running hither by returning thither, but one conjoined to the essence reaches the place of indifference where there is an absolute identity of opposites in virtue of their opposition.

Worship is thus compared to the faculty of the dream imagination; just as the dreamer demonstrates the ability "to combine two opposites in one subject" (*leḥabber shenei hafakhim be-nose eḥad*), since the "root of the dream" is from the aspect of the supernal perimeter (*ha-maqqif elyon*) wherein opposites are no longer distinguishable, so only the worshipper, completely divested of corporeality, is in the position to maintain the corporeal. As if in a dream, we must take hold here of the convergence of opposites: the world is constituted as virtually something by the one who has become nothing actually.[76] Embedded deeper in the comparison of worship to the dream is the discernment that pious life, at least as it is construed (mono)theistically, entails a form of dissimilitude, perpetuating the charade of a dialogic encounter between a personal deity and a personal self. Truth appears, finally, through the mask of this untruth, the mask unmasked as the face that is the mask through which one can see the face.

In an extraordinarily rich discourse from 29 Av 5714 (August 28, 1954), Schneerson develops the somatic understanding of conjunction (*devequt*) and annihilation (*biṭṭul*) as a homiletical explication of the verse "Follow the Lord your God, fear him, observe his commandments, heed his voice, worship him, and cleave to him" (Deut 13:5).[77] Here I will offer only some of the salient points that are most relevant to the topic at hand. The line of worship (*qaw ha-avodah*), which comprises both sacrifices and prayer, given the rabbinic tradition that the latter was instituted in place of the former,[78] involves the "elevation from below to above." The structure of the morning liturgical service is explicated as a roadmap of the soul's ascent: the beginning of prayer, which precedes the gesture of blessing (*berakhah*), is a verbal act of thanksgiving (*hoda'ah*), which signifies the assent of faith in the truth without comprehension,[79] an acquiescence that functions as the prayer before prayer, the prayer, that is, that makes prayer possible in the face of what reason deems impossible, and then there is a gradual advance to the nullification of self connected to the declaration of the oneness of God (*qeri'at shema*) and the silent prayer of the eighteen benedictions (*shemoneh esreh*).[80] One might think of this as a spiritual climax, but it is followed by the supplication prayer (*nefilat appayim*), which marks the need for the mind to be engaged again with corporality (*gashmiyyut*) and materiality (*ḥomriyyut*). Although there is a danger of falling from the heightened state of consciousness, the paradox must nonetheless be embraced: it is precisely when one reenters the physical world that one is most fully conjoined to the divinity that transcends the world. Schneerson marks the difference in the levels of attainment by noting that the conjunction connected to prayer is such that the worshipper becomes a vessel to receive the light, but he is still an independent entity; by contrast, the conjunction that is connected to the supplication is an act of incorporation (*hitkallelut*) whereby the worshipper and the worshipped are one thing in actuality. Alternatively expressed, the nullification of the former (*biṭṭul di-shemoneh esreh*) provokes the "sacrifice of the self in potential, the sacrifice of self from the perspective of the soul, and it does not relate to the body," whereas the nullification of the latter (*biṭṭul di-nefilat appayim*) induces the "sacrifice of the self in actuality, and from the perspective of the body."[81] It is precisely by returning to the corporeal that one can claim to be wholly incorporated into the incorporeal and, as a consequence, to have the capacity to draw down the effluence of light into the world. The prototype mentioned by Schneerson is the Beshṭ, concerning whom it is reported that "when he had an ascent of the soul, he would be divested from all the corporeality of the material life of his body, as one who actually expired, for this is the sacrifice of self in actuality and from the perspective of the body . . . and, analogously, such is the nullification and sacrifice of self of the supplication."[82] What the Beshṭ accomplished by distancing himself completely from the body, others are impelled to achieve by going back to the body, albeit through the sacrifice of the body.

Enlightened Body and the Eschatological (In)corporation

It is correct to emphasize that Ḥabad masters have affirmed the physical, even to the point of imagining an eschatological future wherein corporeality will be elevated over spirituality, and the soul will receive from and be sustained by the body.[83] As Schneerson put it in a letter written on 11 Ṭevet 5716 (December 26, 1955), "In the future-to-come, the soul will receive its vitality from the body in which the higher [element] will be more elevated, for it descends precisely more and more until [it reaches] the body, but now it is in concealment and in the future-to-come the truth will be revealed in this as well, and this is the level of 'And Esther was taken' (Esther 2:16)—the Community of Israel, which is called 'Esther' in the time of exile—'to the king'—the king of the world—'Ahasuerus'—for the end and the beginning are his—'in the tenth month, which is the month of Ṭevet' (Esther 2:16)."[84] In the first chapter, we saw that one of the reasons Purim emblematizes the utopian holiday is that on this festival eating and drinking are granted supreme importance as features of proper worship, an intensification of the Ḥasidic emphasis that the body is the means through which one transcends the limitations of the body. This is the intent of the scriptural exegesis in the aforecited passage: the figure of Esther, who is identified as the "Community of Israel"(*keneset yisra'el*), that is, *Malkhut*, the last of the ten *sefirot*, is lifted up (literally, "taken") to the Infinite, signified by Ahasuerus, the king of the world to whom beginning and end belong.[85] The elevation of Esther to Ahasuerus is the correlative gesture to the descent of the soul to the body. The supremacy of the latter in relation the former, which is the distinguishing feature of the messianic epoch, indicates that the material is the veil through which the light is (un)manifest. Explicating the rabbinic gloss that the month of Ṭevet in which Esther was appropriated by Ahasuerus (Esther 2:16) is the "month that the body derives pleasure from the body" (*yeraḥ she-neheneh guf min ha-guf*),[86] Schneerson notes that, at present, the body above, that is, the essence (*eṣem*) and substance (*mahut*) of the divine, is sustained by the body of the Jew below,[87] but, in the future, the aspect we denominate as soul will derive its life force from the aspect we denominate as body, a contraversion that is also expressed in gender terms as the female encircling the male, *neqevah tesovev gaver* (Jer 31:21),[88] that is, the feminine capacity to receive rises above the masculine potency to bestow.[89] This is the esoteric import of the special connection between Jewish women and the miracle of Purim,[90] instantiated in the talmudic decree that women are obligated in the reading of the scroll of Esther, even though it is a positive commandment dependent on time, the genus of law from which they are generally exempt, according to rabbinic jurisprudence.[91] The rationale offered for this exception is that "even they were in that miracle" (*af hen hayu be-oto nes*).[92] Commenting on this ruling in the talk delivered on Purim 5717 (March 17, 1957), Schneerson noted that the word *even* (*af*) implies that women are inferior to men, but the scriptural account emphasizes that the miracle is linked especially to Esther.[93]

The true intent of the rabbinic diction can be discerned from the Ḥasidic insight proffered by Shneur Zalman regarding the conduct of Esther, "she did everything on her own without the advice of Mordecai."[94] Ostensibly, this assertion inverts the power dynamic that one would have expected, the female heeding the male, and this should have especially been so in the case of Esther, whose name conveys a sense of concealment (*hastarah*). Schneerson draws the implications: "The lesson from this for our time, when we are found in the state and the condition of 'I will keep my countenance hidden' (Deut 31:18), in the abundant darkness of the time of exile, is that there are matters that the women of Israel must do based on their own minds; on the contrary, the husband must act in accord with the opinion of the wife (in these matters)."[95] As we learn from the continuation of the talk, the affairs allocated to the woman's control are domestic in nature. Prima facie, these would seem to be more internal, as they pertain to the upbringing of the family and the maintenance of the household, but symbolically they are more external, as they are mundane when compared to more lofty issues. Yet, the lesson to be learned is that spirituality, indeed the "spirituality of the spirituality" (*ruḥaniyyut she-be-ruḥaniyyut*), cannot be accessed but through corporality.[96]

To the extent that this was the role of Esther in the original Purim narrative, this holiday anticipates the reversal of the male/female dichotomy and the corresponding spiritual/material distinction that is emblematic of the messianic era, and, consequently, the special role associated with this day apportioned especially to Jewish women in the generation of the footsteps of the Messiah.[97] Philosophically, the elevation of the sensual on Purim attests to the Lurianic mystery of *ṣimṣum*, the immeasurable taking on measurable form, rendered figuratively as the "royal garb" (*levush malkhut*) worn by Ahasuerus, the donning of the garment, which symbolizes the exercise of sovereignty in relation to the world.[98] Through this act we come to learn "the greatness of the level of corporality, including the physical body, to the point that within it is the potency of the essence [*koaḥ ha-aṣmut*] even more than in the world of emanation [*olam ha-aṣilut*]."[99] The ascent of the body, and by extension the delimiting of the feminine as the potential of the limitless, which cannot be delimited, is a cluster of themes repeated throughout the duration of the Rebbe's leadership. It would be too onerous to cite all or even a significant percentage of the relevant sources, but, to substantiate the point, I will mention one passage from a talk delivered on 25 Ḥeshvan 5752 (November 2, 1991): "The matter of the Messiah is the 'final redeemer'—for he comes at the end of the toil (*Malkhut*, the end of the *sefirot*), at the end of the time of exile. . . . The light of the recipient [*or ha-meqabbel*] reaches and flows from a gradation that is higher than the light of the donor [*or ha-mashpi'a*], for in the true and perfect redemption it will be revealed that the 'female encompasses the male,' the level of the body of the Jew (vis-à-vis his soul), for the power of the essence is found precisely in it, to the point that in the future-to-come the soul will be sustained by the body."[100]

It is misleading, in my judgment, to allege on the basis of this reversal that Ḥabad pietism advocates a kind of "antispiritualism" that broke with the acosmic or pantheistic quietism of the Maggid of Międzyrzecz .[101] There is little reason to doubt, however, that the sway of Ḥabad thinking is predicated on the belief that the quest for the pneumatic must be sought in the somatic, that the eschatological vision occasions an inversion of the present order, that the root of materiality is positioned higher than the root of spirituality, a matter that is expressed as well in terms of a transposition of gender stereotypes, the female rising above and encircling the male. The cosmological implications of this inversion are made explicitly and succinctly by Schneerson, "the perfection of nature [*ha-sheleimut de-ṭeva*] is such that it will be discerned openly that nature is divinity [*ha-ṭeva hu elohut*]."[102] This comment seems to suggest a worldview in which the difference between divinity and nature is erased, in a manner that strikes me as a reversal of Spinoza's notorious maxim *Deus sive Natura*, "God or nature," that is, Schneerson's words imply the divinization of nature rather than the materialization of God.[103] Upon closer examination, however, it becomes clear that the discernment that nature is divinity is based on preserving the identity of their nonidentity in the nonidentity of their identity, a point that we have already encountered in our appraisal of apophatic panentheism in the previous chapter. Ontologically, God is not reduced to nature nor nature to God; the one is the other in virtue of the one not being (an)other. Epistemologically, the cogitation of the extended can be imagined only from the standpoint of the externalization of the cogitated.

To apprehend this paradox, one must bear in mind that Schneerson's statement needs to be evaluated in terms of the sentiment discussed above, whereby the physical is deemed meaningful only to the degree that it serves as an instrument for the spiritual, becoming the vessel to receive the light. As the RaShaB observed, just as the internal form, or the light of the Torah, must assume the shape of the letters, which are the external form,[104] so, too, the Jewish body is the external form most suitable to be the vessel to receive the divine soul (*nefesh elohit*), which is the human soul (*nefesh ha-adam*) in the most exacting sense. "The divine soul that is garbed in it is the true form, and this is the vitality that sustains him, and it is known that, with respect to Israel, the vitality of their bodies is from the divine soul, but it is garbed in the natural vital soul [*nefesh ha-ḥiyyunit ha-ṭiv'i*]. The righteous, who have purified the natural soul such that it is contained in the divine soul, all of their vitality is from the divine soul, and hence their bodies are formed in this image, so that it will be a vessel for the light of the divine soul."[105] The instrumentality presumed here, which is the unique destiny of the Jewish people, is predicated on the presumption that the body bearing the divine soul is the body in the truest sense. This body is not the corruptible flesh, but the textual body, the body whose limbs are made up of the letters of the Torah, which is God's name. From the Ḥabad vantage point, enfleshment of the spirit is to be grasped from the standpoint of this hyperliterality.

Many passages from Schneerson's oeuvre could be cited to illustrate that this was his view, but, in order to show that this was not an opinion he discarded with the passage of time, I will mention three representative texts, the first two from relatively early dates and the last from a late date. The first passage is from Schneerson's ruminations connected to Ḥanukah 5696 (1935):

> The externality of the Jewish person—"in all your ways know him" (Prov 3:6), the six days [in which] you should do all your labor (Exod 20:9). The interiority—*ḥabad* [*ḥokhmah binah da'at*], which relates only to divinity . . . the day of Sabbath. The interiority of the interiority—the power of self-sacrifice, the eight days [of Ḥanukah] that are even above the day of Sabbath, by way of [the explanation that] circumcision is on the eighth so that one Sabbath will transpire [in the infant's life]. By means of this is its eternality, to the point that, consequently, they light the candles also in their sacred courtyards.[106]

Utilizing a temporal calculus, Schneerson delineates the three dimensions of the Jew's existence: the six weekdays correspond to the external (*ḥiṣoniyyut*), the seventh day, the Sabbath, to the internal (*penimiyyut*), and the eighth, represented by the festival of Ḥanukah, to the internal of the internal (*penimiyyut ha-penimiyyut*). The superiority of the eighth to the seventh is linked to the rabbinic explanation for the timing of circumcision, so that the newborn Jewish body can pass through one Sabbath uncircumcised.[107] There is, however, a more profound intent implied by the number symbolism connected to these two rituals: just as circumcision is the covenantal mark imprinted on the body that points to what is beyond the body, so the lights of Ḥanukah symbolize the most interior aspect, and yet they must be lit on the outside to publicize the miracle. To understand this reversal is the key to grasping the valorization of the corporeal in Ḥabad eschatology.

The second text is from the Rebbe's talk connected to the day of Purim 5719—in that leap year, the holiday was celebrated on the fourteenth of Adar II (March 24, 1959).[108] In the first part of the talk, Schneerson discussed, inter alia, the distinctiveness of the Jewish people and their holiness vis-à-vis the other ethnicities. The distinction is clarified by summoning the interpretation of the verse "The Jews enjoyed light and gladness, happiness and honor" (Esther 8:16) attributed to R. Judah, light is the Torah, gladness the festivals, happiness the rite of circumcision, and honor the phylacteries.[109] In the Rebbe's rendition, these constitute the four signs (*zeichnis*, *otot*) that mark the difference between Jews and non-Jews, a difference mandated by the need "to separate Israel and the nations" (*lehavdil bein yisra'el la-ammim*).[110] Ostensibly, the signs do not relate to the matter of the soul, since the Jewish soul (*yidishe neshome*) is substantially different from the soul of the non-Jew, and there is no need to mark the disparity between things if they are not palpably similar. The markings of difference, therefore, would seem to relate to the physical, as there does not appear to be a discrepancy between the Jewish and non-Jewish body—just as with respect to the four matters delineated by R. Judah there is a superficial similarity between Jews and non-Jews, the latter recognize the wisdom of the Torah in concord with their intellectual capacity, they have their own festivals, some of them are circumcised, and some of them wear a sign like phylacteries to indicate their identity and allegiance. But this is only on the level of external appearance because, in truth, the Jewish body is not the same as the body of the non-Jew; the former, in contrast to the latter, is holy (*der yidisher guf iz koydesh*).[111] The special holiness affixed to the Jewish people, a priestly ideal that exercised great influence on the religious self-perception of Jews through the centuries, is related in Ḥabad to the belief (itself based on much older sources) that Jews uniquely bear the divine soul (*nefesh elohit*), which is the "portion of the divine from above" (Job 31:2). In virtue of this psychic distinction, as Shneur Zalman already made clear,[112] the animal soul (*nefesh bahamit*) is different in the case of the Jew, and Jews are thus obligated to be holy (*heylik*) even with respect to material things (*gashmiyusdike zakhen*). That sense of holiness, as we have already noted, stipulates sanctification rather than suppression of the physical.[113]

The positive valence conferred on the body in the seventh Rebbe's teaching should be viewed from this perspective. It would be erroneous, however, to present this as evidence for a categorical affirmation of the physical, an uplifting of the flesh. The body that is confirmed is the body composed of the letters of the name, the Jewish body, which is viewed as substantively different from the Gentile body, a divergence that is not completely overturned even in the messianic moment, as I will argue in chapter 6. The ascetic dimension of the embodiment, to which spiritual significance is assigned, is underscored in the continuation of Schneerson's talk, when he comments further on the rabbinic interpretation of the word happiness (*sason*) as an allusion to circumcision (*milah*), one of the physical signs that marks the difference between Jew and non-Jew. Schneerson notes that there are Gentiles who also circumcise themselves, but he insists that the circumcision of the Jew is performed in "an altogether different manner" (*ingantsn oyf ander oyfn*).[114] The scriptural verse cited in the talmudic passage to buttress the explanation of *sason* as *milah* is "I rejoice over your speech, as one who obtains great spoil" (Ps 119:162)—an exegesis based on the connection between *milah*, which can also mean "word," and *imratekha*, "your speech." Two things are implied in this verse: first, circumcision has a special joy (*spetsiele freyd*) and, second, this rite is comparable to taking great spoil from an enemy. To clarify these matters, Schneerson refers to the view of Maimonides that the cut of circumcision weakens one's desires for this world (*tayves fun olam ha-zeh*). To be precise, Maimonides argued that the reason for circumcision is that it weakens the male organ and decreases sexual lust beyond what is necessary for procreation.[115] In the Rebbe's adaptation, sexual desire is taken as a metonym for physical appetite in general. His explanation reveals the reworking of the Maimonidean perspective in kabbalistically inflected language: "This world with its multiple pleasures and desires is called the 'world of the shells' [*olam ha-kelipos*], which is the great enemy of the Jew. When a Jew weakens the desires of this world and, moreover, when he seizes all the desires of this world and rescues them for holiness . . . by means of this he takes from the enemy the great spoil, and from the most excellent he gives over to holiness; hence his joy is a great bliss." And it is precisely with respect to this ascetic dimension that Jewish circumcision is distinguished from circumcision of non-Jews. For Gentiles, since there is a more natural link between their comportment and the physical world, the operation of circumcision causes them great pain, whereas, for Jews, since there is an inherent animus between them and the physical world, the same act causes them immense delight. "The separation from the pleasures of this world creates happiness for him, since the interiority of the substance of the Jew [*der penimiyyusdike mahus fun a yiden*] is not pleasure from this world [*der geshmak fun olam ha-zeh*], but, by contrast, delight in godliness [*der geshmak in gottlichkeit*]. This world is the material—the ass that is 'your enemy,' and the taking of the spoil from the enemy causes the Jew to have the greatest bliss."[116]

The language here is unambiguous: the corporeal realm is portrayed as the world of the shells or as the other side (*siṭra aḥara*), standard kabbalistic locutions for the force of impurity. The non-Jew derives gratification from the world of physicality, the Jew from divinity, since the essence of his body is to be a vessel for the light, and thus matter (*ḥomer*) for him is the obstinate enemy, figuratively, the ass (*ḥamor*) against which he must struggle. But, as I have already noted, the task is not to slaughter the ass but to saddle it, not to break the body but to purify it, to transform materiality (im)materially.[117] The point is illumined further in the continuation of the talk in which Schneerson delved deeper into the rite of circumcision and the nature of body.[118] In the case of the Jewish male, the mark of circumcision is identified as the divine image (*ṣelem elohim*) in virtue of which he is called *adam*, that is, the true nature of what is to be human is linked to circumcision, which empowers the Jew over the beastly nature of the other nations, who are not considered to be in the category of human in the fullest sense.[119] The verse "Thus shall my covenant be marked in your flesh as an everlasting pact" (Gen 17:13) indicates that the sign is cut in the flesh to remind the Jew that he must act in sync with the divine will "not only when his soul is found above, but also in its descent into the body and the animal soul in this corporeal and material world." Again, a military image is invoked: the divine soul must fight against the body and the animal soul to fulfill the will of God, the soul must navigate its way through the forces of impurity. The way of combat, however, is not to eradicate the sensual, for this would not constitute being a "great spoil" taken from the enemy. The nature of spoil requires the act of taking, a gesture of appropriation, making the other one's own by making one's own the other, that is, transforming body into consciousness and consciousness into body. Echoing the teaching transmitted in the name of the Besht̩, Schneerson emphasized that the edict is "in all your ways know him" (Prov 3:6). This is the great spoil, the burden to hoist the body, to elevate matters of this world to holiness.

The second text is part of a discourse delivered following the afternoon prayers on the fast day of 10 Ṭevet 5750 (January 7, 1990). Schneerson quotes the view of Shneur Zalman that the essence of the reality of the Jew is the soul, which is consubstantial with the divine in actuality (*ḥeleq eloha mi-ma'al mammash*), and hence the body assumes an inferior status (*nafsham iqqar we-gufam ṭafel*).[120] Yet, the telos of human existence can only be revealed through corporeal worship (*avodat ha-guf*) and thus it is correct to assert that this mode of service is superior to worship through the soul (*avodat ha-neshamah*), an idea bolstered by the principle that the lower a thing is below, the higher its root above (*davar she-hu taḥton be-yoter shorsho lema'lah be-yoter*). After establishing these points, Schneerson commented, "And it is this way with respect to the body that is above [*ha-guf she-lema'lah*]—for by means of worship through the body one reaches above to the gradation that is called by the name *body,* which is higher than the gradation that is called soul. And in greater depth—in contrast to the gradation that is called soul, worship through the body inestimably augments the body that is above."[121]

The supremacy of the body is related directly to the homology between the body below and the body above, an axiom of medieval kabbalistic symbolism that exerted a great influence on Ḥasidism in general and on Ḥabad in particular. The limbs of the human body correspond isomorphically to the sefirotic emanations, which are configured in the corporeal form of the primordial anthropos. The ascription of a body to God on the part of kabbalists is not to be taken literally, as if the divine were composed of a measurable and tangible body, but hyperliterally, that is, the imaginal body of the divine—the body that is constituted in the imagination—is made up of the letters of the Hebrew alphabet, which are contained in the Tetragrammaton, the mystical essence of the Torah. The true nature of human embodiment partakes as well of this textual embodiment, that is, the deportment of the human—idealized in the Jew—is to elevate the somatic *adam*, the "dust of the earth," *afar min ha-adamah* (Gen 2:7), to the pneumatic *adam*, "I will be likened to the most high," *eddammeh le-elyon* (Isa 14:14).[122] Thus, even though the soul is the essence, corporeal worship is privileged not only because it affords one the opportunity to augment the imaginal body above theurgically through ritual performance with the physical body below, but because this is the means by which the latter is transfigured into the spiritual or etheral body.[123] This, it will be recalled, is offered by Shneur Zalman as the mystical meaning of the scriptural notion of Israel's election. From the standpoint of appearances, the physical body (*guf ha-ḥomri*) of the Jew seems to be identical to the bodies of the other worldly nations. But this resemblance is only on the level of semblance. When looked at from the standpoint of the essence, the Jewish body is distinguished from the bodies of all other nations, as only the Jew has been endowed with the means to transpose coarse corporeality into the immaterial materiality, the body that is the text, which is the name of God, and hence the Jewish body is capable of drawing the light of the Infinite into the world, which is the aim of creation.[124] Emancipation is tantamount to becoming cognizant of this sense of embodiment that connects the sensible and the suprasensible. The conjunction between the lower body and upper body also points to the transition from *golah* (exile) to *ge'ullah* (redemption), as the difference between the former and the latter is the letter *alef*, which can be broken orthographically into an upper *yod* and a lower *yod* connected by a *waw*, the numerical value of which is twenty-six (10 + 10 + 6), which is also the value of the four letters of YHWH (10 + 5 + 6 + 5). The contrast between exile and redemption, therefore, consists of nothing but the *alef*, which signifies the name, the divine body, the supernal prototype of the body politic of Israel.[125]

This, I propose, is the esoteric significance of the higher valence ascribed to the body in Schneerson's eschatological teaching. Here it is worthwhile to recall a comment he made in the introduction to the publication of Yosef Yiṣḥaq's *Qunṭres Ḥag ha-Ge'ullah 12–13 Tammuz* in 1951: "The explanation of redemption—the exit from the constriction of the measurement and boundary of the corporeal and physical matters and of the body and the animal soul. But it is incumbent on us to prepare to become a vessel to receive this emanation, to gather it in the interiority, and, as a consequence, to make it actual, in thought, speech, and action."[126]

In this brief remark, one can find the essential import of Schneerson's messianic doctrine: salvation consists of overcoming the limitation of the physical body, so that the material nature may become a container for the divine illumination that is above nature. In the process of receiving, the internal is externalized and the external internalized. Enlightenment, therefore, does not bespeak the dissolution of the corporal, but rather an altered state of consciousness wherein the somatic is suffused with the radiance of the essence. In a talk from 11 Shevaṭ 5721 (January 28, 1961), Schneerson explained that since the future redemption is characterized as the aspect that is without boundary (*beḥinat beli gevul*), the worship that is apposite to it must also be beyond delimitation (*avodah le-lo hagbalot*), for only through this form of service is it possible to "draw down and reveal the limitless light [*ha-or ha-bilti mugbal*] by means of which the darkness is transformed into light [*ithapkha ḥashokha li-nehora*]."[127] The point is elucidated by reference to the talmudic dictum reported by R. Samuel ben Naḥman in the name of R. Yonatan, "everyone who went out to war on behalf of the house of David wrote a bill of divorce for his wife."[128] The "war on behalf of the house of David" is explained as a battle with "those who fight against the disclosure of the Messiah," and the requirement to write a bill of divorce for one's wife is interpreted more broadly as a stipulation to desist from "matters of the world, even for things that are permissible. . . . This is also the issue of 'sanctify yourself in what is permitted to you'[129] . . . to abstain (*opzogn zikh*) from these matters, also from permissible things, and even from matters that are suitable to him according to the Torah . . . for this is the conduct that is above boundary."[130] The combat that is required to bring about the messianic revelation demands giving up matters that pertain to the physical realm, even matters that are, strictly speaking, permissible under the law. "One must renounce and resist all these things with peril, to give oneself over entirely to the war of the house of David, in order to fulfill the supernal will so that the house of David will be victorious, and the disclosure of David will issue from the house of David."[131]

The corporeality that is affirmed by Schneerson cannot be understood simplistically as an endorsement of the material body. As he put it in a talk delivered on 19 Kislev 5725 (November 24, 1964): the soul can be revealed in the body in two ways. The first way is for the soul to dominate and subjugate the body, but it still feels as if the latter has an independent existence; the second way is for the soul to be revealed in the body to the point that the latter has no independent existence at all, but is rather "unified with the soul in absolute substantiality and nullification" (*meyuḥad im ha-nefesh be-takhlit ha-hit'aṣṣemut we-ha-biṭṭul*). The second approach characterizes the vitality of the soul of the Jewish people in its most elemental nature, for

> they are called *adam*[132] in accord with "I will be likened to the most high" [*eddammeh le-elyon*] (Isa 14:14), for their corporeal vitality is also from the divine soul [*nefesh ha-elohit*]—for the whole matter and reality of the Jewish body [*guf ha-yisra'eli*] is that it is a vessel for the soul, so that the soul can carry out the will of the blessed holy One, which is garbed in the practical commandments . . . this is precisely by means of the physical limbs of the body. . . . For the whole purpose of the existence of the Jewish man [*ha-ish ha-yisra'eli*] is only that he will be a tabernacle for the blessed One.[133]

There is no adoration of the physical in any brute material sense, no tint of a hedonistic adulation of sensuality. On the contrary, the body that is valorized as superior to the soul is the transformed body, the body whose autonomous existence vis-à-vis the soul is nullified. The two forms of the soul's relationship to the body are correlated with two kinds of worship, the former designated by the rabbinic instruction that "all your actions should be for the sake of heaven" (Avot 2:12) and the latter by the scriptural command "in all your ways know him" (Prov 3:6).[134] The body can become a means by which to know God when it is no longer considered as ontically independent of the soul, which is truly a portion of the divinity above. The corporeal matter is deemed holy exactly when it is so thoroughly annihilated and assimilated in divinity that the materiality within it is not felt at all. When the Jew eats, for example, he pronounces a blessing to draw down the divine influx on the edible object, and he should sense nothing but the matter of God's kingship in the world (liturgically enacted in the words *elohenu melekh ha-olam*).[135] From the example of eating, we can extrapolate the general principle: all sensual acts are to be divested completely of carnal pleasure. The Alter Rebbe is presented as the model: "he did not feel his corporeal existence, for all of his substance was his divine soul."[136] To be considered a "servant of God," *oved elohim* (Mal 3:18), a title of great esteem in Ḥabad literature, one must "conquer oneself and alter one's routine," and "even though the body is in its physical condition, by means of this one conquers the physical body by force."[137]

It may be beneficial to express this in Husserlian terms as the overcoming of the sensuous by the supersensuous, the merely physical by the material, the idealization of the body through "a particular mode of interpretation, or an intentional modification of the apprehension of the world."[138] It might seem farfetched to juxtapose Husserl and Ḥabad, but in the thinking exemplified by the latter, obviously indebted to much older sources, body is *res materialis*, an object of interpretive understanding, a mental construct, that transforms corporality into corporeity.[139] From this standpoint, the term *gashmiyyut* should be translated as materiality in contrast to physicality (*ḥomriyyut*). In spite of the great chasm separating Husserlian phenomenology and Ḥabad pietism, a common element is the assumption that the material is an already interpreted body, a body not only constituted in but as consciousness, a body that is as much eidetic as it is somatic. In a somewhat ironic twist, the very interpreters who emphasize Schneerson's affirmation of the corporeal end up reifying the hierarchy they say he overcame. That is, they are still operating with the Cartesian idea of body as *res extensa* set against the soul as *res cogitans*. Consider, for example, the following assessment: "The virtue of the physical does not lie in its potential sublimation or spiritualization—in transcending, that is, denying its natural physical self; rather . . . unique spiritual value lies in the physical specifically *because* it is physical."[140] I concur that the force of the Ḥabad orientation, especially conspicuous in the teachings of the seventh Rebbe, is not an unreserved ascetic rejection of the corporeal for the sake of the spiritual, but I do not think it is correct to say that the "spiritual value" of the physical is because it is physical. This tautology fails to take into account that the body that is affirmed in Ḥabad philosophy is the body that has been transfigured by its incorporation into the name that is the Torah, the primordial parable in which the light of the Infinite is garbed, as we discussed in the final section of chapter 1. To be sure, this is not to sublimate the material or to spiritualize it, but it is to diffuse it in a different light, to view the body hyperlinguistically, since all reality is considered to be a manifestation of the hidden name, an investiture of

YHWH, a permutation of the Hebrew letters contained therein. The body that is glorified, therefore, is an ascetic body, a somatic body that has been purified and transformed into a semiotic body. As the fifth Rebbe put it: "The disclosure vis-à-vis the other [*ha-gilluy el ha-zulat*] is by means of the letters of speech [*otiyyot ha-dibbur*], that is, by means of the letters garbing the light that is hidden in the letters, as the letters in essence are the aspect of concealment [*ha-otiyyot be-eṣem hem beḥinat he'lem*] . . . for they garb, cover, and conceal the light and by means of this there is disclosure."[141] Expressing the same idea in slightly different terms, the sixth Rebbe observed: "What is garbed in the worlds in their interiority to sustain them are only the letters of the speech of the aspect of *Malkhut* . . . from *alef* to *taw*, and they reveal merely the external illumination, and even this in constriction after constriction."[142] The insight regarding the insubstantiality of all things other than YHWH, the power of infinity—"for everything is actually as nothing and naught in relation to his substance and his essence" (*she-ha-kol ke-ayin wa-efes mammash legabbei mahuto we-aṣmuto*)[143]—serves to anchor the mandate to transmute the corporeal body into the textual body by augmenting the effluence of the infinite light in the cosmos, the paradoxical ideal of delimiting the limitless, of determining the indeterminate, of creating a temporal-spatial habitation (*dirah*) for the divinity that is beyond time and space, the mystical gnosis of the *coincidentia oppositorum*, the identity of Elohim and YHWH, nature and what is above nature.[144]

4

MESSIANIC TORAH
Hypernomian Transvaluation

The one engaged in a ritual commandment is exempt from the ritual commandment.

—BABYLONIAN TALMUD, SUKKAH 26A

Overturning Opposites and the Transmutation of Darkness Into Light

THE SECRET OF THE SECRET, *RAZA DE-RAZIN*, THAT ONE may elicit from the teachings of the seventh Rebbe is predicated on understanding redemption in the contemplative terms I outlined in chapter 2, a state of enhanced spiritual consciousness characterized as the discernment of the underlying unity of all things. This recognition, however, does not entail the monistic absorption of all difference in the undifferentiated and disembodied One. It is rather the perception of the ultimate indifference, the embodied emptiness, the nothing that is everything in virtue of being nothing. The mystical vision allows one to see the true object of salvation behind the rhetorical screen of a personal redeemer, the luster of the infinite essence, the nonbeing in and through which the multiplicity of beings are conceived in their meontological interdependence. Rendering the biblical reference to waging battle against one's enemies as an allegorical portrayal of the internal psychological struggle with the evil inclination and the animal soul, Shneur Zalman had already observed, "And this is 'When you go out to war' (Deut 21:10), that is, the war of the soul against the setting of one thing against its opposite [*milḥemet ha-nefesh be-zeh le'ummat zeh*], then you will be 'over your enemies' (Deut 21:10), this is the aspect of the disclosure of the point of the heart [*gilluy nequddat ha-lev*], which is from the aspect of surrounding all the worlds [*sovev kol almin*], above your enemies, for the enemy from below has no power or grasp there . . . and, as a consequence, 'you take some of them captive' (Deut 21:10), for evil is transformed into good [*nithappekh ha-ra le-ṭov*]."[1] Interpreting the overturning of attributes (*hafikhat ha-middot*) affirmed in this text, the seventh Rebbe noted that "in relation to the illumination of the point of the heart there is opposition [*legabbei he'arat nequddat ha-lev yeshno mi-neged*] . . . which is not the case with respect to the essence of the point of the heart, the aspect of *yeḥidah*, corresponding to which there is no opposition [*she-ein kenegdah le'ummat zeh*] . . . and hence the nullification of opposition [*ha-biṭṭul di-le'ummat zeh*] that is by way of the disclosure of the essence of the point of the heart [*gilluy aṣmut nequddat ha-lev*] . . . for by means of this disclosure there is no place from the outset for the existence of opposition [*ha-meṣi'ut di-le'ummat zeh*]."[2] The two forms of worship alluded to in Schneerson's comment correspond respectively to *itkafya* and *ithapkha*,[3] the former presupposes duality (marked linguistically by the phrase *zeh le'ummat zeh*) and the volitional obedience to the law (*torah u-miṣwot*) necessary to triumph over that duality, the latter the unity and complete annihilation of the will in a gesture of self-sacrifice (*mesirat nefesh*) that effaces all difference.[4] As Schneerson put it: "By means of the worship whose beginning is the receiving of the yoke, a man can attain overturning [*ithapkha*] from subjugation [*itkafya*], for evil is not only subservient to good but it can be changed into good, and this is the true purpose of man."[5] It goes without saying that this possibility would challenge the dichotomy that serves as justification for lawful observance. What is noteworthy is that the potential to trespass the law is circumscribed within its contours, since the identity of God and Torah, a basic kabbalistic tenet uniformly posited by Ḥabad masters, implies that Torah in its ultimate nature is the infinite unity that betrays the coincidence of opposites.[6] In Schneerson's own words:

> The essence of the Torah, which is unified in his essence, blessed be he, is expressed specifically in the fact that it is an antidote [literally, "spices," *tavlin*] for the evil inclination,[7] since the power to season [*letabbel*] the evil inclination and to transform it to good is precisely from the side of his essence, blessed be he. And the explanation of this: insofar as all the disclosures, even the most elevated, are classified in the category of light

> and disclosure, the existence of evil—the opposite of light—is opposed to them, and hence they do not have the capacity to transform it into good (but rather to battle against it until it is entirely abrogated). Only his essence, blessed be he, which is simple in the utmost simplicity and is devoid of all forms, and no opposite is appropriate in relation to it, has the capacity to change it and to transform it into good. Also, with respect to the aspect of the Torah that is united with his blessed essence, it is said, "toying before him" (Prov 8:30), the bemusement (and joy) that is above comes by way of the purification [*berur*] and rectification [*tiqqun*] of the darkness—the darkness transmuted into light. And this is "toying before him:" precisely through the aspect of the darkness being transmuted into light—"toying"—which is in the Torah; its interiority is expressed as it is united with the interiority of the light of the Infinite, blessed be he—"before him."[8]

What we may call the hypernomian precept, encapsulated in the slogan *ithapkha ḥashokha li-nehora*, the "darkness will be transmuted into light"—which is to say, the epistemic realization that the divergence of the two is merely from the standpoint of appearance and not as they are in the essential reality[9]—is the measure of salvation (*yeshu'a*).[10] It follows that the soteriological task entrusted to the Jews, which epitomizes the model of all human endeavor, even as it must be executed in the arena of history by this particular ethnicity, is "to come to the supreme state of overturning opposites" (*mehafkhim et ha-inyanim de-zeh le'ummat zeh*). The ideal is illustrated textually from the fact that Pharaoh, the archetype of evil, personally assisted in liberating the children of Israel from exile. Insofar as the agency of deliverance from darkness was the power of darkness, the exodus from Egypt can serve as "preparation for the principle of the matter of redemption,"[11] which likewise will come about through a transgressive piety wherein the distinction between sacred and profane will be blurred.

Equanimity, Holy Folly, and Self-Sacrifice: Worship Beyond Worship

In a talk given on 26 Ṭevet 5721 (January 14, 1961), Schneerson articulated a similar idea in noting that the exodus from Egypt was a "spiritual redemption" (*ge'ullah ruḥanit*) and not merely a "physical liberation" (*ge'ullah gashmit*). With respect to the former, a further distinction between a literal and an esoteric application is to be made. On the surface, it relates to the "giving of the Torah and its commandments," but its true intention is the "disclosure and knowledge of the name YHWH,"[12] a revelation that is indicative of the "substance of the attribute of truth" (*mahutah shel middat ha-emet*), the "absence of change" (*he'der ha-shinnuy*). Schneerson connects this idea with the rabbinic tradition that the seal (*ḥotam*) of God is truth (*emet*), for it is composed of *alef*, *mem*, *taw*, the first, middle, and last letters of the Hebrew alphabet.[13] This tradition, which is buttressed by citation of the scriptural verses "I am the first and I am the last, and there is no God besides me" (Isa 44:6) and "For I am the Lord, I have not changed" (Mal 3:6), attests to the indifference (*hishtawwut*) of the essence wherein all things "are equal and there is no variation" (*be-shawweh u-veli shinnuy*). Symbolically configured, the exodus from Egypt (*miṣrayim*) is a "true exit from all constrictions [*meṣarim*] and limitations [*gevulim*]," an attainment of psychic equanimity, the "absolute abnegation [*biṭṭul ha-muḥlaṭ*] to his blessed will without any deviation," which engenders a form of worship that is "above all distinctions." The "point of nullification" (*nequddat ha-biṭṭul*) that is "beyond boundary and change," the extinction of self in the face of the emptiness that is the matrix of all becoming, is the true implication of the Ḥasidic eschatology endorsed by Schneerson and his predecessors: "Just as it applies to the redemption from Egypt, so it applies to the future redemption, for the content of the matter of redemption is not only the physical redemption, and also not simply the spiritual redemption, but the disclosure of the name YHWH."[14] Significantly, most scholars who have commented on the messianism of the seventh Rebbe have focused on the two phases, the physical and the spiritual, the historical and the contemplative. However, as this text attests, there is a third dimension, the secret of the secret, which relates to the disclosure of the name, the compresence of the three temporal modes in the eternality of the nondifferentiated essence, revealed in the concealment of its concealment. Messianic consciousness is the reinscription of the particularity of the world of contingency by its overcoming, returning to the light of the Infinite as it was and is before the primal withdrawal, the luminosity in which the capacity to illumine and the capacity not to illumine are one in actuality. Redemption, therefore, can be understood as the transformation of darkness into light by apprehending the shimmer of the illimitable immaterialty glistening through the shadowy pretense of the material cosmos.[15]

One of the most striking ways that the hypernomian ideal is expressed is in terms of the altered status of the pig in the messianic future. The presumed etymological basis for this contention, the explanation of the name *ḥazir* as the impure animal that will revert in the future (*atid laḥazor*) to being pure, is found in a variety of medieval sources, some of which transmit it as a dictum from the formative rabbinic period.[16] Drawing out the implications of this motif, Shneur Zalman commented: "As the rabbis, blessed be their memory, said with regard to the pig that in the future it will revert and be purified, that is, in the future-to-come, death will be forever destroyed, and then the essence of the Infinite will be revealed, and the pig as well will be capable of ascending."[17] With the obliteration of the force of evil in the eschaton, expressed in the language of the permanent annihilation of death (based on Isa 25:8), the pig will itself be transformed from an impure to a holy being.[18] According to a second passage, the change in status of the pig signifies the purification of the seventy non-Jewish nations of the world:

> Thus in the future, it is written "For then I will make the nations pure of speech" (Zeph 3:9), that is, even the idolaters will be purified, for regarding the future it is written "I will remove the spirit of impurity from the earth" (Zech 13:2), and it is written "The glory of the Lord shall appear, and all flesh [as one, shall behold that the mouth of the Lord has spoken]" (Isa 40:5), "And men shall enter caverns in the rock because of the fear of the Lord" (Isa 2:19), for the entire aspect of evil will be purified, and darkness will be transformed to light, and bitterness to sweetness, to the point that all flesh will bow down and prostrate, and this is the matter of the pig reverting in the future to be pure. . . . This purification comes about precisely through engagement with the Torah, for the reason that it is called *torah* is from the expression *hora'ah*, to differentiate between the impure and the pure, and there is a directive that makes ritually fit and purifies what appears to be forbidden and impure, or, conversely, one that prohibits what appears to be ritually fit, and hence the matter of the purifications is verily to transform the darkness into light.[19]

Since the pig is the root of the force of impurity above, when all aspects of evil have been purified in the future and there is no more refuse in the world, the pig will also be restored and transformed into good.[20] The hypernomian implications of this image are brought into sharp relief in these words of Dov Baer:

> All of this is especially in the aspect of the world of rectification [*olam ha-tiqqun*] in which the light must dwell in the vessel and through contractions by means of the wisdom of the Torah, which comes to purify and to separate good and evil. However, in the aspect of the supernal perimeters [*maqqifim elyonim*] of the aspect of chaos [*beḥinat de-tohu*] that was prior to the world of rectification, which are the highest lights that could not come to be at all in the delimitation of vessels, there the impure can ascend like the pure . . . for there it says "darkness is not dark [for you; night is as light as day; darkness and light are the same]" (Ps 139:12). Since it is called the perimeter [*maqqif*], it is the aspect of the encompassing that is above the category of the concatenation [*sovev she-lema'lah mi-geder ha-hishtalshelut*], for before him in actuality everything is considered as naught [*qameih mammash kolla ke-lo ḥashiv*], and he renders identical the great and the small, the donor and the recipient. . . . If so, the impure animals can also ascend there to be a sacrifice and an offering, for there is no difference at all between the impure and the pure, and before him the darkness is as light, the two of them identical in actuality, as it is written, "Who can produce a pure thing out of an impure one, if not the One?" (Job 14:4), that is, who can make the impure thing to be like the pure thing, such that the pure thing arises from the impure thing in actuality, as the impure thing that is purified, if not the One, the aspect of the simple unity [*aḥdut peshuṭah*] that is in the aspect of the universal perimeter [*maqqif kelali*] that is above the concatenation? . . . It is, for example, as they said, "In the future, the pig will be pure, for it will revert to becoming permissible," and as it written, "the pig of the wild will gnaw at it" [*yekharsemennah ḥazir mi-ya'ar*] (Ps 80:14), with a suspended *ayin* [in the word *mi-ya'ar*], for, in the future-to-come, all the evil and the refuse will be purified entirely, and that which is refuse, like the pig, will also ascend . . . and it will be purified of its impurity. . . . And a true illustration of this matter is the issue of veritable repentance when the evil and impurity change themselves into the good and the pure, and this is exceedingly above the essence of the Torah, which is only to purify and to separate the good and the evil . . .

> and not that the impure itself will be pure, as the impure is to be differentiated and it does not ascend above at all by means of the Torah, but rather by means of repentance, which is above the aspect of the rectification [*tiqqun*] of the Torah, for the impure and the evil as they are in themselves will also be transformed into the pure and the good.[21]

Following his predecessors, the seventh Rebbe also affirms the tradition about the swine to confirm that the messianic epoch is marked by the revelation of the infinite unity as a *coincidentia oppositorum*, a state wherein evil will be changed to good, impure to pure, and guilt into innocence.[22] The metamorphosis of one thing into its opposite is correlated with the act of repentance, which surpasses the perfection of the Torah, as the latter consists of separating the opposites and not unifying them. The future, then, culminates in an ontological transubstantiation and an axiological transvaluation—the epitome of impurity, the pig, will be elevated in its status to a pure entity that can be offered as a sacrifice.

The ultimate goal of pietistic devotion, the humbling of self, is to reach this state of metaphysical indifference where darkness and light are identical in the identity of their opposition. One of the more captivating ways in which Schneerson expresses this idea is his comparison of Purim and the epiphany at Sinai. An early formulation of this assessment appears in the talk he delivered on Purim, 14 Adar 5713 (March 1, 1953): "Purim is on a higher level than the giving of the Torah, as is understood from what is written 'And the Jews received what they had begun to practice' [*we-qibbel ha-yehudim et asher heḥellu la'asot*] (Esther 9:23), that is, with respect to the giving of the Torah, there was only a beginning . . . but with respect to Purim, there was a 'complete reception' [*qabbalah gemurah*]. From this we can understand that the giving of the Torah and Purim belong together, for they are one matter, but Purim is on a higher level."[23] The superiority is further explained—based on a teaching of the Alter Rebbe[24]—in terms of the fact that both events entailed self-sacrifice, but in a fundamentally different way.[25] In the case of Sinai, the sacrifice was only in potential and from the perspective of the soul above, according to the rabbinic dictum that with the utterance of each commandment, the souls of the Israelites departed,[26] whereas, in the case of Purim, the sacrifice was in actuality and from the perspective of the body below, as the peril recorded in the scriptural narrative was one of total extermination.[27] Precisely because the physical well-being of the Jewish people was threatened, the overturning of the fate had to come about through Esther, the feminine correlate to the attribute of *Malkhut*, which is the potency of the Infinite. Interestingly, the very last discourse officially released by the seventh Rebbe (two weeks before his stroke) in conjunction with Purim Qaṭan, 14 Adar I 5752 (February 18, 1992), but delivered on the Sabbath of 10 Adar 5741 (February 14, 1981),[28] rehearses the contrast made between the form of disclosure of divinity when the Torah was revealed at Sinai and the disclosure in the time of Haman and Mordecai. Expanding a talk that the sixth Rebbe gave on Purim Qaṭan, 14 Adar I 5687 (February 16, 1927),[29] Schneerson noted that, in the case of Mordecai, who is portrayed as the Moses of his generation, in line with the principle of *itpashṭuta de-moshe be-khol dara*,[30] study of the Torah and execution of the commandments were bound to a more arduous form of self-sacrifice. From this example a general principle can be adduced: the concealment that is intrinsic to exile actually provides the pretext for a higher type of disclosure. We may infer further that the eradication of self enacted on Purim is a superior mode of worshipping and fulfilling the will of the divine than the ritual observance that is linked to the Sinaitic revelation.[31]

In a discourse from 27 Ḥeshvan 5723 (November 24, 1962), Schneerson utilized the mystery of divine self-concealment (*ṣimṣum*) in Lurianic kabbalah to explain the expression "realizing the will of God" (*osin reṣono shel ha-maqom*): just as the Infinite had to delimit its boundless light to create a space (*maqom*) for the semblance of independently existing worlds, the inceptual clearing that is the disclosive concealment of the plenitudinal void, so when one fulfills the will of God, one draws the will (*raṣon*), which is the aspect of "surrounding all worlds" (*sovev kol almin*), to the place (*maqom*), which is the aspect of "filling all worlds" (*memalle kol almin*). Through observing the commandments (*ha-pe'ulah de-ma'aseh ha-miṣwot*), one can join and unite the constricted light (*or meṣumṣam*) of divine immanence with the transcendent (*memalle be-sovev*), but to draw down from the will, the aspect of transcendence (*beḥinat ha-sovev*), what is required is the intention of the heart (*re'uta de-libba*), which is the matter of loving God with all one's might (Deut 6:5).[32] Schneerson is careful not to speak of a clash or conflict between the two forms of worship, but there can be no question that the mandate to do the will of God (*la'asot reṣono shel maqom*) cannot be accomplished simply by ritual action (*ma'aseh ha-miṣwot*).[33] I think it entirely appropriate to describe the former as the hypernomian complement to the nomian character of the latter. Ceremonial performance (*avodah de-torah u-miṣwot*) is marked by the setting of restrictions (*ṣimṣumim*) and boundaries (*hagbalot*), whereas worship of repentance (*avodat ha-teshuvah*) or self-sacrifice (*avodat ha-mesirat nefesh*), which is the true significance of liturgical worship (*avodat ha-tefillah*), traverses the determination of measure (*medidah*) and limit (*hagbalah*).[34]

The full force of the hypernomian underpinnings of this distinction can be grasped from an examination of another elemental Ḥabad concept employed by Schneerson, *sheṭut di-qedushshah*, "holy folly," which is contrasted with *sheṭut di-le'ummat zeh*, "insolent folly." The former expression denotes the suprarational abandon (*lema'lah mi-ṭa'am wa-da'at*) that leads one to the highest form of worship, the intention of the heart fully realized in the abolition of self, whereas the latter term is the irrational recklessness that leads to aberrant behavior, the spirit of folly inflamed by the demonic shell (*qelippah*) covering the divine light. The task of the observant Jew, which is emblematized in the service of the Tabernacle, as its components were made of acacia wood (*aṣei shiṭṭim*), playfully linked to the motif of idiocy (*sheṭut*), is to transpose the folly of sin wherein darkness and light are oppositional to sacred folly wherein darkness and light are no longer distinguishable as opposites. A critical passage that articulates this notion is the following exegesis of the RaShaB of the verse "You shall make the planks for the Tabernacle of acacia wood, upright" (Exod 26:15):

> Acacia wood [*shiṭṭim*] is from the word *sheṭut*, and there is insolent folly [*sheṭut di-le'ummat zeh*] and holy folly [*sheṭut di-qedushshah*]. The insolent [folly] is the matter of "a person does not commit a transgression unless a spirit of folly [*ruaḥ sheṭut*] enters into him,"[35] which covers the truth, the truth that is the divine spark . . . and there is the aspect of the holy folly . . . and this is the will that is above reason and knowledge [*ha-raṣon she-lema'lah mi-ṭa'am wa-da'at*] . . . and in [this] moment they transformed the insolent folly to holy folly. And this is [the meaning of] "You stand this day [all of you, before the Lord your God]" (Deut 29:9)—you stand in the aspect of the will that is above reason and knowledge . . . and this is [the meaning

> of] "You stand this day, all of you," all of you equal, for in the will that is above reason and knowledge there are no distinct partitions . . . above reason and knowledge there is no division.[36]

In another discourse, the RaShaB repeats that the goal is to transform impudent madness (the foolishness of the evil inclination, the compulsion for contravention that is beneath reason and knowledge) into sacred madness (the foolishness of the good inclination, the spirit of prophecy that is above reason and knowledge), but in that context he also identifies the sublime lunacy as the "worship that is from the side of the essence of the soul" (*ha-avodah she-mi-ṣad eṣem ha-neshamah*).[37] An echo of this formulation is found in *Ba'ti le-Ganni*, the celebrated discourse of Yosef Yiṣḥaq connected to the day of his demise on 10 Shevaṭ 5710 (January 28, 1950).[38] The relevant passage from this treatise was often cited and analyzed by the seventh Rebbe, including in his own address on 10 Shevaṭ 5711 (January 17, 1951): "The work of the seventh generation is to draw down the *Shekhinah* in actuality, to overturn the folly of the animal soul [*lahafokh sheṭut de-nefesh ha-bahamit*] . . . to make from this and to change it into the folly of holiness [*sheṭut di-qedushshah*]."[39] Another text that is important for our purposes appears in a discourse from a few days later, on 13 Shevaṭ 5711 (January 20, 1951). In that context, Schneerson cites his father-in-law to elucidate the notion of "holy deceit" (*mirmah di-qedushshah*), personified biblically in Jacob's taking the blessings of the firstborn from the hands of Esau, which he connects with the act of self-sacrifice (*mesirat nefesh*) that is above reason: "According to this we can understand with respect to the Torah in general, and, in particular, the interiority of the Torah . . . that there is a superior way that is reached in the manner of the holy deceit . . . for the intention is to turn insolent folly into holy folly, for, by means of overturning insolent folly, we reach the level that is greater than the worship by reason and knowledge, the holy folly that is above holy reason and knowledge [*sheṭut di-qedushshah she-lema'lah mi-ṭa'am wa-da'at di-qedushshah*]."[40] In the continuation of the discourse, the holy madness is identified as the "worship of self-sacrifice," which is "aroused precisely by means of the concealment and hiddenness of the world, the body, and the animal soul."[41] I surmise that with this statement Schneerson affirms an ascetic orientation—albeit an asceticism that is expressed through and not by rejecting the body—that is characteristic of messianic redemption: the highest level of achievement, which corresponds to the esoteric meaning of the Torah, comes about by the act of self-sacrifice, a negation of egocentricity (*yeshut*) that is above the demands and understanding of intellect, the worship of repentance that leads one beyond the nomian framework of halakhah, insofar as it presumes that the distinction between compliance and defiance, worthiness and culpability, must be transcended.

Esoteric of the Exoteric: Messianic Torah and the Law Before the Law

To avoid potential misunderstanding, let me be clear that I am not suggesting that in Schneerson's teaching (at any point) the esoteric is at odds with or in contradiction to the exoteric.[42] On the contrary, he consistently viewed the hidden and manifest as two sides of one coin, an idea conveyed, for instance, by the expression *torat yhwh temimah* (Ps 19:8), that is, the complete Torah comprises *torah ha-nigleit* and *torah ha-ḥasidut*. Schneerson emphasized, accordingly, that the imparting of the Torah was a one-time occurrence, for "even the interiority of the Torah that will be disclosed in the future was already bestowed in the giving of the Torah."[43] The need to make this point, we suspect, is related to the fact that the esoteric matters to be revealed in the messianic future are depicted as the "new Torah"—based on the rabbinic rephrasing of *ki torah me-itti teṣe*, "for the teaching will issue from me" (Isa 51:4) as *torah ḥadashah me-itti teṣe*, "a new teaching will issue from me"[44]—but the sense of newness here has to be understood, as I put forward in the introduction, as genuine repetition, the iteration of what has not yet been said. The fourth Lubavitcher Rebbe pithily captured the paradox in explaining why the offering on Pentecost includes loaves of bread, the ingredient that is banned on Passover: "This is by way of the new Torah that will be in the future-to-come, for there is something of it in the bestowing of the Torah [at Sinai]; if this were not the case, whence could there be innovations? Is it not the case that 'there is nothing new under the sun' (Eccles 1:9), and this will be in the coming of the Messiah, let it be speedily in our days, for then the sun will still be, but part of it was already in the bestowing of the Torah."[45] The new Torah to be recovered in the future, which includes as well the novel interpretations proffered by the Ḥabad masters,[46] refers primarily to the "explanations of the internal law" (*ṭa'amei torah ha-penimit*), the mystical secrets, which were already given in the past, albeit covertly;[47] hermeneutic originality, therefore, is an act of renewal (*hitḥaddeshut*), the uncovering of what has been concealed, rather than the fabrication of something that has no precedent.[48] From that point of view, the external and internal should not be separated, as the latter, which is fully exposed to the eye only in the future, is enclothed in the former.[49] As Schneerson put it in the talk from 19 Kislev 5711 (November 28, 1950), the activity of the study of Ḥasidism, which is the disclosure of the interiority of the Torah, together with the study of the revealed aspect of the Torah should be "in the manner that they become one reality in actuality . . . for by means of the study of Ḥasidism the desire is augmented, and through this also the understanding and comprehension of study of the revealed."[50] According to another deep-rooted metaphorical sketch often utilized by Schneerson, the two aspects correspond respectively to the body and the soul, and just as the latter is garbed in the former, so the person must study the external (*galya*) and the internal (*penimiyyut*), which are one Torah. By means of studying this single reality, the embodied soul—or the ensouled body—can become truly integrated by unifying with the One, signified by the "I" (*anokhi*) of the first word of the Decalogue (Exod 20:2),[51] a term that symbolically denotes the inner aspect of *Keter*,[52] the incomposite will (*raṣon pashuṭ*) of the Infinite that is above reason (*lema'lah min ha-ṭa'am*), the aspect of "essentiality" (*aṣmiyyut*) in which a thing and its opposite are indistinguishable, in contrast to the lower form of will in which a thing and its opposite can be differentiated from the perspective of reason and knowledge (*mi-ṣad ha-ṭa'am wa-da'at*).[53] Schneerson insisted, therefore, that the program of Torah study for students of Tomkhei Temimah should aim at the "unity of the revealed and the inwardness of the Torah" (*iḥud nigleh u-penimiyyut ha-torah*).[54] Even though the study of Ḥasidism is what is distinctive about the Lubavitch curriculum, the seventh Rebbe was unambiguous about the need to preserve both dimensions, a point that he illustrated by comparing the esoteric with salt and the exoteric with bread—without the latter the former is of no avail.[55] In Schneerson's mind, dedication to the two dimensions of Torah is the way to prepare for the disclosure of the messianic Torah (*gilluy torato shel mashiaḥ*).[56] As he puts it in another passage, the revelation of the essence in the future comes about through the worship (*avodah*) of the Jew during exile—in the form of Torah study and commitment to ritual practice, which facilitates the "breaking and nullification of the concealment [*shevirat u-viṭṭul ha-he'lem*] that is from the manifold darkness."[57] In the discourse delivered on 19 Iyyar 5734 (May 11, 1974), which is centered around a passage from the Idra Zuṭa section of the *Zohar* (3:288a), Schneerson emphasized that when one studies the exoteric aspect of Torah with the appropriate comprehension, one is also bound to the esoteric aspect (*satim de-orayyta*), and through it one is conjoined to the hidden dimension of the divine, since God and Torah are one essence.[58] According to the seventh Rebbe, reflecting the view of previous Ḥabad masters, which was based on older kabbalistic lore, the "substance of Torah" consists of the fact that "it is thoroughly unified in the light of the Infinite, blessed be he, which is garbed in it with the utmost unity. Therefore, just as all the worlds are actually like nothing vis-à-vis the Infinite, so they are vis-à-vis the Torah. . . . However, from the perspective of its essential point, which is unified with the light of the Infinite, blessed be he, it also comprises all the species of gradations and perfection in the world and through its agency is the efflux of vitality."[59]

The same idea is expressed in a different symbolic register in the discourse from 27 Tishrei 5719 (October 11, 1958), the first Sabbath after the festival of Tabernacles, when the reading of the Torah scroll in the synagogue practice begins again with the commencement of Genesis: "This is the matter of betrothal [*erusin*] and marriage [*nissu'in*] in the Torah, for now is the aspect of engagement exclusively, and in the future there will be the aspect of marriage. . . . The revealed Torah is the aspect of engagement, and the interiority of the Torah is the aspect of marriage. And thus the essence of the disclosure that is disclosed now is the revealed of the Torah, and in the future there will be a disclosure of the interiority of the Torah."[60] The revelation of the Torah at Sinai, which is in the status of engagement, is linked to the exoteric, whereas the revelation in the messianic era, which will be the marriage, is associated with the esoteric.[61] Schneerson's comment weaves together various threads from previous Ḥabad texts. To cite one reference that seems especially significant, Shneur Zalman wrote in his explication of the nuptial blessings (*birkat nissu'in*) included in his expansive commentary on the prayer book:

> The revelation of the Torah was the aspect of betrothal [*erusin*] exclusively, for it is called "his wedding" (Song of Songs 3:11), and not the aspect of marriage [*nissu'in*], for the aspect of marriage will be specifically in the future with the coming of the redeemer . . . but now there is only the aspect of betrothal. And this distinction between engagement and marriage is the matter of the distinction between the aspect of interiority and the aspect of exteriority, for in the revelation of the Torah, even though there was a disclosure of the light of the Infinite in the wisdom that is in the Torah, in the ten commandments, this light was exclusively from the aspect of exteriority, and hence the Torah was given then only in the aspect of exteriority, and that is the revealed part [*ḥeleq nigleh*] of the Torah, for the Torah is hidden and revealed, as is known, but the aspect of the interiority of the Torah, which is the entire aspect of the secret hidden in the revealed that is in the Torah, which is called the reasons of the law [*ṭa'amei torah*], as is known, was not revealed at all at the time of the revelation of the Torah on Mount Sinai.[62] Specifically in the future will the light of the interiority of the reasons of the Torah be disclosed entirely, for in the future will be the disclosure of the light of the Infinite in the Torah from the aspect of the interiority of the light of the Infinite.[63]

As Shneur Zalman contends elsewhere, the commandments will not be nullified in the messianic future, but they will be purified in the aspect of the interiority of the Torah that will be revealed at that time, to the point that ritual observance will bring about the knowledge (*da'at*) through which one is "comprised in the light of the Infinite" (*nikhlal be-or ein sof*).[64] The actual ritual practice (*ma'aseh ha-miṣwot*) may be compared to the body of the Torah, and the rationales of the commandments (*ṭa'amei ha-miṣwot*) to the soul.[65] The term *hypernomian* that I have adopted is meant to position the spiritual ideal in the chasm between the affirmation of law and its negation. Even this formulation is decidedly linear, and we would do well to restate the matter in curvilinear terms, which strike me as hermeneutically more appropriate: the law derives its significance precisely from the possibility of the law being transcended, but the transcendence of the law is only possible by upholding the law. Alternatively expressed, if the line of the law is not firmly instituted, it cannot be violated. We should not be surprised, therefore, to find that in the section of the first part of *Tanya* that immediately succeeds the depiction of the eschatological goal as a disclosure of the divine light without any garment, Shneur Zalman makes a point of underlining that the "ultimate perfection of the messianic days and the resurrection of the dead, which is the revelation of the light of the Infinite, blessed be he, in this physical world, is dependent on our action and our worship all the time of the duration of the exile, for that which brings about the reward of the commandment is the commandment itself, since by performing it the person draws down the revelation of the light of the Infinite, blessed be he, from above to below, to be garbed in the corporality of this world."[66]

In another passage, Shneur Zalman articulates this ideal in eschatological terms: "The aspect of the corona [*aṭarah*] on the head from the commandments and the letters of the Torah is in the aspect of the supernal will [*ha-raṣon ha-elyon*] that is above *Ḥokhmah*, as it will be in the future, as it is written '[Your master] will no longer be covered etc.' (Isa 30:20) and 'Your eyes shall see etc.' (Isa 52:8), that is, the aspect of the supernal will in every commandment will be revealed and from it will be made the aspect of the corona, for the aspect of a garment [*levush*] is only in the aspect of the purifications [*berurim*] that are in *Ḥokhmah*, which is not the case after the purification."[67] In chapter 5, I will discuss at length the image of the corona and the gender transformation implied thereby, but it is pertinent here to note that, when the matter is cast theosophically, the higher aspect of nomian rituals relates to the supernal will, the aspect of *Keter*, which is represented figuratively as the corona that supersedes the level of the garment, which is aligned with *Ḥokhmah*. We may assume that *Ḥokḥmah* should be identified as the Torah and *Keter* with the will that is above the Torah. The task of purification, which is realized through halakhic observance, relates to the former, since the law is predicated on the binary opposition of pure and impure, good and evil, whereas the latter is beyond such division and therefore beyond the task of purification. In this sense, the corona is superior to the garment, disclosure to concealment.

Dov Baer offers a similar explanation in the concluding section of his *Imrei Binah*. The way of the commandments (or the specific example of prayer, which is emblematic of ritual practice more generally) is contrasted with the way of the Torah: the former requires a vessel, that is, a corporeal container, and it is therefore associated with temporal life (*ḥayyei sha'ah*), whereas the latter is at root a radiance that does not require any vessel and therefore associated with eternal life (*ḥayyei olam*). In spite of this distinction, the commandments themselves will be transmogrified:

> The commandments come verily in a vessel as prayer, but in the future-to-come it is written, "[Your master] will no longer be covered etc." (Isa 30:20), for the light apparently will be without any vessel at all [*be-lo keli kelal*], that is, far above the aspect of the vessels of the commandments [*ha-kelim de-miṣwot*]. And, in truth, the essence of the world-to-come is that "every eye [shall behold the Lord]" (Isa 52:8), and it comes from the commandments of the present, as it says with respect to the community of Israel, they have a share in the world-to-come, as it says, "all of your nation is righteous" (Isa 60:21),[68] and [one may be called] righteous only through the fulfillment of the commandments in actuality. . . . The matter, in truth, is that with regard to the future it is written "a woman of valor is a crown of her husband" (Prov 12:4), for the commandments, as well as prayer, are called the precepts of the king, which are in the aspect of *Malkhut*, and they will ascend above the aspect of *Ze'eir Anpin*, her husband, as is known.[69]

A decisive distinction is thus made between the status of ritual in the present age and in the messianic future. In the former, ritual is depicted as a vessel that contains the abundance of light that issues from the Infinite, whereas in the latter ritual ascends to its "source above in the aspect of the essence of the light,"[70] an ascent rendered figuratively as *Malkhut*, the last of the emanations, rising to the level of *Keter*, the first, in the image of the "woman of valor" (*eshet ḥayil*), who is the "crown of her husband" (*aṭeret ba'lah*). Eternal life surpasses the need for any vessel, but the path that leads to that shore is through the vessel, just as the way beyond language is language. The end, we might say, is the instrumental conquest of instrumentality—the vessel is itself transformed into light and hence absolved of its function to receive the light, which is cast as well in terms of the gender transposition, marked by the woman assuming the role of crown in relation to her husband. I will examine this motif more carefully in the next chapter, but suffice it to recapitulate that the reversal of the gender hierarchy is one of the crucial ways that the hypernomian dimension is charted.[71]

According to the formulation in another one of Dov Baer's treatises, insofar as the "essence of the matter of the commandments" is the overflow of the aspect of delimitation within the divine, technically referred to in the zoharic idiom as "the superfluity of the disclosure according to the measure of the line-of-measure," it follows that what is disclosed below, even actions without intent, is "superior to the disclosure that is inward." The example adduced to illustrate the point is "the king, who is revealed in the courtyard of his palace, wherein his essence is more revealed than when he is disclosed in his palace before the ministers that are closest to him."[72] Inverting the logic of one of the standard tropes used to depict the supremacy of the internal to the external in the esoteric calculus,[73] Dov Baer suggests that the disclosure is more profound in the arena where ostensibly there should be greater obfuscation: the external courtyard, as opposed to the inner chamber, is the place of the king's maximum exposure. The proper alignment pertains to the future, when the inversion will be inverted, and the exposure is most conspicuous—indeed, as we have seen, the full exposure entails a divestiture of all exposure—in the spot that is most hidden. To recount the matter in the cosmological terms that we surveyed in detail in the second chapter, the veil of nature is unveiled and the light of divinity wholly exposed in the unveiling of the veil; expressed onomastically, the name YHWH is revealed as it is in its own essence, albeit an essence whose essence it is to be lacking any essence, rather than by being hidden in the mantle of the name Elohim.[74] The final state, accordingly, is one in which all garments will be discarded and all occlusions occluded, the unconcealment of the concealment, the withholding of withholding.

The manner in which the will of the divine is fulfilled in the present is fundamentally different from the manner in which it is fulfilled in the future. In the case of the former, which is referred to as the "mundane prayer" (*tefillat ha-ḥol*), it is appropriate to speak of "labor" (*mela'khah*) or "work" (*avodah*), because it is "for the sake of some rectification [*tiqqun*] or purification [*berur*] to transform evil into good or to purify the good," whereas, in the case of the latter, the Sabbath prayer (*tefillat ha-shabbat*), fulfilling the divine will is completely beyond the need of purifications and entirely outside the category of labor or work, since all the holy sparks have been separated from the demonic shells, and thus the only service that is appropriate is the contemplative ideal of the "essential realization from the perspective of the essentiality of the light of the Infinite [*hitpa'alut aṣmiyyut mi-ṣad aṣmiyyut or ein sof*] as it is and not from the perspective of the concatenation at all."[75] The form of worship that is commensurate with the Sabbath, which portends the world-to-come, is a state of expanded consciousness (*moḥin de-gadlut*), the apophatic delight (*ta'anug*), linked to the essence encoded in the name YHWH, is above the mundane or exilic work of purifications (*avodat ha-berurim*) and therefore supersedes the limitations of the law.[76] To cite from the conclusion of Dov Baer's *Imrei Binah*, "Concerning the future-to-come, it is written '[Your master] will no longer be covered etc.' (Isa 30:20), for the light shall be without any vessel at all, that is, apparently way above the aspect of the vessels of the commandments. In truth, the essence of the world-to-come . . . issues from the commandments of the present . . . as the matter is known, in truth, that concerning the future-to-come, it says, 'a woman of valor is a crown of her husband' (Prov 12:4), for the commandments, which are called the 'edicts of the king,' and similarly prayer, are in the aspect of *Malkhut*, and they ascend above the aspect of *Ze'eir Anpin*, her husband."[77] The crowning moment of the eschaton is dependent on ritual observance, but it is clearly exceeded to the extent that the illumination cannot be contained in a vessel. The surpassing of the nomian is the pragmatic meaning of the scriptural image of seeing the master without any garment.

The hypernomian ideal of removing the cloak is explored in a discourse of the seventh Rebbe, which is a meditation on the following comments of Shneur Zalman:

> "Your master will no longer be covered' (Isa 30:20), for the garments cover the internal matters [*ha-levushim mekhassim al ha-penimiyyim*] to the point that one cannot distinguish between good and evil, as it is with the foolish man who speaks words of wisdom that he received from a sage, and it appears to everyone that he is a great sage, or, with respect to a good act done by a bad man, it appears to everyone that he is essentially good, for a power emanates in the garments of thought [*maḥashavah*], speech [*dibbur*], and action [*ma'aseh*], to beautify the internal, as a most despicable man whose splendid garments verily beautify him. . . . But the

> matter of "Your master will no longer be covered" is that the [names] YHWH and Elohim will be [as one] and the garments of [the worlds of] creation, formation, and doing will no longer conceal. Similarly, "your master," the attributes [*middot*] and consciousness [*moḥin*] of the Community of Israel, will not be beautified in garments, but they will be purified [*berurim*] as they are in truth.[78]

Explicating these words, Schneerson asserted that there is a distinction between worship in the present and worship in the future. In the present, worship takes the form exclusively of the "garments of thought, speech, and action" (*levushin de-maḥashavah dibbur u-ma'aseh*), whereas in the future, it will be in the form of the "purification of the attributes" (*berur ha-middot*) and the "purification of consciousness" (*berur moḥin*). The garments, which are identified more specifically with the traditional 613 commandments, beautify the internal powers (*koḥot penimiyyim*)—the attributes (*middot*) and consciousness (*moḥin*)—but they fall short of the final clarification, about which it is prophesied that the master will no longer be covered. Schneerson explains the matter by recalling the distinction that Maimonides made in the *Guide of the Perplexed* between truth and falsehood, on one hand, and good and evil, on the other. The former is a matter of intellectual cognition, which was found in human nature before the sin in the Garden of Eden, whereas the latter is a matter of convention, a distinction that applies only to things generally accepted as known rather than to matters proven to be rationally true.[79] In Schneerson's reformulation, truth and falsehood, which are apprehended by intellect, relate to matters connected to divinity; good and evil, which come about as a result of sensation and desire, relate to matters that are not connected to divinity. The act of beautification of the internal powers by the "garments of the Torah and the commandments" can be viewed from these two vantage points, but neither one is identical with the innermost reality (*meṣi'ut amittit*), which is beyond the rational distinction of truth and falsehood—and surely beyond the conventional distinction of good and evil. Nevertheless, it is through these very external garments that the core and the interior (*ha-tokh we-ha-penimiyyut*) are beheld, an idea that Schneerson links to the well-known rabbinic saying *mi-tokh she-lo lishmah ba lishmah*,[80] if one observes the Torah for an ulterior motive, such a person will eventually observe it for its own sake.[81]

Broken Tablets and the Overflowing Excess of Law

The interplay between the hypernomian and nomian is underscored in a particularly poignant way in a discourse on 29 Av 5714 (August 28, 1954). The inspiration for the seventh Rebbe's remarks was the decoding of the word *elul* in the *Megalleh Amuqot* of Natan Neṭa Shapira of Cracow as an acrostic for *aron luḥot we-shivrei luḥot*, "the ark of the tablets and the broken tablets."[82] In response to the hypothetical question regarding the connection between the month of Elul and this encoding, Schneerson explains:

> Even though it is known that the matter of repentance is above the Torah, the matter of repentance is also known specifically from the Torah, that is, the Torah discloses the matter of repentance. And this matter is alluded to [by the fact] that the broken tablets were placed in the ark together with the tablets. The "broken tablets"—this is the matter of repentance [*shivrei luḥot—hu inyan ha-teshuvah*]. Thus we find that there is an advantage in the matter of the breaking of the tablets, and the blessed holy One said to Moses our master, "Congratulations that you broke [them]."[83] More than this is what is found in the Yerushalmi,[84] that the blessed holy One said to him that he should break them—in accord with the advantage of those who repent over the righteous, for "in the place where those who repent stand those who are completely righteous cannot stand." And this is [the import of the notion that] the broken tablets (the matter of repentance that is above the Torah) were placed in the same ark in which the tablets (the matter of the Torah) were resting, for the matter of repentance (which is above the Torah) is also disclosed specifically by means of the Torah, and thus the righteous (whose matter is the Torah) disclose and illustrate the order of repentance. It follows that the preparation of the month of Elul relates to these two matters, the matter of repentance (the broken tablets) and the matter of the Torah (the tablets), and in a way that these two matters are bound to one another.[85]

The author of *Megalleh Amuqot* decodes the name of the month Elul as an acrostic that alludes to both sets of tablets that were given to Israel, the first destroyed by Moses after he came down from the mountain and beheld the Israelites worshipping the golden calf and the second set that replaced the first. The connection of this theme to Elul is based on the rabbinic chronology according to which the first tablets were smashed on the seventeenth of Tammuz and the second were given to Israel on the tenth of Tishrei, which is Yom Kippur, the fortieth day counting from the first of Elul when Moses ascended the mountain a third time (the second time he ascended for a period of forty days beginning on the nineteenth of Tammuz, beseeching God to forgive the Israelites). Schneerson cleverly misreads the remark of Natan Neṭa Shapira, for in his mind the acrostic conveys the notion that both the broken tablets and the tablets that are intact are enclosed in one container, a misreading that allows him to develop the crucial idea that the Torah and repentance, respectively the tablets and the broken tablets, are bound together.

What is vital for my argument is the manner in which Schneerson connects the image of the shattered tablets to repentance, which is explicitly described as being above the law (*lema'lah me-ha-torah*). The contrast between worship through repentance (*avodat ha-teshuvah*) and worship through the Torah and the commandments (*avodat torah u-miṣwot*) was already made by Shneur Zalman. Playing with the derivation of the word *teshuvah* from a trilateral radical that means to return, the Alter Rebbe taught that repentance entails the act of "restoring the soul to its source and its root" (*lehashiv et ha-neshamah li-meqorah we-shorshah*),[86] an integration into the Infinite in which the dichotomies that are basic to the nomian standpoint of the Torah are overcome. The tasks correlated with the Torah and repentance vary accordingly: the goal of the former is to purify good from evil (*levarer ha-ṭov me-ha-ra*), whereas the goal of the latter is for evil to be transformed into good (*nehpakh ha-ra le-ṭov*).[87] Repentance rests on the possibility of the sinner converting guilt into innocence, a conversion that, strictly speaking, lies beyond the strictures of law. Expressed ontotheologically, the source in the divine whence repentance issues forth is a level that supersedes the dichotomies presupposed by the law, the infinite will wherein the distinction between right and wrong is no longer operative. This idea resonates with and is often exegetically supported by the talmudic teaching that the supremacy of penitence lies in the fact that it has the power to transmute acts of intentional wrongdoing (*zedonot*) into merits (*zekhuyyot*).[88] The broken tablets are connected, therefore, with contrition, for the exacting measure of law must be suspended if one is to be forgiven.

I reiterate that I am not suggesting that the view implied in this distinction is either openly or clandestinely antinomian; it is forbidden to cancel or to add to the law.[89] The surplus that exceeds the law—in my terminology "hypernomian"—is itself grounded in the nomos, and thus it is not in opposition to the law. The exemplar for the eschatological ideal is none other than Moses, the lawgiver par excellence. The Torah that he received was for the sake of purifying the Tree of Knowledge of Good and Evil, but before his death, when he ascended to his source in the essence of the infinite light, he attained the level of repentance, by means of which the darkness is converted into the light. Analogously, the Messiah will inspire the Jews to repent, so that he may elevate them "to their first source in the essence of the light of the Torah and the commandments as it is in the light of the essence of the Infinite, for from there it is possible to transform the supernal darkness into light."[90] The brilliance that transcends the dyadic foundation of the law is the light of the Torah and the commandments. As the matter is expressed by Schneerson, "repentance is above the Torah, and hence repentance is beneficial with respect to a matter that blemishes the Torah, but even so the matter of repentance itself is taken from the Torah."[91] In another talk, Schneerson mused, "Whence do we know about the commandment of repentance?—From what it says concerning it, 'the Torah is a light' (Prov 6:23); hence it reveals all the matters, even those that are beyond the Torah."[92] In the verse from Proverbs, commandment is compared metaphorically to a lamp (*ner*) and Torah to the light (*or*): the former symbolizes the luminosity that partakes of division, the latter, the luminosity that is indissoluble. Insofar as the indivisible comprehends everything divisible, we can speak of Torah disclosing even what is above Torah, that is, what is beyond-the-law is revealed through the law, as what is unspoken can be heeded only through what is spoken, and what is invisible can be envisioned only through what is visible. In the final analysis, the Torah, immense as it might be, still falls under the category of what is measurable and delimited,[93] whereas repentance is immeasurable and limitless and thus stipulates a higher mode of worship accessible to the Jewish people, for the "souls of Israel are above the Torah, as is known in the matter of the thought of Israel preceded everything,[94] including the thought of the Torah."[95]

The apocalyptic vision of the seventh Rebbe, I submit, is predicated on this hypernomian orientation, which is connected to the mystical attainment of nondifferentiated oneness—theosophically, this corresponds to the source of the Messiah in the interiority of the Ancient One (*penimiyyut attiq*), the inwardness of *Keter*, which is also identified as the aspect of *Ein Sof* that is in the head-that-is-not-known (*reisha de-lo ityeda*), the gradation of wonders (*nifla'ot*) above the Torah that emanates from the source of Moses, the first and final redeemer, in the interiority of Wisdom (*penimmiyut ha-ḥokhmah*) or the interiority of the Father (*penimmiyut abba*),[96] and psychologically to *yeḥidah*, the highest gradation of soul, wherein good and evil are indistinguishable, and hence it is possible, indeed necessary, for one thing to morph into its opposite. It is of interest to note that in the *Qunṭres Inyanah shel Torat ha-Ḥasidut*, Schneerson, building on a passage from Shalom Dovber's discourse on 19 Kislev 5670 (December 2, 1909),[97] demarcates the core of Ḥasidic spirituality in precisely these terms: "The essential point of Ḥasidism is . . . the drawing down of new light from the aspect of the interiority of *Keter*, and even higher, the drawing down of the aspect of the inwardness of *Attiq* itself, the aspect of the Infinite that is found in the head-that-is-not-known."[98] The pneumatic coordinate that corresponds to this divine gradation is *yeḥidah*, the "essential point of the soul," which is presented as unique to the Jewish people[99] and associated especially with the Messiah[100] but, at the same time, described as the "incomposite unity devoid of any relationship to particulars," the "essence of the point of vitality that is above the category of configuration [*geder ṣiyyur*],"[101] the property of the soul that has no form, since it is bound "to divinity from the perspective of divinity" (*hitqashsherutah le-elohut hu mi-ṣad elohut*) and hence "through it one can sense the truth of the substance of the supernal Will as it is in its simplicity whose end is the will itself" (*nirgash bah amittat mahuto shel raṣon ha-elyon kemo she-hu bi-feshiṭuto asher takhlito hu ha-raṣon aṣmo*).[102]

Abolishing (In)difference and the Encroachment of Boundary

Here we come to the basic paradox that underlies the messianic teaching proffered by Ḥabad philosophy: the dimension of the Godhead that effaces difference, the "essence of the light of the Infinite" (*aṣmut or ein sof*), can be discerned only by the Jew, since the Jew alone possesses *yeḥidah*, the facet of the "soul that is unified in his essence" (*ha-neshamah ha-meyuḥedet be-aṣmuto*).[103] Exclusivity may well serve the end of excluding exclusivity, but it is nonetheless an ascription that is exclusive—the very attribute in which all distinctive attributions are removed is attributed distinctively to one ethnic group.[104] In spite of, or perhaps on account of, this apparent inconsistency, the soteriological paradigm is clear: the soul of the Messiah is tied especially to the disclosure of *yeḥidah*, the simple oneness wherein all opposition is transcended. Redemption, accordingly, is characterized elsewhere by Schneerson in the following terms: "The truth of the matter of 'He redeems my soul intact' [*padah ve-shalom nafshi*] (Ps 55:19) is that the adversary is abolished entirely [*ha-menagged mitbaṭṭel legamrei*] . . . and this by way of the disclosure of *yeḥidah*. . . . Since the aspect of *yeḥidah* has no opposite [*ein kenegdah le'ummat zeh*] . . . through the disclosure of *yeḥidah* the opposition is of itself nullified."[105] In a state where opposites coincide, where there is perfect unity purged of any otherness, the binary distinction basic to the nomian system, the contrast between right and wrong, permitted and prohibited, breaks down.

It is of interest to recall the citation in Schneerson's commentary on the Passover Haggadah of a discussion in Ḥayyim Ibn Aṭṭar's *Or ha-Ḥayyim* (in his comments on Num 9:14) regarding whether or not a convert has the obligations of the festival, since the convert did not experience the exodus of the ancient Israelites. The opinion that is proposed for the inclusion of the convert embryonically contains the seeds of the seventh Rebbe's own messianic credo: "Our exit from Egypt was an eternal redemption [*ge'ullat olam*] also for the soul of the convert, even though this was not explicit [*be-nigleh*], it was implicit [*be-nistar*], for the source of holiness is one [*ki shoresh ha-qedushshah eḥad hu*]."[106] In that unifying root of holiness, the partition between one who is natively a Jew and one who converts to Judaism cannot be upheld. Although the words of Ibn Aṭṭar do not affirm the bolder claim that the ontological difference between Jew and non-Jew is completely erased, the phenomenon of conversion problematizes an absolute distinction along these ethnocentric lines,[107] a point to which I shall return in chapter 6. The more extreme implication, however, seems to be implied in a passage from Schneerson's private notebooks that were published posthumously with the title *Reshimot*. In the relevant text, which was penned in 1942, Esau and Jacob are portrayed as mirror opposites: the former's participation in holiness (attested in the rabbinic teaching that he inquired about how one prepares the straw to fulfill the commandment of tithing the produce of the field)[108] is purely for the sake of the corporeal, whereas the latter engaged in physical matters only for the sake of spirituality and holiness. The claim that Esau has a share in holiness is linked, moreover, to the kabbalistic notion that the shell precedes the fruit.[109] Menaḥem Mendel's interpretation subverts the original intent of this teaching, which presumes a dichotomous split between the impure shell and the holy core. The seditious element is accentuated by the fact that Schneerson also modifies the assertion that in the eschatological future the shell of Esau will be extinguished by making a distinction between the stubble (*qash*), which is the part of Esau that is unredeemable, and the straw (*teven*), the indestructible part that is always connected to holiness.[110] What is imperative to emphasize is that, already at a relatively tender age, Menaḥem Mendel resisted an absolute dualism by insisting that a facet of Esau, who represents the demonic other side (*siṭra aḥara*), continuously receives illumination from the side of holiness. The messianic ideal is predicated on discerning that aspect, which effectively neutralizes the underlying basis for the halakhah, the seemingly intractable difference between sanctified and defiled, and its sociocultural manifestation in the need to maintain the boundary between Jew and Gentile.

To provide another illustration of this point, I call the reader's attention to a discourse from 25 Av 5722 (August 25, 1962). Commenting on the verse "See, this day I set before you blessing and curse" (Deut 11:26), Schneerson remarked:

> The reason for bestowing the blessing and the curse is so that there would be possibility of choice . . . for thus the blessed holy One gave authority and power to the other side—for from its own side it has no reality at all—to lift itself over and against the holiness of the divine soul, so that a person can bring it down precisely by means of his worship and through his choice. . . . And just as it is in man, so it is, as it were, above—for granting a place to evil has an aspect that is more superior. On the contrary, with respect to the gradation that is absolutely incomposite [*peshuṭah be-takhlit*] and devoid of all images [*mushlelet mi-kol ha-ṣiyyurim*], no adversary is appropriate in relation to it [*ein shayyakh shum menagged elaw*], and the abroga-

> tion of the existence of evil there is only from the perspective of his choice, blessed be he. As it is written, "After all—[declares the Lord]—Esau is Jacob's brother" (Mal 1:2)—the two of them are equal [*sheneihem be-shaweh*], but through his free choice—"I have loved Jacob and I despised Esau" (Mal 1:2). From the perspective of this choice evil was absolutely annihilated and broken, more so than the aspect of the disclosures. And it is in this manner with respect to man: when he chooses the good, and he arouses his *yeḥidah*, he destroys the existence of evil.[111]

Reflecting a long-standing approach in kabbalistic sources to deny an autonomous ontological status to the other side, Schneerson sees evil as a means to foster greater attainment on the part of an individual who freely chooses life over death. In their ultimate source, however, there is no difference between the two, just as Jacob and Esau, professed rivals, are twin brothers that emerged from the same seminal drop inserted in one womb. With respect to the absolutely incomposite One, and its corresponding pneumatic element designated *yeḥidah*, opposites are no longer distinguishable (presumably, not even as opposites that are no longer distinguishable).

Let me emphasize again that I am not suggesting that Schneerson advocated an antinomian abrogation of ceremonial law. On the contrary, he frequently alleged that the rudimentary task for the Jew is to conform to the traditional rituals, an idea expressed with the slogan *ha-ma'aseh hu ha-iqqar*, "action is the mainstay," a paraphrase of an archaic rabbinic dictum.[112] Indeed, the democratization of the body politic of Israel rests on this very assumption, since the simplest and most sophisticated Jews are equally bound by this principle.[113] Although the exposure of secrets through study is privileged, he would have surely agreed with the assertion that without prayer, which metonymically signifies ritual observance more generally, one could study the tenets of Ḥasidism and accomplish the very antithesis of what is required and expected.[114] There is thus no challenge here to Schneerson's commitment to the world of rabbinic halakhah, which might suggest superficial comparisons to hackneyed portrayals of some earlier forms of Jewish utopianism, most notably, Christianity, Sabbatianism, and Frankism. But what I am arguing is that in characterizing the redemptive moment as a *coincidentia oppositorum*, he (as others before him) conceived of this world as yielding its own surpassing at the limit of its foundation. The metalogic of the apocalyptic expectation leads invariably to an overstepping of boundary, to a realization that, in the infinite light, life is death, good is evil, holy is impure. In this regard, Schneerson was in sync with a much older perspective articulated by Jewish masters of esoteric lore: the axiological conditions to distinguish right and wrong are transfigured by the discrimination that in the foundation of the limit opposites are the same in virtue of being different.[115] The indifferent (as opposed to undifferentiated) oneness of the Infinite precludes the possibility of an unadulterated alterity, as every other is comprised within the indifference of the same. In this nondual state, the human will is so aligned with the divine will—freedom and necessity utterly converge—that acquiescence to ritual is no longer predicated on command and obligation; on the contrary, in the absence of contrariness, keeping within the confines of the law entails extending beyond its periphery. The theme is connected by Schneerson to the fact that the Davidic Messiah comes from the seed of Pereṣ (Ruth 4:18–22), whose name etymologically denotes breaching the womb before his twin brother Zeraḥ (Gen 38:29). Additionally, the sense of rupture turns on the fact that Pereṣ was conceived through the illicit conjugation of Judah and Tamar. In the Ḥasidic interpretation, Tamar signifies the act of self-effacement, which is identified as the necessary condition for the birth of the savior.[116] Notwithstanding the canonical validation of the scriptural story, the transgressive element should not be ignored. Indeed, we might say that the narrative account of virtue coming forth from vice instructs one about the ultimate coincidence of opposites indicative of messianic consciousness. Influenced by the view of previous Ḥabad masters, especially the Mitteler Rebbe and the RaShaB, Schneerson understands joyfulness as an act of encroachment (*poreṣ gader*), since it induces disclosure of what had been concealed and thus advances beyond the previously determined border.[117] In the present, the concatenation of worlds can be sustained only by a diminution of the light, but in the future there will be a manifestation of

> the aspect of the great bliss that is in the essence of the Infinite, blessed be he, in actuality, and precisely by means of this the concealment that is the essence, which is called the concealed of the concealed, will be revealed, for it will not be drawn forth in the aspect of the overflow, in the aspect of donor and recipient [*mashpi'a*

> *u-meqabbel*] as it is now, which entails many withdrawals [*ṣimṣumim rabbim*], but rather, since the essential bliss breaches the boundary . . . it shines from the aspect of the essential light of the Infinite in actuality . . . and then it will shine its essential light equanimously below as well in actuality as it is above in the substance and essence of the blessed One, without any change or differentiation.[118]

In a similar vein, Schneerson notes that the infringement of the breaking forth connotes the ubiquitous revelation of the divine light in the future, an illumination that fills the whole world, as it was at the moment of creation, and therefore cannot be contained, a profligation of spirit, the squandering (*bizbuz*) of the "treasures of the king" buried in the interiority of *Keter*, which is necessary to secure victory (*niṣṣuaḥ*) over wanton self-indulgence through the sacrifice of self.[119] The worship apposite to the eschaton, accordingly, is "above measurement and limitations" (*lema'lah mi-medidah we-hagbalah*), and the bliss associated with it is similarly characterized as that which breaks through the boundary,[120] "for by means of this elation all the boundaries are nullified, and 'The one who makes a breach [*ha-poreṣ*] goes before them' (Mic 2:13) applies to the Messiah, concerning whom it says, 'This is the progeny of Pereṣ' (Ruth 4:18) . . . and then the matter of the 'female encircling the male' (Jer 31:21) will be established, since the rank of the body in each and every Jew will be felt . . . the rank of the body from the perspective of itself—for in it precisely is the disclosure of the essence."[121] The very name of the Messiah, therefore, bears within itself the connotation of infraction,[122] an inevitable consequence of understanding the unity of the essence as the coincidence of opposites.

The historical realization of the ultimate coalescence is reserved for the end-time. The preparation, however, is unfolding in the present through the dissemination of the mystical truths embedded in the Torah. Redemption, on this count, is the fulfillment of revelation. Thus Schneerson described the Sinaitic theophany in a brief discourse on the eve of the new month of Sivan 1953, several days prior to the festival of Pentecost: "In the general matter of the giving of the Torah, there is a response to those who have claims against the study of the hidden aspect [*nistar*] of the Torah, for in the time of the giving of the Torah, the matter was reversed, the exoteric aspect of the Torah was hidden and the esoteric aspect of the

Torah was revealed [*she-nigleh de-torah hayah nistar we-nistar de-torah hayah nigleh*]."[123] Just as in the event of revelation, so in the advent of redemption we find a hermeneutic inversion: the esoteric is revealed and the exoteric concealed. That the concealed is disclosed does not mean, however, that the disclosed is concealed; the exposure of the spirit of the law does not call for the abrogation of its body. On the contrary, by the principle of the coincidence of opposites, external and internal are indifferently identical. In the present, the manifest reveals the latent; in the future, the latent reveals the manifest. As Schneerson put it in another talk from the same year, hearkening to the esoteric meaning (*nistar de-torah*) does not demand that one forget the exoteric (*nigleh de-torah*), for in every matter of Torah study "we reveal the interiority and hidden in it (for the revealed Torah and the interior Torah are not two laws, God forbid, but the interiority of the Torah is the interiority and soul of the revealed Torah)."[124] To separate the concealed and the revealed aspects of the Torah is to create a division within the divine equivalent to committing an act of idolatry, and since Judaism and idolatry are by nature antithetical, the Jew cannot take hold of the revealed unless there is also an appropriation of the concealed.[125] In the *Quntres Inyanah shel Torat ha-Ḥasidut*, Schneerson had already observed that the objective of Ḥasidism is to expose the secret core from within its external husk. This does not come about by discarding the husk, as if a naked truth could be seen, but rather by gazing upon it through the curtain of textual flesh. He insists, therefore, that the distinction between exoteric and esoteric should not be construed in binarian terms: "all the matters in the interiority of the Torah are also expressed in the revealed Torah."[126] The discernment of the overlapping of the literal and the symbolic presages the perception of the simple complexity or complex simplicity beyond discrimination that is endemic to messianic consciousness, envisioning the metaphysical in the physical, the immaterial in the material.

Eradicating the Law and the Torah of the Tree of Life

The *secret of the secret* elaborated by Schneerson is to be fathomed from the space of the transposition of outside and inside. As he put it in a letter dated 5 Nisan 5715

(March 28, 1955): "In the future redemption, the inner soul of the Jew will be united . . . with the external soul, for this is the vessel for the disclosure of the unity of the hidden aspect of the Torah and the manifest aspect, and for the unity and disclosure of the hidden aspect of the blessed holy One, and the manifest aspect of the blessed holy One, for this is the matter of the complete and true redemption."[127] Underlying this comment is the kabbalistic identification of God and the Torah[128] and, even more specifically, the zoharic passages wherein an analogy between the name and the Torah is drawn based on the assumption that both display the dual character of the hidden and the manifest.[129] The new Torah, implanted in the past but implemented in the future, betokens the disclosure of the infinite essence through the garment of the finite universe, the investiture that renders invisibly visible the specter of the visibly invisible.[130] The external and the internal, on this score, may be denoted as opposites juxtaposed in their opposition.[131] According to the principle of the concatenation of worlds within the Infinite, which is also depicted as the emanation of the Torah from above to below, there is a correspondence between the ontic and the semantic, that is, the four worlds in the chain of becoming—emanation (*aṣilut*), creation (*beri'ah*), formation (*yeṣirah*), and doing (*asiyyah*)—are correlated respectively with the four levels of meaning in the text—the esoteric (*sod*), the figurative (*remez*), the homiletical (*derush*), and the literal (*peshaṭ*).[132] Just as the three lower worlds are enfolded within the first, so all the layers of meaning are included in the former, which is identified as the Ḥasidic teachings of the Beshṭ.[133] For Schneerson, this is the mystical intent of the rabbinic dictum "Great is study that leads to action,"[134] that is, the performance of the commandments (*pe'ulat ha-miṣwot*), which is the task of the Jew in the world, is the final realization of the innermost dimension of the law (*penimiyyut ha-torah*). In the messianic future, the hierarchy is inverted, for action (*ma'aseh*) will be greater than study (*talmud*), as the latter is a matter of understanding (*farshtend*), which is inherently limited, whereas the former is a matter of purity (*temimut*), the "heartfelt and earnest worship" (*hartsiger ernster avoyde*), which is based on the unlimited feeling of faith (*gloybn*).[135] The point is further highlighted by the observation that the *Tanya*, the fountainhead of Ḥabad Ḥasidism, is based on the verse "No, the thing is very close to you, in your mouth and in your heart, to observe it" (Deut 30:14).[136] Shneur Zalman's treatise is likened to the Oral Torah that explicates the Written Torah, which is epitomized in the passage previously cited. In line with kabbalistic theurgy from its inception, at least as far as philological scholarship is capable of tracing the historical record, figurative interpretation is presented here as enhancing rather than undermining or replacing literal observance.[137]

From another vantage point, however, the secrets and rationales do not relate to ritual practice as such, since in the messianic state there is no longer a viable distinction between permissible and forbidden. Thus, we read in the continuation of the aforementioned discourse: "This is also the matter of the teaching of Ḥasidism, the interiority of the Torah, which corresponds to the world of emanation—for in the world of emanation 'evil cannot abide with you' (Ps 5:5), as there all matters (including the matter of 'this corresponding to this') are in the manner of being entirely good [*kullo ṭov*]. And it is necessary to act with respect to the matter of 'this corresponding to this' as it literally is, so that it will be transformed to become 'this corresponding to this' as it is in the world of emanation, in the interiority of the Torah."[138] The disclosure of the inwardness of the Torah, the messianic diffusion triggered by the constrictions of exile,[139] is linked to the world of emanation in which there is no more binary opposition. In this state, the duality, which is designated by the idiom "this corresponding to this" (*zeh le'ummat zeh*), is transformed into the underlying unity of opposites, which is signified by the expression "entirely good" (*kullo ṭov*), an allusion to the rabbinic characterization of the world-to-come as a "world that is entirely good" (*olam she-kullo ṭov*), anchored exegetically in the verse "so that you may fare well and have a long life," *lema'an yiṭav lakh we-ha'arakhta yamim* (Deut 22:7).[140] In the Ḥasidic interpretation, the utopian ideal of the world that is entirely good implies that evil itself is transmuted into good, and, as a consequence, guilt is transmuted into innocence, in accord with the rabbinic depiction of repentance.[141]

Utilizing the language of the later strata of zoharic literature, the *Ra'aya Meheimna* and the *Tiqqunim*,[142] Schneerson elaborated the hypernomian potential of the messianic Torah in a discourse connected to the second day of Pentecost, 7 Sivan 5751 (May 20, 1991). The revealed aspect of the law (*nigleh de-torah*) corresponds to the Tree of Knowledge of Good and Evil, and hence its primary concern is the purification of good from evil in the world, the separation of the forbidden and impure from the permissible and pure, the distinguishing of truth from falsehood; the hidden aspect of the law (*nistar de-torah*), by contrast, corresponds to the Tree of Life, and inasmuch as the binary of good and evil has been surmounted, the objective of the laws that derive from this source is no longer to maintain a boundary between opposing forces, but rather to unify the supernal unifications (*leyaḥed yiḥudim elyonim*).[143] This is not to say that the rituals will be abrogated, but rather that the purpose of fulfilling them will have been altered; instead of observing the law "to purify the purifications" (*levarer berurim*), the goal is "to fulfill the commandments through the supernal intentions [*leqayyem ha-miṣwot be-khawwanot elyonot*], the interiority of the commandments and their hidden reasons [*penimiyyut ha-miṣwot we-ṭa'ameihem ha-nistarim*]."[144] The full implication of the hypernomian perspective is here laid bare by insisting that the fulfillment in the future is not dependent on the performative dimension, but on the intentionality, which shifts from complying to the ritual laws in order to purify the world to doing so for the sake of realizing their esoteric meaning by facilitating the higher modes of unity within the Godhead. The intricacy of Schneerson's position is made clearer in his attempt to affirm the continued existence of evil in the messianic period, though the latter can arrive only after all the evil has been purified and separated from the good: "It is known that also in the days of the Messiah, when the work of the Jews in purifying good from evil will be completed, and they will attain the perfection that was before the sin of the Tree of Knowledge, there will still be the existence of evil in the world,[145] and hence there remains the need for cities of refuge in order to negate the possibility of an inadvertent matter that might be an outcome of the existence of evil in the world (just as before the sin of the Tree of Knowledge there was the possibility for the transgression through the existence of evil in the world)."[146] The process of purification will reach its termination in the eschaton, but there remains the possibility for evil, albeit an evil that can produce only an involuntary sinful act (*bilti raṣuy*), which explains the need for maintaining cities of refuge—the scriptural notion of setting up physical localities where one who has killed unintentionally may flee to escape from a potential blood avenger (Num 35:9–15, Deut 19:1–10)—even in the eschatological future.

> This matter (the nullification of the possibility of an inadvertent matter) is achieved by means of [the directive] "then you shall add three more towns" (Deut 19:9),

> the addition of a new type of cities of refuge [*arei miqlaṭ*], the novel revelation of "words of Torah offer protection" [*divrei torah qolṭin*][147]—for this is the matter of "a new Torah will issue from me" [*torah ḥadashah me-itti teṣe*],[148] the revelation of the rationales of the Torah, the interiority of the Torah, for the interiority of the Torah is above the relevance of purifying good and evil, and thus it protects the person in the manner that it nullifies even the possibility of the inadvertent matter. . . . And this matter will be by means of a revelation of a higher level of the Torah . . . "a new Torah will issue from me," the rationales and secrets of Torah, for since they are above what applies to purifying the world, through their agency even the possibility for inadvertent matters is nullified.[149]

Those who attribute the word *antinomian* to Schneerson's messianic vision need to attend carefully to passages such as this one where he was unambiguous about adherence to the law in the future.[150] The new Torah is identified with the rationales and secrets of the commandments, whose purpose is no longer to purify the world, since there is no more evil to expunge. Nevertheless, the capacity for contravention persists, as is attested by the example of accidental murder, and thus the nomian feature of the Torah has not been totally dismantled. Indeed, the seventh Rebbe even made a point of citing a passage from Shneur Zalman in which he distances himself from the talmudic dictum (transmitted in the name of R. Joseph) that "the commandments will be abrogated in the future-to-come" (*miṣwot beṭelot le-atid lavo*)[151] by insisting that the verse "And in that day, a great ram's horn shall be sounded" (Isa 27:13) indicates that the obligation to sound the ram's horn (*shofar*) on Rosh ha-Shanah will endure in the future, though the object itself will be of a different kind.[152] From the specific example, Schneerson adduces the larger principle regarding the immutability of the ritual law, a viewpoint that likely reflects the influence of Maimonides. But those who would deny the radical potential of his teaching with regard to the status of the messianic law must also be more assiduous in considering his precise words. In the new Torah, which stems from the Tree of Life, the halakhah will be fundamentally transformed—in the absence of binary opposition, there will be no need to separate the sacred and the profane and, consequently, upholding the lawfulness of the law will not be dependent on the possibility of intentional wrongdoing. The new Torah partakes of the Infinite and hence defies the limits of all demarcation. This is the import of *torah ḥadashah me-itti teṣe*, "a new teaching will issue from me," that is, "from me"—from the substance and essence of the divine, which are beyond any "true boundary."[153] According to another locution adopted by Schneerson, the eschatological future is the "day that is entirely Sabbath" (*yom she-kullo shabbat*),[154] for the seventh day succeeds the purifications (*berurim*) that were achieved during the six days of the week, which correspond to the six millennia, by means of Torah study and ritual observance. This is the esoteric connotation of the rabbinic maxim[155] that only one who prepares before the Sabbath can eat on the Sabbath.[156] But, as the Alter Rebbe already commented,

> In the future-to-come, there will be the day that is entirely Sabbath, that is, the aspect of emanation will ascend, and not like it is in the present, for after Sabbath there must be the weekday, the aspect of emanation purifies [the worlds of] creation, formation, and doing, but in the future-to-come, the aspect of emanation will ascend and it will no longer need to purify [the worlds of] creation, formation, and doing, for [concerning that time it is said] "I will remove the spirit of impurity" (Zech 13:2), death will be destroyed (Isa 25:8), "a woman of valor is a crown for her husband" (Prov 12:4), and "the female encircles the male" (Jer 31:21).[157]

To have attained the day that is completely Sabbath implies that there is no more distinction between the profane and the holy, that the sacred time will not be succeeded by the return of mundane time. But if there is nothing but Sabbath, it is not meaningful to speak of preparing for the Sabbath.

The hypernomian implications of the rabbinic eschatological image are drawn explicitly by Dov Baer:

> In the future-to-come, the Tree of Good and Evil will be eradicated, and then the commandments will be nullified, and this is the day that is entirely Sabbath. . . . Therefore, the day that is entirely Sabbath is not at all in the category of the commandment of Sabbath, for in the future-to-come the commandments will be nullified, as everything will have been purified, as it says in the *Ra'aya Meheimna*,[158] the Tree of Knowledge of Good and Evil will be removed from the world, for the

> spirit of impurity will be completely eliminated from everything, and the aspect of the purification of good and evil will not be possible at all, and on this foundation are established all the practical commandments, "to turn away from evil and to do good" (Ps 34:15), to separate the impure and the pure.[159]

To appreciate the radical nature of what is implied in this passage, let me cite another one in which Dov Baer offers a view that directly contradicts the hypernomian perspective. The leitmotif of the text is an elucidation of the principle "the end of action is what arose first in thought" (*sof ma'aseh alah be-maḥashavah teḥillah*),[160] which, we are told, can be inferred

> also from the world-to-come, which is naught but the fulfillment of the commandments through the physical and not through the spiritual, for even in the days of the Messiah the essence of the perfection will be only through the fulfillment of the commandments in actuality [*be-fo'al mammash*], even though it will be after the purification of the Tree of Knowledge, as it has been explained in another place with respect to the matter "There the commandments of your will shall be done before you,"[161] for the commandments are not nullified in the future-to-come. Thus, the commandments that come to us, "which are revealed to us and to our children" (Deut 29:28), to observe and to fulfill in actuality, are more elevated because the end of action in the physical is precisely what arose first in thought.[162]

In spite of the opinion expressed in this text, the preponderance of evidence to be culled from Dov Baer's works demonstrates conclusively that he did not shy away from the more insurgent view regarding the abrogation of ritual practice in the world-to-come, which is consequent to the resurrection of the dead, even as he maintained its persistence in the messianic era that precedes it.[163] Thus, in another context, elaborating an exegesis already found in the discourses of his father,[164] Dov Baer links this idea to the verse regarding the Hebrew slave, "he shall serve six years; in the seventh he shall go free, without payment" (Exod 21:2):

> "In the seventh" is the seventh millennium, which is the world-to-come, the seventh year in general that is called the Sabbatical of years, for the world exists for six mil-

> lennia,[165] and it is beyond the worship of the purifications of the Tree of Knowledge of Good and Evil . . . since it is in the aspect of the light of the essence of the Infinite, blessed be he, which is above all the concatenation . . . and then the ascents and descents are not possible at all, and it is called the eternal rest. Therefore it is called the day that is entirely Sabbath, for it is entirely elongated in the life of the eternal world. And thus he goes free in the seventh without any payment, that is, without any commandments, in accord with the dictum "the commandments are nullified in the future-to-come," for there is no need at all for worship and purification, and then is the reward for the commandments.[166]

Ritual servitude is necessary to carry out the task of purification, but it is a form of enslavement, and the freedom therefrom consists of being delivered from the worship determined by the gauge of the law.[167] The rabbinic idea that the world-to-come is the place where one reaps the rewards for observing the commandments in this world is interpreted to mean that submission in the present is superseded by the recompense of the future,[168] which consists of the disclosure of the essence.[169] The limit of the law is delineated by the possibility of its being extended to the limitless—the eschatological ideal of the Sabbath is not comprised in the code of Sabbath regulations, as it is a time of utter rest when all forms of labor have been abolished, hence it would be gratuitous to prohibit labor by decree. From the example of Sabbath, we can extrapolate more generally on the rationale for all the ceremonial obligations: with the elimination of impurity as an independent force, there is no need to separate pure and impure, and, as a consequence, the purpose of fulfilling the law on these grounds has been rendered superfluous. The lawfulness of the law gives way to the deeper intent of the law, the unmasking of the essence divested of the investiture of ceremonial praxis. To cite Dov Baer once more: "As is known in the matter of 'Your master will no longer be covered etc." (Isa 30:20), and therefore the commandments will be nullified in the future, for the name YHWH will be revealed in its essence, without the garment of the commandments, but the aspect of the Oral Torah that is the halakhah will not be abolished in the future, since it is the essence of the disclosure of the interiority of the will, the source of the wisdom of the Written Torah."[170] In my judgment, this is the crux of the seventh Rebbe's teaching concerning the messianic Torah.

One might be tempted to argue that my analysis fails to take into account that the rabbinic dictum "the commandments are nullified in the future-to-come" applies to the period of the resurrection of the dead and not to the days of the Messiah.[171] We have noted this distinction in the Mitteler Rebbe, but it is enunciated as well in a parenthetical remark in the section from the Alter Rebbe's *Iggeret ha-Qodesh* that begins with the citation of a passage from the *Ra'aya Meheimna*,[172] wherein a contrast is drawn between kabbalistic lore and the laws of what is forbidden and permissible: the former derives from the Tree of Life and the latter from the Tree of Knowledge of Good and Evil. During the period of exile, the Tree of Knowledge reigns, and the sages are preoccupied with halakhic matters, but, in the days of the Messiah, the Tree of Life reigns, and they are released from this concern.[173] There is no question that the contrast in the zoharic text is between the present and the messianic future, and the rationale for ritual observance becomes obsolete in the latter when the Tree of Life, as opposed to the Tree of Knowledge, will sustain the Jewish people. In introducing a distinction between the period of the Messiah and the time of the resurrection of the dead, Shneur Zalman deviates from the text he was explicating. Let me cite his exact words:

> When the *Shekhinah* departs from the shell of splendor [*qelippat nogah*],[174] after the purification of the sparks has been completed, and the evil separates from the good, and "all evildoers will be scattered" (Ps 92:10), and the Tree of Good and Evil will not reign when the good goes out from it. Consequently, there will not be engagement with the Torah and the commandments to purify the purifications but rather to unify additionally the supernal unifications, to draw down the upper lights further from the emanation. . . . And everything will be in accord with the interiority of the Torah, to fulfill the commandments by means of the supernal intentions, which are directed to the upper lights, for the root of the commandments is above in the Infinite, blessed be he. (And what the rabbis, blessed be their memory, said, "the commandments are nullified in the future-to-come," relates to the resurrection of the dead, but in the days of the Messiah prior to the resurrection of the dead, they are not nullified.) Therefore, the essence of the engagement with the Torah will be as well with respect to the interiority of the commandments and their hidden explanations.[175]

In an effort to circumvent an antinomian interpretation, Shneur Zalman modifies the words of the zoharic text in light of a key doctrine culled from the Lurianic kabbalah. Specifically, when all of the sparks are purified from the shells there is no more need for the binary distinction between the permissible and the forbidden. Although this presents a major challenge to the nomian framework of the biblical-rabbinic law, it does not mean that there is an outright rejection of the law; on the contrary, we can still speak evocatively of the fulfillment of the law, but it is of a fundamentally different nature—the law is fulfilled not by ritual action, whose purpose it is to separate good and evil, but by the proper intention related to the internal and esoteric meaning of the laws, which results in drawing down the light of the Infinite in an augmented fashion. This is the mystical import of the rabbinic teaching that the commandments will be nullified in the future, that is, their exterior performance, but not their interior intentionality, will be abrogated. On this reading, the parenthetical remark actually obfuscates what I propose to have been the original gist of the passage.[176] If we were to remove that remark, then the text would read: "And everything will be in accord with the interiority of the Torah, to fulfill the commandments by means of the supernal intentions, which are directed to the upper lights, for the root of the commandments is above in the Infinite, blessed be he. Therefore, the essence of the engagement with the Torah will be as well with respect to the interiority of the commandments and their hidden explanations." It is important to recall a passage from the first part of *Tanya*,[177] in which Shneur Zalman affirms that the purpose of observing the positive and negative commandments is to provoke the disclosure of the divine glory, as it was at the revelation of Sinai, which together constitute the "telos of the days of the Messiah and the resurrection of the dead" (*takhlit yemot ha-mashiaḥ u-teḥiyyat ha-metim*)—the two are lumped together as the time frame of the redemption. Furthermore, as we have already seen, this is precisely the language deployed by Schneerson to depict the messianic secret regarding the hypernomian transvaluation of the law, the affirmation of a law beyond the polarity of lawful and lawless. I note as well that the expression *atid lavo*, the "future-to-come," is used as a catchphrase to designate the various eschatological stages and thus, to some extent, the distinctions between the messianic era, the seventh millennium, the resurrection, and the world-to-come are obscured.[178] Even if it can be demonstrated that Schneerson consistently deferred the nullification of the laws until the period of the resurrection,[179] the messianic epoch (anticipated in the present and therefore already experienced as part of the present) betrays a fundamental change occasioned by the restoration of evil to the good. The nature of halakhic observance must be modulated in light of surmounting this duality.

5

FEMALE ENCIRCLES MALE

Gender Transposition

Greater is the promise made by the blessed holy One to the women than to the men.

—BABYLONIAN TALMUD, BERAKHOT 17A

Transposition of Gender: Ascent of Malkhut *to* Keter

ACCORDING TO ḤABAD TRADITION, THE BESHṬ INSTITUTED A third meal at the closing hours of the last day of Passover known as the messianic banquet (*se'udat mashiaḥ*).[1] The rationale for this custom is obvious enough: this festival commemorates the initial redemption, the exodus from Egypt, that came about through the agency of Moses, the first redeemer, and thus its termination is an auspicious moment to experience proleptically the future redemption to be wrought by the Messiah, the final redeemer,[2] in accord with the rabbinic dictum "In Nisan they were redeemed and in Nisan they will be redeemed."[3] Given the charged spirit of this practice, it is not surprising that the Lubavitch masters used the occasion to communicate messages of an intensely apocalyptic nature. I shall return to this matter at a later juncture of the book, but suffice it here to note the remark of the sixth Rebbe in the talk that he delivered on 22 Nisan 5702 (April 9, 1942): "Every Jewish man and every Jewish woman must know the gravity of the time [*reṣinut ha-zeman*]. The Creator, blessed be he, is shattering the chains of exile and the illumination of the complete redemption will be soon, but this of necessity can only come about through repentance. . . . The work of arousal must be done with extreme haste and it is forbidden to defer it; the fool procrastinates until tomorrow, the wise one will act immediately."[4] Two years later on the same day, he said, "The last day of Passover is the disclosure of the Messiah [*ha-gilluy shel mashiaḥ*], and the preparation for such is repentance, for every disclosure requires preparation."[5] The urgency of both statements is palpably evident and likely reflective of the experiences endured by the sixth Rebbe on leaving Europe and resettling in America. What is also striking is the inclusion of men and women in the charge to carry out the work of repentance in order to accelerate the coming of the Messiah, an inclusion based on the fact that the corpus of Israel, the first-born of God, comprises both male and female. As we shall see, the seventh Rebbe ventured one step further by emphasizing that women are the principle agents that will bring about the future redemption. It goes without saying that the traditional patriarchy is not overthrown by Ḥabad eschatology, either in theory or in practice, and on occasion one comes across explicit misogynist language that preserves the conventional biases,[6] but what we do find is that the vision of the end is predicated on transposing the accepted coordinates of the gender dimorphism, a shift in attitude toward women within the admittedly male dominated culture, a move that was, in some respects, prescient of changes that have and will likely continue to take place within orthodox communities.

As I noted in chapter 3, the transposition is expressed by the elevation of the body over the soul, a reversal of the prevailing hierarchy affirmed on numerous occasions by Schneerson. One conspicuous example comes from an edited sermon delivered in 1960. In explicating the difference between worship of the heart and worship with the heart, the seventh Rebbe comments on the verse "And from my flesh I beheld God" (Job 19:26):

> You must understand that the essence is the soul, and it says "And from my flesh I beheld" because there are two kinds of vision, intellectual vision [*re'iyyah sikhlit*] and sensible vision [*re'iyyah muḥashit*]. The intellectual vision is related more to the soul, the sensible vision more to the body. This distinction applies as well to the matter that is seen, for in everything there is body and soul, in corporeal matters there is also a soul and in spiritual matters there is a body. Therefore it says "And from my flesh I beheld God," for the intent of "I beheld God" is a sensible vision of divinity.[7]

To comprehend this matter properly, one must bear in mind that Schneerson envisioned redemption as bringing about a state that is inherently "beyond nature" (*lema'lah min ha-ṭeva*), a beneficence issuing from the mercy (*ḥesed*) of the "light that is above the worlds" (*ha-or she-lema'lah me-ha-olamot*).[8] Thus, in the celebrated pamphlet on the essence of Ḥasidism, to which I have referred several times, Schneerson asserts that in the time of the Messiah the "aspect of divinity that is above nature will then be revealed," a comment glossed with the observation that in the future the Tetragrammaton will be pronounced as it is written, "for in the entire world there will be a disclosure of the aspect of the name YHWH—he was, he is, and he will be as one—which is above time and place, in the pattern of the disclosure that was in the Temple."[9] The messianic task is expressed in the language of Lurianic kabbalah that became so prevalent in Ḥasidic teaching—to liberate the sparks of the divine from the material shells, but, from the vantage point of Ḥabad's acosmic naturalism, this process induces the transmutation rather than the obliteration of the physical, that is, the theurgic task for the pious Jew is not simply to release the spiritual luminosity from the corporeal encasement,[10] but it is rather to discern epistemically that there is no ontic difference between the latter and the former. As Schneerson put it in a discourse from the last day of Passover, 22 Nisan 5738 (April 29, 1978), a text that was edited by his own hand, "by means of every spark that is purified, the world becomes more refined, until the termination of the purifications when the world will be a vessel for the disclosure of divinity that is above the worlds [*yihyeh ha-olam keli le-gilluy elohut she-lema'lah me-olamot*], for the principle is that the nature of the world is a vessel for that which is above nature [*she-ha-ṭeva de-olam yihyeh keli li-lema'lah me-ha-ṭeva*]."[11] Schneerson invokes the paradox—what we perceive is merely a veil for what cannot be revealed except in the manner that it is concealed—to explain the halakhic ruling that the narrative about the exodus from Egypt must be mentioned even in the days of the Messiah: the liberation from physical enslavement reminds us that the future redemption will not be based on the eradication of the corporeal but on the realization that from the godly perspective "spirituality and materiality are identical" (*ruḥaniyyut we-gashmiyyut shawin*).[12] I have already discussed the intent of this statement in chapter 2, and in this context I will simply regurgitate that the difference between redemption and exile, enlightenment and ignorance, is discriminating their lack of difference, a discrimination that arises from the discernment of the paradoxical identity of opposites, that the spiritual is the material, the concealed is the revealed. "The ultimate purpose of the exile—to transform darkness into light, so that the exile itself will be transformed into redemption."[13] The depiction of the world as a vessel for divinity may still seem to imply a dualism, but it is, in truth, an undermining of that dualism, since the intent is to communicate that the face beyond nature can be disclosed only through the mask of nature. It follows that the most ethereal aspect will be manifest in the most mundane, the brightest light in the darkest pit. The "matter of the rectification" (*inyan ha-tiqqun*), therefore, points to "the aspect of *Keter* that is above the aspect of the order of concatenation [*beḥinat seder ha-hishtalshelut*] . . . and hence it comes especially in matters that are linked to the earth."[14] Based on the principle that the lowest has its source in the highest[15]—sometimes expressed as the rootedness of *Malkhut* in *Attiq*, the inward property of *Keter*, the head-that-is-not known,[16] according to the zoharic locution, or, in the language of the description of the *sefirot* in *Sefer Yeṣirah*, "their end is fixed in their beginning, and their beginning in their end"[17]—the eschatological ideal affirms that the one is an expression of the other, implying thereby a transposition of upper and lower, a transformation of male and female, the power to bestow and the capacity to receive, which is frequently linked exegetically to the verse "a woman of valor is a crown of her husband," *eshet ḥayil aṭeret ba'lah* (Prov 12:4).[18] Consider the following formulation in Schneerson's exposition of the words from the *Lekha Dodi* hymn composed by the sixteenth-century Safedian kabbalist, Solomon Alqabeṣ, "Come my Beloved, to meet your Bride, let us receive the face of Sabbath," delivered on Shabbat Ki Teṣe, 13 Elul 5714 (September 11, 1954):

> The matter is that the root of *Malkhut* is higher than the root of *Ze'eir Anpin*, for the root of *Ze'eir Anpin* is from the exteriority of *Keter* and the root of *Malkhut* is from the interiority of *Keter*. Even though it is also said with respect to *Ze'eir Anpin* that *Ze'eir Anpin* is united with and depends on *Attiqa*,[19] it is known that the intention of this is not to *Attiq* itself (but only to the exteriority of *Attiq*), which is not the case with the root of *Malkhut*, which is in the interiority of *Attiq*, the head-that-is-not-known [*reisha de-lo ityeda*]. Even so, on account of her descent below, her root is

> concealed, and the disclosure of the root of *Malkhut* is by means of *Ze'eir Anpin* precisely. . . . Since this emanation [*hamshakhah*] is from the side of *Malkhut*, by means of this we reach the root of *Malkhut*, which is above the root of *Ze'eir Anpin*, to the point that *Malkhut* bestows upon *Ze'eir Anpin*, "a woman of valor is a crown of her husband" (Prov 12:4). . . . And this is "Come my Beloved, to meet your Bride, let us receive the face of Sabbath," this is the request of the souls of Israel, that the emanation of *Ze'eir Anpin* would be upon *Malkhut*. The beginning of the emanation is "Come my Beloved, to meet your Bride," walking alone,[20] and by means of this "let us receive the face of Sabbath," for this is an internal emanation [*hamshakhah penimit*], "the face of Sabbath," for the aspect of the interiority of *Malkhut* is disclosed as she is rooted in *Attiq*. Therefore, the word *receive* is in the plural, for *Ze'eir Anpin* also receives from the root of *Malkhut*, "a woman of valor is a crown of her husband." Just as it is above in *Ze'eir Anpin* and *Malkhut*, so it is in every donor and receiver [*mashpi'a u-meqabbel*], for by means of the receiver something is added to the donor . . . and especially in the case of the groom and bride below, as it is precisely by means of the inner emanation that "a woman of valor is a crown of her husband," and "everything is from the earth" (Eccles 3:20).[21]

The eschatological elevation of *Malkhut* to *Keter*, proleptically realized on Sabbath, is a motif well attested in older kabbalistic literature.[22] It strikes me, however, that there is a nuance in the Ḥabad reworking of this theme that offers an alternative understanding of the reversal of the gender polarity implied thereby. To appreciate this component of Ḥabad messianism, which has significant sociopolitical implications, we need to recall the principle at work in the kabbalistic symbolism: masculinity and femininity are correlated respectively with the power to overflow and the capacity to receive, the effusiveness of mercy and the constriction of judgment. While these associations, contingent to the traditional symbolic matrix, are absolute and fixed, the gender dynamic is relative and fluid, as everything has the ability to function as both male and female. That the gender attributions are not to be understood exclusively in anatomical terms is confirmed, for instance, in the comment of Shneur Zalman, "Every Jewish spark is in the feminine aspect [*beḥinat nuqba*] vis-à-vis the blessed holy One, to ascend and to see the light of the Lord, each one in accord with its level."[23] *Every Jewish spark*, men and women, are gendered as feminine in relation to the divine. This is not to suggest that sex as a physiological taxon and gender as a cultural marker never coincide in Ḥabad, such that symbolic structures reflect and reinforce sociological patterns and vice versa—there is plenty of evidence to the contrary. My point is rather that, in spite of this concurrence, it is necessary to distinguish them, to view the gender properties more broadly as functional rather than restrictedly as ontological. It is imperative to keep in mind that the seventh Rebbe's comments about masculinity and femininity should be interpreted in this vein.

The conceptual basis for the gender metamorphosis indicative of the eschaton, the turning of the recipient (*meqabbel*) into the donor (*mashpi'a*),[24] is pinpointing the root of *Malkhut* in the highest aspect of the Godhead, the head-that-is-not-known,[25] or even within the essence of the Infinite itself,[26] the potential for lack lodged in the marginal center of the plenum, a potential expressive of judgment, the quality of limitation and boundary that makes possible the dissemination and expansion of the limitless and already infinitely expanded light, a concealing that discloses the concealing in concealing the disclosing. The critical verse from Proverbs, *eshet ḥayil aṭeret ba'lah*, signifies the reincorporation of the female in the male,[27] an integration that results in the restoration of the former to her source in the Infinite, the "interiority of *Malkhut*," which is revealed in the manner that "she is rooted in *Attiq*," a transpositioning that renders her superior to the male counterpart, referred to technically as *Ze'eir Anpin*.[28] Redemption, as Sabbath, has two phases, the first entails the heteroerotic yearning of the male to be upon the female, but the second inverts this desire, as the female is set like a diadem atop the head of the male, the woman imparting to the man after having become a part of the man.[29] It is of interest to note, in passing, that in a discourse delivered in Kislev 5689 (1928) honoring the wedding of Ḥaya Mushqa to Menaḥem Mendel, Yosef Yiṣḥaq related the idea of gender transformation to the ritual gesture of the bridegroom covering the bride with a veil prior to entering the nuptial canopy (*ḥuppah*):

> And the matter is that in every ascent of the receiver to the donor [*aliyyat ha-meqabbel el ha-mashpi'a*], there must first be the emanation of the donor in the

> aspect of exteriority that is within him to the aspect of exteriority of the receiver, so that by means of this emanation the receiver can lift itself and ascend to be closer to the level of the donor, and then it will receive the inner emanation from the donor. The bridegroom and bride are in the pattern of the supernal *sefirot*, *Ze'eir Anpin* and *Malkhut*. . . . The honor of the bridegroom is the love of the blessed holy One for the Community of Israel and the honor of the bride is the love of the Community of Israel for the blessed holy One, and the canopy is the emanation of the essence, and prior to the canopy the bridegroom covers the bride with a veil [*ṣa'if*], which is the drawing near of the exteriority of the donor to the exteriority of the receiver on account of the overflow and the reception of the interiority.[30]

When the bride receives from the internal aspect of the bridegroom, the line between donor and recipient, usually valorized respectively as male and female, is blurred, as the one that receives is converted into the one that bestows, a conversion intimated by the verse "a woman of valor is a crown of her husband."[31]

The eschatological orientation enunciated here is repeatedly emphasized in Ḥabad literature, beginning with Shneur Zalman.[32] For example, the trope is summoned to account for the discrepancy between the poetic sealing of the last two of the seven wedding blessings, *mesammeaḥ ḥatan we-khallah*, "to gladden the bridegroom and the bride," and *mesammeaḥ ḥatan im ha-kallah*, "to gladden the bridegroom with the bride." The former is ascribed to the present and the latter to the future. In the present, the erotic pairing is such that the feminine, *Malkhut*, is in the posture of a vessel that receives from her masculine counterpart, *Ze'eir Anpin*, but in the future she will ascend to be a crown on his head, the feminine will be transformed from the one receiving the light to one bestowing that light, and the masculine from the one bestowing the light to one receiving the light.[33] We can delineate two elevations of *Malkhut* in the future, the one whereby she is rendered equivalent to *Ze'eir Anpin*—the two kings, sun and moon, making use of a single crown, according to the talmudic legend regarding the diminution of the lunar light[34]—and the second that renders the female superior to the male, insofar as *Ze'eir Anpin* will receive from *Malkhut,* in the aspect of the crown (*aṭarah*), the supernal will (*raṣon ha-elyon*), that will be disclosed without garment (*beli levush*) after all the purifications (*berurim*) of the sparks of light from the demonic shells are completed.[35] The parabolic import of the verse "a woman of valor is a crown of her husband," therefore, is that the tenth emanation, *Malkhut*, ascends to the aspect of the first, *Keter*, an encircling of the line, the (re)trace of light to its source. Underlying the eschatological idea is the previously mentioned principle regarding the *sefirot*, enunciated in *Sefer Yeṣirah*, the beginning is fixed in the end and the end in the beginning.[36]

The point is elaborated in a second passage from Shneur Zalman. I will cite the part most germane to our interests, as it provides the foreground against which other relevant remarks are to be evaluated:

> In the future, it is written "a woman of valor is a crown of her husband," that is, the aspect of *Malkhut*, which is called "a woman of valor" [*eshet ḥayil*], will be "a crown of her husband" [*aṭeret ba'lah*], which is *Ze'eir Anpin*. . . . In the future, the aspect of this crown [*aṭarah zo't*] will come to him [*Ze'eir Anpin*] especially from the aspect of *Malkhut*, which is called "receiver," for the light of *Malkhut* then ascends upward, above the aspect of *Ze'eir Anpin*, for "their end is fixed in their beginning," and precisely the end of action [*sof ma'aseh*] arose initially in thought [*alah be-maḥashavah teḥillah*].[37] . . . And, since it is so, we can understand the matter of their saying, blessed be their memory, regarding the days of the Messiah,[38] "In the future, the righteous will say before them 'holy' [*qadosh*]," for the root of the soul of the righteous is in the aspect of *Malkhut* that ascends above in the aspect of *Keter*, which I called "their beginning." . . . And through this we can understand why we now say "to gladden the bridegroom and the bride" [*mesammeaḥ ḥatan we-khallah*] and in the future "to gladden the bridegroom with the bride" [*mesammeaḥ ḥatan im ha-kallah*], for now is the aspect of *Malkhut*, which is called "bride" [*kallah*], and she receives from the aspect of *Ze'eir Anpin*, which is called "bridegroom," and thus the joy is first in the bridegroom and afterwards the bridegroom gladdens the bride [*he-ḥatan mesammeaḥ le-khallah*], for her efflux comes to her from the aspect of *Ze'eir Anpin*, by means of the consciousness [*moḥin*] that he receives from the light of *Imma*, as we said above in explaining [the verse] "wearing the crown that his mother [gave him on his wedding day]" (Song of Songs 3:11). In the future, however, it says, "a woman of valor is a crown of her husband," for *Malkhut* shall ascend to *Keter*, and her gradation will be above the aspect of *Ze'eir Anpin*. Then it

will be said "to gladden the bridegroom with the bride" [*mesammeaḥ ḥatan im ha-kallah*], that is, the essence of the joy will be from the bride, which is the aspect of *Malkhut*, the end of all the gradations, for "their end is fixed in their beginning," and from the bride shall come the light of the overflow of this joy to the bridegroom.[39]

One could dedicate a whole essay, perhaps even a monograph, to explicating this text, but suffice it to underline that the contrast between the present and the future is set in terms that bespeak a significant shift in the gender dynamic. To be sure, we should not expect, and we do not get, a total uprooting of the dimorphic hierarchy, to the point that it is no longer cogent or possible to speak of male or female, as we find, for example, in a passage from the Ḥasidic master Qalonymus Qalman Epstein:

All of the worlds, and all of the created beings, are in the aspect of male and female, the aspect of overflowing and receiving, for the higher world overflows to the world that is below it. . . . But in the future everyone will rectify the part of his soul unto its source, and the holy sparks will be uplifted, and the external matters will be utterly annihilated, and then the light of the resplendence of his divinity will be manifest in all the worlds, and the circle and line will be equal, and then there will be no aspect of male and female, for they will all comprehend the light of his divinity equally.[40]

By contrast, note the concluding part of Shneur Zalman's remark. In the present, when the relation of male and female is labeled the time of engagement (*erusin*), the light comes only from the external, and hence the interior dimension is in the form of the encompassing light (*or maqqif*), a point symbolically enacted as well in the fact that at the time of betrothal (*qiddushin*) the bride utters the formula silently as a circular ring, which emblematizes the "aspect of annihilation in the silent prayer" (*beḥinat biṭṭul bi-ṣelota de-laḥash*), is placed on her finger. This gesture is appropriate in the present time of exile, since *Malkhut* is inferior (*ṭafel*) and, in fact, "completely annihilated vis-à-vis the bridegroom," and thus her voice is not heard independently. In the future, however,

when the aspect of *Malkhut* will ascend to *Keter*, and she will be a crown of her husband, then she will be the aspect of bestowing on *Ze'eir Anpin*, her husband, and

> then she will have the aspect of the voice expanding by itself [*qol hitpashsheṭut bifnei aṣmo*], and this is the "voice of the bride" [*qol kallah*]. . . . In the future, in particular, *Malkhut* will ascend in the aspect of *Keter*, and she will receive from the inner aspect of the light of the Infinite, which is the aspect of marriage [*nissu'in*], that is, she becomes a vessel unto herself [*keli bifnei aṣmah*], and thus *Malkhut* perforce will have the aspect of an expanding voice [*qol be-hitpashsheṭut*]; on the contrary, from *Malkhut* will come the light of the overflow to the aspect of *Ze'eir Anpin*.[41]

The facility of *Malkhut* to function like a male, for the recipient (*meqabbel*) to become the donor (*mashpi'a*), derives from her being female quintessentially, that is, she brims over when she becomes a vessel unto herself—no longer a vessel to receive, but a vessel to overflow. In that regard, the female attains a status more elevated than the male, rendered figuratively in the image of the woman of valor positioned as a diadem on the head of her husband, "for the light of the Lord that is revealed within her now is called 'her husband,' but in the future it will be on a higher level. Therefore, it is written, 'The maiden of Israel has fallen and she will not continue to rise' (Amos 5:2), that is, the aspect of rising and ascending will not be appropriate to her, for precisely below the light of God will be intensely disclosed. And this is on account of the fact that the darkness is transformed into light, and not merely the subjugation of the other side, when it is annihilated and subdued."[42] The gender transposition of the future corresponds to the transformation of the dark into light, which is superior to the eradication of the dark by the light, but there is still a rationale to speak of dark and light. For the Alter Rebbe, the equalization of the difference between male and female signifies that the female will rise above the male and not that the difference would be completely effaced.

Overturning the Encircling

The philosophical import of the transposition is developed further by Dov Baer in a manner that imprinted the course of Ḥabad thought and practice. For instance, in the discourse celebrating the marriage of his daughter, Sarah, on 15 Av 5586

(August 18, 1826), he observed that the image of the woman encircling the man as a crown—an image anchored in the scriptural expression *neqevah tesovev gaver* (Jer 31:21)[43]—marks the containment (*hitkallelut*) of male and female in the incomposite unity (*aḥdut ha-pashuṭ*), the nondifferentiated One, which is the substance (*mahut*) and essence (*aṣmut*) of the divine that is "above the aspect of donor and recipient" (*mashpi'a u-meqabbel*).[44] It appears from this passage that the ultimate eschatological ideal calls for an eradication and not simply a reversal of the gender hierarchy, that is, it is not only the case that the receiver is transposed into a donor, and the donor into a receiver, but the unity that is realized is altogether beyond the binary distinction of donor and receiver. It is for this reason that Dov Baer relates this image to the supreme aspect of the divine, which is called (based on 1 Sam 15:29) the nonhuman (*lo adam*).[45] I shall discuss this theme in chapter 6, but it suffices here to underscore that the gender transposition is connected more generally to a transcending of anthropomorphic imagery. Inasmuch as the highest affirmation of the anthropos is the negation of the anthropos, it follows that the notion of androgyny implied in this nonanthropomorphic totality would not invariably constrict the feminine to a phallic prism, as is typical of androcentric systems of semiosis including, as I have argued, older forms of kabbalistic speculation. Simply put, to traverse the prejudices of the traditional gender construction, one must imagine a body that is devoid of imaginal embodiment, the nonhuman that is human precisely in virtue of resisting the form of any somatic confabulation.

This alternative figure of the androgynous—indeed the androgyne beyond androgyny, neither male nor female because both male and female—is affirmed by the seventh Rebbe, but in his case as well one can detect the tension between the obliteration of the male-female binary, on the one hand, and the inversion of their relationship, on the other hand. Although we can readily assume that he was cognizant of the passages I have mentioned, as well as many others where this idea is addressed, I would suggest that his words are indebted especially to Shalom Dovber's depiction of the "unity of the male and female" (*yiḥud zakhar u-neqevah*) as the "disclosure of divinity" (*gilluy elohut*), a matter that is most fully realized "when the root and source of *Malkhut* is revealed as she is essentially in the aspect of the Infinite [*she-yitgalleh shoresh u-maqor ha-malkhut kemo she-hi bi-veḥinat ein sof aṣumah*], which is above the level of the root and source of the aspect of *Ze'eir Anpin*. . . . This will be the aspect of the unity of male and female after the root and source of *Malkhut* will be disclosed as it is above the aspect of *Ze'eir Anpin* . . . for the matter of the unity will be the aspect of *Malkhut* bestowing upon *Ze'eir Anpin*."[46] The unity to be realized in the future, an ideal that the RaShaB derives eisegetically from the prophetic oracle "In that day, living water shall issue from Jerusalem" (Zech 14:8), transvalues the gender appropriations by reversing the position of male and female:

> This is also the import of what is said that she will be the "crown of her husband" [*aṭeret ba'lah*], increments of light will be drawn forth from the aspect of *Malkhut* that is within *Ze'eir Anpin*. . . . According to this, it can be said that the aspect of the unity of male and female will then be the opposite of what it is now, as *Malkhut* receives from *Ze'eir Anpin*, but then *Ze'eir Anpin* will receive from the aspect of *Malkhut*. Even though the truth is so, nevertheless it is impossible to say that *Ze'eir Anpin* will be a recipient only [*meqabbel levad*] and that *Malkhut* will be in the aspect of donor only [*mashpi'a levad*]. From what is written, "a woman of valor is a crown of her husband," it can be inferred that even when she is in the aspect of a diadem [*aṭarah*] on his head, he is still called "her husband" [*ba'lah*] in the aspect of bestowing [*mashpi'a*] upon *Malkhut*. It follows that it must be said with respect to the matter of the unity of male and female that from one perspective *Ze'eir Anpin* is in the aspect of bestowing upon *Malkhut*.[47]

Lest one think of the messianic moment as an absolute erasure of the gender schism, the RaShaB is careful to point out that there is still a polarity at play in the future, but both genders are assigned an active role—just as the male bestows on the female, the female bestows on the male—rather than one being active and the other passive. This claim is surprising, however, for if the "aspect of the root of *Malkhut* is revealed as it is essentially in the aspect of the Infinite," why would the "matter of the efflux from *Ze'eir Anpin* to *Malkhut*" still be relevant? If the identity of *Malkhut* and the Infinite, which is the elevated element of the feminine, has already been revealed, how are we to understand the continued need for the female to receive from the male?

In response, the RaShaB goes into detail about the theosophic implications of coital coupling, the exposition of which lies beyond my immediate concern. However, I will note some crucial points. The female is privileged over the male, as the power to generate new beings is linked specifically to the woman's orgiastic fluid, the "drop of feminine waters" (*tippat mayyin nuqvin*). This capability, however, is within her clandestinely—in her "root" and "source," she bears the "aspect of the essential concealment of the Infinite [*beḥinat he'lem ha-aṣmi de-ein sof*], which is entirely beyond the category of disclosure."[48] Concealment is associated with femininity, indeed the feminine aspect of the Infinite, and disclosure with masculinity.[49] The male is accorded procreative agency—the power to reveal the essence in actuality is tied physiologically to the semen, the "drop of masculine waters" (*tippat mayyin dukhrin*), the stimulus for conception and birth. But supremacy is assigned to the female. Thus the future is distinguished from the present because the

> aspect of the power of the essential concealment of *Malkhut* will be revealed as it is from the perspective of the essential concealment of the Infinite [*yitgalleh beḥinat koaḥ ha-he'lem ha-aṣmi de-malkhut kemo she-hu mi-ṣad ha-he'lem ha-aṣmi de-ein sof*]. . . . Now the aspect of the power of the essential concealment does not shine openly, but only the aspect of the power of disclosure, and the essential power is concealed. In the future-to-come, however, by the power of disclosure, the aspect of the power of the essential concealment will shine verily in the aspect of disclosure [*al yedei koaḥ ha-gilluy ya'ir beḥinat koaḥ ha-he'lem ha-aṣmi bi-veḥinat gilluy mammash*].

The future, as we have now seen at several points along the way, is marked by the promise of a complete unveiling, the disclosure of the essential concealment. But how can the essential concealment be disclosed and remain the essential concealment? Surely it seems plausible only as the concealment that abides in its unconcealment. What is unveiled, then, is the veil.

The future, as the present, will exhibit the heteroerotic pairing of male and female, but there is a change in the nature of the eros and the respective values assigned to the two genders. In the present,

> the efflux of *Ze'eir Anpin* is the essence, for it shines openly, while the efflux of *Malkhut* is concealed. In the future-to-come, however, she will be in the aspect of "a woman of valor is a crown of her husband," that is, the root of *Malkhut*, which is the aspect of the essential concealment of the Infinite [*beḥinat ha-he'lem ha-aṣmi de-ein sof*], will shine and will proceed in her essence in *Ze'eir Anpin*, and by means of *Ze'eir Anpin* there will be a disclosure of the essence. Consequently, the aspect of *Ze'eir Anpin* will receive from the aspect of *Malkhut*, and he will also bestow, as the aspect of the essential concealment of the Infinite will shine by means of the disclosure below.[50]

Throughout the duration of his leadership, Schneerson reiterated this eschatological teaching. I will refer only to a selective sampling of relevant examples that substantiate the claim. The first text I will adduce is from the discourse on Simḥat Torah, 23 Tishrei 5713 (October 12, 1952). The homily begins with the assertion that the "ultimate intention" (*takhlit ha-kawwanah*) in reality is that the two aspects of the divine manifest in the system of concatenation (*kelalut ha-hishtalshelut*), the transcendent (*sovev kol almin*) and the immanent (*memalle kol almin*) are unified. Alternatively, this unity can be expressed as the paradoxical identity of concealment and revelation, for the very matter of the "nullification of something into nothing" (*biṭṭul ha-yesh el ha-ayin*) is "the preparation for the disclosure of the aspect of the essence of the Infinite" (*hakhanah le-gilluy beḥinat aṣmut ein sof*). The "ultimate purpose" of God desiring to have a "habitation in the lower beings" (*dirah ba-taḥtonim*), which, as I have underscored in the introduction, was understood as the principal messianic task of the seventh generation,[51] comes to fruition in the apophatic realization that there is no thing outside nothing, that the finite world itself is consubstantial with the insubstantiality of the infinite essence. We are told, moreover, that this unification comes about through *Malkhut*, for she is distinguished from the other *sefirot*, insofar

> as all of them emanate so that there will be something from nothing [*lihyot me-ayin yesh*], that is, they emanate so that there will be the aspect of emanation and disclosure . . . and by means of the emanation the disclosure of divinity in created beings is realized . . . which is not the case with respect to the *sefirah* of *Malkhut*,

> which does not occasion manifestation in created beings, but, on the contrary, it actualizes the matter of concealment [*he'lem*], and it brings about the nullification of something into nothing, that is, the rest of the *sefirot* are manifestations in relation to the other [*gilluyim el ha-zulat*], that is, they bring about something from nothing [*mehawwim me-ayin le-yesh*], whereas the *sefirah* of *Malkhut* actualizes the nullification of something to nothing [*po'elet biṭṭul ha-yesh el ha-ayin*].[52]

The inherently privative nature of *Malkhut* is expressed figuratively in the portrayal of her as the "essential point that has no form" (*nequddah aṣmit she-ein bah ṣiyyur*), a state that is linked as well to her being the point situated beneath *Yesod*.[53] By contrast, we can speak of *Malkhut* as having a form when we think of her in relation to the lower worlds in the chain of becoming. This aspect is designated by the expression *malkhut she-be-malkhut*, the "kingship that is within the kingship," but the essence of *Malkhut* is in her possessing no essence, her being consists of her not being, that is, she is the archetypal lack, the privation that is the nullification of all existence. This quality of *Malkhut* is associated with *Keter*, as the latter is also described as an "essential point that has no form," the nothing that subsists in ultimate annihilation (*be-takhlit ha-biṭṭul*). Schneerson concludes, therefore, that the

> annihilation of the attribute of *Keter* is disclosed especially in the attribute of *Malkhut*, as it is known that the supernal Crown [*keter elyon*] is the crown of kingship [*keter malkhut*]. And thus the attribute of *Malkhut* is also a point that has no form, since it is the annihilation in the extreme [*she-hi be-viṭṭul be-takhlit*]. And the root of the matter of the point that has no form is the point of the trace that is prior to the withdrawal [*nequddat ha-reshimu she-lifnei ha-ṣimṣum*], for the point of the trace is not a source for the concatenation, and similarly it is not the remainder of the light from before the withdrawal . . . but it is the general residue of the light of the Infinite prior to the withdrawal [*roshem be-alma me-or ein sof she-lifnei ha-ṣimṣum*]. Therefore, this is a point that has no form, and it is in annihilation and ascent in relation to those that are above it.[54]

Malkhut is distinguished from all the other *sefirot*, insofar as a form can be ascribed to them in their bringing forth something from nothing by disclosing divinity in the world, whereas the nullification of something into nothing occurs through *Malkhut* and, consequently, concealment (*he'lem*) rather than disclosure (*gilluy*) is attributed to her essential nature. The perplexity of apophatic embodiment comes to full light here: even the aspect of *Malkhut* denoted the "kingship of the kingship" (*malkhut de-malkhut*), the aspect related to providence in the standard three worlds of kabbalistic cosmology, creation (*beri'ah*), formation (*yeṣirah*), and doing (*asiyyah*), is interpreted as an expression of "actualizing the concealment in created beings [*po'elet he'lem ba-nivra'im*] and actualizing in created beings the matter of annihilation and ascent to the essential concealment [*u-fo'elet be-ha-nivra'im inyan ha-biṭṭul we-ha-aliyyah le-he'lem ha-aṣmi*]."[55]

The reader will readily agree that, in an effort to explain how the concatenation of being proceeds from the "essential concealment" (*he'lem ha-aṣmi*), the concealed essence that is *Ein Sof*, an essence whose essence is perpetually concealed—and never more so than when it is revealed—and therefore never essentialized, language is stretched to the limit of the inarticulate. We must think the ground of all becoming, the light of the Infinite, without regard to the metaphysical conception of substance, for this ground gives way by keeping back, extending forward in withdrawing. From the vantage point of this dialectic, whose roots go back to some of the earliest kabbalistic texts from the thirteenth century,[56] concealment is precisely what makes disclosure possible, since what is disclosed can only be disclosed to the extent that it is concealed.[57] The (il)logic of the paradox is pristine: the quality of lack, *he'lem*, endows meaning to the very conception of worldhood, *ha-olam*, the hidden manifestation that is the manifest hiddenness of the divine. What is crucial to emphasize is the emplacement of this principle in *Keter* and *Malkhut*, the first and last of the sefirotic gradations, the inaugural egression of nothing into something and the futural regression of something back to nothing, a mirroring that inflects a closing of the circle, as it were, albeit an open circle, as beginning and end are wholly fragmentary, an assumption expressed by the arresting image of the point that has no form, which is applied to both termini. The ontological source for the point that has no punctiform extensionality is depicted paradoxically as the "point of the trace prior to the withdrawal" (*nequddat ha-reshimu she-lifnei ha-ṣimṣum*)[58] or as the "general residue of the light of the Infinite prior to the withdrawal" (*roshem be-alma me-or ein sof she-lifnei ha-ṣimṣum*), that is, the residual point of light that precedes any residue is produced by the contraction of light within the Infinite.[59] It is precisely this point—the vestige before there is anything of which it might be considered a vestige, the trace that may be considered originary precisely because there can be neither a trace of the origin nor an origin of the trace, a trace that perforce (re)traces itself, the trace of the trace[60]—that underscores the intrinsic quality of *Keter* and *Malkhut* as negation—the trace (*reshimu*) is correlated with concealment (*he'lem*), the line (*qaw*) with disclosure (*gilluy*)[61]—the primeval condition before time to be realized again at the end of time.

In a passage from a homily delivered on Shabbat Ḥanukah, 26 Kislev 5733 (December 2, 1972), Schneerson discussed the messianic alteration in terms of a distinction between the "seventh ascent," which is ascribed to the aspect of *Malkhut* as she is in herself (*mi-ṣad aṣmah*), and the "sixth ascent," which applies to the aspect of *Malkhut* as she is bound to the phallic foundation (*qeshurah li-yesod*).[62] The final state entails a transfiguration of the corporeal, which is at the same time a transvaluation of gender:

> Just as *Malkhut* extends to the worlds of creation, formation, and doing, which is the matter of the potency of the agent in the recipient [*koaḥ ha-po'el ba-nif'al*], it will also be there in disclosure [*be-gilluy*] . . . for YHWH as well will be disclosed in the world from its essence, to the point that "the glory of the Lord shall be revealed, and all flesh, as one, shall behold, for the mouth of the Lord has spoken" (Isa 40:5), for also in the corporeal flesh [*ha-basar ha-gashmi*] the word of the Lord will be disclosed [*devar yhwh be-gilluy*], to the point that in the future-to-come the soul will also be sustained from the divinity that is in the body [*tihyeh gam ha-neshamah nizzonah me-ha-elohut she-be-ha-guf*].[63]

In distinguishing two aspects of *Malkhut*, and in assigning a higher value to the facet of *Malkhut* that is not dependent on *Yesod*, the seventh Rebbe was both affirming the prevailing stereotype and undoing it: the feminine is still connected to the body in the future, but the corporeal becomes more visibly the site of the incorporeal, the physical is transmuted vis-à-vis the mental, and it is discerned that the difference between the one and the other is in the discernment of the indifference of the one in relation to the other.

Malkhut Within Malkhut/Secret of the Secret

In a discourse delivered on 12 Nisan 5740 (March 29, 1980), Schneerson offered two explanations of the statement in *Pirqei Rabbi Eli'ezer* that before the world was created God and his name alone existed.[64] Either the *world* denotes the physical cosmos and the *name* the ten *sefirot*, or the *world* denotes the realm of emanations and the *name* that which is contained in the Infinite (*ha-shem ha-kalul be-ein sof*), which is identified as "the aspect of delimitation in that which has no limit [*beḥinah shel hagbalah be-tokh mah she-ein lo gevul*], the root for there being a world [*shoresh lihyot olam*], for there being the aspect of the other in relation to the Infinite that bears everything [*lihyot beḥinah zulat legabbei ein sof ha-nose et ha-kol*]."[65] The origin of otherness within the nondifferentiated One, which is the substratum of everything and therefore can entertain no genuine other, the potentiality for there to be both a world that is emanated and a world that is created, the aspect of the name comprised in God's unnameable essence, is engendered as the feminine. Analogously, the eschaton is described as the nullification of concealment (*biṭṭul ha-he'lem*), since the final shell that obstructs the light will be shattered and hence all flesh shall behold the glory.[66] Following his predecessors, Schneerson depicts the messianic redemption as the "disclosure without any garment" (*gilluy beli shum levush*),[67] a disclosure that issues from the aspect of the interiority of *Attiq*, in contrast to the exodus from Egypt wherein the disclosure of the divine presence was through being garbed in the aspect of *Malkhut*. But what kind of disclosure can there be if there is no garment, no form through which the formless can be seen? Here the paradox turns on itself: the disclosure divested of all enclothing, the showing of the unconditional, is nothing other than the world that appears in its conditioned phenomenality, and hence the concealed is revealed as the concealed that is revealed as the concealed. Alternatively expressed, things of nature will be so pure that they will be perceived exclusively as vessels for the manifestation of divinity (*kelim le-gilluy elohut*), vessels so refined that they are themselves the light of the essential concealment.[68] The corporeal entities will then reflect the status of the vessels that are "in the aspect of the disclosure of the concealment [*beḥinat gilluy ha-he'lem*], for they reveal the concealment that is prior to the withdrawal [*megallim et ha-he'lem she-lifnei ha-ṣimṣum*]."[69] The symbol of the point of the trace (*nequddat ha-reshimu*), the geometric representation of the disclosure of the hiding that is the hiding of the disclosure, provides the ideational principle against which claims made about the higher status accorded the feminine in the future must be evaluated.

The supremacy of the feminine is also related to the aspect of *Malkhut* that is within *Malkhut*, a doubling of the double. In Schneerson's words from a discourse delivered on 5 Iyyar 5751 (April 19, 1991), "And *malkhut she-be-malkhut* is the disclosure of 'your kingship is the kingship of all worlds' [*malkhutkha malkhut kol olamin*] (Ps 145:13)—'your kingship' precisely, the *Malkhut* of *Ein Sof* that was prior to the withdrawal [*ha-ṣimṣum*] (which is bound to *Keter* and the interiority of *Keter*, the supernal crown [*keter elyon*], which is the crown of kingship [*keter malkhut*])[70] which emanates, is disclosed, and becomes the kingship of all worlds."[71] In the "aspect of the kingship of the Infinite" (*malkhut de-ein sof*), the "final aspect of the light," there is "concealment and withdrawal [*he'lem we-ṣimṣum*], and there remained only the aspect of the kingship of the kingship [*malkhut de-malkhut*], as it says in the *Eṣ Ḥayyim*,[72] as if it spoke of the kingship of the kingship of the Infinite [*malkhut de-malkhut de-ein sof*]."[73] *Malkhut* that is within *Malkhut* is the aspect of the kingship of the Infinite, the final facet of the light that bears the seeds of becoming the kingship of all worlds, the disclosure of light in the whole of creation, which renders it as the place wherein the divine is concomitantly revealed and concealed, concealed precisely because revealed, and revealed because concealed. The paradox was already articulated by Shneur Zalman:

> The purpose of the creation of the worlds from nothing to something [*me-ayin le-yesh*] was so that there would be something, and that something would be nullified [*yihyeh ha-yesh baṭel*], and this is the attribute of his kingship [*malkhuto*], blessed be he, for there is no king without a nation. "Your kingship is the kingship of all worlds," for the worlds [*ha-olamot*] and the concealment [*he'lem*] are only from the aspect of "your kingship," and the purpose of the concealment is only to reveal his

> kingship, blessed be he, and with the revelation of the glory of his kingship, blessed be he, is the nullification of something [*biṭṭul ha-yesh*] in relation to the aspect of his kingship that is unified verily within the Infinite, blessed be he, and all this is because it thus arose in his will so that there would be spiritual repose in the nullification of something and the subjugation of the other side [*naḥat ruaḥ be-viṭṭul ha-yesh we-itkafya de-siṭra aḥara*].[74]

The aspect of what is disclosed, the very notion of worldhood (*olam*), comes to be seen from the vantage point of the concealment (*he'lem*) within the Infinite—*malkhut ha-meyuḥedet bo be-ein sof*—the withdrawal before the withdrawal of withdrawal, the withdrawal that makes possible the turning of something back to the nothing whence the something came to be, the overturning of the (demonic) alterity, the root of differentiation in the nondifferentiated One. Here we come again to the alchemic and hermetic mystery of the *coniunctio oppositorum*, the coalescence of beginning and end, or in the oft-cited language of *Sefer Yeṣirah* describing the ten *sefirot*, their end is fixed in their beginning and their beginning in their end—*keter elyon*, the first, is *keter malkhut*, the last.

In consonance with the rhetorical formulations of his predecessors, Schneerson enunciated the messianic change in gender terms, often encoding it in the scriptural formula *neqevah tesovev gaver*, the "female encircling the male" (Jer 31:21).[75] As he put it, for example, in the talk delivered on 25 Ḥeshvan 5752 (November 2, 1991): "Now *Ze'eir Anpin* is above *Malkhut*, for *Ze'eir Anpin* bestows upon *Malkhut* . . . but in the future-to-come the aspect of *Malkhut* will be revealed as she is from herself, for she will receive from the light of the Infinite itself, as it is written, 'And the light of the moon will be like the light of the sun' (Isa 30:26), since the moon will shine from itself like the sun. Moreover, it will be revealed that the root of *Malkhut* is above the root of *Ze'eir Anpin*, and then *Malkhut* will be above *Ze'eir Anpin*, 'a woman of valor is a crown for her husband' (Prov 12:4)."[76] Several weeks later, on 16 Kislev (November 23), Schneerson returned to this theme. In that context, he emphasized that the prophetic pronouncement that the lunar light will shine with the intensity of the solar light, as well as the kabbalistic dictum that God and Israel will be one, attest to a unity still based on a binary, the feminine recipient is elevated to the status of the masculine donor. There is, however, a higher unity to be realized, a unity beyond the division of donor and recipient. In his own words: "*Kislev*—this comprises two words *kes lo*.[77] *Kes*—from the expression covering [*kissuy*] and concealment [*he'lem*], and *lo*—its numerical value is thirty-six [*lamed* + *waw* = 30 + 6], the numerology of the word *elleh* [*alef* + *lamed* + *he* = 1 + 30 + 5], which instructs about disclosure [*gilluy*] . . . and the conjunction of the two of them is in one word—*kislev*—this instructs about the conjunction of concealment and disclosure, that is, the essence . . . will be disclosed not in the manner of donor and recipient but in the manner that they will be one in actuality."[78] We may conclude, therefore, that the inner dialectic of Ḥabad thinking, along with the influence of the changing social reality of America in the second half of the twentieth century, led Schneerson to affirm a notion of unity that transcends gender dimorphism. The coupling of the masculine and feminine eventuates in a unity that does not entail the androcentric restoration of the female to the male, but a genuine sense of there being neither male nor female, that is, a model of androgyny that does not subject the feminine to the reign of the phallus.

In contrast to his predecessors, however, the seventh Rebbe did not treat the messianic elevation of the feminine simply as a theoretical issue; not only did he often stress that the "true and complete redemption" will come about on account of the merit of righteous Jewish women,[79] but he would emphasize the superiority of women, inasmuch as they are symbolically correlated with *Malkhut*, which is rooted in an aspect of the essence that is higher than the source of her male counterpart, *Ze'eir Anpin*.[80] The anticipation of this future was enough for him to justify practical changes on its basis, changes that may fall short of a full-blown egalitarianism but that nevertheless portend a progressive approach within an ultraorthodox environment.[81] Following the opinion of his father-in-law,[82] Schneerson argued that women were to be included not only in the duty to study the halakhic issues relevant to their ritual obligations, as Shneur Zalman had argued,[83] but also in the mystical dimensions of the Torah, which were to be revealed more fully in the time of the redemption.[84] In a letter dated 29 Ṭevet 5714 (January 4, 1954), Schneerson encouraged the study of *Tanya* by women, even if not in an orderly fashion, on the grounds that the commandments binding on women—all the prohibitions, the injunctions that are not time bound, and the six perpetual commandments delineated in the thirteenth-century *Sefer ha-Ḥinnukh*, to believe in God, not to believe in any other power, to unify him, to love him, to fear him, and not to stray after one's desires—cannot be fulfilled properly without knowledge of Ḥasidic teachings.[85] Many years later, in a discourse on messianic matters delivered on 3 Iyyar 5750 (April 28, 1990), Schneerson emphasized that the study and dissemination of the "interiority of the Torah as it is revealed in the teaching of Ḥasidism" is mandatory for every Jew, man and woman, for even the latter "are obligated in the study of Ḥasidic teaching in which matters pertaining to the faith in God, the love of him and the fear of him, are explained."[86] In addition to advocating that Jewish women should study Torah in both its exoteric and esoteric senses, Schneerson promoted the idea that the responsibility for educating young children fell especially on Jewish women.[87] I will refer here to one discourse in particular, delivered on Purim 5713 (March 1, 1953), for in that context Schneerson explained this conviction in terms of the complex view on gender construction we have been examining: "the matter of the woman is the attribute of *Malkhut*, concerning which it says 'a woman of valor is a crown for her husband,' for this is from the perspective of the privileged status of the attribute of *Malkhut*, which is rooted in the essence [*mushreshet be-aṣmut*]. The matter of the schoolchildren,[88] the essence of the existence of the people of Israel, is the level of the body—this touches on and is bound to the essence [*noge'a we-qashur im ha-aṣmut*]."[89] Women bear the pedagogical burden, for they correspond to *Malkhut*, which is enrooted in and therefore must be envisioned from the essence of the Infinite—we note again the profound paradox that the sefirotic attribute signifying privation is precisely the marker of the essence, the substance that is substantially insubstantial. There is no reason to doubt the literalness of Schneerson's view regarding the educational task assigned especially to women, but neither should the figurative implications, which he draws explicitly, be ignored: the schoolchildren represent the corporeal, and therefore the symbolic intent of his teaching involves harnessing the finite to the Infinite. As we have seen already, the dialectic embraced by Ḥabad leads to the perception that the physical and spiritual are not in binary opposition. Reporting some of his dreams and visions in his personal diary on 12 Kislev 5705 (November 28, 1944), Schneerson expressed this matter in terms of the interpretation he heard from the RaShaB of the scriptural narrative concerning Abraham's servant choosing Rebekah as a spouse for Isaac. Rebekah is distinguished from the rest of the "daughters of the townsmen" who stood by the "well of water" (Gen 24:13). These women represent the "souls as they are in *Malkhut*, they 'come out to draw water'—Torah—but without vessels." By contrast, it says of Rebekah that she "came out with her jar on her shoulder" (Gen 24:15), that is, the vessel (*keli*), which denotes the attribute of that which encompasses (*maqqif*). In the continuation of the narrative, it is related that Rebekah "went down to the spring" (Gen 24:16), that is, "she went into the interiority of the seventy aspects of the Torah" (the word *ayin* connotes both "spring" and the number seventy),[90] and she "filled her jar, and came up" (Gen 24:16), that is, "she drew the inner potency to that which encompasses, for she made the encompassing the inner, an elevation of the corporeal, the disclosure of the corporeal gradation." As a consequence of transposing the inner (*penimi*) and the encompassing (*maqqif*), Rebekah raised the corporeal to the level of the spiritual, and she thereby attained the rank of the "worship of Abraham," which is encapsulated in the words *el olam,* "God of the world" (Gen 21:33),[91] an idiom that signifies (when read in the appositive)[92] that "God is the world and the world is God."[93]

Messianic wisdom is brought about by this epistemological awakening. As Schneerson put it in the *Quntres Inyanah shel Torat ha-Ḥasidut*: "The matter of the unity that 'there is none beside him' (Deut 4:35) is not that the worlds have no being, but rather that the worlds themselves as they are found in their being (and delimited by the taxonomy of time and space) are united in the ultimate unification in the essence of the light of the Infinite, blessed be he [*meyuḥadim hem be-takhlit ha-yiḥud be-aṣmut or ein sof barukh hu*]."[94] Discerning that the worlds are united in the essence of the Infinite fosters a destabilization of the distinction between outside and inside. Schneerson articulated this idea by means of a clever exegesis of the response that the Beshṭ reported having heard from the Messiah regarding the latter's eventual arrival.[95] "The whole time that the wellsprings are only in [the aspect of] the 'face' [*panim*], they do not yet express the truth of their substance. Since the preparation and the instrument for the coming of the Messiah is the essence of Ḥasidism, it is especially necessary to spread the wellsprings outwards [*lehafiṣ et ha-ma'yanot ḥuṣah*]—to the point that the 'outward' [*ḥuṣah*] is transformed into the 'wellsprings' [*ma'yanot*]—for by means of this the essence of the wellsprings is expressed, and then 'the man will come'—that is, the King Messiah."[96] The coming of the messianic redeemer is made dependent on the realization that the wellspring does not actualize its potential until it overflows to the outside and thereby problematizes a hard-and-fast distinction between inner and outer, the spiritual core and the physical shell. One who is enlightened comprehends that "the opposition between the world (exile) and redemption is only an external matter, and its nullification is through the disclosure of the true matter of the world—*Malkhut*."[97] In the subversion of the distinction between exile and redemption, the concealment of revelation and the revelation of concealment, lays the secret of the secret, the obviously obscure secret that is obscurely obvious.

APOCALYPTIC CROSSING

Beyond the (Non)Jewish Other

A Gentile does not die,
for he has never lived in order that he may die.
He who has believed in the truth has found life,
and this one is in danger of dying, for he is alive.

—Gospel of Philip

In God We Trust: America as the Spiritual Superpower

There is no question that the environment of America had a profound impact on the Ḥabad-Lubavitch Ḥasidism under the leadership of the seventh, and presumably last, Rebbe. One of the areas where this effect is most conspicuous is with reference to the attitude toward the Gentile nations. The sixth Rebbe had already expressed gratitude for the freedom to practice Judaism in this country in contrast to the persecutions and hardships suffered in Russia.[1] It goes without saying that his outlook was more complex, as is attested, for instance, by his decision to return to Europe after his first visit to the United States, the purpose of which was to muster aid for Russian Jewry and to strengthen American Jewry.[2] Although America did provide a haven for Yosef Yiṣḥaq and members of his family and entourage to escape the havoc of Nazi persecution, like many rabbinic sages from Europe, he was concerned that the material abundance indicated a spiritual depravity, that the very opportunities that made it appealing also presented a unique challenge to the preservation of tradition. Thus, in the beginning of the pamphlet *Qol Qore,* which appeared for the first time in America on 29 Iyyar 5701 (May 26, 1941), Yosef Yiṣḥaq remarked that in the "old country" the fires were burning to consume the body of the Jewish people (*yiddishen guf*), whereas in the "new country," the Jewish soul (*yiddishe neshomoh*) was threatened with extinction.[3] A similar sentiment was expressed in a talk the sixth Rebbe gave on the second day of Pentecost, 7 Sivan 5703 (June 10, 1943): the situation in America was deemed to be worse than under Tzar Nicholas in Russia, for, in the latter, the wish was to murder Jews physically, but, in the former, to uproot them entirely from the faith.[4] The matter is also depicted in terms of a well-known rabbinic recasting of a biblical typology: the destiny of Jacob is linked to the world-to-come, the fate of Esau to this world. Inasmuch as the people of Israel are involved in mundane matters solely for the sake of Torah, their material needs are fulfilled on the basis of unwarranted divine grace (*ḥesed ḥinnam*); American Jews, however, are not at ease with this sense of munificence, and thus they are in "partnership" with non-Jews in pursuit of physical desires and pleasures.[5] In the following month, on *Ḥag ha-Ge'ullah,* 12 Tammuz (July 15), the point was repeated in a brief but poignant way: "Here in America, it is not only that new melodies are not created, but the old ones, too, are forgotten."[6] One would readily agree that these are rather dismal assessments about American Jewry. There are occasional asides in which Yosef Yiṣḥaq extols the Jews of America,[7] but on the whole he is rather grim regarding their religious fortitude. The seventh Rebbe emphasized that his predecessor was far more optimistic about America, noting, for instance, that he rejected the more conventional view of European rabbis that this was not a place where orthodox Jewry could flourish; indeed, with respect to the possibility of establishing a vibrant context for a traditional life of Torah and ritual, the Friediker Rebbe apparently insisted that America is "not different" (*nit andersh*) from other places.[8] Schneerson's comportment, however, is fundamentally different. From the beginning of his leadership until the last years of his life, he maintained his father-in-law's deep conviction concerning the imminent coming of the Messiah, which logically implies a continued sense of physical dislocation and temporary belonging, but he also felt great possibilities in the American landscape to promote the cause of Judaism and to spread the teachings of Ḥasidism worldwide. When the Messiah comes, he declared on 7 Kislev 5712 (December 6, 1951), we will be able to say with "justified pride" (*barekhtiktn shtolts*) that the Jewish youth of America were the soldiers in the army responsible for carrying out the mission of bringing the redemption.[9] Moreover, the freedom of worship secured by the American constitution would operate as a lynchpin in his overall post-Holocaust messianic strategy. In the talk from 26 Nisan 5717 (April 27, 1957), Schneerson stressed that, in the present, the situation of Jews in America takes precedence over the situation of Jews in the state of Israel, and, while this will change in the future, even then the "land of Israel will spread to all the lands" and this includes America as well.[10] As I argued in chapter 3, one must acknowledge Schneerson's commitment to religious Zionism, but it is also necessary to take into account the fact that he affirmed a conception of the land that is decidedly diasporic, inasmuch as the boundary of what constitutes the land extends to the entire globe of the earth. In the nonlocalized space of the messianic ideal, the mental zone of nonlocality, America occupies a special place.

Over the course of time, we find pronouncements on the part of Schneerson indicating that he applauded actions and words by the government and even the president in accord with his spiritual vision, for example, the ruling to allow the lighting of the Ḥanukah menorah in public places.[11] The mystical import of this activity is to maximize the dispersal of the divine light to Jews, but more particularly to non-Jews, an idea that is linked to the rabbinic injunction to light the candles of Ḥanukah "in the entry to one's house from the outside" (*al petaḥ beito mi-ba-ḥuṣ*),[12] that is, the essence of this gesture is to illumine spiritually those who are positioned on the exterior.[13] The seventh Rebbe appealed to and upheld the rabbinic maxim *dina de-malkhuta dina*,[14] which accords legitimacy and authority to the rule of the land where one lives in matters that do not conflict with the regulations of the Torah, but, beyond this principle of pragmatic expediency, he viewed America in a special way and thus believed that there was an inherent affinity between American and Jewish law. After all, this was the country where his predecessor, fleeing from the ravages of the Second World War, found refuge and was able to establish headquarters for the Lubavitch movement. In the talk given by the seventh Rebbe on 12 Tammuz 5743 (June 23, 1983), the day celebrating the discharge of the sixth Rebbe from Soviet prison, America and its leadership were singled out for securing his escape.[15] Schneerson took the opportunity of the moment to express gratitude to the current American president, Ronald Reagan, though his name is not mentioned explicitly: "Even though the president of the nation today is not the same as the president of the nation in those days—he nonetheless fills his place with respect to everything connected to the responsibility and office of the presidency of the nation."[16] The intent of Schneerson's logic is made explicit in the continuation: just as the sixth Rebbe was emancipated from Soviet oppression and allowed to emigrate to the United States—an event that is referred to somewhat allusively as "his exiting from the boundaries of that nation"—through the intervention of the American government, including the executive branch, so the current president should continue to pressure Soviet authorities, by way of diplomacy rather than through military victory, to venerate the inalienable right of every Jew "behind the iron curtain" to be free and live where he or she wants to live.[17]

Ever mindful of the dynamics of realpolitik, Schneerson implored those who might have connections to people in government to persuade them that they should do all they could to help secure the liberation of Soviet Jews, citing as exegetical support the words of Mordecai addressed to Esther, "And who knows, perhaps for just this moment you have attained to royal position" (Esther 4:14). The liberation of the sixth Rebbe and his emigration to the United States became the prototype of the struggle for Soviet Jewry. In Schneerson's mind, this twist of fortune was not simply fate but an expression of individual providence (*hashgaḥah peraṭit*).[18] The superpower status of America is directly related to the fact that it is distinguished among all modern nations in placing "exceptional emphasis" on faith (*emunah*) and conviction (*biṭṭaḥon*) in God, a propensity exemplified in the slogan "in God we trust," which is linked especially to the nation's currency. The content of these words relates to "faith in the Creator of the world, and not faith [*emunah*] alone, but 'trust'—faith of conviction [*emunah shel biṭṭaḥon*], that is, they place absolute trust [*emun muḥlaṭ*] in the Creator of the world, and they have faith in him."[19] Schneerson shows here, as he was wont to do, a finely attuned sensitivity to mundane matters. He astutely discerns the underlying importance of religious fervor in the American terrain—one must still wonder if a person who did not explicitly profess belief in God by invoking the divine in political jargon, let alone someone who openly denied or expressed doubt concerning the existence of God, could stand a chance of running for the presidency. The picture of America proffered by Schneerson, and the presidential comments to which he refers, bolstered his messianic vision. All Israel will be united, but beyond Israel the "matter of peace" will spread through the civilized world. The agency that shall bring this about is observance of the seven Noahide laws, the rabbinic category to denote the universal laws that are binding on any human society.[20] The matter is expressed most elaborately in a letter to Reagan dated 25 Nisan 5742 (April 18, 1982), which was a response to Reagan's letter from April 2, 1982, informing the seventh Rebbe that in honor of his eightieth birthday he was issuing a proclamation for a "National Day of Reflection" (April 4, 1982):

> By focusing attention on "the ancient ethical principles and moral values which are the foundation of our character as a nation," and on the time-honored truth that "education must be more than factual enlightenment—it must enrich the character as well as the mind," while reaffirming the eternal validity of the G-d given Seven Noahide laws (with all their ramifications) for people of all faiths—you have expressed most forcefully the real spirit of the American nation. More than ever before the civilized world of today will look to the United States of America for guidance as behooves the world's foremost Super Power—not merely in the ordinary sense of this term but, even more importantly, as a moral and spiritual Super Power, whose real strength must ultimately derive from an unalterable commitment to the universal moral code of the Ten Commandments. Indeed, it is this commitment to the same Divine truths and values that, more than anything else, unites all Americans in the true sense of E Pluribus Unum.[21]

Reflecting back to Reagan the language of the proclamation, which we can plausibly assume was crafted with the help of Lubavitchers, the seven Noahide laws are depicted as the "moral code" binding on all Americans "regardless of religious faith."[22] From Schneerson's perspective, adherence to these laws on the part of non-Jews purifies their corporal and cerebral state of being. Salvation (*haṣṣalah*), therefore, is not exclusively for the Jews but for the world in its entirety.[23] Here, too, Schneerson cites Maimonides as his authority: "He who fulfills one commandment tips himself and the whole world to the scale of merit, and he brings about for himself and for them redemption and deliverance."[24] As he made clear in a talk he delivered on 19 Kislev 5747 (December 21, 1986), "In

God we trust" bespeaks the utopian ideal of all nations worshipping together so that the attribute of kingship will be properly ascribed to God.[25]

Seven Noahide Laws: Including the Excluded

Perhaps nothing expresses more lucidly the zeal, and to some extent, audacity of Schneerson's messianic ambition than the drive on the part of the Lubavitch movement under his supervision to spread the knowledge of and gain compliance to the seven Noahide laws among Gentiles. This undertaking should not be construed as missionary activity, since there is no interest in conversion; indeed, as I will discuss later in this chapter, the convert is understood to be an alienated Jewish soul returning to the fold rather than a non-Jew becoming Jewish. The target audience for the missionizing tendencies on the part of Ḥabad is secular Jews. Still, the aspiration to spread the seven Noahide laws comes closest to something akin to a proselytizing program on the part of Lubavitchers insofar as it reflects an aspect of their religious vision that entails shaping the beliefs and practices of non-Jews for the sake of redeeming the world.

As is the case with so many crucial ideas, the emphasis to exact a commitment to the seven Noahide laws by non-Jews was seen as an integral part of the sixth Rebbe's messianic task. Specifically, the release of Yosef Yiṣḥaq from Soviet prison on 12 Tammuz 5687 (July 12, 1927) was interpreted as a reaffirmation of his duty "to unify all the people of Israel by means of the dissemination of the Torah and Judaism, which includes the spreading of the fulfillment of the commandments of the sons of Noah in all of the world in its entirety."[26] The universalist objective is part of the vocational particularity. The significance of the seven Noahide laws in Schneerson's teachings has been noted by a number of scholars, but the topic has been treated in isolation from the larger and more complex issue concerning his philosophical stance on the question of alterity and the status of the non-Jew. Many have claimed, apologetically in my view, that the campaign of the seven Noahide Laws illustrates not only a more conciliatory attitude toward Gentiles but a weakening of traditional ethnocentrism. While I do not deny that there is an interesting shift in Schneerson's rhetoric, I submit that a careful scrutiny of the various articulations of this idea leads to the conclusion that the boundary separating Jew and non-Jew is not completely obliterated or even substantially blurred; on the contrary, the ostensible narrowing of the abyss only widens it further.

One passage, in particular, is worthy of citing, as the matter of the Jew's responsibility to proliferate the knowledge and observance of the seven Noahide laws on the part of non-Jews is framed in gender terms. The relevant comment is from a discourse delivered on 21 Kislev 5745 (December 15, 1984):

> It is known and it has been explained in a number of places that the blessed holy One created the world in a manner that every created being is both a donor [*mashpi'a*] and a recipient [*meqabbel*], for it is not possible for a discriminate entity to be exclusively in the aspect of donor or in the aspect of recipient. As it pertains to our matter, since the responsibility of the Jew is to influence and to cause the non-Jew to receive the commandments given to the sons of Noah, it follows that the Jew is the donor and the non-Jew the recipient. But since it is not possible for a discriminate entity to be exclusively in the aspect of recipient—the blessed holy One caused the non-Jew to bestow on the Jew in matters of a livelihood.[27]

Utilizing the standard binary of the donor and the recipient, which, as we discussed in the previous chapter, is engendered as male and female, the hierarchical supremacy of Israel is expressed by the fact that even the more active role assigned to the non-Jew is tied to benefiting Jews in material matters. Another text, in which the disharmony is heard even more sharply, is taken from a talk given on 26 Av 5745 (August 13, 1985). Predictably, Schneerson insists that the Jews must not be swayed by the nations in which they are entrenched. The reason for the diasporic existence is to accentuate the chosenness of the Jewish people and the fact that they are a living example for the nations of the world, especially to endorse the seven Noahide laws. Schneerson makes a point of singling out America as an auspicious place where Gentiles respect the Jews and help them establish their own social and educational institutions.[28]

An honest appraisal of this passage, as well as others that could have been cited, leads inevitably to the conclusion that the other nations are treated as a means to benefit the Jews,[29] an idea supported exegetically by the verse "Kings shall tend your children, their queens shall serve you as nurses" (Isa 49:23).[30] Even the demand that they fulfill the seven commandments of Noah is merely an aspect of this instrumentality. This is not to deny that Schneerson, following Maimonides,[31] whom he cites quite frequently, did impart soteriological significance to the observance of the non-Jews. More specifically, the goal of transposing the world into a habitation for the divine is realized when the Jews fulfill the Torah, and the Gentiles the seven Noahide commandments.[32] Nevertheless, the hierarchy is not effaced, a crucial point that has not always been appreciated by scholars. Those who wish to speak of a partnership between Jews and Gentiles in the business of redemption must avow the terms of that collaboration without defensiveness or dishonesty. The seventh Rebbe's effort to promote the observance of the seven commandments on the part of non-Jews was certainly laudable, but a careful analysis of his remarks on this topic indicates that they only reinforced the deleterious alterity implied in his portrayal of the non-Jew as the other to the other who is the Jew. By including the excluded in the claim to exclusivity, the exclusivity is rendered even more inclusive.

Israel's Humanity: Jewish Particularity as Idiomatic of Self-Nullification

As I have noted at several intervals of this book, foundational to Ḥabad's philosophic orientation is the presumed ontological difference in the constitution of the Jew and the non-Jew, both psychically and somatically, a point sorely missed by those who uncritically use the term *ethical* to characterize the spiritual pietism of Ḥabad.[33] While hardly unique to this corpus, each of the seven masters in the Lubavitch dynasty has accepted such a view, apologetic denials on the part of some scholars and practitioners notwithstanding. The textual evidence to support this assertion is overwhelming and it would be impractical to offer even a small percentage of the sources that substantiate the point. A striking way that this dogma has been expressed is the claim that non-Jews possess an animal soul that derives from the demonic, whereas Jews possess a divine soul that equips them with the capacity to uplift their animal soul and to transform it into a vessel for holiness. Formulated in more technical terminology, Jews alone are said to be endowed with the aspect of soul known as *yeḥidah*, in virtue of which the individual can be reincorporated into the incomposite unity of the nondifferentiated One (*yaḥid*).[34] A distinctive rank is accorded the Jews, as it is reputed that only they have the facet of the divine that is enrooted in the essence of the Infinite, the "inner point of the heart" (*nequddat ha-lev penimit*)—they are not just of a similar substance, they are of the same substance (a doctrinal principle attested in the dicta *yisra'el we-qudsha berikh hu ḥad* and *yisra'el we-qudsha berikh hu kolla ḥad*)[35]—and therefore they are the only ones capable of being bound to and absorbed in the transcendent light beyond the delimitation of the concatenation of worlds.[36] Even the pious Gentiles, who concur that God creates the world *ex nihilo*, can comprehend only the existence (*meṣi'ut*) of the divine but nothing of its substance (*mahut*), and since the light of the Infinite is completely concealed from them, they do not have the capacity to cultivate the ultimate experience of ecstasy through the "realization of the nullification of their existence" (*hitpa'alut ha-biṭṭul mi-meṣi'utam*).[37] The Jews singularly have the prominence to suffer the experience of self-sacrifice (*mesirat nefesh*), to be affixed to the supernal knowledge (*da'at elyon*) that is above reason,[38] to attain the metanoetic state labeled variously as the "conjunction" (*devequt*), "bonding" (*hitqashsherut*), or the "unification" (*yiḥud*) of the "essence with the essence" (*eṣem ba-eṣem*),[39] and it is thus through them that "the darkness is also transformed into light, and it is revealed to them as it will verily be in the world-to-come."[40]

On this score, it is relevant to recall that the term to designate the Jew, *yehudi*, is related by Shneur Zalman to the declaration of Rachel *ha-pa'am odeh et yhwh*, "This time I will praise the Lord" (Gen 29:35), the scriptural explanation of the name of Judah (*yehudah*). The essence of what it is to be a Jew is connected to the gesture of expressing gratitude to God (*hoda'ah*),[41] which, conceived mystically, is the "aspect of nullification in the light of the Infinite" (*beḥinat ha-biṭṭul le-or ein sof*).[42] That the inimitable power of the Jew is linked to the liturgical utterance is an idea affirmed in classical rabbinic sources, but its deeper meaning, according to Ḥabad philosophy, concerns the annihilation of self in what I have called the *inessential essence*, the essence that defies any essentializing but as the essence that cannot be essentialized. This, too, is the meaning elicited from the scriptural term for "Hebrew," *ivri*, which is linked to the verse "In ancient times, your forefathers lived beyond the river," *be-ever ha-nahar yashvu avoteikhem me-olam* (Josh 24:2): the root of the Jewish soul is from beyond the river, that is, from the essence, the concealed thought and the infinite will that transcend the concatenation of the worlds.[43] The biblical depictions of the people of Israel as the children of God (Deut 14:1) or as the firstborn (Exod 4:22) are related similarly to the "essential connection to the divine" (*hitqashsherut aṣmit le-elohut*) alleged on the part of the Jews, an indigenous bond that facilitates their incorporation within the essence.[44] Summarizing the point, Schneerson remarked that the soul of each and every Jew is a "portion of the divine from above in actuality [*ḥeleq eloha mi-maʿal mammash*], a portion of the essence by means of which they grasp the essence, and when the worship is from the side of the essence of the soul, which is the matter of nullification and acceptance of the yoke, then all the matters of worship are equaniminous."[45] In an important letter to David Ben Gurion, the first prime minister of the modern state of Israel, written on 8 Adar I 5719 (February 9, 1959), the seventh Rebbe categorically rejected the idea of a "secular Jew," since Jewish identity is intricately linked to the pneumatic connection of the Jew, regardless of his or her allegiance, to the divine essence. He recognizes that there are righteous individuals among the nations of the world, but, as the nomenclature indicates, they are from the nations of the world and hence they cannot be on the same footing as Jews.[46] There is no corroboration that Schneerson ever discarded or ameliorated this viewpoint.

One should be struck straightaway by a blatant contradiction: on the one hand, the intrinsic nature of the Jew, in contrast to the non-Jew, is tagged as the ability to be integrated in the essence, but, on the other hand, in that essence, opposites are no longer distinguishable, whence it should follow that the division between Jew and non-Jew should itself be subject to subversion. I shall return to this matter, but suffice it here to note that even if it is acknowledged that the overcoming of difference is the purpose of the path, the path to get beyond the path is tendered as the unique responsibility of the people of Israel, since only they are thought to be conterminous with the divine, and hence only they are fully entrusted with the task of transmuting the animal craving for the pleasures of this world into the all-consuming hankering for and delight in God. The matter is expressed succinctly in the following saying of Yosef Yiṣḥaq included by the seventh Rebbe in *Ha-Yom Yom*, the collection of aphorisms arranged according to the days of the year:

> There are two ways, the way of nature [*derekh ha-ṭeva*] and that which is above nature [*lema'lah min ha-ṭeva*]. The blessed holy One created the world to appear as if it were in the way of nature—in the eyes of the flesh—and this is the way of Elohim. The law and the commandments [*torah u-miṣwot*] are the way of YHWH, the drawing down of that which is above nature into nature, on account of which the blessed holy One overflows to Israel from that which is above nature into nature.[47]

The two ways, nature and what is above nature, the physical and the metaphysical, correspond respectively to the two names of God, Elohim and YHWH. To ordinary sense perception, the world appears as if it were the way of nature, but, in truth, as we discussed at great length in chapter 2, the world is naught but the (dis)similitude through which the divine essence is revealed as what is hidden. Schneerson offered the following concise account of the intricate mystical cosmology, "The emanation of the boundless is actualized in the bounded, for in the garments of nature, too, we can see the blessing of the Lord and the felicity that is above nature."[48] The ritual observance of the Jewish people is the primary means by which a habitation is made for God in the world, so that the light beyond nature can be drawn into nature. The ideal of self-abnegation is customarily presented, therefore, as the mystical exegesis of the verse *ner yhwh nishmat adam*, "the human soul is the lamp of the Lord" (Prov 20:27), which is applied specifically to Israel based on the older rabbinic idea that the word *adam*, in its most exacting sense, refers to the Jews and not to the nations of the world.[49] Just as it is the nature of the flame to illumine and to rise upward, so the desire of the soul of every Jew (even if a particular individual is unaware) is to ascend and be conjoined to its source as well as to augment the light in the world.[50] To cite one of countless passages in which Schneerson makes this point: "Therefore Rosh ha-Shanah is precisely the day that he created the first Adam [*adam ha-ri'shon*], for this power (to draw the disclosure of the essence of the light of the Infinite that is above the worlds, so that this expansion will be in the world) is in Israel especially, 'you are called *adam*,'[51] in the name of the first Adam. . . . Since the root of the soul of Israel is in his essence, blessed be he, their capability is to draw into the world the disclosure of the essence of the light of the Infinite."[52] Note that the biblical account of the creation of Adam is translated ethnocentrically—the text is interpreted as a reference to the Jew, who is the exemplary human being. Moreover, as we have seen in chapter 3, the term *adam* is related linguistically to the expression *eddammeh le-elyon* (Isa 14:14), which denotes the correspondence between the human below and divine anthropos above.[53] That this is confined to the Jews is well attested in Ḥabad sources. I will mention one passage from the Alter Rebbe, which may be taken as emblematic: "Therefore 'you are called *adam*,' for the meaning of *adam* is *eddammeh le-elyon*, and it is written 'Israel in whom I glory' (Isa 49:3)."[54] The credo is repeated routinely by the seventh Rebbe. To approach his worldview unapologetically, this is the place where one must begin: of all ethnicities, the Jews, idiosyncratically, are isomorphic with the amorphic essence, and thus they alone are capable of apprehending the imaginal body of God from their embodied mindfulness.[55]

Early on, Schneerson offered a strident expression of this belief: "The Jewish man [*ish ha-yisra'eli*] is constituted by two lines . . . the natural qualities, too, are composed of good and evil, which is not the case with respect to the nations of the world, for they have no good at all."[56] One might propose that such a rash formulation was reflective of youthful intemperance, but it must be remembered that the opinion expressed by the young man was not eccentrically his own. Indeed, in the opening chapter of the first part of *Tanya*, we find the infamous distinction between the animal soul of the Jews and the animal soul of the idolatrous nations: the former derives from the shell of the radiance (*nogah*), which is from the Tree of Knowledge of Good and Evil, whereas the latter derives from the remaining three impure shells "in which there is no good at all."[57] It is not only that the Jews alone possess a divine soul, but even their animal soul is unrivaled and superior to other ethnic identities. To some extent, this view is modified by the Ḥabad-Lubavitch masters in accord with the Ḥasidic teaching, which is partially anticipated in medieval kabbalistic lore, that there is no evil without an admixture of good, and hence the redemptive obligation is to ignite the spark of light encased in the shell of darkness in order to restore the darkness to the light. This enterprise is portrayed by Schneerson with special reference to Esau or Edom, which, following a long-standing exegetical tradition, is a figurative trope for Christianity:

> This is also the content of the work of Israel in this last exile, the exile of Edom, to purify also this evil of Esau (the father of Edom) until the time of the end when the good hidden in him will be revealed. . . . And by means of this Edom, too, is transformed into good—as the sages, blessed be their memory, said, "In the future, the pig will become pure"[58] (which alludes to Edom, "the pig is Edom"[59]), to fulfill the promise "For the liberators shall march up on Mount Zion to wreak judgment on Mount Esau, and dominion shall belong to the Lord" (Obad 1:21), quickly in our days in actuality.[60]

I shall return below to the image of the kosher pig, as it were, and the apocalyptic theme of the othering of the non-Jew, the Jewish other, that it implies, but the crucial point to underscore here is that Schneerson, following the teaching of his predecessors, which can be traced to much older sources, accorded ontic singularity to the Jewish people. The rich tradition that informed his thinking notwithstanding, the specific exigencies of his moment cannot be denied. In the wake of the mass destruction of European Jews, and the relocation of many refugees to the liberal, democratic society of America, where the powerful forces of secularism and assimilation obviously posed a challenge to those who sought to protect and promulgate orthodox beliefs and actions, the necessity to emphasize even more stridently the irreducible character of the Jew is surely understandable.[61] Claims to the superiority of the Jew in a post-Holocaust world might seem counterhistorical, but their power derives precisely from this fact.

Numerous texts articulate this perspective. Consider the following passage from the talk of 28 Tammuz 5713 (July 11, 1953):

> Since the [world of] emanation is the aspect of the face, the matter of forgetfulness does not apply there, which is not the case in [the worlds of] creation, formation, and doing, which are the aspect of the back, and there the matter of forgetfulness is appropriate. This is the variation in the worlds, which is not so [with respect to] the souls of Israel, for just as below they are the aspect of the interiority, so it is written

> [about] the souls of Israel that arose in [divine] thought, that is, in the most supernal level of thought, "face to face the Lord spoke with you" (Deut 5:4), for by means of the fact that the Lord spoke with them, the interiority of Israel became the interiority that is above.[62]

Schneerson never wavered from the conviction that the "soul of each and every one from Israel is a portion of the Creator and it is bound to him, and by means of this it possesses superior spiritual powers."[63] The pietistic paradigm of self-annihilation (*biṭṭul aṣmi*)—the catalyst that makes possible the disclosure of the concealment—rests on the consubstantiality of the Jewish soul and the essence.[64] The Jew, as it were, has what it takes to be nothing, the ember of infinity compressed in the point of the heart, the simple complex of a complex simplicity. The Torah, which in its full incarnation is given chiefly to Israel, is this measure that cannot be measured, the intermediary bond through which the opposites, God and human, nature and what is beyond nature, coalesce in the sameness of their difference.[65] In Ḥabad, accordingly, we have a mystical discipline predicated on a nonegocentricist philosophy that is at the same time culturally ethnocentric. One might have expected the two to have been coupled, such that the breeding of egocentricity on the psychological plane is the efficient cause that engenders the propagation of ethnocentricity on the anthropological.[66] But it is also possible, as the example of Ḥabad illustrates, to decouple the two.

The special connection that the Jew has to the essence is to be enacted ideally in the mundane by adhering to the law, as Schneerson's mantralike repetition of the slogan *ha-ma'aseh hu ha-iqqar*, "action is the mainstay,"[67] clearly indicates. Although functionally dependent on its execution in the social arena, the allegation, theoretically, is an ontological one, and hence this special status is thought to be innate in each individual Jew, irrespective of his or her fidelity to traditional dogma and/or ceremonial practice.[68] The glimmer of the infinite light, the *pintele yid*, has to be activated, but it is believed to exist equally and uniquely in the heart of every Jew. The seventh Rebbe was fond of citing a dictum attributed to the Mitteler Rebbe, "When two Jews come into contact, there is between them two divine souls [*shenei nefesh elohit*] and one animal soul [*nefesh aḥat bahamit*],"[69] that is, the physical body is a substratum for the divine soul, which is the distinguishing mark of identity. The alliance of Jews facilitates the conquest of the somatic by the spiritual;[70] the idea of the Jew's triumph over nature is supported by the halakhic principle of "one thing being nullified by two" (*ḥad bi-terei baṭil*), even to the point that "something prohibited might be transformed into something permissible" (*nehpakh ha-issur lihyot heter*).[71] We note, yet again, that the hypernomian axiom, the transmutation of the forbidden into the permitted, is rooted in a dictate of the law.

As Schneerson put it in the talk delivered on the night after the Sabbath, 20 Kislev 5717 (November 24, 1956), the second day celebrating the festival of the nineteenth of Kislev,

> This is the level of the Jew, who is called "Israel," according to the verse "for you have striven with beings divine and human, and have prevailed" (Gen 32:29)—he conquers all the matters of nature, as this is the matter of Elohim, which is numerically equal to *ha-ṭeva*, and he elevates them to his level, beginning with the joining of the body, which is "dust from the earth" (Gen 2:7), to the soul, which is hewn from beneath the throne of glory and emanates from his thought and wisdom, blessed be he. And through this intermediary—Israel—the blending of the emanation of the blessing of the blessed holy One in the measured and delimited world is realized.[72]

The presumption that every Jew bears this distinction is precisely what fueled Schneerson's determination to spread orthodoxy to secular and estranged Jews. I see no evidence that the seventh Rebbe challenged the view of his predecessors, which restricted mystical gnosis to the Jews. It is true that Schneerson accepted the Maimonidean hypothesis that the future redemption entails the diffusion of the knowledge of God for Jews and non-Jews. But this does not efface the incongruity. Indeed, an unbiased examination of the material proves that precisely in contexts where Schneerson affirmed the eschatology of Maimonides, he was careful to emphasize as well the kabbalistic theme of Israel's meontological identity with God.[73] Even when Schneerson agrees to Maimonides's view that the scriptural notion that Adam was created in God's image (*ṣelem elohim*) refers to the faculty of reason, which presumably should not be ethnically exclusive, he qualifies this (in a manner reminiscent of Judah Loewe of Prague, the Maharal)[74] by demarcating a difference between the rational soul of the Jew and the rational soul of the non-Jew. Thus, for example, in the talk from 25 Sivan 5737 (June 11, 1977), Schneerson elaborated on discourses by the third and sixth masters,[75] explaining the dictum transmitted in the name of R. Aqiva, "Beloved is man [*adam*] that he was created in the image, an extra love is made known to him that he was created in the image, as it says 'in the image of God he made man' (9:6). Beloved is Israel for they are called sons of God, an extra love is made known to them that they are called sons of God, as it says 'you are sons of the Lord your God' (Deut 14:1)."[76]

> The rational soul (which is the matter of the divine image) in the Jew is not comparable to the rational soul in the Gentile . . . for the rational soul of the Jew is in a manner different than the rational soul in the human species . . . for Israel is called "sons of God," as they have a divine soul, and thus their rational soul is also in another manner than the rational soul in the human species. And the principle difference between them is that the intellect of the divine soul is humble . . . it can attain nullification, which is not so in the intellect of the world (the rational soul) that effectuates being . . . and it can lead to arrogance . . . when it acquires an intellectual matter.[77]

In the continuation, Schneerson emphasized that the body of the Jew is also to be distinguished from that of the non-Jew, insofar as only the former can be considered holy. The psychic and somatic superiority are due to the fact that Israel alone received the Torah, the "cherished vessel" (*keli ḥemdah*) by means of which the world is created.[78] The talk ends with a citation of Maimonides's eschatological vision of all nations worshipping the one God, but this in no way undermines the fundamental discrepancy of Jew and Gentile. On the contrary, what they will share in common highlights the gap that separates them. The same can be said about the endeavor to propagate the seven Noahide laws to non-Jews: its rests on the irreducible difference between Israel and the other nations, a point neglected by scholars who have previously weighed in on this issue. Hagiographic presentations of Schneerson's ideas notwithstanding, a critical evaluation must begin with acknowledging the basic precept of Ḥabad religious philosophy regarding the unassimilable singularity of the Jews vis-à-vis other ethnicities. One cannot leap ahead if one is not willing to step back.

Messianic Anthropos: Beyond Theopoetic Metaphoricization

One might contend that the seeds to undermine this perspective are found in Ḥabad teaching as well, since the supernal mindfulness is knowledge of the essence, which is characterized as the nondifferentiated light of the Infinite, a *coincidentia oppositorum* where there is no longer any basis to distinguish binaries, including that of the light and the darkness, Jacob and Esau, the Jew and the non-Jew. This state of indifference, however, is itself caught in the snare of ethnocentricity, and hence we would be more precise in rendering the Ḥabad approach as thinking of the non-Jew, the other to the Jew, as still a Jewish other, the other that is other to the other, which is precisely what makes any semblance of identity possible. I make no effort to defend or rationalize this conception of alterity, but I would suggest that there is a principle at work here that may have a wider resonance and relevance. We seek to recover from this admittedly constricted ideational matrix a logic that will preserve difference in sameness by keeping to the same difference. Without denying the demonstrably detrimental attitude that has informed Ḥabad's construction of the non-Jewish other, we still insist that the negative predilection has the capacity to yield a positive principle, indeed what may be called the quintessential ethical imperative of an egalitarian sociality: what secures our equality is our diversity.

Shneur Zalman ascribed this very characteristic to the adamic nature that is linked distinctively to the Jews. Speaking about the forms of the chariot envisioned by Ezekiel, he noted that the face of the lion was to the right and the face of the ox to the left (Ezek 1:10), "but in the aspect of the human there is no right or left, for it is their inner aspect that comprises them together, and therefore it is called *adam*, 'I will be likened to the most high' [*eddammeh le-elyon*] (Isa 14:14), that is, to the aspect of the supernal anthropos that is upon the throne, which is called the 'anthropos of emanation' [*adam de-aṣilut*]."[79] The divine anthropos is identified specifically as the Jew, but the face of the human is said to be beyond duality—situated neither to the right nor to the left because it comprises both left and right—and therefore the distinction between Jew and non-Jew must be surpassed in the discernment that the (non)Jew is the same to the other that is the same other.

As Shneur Zalman put it in another context,

> It is written "upon the semblance of the throne, there was the semblance of the appearance of a human" (Ezek 1:26), "the appearance of a human" [*ke-mar'eh adam*], through the register of the imagination [*be-kaf ha-dimyon*], for the way and order of the concatenation from world to world . . . is in the aspect of a human in three lines, the right and left hands, and the middle is the body. . . . And by bearing the throne, the beasts bear the appearance of a human that is "upon it from above" (Ezek 1:26), to the aspect of "for he is not human" [*ki lo adam hu*] (1 Sam 15:29), above the aspect and category of the concatenation, to draw down from there a new light to the aspect of the human that is upon the throne.[80]

The enthroned anthropos envisaged by the prophet figuratively symbolizes the manifestation of the infinite light in the structure of the worlds, but the light itself is beyond that form, indeed, it is the meta/figure, the figure without figure, the supernal anthropos (*adam ha-elyon*), the not-human (*lo adam*), which is "above the aspect of the anthropos" (*lema'lah mi-beḥinat adam*).[81] The boundless light is connected as well with the zoharic depiction of *Attiqa Qaddisha*, the highest dimension of the Godhead, as lacking any left side,[82] that is, "there is no division of gradations at all and therefore there are no changes there at all. And this is what Samuel said to Saul, 'The eternality of Israel does not deceive or have remorse' (1 Sam 15:29)."[83] It is important to heed the scriptural context: Samuel informs Saul that he cannot reclaim the monarchy from David, since the kingship of David, the promise of the messianic reign, derives from the aspect of the divine that is the "eternality of Israel" (*neṣaḥ yisra'el*), the aspect of the not-human (*lo adam*) that transcends the aspect of the human whence Saul derived his regal power. With this we come to what might certainly appear to be a grave inconsistency in Ḥabad thought. On the one hand, the light of the Infinite, which is called "not-human," is above the bifurcation of right and left[84]—a point exemplified as well by the claim that there is no distinction between the masculine donor and the feminine recipient (*she-ein sham beḥinat hitḥallequt mashpi'a u-meqabbel kelal*), a concurrence that is acclaimed to exceed rational comprehension[85]—but, on the other hand, it is only through the revelation of the Torah that there can be a disclosure of this light in the shape of the anthropos (*ṣiyyur adam*) that is peculiar to Israel, and, consequently, the attainment of the higher level in which the anthropomorphic depiction of the divine is surmounted is spearheaded solely by the Jewish people.[86]

That this is the implication of the eschatological awakening is proffered in a remarkable way in the following comment of Dov Baer:

> It is known that [the nature of the] human [*adam*] [is linked to] "I will be likened to the most high" [*eddammeh le-elyon*] (Isa 14:14), and the very opposite of this will be in the Messiah, about whom it is written, "My servant will be enlightened" [*yaskil avdi*] (Isa 52:13), and his root is in the essence of the light of the Infinite, the essential attributes above the aspect of the human, as its says "very" [*me'od*] (Gen 1:31). Nonetheless, it will be precisely in the aspect of the human, for presently the aspect of the human comes in the aspect of the delimited consciousness [*hagbalah de-moḥin*] of *Abba* and *Imma* in *Ze'eir Anpin*, in a diminished state [*be-qaṭnut*], and *Arikh Anpin* is also in the aspect of constriction [*ṣimṣum*] vis-à-vis the essence, but in the future-to-come, all the lights of the ten *sefirot*, which are verily in the essence, will appear in the aspect of the human that is without boundary at all [*beḥinat adam she-hu beli gevul kelal*], as it is written about him, "[You are] My son, I have fathered you this day" (Ps 2:7), just as he is in the substance and the essence in actuality [*kemo she-hu be-mahut we-aṣmut mammash*].[87]

In the premessianic epoch, the divine light assumes the shape of an anthropos, buttressed by the etymological derivation of *adam* from *eddammeh le-elyon*, a double-edged sword that cuts two ways—anthropomorphically, the quality of being human is to be assimilated within the essence beyond, although, theomorphically, what is beyond essence is imagined in human terms. The imaginal bodies, in and through which the light is incarnate, are the figural constructs (*parṣufim*) specified in some passages of the zoharic corpus and developed further in Lurianic kabbalah, the states of consciousness delineated as *Arikh Anpin*, *Abba*,

Imma, and *Ze'eir Anpin*, to which we should add *Nuqba*, the feminine counterpart, which for some reason is not specified here independently. In the diminished state—figuratively rendered as the exile of God, the exile of world, and the exile of human—the sefirotic light is fashioned in the imagination as an anthropos, in mythopoeic language that conjures the portrait of a divine family; in the messianic future, however, the light will appear in the "aspect of the human that is without boundary at all."

How are we to confabulate an anthropomorphic form that cannot be circumscribed in the periphery of any fixed borders? As expansive as one's imagination might be, this can be imagined only as unimaginable, the figure of the metafigure, the infinite essence that is the nonhuman.[88] The excess of this lack is encoded in the word *me'od*, in the refrain at the conclusion of the sixth day of creation, "and it was very good," *we-hinneh ṭov me'od* (Gen 1:31). From the fact that the word *me'od* has the same consonants as *adam*, we can deduce the double bind of the imagination: the possibility of expanding beyond the image of the human is communicated by the word that denotes the human image. Furthermore, we are told that the anthropos without dimensions, and, consequently, the representation that is incapable of representation, is linked to the Messiah, whose root is in the "essence of the light of the Infinite," which comprises the "essential attributes above the aspect of the human" (*middot ha-aṣmiyyim she-lema'lah mi-beḥinat adam*).[89] Schneerson extended this insight by noting that the rabbinic insistence that the Jews alone are called *adam* implies that they "are like one human that is above division [*lema'lah me-hitḥallequt*]. . . . Therefore, their integration [*hitkallelut*] is in a manner such that you do not find in them a beginning and an end."[90] There is a complete homology, then, between the essence, the Messiah, and the Jewish polity: just as the essence is devoid of essence, so the messianic constellation of Israel is above visual and verbal anthropomorphization. In the distended consciousness, we meander beyond the theological desire to imagine the divine as human, since the human is thought to be divine, at the margin of what it is to be human, the figure of the savior, and hence the need to specularize that human through the culturally specific prism of Israel is called into question, even though we must candidly admit that the masters of Ḥabad-Lubavitch have consistently maintained that only the soul-root of the Jew is in this facet of the divine that is the not-human. In the talk delivered on 11 Shevaṭ 5728 (February 10, 1968), [91] which was an explication of the eighteenth chapter of Yosef Yiṣḥaq's *Ba'ti le-Ganni*,[92] Schneerson (paraphrasing the aforementioned distinction that Shneur Zalman made between the attributes of kingship bestowed respectively upon Saul and David) remarked that the royalty of Saul is aligned with the aspect of the anthropos, that is, the representation of the divine in the theistic image of a human persona, whereas the royalty of David, which is the messianic potency, is rooted in the aspect of *Attiq*, or the interiority of *Keter*, the will that is "above light and disclosure," the dimension of the Godhead that "likewise is not in the category of the shape of the supernal anthropos" (*she-eino gam be-geder ṣiyyur adam ha-elyon*), but it is rather the "aspect of the not-human, which is above the elevation of the human as well" (*lo adam she-hu lema'lah gam me-ha-illuy de-adam*). Revisting this point in talk delivered on 11 Shevaṭ 5748 (January 30, 1988), which was an elucidation of the same chapter of *Ba'ti le-Ganni*, Schneerson noted that the aspect that is called *Attiq* is separate from the image of an anthropos—indeed the term itself connotes removal—but it is still linked to the aspect of the anthropos.[93] On the ladder of the contemplative ascent, it is necessary to climb from *Malkhut* to *Ze'eir Anpin*, and from *Ze'eir Anpin* to *Keter*, and from *Keter* to *Attiq*, and from *Attiq* to the summit of the Godhead that completely transcends the emanation, "since in the aspect of 'for he is not human' as well there is the matter of form" (*ki gam bi-veḥinat ki lo adam hu yeshno inyan shel ṣiyyur*).[94] The ascent culminates in an atheological showing, the disclosure of the concealment that is beyond figurative symbolization, the essence of the Infinite, the utter transcendence that is so entirely removed that it is removed from the very notion of removal, insofar as removal itself implies something from which to be removed, but the way to this anthropomorphic and theomorphic disfiguration—the human that is not-human and therefore the God that is not-God—is through the configuration of the divine anthropos that is limited to Israel. It is in this sense that the Torah is delegated the intermediary that connects the emanation and that which is above the emanation (*memuṣ'a bein lema'lah me-aṣilut we-aṣilut*).[95]

According to Shalom Dovber, as we discussed in chapter 2, the future vision is a "seeing of the substance itself," which is distinguished from ordinary prophetic vision, insofar as the latter is mediated through the anthropomorphic image.[96] Emulating Moses, the enlightened mind beholds the substance as it is in its insubstantiality; in this beholding, one takes hold of the aim of knowledge, which is to know that one does not know.[97] In the end, as many mystic visionaries have ascertained, to see the effulgence is to see the darkness, to comprehend that in the supernal light (*or elyon*)[98] the two are indistinguishable,[99] a vision that cannot be seen but in the seeing of its (un)seeing. As Shneur Zalman put it,

> That which is revealed is called "light" and that which is above disclosure is called "darkness." Accordingly, whatever is in the higher level is referred to in relation to us as darkness, but from above to below it is the opposite, for, regarding what is more revealed, the comprehension is more in the category of darkness vis-à-vis the light of the Infinite, blessed be he, in his essence and his glory, as it is written in the *Zohar,* with respect to the supernal Crown (*keter elyon*),[100] "Even though it is the resplendent light and the radiant light, it is black vis-à-vis the Cause of Causes," and everything is darkened before him.[101]

Referring to the same zoharic passage, the seventh Rebbe commented, "So it is with respect to the higher gradations, the closer one approaches to the aspect of the infinite essence [*aṣmut ein sof*], the more it is itself in the aspect of the nullification of existence [*beḥinat biṭṭul ha-meṣi'ut*] and in the aspect of darkness [*beḥinat ḥoshekh*]."[102] To attain this apophasis, the mind must venture past all that is implied in the motto repeatedly invoked by the seven Ḥabad masters, *adam eddammeh le-elyon*, that is, one must traverse the threshold of theism itself. The biblical phrase, accordingly, assumes a different meaning in the enlightened state: for the archetypal "human" (*adam*) to become like the "supernal One" (*elyon*), it is necessary that one become not-human (*lo adam*) through the eradication of one's will.[103] The quietistic divestiture of self by which the human becomes divine corresponds to ridding the imagination of images that configure the divine as human. This is the intent of the ideal visualization of the essence without any garment: to see with no veil is to see that there is no seeing without a veil, but in this seeing the mind lets go of the fanciful urge to posit a face beyond the veil.

Redemption is characterized, accordingly, as the collapse of antinomies, conveyed in the Ḥabad lexicon as *zeh le'ummat zeh*, "this corresponding to this." Needless to say, this would include the blurring of the discord between Israel and the nations. When considered geopolitically, the ramifications of the coming of the Messiah would have to extend to all nations, a point that is regularly supported by reference to the verse "Strangers shall stand and pasture your flocks, aliens shall be your plowmen and vine-trimmers" (Isa 61:5). Since this boundary will be blurred, the Jews will be able to converse openly about the wisdom of the Torah, fulfilling the prophecy "For the land shall be filled with devotion to the Lord, as the water covers the sea" (Isa 11:9).[104] Schneerson's view, as he explicitly notes, is based on the opinion of Maimonides that the sages and prophets have not desired the days of Messiah for any material or political power, but only so that "they would be free [to study] Torah and its wisdom" and on account of which "they would merit the life of the world-to-come."[105] Schneerson also follows the conjecture of Maimonides that at that time there will be peace among the nations and "the occupation of the whole world will be solely to know the Lord, and, therefore, Israel [will consist of] great sages, who know the concealed matters and who comprehend the knowledge of their Creator in accordance with human potential."[106] Prima facie, it seems that the seventh Rebbe did affirm a universal knowledge of the divine that effectively would do away with the distinction between Jew and non-Jew. Upon closer examination, however, it becomes apparent that the chasm separating Israel and the nations is not entirely bridged. Just as we noted above that the Alter Rebbe accredited the righteous Gentiles with the ability to discern the existence, but not the essence, of the divine, so the seventh Rebbe appropriates the Maimonidean language to articulate that the eschaton is marked by such an unobstructed epiphany that even the non-Jews will know that the corporeal existence of the world is not ontically autonomous. Schneerson explains the Maimonidean position by linking the messianic description to the metaphysical tenet established at the beginning of the *Mishneh Torah*, all things in heaven and earth are said to exist on account of the truth of the existence of the First Existent (*maṣuy ri'shon*),[107] which he interprets panentheistically. In spite of the significant level of philosophical attainment that Schneerson assigns to the non-Jew, to know that there is naught but God and hence to perceive the elevation of the world to divinity, a critical difference is still maintained: only the Jew is capable of knowing the gradation of Godliness that utterly transcends the ontic chain, the aspect of the divine that has no connection to the universe, the name YHWH, encrypted acrostically in the opening words of the Maimonidean code, *yesod ha-yesodot we-amud ha-ḥokhmot*, "the foundation of all foundations and the pillar of all wisdoms," the essence that is beyond the taxonomy of the First Existent. There is no intimation of the possibility of non-Jews achieving this (un)knowing, which is contingent on the absolute annihilation (*takhlit ha-biṭṭul legamrei*) of the self, a state of monopsychic absorption in the light of the essence, which is instantiated in the Torah, akin to that of the Jews.[108]

In line with the *via negativa* of Maimonides, the Ḥabad interpretation of the salvational wisdom, as we have seen, implies that the objective of Jewish monotheism is to divest the mind of the theopoetic temptation to portray God anthropomorphically and anthropopathically.[109] However, at play as well is the kabbalistic depiction of the Infinite as the coincidence of opposites, an idea that stretches momentously beyond the perspective of the medieval sage, especially in the challenge it presents to the axiological dualism, which justifies and sustains the sociopolitical reality of the Jews as an autonomous community. Indeed, Maimonides is on record as affirming that in the messianic age nothing of the natural order will be obliterated.[110] It is plausible to theorize that this applies to the law of noncontradiction, for the very concept of nature accepted by Maimonides would not be intelligible unless we presume this principle. I see no reason to suppose that Maimonides thought this constraint would be abrogated in the future.

In Ḥabad soteriology, this law is surpassed in the identification of opposites, to the point that we can no longer differentiate between good and evil. The eschatological surplus is encapsulated in the rabbinic designation of the future as a "world that is entirely good" (*olam she-kullo ṭov*)[111]—"goodness" is no longer a correlative term, as it has incorporated evil within itself. The position of the previous Ḥabad masters as regards the dissemination of the secrets in messianic times, the revelation of the new Torah, is thus paired by Schneerson with the Maimonidean opinion that knowledge of God will fill the land and all the nations shall come to listen to the Messiah, yielding the claim that the mysteries will be expounded publicly, presumably even before non-Jews.[112] Not only is the broadcasting of the esoteric seen as a propadeutic to accelerate the redemption, but redemption is depicted as the wholesale dispersion of the mysteries of the Torah, an overt breaking of the seal of esotericism. But it is precisely with respect to the explicit claims about the disclosure of secrets that the scholar must be wary of being swayed by a literalist approach that would take the seventh Rebbe at his word. There is no suggestion of willful deceit on the part of Schneerson, of an intention to falsify, but there is an appeal to the wisdom of the tradition pertaining to the hermeneutic duplicity of secrecy: the secret will no longer be secret if and when the secret will be exposed to have been nothing more than the secret that there is a secret. To discover the secret that there is no secret is the ultimate secret that one can neither divulge without withholding nor withhold without divulging.

Blessed Is Mordecai and Cursed Is Haman: Mystical Transvaluation of Tradition

Given the preponderance of textual evidence to support the radical separation of Jew and non-Jew, the exceptions are all the more noteworthy. In presenting the literary verification of this view, it should be borne in mind that one cannot make assumptions about actual behavior purely on the basis of doctrine. To mention one anecdote, let us consider the entry in Schneerson's diary from August 1932. He reports having been walking with his father-in-law when a funeral of a non-Jew was taking place. Schneerson writes that when the coffin passed by the sixth Rebbe tipped his hat and said, "this is for the sake of honoring the dead."[113] A small gesture, to be sure, but one that speaks loudly and should give us pause when we think about the causal relation between official ideology and social practice. Notwithstanding the view expressed in *Tanya* and reiterated in countless other sources, reverence for the deceased body of a Gentile was in order at that moment, and Yosef Yiṣḥaq obliged. I do not mean to insinuate that ideas have no part in shaping behavior, but I am proposing that one must be open to the possibility of a disjuncture.

As it happens, that possibility looms most conspicuously at the precipice to which the pietistic path leads, the ideal of equanimity whereby the dissonance between good and evil is defused. The collusion of opposites patently presents a theoretical challenge, since the overcoming of binaries in the Infinite would belie the rigid dualism separating Jew and non-Jew that is presupposed by the halakhic standpoint. An interesting passage that displays the sensitivity to this issue is found in Dov Baer's *Sha'arei Orah*: "The joy of Purim is above the concatenation, and this is the matter of 'until one does not know'[114] . . . the intention is not that there is equanimity [*hishtawwut*], God forbid, for Haman is forever cursed and Mordecai the Jew blessed, but the principle of the matter in the gradation that is above the concatenation is the replica of the gradation that is above wherein the darkness is like the light."[115] The festival of Purim, as we discussed in chapter 1, is distinguished from other holidays insofar as the joy commensurate to it relates symbolically to that which is beyond all differentiation and particularity, a level of attainment that is captured in the talmudic dictum that one must drink enough wine on Purim so that it is no longer possible to distinguish between "cursed is Haman" and "blessed is Mordecai," expressions that are numerically equivalent. Dov Baer recoils, however, at the categorical effacing of boundaries implied by this tradition, and thus he underscores that equanimity, the indifference that is the defeat of all difference, is not the intention of the ritual practice ordained by the rabbinic authorities. As he emphasizes elsewhere,[116] the root of the Jew is "from the perspective of the essence of the Infinite in actuality," but the root of the idolatrous nations is "from the first contraction [*ha-ṣimṣum ha-ri'shon*], which is after the withdrawal of the light, and it is comprised in the luminosity that is called the vacant place [*maqom panuy*], as this is the source for the root of the aspect of separation and division." The possibility of messianic rectification for the non-Jews in the end is secured by the fact that a trace (*reshimu*) of the light remained concealed in that space in the beginning. In the future, souls of the non-Jews will be restored to the vacant place, which is the void (*tohu*) and the emptiness (*efes*). This is the esoteric meaning of the verse "All of the nations are as naught [*ke-ayin*] in relation to him, he considers them as if they were from the void and the nothing [*me-efes wa-tohu*]" (Isa 40:17). Here philological attunement is critical: the very same words used to designate the essence that is prior to the withdrawal are used to designate the vacuum that arises as a consequence of the withdrawal. Dov Baer, however, is careful to distinguish the two: the former is the "true divine nothing" (*ayin ha-elohi ha-amitti*), which is the "source of everything" (*meqora de-kholla*), the "true being" (*yesh ha-amitti*), whereas the latter is the "actual nothing" (*ayin mammash*), which appears "as if it were not in existence at all" (*ke-illu eino bi-meṣi'ut kelal*). While this distinction may seem pedantic, it is the basis for upholding the rabbinic claim that the term *adam* applies exceptionally to Israel, a philological point that, as we have seen, exerted a profound influence on kabbalistic anthropology. The non-Jew, even when purified, can only reach the level of incorporation into the externality of the human form (*hitkallelut de-adam be-ḥiṣoniyyut*), which is associated with Elohim, the attribute of judgment, but not the interior aspect (*beḥinah penimit*), signified by YHWH, the attribute of mercy, since they were separated from the "essential unity" at the time of the first contraction and they derive from the void that is "considered as if it were not in actuality" (*she-ke-lo mammash ḥashiv*), the negative that dissimulates as the negative, which is to be distinguished from the prerogative of the Jew to affirm the negative in its fecund positivity. This is the kabbalistic intent of the rabbinic teaching that the term *adam* applies most properly to the Jews and not to the idolatrous nations.

Something of the initial break—the inaugural division within the indivisible, which engenders the beginning that conceals the origin—cannot be rectified. Hence, even though the future is described as a time when all the holy sparks will be liberated from the demonic shells and evil will be annihilated from the world, an element of contrariness will endure: Haman, who is from the seed of Amaleq, will always be cursed and Mordecai the Jew will always be blessed. What, then, does the numerical equivalence of the two expressions convey? In the essence above the concatenation of worlds, and this includes the first act of contraction, opposites are truly identical—darkness is indistinguishable from the light that is luminous to the extent that it is dark, which is to say, the light that is neither luminous nor dark. However, in the mind of the Mitteler Rebbe, and this should not be viewed as idiosyncratic, the possibility of attaining this gradation is assigned peculiarly to the Jewish people. As conceptually difficult and spiritually limiting as this may sound, we must accept that the mystical logic advanced by Ḥabad allows us to speak of a *universal singularity* only if we are willing to admit that the universal, which entails the effacing of boundaries, is the specific dispensation of one ethnic faction. The messianic calling of the Jew, then, would be to sponsor the truth that Jew and non-Jew are identical in virtue of being different. In a manner resonant with Levinas, ethnocentricism is the condition that secures the viability of a genuine alterity, since the notion of an "absolutely universal," the principle that grounds the sense of respect for and responsibility toward the irreducible other, "can be served only through the particularity of each people, a particularity named enrootedness."[117] Simply put, otherness is what makes the other the same; what I share with the other is that we are different. An obvious point of divergence between the approach of Ḥabad and that of Levinas would turn on the question of ontology. Although Levinas was conversant with at least some kabbalistic sources that demonstrate affinity with the Ḥasidic orientation, including, ironically enough, the *Nefesh ha-Ḥayyim* of Ḥayyim of Volozhyn,[118] the disciple of the premier Lithuanian opponent to East European Ḥasidism, Elijah ben Solomon, the Gaon of Vilna, he squarely rejected the ontologizing of Israel's election, which renders the distinctiveness of the Jews a matter of inborn nature.This is not to deny that Levinas spoke of the "ultimate essence of Israel," a "carnal essence" that is "prior to the freedom that will mark its history" and that "derives from its innate predisposition to involuntary sacrifice, its exposure to persecution." The "original responsibility" for the Other (*l'Autre*), therefore, is rooted in this "invisible universality," which is borne singularly by the nation that embodies suffering in the world.[119] I concur with the critique of Judith Butler that, for Levinas, "the Jew" is a "category that belongs to a culturally constituted ontology (unless it is the name for access to the infinite itself), and so if the Jew maintains an 'elective' status in relation to ethical responsiveness, then Levinas fully confuses the preontological and the ontological."[120] The ascription of the unparalleled ethical role to the Jewish people based on being exclusively persecuted is problematic, and, regrettably, at times this has been used to justify persecution of others on the part of Jews, rationalizing acts of aggression in the name of self-defense.[121] Despite the validity of this criticism, it is still legitimate to distinguish the connotation of the expressions *ontological* and *preontological* as they relate to Levinas and their connotation when applied to Ḥabad. On Levinasian terms, chosenness is a function of acting, a matter of historical destiny shaped by temporal contingencies, not an eternal condition of transhistorical being; for the Ḥabad masters, by contrast, Israel's election is precisely the latter, a feature of the inherent ipseity of the Infinite, and thus ethics cannot be severed from ontology. We can propose a coincidence of opposites in the absence of opposites to coincide, but this only reinforces the othering of the other. When there is no other, the other persists as not (an)other, and therefore it is not sufficient to envision a unity in which there is neither one nor the other.

The point is illustrated convincingly with another passage from Dov Baer. In discussing the nature of the future, he observes that many of the critical verses that speak of the eschatological vision (Isa 2:2, 11:9, 40:5, Zeph 3:9) imply that the nations of the world are included. In chapter 4, we had the occasion to mention a passage from Shneur Zalman in which he quotes some of these same texts, whence he concludes without qualification that the inequity between Israel and the seventy nations of the world will be abolished in the messianic epoch.[122] The seventy nations or, more specifically, the seventy archons attached to them, correspond to the seventy powers on the side of holiness, which are connected as well to the number of persons that were Jacob's issue (Exod 1:5). As a consequence of the obliteration of evil, the seventy forces will be elevated to their source, the seven supernal attributes from *Ḥesed* to *Malkhut*, and the corresponding seven kings of the world of chaos (or the seven primordial kings of Edom) that fell in the breaking of the vessels will be rectified, an idea that is linked orthographically to the suspended *ayin* in the last word of the expression *yekharsemennah ḥazir mi-ya'ar*, "the pig of the wild will gnaw at it" (Ps 80:14),[123] the letter, incidentally, that marks the middle of this biblical book.[124] In some contexts, Dov Baer seems to posit a view similar to his father, and thus he characterizes the future as the unconditional destruction of every source of unholiness and the uncompromising purification of evil. The total transformation of darkness into light is the condition that fosters the indiscriminate manifestation of the divine presence to all flesh, Jews and non-Jews alike.[125] Occasionally, however, he insists otherwise. In one passage, for instance, he declares that

> there will still be a great variance between Israel and the nations of the world, for with regard to Israel it is said, "you, O Lord, will be seen in plain sight" (Num 14:14) . . . for the Jews will see with their eyes [*ayin be-ayin*] the essence of the

> light of the Infinite, blessed be he, in actuality, without any garment of concealment at all, but rather as it is above in actuality, it will come to them in the disclosure below. Therefore, the worship of Israel then will be in the aspect of the enlarged consciousness [*moḥin de-gadlut*], insofar as they will be sustained from the splendor of the essence of the light of the Infinite in actuality, as their contemplation will be of the essence in actuality, which is above the concatenation of transcendence and immanence.[126]

What is given with one hand is taken away with the other, or, to be even more precise, the hand that gives is the hand that takes away: the Jew alone is capable of contemplating the essence within which the dissimilarity between Jew and non-Jew is transcended. The identity of difference is apperceived through the speculum of the difference of identity.

Incongruous as it may seem, the ultimate vision casts a spotlight on the blind spot in the system on the whole. By dint of its own paradoxical logic, the attempt on the part of the Mitteler Rebbe to avoid saying that the disproportion between the other nations and Israel is completely redressed is not viable. We could even grant the exception Dov Baer made with respect to Amaleq, an idea repeated by other masters of the Ḥabad tradition,[127] including the seventh Rebbe,[128] for this force derives its power from the demonic shell that stands in opposition to the attribute of knowledge (*da'at*)—that is, the force of Haman or Amaleq signifies the lower and nefarious form of knowledge, the spirit of folly, disbelief, and lust that covers the divine spark, which is to be distinguished from but yet correlated with the supernal knowledge that is beyond knowledge.[129] Amaleq is designated the paramount of the evil attributes, as it personifies the qualities of insolence and arrogance, a deportment compared figuratively to "royalty without a crown" (*malkhuta be-lo taga*),[130] the antithesis of diffidence and modesty, which are the means by which one becomes an adequate container to hold that which cannot be contained.[131] As Shneur Zalman already argued, Amaleq is described on the part of Balaam, the prophet of Moab, as the first and the last of the nations (Num 24:20), which correspond in the demonic side respectively to the divine qualities of transcendence and immanence, and, precisely on account of this correlation, this nation will be unreservedly destroyed in the messianic future.[132] The Alter

Rebbe, however, was not consistent; he also spoke of the future as a time when "Amaleq, too, would be purified, since it would be transformed from the ultimate something to the ultimate nothing." Curiously, in the continuation of this very passage, he claims that there is no rectification for Amaleq, and hence the scriptural mandate is to erase his name to the point of "complete extermination" (*biṭṭul legamrei*).[133] It is reasonable to surmise that the inconsistency is not due to scribal emendations but to the complexity of this issue, the realization that affirming the possibility of the rectification of Amaleq poses a challenge not only to the archaic notion that this nation, the earthly manifestation of the demonic, is the nemesis to Israel in the world that must be extinguished[134] but also to the later rabbinic exegetical tradition (linked to Exod 17:16) that neither the name of God nor his throne is complete until the memory of Amaleq is expunged,[135] an idea that had considerable influence as well in the history of kabbalah from a relatively early period.[136]

Following the lead of his father,[137] Dov Baer distinguished between two aspects of Haman, the Haman of the shell, which is the insolence and arrogance that will be obliterated, and the Haman of holiness that is salvaged, which is the exaltation and elevation of the heart in the worship of God.[138] In another context, Dov Baer addresses the point even more plainly: the chief of the seven evil nations is identified as Amaleq, which is said to have an anthropomorphic form (*ṣiyyur adam*) that parallels the pattern of the *sefirot*; these seven attributes, we are told, are not "entirely evil," for if one were to remove the shell of Amaleq, which is their source of vitality,[139] they could be transformed into good. Commenting on the biblical pronouncement that Amaleq will "perish forever" (Num 24:20), Dov Baer remarked that "it is not purified at all until the spirit of impurity is eradicated." He undoubtedly wanted to have his cake and eat it too, so to speak, to affirm that Amaleq is the embodiment of an irredeemable evil and yet to insist that there is no evil that does not have the capacity of being redeemed. As he says in the continuation, there is a debate between one group that speaks of the model as bearing iniquity (*nose awon*) and a second group that speaks of conquering iniquity (*kovesh awon*); the former refers to the actualization (*hitpa'alut*) of the attribute in its essence, which is not complete evil, and thus there is always the possibility of transforming desire into something divine, whereas the latter refers to the garbing of the attribute in thought, speech, and action, which is a complete evil, and therefore it must be eliminated.[140]

The views regarding Amaleq correspond to the two approaches to the problem of evil that can be traced to at least the thirteenth century, the monistic and the dualistic; the former proclaims that, in the end, the evil is restored to the good, since it emerged therefrom at the beginning, whereas the latter forecasts an obliteration of evil, even as it admits that the ultimate source for evil is the good.[141] To maintain that the disparity between Haman and Mordecai persists makes sense if we assume that the people of Amaleq are an exception to the messianic vision of the purification and transformation of all the nations; their fate is one of annihilation—an idea linked exegetically to the scriptural directive to the Israelites to wipe out the memory of Amaleq (Exod 17:14, Deut 25:19) as well as to the aforementioned oracle of Balaam, "A leading nation is Amaleq; but its fate is to perish forever" (Num 24:20)—which suggests an aspect of incorrigible evil. As the fourth Lubavitcher Rebbe put it, Amaleq is the "evil empire" that cannot be purified, and hence "its demolition is its rectification" (*shevirato zehu tiqquno*).[142] One could make the argument that the disclosure of the light of the Infinite is facilitated by the destruction of Amaleq at the end, for this is the venomous complement to the ideal of nullification, which is the unequaled calling of Israel. That is, in order for there to be the revelation of the divine (*gilluy elohut*), the force that represents the concealment of the divine (*hester elohut*) must be exterminated.[143] Even if we accept this, however, it would have to be admitted that there is a salient distinction between the two types of *biṭṭul*, the one is an actual abolition with a negative connotation and the other is the mystical trope of diminution.[144] In the final analysis, it is not coherent to say, on the one hand, that the messianic future heralds the unconcealment of the essence in which opposites will be overcome and to aver, on the other hand, that the non-Jew, or at the very least the segment of the non-Jewish population represented by Amaleq, is incapable constitutionally of apprehending this truth. Indeed, in spite of the concerted effort on the part of the Ḥabad masters to uphold difference in the face of the indifferent, it is precisely in this component of their mystical scheme that one can unearth the seeds for the undoing of its axio-ontological framework.

I will cite and analyze a passage from Shalom Dovber that is illustrative of the conceptual point. The fifth Lubavitcher Rebbe explains that the verse "For then I will make the nations pure of speech" (Zeph 3:9) applies to the eschatological future,[145] for then the evil forces

> will be entirely transposed in the essence of their being . . . the evil will be transformed into good . . . and the disclosure will be in the aspect of *Malkhut*-that-is-within-*Malkhut*, the aspect that is the very last in *Malkhut*. . . . In the future, when there will be a disclosure of the aspect of *Malkhut* within *Malkhut* itself, then those who have no nullification at all, that is, they have no divine sentiment by which they would be aroused and elevated to the aspect of running [to and fro] and the attachment [to the Infinite]. . . by means of the disclosure of the future, they will be elevated and comprised within the holiness.[146]

The contrast between present and future is depicted here specifically from the angle of the transformation of the status of the non-Jew. In the present, even at the most felicitous time, such as the reign of Solomon, when the Jerusalem Temple was constructed, the evil forces persist in opposition to the good, and thus the nations do not have the facility, or, literally, the "divine feeling" (*hergesh elohi*), to be aroused and to ascend to the Infinite. In the future, however, there will be a disclosure of the "kingship-that-is-within-the-kingship" (*malkhut she-be-malkhut*),[147] a phrase that signifies the terminal aspect of the final gradation, the outermost limit, one might say, which leads one back to the uppermost limit, the beginning, the aspect of the "kingship-that-is-within-the-kingship-of-the-Infinite" (*malkhut she-be-malkhut de-ein sof*),[148] the aptitude for alterity in the essence that subsumes alterity under the stamp of alterity, the essence that is void of essence. When this aspect will be disclosed, it will summon the restoration of evil to good, which, in turn, will empower non-Jews, the imprint of the other, to rise spiritually, to be bound, as the Jews, to holiness through the sacrifice of egocentricity (*biṭṭul ha-yesh*), to fulfill the infinite will, marked metaphorically by the description of the motion of the beasts seen by Ezekiel, running hither and thither. Unquestionably, this portends a trespassing of boundaries, a degree of integration that compels the disintegration of Israel's preeminence.

The potential of the messianic politics that may be culled from this text (and from Ḥabad thought generically) is such that the supreme anthropos is a third term between Jew and non-Jew, that is, the human that is both and thus neither Jew nor non-Jew. In the continuation of the discourse, the RaShaB adds that the radical change of the future can also be expressed in terms of "the corporeal becoming divine in actuality" (*yihyeh ha-gashmi elohut mammash*), which comes about "by means of the aspect of *Malkhut*-that-is-within-*Malkhut*, for this is the aspect of the faculty of the agent in that which is acted upon, for it is concealed and it is garbed in the aspect of actual being. Thus, by means of the disclosure in the aspect of *Malkhut*-that-is-within-*Malkhut*, the corporeal will be in the aspect of divinity in actuality."[149] Significantly, attributing to the non-Jew the demeanor that is normally reserved for the Jew is parallel to the transubstantiation of corporeality into divinity, the mystery of the concretization of the divine light in the material substratum, expressed in stock medieval philosophical terms[150] as the potency of the agent being present in that which is acted upon (*koaḥ ha-po'el ba-nif'al*),[151] the manifestation of the essence of the light (*gilluy or be-aṣmuto*) by its "being hidden and garbed in the aspect of actual being" (*mit'allem u-mitlabbesh bi-veḥinat ha-yesh be-fo'al*). As I have argued in the preceding chapters, this does not imply a reduction of one term to the other; the statement that "the corporeal will be in the aspect of divinity in actuality" (*yihyeh ha-gashmi bi-veḥinat elohut mammash*) is neither pantheistic nor acosmic; what it does denote is the panpsychic phenomenon referred to as the "wondrous enigma" (*hafle wa-fele*),[152] the invisible assuming the spectral of visibility,[153] a coincidence of opposites wherein the identity of God and world, the mental and the material, is determined in the sameness of their difference. Similarly, with regard to the relationship of Jew and non-Jew: the one, as the other, is not other in virtue of being other.

Beyond the River: Transcendence and the Singular Universal

Much evidence can be adduced from the writings and discourses of the seventh Rebbe that confirms his conformity to the conception of alterity outlined in the previous section. Like his predecessors, he ascribed to the Jews a unique role in the messianic assignment to redeem the world, often expressed in the traditional liturgical idiom, "to rectify the world in the kingdom of the Almighty" (*letaqqen olam be-malkhut shaddai*),[154] and thus he, too, imagined an end-time in which the gulf separating Jew and non-Jew would be appreciably narrowed.[155] It is particularly the proliferation of the study of the interiority of the Torah on the part of the Jews—to the point that there will not remain even one Jew who is not acquainted with the teaching of Ḥasidism—that facilitates the eschatological change in the status of the non-Jew.[156] The cosmological underpinning of the apocalyptic sensibility is transparent enough: the world is a "unified reality," since it was created by a "singular and united" God, and therefore "all human beings and all the things in the world are bound to each other."[157] Schneerson was, no doubt, influenced by (and on occasion even directly cites)[158] the words of Maimonides from the uncensored version in the section on the laws of kingship toward the end of his halakhic compedium. According to this text, Jesus and Mohammed are described as being entrusted with the chore of "paving the way for the messianic king, to prepare the world in its entirety to worship the Lord together, as it says, 'For then I will make the nations pure of speech' (Zeph 3:9)."[159] This biblical verse is invoked by Schneerson to mark the disruption of the partition that separates the Jew and non-Jew; in the future, all the nations, even the sparks that are presently submerged in the depths of darkness, shall be restored to the light of holiness.[160] Departing from Maimonides, the Ḥabad approach privileges Judaism as the agent to purify the other two Abrahamic faiths, the attribute of judgment associated with Edom (Christianity) and the attribute of mercy associated with Ishmael (Islam).[161] Be that as it may, if we take seriously Schneerson's insistence that the one who is truly pious (*ḥasid amitti*) has no concern for boundaries,[162] it follows that the spiritual ideal would necessarily entail venturing beyond the discordant demarcations of the law. As he put it in a talk from 12 Tammuz 5713 (June 25, 1953), "Since the root of the disclosure of the Messiah is from the aspect that is above boundary, it follows that the emanation below in the world will also be in the manner of unity and the lack of division—and thus the action of the Messiah will be in the manner of rectifying the world completely to worship the Lord together, as it says, 'For then I will make the nations pure of speech, so that they all invoke the Lord by name and serve him with one accord' (Zeph 3:9), and as it says, 'And the Lord will be king over all the earth; in that day there shall be one Lord with one name' (Zech 14:9)."[163]

I spoke a moment ago of disruption of the partition and not its dismantling, for, as I have already clarified, Schneerson did not abandon entirely the ethnocentrism of his predecessors. It would be intellectually misleading to say that his teachings are exempt from the prejudicial ontology of the kabbalistic tradition or that he was unaware of the potentially subversive repercussions of the messianic characterization of the infinite essence. Earlier I noted that the special connection of the Jew to that essence is linked etymologically to the title *ivri*, which denotes the one who dwells on the other shore, the shore beyond the river. But if that shore is a metaphor for the division beyond divisions—the shore, that is, without a shoreline—then it must be the source of both Jewish and non-Jewish souls. The point was made by Schneerson in the following comment on Josh 24:2 (or, more accurately, on the section of the traditional Passover Haggadah in which this verse is cited) from a talk delivered the second night of Passover, 16 Nisan 5720 (April 12, 1960):

> The matter of the river is what is written, "And the river goes forth from Eden to water the garden" (Gen 2:10), for Eden is the aspect of *Ḥokhmah*, and the river is the aspect of *Binah*, and this is the matter of *Maḥashavah*, for just as the waters of the river never cease, so thought does not stop, and it flows perpetually. However, the root of the souls are above the aspect of *Maḥashavah*, and this is what is written "your forefathers lived beyond the river," that is, above the aspect of the river. And this is also the explanation of the saying that "Israel arose in thought,"[164] "arose" precisely, for they are in the highest aspect of thought. This is also what is written in the *Zohar* on the verse "On the day of the first fruits" (Num 28:26), for, of all the nations of the world, Israel was the most ancient and the first fruits of the blessed holy One,[165] and the meaning of "ancient" [*qadmonim*] is that their source is in the primeval thought of the primordial anthropos [*maḥashavah ha-qedumah de-adam qadmon*]. Indeed, the dictum of the Maggid[166] that the primeval thought of the primordial anthropos is the aspect of universal light (the universal crown) that comprises all the concatenation equanimously [*or kelali* (*keter kelali*) *ha-kolelet kol ha-hishtalshelut be-hashwwa'ah aḥat*] is well known. It follows that there is also the place for the nations of the world,[167] and hence it says that [the Jews] were in the aspect of first fruits, for in the primordial anthropos they were in the highest aspect, in the aspect of the interiority of the primordial anthropos. And even higher, the source of the souls is in the aspect of the letters that are in

> the essence of the light of the Infinite before the withdrawal, according to the saying[168] "he engraved engravings in the supernal luster."[169]

Contextually, the biblical description of the forefathers of Israel having resided "beyond the river" refers to the Euphrates, but it is interpreted mystically as an allusion to the innermost essence, the being-event beyond the concatenation of the chain of becoming, the alterity of alterity, one might say, the other par excellence, the other above any and every specification and therefore other vis-à-vis its own otherness. Since this essence is, according to the locution transmitted in the name of the Maggid of Międzyrzecz, the "universal light" that contains the multiplicity of differentiated beings in a nondifferentiated oneness, it must be the source of both Jew and non-Jew. The paradoxical truth may be elicited from the fact that, on the one hand, it is Teraḥ, Abraham's non-Hebrew father, who occupied the position beyond the river, and yet, on the other hand, being so positioned is proffered as the distinctive disposition of the Hebrew. The non-Jew inhabits the place reserved for the Jew.[170] Dialogically, the other to the other secures the irreducibility of the other. The essence, therefore, is demarcated as the "impossibility of impossibilities" (*nimna ha-nimna'ot*), since it bears opposites (*nose hafakhim*) in a manner that defies the logic of noncontradiction.[171] Schneerson stays faithful to the teaching of the previous masters, however, going back to the Alter Rebbe, by insisting that even in this indiscriminate essence a discrimination can and must be made between Jew and non-Jew: the ontological root for the soul of Israel is located in the highest aspect of the essence, which is designated the "primeval thought of the primordial anthropos" and the "letters that are in the essence of the light of the Infinite."

As contradictory and inscrutable as this may seem, the path of Ḥabad leads us notionally to posit that in the place of indifference, where opposites collide, a difference can still be made, the paradox conveyed by the arresting image of letters in the infinite essence.[172] We touched on this theme briefly in chapter 1, and here it is only necessary to underscore that Israel is distinguished to the extent that it is rooted in the primeval thought, indeed, identical with the primordial Torah, which is the light of the Infinite. The Jew, in other words, is the sign of difference within indifference, the consummate mark of the other, the other to the other, the singular universal. The possibility of messianic rectification, and the universal singularity implied thereby, is predicated on the paradoxical emplacement of the non-Jew in the light of the essence, but in such a way as to safeguard the inequality with the Jew. The "spiritual vocation" of the Jew is not in principle open to all, as it has been recently argued, and even the phenomenon of conversion, which ostensibly challenges this assumption or at the very least mitigates against a simplistic biological explanation for the inequity of Jew and non-Jew,[173] is possible because of the ontological difference. I consent to the contention that conversion is an important trope to articulate a critical aspect of the ecstatic experience. I do not think, however, that it alleviates the imbalance between the respective somatic and pneumatic conditions of the Jew and non-Jew. Such a claim fails to take into account either the mechanics of conversion or the contours of embodiment as they are understood generally in kabbalistic sources and particularly in the thought of the Ḥabad masters. I have already discussed the latter at great length in chapter 3 and here I will only reiterate that the conception of body affirmed in Lubavitch thought is semiotic and not anatomic. If we understand embodiment in this hyperlinguistic sense, then it is accurate to inscribe the distinction between Jew and non-Jew physiologically. Apropos of the former, it can be said briefly that conversion does not involve undergoing a transubstantiation to become part of the other in relation to which it is the same, but rather a process of return, the restoration of the other to the same in relation to which it is the other.

In the talk delivered on 11 Shevaṭ 5718 (February 1, 1958), Schneerson refers to Ḥayyim Joseph David Azulai's observation that the talmudic expression[174] is the "convert who converts" (*ger she-nitgayyer*) rather than the "non-Jew who converts" (*goy she-nitgayyer*) to indicate that the soul of the convert was present at Mount Sinai, even though it may be many years before the actual conversion takes place.[175] Going considerably beyond this explanation, which builds on the rabbinic idea that the souls of all converts were present together with all future generations of native-born Israelites at the Sinaitic theophany,[176] Schneerson insists that, technically speaking, "it is never the non-Jew who converts, for the one who converts does so because there is a holy spark within him, but for some reason it fell into a place to which it does not belong, and when he converts—after several prompts and attempts—then the holy spark is liberated and it joins the 'torch' and the 'light,' that is, the Torah, the commandments, and the blessed holy One."[177] The professed redundancy communicates that conversion is akin to a gnostic drama of emancipation of the spirit: the convert to Judaism is already a Jew—one is to become what one has formerly been—and thus conversion is a reversion, a release of the spark of holiness from its imprisonment in a foreign body.[178] To convert, therefore, is not to affirm a genuine sense of difference, to cross a boundary, but rather to reclaim part of the self that has been lost, to go back to one's origin.

Elaborating on this theme in the talk from 15 Shevaṭ 5743 (January 29, 1983), Schneerson noted that the adage "the convert who converts is compared to a newborn infant" (*ger she-nitgayyer ke-qaṭan she-nolad damei*) indicates that the convert is not an "entirely new reality" (*meṣi'ut ḥadashah legamrei*) but rather she or he is like a baby that existed prenatally before entering the world.[179] To state the matter in more technical terms, the souls of converts to Judaism are identified as the holy sparks that were scattered as a consequence of the breaking of the vessels in the seventy nations and displaced to the shell of *nogah*, the innermost of the four shells, the one in closest proximity to the core, the shell that consists of the duality of good and evil.[180] Using this criterion, converts are treated as lower than those who are thought to be Jewish indigenously—the root of the Jews is "in the aspect of truth," the central pillar or the attribute of compassion (*raḥamim*), and thus the destiny of Israel is to "receive the aspect of the truth of the light of the Infinite," whereas the root of the converts is "beneath the wings of the *Shekhinah*,"[181] the proselytes from Ishmael (Islam) derive from the right wing of mercy (*ḥesed*) and the ones from Edom (Christianity) from the left wing of judgment (*din*), and thus they receive the light only by way of the lateral lines.[182] In spite of this discrepancy, they are nevertheless implanted in the same divine substance.[183]

The prospect of conversion only reinforces the paradoxical attribution of difference within the indifference. As the seventh Rebbe put it in the talk on the second day of Pentecost, 7 Sivan 5720 (June 2, 1960), the Jews have the ability to ascend "to the root and source of the soul in the aspect that is above the chaos and the rectification, and hence, even though 'Esau was a brother to Jacob' (Mal 1:2), to the point that he does not know which of them he desires, 'he loved Jacob' in particular."[184] In a treatise prepared for 18 Elul 5727 (September 23, 1967), the day that commemorates the return of the sixth Rebbe to America, Schneerson analogously observed: "The matter of 'for [the Lord your God] loves you' (Deut

23:6) is the essential love of the blessed holy One for Israel, for even though in the gradation above the concatenation, it says 'and Esau was a brother to Jacob,' nevertheless 'he loved Jacob' particularly. And this is 'the Lord your God,' even though in YHWH, which is above (the light of the Infinite that is above the concatenation), everything is identical, still by means of a disclosure of the essential love of the blessed holy One for Israel, YHWH, which is above, is 'your God' precisely."[185] The Jewish soul, which is rooted in the essence, has the competency through ritual observance to transform curse into blessing and the power through repentance to turn iniquities into virtues. At an earlier point in this chapter,[186] I cited a passage in which this exploit is portrayed with special reference to Esau or Edom, depicted metaphorically as the pig, the animal that symbolizes the force of impurity paradigmatically. The salvific work of Israel in the "last exile," which is the "exile of Edom," is to purify the evil of Esau, so that the good hidden in him will be revealed, the "lights of chaos" (*orot de-tohu*), which is the source of his soul,[187] and, consequently, the pig will be restored to holiness. And yet, in the light of the Infinite, which is above binary opposition, God harbors a special love for Israel, which distinguishes them from all other nations.

The possibility of the destabilization, if not undermining, of traditional biases is implied in the vision of the messianic unity, the consciousness of the light that is beyond the division into light and dark. Let us consider a discourse delivered on 23 Elul 5712 (September 13, 1952).[188] The focus of the homily is the Holy of Holies in the Jerusalem Temple, the innermost sanctum, long regarded in the tradition to be the most sacred spot in the physical universe. This locale is dubbed the "place that is above place" and the "time that is above time"[189]—place and time cannot be conceptually differentiated or experientially disentangled. What is most remarkable is Schneerson's claim that the rabbinic tradition that the Torah scroll was placed in this space signifies the fact that holiness emanates outward from the inner core until it reaches the nations of the world wherever they are, so that they "will detect the time and place that are above time and place" (*zoln visn az zeman u-makom iz lemalah mi-zeman u-makom*). The text both affirms and subverts the dualism of the sanctity of Jews and the impurity of non-Jews; the latter are identified as "aliens" (*zarim*) on the outside, but they have the capacity to acquire the gnosis from within, to enter the Holy of Holies, the inner point, the *axis mundi*, where time is above time and place is above place.[190] From this relatively early date, the seventh Rebbe was pondering the manner in which non-Jews can participate in the holiness attributed to the Jews. The prophetic promise "and all flesh together shall see that the mouth of the Lord has spoken" (Isa 40:5) includes Jews and non-Jews.[191] This vision only intensified in the years of his leadership. The status of the nations of the world in Schneerson's messianic agenda has been discussed mostly from the vantage point of his crusade to inspire the non-Jews to fulfill the seven Noahide laws. In my judgment, the scope of this discussion should be expanded. The matter of the seven Noahide laws, while surely important, is not the only relevant topic to assess Schneerson's complex views on the subject of non-Jews.

In the final analysis, there is a tension in Schneerson that was never fully resolved. In a letter from 14 Av 5719 (August 18, 1959),[192] he discussed the uniqueness of the Sinaitic revelation for the Jewish people, contrasting it explicitly with Christianity and Islam. Addressing the more general question of the difference between Jews and non-Jews, he begins by referring to the ruling of Maimonides that the righteous of the nations have a portion in the world-to-come,[193] but he then goes on to acknowledge that Jews have more possibilities than the other nations. In response to the question why this is so, he confesses that it is not rationally comprehensible: "The main explanation is that we do not know the ways of the Creator and his reasons in a distinct manner." Having conceded this basic point, he does go on to compare the different nations to the various parts of a body, and just as the latter have discrete functions, so the former. The special role accorded Israel is justified by the comparison of Israel to the heart,[194] a position famously articulated by Judah Halevi in the twelfth century and one that greatly informed the kabbalistic sensibility through the ages.[195] The attempt to synchronize Maimonidean universalism and mystical individualism may be considered typical of the hybridity that shaped the seventh Rebbe's orientation throughout his life. I do not sense any appreciable modifications with the progression of time. The coalescence of these disparate intellectual currents produced a curious, and not altogether coherent, apocalyptic disbanding of the dyadic clash between Jew and non-Jew, but in such a way that the one remains other to the other, and thereby indifferently the same.

POSTFACE
In an Instant—Advent of the (Non)event

Yeder tog zugt epes . . . yeder tog iz a tog.

—FRIEDIKER REBBE

Let me forget about today until tomorrow.

—BOB DYLAN

I BEGAN TO WRITE THIS POSTFACE AS THE PREFACE, but soon realized what I initially conceived of as the entry was, in fact, the exit. To ascertain that wisdom may have been the point of this journey. It is reported that Simḥah Bunim of Przysucha (1765–1827) explained that the intent of the rabbinic dictum that "a person must always enter the synagogue through two doors"[1] is to learn that through one door we depart from this world (*olam ha-zeh*) and through the other door we enter the supernal world (*olam ha-elyon*).[2] The distinction between the two worlds may be a traditional taxonomy that has lost its relevance, at least if it is understood literally, but it is possible to translate the philosophic import of this insight into a contemporary register. Prayer, topographically, requires two doors, one to exit and the other to enter; symbolically, the former signifies the habitual frame of ordinary-mindedness and the latter an alternative state of transcendental awareness, the openness to being open to what remains open precisely because there is no-what to open. Reversing the commonsense order, the first portal through which one enters is the way of departure, and the second through which one departs is the way of entry; the wise of heart, however, know that the way in and the way out are indifferently the same.

Messianic Hope and the Truth of Untruth

In a celebrated passage from his commentary on Judah Halevi's poem *yonat reḥoqim naggeni heṭivi*, which he renders as *Die Frohe Botschaft*, Franz Rosenzweig remarked as follows:

> For the expectation of the Messiah, by which and for the sake of which Judaism lives, would be an empty theologoumenon, a mere "idea," idle babble,—if it were not over and over again made real and unreal, illusion and disillusion in the form of "the false Messiah." The false Messiah is as old as the hope of the genuine one. He is the changing form of the enduring hope. Every Jewish generation is divided by him into those who have the strength of hope not to be deceived. Those having faith are better, those having hope are stronger. The former bleed as sacrifices on the altar of the eternity of the people, the latter serve as priests before this altar. Until the one time when it will be the reverse, and the faith of the faithful becomes the truth, and the hope of the hoping becomes the lie. Then—and no one knows whether this "then" will not happen even today—then the task of those who hope comes to an end, and the one who still belongs to the hopeful and not to the faithful when the morning of that day breaks, risks the danger of being rejected. This danger hangs over the apparently unimperilled lives of those who hope.[3]

With characteristic brilliance, Rosenzweig captured a profound dimension of Jewish messianism. In the annals of Jewish history, apocalyptic anticipation of redemption has often been intertwined with the phenomenon of a false Messiah. Indeed, the false Messiah is, in Rosenzweig's provocative formulation, the *changing form* of the enduring hope in a genuine Messiah. Beyond the contours of a historical argument, it can be argued, philosophically, that the faith to believe in a savior is severely compromised if the strength of hope not to be deceived by a false one has been diminished, but it is the very hope not to be deceived that makes the matter of trust possible. It is germane to recall here the comment of Rosenzweig in the *Star of Redemption* that divine truth (*göttliche Wahrheit*) "hides from the one who reaches for it with one hand only. . . . It wants to be implored with both hands. To the one who calls to it with the double prayer of the believer and of the unbeliever, it will not be denied."[4] Just as genuine worship requires belief and unbelief, so messianic expectation is as much dependent on what is presumed to be real as on what is resolved to be so; one might even go so far as to say that the line separating fact and fiction in this domain cannot be sharply drawn. To be sure, Rosenzweig was still trying to hold on to something of a distinction between the actual and the imaginary, and thus he insisted that, when the end comes, the hope of the hopeful will give way to the faith of the faithful, and only then will those who retain the capacity to lend credence to a pretender run the risk of being rejected. The openness to the future depends on a hope dialectically entwined with the possibility of being deluded.[5]

But, we are compelled to ask, how does Rosenzweig, finally, understand the end and the possibility of its coming? It is worth recalling that in the continuation of the passage, Rosenzweig recounts the comment that Hermann Cohen purportedly once made to him, "I am still hoping to experience the beginning of the Messianic time." Steven Schwarzschild has expressed doubt regarding the veracity of this attribution, and this suspicion seems reasonable to me given Cohen's steadfast and unambiguous rejection of a personal Messiah and his affirmation of an asymptotic conception of messianism, but for our purposes this is not important, since the remark of Rosenzweig sheds much light on his own eschatological sensibility, and this is our main concern.[6] Apropos of the preceding discussion, Rosenzweig explains that the "false Messiah" to which Cohen succumbed was his conviction that Christians would convert to the "pure monotheism" of his understanding of Judaism, the evidence for which he sought in contemporary liberal Protestant theology. Rosenzweig reports having been surprised by the vehemence of Cohen's desire, but he did not dare profess any reservation concerning the signs proffered by his teacher, nor did he have the heart to tell him that from his standpoint no date could be named. He merely responded that he did not believe he would experience it in his life. When pressed, however, by Cohen to offer some time frame, Rosenzweig answered, "Only after hundreds of years," to which Cohen, thinking that Rosenzweig said "only after a hundred years," desperately replied, "Oh, please say fifty!"[7] Rosenzweig's refusal to select a specific date does not simply bespeak deferral of the goal, but the more paradoxical discernment that the goal can only be attained by its never being attained, that the path to the way gives way to the undermining of the way. Rosenzweig's eschatology is marked by the irony that captures the inherent dialectic of the Jewish apocalyptic proclivity: on the one hand, redemption is predicated on a diremptive temporality that assures the possibility of the future being realized in the present, but, on the other hand, the future that is realized is precisely what remains constantly to come. Gershom Scholem came to the same conclusion when he noted that the messianic idea in Judaism is "anti-existentialist," since it has "compelled a *life lived in deferment*, in which nothing can be done definitively, nothing can be irrevocably accomplished." The consolation of Jewish messianism can never be realized except as calamity, and hence its "greatness" is also its "constitutional weakness."[8] In the manner of the seventh beggar in Naḥman of Bratslav's renowned tale, the beggar without feet, the consummate dancer, who is the one beggar not to arrive at the wedding celebration, the Messiah is the one that comes by not-coming, the one that is present in the absence of being present.[9] I am also here reminded of the observation of Kafka, "The Messiah will come only when he is no longer necessary; he will come only on the day after his arrival; he will come, not on the last day, but on the very last."[10] What is the distinction between the *last day* and the *very last day*? Evidently, the last is not final enough. The very last day is the day after the last, a day that cannot come forth in the ebb and flow of time any more or less than the very first day, the first that would have to come before the first. Time and again, Jews have had to confront the belatedness of the messianic drive. In the hypernomian terms that I explored in chapter 4, the fulfillment of the law portends the overcoming of the law that has been fulfilled. The utopian impulse, as it has taken shape within the multifaceted matrix of rabbinic Judaism, requires the resolute adherence to a singular tradition that marks its bearers as a chosen people set apart from other ethnicities, but the actualization of the ideal blurs the boundary between Jew and non-Jew to the point of contesting the very claim to that singularity.

Is it possible for a Jewish Messiah to be anything but false? Has not the historical record proven definitively that every person proclaimed the redeemer is eventually judged to be an impostor, even in the case of messianic factions that have had sociopolitical impact, most notably the apocalyptic movement surrounding the figure of Jesus that eventually evolved into the world religion of Christianity?

If we factor in events that unfolded in the twentieth century after Rosenzweig's demise, the argument is considerably strengthened. Some orthodox Jews may still harbor the traditional belief in a personal Messiah, and some religious Zionists may yet suppose that the establishment of the modern state of Israel in 1948 was a harbinger of the end of exile and the beginning of redemption, a process that, presumably, will reach its culmination with the restoration of all Jews to the land and the construction of the third Temple in Jerusalem, but I would surmise that the vast majority of Jews involved in some kind of observance (and, needless to say, the many more secular Jews estranged from any observance) have lost their ability to be lured by the posturing of a pseudo-Messiah and hence their faith in the authentic one has been inexorably weakened, if not completely eradicated. For most practicing Jews, I would contend, there remains a volatile place where the lines of the political and theological meet, but it is a site of deep-seated skepticism, as scores of these practitioners presently lack any real confidence that there is one who is coming.

The assessment of Rosenzweig, however, is more than a historical judgment. His reflections give voice to what I think of as the tragic optimism coiled within the recesses of Jewish utopianism and the distinctive sense of (a)temporality implied thereby: the promise of a future—the tomorrow that can happen today, even at this very moment—may be construed as a source of unending sanguinity, but it cannot be disentangled from the inevitability of its failure. The possibility of the future's coming to be lies in its already having been the past that can never come to pass as anything but the present that is always passing in its own future as the past. The hope delineated therein cannot be separated from the hopelessness that the hope can never be realized except as the task of remembering the future that persistently stays behind as the past that provisionally stretches ahead.[11] One might counter that it is equally plausible, indeed preferable, to demarcate what I have described as a place of illimitable hope, the interminable interim of futurity, in a manner that accords with Derrida's achronic conception of the future (*l'avenir*) as the "coming" (*venire*) of "the event of a novelty that must surprise, because at the moment when it comes about, there could be no statute, no status, ready and waiting to reduce it to the same."[12] The "invention of the other," Derrida insists, "is not opposed to that of the same, its difference beckons toward another coming about, toward this other invention of which we dream, the invention of the entirely other, the one that allows the coming of a still unanticipatable alterity, and for which no horizon of expectation as yet seems ready, in place, available." Even though the future is incalculable and aleatory—one happens upon it in an encounter that escapes all programming—one must still prepare for it. The term *invention* is employed by Derrida to convey just this sense of getting ready for what cannot be anticipated—or, better, what cannot be anticipated except as what cannot be anticipated—to let the wholly other (*tout autre*) come in its irreducible otherness. "The invention of the other, the incoming of the other, is certainly not constructed as a *subjective genitive*, and just as assuredly not as an objective genitive either, even if invention comes from the other—for this other is thenceforth neither subject nor object, neither a self nor a consciousness nor an unconscious. To get ready for this coming of the other is what can be called deconstruction."[13] It is surely instructive that from Derrida's perspective, the deconstructionist method is understood as the invention of the inventable other.[14] The comparison, as he makes clear, highlights the opening of the future, which makes possible "the adventure or the event of the entirely other to come"—an entirely other "that can no longer be confused with the God or the Man of ontotheology or with any of the figures of this configuration"[15]—as the iteration of the different (the other is not the new, unless we understand novelty as a form of "reiterative simulation")[16] that is written continually like a text and therefore "open to a non-finite series of re-deployments and re-reading."[17] The thematic connection that links deconstruction and the writing of the future is unquestionably informed by the Jewish messianic ideal.[18] In a passage from *Specters of Marx*, the influence is patently acknowledged: "Well, what remains irreducible to any deconstruction, what remains as undeconstructible as the possibility itself of deconstruction is, perhaps, a certain experience of the emancipatory promise; it is perhaps even the formality of a structural messianism, a messianism without religion, even a messianic without messianism, an idea of justice—which we distinguish from law or right and even from human rights—and an idea of democracy—which we distinguish from its current concept and from its determined predicates today."[19] At a later period, Derrida elaborates his atheological appropriation of the Jewish utopianism by referring to "messianicity without messianism," by which he intends the "opening to the future or to the coming of the other as the advent of justice, but without horizon of expectation and without prophetic prefiguration. . . . Possibilities that both open and can always interrupt history, or at least the ordinary course of history."[20] This "spectralizing messianicity beyond all messianism"[21] indicates how far removed Derrida's eschatological stance is from traditional forms of Jewish messianism. Nevertheless, he does retain something of the latter, even translating this faith into the temporal underpinning of the method of deconstruction. As he puts it, "There has to be the possibility of someone's still arriving, there has to be an *arrivant* . . . someone absolutely indeterminate . . . who may be called the Messiah."[22]

It is noteworthy that Luce Irigaray concluded her contribution to a conference on the work of Derrida, which convened on August 10, 1980, by speaking of the prophets, who will know that "if anything divine is still to come our way it will be won by abandoning all control, all language, and all sense already produced. . . . These predecessors have no future. They come from the future. In them it is already present."[23] Commenting on this passage, Catherine Keller, correctly in my judgment, observed that Irigaray's admonition to "cut free of every endtime calculus," much like Derrida's "messianicity without a messiah," "trembles with apocalyptic codes."[24] Indeed, the very notion of an apocalyptic code rests on the presumption regarding a calculus capable of predicting the unpredictable, the prospect of expecting the unexpectable. To "come from the future," accordingly, is to "have no future;" it is to be "already present," to have always been coming. There is hope in this unsettling of temporal tensiveness, the irreducible sense of newness implied by the "forever differing alterity" of "what is to come,"[25] the obfuscation of borders that separate yesterday, today, and tomorrow; the future "still comes" from its past, and it is thus the "subject of an incalculable present tense."[26] But, at the same time, one must not lose sight of the fact that within certain ideological contexts a sense of despair might proceed from the awareness that the future can never come as it must always be coming, that it can only be, as Derrida put it, for ghosts.[27] The separation of eschatology and teleology implied by Derrida's sense of the "messianic extremity," the eschaton "whose ultimate event (immediate rupture, unheard-of-interruption, untimeliness of the infinite surprise, heterogeneity without accomplishment) can exceed *at each moment*, the final term of a *phusis*,"[28] can hardly be accounted a source of inspiration to the person who still adheres to the soteriology of a particular liturgical community. For such an individual, it may simply not be enough—or perhaps it is too much—to bear the truth that the promise will yield nothing but the promise of a promise.

Rosenzweig's response to Cohen, I submit, issues from a similar sentiment, the mixture of hope and grief. I am not oblivious to the fact that there are decisive differences between the thinkers I have mentioned, not least of which is Rosenzweig's theocentric framing of redemption in terms of revelation, a point Derrida explicitly denies. Lest there be any confusion, Derrida writes unequivocally that his "structural or *a priori* messianicity" does "without the dating of a given revelation."[29] Notwithstanding this disparity, and many others that could have been chronicled, Rosenzweig, Scholem, Derrida, and Irigaray are all keenly attuned to the paradox that the possibility of the future's coming is predicated on the impossibility of its arrival. Rosenzweig, Scholem, and Derrida think this matter more closely to the bone of Judaism and its messianic ideal. Like Kafka, they perceive the indeterminacy of the future to be both a source of expectation and of disappointment.

Messianic Secret and the Duplicitous With/holding

Although it might appear improbable, I would suggest to the reader that thinking of the eschatological hope as the possibility of the impossible—the possible whose possibility consists of its being impossible—can serve as a valuable lens through which to examine the religious philosophy of Menaḥem Mendel Schneerson. Much of the scholarly and popular attention to Schneerson has been focused on whether or not he identified himself as the Messiah. While this interest is surely understandable, both textually and anthropologically, in my opinion, it obscures the crucial question concerning the nature of the messianism he promulgated. On the surface, this line of inquiry seems gratuitous for two reasons. First, his writings, discourses, and actions are replete with references to a personal Messiah, the righteous redeemer who would come and lead the Jewish people out of exile to the land of Israel, and since there is no evidence that he ever deviated from the strictures of rabbinic orthodoxy, there should be no reason to cast doubt on his explicit assertions. Second, as I noted in the introduction, a distinguishing feature of Ḥabad ideology, in consonance with the more general drift of Ḥasidism as a spiritual phenomenon, is the ostensible commitment to divulging mystical secrets, the interiority of the law, the spreading of the wellsprings outward to circulate the mysteries that impart the knowledge of divinity mandatory for proper worship. Prima facie, it would appear that Ḥabad breaks the code of esotericism upheld (in theory if not unfailingly in practice) by kabbalists through the centuries. There is little question that this is the self-understanding endorsed by the seventh Rebbe as well, consequently there would be no justification to suspect him of insincerity. However, the historical picture is far more complex. One should never forget that Schneerson was heir to a hoary esoteric tradition according to which things are not always as they seem to be, nor do they always seem to be what they are. As we discussed in chapter 1, the role of secrecy in his teaching endures both in content and in form. Even though he was overtly dedicated to the indiscriminate diffusion of esoteric matters, Schneerson remains beholden to the hermeneutic principle attested in much earlier sources: a secret can only be divulged as secret if it is a secret that is divulged. To be revealed as secret, the secret revealed must be concealed, but to be concealed as secret, it must be revealed. Therefore, we can speak of an inherent duplicity in the dissemination of the secret, the enfolding of the secret as secret, the withholding of the exposure in the exposure of the withholding.[30] For Schneerson, as for many masters of Jewish esoteric wisdom that preceded him, the ploy of secrecy is especially operative in the ambit of messianic speculation. If one bears this in mind, then it should not be difficult to heed the argument that employing the standard ways of referring to the Messiah does not necessarily mean allegiance to a literal interpretation.

We have arrived at the spot where my approach diverges most conspicuously from the work of others. In my judgment, Schneerson was intentionally ambiguous about his own identity as Messiah, since the key aspect of his teaching involves cultivating a modification in consciousness with respect to this very issue. Simply put, the image of the personal Messiah may have been utilized rhetorically to liberate one from the belief in the personal Messiah. The millenarian enthusiasm that fueled Schneerson's mission from its inception is about fostering the "true expansion of knowledge" (*harḥavat ha-da'at amittit*),[31] an alternate angle of vision, an epistemological shift (paralleled with a change in cosmological orientation) marked by progressively discarding all veils in the effort to see the veil of truth unveiled in the truth of the veil. If reality is, as we probed in detail in chapter 2, a "coalescence and unification of opposites" (*hitkallelut we-hitaḥadut ha-hafakhim*),[32] the original nonground (*ein sof*), the essence (*aṣmut*) that is neither light nor dark, as both light and dark are nullified in the sameness of their indifference[33] (*ha-or we-ha-ḥoshekh bi-veḥinat ha-biṭṭul be-hashwa'ah aḥat*),[34] then the logic vital to uphold the binary distinctions that are basic to the social and communal fabric of the Jewish tradition—holy and profane, permissible and forbidden, Jew and non-Jew—is to be transcended. We explored this matter in detail in the preceding chapter, but let me here mention Schneerson's talk from 11 Shevaṭ 5721 (January 28, 1961). The future redemption, in contrast to the exodus from Egypt, is described as a manifestation of the aspect of boundlessness (*beḥinat beli gevul*), and hence the praxis that is preparation for it must partake of the same quality, worship of repentance (*avodat ha-teshuvah*), which is distinguished from worship of the law and commandments (*avodah de-torah u-miṣwot*), a form of service that is bound by the canon of the obligatory and deplorable. As we discussed in chapter 4, the worship appropriate to the messianic epoch entails the ecstatic state of frenzy referred to as the "folly of holiness that is above reason and knowledge" (*sheṭut di-qedushshah she-lema'lah mi-ṭa'am wa-da'at*), which is described further by the seventh Rebbe as an ascetic turning away from mundane matters, even if permissible by the law.[35] In the talk given on Saturday evening, 10 Shevaṭ 5730 (January 17, 1970), the anniversary of his father-in-law's death, Schneerson emphasized that worship of repentance is apposite to the generation of the footsteps of the Messiah, for this is a form of service that emerges from the "perspective of constriction, bondage, and suffering," and therefore it alone can engender an expansion beyond boundary and limitation, a disclosure of the divine glory that is no longer "through the withdrawals, concealments, and garments above," an unmasking of the glory (Isa 30:20, 40:5).[36] Elaborating the theme in a talk delivered on the eighth day of Passover, 22 Nisan 5747 (April 21, 1987), the prolepsis of the future redemption and therefore the day on which the messianic banquet is held,[37] Schneerson noted:

> All the revelations of the future-to-come [*gilluyim di-le-atid lavo*] are dependent on our actions and on our worship during the whole duration of the exile. From this can be understood that the disclosure of the splitting of the river [*ha-gilluy di-veqi'at ha-nahar*] is also in the present. And it must be said that this is by means of the worship in the aspect of *yeḥidah*, for the distinctive matter of the Messiah [*inyano ha-meyuḥad shel mashiaḥ*] is what is in the aspect of *yeḥidah*. And the matter of worship can be understood from this, worship in the aspect of *yeḥidah*, "to unify you" [*leyaḥedkha*], which is connected to the single One of the world [*ha-qeshurah im yeḥido shel olam*]. This matter is revealed on the last day of Passover.[38]

There is much to extract from this passage, but let me just emphasize the characterization of worship in the messianic epoch as the worship of the aspect of *yeḥidah*, the source of the Messiah in the divine physiognomy and the dimension of the soul unique to the Jewish people, in virtue of which they can be ontically united with the one true essence. The eschatological consequence of the monotheistic mandate to unify God, therefore, is that the Jewish soul will be bound to and incorporated within the "single One of the world," that is to say, the One that is singularly the phenomenal world of multiplicity to the degree that the latter is (not) the One (*yaḥid*) in which there is no more division, the One about which it is even too limited to say it is one. In this nondual (meta)consciousness, the contrast between truth and untruth is itself no longer viable, and thus the axiological basis of the nomian perspective would have to be subjected to radical transvaluation. The messianic Torah is expressive of this transvaluation, the Torah of the Tree of Life, in contrast to the Torah of the Tree of Knowledge, the law that is above the law and the commandments, the new Torah that exceeds the distinction between innocence and guilt.[39] The form of worship suitable to this law(less) law, the lawfulness beyond the law, derives from the interiority of the immeasurable will in which all restrictions are abrogated.[40]

The story of the seventh Rebbe, according to this enframing, provides yet another illustration of the paradox articulated by Rosenzweig: faith in a legitimate Messiah is unsustainable without a hope that may—indeed must—incriminate one in believing in an illegitimate Messiah, if that hope itself is to be incontrovertible. From this slant, the pledge about the messianic future is, invariably, a put on, the putting off of what is forthcoming. At the most extreme, one might be tempted to think of the eschatological drama as a cover-up, a dogmatic cloak in which to envelop the truth that there is no Messiah for whom we must wait, the cloak that lays bare the final divestiture of the cloak, the pretense of describing the end as the full disclosure of the essence without any garment, a seeing of the divine light as it is manifest in the garb of the material world, which (dis)appears, finally, to reveal its concealment. The concluding exposé at the fringe of time is the hierophany of this occlusion, anchored exegetically in the verse "You have come to see that the Lord alone is God, that there is none beside him" (Deut 4:35), that is, to fathom that there is no reality but the nondifferentiated One.[41]

The tragedy of Schneerson's messianic campaign can be gauged by the rituals performed by some of his followers to render his absence present, a denial of the facticity of his mortality based on a construction of time that blurs the past and the present in the hopes of compelling an appearance in the future.[42] Ironically, such behavior, which ensues from a literalizing of the seventh Rebbe's apocalyptic lingo, perpetuates the exilic consciousness that his teaching sought to overcome. What is seemingly lost to those who follow this path is the realization that true vision consists of seeing the invisible in the visible, and not of seeing the nonvisible as visible. This is the import of Schneerson's insistence that the Messiah is already here and all that is necessary is for people to open their eyes in order to greet him.[43] Postmortem apparitions of the seventh Rebbe, by contrast, are indicative of a profound spiritual blindness.

In No-Time: Immediately and Without Delay

It is undeniable that Schneerson preached sincerely that one must prepare for the occasion of the messianic coming, even following Maimonides by classifying the act of waiting as a positive commandment mandated by the Torah,[44] and thus he desperately and recurringly urged his followers to believe in the possibility of the realization of the promise at any moment, epitomized in the Yiddish incantational chant *ot ot kumt moshiach*, "Verily, verily, let the Messiah come,"[45] or, in its English equivalent, "We want moshiach now."[46] Existentially, however, this *now* is an occasion that can never take place, a (non)event that defies temporal location—if it is to come, it is because it presently is what has already been. To substantiate this point, it is imperative to recall that the Ḥabad conception of time is such that the quintessential aspect of temporality is the moment in which there is a compresence of past, present, and future, an idea that is adduced as the metaphysical import of the Tetragrammaton, the most sacred of God's names. I will mention one passage from the Ṣemaḥ Ṣedeq that may be taken as illustrative of the manner in which the moment is pinpointed as the convergence of time and eternity in the confluence of the three temporal modalities.[47] Commenting on the verse "Let the name of the Lord be blessed now and forever" (Ps 113:2), the third Rebbe explained:

> *Malkhut* is called "now" [*attah*], the "moment of the Lord" [*et h*], for the root of time begins in her, as it is written in *Liqquṭei Amarim*, part 2,[48] concerning the matter of "he reigns [*melekh*], he reigned [*malakh*], and he will reign [*yimlokh*],"[49] and thus she is also called "temporal existence" [*ḥayyei sha'ah*]. . . . Therefore, *Malkhut* is called . . . "now," which is in the present tense [*howeh*], and its meaning is a minute moment [*rega qeṭannah*], concerning which the expression *now* applies, which is not the case when there is some temporal extension [*yumshakh zeman mah*], for the expression *now* does not apply, as there is also past, future, and present. However, *now* is naught but a "little while" [*rega qaṭan*][50] in which the language of now, that is, this second [*zo ha-rega*], is possible. In relation to the Infinite, blessed be he, all the days of the world, and the six millennia, which are the six attributes that emanate from *Malkhut*, are only like the minute moment.[51]

A thorough analysis of all that is intimated in this citation lies beyond our immediate concern. But what is critical to our discussion of the propinquity of the end in Schneerson's messianic teaching is the depiction of the now offered by his namesake, which is linked theosophically to *Malkhut*, as the present that is not subject to the triadic dissection of the timeline. We can speak of that now, therefore, as an atemporal present in which the three temporal modalities of past, present, and future coalesce, just as we say of the divine that he reigned, he reigns, and he shall reign—not sequentially but concurrently, since God is entirely above time and the chain of concatenation. The paradox is symbolically embedded in the word *attah*, whose consonants (*ayin*, *taw*, *he*) can be rearranged to spell *et h*, that is, the "moment of the Lord" (the letter *he* is one of the stock metonyms for the full name YHWH), an expression that invokes the conjunction of the unlimited in the delimited, the everlasting in the transitory. From the standpoint of the Infinite, all time is comprised in the "little while" (*rega qaṭan*), the smallest of demarcations, the infinitesimal point that contains all difference indifferently.[52] It is not coincidental that Schneerson spoke of the coming of the Messiah in terms of this *rega qaṭan*, the interlude of time that cannot be measured in time, in and through which "we will exit from slavery to freedom and to the great light, in the true and complete redemption through our righteous Messiah."[53] The insinuated tenselessness of the intersection of the three temporal modes in this moment renders it meaningless to speak of the now in terms of the passage of time. If, however, we cannot speak of time passing, then it is not feasible to imagine that present, the future that is now, as anything but impossibly possible, that is, possible only as impossible. Is this not the intimation of Schneerson's entreaty regarding the Messiah's arrival, *tekhef u-mi-yad mammash*, "immediately and without delay in actuality"? Would it not have been sufficient to say either *tekhef mammash* or *mi-yad mammash*? The rhetorical rationale for the repetition is evident—and especially if we bear in mind that the Hebrew *tekhef u-mi-yad* (as utilized in the seventh Rebbe's messianic proclamations) is likely a translation of the Yiddish *ot ot*[54]—but I think it relevant still to wonder if there is something conceptual to deduce from the doubling. In the earlier years, he would typically express his millennial impatience by using such phrases as "quickly in our days" (*bi-meherah be-yamenu*),[55] "verily soon" (*be-qarov mammash*),[56] or in the language of his father-in-law, "forthwith to repentance, forthwith to redemption" (*le'altar li-teshuvah le'altar li-ge'ullah*);[57] in later years, however, his oratory intensified in accord with the elevated doggedness of his desire, epitomized, as we have seen, in the plea "immediately and without delay in actuality" (*tekhef u-mi-yad mammash*). Seemingly, "immediately" is not soon enough, and hence it must be qualified by "without delay." But what is more immediate than immediately? Is there an interval between "immediately" and "without delay?" *Tekhef u-mi-yad mammash*—what Shneur Zalman referred to as the "actual instant" (*rega mammash*), the moment, in which the infinite will is to be executed,[58] ought to come about without any further deferral,[59] not even for a split second. The quality of that instant, too instantaneous to be arrested by any instance of time, may be discerned from another passage where Shneur Zalman spoke of one's ability to transform darkness into light by means of repentance in "one second" (*be-rega aḥat*),[60] which derives from "the horizon of the supernal Crown" (*ha-maqqif de-keter elyon*), the aspect of the "I" (*anokhi*)[61] that is "revealed below, expressly now, for before him darkness is as light, the one who makes everything equal."[62] The quality of divine forgiveness, similarly, is said to spring "from the attribute of mercy," which cannot be demarcated by "any boundary or limit," since it is "the aspect of the Infinite . . . and vis-à-vis the Infinite there is no difference between a small and a large number, as before him everything is considered nothing in actuality."[63] Insofar as the bringing of Messiah was thought to be dependent on repentance, and the latter "is not in the aspect of time at all but above time,"[64] we can assume that redemption as well must come forth in the moment that is, at once, too small and too large to be calculated temporally. As Shneur Zalman put it in another homily, "In the future, the light of the Lord will be revealed in a great and powerful revelation, the drawing forth of his blessed divinity, and his essence and his substance, from the aspect of 'For I am the Lord, I have not changed' (Mal 3:6), he was, he is, and he will be [*hayah howeh we-yihyeh*], in one moment [*be-rega eḥad*], and all the flesh shall see with the eyes of the corporeal intellect [*einei ha-sekhel gashmi*] that our God [*elohenu*] will be in this aspect . . . and this revelation will take place specifically in the lower beings below."[65] The comportment of the future disclosure, the unveiling of the veiling, partakes of the collapse of the threefold division of time in the realization of the compresence of past, present, and future in the divine essence, the connotation of the Tetragrammaton, in one moment, the moment that is one and therefore outside the parameter of partition. The mode of comprehension (*hassagah*) that is fitting to that future, the "contemplation of the substance and essence of the light of the Infinite" (*histakkelut be-mahut we-aṣmut or ein sof*), is a direct and immediate "vision of the intellect" (*re'iyyat ha-sekhel*) that occurs "in one moment" (*be-rega eḥad*) and not in a temporal sequence characteristic of our sensory perception and mental apprehension.[66]

The esoteric implication of the appropriation on the part of the last two Ḥabad masters of the talmudic view that all "appointed times" for the messianic coming had already passed, and hence the matter is dependent on repentance,[67] is that redemption cannot be circumscribed within time. The absolute nonbeing of the event, accordingly, demands instantaneous action, since at any point in time it is pertinent to speak of bringing about the coming of the Messiah "immediately and without delay."[68] Reflecting this sense of the exigency of time, Yosef Yiṣḥaq stressed that "the fool postpones until tomorrow, the wise one acts right away."[69] The seventh Rebbe well understood the message. Exploiting an earlier midrashic depiction of God's precision and punctuality in the first redemption,[70] in the last years of his life, he would frequently apply to the final redemption the words *de-lo ikkevan afillu ke-heref ayin*, "he should not delay even for the blink of the eye."[71] The portal through which the future is cajoled to come must be less than a blink of the eye, the nanosecond that is denoted elsewhere as the "original moment" (*rega ri'shon*) of creation, which is as well the hour of redemption, the fiftieth day following the discharge from Egypt, the "aspect that is above the boundary of time but revealed in time . . . in time though not in time."[72] The paradox "in time though not in time," *bi-zeman akh eino bi-zeman*, indicates that this moment, in which the lines of creation, revelation, and redemption all meet, cannot be measured temporally, no matter how refined our tools of analytic computation, and hence, mathematically, there is no way to think of its occurrence but as the occurrence of what cannot occur save in the nonoccurrence of its occurrence.

Further verification of my conjecture can be found in the talk delivered on 24 Tammuz 5745 (July 13, 1985). On account of the release of Yosef Yiṣḥaq from Soviet prison on 12–13 Tammuz 5687 (July 12–13, 1927), this month is labeled the "month of redemption of the honorable and holy Admor, the prince of our generation."[73] The emancipation of the sixth Rebbe is understood typologically as a prognostication of the future liberation, which is to occur in the following month, according to the talmudic tradition that the Messiah was born on the ninth of Av, the day that both Jerusalem Temples were destroyed.[74] The feature of that deliverance, moreover, is connected by Schneerson to his father-in-law's motto regarding the proximity of redemption based on repentance, *le'altar li-teshuvah le'altar li-ge'ullah*. Noting that the essence of the worship is to speed up the coming of the redemption, "immediately and without delay," and even more rapidly, as the word *now* implies, Schneerson asks the hypothetical question "This pronouncement—

'forthwith to repentance, forthwith to redemption'—was made before so many years, and even so it has still not come, and hence the explanation of 'forthwith to redemption' necessarily cannot be in the manner of immediately and without delay in actuality [*de-tekhef u-mi-yad mammash*]!"[75] Schneerson responds that this query is asked by the "old and foolish king" (Eccles 4:13) and his emissaries, that is, the evil impulse and his minions.[76] There is no doubt that the intent of the sixth Rebbe when he avowed *le'altar li-teshuvah le'altar li-ge'ullah* was that the redemption should come "immediately and without delay," but on account of our transgressions we have not been worthy to see its realization. As a consequence, he had to keep announcing it, placing special emphasis on *le'altar*, "forthwith," or, literally, "on the spot." Analogously, the seventh Rebbe had to assert relentlessly the slogan of Yosef Yiṣḥaq together with *moshiach now* and *tekhef u-mi-yad mammash*. The nonoccurrence in no way effects the belief in the possibility of the advent of the future; on the contrary, insofar as that advent is not an event that can materialize in time, the nonoccurrence is, strictly speaking, what guarantees its occurrence. The point is underscored by the fact that the catalyst for redemption is repentance, which "is not worship that demands the duration of time [*meshekh zeman*], but rather, as in the words of the *Zohar*,[77] 'in one moment and in one second' [*be-sha'ta ḥada u-ve-rig'a ḥada*], in the second that is as [long as it takes to utter] the word![78] The content of the worship of repentance is, indeed, that he receives on himself the fulfillment of all matters of the Torah and its commandments, but nonetheless there is here no division into 613 components—the 613 commandments of the Torah—and not even into two components, but rather solely one point. Therefore it is not bounded in time, but only 'in one moment and in one second'."[79] The time of repentance is the second that is not confined by past or future, the instant in which the individual, who is not hemmed in by the burden of retention or the buoyancy of protention, can be suddenly transformed from being completely wicked to being completely righteous. To traverse abruptly from one extreme to its opposite is possible only in the space wherein opposites coincide in the sameness of their difference, a space that cannot be measured chronoscopically. Correspondingly, the time of redemption is this timeless moment, which cannot transpire temporally and therefore must always be capable of occurring (in)temporally—this is the nuance of Schneerson's "immediately and without delay."

As another illustration of the point, I will translate the continuation of the aforecited passage from the end of the talk delivered on the last day of Passover, 22 Nisan 5747 (April 21, 1987).

> And it must be added that the worship itself ought to be according to the order of the verse . . . "He turned the sea into dry land, they crossed the river on foot" (Ps 66:6), at first, the work of the splitting of the sea . . . and afterward the work of passing the river (the revelation of the future-to-come), the last day of Passover. By means of the worship in all this, we come immediately and without delay [*tekhef u-mi-yad*] to the matter of "they crossed the river on foot," [the word *ya'avru*, "they crossed," can be vocalized] in the future tense [*ya'avoru*, "they will cross"], the future that comes immediately and without delay . . . in the manner of "he should not delay even for a blink of the eye" [*de-lo ikkevan afillu ke-heref ayin*]. From the exodus out of Egypt they danced immediately to "I will show him wondrous deeds" (Mic 7:15), until "we therefore rejoice in him" (Ps 66:6), "in him"—in his essence [*be-aṣmuto*], and so shall it be for us, that he should not delay even for a blink of the eye, and from the [recitation of the] prophetic portion on the last day of Passover [Isaiah 11], by way of the future redemption, we will dance to the future redemption, in the manner of "he should not delay even for a blink of the eye." And what is written will be fulfilled, "For the earth will be filled with the knowledge of the Lord as the waters cover the sea" (Isa 11:9), and beyond this in the true and complete redemption through the Messiah our righteous one.[80]

A central theme in Ḥabad apocalypticism, especially prominent in the sixth and seventh masters, is the correspondence between the first and the final redemption, a conceptual pairing attested prophetically (Mic 7:15) and expanded midrashically through the ages. The association suggests that the scriptural account of the exodus from Egypt can be interpreted typologically as a sign of the future deliverance,[81] though the affinity also afforded the opportunity to underline differences. Ritualistically, Passover embodies the two as bookends, the beginning of the holiday commemorates the release of the ancient Israelites from Egyptian slavery and the end of the holiday heralds the coming of the Messiah, what I have called the event of the (non)event, which must be distinguished from the nonevent of the event. Two miracles, both signposted in the verse from Psalms, are correlated respectively with the two moments of salvation, the splitting of the sea with the first and the crossing of the river with the last.[82] The latter, as the former, is characterized as the disclosure of the light of the Infinite in which opposites merge, in which the spiritual and the material, the light and the dark, the concealed and the revealed, are conjoined in a state of absolute indifference.[83] Prayerfully, the seventh Rebbe expressed his yearning that just as in the exodus there was no delay in God's activity, not even for a blink of the eye, and the Israelites "danced immediately" to the point of being shown wonders and rejoicing in the essence, so, in the present, the Jews should dance immediately from reciting the prophetic portion on the eighth day of Passover, the eleventh chapter of Isaiah, to the future redemption. One might protest that the enunciation is circular, "by way of the future redemption, we will dance to the future redemption," but it is the circularity that reveals the truth about the time swerve that constricts the future into the present and extends the present into the future, a line that is a circle. The image of crossing the river is a particularly apt metaphor to convey the bridging of time—itself a gesture of metaphoricity that narrows the gap between what is imagined to be real and what is really imagined—conjured by the seventh Rebbe's begging God to act immediately and without delay; in the very petition, there is more than expectancy—there is a sense in which it is here already. As he put it with an augmented sense of coercion after the evening prayers on the night of 11 Shevaṭ 5750 (February 5, 1990), "Let it be your will that by means of all these things we will merit in all of Israel, immediately and without delay in actuality, immediately and without delay in actuality, immediately and without delay in actuality, the true and complete redemption. And especially when we are standing in the end of the time of the footsteps of the Messiah, verily in the end of the end—the footsteps of the footsteps of the Messiah, and hence this moment is in actuality the last moment of exile, and immediately succeeding it is the first moment of the true and complete redemption."[84]

Lest one presume that the urgency was due exclusively to Schneerson's own advancing age, consider the following comment from the talk on the last day of Passover, 22 Nisan 5714 (April 25, 1954), just a few years after he accepted the role as the seventh Rebbe: "The matter of the drawing down of the Messiah on the last day of Passover—this continues in each and every generation, and in each and every year, and especially in the most recent time, in the footsteps of the Messiah. . . . And especially now 'when all the predicted times have come to an end and the matter is dependent on repentance'[85]—and repentance occurs 'in one moment and in one second.'[86] . . . One should not fret from the concealments and obscurities, since in one moment, and in a second, it is possible to effectuate the redemption."[87] This text, and countless others that could have been cited, should give one pause against thinking narrowly of Schneerson's apocalyptic fervor in temporal terms, at least not a linearly construed temporality. Particular episodes on the stage of world history (such as the fall of the Soviet Empire and the Persian Gulf War) obviously played a part in eliciting responses, and his living words, as they can be elicited from the textual, audio, and video records, were on every occasion transmitted in the moment—therein lies their performative power, to be always of the moment, always the same because always different. Despite the viability of this claim, a careful examination of those records shows that from the start Schneerson was driven by the messianic ardor of his predecessor, an eagerness, no doubt, inspired in the last decade of his life by the dark shadows hovering over millions of European Jews during the Second World War. Schneerson carried this exuberance forward, finding ways to implement it in historical time, even though the moment itself is not of this time, and thus, potentially, it can come to fruition at any time.[88]

Recollecting the Future/Anticipating the Past

To apprehend the apocalyptic predilection of the seventh Rebbe of Lubavitch, we must seriously engage his reflections on the nature of time and eternity, specifically the collapse of this binary in the discernment of the eternality of the temporal and the temporality of the eternal. Indeed, the breakdown of this binary is essential to Schneerson's presentation of the possibility of experiencing the advent of the future even before the event of its arrival. Appropriating a distinction in the exegesis of Exod 13:14 found in several midrashic compilations,[89] but mediated primarily through the Pentateuchal commentary of Rashi,[90] Schneerson differentiates the "tomorrow that is now" (*maḥar she-hu akhshav*) and the "tomorrow that will be subsequently" (*maḥar she-hu le'aḥar zeman*).[91] The latter is a measurable marker of time (*shi'ur shel zeman*), the tomorrow that shall come at a later temporal juncture, but the former is a marker of contingency that is independent of any fixed temporal demarcation (*seder zemannim*), a tomorrow that is now, as it can be at any moment, if the ontic-existential conditions necessary to bring about a particular change are properly met. Commenting on a dictum attributed to the Alter Rebbe, "Even if there were one righteous man who effected a complete repentance in his generation, the Messiah would come," Schneerson added, "There is no need to wait for an appointed time, but rather our righteous Messiah can come immediately and without delay [*tekhef u-mi-yad*]—even in the night!"[92] In the same vein, the tomorrow that is now is spoken of as "the time that comes immediately" (*ha-zeman ha-ba tekhef*), but this is not a matter of the future (*atid*) that serially succeeds the present (*howeh*), as much as it is a sense of immediacy of what is to come next (*aḥar kakh*), a future that is already in the present. In a talk from 12 Sivan 5751 (May 25, 1991), Schneerson observed that the scriptural depiction of the eschaton, "For the new heaven and the new earth that I am making" (Isa 66:22), "is not only in the future tense, but it is in the present, to the point that in the succeeding moment, it will already be in the past, since [it says] 'behold, this one has come' (Song of Songs 2:8), he has already arrived."[93] In what may have been his last vocal announcement on the matter, Schneerson declared, "The Messiah will come very soon, and it is not only that he is about to arrive, but he is already on the way."[94] It would appear that this apocalyptic sensibility ascribes to each Jew the contradictory duty of living in two time zones, the time of the exilic present and the time of the redemptive future.[95] But this fails to comprehend the depth of the paradox implicit in the messianic waiting: to be on the way is to be already present, albeit as what is still absent. As Schneerson expressed it on 6 Ḥeshvan 5752 (October 14, 1991):

> There is nothing more for which to wait, since all the matters of worship have been completed, and they have already repented, the matter is dependent solely on the coming of the Messiah himself. . . . All that is necessary is that the Messiah should actually come in reality [*be-fo'al mammash*], "one should point with one's finger

> and say *this*,"[96] this is our righteous Messiah. . . . The essence is that this should be . . . immediately and without delay in actuality [*tekhef u-mi-yad mammash*], as I have said and repeated many times, it is not only that the terminus of the redemption is to come, but that the redemption is already standing at the entrance of the door, and it is waiting for each and every Jew to open the door and to usher the redemption into the room![97]

Here again I note a striking affinity between Schneerson and Rosenzweig. Commenting on Halevi's poem *yashen we-libbo er*, translated as *Auf*, Rosenzweig described the final vision as one in which "only the purely present future [*rein gegenwärtig Zukunft*] speaks, the call, the 'Be ready' of the hour that has come, finally come."[98] Is it not gratuitous to write of an invocation to beseech others to be ready for an hour that has come? Would it not be more sensible to expect that the future for which one is summoned to be ready is the future that is to come, not one that has "finally" come? And yet, messianic hope—in the notorious articulation of Walter Benjamin, the decree to remember the past incumbent upon the Jew, which turns "every second" into a narrow gate "through which the Messiah might enter"[99]—hinges on the paradox of preparing for the onset of what has transpired, the *purely present future*, the future that is already present as the present that is always future, the *tomorrow that is now precisely because it is now tomorrow*.

The temporal paradox has a spatial application, as may be seen from Schneerson's view, based on an earlier tradition, that the third Temple is already built in heaven, presumably by the hands of God (an idea linked exegetically to Exod 15:17 and to Ps 90:17), and it is just a matter of waiting for it to come down to earth.[100] Without denying the earnestness of the seventh Rebbe's utilizing this language literally to designate an actual edifice, indeed one he considered to be everlasting,[101] it is nevertheless clear that he also interpreted the image figuratively, inspired by the midrashic rendering of the verse "And let them make me a sanctuary that I may dwell among them" (Exod 25:8)—the divine indwelling is dependent on the worthiness of the people of Israel and not on the physical space as such.[102] Accordingly, the talmudic dictum that "every generation in which the Temple is not built, it is considered as if it destroyed it" implies that each Jew has to build the Temple in his or her own being—the purification of the "inner sanctuary" (*miqdash penimi*) that is lodged in the heart—or within the province of one's own home, to create thereby a habitation for the divine in the mundane.[103] "And in the manner that in each and every moment 'the Temple should be built in his days'—by means of this one adds another element and another detail to the coming of the Messiah, and one draws a little closer the third Temple, which is constructed and perfected above, and it is necessary only to bring it down, so that it will be below ten handbreadths."[104]

Often referring to the teaching of his father-in-law,[105] Schneerson likewise affirmed that the Messiah for whom we are waiting is actually waiting for us, as he has already come, standing behind the wall, and all that is required to apprehend his occluded presence is a new way of seeing and a new way of hearing occasioned by each Jew truly repenting,[106] a "polishing of the buttons" on their uniforms, according to the military image deployed by the sixth Rebbe in his talk on Simḥat Torah 5689 (October 7, 1928) and repeated regularly by the seventh Rebbe.[107] As early as 26 Tishrei 5711 (October 7, 1950), Schneerson expressed the matter as follows: "Concerning the light created on the first day, which was good, the sages, blessed be their memory, said that it was hidden for the righteous in the world-to-come,[108] and the saying of the Beshṭ is known,[109] 'Where did they hide it?—In the Torah,'[110] that is, the light that will be in the future-to-come is hidden now in the Torah, and from this it is understood that by means of the Torah we can reach even now the disclosure of the light for the future-to-come."[111] In spite of the tireless reiteration of this belief through the years, Schneerson did not deviate from this commitment to the viability of someone experiencing the light of the future hidden in the past by studying the sacred text in the present, a compresence of the three temporal modes in the noetic consciousness that is at the core of the messianic zeal he sought to instill in the hearts of his ḥasidim. Thus, in a talk from 14 Tammuz 5751 (June 26, 1991), he remarked:

> This is the essence—that this matter should be hastened and it should bring immediately and without delay in actuality [*tekhef u-mi-yad mammash*] the realization of the stipulation "soon shall it be heard" [*meherah yishshama*], and not only "be heard" in the future tense, but in the present tense, so that immediately and without delay, in the present, we will hear "in the towns of Judah and the streets of Jerusalem . . . the voice of the bridegroom and bride" (Jer 33:10–11), all the

> five voices[112] and all the ten expressions of joy, in the true and complete redemption through the Messiah our righteous one. And as it has been uttered quite a few times, immediately and without delay.[113]

The waiting, here conceived, transposes the future into the present with the previously uttered but still urgent summons that the future come instantly, immediately and without delay in actuality. In the conclusion of a talk from 22 Shevaṭ 5752 (January 27, 1992), the fourth anniversary of the death of his wife, Schneerson offered the following prayer: "Let it be your will—and this is the root of all roots—that this should occur for us in reality, immediately and without delay in actuality, and it should come to us especially from the twenty-second of Shevaṭ, 'By you shall Israel be blessed' [*bekha yevarekh yisra'el*] (Gen 48:20)[114]—for by the merit and recompense of the righteous women all of Israel will be redeemed already in the true and complete redemption."[115] To "be redeemed already," *yig'alu kevar*, is a grammatical hybrid that signifies the ontic curvature of time by which future and present are looped together, so that the longing for the former would not be tenable without staging the subterfuge that the (un)fulfillment of the promise could elapse at any moment. We are thus implored (perpetually it seems) to bring the Messiah by doing "at least a little more."[116] But can this condition ever be met? Can there be an *at least* that is not a *little more*, a *little more* that is not an *at least*? The open secret, repeatedly and variously, revealed by the seventh Rebbe, a secret most hidden because so exposed, lingers in the chiasm between "at least" and "a little more."

It would be ludicrous to deny that Schneerson's writings and discourses are suffused with the jargon of the traditional eschatology; ostensibly, his conception of the "true and complete redemption" included the belief in the coming of the Davidic Messiah, the resurrection of the dead, and the building of the third Temple.[117] This is obvious, and one could (as some have already done) fill many volumes copying and explicating the relevant citations. The assignment I set for myself has been different, to investigate whether, beyond the didactic veneer, one can glimpse a postmodern posture that resonates with the satirical wisdom of Kafka: the Messiah will come on the day after he has arrived, on the day after he is needed, not on the last day, but on the very last day. The *very last day*, imagined as what cannot be imagined. It is not for naught that Schneerson taught that Purim is the messianic festival par excellence. Building on rabbinic and kabbalistic sources, including most importantly the Ḥabad-Lubavitch masters who preceded him, he depicts Purim as the holiday that venerates the turning of one thing into its opposite, and hence it is a foreshadowing of the redemption in which the true unity, the transcendence of dipolar opposition in the essence beyond all duality, even the duality of duality and nonduality, will be disclosed. The messianic truth is epitomized in the rabbinic directive to drink until one no longer knows the difference between "blessed is Mordecai" and "cursed is Haman."[118] The numerical equivalence of the two expressions—both tally up to 502—indicates that, in the essence, opposites are not oppositional, as they are identical in virtue of their opposition. One acquires this knowledge when "one no longer knows," *ad de-lo yada*, that is, when one executes the sacrifice of self (*mesirat nefesh*) in true worship of the heart (*avodat ha-lev*), one is utterly beyond the logical antinomies of discursive knowledge (*lema'lah mi-ṭa'am wa-da'at legamrei*).[119] The Purim slogan *ad de-lo yada* corresponds, therefore, to the talmudic tradition that the Messiah is one of three things that comes when one is inattentive, literally, by way of the "removal of knowledge" (*be-hessaḥ ha-da'at*).[120] Interpreted mystically, the (un)mindfulness—the agnosticism of the gnostic—signifies that "the true and complete redemption" derives from the "gradation that is wholly beyond knowledge" (*darga she-lema'lah min ha-da'at legamrei*). Thus, prophetically, the messianic future is described not only as a time when the earth will be filled with the knowledge of God but also as a moment in which the water shall cover the sea (Isa 11:9), a paradoxical image that is meant to lead thought beyond the limit of thought.[121] Water covering water—here we come to the brink of consciousness, where difference dissolves in the dissolution of the difference between difference and nondifference. The means by which the mind(less) may cross that threshold is sacrifice of self through faith and devotion.

Crossing the Crossing and the Disbanding of Dichotomies

On Purim, there is a special significance to the matter of this sacrifice, as may be ascertained from Schneerson's use of the zoharic decoding of *yom kippurim* as *yom ke-purim.*[122] Yom Kippur will become like the day of Purim. But how can the celebration of the sensual, to the point of debauchery, represent a higher form of surrender than the austerity of ascetic renunciation associated with the Day of Atonement? Purim, in its narrative and ritual, encapsulates an inversion of soul and body, a metaphysical turnabout, which in some respects (in spite of the continued dominance of the patriarchy of orthopraxis)[123] threatens the phallogocentric essentializing of the tradition and the dichotomies produced thereby—visible/invisible, external/internal, corporeal/incorporeal, feminine/masculine. The secret meaning conveyed by Purim is the overturning of opposites: through the body, the soul is sustained. In the unity represented by this day, the two are neither different nor identical; they are differently identical in a manner that is identically different, a knowing that exceeds the bounds of knowing by the phallic axis of duality. Purim serves as an apt model for the future redemption, insofar as it enacts the interplay of metaphoric dissimilitude, encoded in the scriptural parlance *we-nahafokh hu*, "and the opposite happened" (Esther 9:1),[124] the (non)appearance of one thing through the guise of the other. The most significant instantiation of this coincidence of opposites—the juxtaposition of the unfamiliar—is in the cosmological paradox that preoccupied the seven Ḥabad masters, the inhabitating of the one true reality beyond any time and space in the spacetime continuum of material nature, the (non)manifestation of the unified infinite light in the differentiated body of the finite cosmos. The insight, the intricacies of which were scrutinized in chapter 2, poses a challenge to both a theistic idealism and a cosmic materialism: God and world should not be viewed in either binarian or monistic terms. What is consistently maintained is that, on the one hand, the universe is the divinity in actuality (*ha-olam hu elohut mammash*), but, on the other hand, the divinity is categorically above the universe (*lema'lah legamrei me-ha-olam*). To be enlightened messianically is to be delivered from the theoretical limitation of thinking of these statements as contradictory, indeed to be delivered from all limitation, including the limitation of the very notion of being delivered from limitation. The one who is wise has surpassed the need to see the divine and the mundane as either identical or nonidentical; they are both, and therefore neither, one or the other.

In his introduction to Shalom Dovber's *Quntres ha-Tefillah*, Yosef Yiṣḥaq noted that the study of *ḥasidut* in general, to which he refers as the "words of the living God" (*divrei elohim ḥayyim*), and specifically engagement with prayer (*hit'assequt bi-tefillah*), constitute a form of "systematic worship" (*avodah mesuddarah*) that cannot tolerate any deception (*nit kein genarte*).[125] In a talk from 18 Iyyar 5704 (May 11, 1944), Lag Ba-Omer, the thirty-third day between Passover and Pentecost, which traditionally marks the cessation of the murder of the students of Simeon bar Yoḥai at the hands of Roman persecutors, the sixth Rebbe elaborated poignantly on the nature of truth. The suitability of that day to the topic is related to the fact that Lag Ba-Omer, when understood symbolically, signifies the "disclosure of the interiority of the Torah" (*gilluy penimiyyut ha-torah*), in contrast to Pentecost, which is the revelation of the external sense (*galya de-torah*).

> Truth is from end to end. The truth is like the matter of the letters *alef mem taw*, beginning, middle, end, for this is the straight line [*qaw ha-yashar*] in worship, the drawing forth of consciousness into the attributes [*hamshakhat ha-moḥin be-middot*], and afterward the necessity to draw them into the garments of thought, speech, and action [*levushei maḥashavah dibbur u-ma'aseh*], and to bring things to actualization in actuality [*be-fo'al mammash*]. The truth must be from end to end, in the street as in the house, and in the house as in the street, so that truth will be from end to end. Hence, this is the blessing, to discriminate the truth and that the truth shall be.[126]

The blessing is twofold, that the truth be detected and that the truth shall exist. Based on the priestly description of the central bar of the Tabernacle (Exod 26:28, 36:33), the truth is described as extending "from end to end." This is elucidated further by appeal to the rabbinic idea that the consonants in the word for truth, *emet*, comprise all the letters of the Hebrew alphabet, *alef* the first, *mem* the middle, and *taw* the end.[127] According to Yosef Yiṣḥaq, this tradition alludes to the linear character of worship, the straight line of emanation that extends from consciousness to the attributes, that is, from the intellect to the sensations,[128] and then to the garments of thought, speech, and action, until the light expands to the corporeal, and all things are actualized in their actuality. In discriminating the truth, the distinction between public and private space is unsettled; one should be in the house as one is in the street, and one should be in the street as one is in the house. The goal of the Ḥasidic regimen is to inculcate this extensive measure of truth, a touchstone that does not allow for any dissimilitude between external and internal, appearance and reality.

> All the efforts of a person are with himself, to arouse the essential potency that is within him, that is, the essential connection to the complete faith to the point that all obstructions and obstacles will be nullified, for the truth is that nature itself is above nature [*ki ha-emet hu de-ṭeva aṣmo hu lema'lah min ha-ṭeva*], but it is the light that is hidden and concealed. Thus the matter of worship is to disclose the truth, and then the light of the efflux that is verily above nature emanates upon him in all of his natural matters, that is, in the vessels of children, livelihood, and sustenance, which are in the way of nature, the light of the efflux of blessing that is above the way of nature emanates in them.[129]

Shneur Zalman had already defined the Ḥasidic lifestyle as an unyielding quest for truth devoid of all delusion, a truth stripped of all embellishment. To see this truth, denuded of its adornment of truth, is to behold the essence, the nothing that is something and therefore nothing, the void of all things fully void—the vision that is proffered as indicative of the end-time. The cognitive disrobing, which would be required to plumb the depths of this emptiness, corresponds sensorily to the curbing of desire, the controlling of the animal soul, stimulated by the intense love of God, which illumines the "inwardness of the point of the heart" (*penimiyyut nequddat ha-lev*), so that one can annul oneself in God's unity (*levaṭṭel be-yiḥudo*) and thereby achieve the "expiration of the soul in actuality" (*kelot ha-nefesh mammash*).[130] Prayer, in its contemplative valence, is the primary means by which one ascends to "the aspect of the essence of the light of the Infinite" (*beḥinat aṣmiyyut or ein sof*), the abyss that is "above the aspect of division" (*lema'lah mi-beḥinat hitḥallequt*), the black hole where light is the extinction of light, since "darkness before him is as light" (Ps 139:12). Through the sacrifice of self, which is portrayed in the zoharic imagery (especially pronounced in Lurianic texts) of the worshipper being assimilated into female waters (*mayyin nuqvin*) that rise from below to stimulate male waters (*mayyin dukhrin*) from above,[131] one "goes out entirely from the vessel and is contained in his essence." The path thus brings one to the "realization without any limit at all" (*hitpa'alut bilti mugbelet kelal*),[132] an attainment in which there can be no deception, as there is nothing to attain, not even that there is nothing to attain.

The Eighth Within the Eighth: No One to Follow

The essential truth, therefore, is neither true nor untrue, for to say that it is either true or untrue would be too limited for the limitless truth of the essence. That which is neither true nor untrue, however, must be both true and untrue, and thus it cannot be subject to either verification or falsification. In seizing this (un)truth, any possibility of a ruse wherein deceit appears as truth is dispelled, even as it undercuts the assurance that truth will never appear as deceit. The "true and complete redemption" consists of being reintegrated into the infinite essence beyond all distinctions, including the distinction between being emancipated and not being emancipated, emancipation, in other words, that emancipates one from the very bind of emancipation. Taking the matter of masquerade one step further, we might say that, insofar as Schneerson thought of the role of the sixth Rebbe in decidedly salvific terms and viewed his own leadership as the seventh Rebbe to be nothing but the completion of what was accomplished by his predecessor, it is valid to wonder whether, at the deepest level, his eschatological doctrine entailed the recognition that a spiritual master, if he be true, must dispose of the mask of mastery.

To set the broader framework for this effacing of boundary, it is apposite to mention again the idea that the virtue of the Messiah consisted of his willingness to teach Torah, and especially the inner meaning, to every Jew, irrespective of status or vocation.[133] In Schneerson's interpretation, the implication of this tradition is that the unity of the Jewish people to be achieved in the future is one in which there will be no more separation into vying groups, and hence the study suitable to that time is above the distinctions imposed by rational comprehension; messianic gnosis, rather, is a vision (*re'iyyah*) through which the "substance of the divine" is revealed "without any division of gradations."[134] The ultimate purpose of the study of the inner secrets of the Torah, in contrast to the study of the external meaning, is to bridge the chasm separating master and disciple, for the one who studies esoteric matters abrogates his own being and is bound thereby to the teacher's essence, even to the point that they become one entity. It is in this sense that each ḥasid can be said to fill the place[135] (*memalle meqomo*) of his rebbe.[136]

Dedicating oneself to this venture may be viewed as a propadeutic for the messianic epoch in which all hierarchies are destabilized. Let us recall the letter from 26 Kislev 5713 (December 14, 1952) in which Schneerson interpreted the tannaitic depiction of the footsteps of the Messiah as a time of depravity in which, inter alia, insolence will increase, scribal wisdom will deteriorate, fearers of sin will be despised, truth will be lacking, the young will disgrace the old, the old will stand before the young, the "son will scorn the father, the daughter will rise up against the mother, and the daughter-in-law against the mother-in-law" (Mic 7:6).[137] As we might expect, Schneerson displays his uncanny aptitude for reversing the original intent of the rabbinic passage; the blatantly negative assessment is turned into a positive:

> In the worship of God, without considering the accounting of one's own position and stature, even as it relates to simple matters of thought, speech, and action, a person has the latitude (*di breytkeyt*) to become one who influences, arouses, and guides the way in his environment, not only with respect to laws but also in the ways of Ḥasidism and in their conduct, and not only with respect to the study of the revealed matters of the Torah but also with respect to the study of the hidden matters of the Torah, the mystery of the mysteries—which are also contained and expounded in the teaching of Ḥasidism. Moreover, those who have acquired the wisdom of the Torah, but they have not up to now merited the light that is in the Torah, which is the teaching of Ḥasidism, but he himself is still a youth, and "the young will disgrace the old." . . . May God, blessed be he, swiftly make us worthy to see with our fleshly eyes how "the Lord your God turned the curse into a blessing for you, for the Lord your God loves you" (Deut 23:6).[138]

The mishnaic lament that the old will be humiliated by the young is converted into a virtue that is evocative of the overturning of the tables that is characteristic of the final days before the messianic era. It is perfectly fitting for the novice to instruct the elderly sage in esoteric matters, a pedagogical transvaluation that parallels the theological promise of the transmutation of the curses into blessings.[139]

A similar note is sounded in a comment of Schneerson in a letter written in the days between Rosh ha-Shanah and Yom Kippur in 5720 (1959) to Louis Finkelstein, talmudic scholar and chancellor of the Jewish Theological Seminary of America. The seventh Rebbe explained, inter alia, that the reversal characteristic of the United States, whereby parents follow and listen to their children and teachers to their students, is one of the signs of the footsteps of the Messiah, the "last generation of exile," that is, the "generation right before the beginning of the redemption," for this is a time in which we are commanded to overcome binary opposition, "to transmute darkness into light and bitterness into sweetness."[140] It is prudent to suppose that, in some measure, Schneerson applied this to himself as well, recognizing that as the leader of the seventh generation, it was incumbent on him to lead by following.

Support for my conjecture can be elicited from a messianically charged talk delivered by Schneerson on Friday evening, 30 Ṭevet 5750 (January 26, 1990),[141] the celebration of the new month of Shevaṭ. The seventh Rebbe noted, when the New Moon falls on Sabbath (*shabbat rosh ḥodesh*), this symbolizes the conjunction of solar and lunar (the Sabbath is the seventh day of the week, which is enumerated according to the sun, and the month is calculated according to the phases of the moon), donor (*mashpi*ʿa) and recipient (*meqabbel*), a coupling of masculine and feminine that anticipates the redemption.[142] The charge of each Jew—men, women, and children are all included—is twofold, to bestow and to receive, and even in the matter of learning Torah the highest level of perfection is for the master (*rav*) to teach the disciple (*talmid*) to receive and to bestow, but this can only be accomplished if the master receives from the disciple even as he gives, since it is the nature of the master to transmit in the effort to diffuse the teaching and in the nature of the disciple to become as nothing in relation to the master so that the teaching will be transmitted.[143] In this manner, each individual learns that in worship, too, the supreme level is to be the donor and the recipient concomitantly (*mashpi*ʿ*a u-meqabbel be-vat aḥat*), to overflow by receiving and to receive by overflowing. Through this coincidence of opposites, the Jewish people fulfill their messianic destiny, which is linked to the constellation of the human form beyond partition, the indivisible point, an organic unity that is not constituted by the composition of parts, a bodily aggregation in which it is not possible to determine who is the head and who is the end.[144]

Let us recall the following passage, near the conclusion of the final discourse distributed by Schneerson on Purim Qaṭan, 14 Adar I 5752 (February 18, 1992), to which we have referred at various points in this book:

> Similarly, as it pertains to the Moses of our generation, my saintly teacher and father-in-law, Admor, the leader of our generation—his work was to arouse and to reveal the faith in every one of Israel from the perspective of the essence of the soul, and this is in a manner that afterward they would carry out their service from their own power, to the point that they would become a permanent lamp [*ner tamid*], in relation to which no change is appropriate, even from the perspective of the revealed powers. By means of this we will merit the true and complete redemption, soon in actuality [*be-qarov mammash*], for then there will be a disclosure of divinity also from the perspective of what is below. And then there will be a bringing of the oil and a lighting of the lamps . . . also in materiality, in the third Temple, in the true and complete redemption by means of our righteous Messiah, soon in actuality.[145]

The customary eschatological motifs are all affirmed in this passage, but what is most important is the emphasis placed on the sixth Rebbe's insistence that Jews must accomplish the soteriological undertaking based on their own power (*be-khoaḥ aṣmam*),[146] which is "rooted in the essence" (*mushreshet be-ha-aṣmut*).[147] When one attains this level of devotion and self-sacrifice,[148] there is no more need for an external master, as the individual is his or her own master. This is the secret of the verse upon which the homily was based, "You shall command the children of Israel to bring to you pure oil of beaten olives for lighting, for to kindle a permanent lamp" (Exod 27:20)—Moses empowers the Israelites with the ability to receive (*mamshikh lahem netinat koaḥ*) by instructing them to give to him (*we-yiqḥu eleikha*). The secret of leadership exemplified by Moses, and, by extension, every leader of the Ḥabad-Lubavitch dynasty, especially the sixth, is centered on the mystery of the gift—taking by offering—that transforms the beneficiary into benefactor and the benefactor into beneficiary. That this was the implication of the last discourse personally edited and dispersed by the seventh Rebbe is hardly inconsequential. It is important to recall as well the much discussed comment of Schneerson in the talk delivered spontaneously after evening prayers on 28 Nisan 5751 (April 11, 1991). After expressing the perplexity regarding the delay of the messianic coming, and sharing his doubt about the desire of the Jewish people for the redemption, he infamously announced to his ḥasidim, "I have done what I can, and from now on you must do all that is in your capacity. And let it be the will [of God] that there will be one, two, or three of you, who may suggest what to do, and how to do it, but the essence is that you should act so that the true and complete redemption will be realized in actuality [*be-fo'al mammash*], immediately and without delay in actuality [*tekhef u-mi-yad mammash*], and through joy and good-heartedness."[149] Many have marveled at the apparent tone of resignation in this statement, but what has not been appreciated is the extent to which the theme of shifting responsibility on others to accelerate redemption is perfectly consistent with the approach of the sixth Rebbe, which informed and fueled the apocalyptic ambition of the seventh Rebbe, the undoing of the master-disciple hierarchy. Consequently, there cannot be a Rebbe succeeding the seventh, for if there is an eighth Rebbe, he is precisely the one whom no one can or should follow.

Even at this late date in his lifetime, Schneerson's penchant for speaking in highly complex symbolic codes has not abated. The hidden meaning is implied in the date of the talk, on the eve of the Sabbath when the section from Leviticus that begins "On the eighth day" (Lev 9:1) was to be chanted liturgically. The aging Rebbe duly highlighted the significance of this number: "The 'eighth' is connected to the matter of redemption . . . the eighth within the eighth (the redemption within the redemption—the ultimate perfection of the redemption)."[150] Factually, this talk was not Schneerson's final public communication, but speculatively it could have been. His career started, as we discussed in the introduction, by applying the midrashic teaching regarding the seven righteous men from Abraham to Moses to the seven masters of the Ḥabad-Lubavitch dynasty. The sevenfold emblematically represents the historical realm, and the eighth, the metahistorical, the infinite that is utterly beyond the manifestation of space and time, the concealment that abides in the unconcealment of the concealed.[151]

Menaḥem Mendel's life was dedicated to completing the work of Yosef Yiṣḥaq by leading the seventh generation to the eighth gradation, or, more specifically, the "eighth within the eighth" (*shemini she-bi-shemini*), an obvious allusion to the messianic epoch.[152] This locution was employed by Schneerson, as well as the previous Ḥabad masters, to refer to the eschatological transfiguration of Haman, the personification of the demonic in the world.[153] The Ḥasidic interpretation builds upon the tradition of Rav, which is transmitted by Ḥiyya bar Ashi, to the effect that a scholar must possess an eighth of pride (*eḥad mi-shemoneh bi-sheminit*), that is, the modicum of self-respect necessary to engage in Torah study.[154] In Ḥabad lore, this image betokens the element of dignity that is necessary to embark on the path of humble worship that culminates in self-abnegation—one must be something to become nothing—a portent of the purification of the attributes of egotism and conceit, which represent the indigenous nature of Amaleq, and their restoration to holiness.[155] It is reasonable to assume, moreover, that the eighth within the eighth also alludes to the older kabbalistic theme (mentioned briefly in chapter 1) regarding the eighth Edomite king, Hadar, whose marriage to Meheṭabel (Gen 36:39) signifies the rectification of the alleged celibacy of the prior seven kings.[156]

There are a number of passages in the Ḥabad corpus wherein the Lurianic identification[157] of the figure of Hadar as both the phallic potency[158] (literally, the foundation) of the primordial anthropos (*yesod de-adam qadmon*) and as the beginning of the world of rectification (*olam ha-tiqqun*) is explicated.[159] The following excerpt from the Alter Rebbe may be considered representative: "It is known that the kingship of the primordial anthropos [*malkhut de-adam qadmon*] was the source of the break with respect to the seven kings . . . for their root was from the aspect of *Malkhut*, but the eighth king was Hadar, and he did not die, for he was above the seven kings of chaos, that is, from the aspect of the foundation of the primordial anthropos, which is called the 'splendor of the body' [*hiddura de-gufa*] that is above the root of the break. Therefore, the rectification [*tiqqun*] and the purification [*berur*] are from him."[160] Drawing out the implications of this claim, the third Lubavitcher Rebbe asserted, "The aspect of the eighth king, Hadar, is the foundation of the primordial anthropos, the aspect that is above the break and the rectification."[161] Expounding this symbolism further, the fourth

Lubavitcher Rebbe observed that this aspect of the Godhead is beyond the opposition of chaos and rectification and hence it is capable of the paradoxical combination of the two, "placing the lights of chaos in the vessels of rectification,"[162] a trope with obvious cosmological and soteriological repercussions.[163] Interestingly enough, the seventh Rebbe applied the symbol of Hadar the eighth king to the sixth Rebbe, insofar as he was the eighth leader from the Besht̩, and thus he is also referred to as the "eighth candle" of Ḥanukah, the gradation of Joseph, the attribute of *Yesod*, the foundation of the world, the rite of circumcision, the holiday of Shemini Aṣeret, the eight-stringed harp of the Messiah,[164] and alluded to as well as the "distinctive one of the eight human princes" (*eḥad we-yaḥid de-shemonah nesikhei adam*).[165] The various symbolic nuances of the number eight were blended together in the following remark that Schneerson made on 25 Kislev 5718 (December 18, 1957), the first day of Ḥanukah, which fell on the Sabbath that year, a remark that may very well be considered the ideational completion of his inaugural address:

> The number eight is above the number seven . . . as in the case of Shemini Aṣeret, for even though it is an independent festival, it is also the continuation of the seven days of Sukkot, and thus it is called the eighth, the eighth in relation to the first. The matter of the number eight is above seven, for the matter of the number seven is the perimeter, and the matter of the number eight is above the perimeter, and this is also what we find with respect to the "seven shepherds and the eight human princes" (Mic 5:4). Moses our master, peace be upon him, is enumerated among the seven shepherds, for he comprises all of them, and the Messiah is enumerated among the eight human princes . . . for Moses is the seventh, and all things sevenfold are cherished,[166] the seventh day, which is Sabbath, is the most cherished of the days, the seventh year is the most cherished, and in each year the seventh month is most cherished . . . and, similarly, in the souls of Israel, Moses is the seventh . . . and hence the Torah was given through him. However, the Messiah is from the eight human princes, for this is a matter that is superior to the seven days of the perimeter, that is, above the concatenation, as is known with respect to the matter of the gradation of the future disclosure, that is, seven instructs about the disclosure of the concatenation . . . but the Messiah is the disclosure that is above the concatenation . . . since

> the Messiah is above Moses.[167] This is also what the rabbis, blessed be their memory, said, the harp of the Temple had seven strings, and that of the days of the Messiah will have eight, for in the future the aspect of the eighth will be revealed. And in the matter of the *sefirot*, the number seven is the matter of the seven attributes, which are the seven days of the edifice, for the attributes belong to the worlds . . . and the aspect of the eighth relates to the *sefirah* of *Binah*, which is above the worlds. . . . This is the difference between the disclosure of the present and the disclosure of the future, for the disclosure of the present is that of the seven strings, that is, from the aspect of the attributes that belong to the worlds, whereas the harp of the future is that of eight strings, and this is the disclosure of the aspect of *Binah*, which is above the worlds.[168]

We may conclude, therefore, that Schneerson's reference to the eighth within the eighth, the redemption within the redemption, alludes to the ogdoad above the heptomad,[169] the light that is beyond the order of concatenation in which the darkness has been transposed into light,[170] the supernal delight (*oneg elyon*) of *Binah*, the world-to-come,[171] a state of equanimity marked by the surpassing of binary opposition, including especially the obfuscation of the barrier separating Jew and non-Jew, a point accentuated by the fact that the last of the Edomite kings is the commencement of the reign of Israel. The ultimate legacy of the seventh Rebbe's messianic aspiration, the encrypted message he wished to bequeath to future generations, lies in proffering an understanding of salvation as the expanded consciousness of and reabsorption in the inestimable essence, whose essence it is to resist essentialization, the moment of eternity for which we await in its fully temporalized sense, the advent of the absolute (non)event. True liberation, on this score, would consist of being liberated from the need to be liberated.

NOTES

Introduction

1. Ḥabad follows a perspective that can be traced as far back as the thirteenth century, when some kabbalists began counting the ten *sefirot* with *Ḥokhmah* or *Maḥashavah*, adding *Da'at* in place of *Keter*. This is not to say that *Keter* does not figure prominently in Ḥabad speculation. As will be noted at several points in this study, and especially chapter 2, *Keter* is described variously as the nothing (*ayin*), the incomposite will (*raṣon pashuṭ*), the infinite light (*or ein sof*), the one in which opposites coalesce. See Hallamish, "Theoretical System," pp. 70–77. The Ḥabad perspective is expressed succinctly by Schneersohn, *Or ha-Torah: Bemidbar*, 1:128: "The ten commandments are correlated with the ten *sefirot*, and it says in *Sefer Yeṣirah* [1:4] 'ten and not eleven,' that is, the interiority [*penimiyyut*] of *Keter* is not in the enumeration of the ten *sefirot*, for it emanates from *Malkhut* of the Infinite, which is one but not in number [based on *Tiqqunei Zohar*, introduction, 17a and sec. 69, 116a]. And this is the matter of the commandment of *anokhi* (Exod 20:2), which instructs about *Keter* [see chapter 4, n. 52], for even though it is in the enumeration of the ten commandments, which are the ten *sefirot*, it is nevertheless called 'the eleventh,' for its interiority is not in the enumeration of the ten *sefirot*." An even more concise expression of the point is offered by Schneersohn, *Sefer ha-Ma'amarim, 5669*, p. 38: "The aspect of the supernal *Keter* is the aspect of the Infinite in actuality [*beḥinat ein sof mammash*], the lowest aspect that is in the Emanator." The dimension of soul that corresponds to *Keter* is called *yeḥidah*, which connotes unity and signifies the consubstantiality between divine and human, at least as it relates distinctively to the Jewish people. See discussion in chapter 6.

2. The *locus classicus* for this terminology is Shneur Zalman of Liadi, *Liqquṭei Amarim: Tanya*, part 1, chapter 3, 7a–b. See Hallamish, "Theoretical System," pp. 78–85, 210–217.

3. There is ample evidence (contra the efforts on the part of some Lubavitch ḥasidim) to demonstrate that the seventh Rebbe strongly opposed several scientific claims that would contradict basic principles of the orthodox rendering of religious faith. For example, consider the criticism of the conception of time according to Einstein's relativity theory in a letter from 14 Av 5707 (July 31, 1947) in Schneerson, *Iggerot Qodesh*, no. 283, 2:224–225. An earlier version was published in *Liqquṭei Siḥot*, 10:176–177. For a critique of Darwinian evolutionism, see the letter from 27 Ṭevet 5713 (January 14, 1953) in Schneerson, *Liqquṭei Siḥot*, 30:259–263. And see the letter from 10 Ḥeshvan 5716 (October 26, 1955) in *Liqquṭei Siḥot*, 10:177–178, which attacks the scientific view that

the world is much older than the traditional Jewish reckoning based on a theory of creation. For a criticism of the tendency in American public schools to promote views that deny creation, miracles, and other matters that are beyond the way of nature, see the passage from a talk in 5721 (1961) in Schneerson, *Liqquṭei Siḥot*, 8:303. For a defense of the traditional dogma of *creatio ex nihilo* against prevailing scientific cosmologies, see the letter from 4 Sivan 5716 (May 24, 1956) to Isaac Halevi Herzog, the chief rabbi of Israel (1936–1959), in Schneerson, *Liqquṭei Siḥot*, 30:265–266, also printed in *Iggerot Qodesh*, no. 4414, 13:145–146. For a similar criticism, see the letter of 14 Av 5719 (August 18, 1959) in Schneerson, *Liqquṭei Siḥot*, 6:318–319. In that context, Schneerson wrote categorically that "all the sciences, even those that are called exact sciences, are based on suppositions that have no foundation but only convention." On the characterization of the scientific method—with the name of Heisenberg explicitly mentioned—as based on probability rather than certainty, see the aforementioned letter to Herzog in *Liqquṭei Siḥot*, 30:264 (*Iggerot Qodesh*, no. 4414, 13:143), and see also Schneerson's response from a letter written sometime in the winter 5726 (1965–66) to a query about science in *Liqquṭei Siḥot*, 33:255, reprinted in *Iggerot Qodesh*, no. 9114, 24:97. For a critique of scientists and philosophers who lack moral rectitude based on faith in God, typified by the German people in the Second World War, see the letter from Pesaḥ Sheni, the "second Passover," 14 Iyyar 5723 (May 8, 1963), in *Liqquṭei Siḥot*, 33:253–254. See also the comment in Schneerson's letter to Elie Wiesel from 25 Nisan 5725 (April 27, 1965) in *Liqquṭei Siḥot*, 33:256 (reprinted in *Iggerot Qodesh*, no. 8969, 23:370) that the biblical concept of worshipping "other gods" can also include those who make the intellect into a god and as the final arbiter of truth. A separate study would be required to do justice to this subject, but in general it can be said that Schneerson's position was that science, and especially technology, should serve as handmaiden to religion, but, at points of conflict, the latter is to be privileged. The rationale for this position is that scientific methodology does not sanction certitude as the measure of proof but only probability. See Branover, "The Lubavitcher Rebbe on Science and Technology," and *A Prophet from the Midst of Thee*, pp. 197–198. I am not persuaded by Branover's conclusion that the Rebḅe's views on this topic should not be considered apologetic. For other references to scholars who have discussed the Rebbe's critique of the theory of evolution and his defense of a literal understanding of the biblical account of creation, see Selya, "Torah and Madda?" pp. 197–198, n. 44. In sum, the position taken by Schneerson is that the truths of science and philosophy corroborate the truths of Torah, but the former should not be considered the primary and final arbiter of truth. The view is summed up in a medieval maxim that Schneerson cited in the name of the Ṣemaḥ Ṣedeq, "Love Plato, love Aristotle, but love truth more than all of them." See Schneerson, *Iggerot Qodesh*, no. 5449, 15:135, printed as well in *Liqquṭei Siḥot*, 30:269. See chapter 1, n. 33.

4. Schneerson, *Iggerot Qodesh*, no. 4306, 13:32.

5. Scholem, *Origins of the Kabbalah*, pp. 312 and 439, n. 174, and discussion in Wolfson, *Language. Eros, Being*, pp. 99–105.

6. Schneersohn, *Sha'arei Orah*, 144b; Elior, *Theory of Divinity*, pp. 37–43. For discussion of the principle of the coincidence of opposites in Ḥabad speculation, see Hallamish, "Theoretical System," pp. 163–174; Elior, *The Paradoxical Ascent to God*, pp. 25–31,

63–72, 97–100; Drob, *Kabbalistic Metaphors*, pp. 20–22, 148–151; and two essays by the same author, "The Doctrine of *Coincidentia Oppositorum* in Jewish Mysticism" and "A Rational Mystical Ascent," posted at http://www.newkabbalah.com.

7. See, for instance, Shneur Zalman of Liadi, *Torah Or*, 28d. The expression *shenei hafakhim be-nose eḥad* recurs often in Ḥabad sources to mark the paradoxical confluence of opposites, at times also troped as *hitkallelut shenei hafakhim be-nose eḥad*, the "containment of two opposites in one subject." See Shneur Zalman of Liadi, *Liqquṭei Torah*, Neṣavim, 2:49a; *Torah Or*, 28c–d; *Ma'amerei Admor ha-Zaqen, 5565*, 1:184–185; Schneersohn, *Torat Ḥayyim: Bere'shit*, 88d, 192d, 221d, 244d; *Torat Ḥayyim: Shemot*, 192a; *Ner Miṣwah we-Torah Or*, 70a, 84b; *Sha'arei Teshuvah*, 14c; Epstein, *Ma'amar ha-Shiflut we-ha-Simḥah*, p. 187; Schneersohn, *Ma'amerei Admor ha-Ṣemaḥ Ṣedeq*, pp. 79–80, 87; Schneersohn, *Be-Sha'ah she-Hiqdimu,* 1:728; Schneerson, *Sefer ha-Ma'amarim 5734–5735*, p. 74; *Torat Menaḥem: Hitwwa'aduyyot 5743*, 1:293.

8. Friedman, "Habad as Messianic Fundamentalism," and "Messiah and Messianism"; Butman, *Countdown to Moshiach: Can the Rebbe Still Be Moshiach?* posted at http://www.torah4blind.org/count.txt; Ravitzky, *Messianism*, pp. 181–206; "The Messianism of Success in Contemporary Judaism"; Elior, "The Lubavitch Messianic Resurgence"; Lenowitz, *The Jewish Messiahs*, pp. 215–223; Dan, *The Modern Jewish Messianism*, pp. 189–203; Idel, *Messianic Mystics*, pp. 242–244; Szubin, "Why Lubavitch Wants the Messiah Now"; Kraus, "'Living with the Times,'" and the recently published revised version, *The Seventh*; Goldberg, "Zaddik's Soul"; Gotlieb, "Habad's Harmonistic Approach," pp. 233–278; Feldman, *Lubavitchers as Citizens*, pp. 33–37; Ehrlich, *Leadership in the HaBaD Movement*, pp. 113–119; *The Messiah of Brooklyn*; Marcus, "The Once and Future Messiah"; Ochs, "Waiting for the Messiah"; Dahan, "'Dira Bataḥtonim'"; Kohanzad, "Messianic Doctrine"; Branover, *A Prophet from the Midst of Thee*, pp. 192–236.

9. Berger, *The Rebbe, the Messiah, and the Scandal*; and the self-acknowledged "insider" rejoinder by Rapoport, *The Messiah Problem*; see also Student, *Can the Rebbe Be Moshiach?*

10. Loewenthal, "The Neutralisation"; see also the anecdotal evidence in Levine, *Mystics, Mavericks, and Merrymakers*, pp. 2–3, 38, 47–48, 84, 105–106, 146, 171–172.

11. Schneersohn, *Sefer ha-Siḥot 5688–5691*, pp. 8, 50. See Schneerson, *Iggerot Qodesh*, no. 4997, 14:237, where it is reported in the name of the sixth Rebbe that "we are found in the end of the footsteps of the Messiah." See also Schneerson, *Iggerot Qodesh*, no. 5968, 16:192, no. 5983, 16:207; no. 7095, 19:68.

12. It would be cumbersome to delineate all the places in which Schneerson speaks of his time as the "footsteps of the Messiah," a belief from which he did not oscillate his whole life. I offer here only a small portion to illustrate the point: Schneerson, *Iggerot Qodesh*, no. 34, 1:57; no. 39, 1:63; no. 40, 1:64; no. 45, 1:72; no. 48, 1:76; no. 84, 1:140; no. 1812, 6:306; no. 2594, 8:339; no. 2886, 9:259; no. 4487, 13:219; no. 4497, 13:230; no. 5647, 15:326; no. 6130, 16:355; no. 6836, 18:348; no. 7082, 19:52; no. 7294, 19:293; no. 7310, 19:310; *Torat Menaḥem: Hitwwa'aduyyot 5711*, 1:180; *Torat Menaḥem: Hitwwa'aduyyot 5715*, 1:203. It should be noted that the Alter Rebbe had already expressed the view that his time was the period known as the "footsteps of the Messiah." See, for instance, Shneur Zalman of Liadi, *Torah Or*, 41a; *Ma'amerei*

Admor ha-Zaqen 5566, 2:565. It is also of interest to consider the anecdotal evidence of Joseph B. Soloveitchik concerning Schneerson's messianic aspirations, reported by his son Haym to Deutsch, *Larger Than Life,* 2:122. According to one remark, the older Soloveitchik expressed his concern that the "Rebbe will turn Lubavitch into a messianic movement," and, according to a second remark, there was trepidation that the "Rebbe has a fantasy that he is Moshiach."

13. Schneerson, *Torat Menaḥem: Hitwwa'aduyyot 5715*, 2:32. For a similar view, see Schneersohn, *Sefer ha-Ma'amarim 5710–5711*, part 2, p. 289. On the one hand, the final exile is distinguished as one in which the concealments of the divine light are greatly augmented, but, on the other hand, precisely on account of that increase, the sense of being tested is also at a maximum, and hence the possibility of self-sacrifice is amplified proportionally. The view expressed by the last two Lubavitch masters regarding the intensification of darkness in the last phase of exile prior to the revelation of the messianic light is a metaphorical amplification of a well-known phenomenological belief that the darkest moment of the night is right before the break of dawn. See Schneersohn, *Be-Sha'ah she-Hiqdimu,* 1:551, where this theme is linked exegetically to the rabbinic tradition that insolence will increase in the footsteps of the Messiah (Mishnah, Soṭah 9:15, and see discussion of this text in the postface at n. 137); see also chapter 1, n. 23.

14. Babylonian Talmud, Sanhedrin 97b.

15. For instance, see Schneerson, *Iggerot Qodesh*, no. 91, 1:164; *Torat Menaḥem: Hitwwa'aduyyot 5714*, 1:210; *Torat Menaḥem: Hitwwa'aduyyot 5751*, 4:170; *Torat Menaḥem: Hitwwa'aduyyot 5752*, 2:90; *Torat Menaḥem: Sefer ha-Ma'amarim Meluqaṭ*, 3:313.

16. Moses ben Maimon, *Mishneh Torah*, Teshuvah 7:5.

17. Schneerson, *Sefer ha-Ma'amarim 5730–5731*, p. 129. See Schneerson, *Torat Menaḥem: Hitwwa'aduyyot 5744*, 1:65. The expression *be-qarov mammash*, which was used repeatedly by Schneerson to express his messianic aspiration, was also utilized with the same intent by the sixth Rebbe. See Schneersohn, *Sefer ha-Siḥot 5688–5691*, p. 68; *Sefer ha-Siḥot 5706–5710*, pp. 149, 150, 180 (*Der Abershter zol gebn a ge'ullah sheleimah be-karov be-fo'al mammash un nit nor be-khoach*, "God should grant a complete redemption soon, in actuality truly, and not just in potentiality"), 182, 343, 387; *Iggerot Qodesh*, no. 2166, 8:19 (cited at n. 46, this chapter); Schneerson, *Iggerot Qodesh*, no. 27, 1:48, no. 33, 1:55, no. 91, 1:165, no. 102, 1:187, no.104, 1:190; no. 242, 2:162; no. 524, 3:185; no. 1282, 5:68, no. 1403, 5:203; no. 1824, 6:319; *Torat Menaḥem: Hitwwa'aduyyot 5710*, p. 114; *Iggerot Qodesh*, no. 2316, 8:71, no. 2323, 8:80, no. 2581, 8:328; *Quntres Inyanah shel Torat ha-Ḥasidut*, p. 23.

18. Schneersohn, *Arba'a Qol ha-Qore me-ha-Admor*; *Iggerot Qodesh*, no. 1447, 5:361, no. 1455, 5:377–378; no. 1865, 6:430; Elior, "The Lubavitch Messianic Resurgence," pp. 388–389. The number of times this expression appears in Schneerson's letters (especially from 1943–45) are so numerous that it would be impractical to cite specific examples. A perusal of the first two volumes of his *Iggerot Qodesh*, however, will prove the point demonstratively. See also Schneerson, *Reshimot*, sec. 147, 4:358. The frequency of Schneerson's invoking his father-in-law's slogan at this relatively early time indicates the intensity of his hope for the imminent arrival of the messianic age, and this should put to

rest those who maintain that the apocalyptic fervor was an outcome of his old age combined with despair over the death of his wife.

19. Schneerson, *Iggerot Qodesh*, no. 1037, 4:314; no. 1481, 5:281, no. 1527, 5:331; no. 1542, 6:16, no. 1564, 6:47, no. 1649, 6:129, and no. 1684, 6:169; *Torat Menaḥem: Hitwwa'aduyyot 5712*, 2:244; *Torat Menaḥem: Hitwwa'aduyyot 5750*, 2:241; *Torat Menaḥem: Hitwwa'aduyyot 5751*, 4:169.

20. Deutsch, *Larger Than Life*.

21. Shandler, "The Virtual Rebbe."

22. For an illuminating study, see Katz, "On the Master-Disciple Relationship in Hasidic Visual Culture," pp. 68–76. Summing up her thesis, Katz writes: "Habad's prodigious visual output was deeply intertwined with its messianism, which further reinforced the centrality of the portrait in Habad culture. While the literary output of Habad leaders had a transcendent influence over Habad culture, the constant and public visual display of Schneerson's image has allowed him to achieve immanence. The influence of the Tanya and the other writings of Habad rebbeim derive their importance in Habad culture as founding documents that shape the theology of the movement, while the image of Schneerson has become indistinguishable from Habad culture. Proximity to the persona of Schneerson and identity with the visual image of Schneerson becomes the *sine qua non* of Habad Hasidism" (pp. 76–78). The argument proffered by Katz may be somewhat overstated, but it seems to me correct to note the transition from a text-centered to an image-centered culture, a pattern that is hardly unique to Ḥabad. In our era, visuality is accorded a privileged position as a carrier of cultural meaning and value.

23. Fishkoff, *The Rebbe's Army*, pp. 80–81; Branover, *A Prophet from the Midst of Thee*, pp. 208–209.

24. Kravel-Tovi and Bilu, "The Work of the Present," pp. 69–70. On the numerological equivalence of *beit mashiaḥ* as 770, which is also linked to the messianically charged word *paraṣta* (Gen 38:29), see Schneerson, *Torat Menaḥem: Hitwwa'aduyyot 5752*, 1:423, n. 92. See chapter 3 at n. 17.

25. *Zohar* 3:71b.

26. Schneerson, *Torat Menaḥem: Hitwwa'aduyyot 5710*, p. 16. Compare Schneerson, *Torat Menaḥem: Hitwwa'aduyyot 5719*, 3:120. On the manner in which the seventh Rebbe dealt with the apparent demise of the sixth Rebbe, see Ehrlich, *Leadership in the HaBaD Movement*, pp. 374, 387–388.

27. Schneerson, *Torat Menaḥem: Hitwwa'aduyyot 5745*, 5:2618.

28. Ibid.

29. For an extensive discussion of the concept of *hillula* in Lubavitch sources, see Goldberg, "Zaddik's Soul," pp. 100–169.

30. Schneerson, *Torat Menaḥem: Hitwwa'aduyyot 5752*, 2:251. It is of interest to recall here Schneerson's remark in a letter from 28 Av 5707 (August 13, 1947) that the "eternality of the Messiah will come to be sometime after he is revealed" (*Iggerot Qodesh*, no. 349, 2:234).

31. Schneerson, *Torat Menaḥem: Hitwwa'aduyyot 5719*, 3:120. On the augmented effectiveness of the righteous one after the death of the body, see Schneerson, *Torat Menaḥem: Hitwwa'aduyyot 5714*, 1:326; *Torat Menaḥem: Hitwwa'aduyyot 5748*, 2:325. This is the conceptual basis for the practice of praying at the grave of the sixth Rebbe (see

ibid., 2:326), which was a personal custom of the seventh Rebbe. Needless to say, after his physical demise, this practice has been transferred to him (see n. 26, this chapter).

32. Babylonian Talmud, Berakhot 18a–b.

33. On Menaḥem Mendel of Vitebsk and Shneur Zalman of Liadi, see Loewenthal, *Communicating the Infinite*, pp. 40–42, 48, 109.

34. Schneersohn, *Sefer ha-Siḥot 5705*, p. 105; Schneerson, *Liqquṭei Siḥot*, 21:449; *Liqquṭei Siḥot*, 26:378. See also Schneerson, *Torat Menaḥem: Hitwwa'aduyyot 5714*, 1:277; and the note in Schneerson, *Qiṣṣurim we-He'arot le-Sefer Amarim Tanya*, p. 118.

35. Shneur Zalman of Liadi, *Liqquṭei Amarim: Tanya*, part 4, sec. 27, 146a–b.

36. See n. 25, this chapter.

37. See also the formulation in Shneur Zalman's letter of consolation to Levi Yiṣḥaq of Berditchev over the death of his son, Meir, included in *Liqquṭei Amarim: Tanya*, part 4, sec. 28, 148a: "Every effort that a man makes with his soul above in the aspect of concealment and hiddenness is revealed and illumines in the aspect of disclosure from above to below at the time of his death."

38. *Tiqqunei Zohar*, sec. 69, 111b–112a, 114a. See also *Zohar* 3:216b (*Ra'aya Meheimna*).

39. Shneur Zalman of Liadi, *Liqquṭei Amarim: Tanya*, part 4, sec. 27, 147b.

40. Scholem, *Sabbatai Ṣevi*, pp. 53–54, 59, 584–586; Giller, *The Enlightened Will Shine*, p. 52; Liebes, *Studies in the Zohar*, pp. 15–17, 73; *On Sabbateanism and Its Kabbalah*, pp. 281–282, n. 79; Goldreich, "Clarifications," pp. 469–473; Wolfson, "The Engenderment of Messianic Politics," pp. 221–223, nn. 58–60, p. 254, n. 158, p. 258; Idel, *Messianic Mystics*, pp. 61–62 (but see, by contrast, the evidence adduced on p. 191 for the notion that the soul of the Messiah is higher than that of Moses); Fine, *Physician of the Soul*, pp. 329–330, 335, 438, n. 35.

41. Schneerson, *Liqquṭei Siḥot*, 39:352; *Torat Menaḥem: Hitwwa'aduyyot 5718*, 3:55. This is not to say that distinctions between Moses and the Messiah were not also drawn in some Ḥabad discourses. See, for instance, Schneersohn, *Sefer ha-Ma'amarim 5669*, p. 39, and further explication in Schneerson, *Torat Menaḥem: Hitwwa'aduyyot 5713*, 3:55–56. See chapter 6, n. 163. On the superiority of Messiah vis-à-vis Moses, see Shneur Zalman, *Liqquṭei Torah*, Ṣaw, 1:17a; Schneersohn, *Ner Miṣwah we-Torah Or*, 89a; Schneerson, *Liqquṭei Siḥot*, 6:254; 16:491; 21:351; *Torat Menaḥem: Hitwwa'aduyyot 5717*, 2:272 (cited in chapter 4, n. 96); *Torat Menaḥem: Hitwwa'aduyyot 5718*, 1:278–279 (cited in the postface at n. 168).

42. Shneur Zalman of Liadi, *Liqquṭei Amarim: Tanya*, part 1, chapter 42, 59a; *Liqquṭei Torah*, Wayyiqra, 1:2a; *Torah Or*, 68c; *Ma'amerei Admor ha-Zaqen 5566*, 2:463; Schneersohn, *Ma'amerei Admor ha-Emṣa'i: Hanaḥot*, p. 271; Schneersohn, *Or ha-Torah: Bemidbar*, 1:134; Schneersohn, *Liqquṭei Torah: Torat Shmu'el 5632*, 2:444; Schneersohn, *Sefer ha-Ma'amarim 5689*, p. 175; *Sefer ha-Siḥot 5688–5691*, p. 167; *Sefer ha-Siḥot 5706–5710*, pp. 242, 347; Schneerson, *Torat Menaḥem: Hitwwa'aduyyot 5711*, 1:266; *Torat Menaḥem: Sefer ha-Ma'amarim Meluqaṭ*, 4:24.

43. Schneerson, *Torat Menaḥem: Hitwwa'aduyyot 5717*, 2:305; *Torat Menaḥem: Hitwwa'aduyyot 5719*, 1:329; *Torat Menaḥem: Hitwwa'aduyyot 5720*, 1:172, 374; *Torat Menaḥem: Hitwwa'aduyyot 5745*, 5:2619.

44. Shneur Zalman of Liadi, *Liqquṭei Amarim: Tanya*, part 1, chapter 42, 59a; Schneersohn, *Liqquṭei Torah: Torat Shmu'el 5632*, 1:46; Schneersohn, *Sefer ha-Ma'amarim 5689*, p. 177; Schneerson, *Torat Menaḥem: Hitwwa'aduyyot 5710*, pp. 121, 184; *Torat Menaḥem: Hitwwa'aduyyot 5711*, 1:236, 251, 266, 269; *Torat Menaḥem: Hitwwa'aduyyot 5717*, 2:305; *Iggerot Qodesh*, no. 1838, 6:332. The link between *yeḥidah* and *yaḥid* is based on the description of the soul as singular in the body (*yeḥidah ba-guf*) and the characterization of God's oneness in his world (*yaḥid be-olamo*) found in older sources. See *Midrash Wayyiqra Rabbah* 4:8, p. 97; *Midrash Devarim Rabbah* 2:37, in *Midrash Rabbah im Kol ha-Mefarshim*, 6:53; *Midrash Tehillim*, 103:4, 217a. On the rabbinic designation of the soul as *yeḥidah*, see *Sifre on Deuteronomy*, sec. 313, p. 355, and references to other sources cited in n. 4.

45. Schneersohn, *Sefer ha-Siḥot 5703*, p. 145.

46. Schneersohn, *Iggerot Qodesh*, no. 2166, 8:19.

47. Schneerson, *Torat Menaḥem: Hitwwa'aduyyot 5712*, 3:41.

48. Schneerson, *Torat Menaḥem: Hitwwa'aduyyot 5718*, 3:55.

49. Schneerson, *Torat Menaḥem: Hitwwa'aduyyot 5710*, pp. 108, 111, 113, 122, 200, 201; *Torat Menaḥem: Hitwwa'aduyyot 5711*, 1:174, 236; *Torat Menaḥem: Hitwwa'aduyyot 5711*, 2:150, 174–175; *Torat Menaḥem: Hitwwa'aduyyot 5712*, 3:41–42; *Torat Menaḥem: Hitwwa'aduyyot 5715*, 1:203, 336; *Torat Menaḥem: Hitwwa'aduyyot 5715*, 2:133; *Torat Menaḥem: Hitwwa'aduyyot 5716*, 2:139, 356; *Torat Menaḥem: Hitwwa'aduyyot 5748*, 2:324; *Torat Menaḥem: Sefer ha-Ma'amarim Meluqaṭ*, 3:42–43.

50. Schneerson, *Torat Menaḥem: Hitwwa'aduyyot 5710*, p. 111.

51. Schneerson, *Iggerot Qodesh*, no. 1838, 6:332–333; *Torat Menaḥem: Hitwwa'aduyyot 5711*, 1:251, 273; *Torat Menaḥem: Hitwwa'aduyyot 5712*, 1:282–283; *Torat Menaḥem: Hitwwa'aduyyot 5714*, 2:262; *Torat Menaḥem: Hitwwa'aduyyot 5716*, 2:339. On the explicit identification of the essence of the Rebbe as the essence of divinity, see *Torat Menaḥem: Hitwwa'aduyyot 5716*, 1:141. See the comments of Garb, *"The Chosen will Become Herds"*, pp. 126–127, 150–151.

52. Schneerson, *Iggerot Qodesh*, no. 1028, 4:304.

53. Schneerson, *Iggerot Qodesh*, no. 1838, 6:332; no. 4147, 12:327; no. 5083, 14:315; no. 5605, 15:2875; no. 8927, 23:314; *Torat Menaḥem: Hitwwa'aduyyot 5710*, pp. 55, 128–129, 184, 200; *Torat Menaḥem: Hitwwa'aduyyot 5711*, 1:267; *Torat Menaḥem: Hitwwa'aduyyot 5711*, 2:213–214, 220; *Torat Menaḥem: Hitwwa'aduyyot 5712*, 2:177; *Torat Menaḥem: Hitwwa'aduyyot 5712*, 3:41; *Torat Menaḥem: Hitwwa'aduyyot 5715*, 1:203. See, however, Schneerson, *Torat Menaḥem: Hitwwa'aduyyot 5746*, 4:35–36. In describing the redemption of the "leader of Israel" (*nasi be-yisra'el*) on 12–13 Tammuz—the birthday of Yosef Yiṣḥaq Schneerson (1880) and the anniversary of his release from imprisonment in Soviet Russia (1927)—Schneerson remarked that the word *nasi* is an acrostic for *niṣoṣo shel ya'aqov avinu*, "the spark of Jacob our father," an idea linked to the belief that the soul of Jacob contains the souls of all the Jewish people, and hence the liberation of the sixth Rebbe amounts to the "redemption of the totality of Israel, and the redemption of all matters of the world, which are for the sake of Israel." This depiction of Jacob is based on the aggadic view that the beauty of Jacob was like the beauty of Adam (Babylonian Talmud, Baba Meṣi'a 84a), and, just as the latter was thought to be composed of all the souls of the future generations of human beings, which are related more specifically to the ethnicity of Israel, so too the former. This empowered Jacob, moreover,

to rectify the sin of Adam. The likely source for Schneerson's formulation is Shneur Zalman of Liadi, *Liqquṭei Amarim: Tanya*, part 4, sec. 7, 111b–112a. Also relevant here is another tradition (transmitted in the name of R. Yoḥanan) that Jacob did not die; see Babylonian Talmud, Ta'anit 5b. See the lengthy note on this matter in Schneerson, *Iggerot Qodesh*, no. 20, 1:36-37, and discussion in *Liqquṭei Siḥot*, 35:223–228. On the application of this aggadic tradition to the sixth Rebbe, see Schneerson, *Torat Menaḥem Hitwwa'aduyyot 5714*, 2:58; *Torat Menaḥem Hitwwa'aduyyot 5723*, 2:114; *Torat Menaḥem Hitwwa'aduyyot 5751*, 2:94; *Sefer ha-Siḥot 5751*, 1:213. On decoding the word *nasi* as the acrostic *niṣoṣo shel ya'aqov avinu*, see Schneerson, *Torat Menaḥem: Hitwwa'aduyyot 5716*, 1:283, where the source is given as Yalles, *Qehillat Ya'aqov*, s.v. Rabbi, 9c. See also Schneerson, *Liqquṭei Siḥot*, 4:1061, n. 18. The tradition that R. Judah the Prince was the spark of Jacob based on this acrostic is found as well in Shapira, *Megalleh Amuqot*, 2:12c; and *Megalleh Amuqot: RN"B*, sec. 83, 61a.

54. Schneerson, *Torat Menaḥem: Hitwwa'aduyyot 5710*, p. 122. See *Torat Menaḥem: Hitwwa'aduyyot 5711*, 1:174.

55. Schneerson, *Torat Menaḥem: Hitwwa'aduyyot 5710*, p. 201.

56. Viṭal, *Sha'ar ha-Gilgulim*, introduction, sec. 20, 19b–20a; *Sefer ha-Liqquṭim*, pp. 146–147; *Liqquṭei Torah*, p. 130.

57. Schneerson, *Torat Menaḥem: Hitwwa'aduyyot 5715*, 1:202–203; *Torat Menaḥem: Hitwwa'aduyyot 5745*, 5:2619–2620.

58. Schneersohn, *Iggerot Qodesh*, no. 72, 1:141. See Schneerson, *Torat Menaḥem: Sefer ha-Ma'amarim Meluqaṭ*, 1:284.

59. Schneerson, *Torat Menaḥem: Hitwwa'aduyyot 5711*, 1:231; *Torat Menaḥem: Hitwwa'aduyyot 5720*, 1:172.

60. This title of honor, which is conferred upon the Ḥasidic master, is literally an acronym for *adoneinu morenu we-rabbenu*, "our lord, our teacher, our master."

61. Schneerson, *Sefer ha-Ma'amarim 5730–5731*, p. 139. See *Torat Menaḥem: Hitwwa'aduyyot 5711*, 1:128; *Iggerot Qodesh*, no. 5605, 15:287.

62. Schneerson, *Torat Menaḥem: Hitwwa'aduyyot 5717*, 2:305. In that context, the Rebbe also mentions the words of the RaShaB that he reportedly uttered several hours before his departure from this world, "I am going to heaven, but I will leave the writings for you" (*Ich gay in himmel di kesavim loz ich fahr aykh*). See Schneersohn, *Iggerot Qodesh*, no. 59, 1:113. On study of a particular master's teaching as a means to unite with him, see the explication of Shneur Zalman of Liadi, *Liqquṭei Amarim: Tanya*, part 1, chapter 5, 9a–10a, in Schneerson, *Torat Menaḥem: Hitwwa'aduyyot 5716*, 2:241. See also *Torat Menaḥem: Hitwwa'aduyyot 5710*, pp. 16–17.

63. *Zohar* 1:27b. In that passage, which is from the *Tiqqunim*, the burial place of Moses is identified as the Mishnah.

64. Menaḥem Naḥum of Chernobyl, *Me'or Einayim*, 2: 511.

65. Schneerson, *Torat Menaḥem: Hitwwa'aduyyot 5710*, p. 108. On Schneerson's worship at his father-in-law's gravesite, see Ehrlich, *Leadership in the HaBaD Movement*, pp. 108–109, 386.

66. The epithet *ba'al ha-ge'ullah* for the sixth Rebbe appears frequently in the words of the seventh Rebbe. See, for instance, Schneerson, *Liqquṭei Siḥot*, 8:345; *Torat Menaḥem:*

Hitwwa'aduyyot 5712, 3:41; *Torat Menaḥem: Hitwwa'aduyyot 5743*, 4:1733–1735; *Torat Menaḥem: Hitwwa'aduyyot 5744*, 4:2207–2208; *Torat Menaḥem: Hitwwa'aduyyot 5745*, 4:2514.

67. Schneerson, *Torat Menaḥem: Hitwwa'aduyyot 5751*, 2:94; *Sefer ha-Siḥot 5751*, 2:595.

68. Babylonian Talmud, Sanhedrin 97a.

69. Schneerson, *Torat Menaḥem: Hitwwa'aduyyot 5711*, 1:236.

70. To be precise, there were four parts to the discourse, two to be published on 10 and 13 Shevaṭ, respectively the anniversary of the deaths of Yosef Yiṣḥaq's grandmother and mother, the third to be published for Purim, and the fourth for 2 Nisan, the anniversary of the death of his father, the RaShaB. The series of discourses is published in Schneersohn, *Sefer ha-Ma'amarim 5710–5711*, part 1, pp. 111–137, 151–155. The original discourses that served as the basis for the later embellishment can be found in Schneersohn, *Sefer ha-Ma'amarim 5682–5683*, pp. 168–196.

71. *Midrash Bere'shit Rabba* 19:7, pp. 176–177. See Shneur Zalman of Liadi, *Liqquṭei Amarim: Tanya*, part 1, chapter 42, 59a.

72. Schneersohn, *Sefer ha-Ma'amarim 5710–5711*, part 1, p. 111. For the earlier version, see *Sefer ha-Ma'amarim 5682–5683*, p. 168.

73. *Midrash Wayyiqra Rabbah* 29:11, pp. 680–681. Compare Schneerson, *Reshimot*, sec. 165, 5:144–145.

74. Schneerson, *Torat Menaḥem: Hitwwa'aduyyot, 5711* 1:194–195, 202. For extensive analyses of the concept of the seventh generation in the messianic activism of the seventh Rebbe, see Kraus, "'Living with the Times'"; and *The Seventh*; see also Kohanzad, "Messianic Doctrine," pp. 85–94.

75. The point was noted (albeit without documentation) by Sharot, *Messianism, Mysticism, and Magic*, p. 205. For a delineation of the similarities and dissimilarities between Shneur Zalman and Menaḥem Mendel, see Ehrlich, *Leadership in the HaBaD Movement*, pp. 153–156.

76. Schneerson, *Torat Menaḥem: Hitwwa'aduyyot 5711*, 2:150; *Torat Menaḥem: Hitwwa'aduyyot 5719*, 1:329. On the centrality of the messianic goal in Schneerson's inaugural talk, see Loewenthal, "Contemporary Habad," pp. 384–385; Kohanzad, "Messianic Doctrine," pp. 19–20.

77. Dahan, "The Last Redeemer"; see also Dan, *The Modern Jewish Messianism*, pp. 194–197.

78. The bibliography on the Beshṭ is quite substantial, so I will here only refer to some of the more recent works where one can find ample reference to other relevant scholarship: Rosman, *Founder of Hasidism*; Etkes, *The Besht*; Elior, *Mystical Origins*, pp. 59–71; Lederberg, *Sod ha-Da'at*. On the depiction of the Beshṭ in Ḥabad, see the evidence adduced by Mondshine, *Shivhei ha-Baal Shem Tov*, pp. 243–260.

79. Feldman, *Lubavitchers as Citizens*, p. xii.

80. Discussion of the various genre of literary sources that preserve the Rebbe's teachings, including the issues of translation, transmission, and censorship, can be found in Kohanzad, "Messianic Doctrine," pp. 24–41.

81. See the comments with regard to Schneerson's letters in English offered by Mindel, *The Letter and the Spirit*, p. ix: "The Rebbe neither wrote nor dictated—in the conventional sense of the term—any of the letters in this volume. Mine was the exclusive and awesome responsibility of rendering his responses, communicated to me in Hebrew and Yiddish, into the English language." With respect to the thousands of letters in Yiddish and/or Hebrew, we have to distinguish between those signed by Schneerson and those signed by a secretary.

82. Schneersohn, *Torat Shalom: Sefer ha-Siḥot*, p. iii. On the relationship of Hebrew to the seventy languages, and the special status of Yiddish, see Schneerson, *Liqquṭei Siḥot*, 21:446–448.

83. It is of interest in this regard to recall the tradition recorded by Schneersohn, *Sefer ha-Siḥot 5703*, pp. 136–137: the Oral Torah denotes the Alter Rebbe's hearing a teaching from the Maggid of Międzyrzecz, whereas the Written Torah refers to his hearing a story. The privilege accorded orality is evident from this taxonomy. In the continuation of this talk, the study of the Written Torah encompasses the dicta of the sages in the aggadic, midrashic, and zoharic corpora, whereas the study of the Oral Torah is related to the "inwardness of matters," which does not designate the hidden mysteries of the kabbalah, but the "inwardness that is in the external, for the revealed is a garment, and there must be an internal knowledge, that is, the study of the Oral Torah will be through the fear of heaven."

84. For a thorough analysis of the seven masters of the Lubavitch sect, see Ehrlich, *Leadership in the HaBaD Movement*. See also the discussion of the "transitional consolidation" of the movement in Ehrlich, *The Messiah of Brooklyn*, pp. 51–80.

85. Schneerson, *Torat Menaḥem: Hitwwa'aduyyot 5714*, 1:276. The expression *ḥag ha-ge'ullah*, the "festival of redemption," is applied to 12–13 Tammuz as well; see n. 103, this chapter.

86. See the passage from an epistle by the RaShaB at the beginning of *Ha-Yom Yom*, an anthology of Yosef Yiṣḥaq Schneersohn's teachings collected and edited by Schneerson, p. 4. See also Schneerson, *Liqquṭei Siḥot*, 5:436; *Torat Menaḥem: Hitwwa'aduyyot 5744*, 4:2207.

87. For example, see Schneerson, *Liqquṭei Siḥot*, 10:101.

88. Needless to say, Jung speaks about the principle of individuation in many places, but the one text that most influenced my own words here is Jung, *Dream Analysis*, pp. 288–289.

89. Jung, *The Archetypes and the Collective Unconscious*, p. 275.

90. Here it is also worthwhile to recall that on the frontispiece of the *Tanya*, beginning with the *editio princeps* (Slavuta, 1796) and continuing in all subsequent editions, the book is described as being "assembled from books and authors of the holy, supernal ones" (*meluqaṭ mi-pi sefarim u-mi-pi soferim qedoshei elyon*). Shneur Zalman already demonstrated the characteristic modesty of the master by casting his thoughts as elicited from previous authorities, thereby minimizing his own innovativeness.

91. Schneerson, *Torat Menaḥem: Hitwwa'aduyyot 5715*, 2:133–134.

92. The point is, quite literally, etched in stone, as the Rebbe is described on his tombstone as "filling the place" (*memalle meqomo*) of his father-in-law. See Schneerson, *Torat Menaḥem: Hitwwa'aduyyot 5715*, 2:133, where the Rebbe explains that *memalle meqomo*

means that a person has all the properties of the one whose place he fills, but he also has a supplement. For more on this expression, see n. 106, this chapter.

93. *Zohar* 1:253a; Viṭal, *Sha'ar ha-Pesuqim*, p. 99; Schneerson, *Torat Menaḥem: Hitwwa'aduyyot 5711*, 1:236; *Torat Menaḥem: Hitwwa'aduyyot 5713*, 2:36; *Sefer ha-Siḥot* 5752, pp. 313–314; *Iggerot Qodesh*, no. 4506, 13:240.

94. Schneerson, *Torat Menaḥem: Hitwwa'aduyyot 5711*, 1:128.

95. Exod 14:8.

96. Schneerson, *Torat Menaḥem: Hitwwa'aduyyot 5711*, 1:202–203.

97. It is worth pondering if the Rebbe considered his father-in-law the Messiah son of Joseph, the savior who, according to the tradition, suffers physical death. If that is so, it would lend credence to those who maintain that he thought of himself as the Messiah son of David, the figure assigned with the task to complete the redemption. On the two messiahs, see Schneerson, *Iggerot Qodesh*, no. 288, 2:234; *Torat Menaḥem: Hitwwa'aduyyot 5723*, 1:323. See n. 112, this chapter.

98. Schneerson, *Torat Menaḥem: Hitwwa'aduyyot 5711*, 1:200–201. Reference is made to the discussion of *histallequt* in the *Iggeret ha-Qodesh* of Shneur Zalman of Liadi (see n. 35, this chapter). See also Schneerson, *Sefer ha-Ma'amarim: Ba'ti le-Ganni*, 1:235, reprinted in *Sefer ha-Ma'amarim 5730–5731*, p. 119.

99. See n. 68, this chapter.

100. The wordplay is based on the comments of the sixth Rebbe in the *hemshekh* for 13 Shevaṭ 5710 (January 31, 1950). See Schneersohn, *Sefer ha-Ma'amarim 5710–5711*, part 1, pp. 119–120.

101. Schneerson, *Torat Menaḥem: Hitwwa'aduyyot 5711*, 1:236. See Schneerson, *Liqquṭei Siḥot*, 25:481.

102. Schneerson, *Sefer ha-Siḥot* 5752, p. 111. See also Schneerson, *Torat Menaḥem: Hitwwa'aduyyot* 5750, 2:174; *Torat Menaḥem: Hitwwa'aduyyot* 5752, 1:420–421.

103. Schneersohn, *Iggerot Qodesh*, no. 386, 2:80. See Schneerson, *Torat Menaḥem: Hitwwa'aduyyot 5710*, p. 125; *Liqquṭei Siḥot*, 8:344–345; and the end of n. 106, this chapter.

104. Schneerson, *Torat Menaḥem: Hitwwa'aduyyot* 5745, 5:2616–2617. See n. 18, this chapter.

105. See n. 74, this chapter. See Tishby, "The Messianic Idea," pp. 37–41; and the comment of Dan, "The Duality of Hasidic Messianism," p. 314, n. 28, that Menaḥem Mendel Schneerson's understanding of the messianic mission of Ḥasidism has affinity to the view of the historian Ben-Zion Dinur. Like Tishby, Dinur took issue with Scholem's well-known thesis regarding the neutralization of messianism in the East European pietism, an approach he shared famously with Simon Dubnow and Martin Buber. See Dubnow, "The Beginnings," pp. 36–45; Buber, *Hasidism*, pp. 6–17, 25–33, 34–59, 112–116; Scholem, *The Messianic Idea in Judaism*, pp. 176–202; Dinur, "The Origins of Hasidism," pp. 90–92. For a critical review of the previous scholarship, see Idel, *Hasidism*, pp. 16–17. On the messianic elements and mystical redemption in early Ḥasidism, see also Schatz-Uffenheimer, "The Messianic Element in Ḥasidic Thought"; "Self-Redemption in Hasidic Thought"; *Hasidism as Mysticism*, pp. 326–339; Werblowsky, "Mysticism and Messianism"; Green, *Tormented Master*, pp. 182–220; Piekarz,

"The Messianic Idea"; Morgenstern, *Mysticism and Messianism*; Idel, *Messianic Mystics*, pp. 212–247.

106. See n. 92, this chapter, where I remarked that the expression *memalle meqomo* is carved on Schneerson's tombstone to depict his relationship to the Friediker Rebbe. In addition to this relationship, as well as the relationship of the Friediker Rebbe to his father, the RaShaB (see following note), the locution is used to describe other relationships, such as the Maggid of Międzyrzecz vis-à-vis the Besht (Schneersohn, *Sefer ha-Siḥot 5701*, p. 136; Schneerson, *Iggerot Qodesh*, no. 7371, 19:373; *Torat Menaḥem: Hitwwa'aduyyot 5718*, 3:53), the Mitteler Rebbe vis-à-vis his father, the Alter Rebbe (Schneerson, *Iggerot Qodesh*, no. 8558, 22:368; no. 8987, 23:400; no. 9053, 24:31; no. 9618, 26:52; *Torat Menaḥem: Hitwwa'aduyyot 5711*, 1:326; *Torat Menaḥem: Hitwwa'aduyyot 5717*, 2:177; *Torat Menaḥem: Hitwwa'aduyyot 5718*, 2:165; *Torat Menaḥem: Hitwwa'aduyyot 5718*, 3:266; *Torat Menaḥem: Sefer ha-Ma'amarim Meluqaṭ*, 2:95, 463, 3:126; *Liqquṭei Siḥot*, 35:261, 292), and the fourth Rebbe vis-à-vis the Ṣemaḥ Ṣedeq (Schneerson, *Torat Menaḥem: Hitwwa'aduyyot 5714*, 3:141). On the use of the expression *memalle meqomo* to refer to each of the links on the chain of the Ḥabad-Lubavitch leadership until the Messiah, see Schneerson, *Liqquṭei Siḥot*, 39:332.

107. Schneerson, *Torat Menaḥem: Hitwwa'aduyyot 5715*, 2:133; *Torat Menaḥem: Hitwwa'aduyyot 5716*, 2:186; *Torat Menaḥem: Hitwwa'aduyyot 5717*, 2:27; *Torat Menaḥem: Hitwwa'aduyyot 5717*, 3:112; *Torat Menaḥem: Hitwwa'aduyyot 5720*, 1:300, 343; *Liqquṭei Siḥot*, 32:23; *Torat Menaḥem: Sefer ha-Ma'amarim Meluqaṭ*, 1:284, 299, 3:126, 4:275. See ibid., 4:25, where Yosef Yiṣḥaq is described as filling the place of Shneur Zalman, as both were released from imprisonment (the former on 12–13 Tammuz and the latter on 19 Kislev) and hence they both are accorded the title "master of redemption" (*ba'al ha-ge'ullah*).

108. Schneerson, *Siḥot Qodesh 5752*, 1:318. See also Schneerson, *Torat Menaḥem: Hitwwa'aduyyot 5752*, 2:282: in the body of the talk, the word *mi-yad* in the entreaty the Rebbe used repeatedly to traverse the temporal divide from the exilic present to the messianic future, *tekhef u-mi-yad mammash*, is decoded as an acronym for Moses, Israel (that is, the Besht), and David. In n. 148, however, the decoding relates to the last three Lubavitch masters: Menaḥem, Yosef Yiṣḥaq, and Dovber. All three constitute the countenance of the Messiah.

109. On the symbolic correlation of the sixth and seventh leaders of Ḥabad respectively with *Yesod* and *Malkhut*, see Kraus, "'Living with the Times,'" pp. 115–123; *The Seventh*, pp. 41–49. The point was also noted by Handelman, "Putting Women in the Picture," posted at http://www.chabad.org/theJewishWoman/article_cdo/aid/16`694/jewish/Putting-Women-in-the-Picture.htm. The author remarks that the essay is adapted from the forthcoming volume *The Chabad Movement in the Twentieth Century*, edited by Yitzhak Kraus and Moshe Hallamish. She estimated that the book would be published by Bar-Ilan University Press in 2005, but I have learned from one of the editors that the date of publication is currently set as 2009. On the symbolic representation of the Rebbe as *Malkhut*, see also Dalfin, *The Seven Chabad Lubavitch Rebbes*, pp. 132–133; Dahan, "'Dira Bataḥtonim,'" pp. 205–234.

110. Schneerson, *Quntres Inyanah shel Torat ha-Ḥasidut,* pp. 16–18. Although all passages from this text are my own translations, I call the reader's attention to an independent rendering published as *On the Essence of Chasidus.*

111. Shneur Zalman of Liadi, *Liqquṭei Amarim: Tanya,* part 2, chapter 7, 81b–82b.

112. On the relationship of *Yesod* and *Malkhut,* with reference to the messianic implications of the latter, see Schneerson, *Torat Menaḥem: Hitwwa'aduyyot 5716,* 3:93–94. Commenting on a distinction made in a zoharic passage (3:204a) between two types of morning, one linked to Abraham, the attribute of *Ḥesed,* and the other to Joseph, the attribute of *Yesod,* the Rebbe noted that in the case of the latter, "there is already a connection to that which receives," that is, the attribute of *Malkhut.* On the connection between Shemini Aṣeret, the eight days of Ḥanukah, Joseph, and the sixth Rebbe, see Schneerson, *Torat Menaḥem: Hitwwa'aduyyot 5723,* 1:324, and *Liqquṭei Siḥot,* 3:835. In the latter context, the seven guests (*ushpizin*), associated with the seven days of Sukkot, are delineated as the Beshṭ, the Maggid of Międzyrzecz, the Alter Rebbe, the Mitteler Rebbe, the Ṣemaḥ Ṣedeq, the Rebbe MahaRaSh, and the Rebbe RaShaB; the Friediker Rebbe, the eighth, corresponds to Shemini Aṣeret, which is related, in turn, to Joseph the Righteous, since his righteousness is related to circumcision and *tiqqun ha-berit,* the rectification of the phallus through resisting sexual temptation. See postface at n. 164. On the identification of the sixth Rebbe with the biblical Joseph, see also Schneerson, *Torat Menaḥem: Hitwwa'aduyyot 5717,* 2:364. On the connection between the eight days of Ḥanukah, the eight human princes (*shemonah nesikhei adam*) mentioned in Mic 5:4, and the messianic rectification, see Shneur Zalman of Liadi, *Torah Or,* 33b–34c. See also Schneersohn, *Torat Ḥayyim: Bere'shit,* 217b.

113. Schneerson, *Torat Menaḥem: Hitwwa'aduyyot 5743,* 4:1735. On the special obligation of Jews in free countries toward Russian Jewry, see *Torat Menaḥem: Hitwwa'aduyyot 5716,* 2:356. Many of the relevant comments of Schneerson pertaining to the lot of the Jews who lived in the Soviet Union are collected in *Diedushka.*

114. Palestinian Talmud, Sheqalim 6:1, 49d; Megillah 1:4, 70d; Soṭah 3:1, 22d; Babylonian Talmud, Pesaḥim 6b; *Mekhilta de-Rabbi Ishmael,* p. 139; *Midrash Tanḥuma,* Terumah, 8. For discussion of this principle of rabbinic hermeneutics, see Heschel, *Heavenly Torah,* pp. 240–243; Schlüter, "The Creative Force of a Hermeneutic Rule."

115. *Sefer Yeṣirah,* 1:7.

116. For an explicit reference, see Schneersohn, *Liqquṭei Torah: Torat Shmu'el 5638,* p. 116, and compare the discussion of the work in Lieberman, *Ohel Raḥel,* 1:93–99.

117. Moses of Kiev, *Shoshan Sodot,* 60b.

118. For a more detailed discussion of this conception of temporality, see the chapter entitled "Linear Circularity / (A)temporal Poetics" in Wolfson, *Alef, Mem, Tau,* pp. 55–117, and especially pp. 107–117, where I engage some Ḥabad texts to articulate my ideas. Needless to say, this discussion could have been greatly expanded. I am presently working on an essay that analyzes the views of time enunciated in Ḥabad thinking, though surely a whole monograph on this topic is in order.

119. Based on the rabbinic idea that Israel is one of the items that arose in the thought of God prior to its having been created. See *Midrash Bere'shit Rabba* 1:4, p. 6.

120. Schneerson, *Torat Menaḥem: Hitwwa'aduyyot 5752,* 2:242–243.

121. Ibid., p. 243.

122. The view of Schneerson can be compared profitably to Deleuze, *Difference and Repetition*, pp. 90–91: "We produce something new only on condition that we repeat—once in the mode which constitutes the past, and once more in the present of metamorphosis. Moreover, what is produced, the absolutely new itself, is in turn nothing but repetition: the third repetition, this time by excess, the repetition of the future as eternal return. . . . The order of time has broken the circle of the Same and arranged time in a series only in order to re-form, a circle of the Other at the end of the series. . . . The form of time is there only for the revelation of the formless in the eternal return. . . . In this manner, the ground has been superseded by a groundlessness, a universal ungrounding which turns upon itself and causes only the yet-to-come to return." As I have suggested elsewhere, the Deleuzian interpretation of Nietzsche's eternal recurrence of the same bears a striking resemblance as well to Rosenzweig and to Derrida. See Wolfson, "Structure, Innovation," pp. 156–159.

123. Elior, *The Paradoxical Ascent to God*, p. xii.

124. Ibid., p. xiii.

125. Ibid. For a more nuanced approach, see Weiss, *Studies in Eastern European Jewish Mysticism*, pp. 202–208; and, more recently, Goldberg, "Zaddik's Soul." On the essentially ahistorical nature of Lubavitch, see also Rigg, *Rescued From the Reich*, pp. 211–212.

126. Shneur Zalman of Liadi, *Liqquṭei Amarim: Tanya*, part 1, chapter 36, 46a–b; *Seder Tefillot*, 132a; Schneersohn, *Sha'arei Teshuvah*, 142d; Schneerson, *Liqquṭei Siḥot*, 9:63–64.

127. Shneur Zalman of Liadi, *Liqquṭei Amarim: Tanya*, part 1, chapter 36, 46a; *Ma'amerei Admor ha-Zaqen 5572*, p. 188; *Ma'amerei Admor ha-Zaqen ha-Qeṣarim*, p. 144; Schneersohn, *Imrei Binah*, part 2, 25d; Schneerson, *Torat Menaḥem: Sefer ha-Ma'amarim Meluqaṭ*, 1:140–141.

128. Schneersohn, *Sefer ha-Ma'amarim 5701*, p. 9.

129. Schneerson, *Torat Menaḥem: Hitwwa'aduyyot 5717*, 2:363. The noetic and gnostic quality of the Rebbe's conception of personal redemption has been emphasized by Kohanzad, "Messianic Doctrine," pp. 22, 52, 123, 148, 154–155, 161, 228–229.

130. For a more extensive discussion of my Heideggerian-inflected hermeneutic of kabbalistic esotericism, see Wolfson, *Language, Eros, Being*, pp. 1–45. See also Steinbock, *Phenomenology and Mysticism*, pp. 149–166. The author includes a philosophically astute, though textually derivative, discussion of the "mysticism of ecstasy" in Dov Baer Schneersohn, pp. 67–88.

131. *Tiqqunei Zohar*, introduction, 17a, and see also sec. 69, 116a.

132. Epstein, *Ma'amar ha-Shiflut we-ha-Simḥah*, p. 159.

133. Epstein, *Ma'amar Yeṣi'at Miṣrayim*, 19c.

134. Badiou, *Being and Event*, pp. 304–305.

135. Ibid., p. 189.

1. Concealing the Concealment

1. A telling example to illustrate the point is the letter written by the Rebbe's father, Levi Yiṣḥaq Schneersohn, on 6 Kislev 5689 (November 19, 1928) in honor of his upcom-

ing marriage a few days later in Warsaw on the fourteenth of that month (November 27). The letter relates the concrete matrimonial issues to the complex kabbalistic symbols, which indicates that there is no justification to impose a distinction between the "real" and symbolic worlds. The text is printed in Schneersohn, *Liqquṭei Levi Yiṣḥaq*, pp. 203–206. For discussion of the historical details surrounding the Rebbe's wedding, see Deutsch, *Larger Than Life*, 2:209–248.

2. Loewenthal, *Communicating the Infinite*, p. 52. As Hallamish, "Theoretical System," noted, Shneur Zalman was influenced by both Cordovero and Luria. See, for instance, the discussion of the doctrine of the *sefirot* on pp. 61–69, and the summary discussion, pp. 392–400.

3. Schneerson, *Torat Menaḥem: Hitwwa'aduyyot 5714*, 1:271. For a similar account, see Schneerson, *Sefer ha-Siḥot 5700*, pp. 80–81.

4. Schneerson, *Torat Menaḥem: Hitwwa'aduyyot 5714*, 1:277.

5. Schneerson, *Torat Menaḥem: Hitwwa'aduyyot 5750*, 2:15.

6. Schneerson, *Torat Menaḥem: Sefer ha-Ma'amarim Meluqaṭ*, 2:36–37.

7. Schneerson, *Torat Menaḥem: Hitwwa'aduyyot 5750*, 2:22.

8. See introduction, n. 66.

9. Schneerson, *Quntres Inyanah shel Torat ha-Ḥasidut,* p. 1.

10. Schneersohn, *Sefer ha-Siḥot 5701*, p. 137.

11. Schneerson, *Torat Menaḥem: Sefer ha-Ma'amarim Meluqaṭ*, 3:126. See Schneerson, *Iggerot Qodesh*, no. 4487, 13:220, and *Torat Menaḥem: Hitwwa'aduyyot 5720*, 1:189–190: "Inasmuch as the interiority of the Torah is a portion of the Oral Torah, for the order of its study must be precisely through understanding and comprehension . . . it is understood that the dissemination and spreading forth of the interiority of the Torah must also be in the manner of understanding and comprehension [*be-havanah we-hassagah*], as it is garbed in the corporeal intellect, in the manner that is appropriate as well to the intellect of the animal soul. . . . We must be occupied with the interiority of the Torah, the matter of the world of emanation, and to spread it in the world below in the manner of understanding and comprehension through the corporeal intellect." From the fuller context whence this text was elicited, it is evident that the publication of the secrets in this intellectual manner is the mission of the messianic redeemer. Thus, in the continuation of the discourse, we read (p. 190): "Since we are in the generation of the footsteps of the Messiah, concerning which [it is said] 'There he stands behind the wall' (Song of Songs 2:9) in actuality—it is appropriate that in order for the drawing forth to be from above there must be worship in like manner below, and this is the worship of 'Your wellsprings will spread outward' (Prov 5:16): 'will spread' [*yafuṣu*]—without measure and boundary, 'your wellspring' [*ma'yenotekha*]—the interiority of the Torah, for this is the matter of the world of emanation, until it also reaches 'outward' [*ḥuṣah*]—in this corporeal world, for this is the inwardness of the matter that the Messiah must fulfill openly before the eyes of all flesh."

12. Schneerson, *Torat Menaḥem: Hitwwa'aduyyot 5718*, 3:54–55 (see postface at n. 136).

13. Wolfson, "Occultation of the Feminine," pp. 113–124, reprinted in Wolfson, *Luminal Darkness*, pp. 258–264; *Abraham Abulafia*, pp. 9–93; *Language, Eros, Being*, pp. 10, 16, 26, 128–141, 220–221, 384.

14. Buber, *Hasidism*, p. 24. In spite of his critical assessment of Buber's interpretation of Ḥasidism, with respect to the "deschematization of the mystery," Scholem concurs. See Scholem, *The Messianic Idea in Judaism*, pp. 228–250, esp. 236–240. Regarding this hermeneutical debate, see Idel, "Martin Buber and Gershom Scholem on Hasidism," pp. 389–403, and references to other scholars enumerated on p. 389, n. 1. On the use of esoteric terminology in Buber's dialogical writings, see Koren, *The Mystery of the Earth*, pp. 209–213, 278–281, 310–311.

15. Elior, *The Paradoxical Ascent to God*, pp. 21 and 222. On the rejection of esotericism on the part of early Ḥabad and the particular impact this had on Dov Baer Schneerson's attempt to clarify the goals of contemplation and ecstasy, see ibid., pp. 193–195.

16. Jacob Joseph of Polonnoye, *Ben Porat Yosef*, 127b–128b. In addition to the Korets version, there are at least two other known versions: the second was first published by Frankel, *Letters from the Besht*, and published a second time from manuscript by Bauminger, "Letters of Our Rabbi Israel Ba'al Shem Ṭov," and the third version published from a different manuscript by Mondshine, *Shivhei ha-Baal Shem Tov*, pp. 229–242. For a critical assessment of the letter, including an English translation based on the Frankel-Bauminger version, see Rosman, *Founder of Hasidism*, pp. 99–113. Significantly, according to this version, the critical passage regarding the dissemination of the Beshṭ's teaching simply reads *ad she-yitpasheṭ toratekha be-khol ha-olam*, which Rosman renders "Once your Torah will have spread throughout the whole world" (ibid., p. 106). The wording from Prov 5:16 about the dissemination of the wellsprings outward, which was so crucial to Ḥabad philosophy, is missing. For analysis of the epistle and a synoptic English translation of the three versions, see Etkes, *The Besht*, pp. 79–91, 272–288. For discussion of the Beshṭ's letter and an English translation based on the standard version, see Lamm, *Religious Thought*, pp. 541–555. For a delineation of some of the other relevant scholarly analyses of the Beshṭ's letter, see Rosman, *Founder of Hasidism*, pp. 245–246, n. 8, and for an account of the place of this anthology of legends in the scholarship on Ḥasidism, see Rosman, *Stories That Changed History*, and references cited in the following note.

17. Jacob Joseph of Polonnoye, *Ben Porat Yosef*, 128a; see Loewenthal, *Communicating the Infinite*, pp. 13–14. Needless to say, the letter of the Beshṭ has commanded much scholarly attention. For relatively recent discussions, which take into account the previous scholarship, see Idel, *Messianic Mystics*, pp. 213–220; *Ascensions on High in Jewish Mysticism*, pp. 143–166; Altshuler, *The Messianic Secret of Hasidism*, pp. 14–28; Pedaya, "The Baal Shem Tov's Iggeret Hakodesh."

18. Schneersohn, *Sefer ha-Siḥot 5701*, pp. 132–139.

19. Schneerson, *Iggerot Qodesh*, no. 3636, 10:304.

20. Schneerson, *Torat Menaḥem: Hitwwa'aduyyot 5711*, 1:110.

21. Ibid., p. 111. See ibid., pp. 117–118, and the passage cited in n. 11, this chapter. On the charge of the Messiah to teach the "new Torah," that is, the secret matters that concern the knowledge of the divine, to the whole nation of Israel, see Schneerson, *Liqquṭei Siḥot*, 32:35, 180. It goes without saying that the seventh Rebbe's view is based on earlier sources. For instance, see Shneur Zalman of Liadi, *Liqquṭei Torah*, Ṣaw, 1:17a; Schneersohn, *Ner Miṣwah we-Torah Or*, 89a–b.

22. Schneerson, *Iggerot Qodesh*, no. 1037, 4:314.

23. Schneerson, *Torat Menaḥem: Hitwwa'aduyyot 5711*, 1:124. The description of the period before the arrival of the Messiah as a time of augmented darkness is a well-attested motif in sources that influenced the seventh Rebbe. For instance, see Shneur Zalman of Liadi, *Torah Or*, 41a.

24. Schneerson, *Torat Menaḥem: Hitwwa'aduyyot 5714*, 1:326; *Torat Menaḥem: Hitwwa'aduyyot 5716*, 2:230. See also Schneerson, *Iggerot Qodesh*, no. 4497, 13:230; no. 5647, 15:326; *Torat Menaḥem: Hitwwa'aduyyot 5711*, 2:213.

25. Schneerson, *Iggerot Qodesh*, no. 1042, 4:319.

26. Schneerson, *Torat Menaḥem: Hitwwa'aduyyot 5711*, 2:306; *Torat Menaḥem: Hitwwa'aduyyot 5713*, 1:180.

27. Schneerson, *Iggerot Qodesh*, no. 2886, 9:259–260. See also Schneerson, *Iggerot Qodesh*, no.7294, 19:293.

28. Based on the language of the twelfth of the thirteen principles of faith articulated by Maimonides, which deals with the belief in the Messiah and the need to wait for him on whatever day he will come (*aḥakkeh lo be-khol yom she-yavo*) even if he tarries.

29. Schneerson, *Torat Menaḥem: Hitwwa'aduyyot 5717*, 2:40. See Schneerson, *Iggerot Qodesh*, no. 4487, 13:219; *Torat Menaḥem: Hitwwa'aduyyot 5720*, 1:150.

30. Schneerson, *Torat Menaḥem: Hitwwa'aduyyot 5719*, 1:187.

31. That is, 5640, which corresponds to 1839/40.

32. *Zohar* 1:117a. See Schneerson, *Liqquṭei Siḥot*, 15:42–48; 35:241; and the fragment from the Rebbe's talk delivered on the last day of Passover, 22 Nisan 5730 (April 28, 1970) printed in Schneerson, *Qunṭres Inyanah shel Torat ha-Ḥasidut*, pp. 25–30.

33. Schneerson, *Liqquṭei Siḥot*, 15:48. On the synthesis of the scientific-technological and the mystical-spiritual elements in Schneerson's messianic orientation, see Loewenthal, "Contemporary Habad," pp. 389–390.

34. Previous discussions of esotericism and Ḥasidism, as one might expect, have often focused on the issue of messianism. Two recent works worthy of note are Altshuler, *The Messianic Secret of Hasidism* and Mark, *Scroll of Secrets*. On the portrayal of Ḥasidism as an esoteric discipline expressed as a piety of secrecy, see Magid, *Hasidism on the Margin*, pp. 1–108. On the transition from the esoteric to the exoteric in the figure of the seventh Rebbe, see Kraus, "'Living with the Times,'" pp. 97–105; *The Seventh*, pp. 36–40; Dahan, "'Dira Bataḥtonim,'" pp. 147–196.

35. Babylonian Talmud, Eruvin 65a, Sanhedrin 38a.

36. Schneerson, *Torat Menaḥem: Hitwwa'aduyyot 5713*, 2:215.

37. Ibid., p. 240.

38. Compare the oral tradition transmitted in the name of the Ṣemaḥ Ṣedeq: each of the four levels of meaning, *peshaṭ*, *remez*, *derash*, and *sod*, contains all four levels, and therefore we can speak of the *peshaṭ* within the *sod*, the *remez* within the *sod*, the *derash* within the *sod*, and the *sod* within the *sod*. The first was revealed by Simeon bar Yoḥai, the second by Isaac Luria, the third by the Beshṭ, and the fourth will be revealed by the Messiah. See *From Exile to Redemption*, 1:17.

39. Schneerson, *Torat Menaḥem: Hitwwa'aduyyot 5714*, 1:305. See Schneerson, *Torat Menaḥem: Hitwwa'aduyyot 5710*, p. 41; *Sefer ha-Siḥot 5752*, p. 319. On the metaphorical depiction of the teaching of Ḥasidism as oil, see Schneerson, *Qunṭres Inyanah shel Torat*

ha-Ḥasidut, pp. 7–8. On the nexus between oil (*shemen*), the number eight (*shemonah*), symbolized by the candles of the menorah and the strings on the harp of the Messiah, and the disclosure of the interiority of the Torah to be realized in the messianic era, see the discourse delivered on the new month of Kislev 5748 (November 22, 1987), printed in Schneerson, *Sefer ha-Sheliḥut 5741–5750*, p. 66. On the disclosure of the eight-stringed harp connected to the Messiah, see Babylonian Talmud, Erkhin 13b; Schneerson, *Iggerot Qodesh*, no. 2316, 8:71; *Torat Menaḥem: Hitwwa'aduyyot, 5716*, 2:252–253. See n. 122, this chapter. For more discussion of the messianic implications of the number eight, see postface, nn. 150–154. I note, finally, that the interiority of the Torah is also compared (on the basis of Babylonian Talmud, Ḥagigah 13a and Moses ben Maimon, *Mishneh Torah*, Yesodei Torah 2:12) to honey; see Schneerson, *Sefer ha-Siḥot 5752*, p. 318.

40. Schneerson, *Torat Menaḥem: Hitwwa'aduyyot 5744*, 2:921–922.

41. Schneersohn, *Imrei Binah*, part 1, 52b–54a.

42. *Zohar* 1:50b, 3:288b; *Zohar Ḥadash*, 8c (*Sitrei Otiyyot*); *Tiqqunei Zohar*, sec. 69, 115a.

43. The novelty of Dov Baer's approach is highlighted by recalling the remark of Shneur Zalman of Liadi, *Seder Tefillot*, 132a: the "reasons for the law" (*ṭa'amei torah*), whose root is in the "aspect of the concealed brain of *Arikh Anpin*," will be revealed in the future when the aspect of the splendor (*nogah*) (see chapter 4, n. 174) will be purified from the admixture of evil, which arose as a consequence of the cataclysm (*shevirah*) occasioned by the death of the first seven Edomite kings. "The purification [*berur*] is not complete until the future, and as long as there is a part of evil in the good, there cannot yet be the disclosure of the aspect of the reason and the supernal delight that is hidden in the commandments below, for the shell obscures." There are many technical kabbalistic motifs at work here, but what is important to emphasize presently is the fact that Shneur Zalman, in contrast to Dov Baer, maintains that the secrets that stem from the most recondite place will be revealed in the messianic future. On the depiction of the concealed brain (*moaḥ setima'ah*), identified further as *Attiq*, as the "supernal will" (*raṣon ha-elyon*) that appears as a "volition without any revealed reason" (*raṣon beli ṭa'am galluy*), see Shneur Zalman of Liadi, *Liqquṭei Torah*, Shir ha-Shirim, 2:48a.

44. *Zohar* 1:45a, 83b, 123a, 141b, 231a, 232b, 2:89a, 142a, 146b, 149q, 165b, 239a, 3:15a, 88b, 144a, 161b, 208a, 288a, 288b, 289b, 290a, 291b, 292a, 294a, 295b; *Zohar Ḥadash*, 65c; *Tiqqunei Zohar*, sec. 19, 41b, sec. 69, 115a.

45. *Zohar* 3:288b, 289b. The head-that-is-not-known (*reisha de-lo ityeda*) denotes the superlative aspect of the divine, also designated as the head-that-is-no-head (*reisha de-law reisha*).

46. Schneersohn, *Sefer ha-Ma'amarim 5689*, p. 176.

47. See, for instance, Shneur Zalman of Liadi, *Torah Or*, 44a–b.

48. Schneerson, *Liqquṭei Siḥot*, 31:177–183.

49. Babylonian Talmud, Megillah 7b.

50. The expression *kelot ha-nefesh*, linked exegetically to Ps 84:3, to demarcate the expiration of the soul that is the consequence of the passionate love of God appears frequently in Ḥabad sources. See, for instance, Shneur Zalman of Liadi, *Liqquṭei Amarim: Tanya*, part 1, chapter 3, 7b, chapter 50, 70b; part 2, introduction, 75b; part 5, 161b; Schneersohn, *Qunṭres*

ha-Tefillah, p. 11. For a corrected text and English translation, see *Tract on Prayer*, pp. 29–31. The terminology is not exclusive to Ḥabad. See, for instance, Levi Yiṣḥaq of Berditchev, *Qedushat Levi*, p. 324: "His worship should be in the aspect that is without limit, the supernal awe, the sacrifice of self [*mesirat nefesh*], and the annihilation of existence [*biṭṭul bi-meṣi'ut*], so that his worship would not be felt by him, but it would be in the ultimate nullification [*be-takhlit ha-biṭṭul*] and the lack of any feeling of self [*he'der hargashat aṣmuto*]. . . . David was in the aspect of nullification before the Lord, in the supernal awe, in the aspect of the annihilation of existence [*biṭṭul bi-meṣi'ut*]. Therefore, he 'whirled with all his might' (2 Sam 6:14), that is, he [experienced] the expiration of the soul [*kelot ha-nefesh*] and the annihilation of existence [*biṭṭul bi-meṣi'ut*], on account of his going out of his vessel [*asher yaṣa me-ha-keli shelo*], and all this because he was 'before the Lord,' and understand." For an earlier text wherein the experience of the love of God is described as the expiration of the soul (*kelot ha-nefesh*), see Baḥya ben Joseph Ibn Paquda, *Sefer Torat Ḥovot ha-Levavot*, Sha'ar Ahavat ha-Shem, chapter 1, p. 410. On the concept of *devequt* and mystical union in Ḥasidic sources, see Scholem, *The Messianic Idea in Judaism*, pp. 203–227; Idel, *Kabbalah*, pp. 49–51, 62–73; *Hasidism*, pp. 107–127; Piekarz, *Between Ideology and Reality*, pp. 150–178; Margolin, *The Human Temple*, pp. 288–342.

51. Schneerson, *Liqquṭei Siḥot*, 32:98–105.

52. Babylonian Talmud, Ḥagigah 14b.

53. For an extensive discussion of the motif of *dirah ba-taḥtonim* in the Rebbe's teaching concerning the seventh generation, see Kraus, "'Living with the Times,'" pp. 37–72.

54. Schneerson, *Quntres Inyanah shel Torat ha-Ḥasidut*, pp. 4, 22; *Torat Menaḥem: Hitwwa'aduyyot 5744*, 2:927. See Schneerson, *Liqquṭei Siḥot*, 4:1119–1120, n. 34. On the theme of *hafaṣat ha-ma'yanot ḥuṣah*, see the extensive analysis in Kraus, "'Living with the Times,'" pp. 109–161.

55. Schneerson, *Torat Menaḥem: Hitwwa'aduyyot 5720*, 1:353.

56. Schneerson, *Ha-Yom Yom*, p. 75. The sixth Rebbe is described in similar terms: he lowered himself by attending to the simplest of matters affecting the Jewish people at times when he would have preferred to be studying the most recondite secrets of the tradition. See Schneerson, *Iggerot Qodesh*, no. 812, 4:57, no. 914, 4:171.

57. Schneersohn, *Sefer ha-Ma'amarim 5708–5709*, part 1, p. 292.

58. Schneerson, *Liqquṭei Siḥot*, 14:177.

59. Shneur Zalman of Liadi, *Liqquṭei Amarim: Tanya*, part 4, sec. 26, 142b.

60. Schneerson, *Torat Menaḥem: Hitwwa'aduyyot 5714*, 1:271–272.

61. Schneerson, *Sefer ha-Ma'amarim: Ba'ti le-Ganni*, 1:232. The text is also published in Schneerson, *Sefer ha-Ma'amarim 5730–5731*, p. 116. On the messianic goal of Schneerson and the teaching of the inner dimension of Torah, see Loewenthal, "The Neutralisation," pp. 70–72.

62. Schneerson, *Sefer ha-Ma'amarim 11 Nisan*, 2:402.

63. An unedited version is printed in Schneerson, *Torat Menaḥem: Sefer ha-Ma'amarim Meluqaṭ*, 2:178–185, and a different version in *Torat Menaḥem: Hitwwa'aduyyot 5743*, 2:727–730.

64. Schneerson, *Torat Menaḥem: Sefer ha-Ma'amarim Meluqaṭ*, 2:180–181; *Torat Menaḥem: Hitwwa'aduyyot 5743*, 2:728–729.

65. This insight is found in the version of the talk in *Torat Menaḥem: Hitwwa'aduyyot 5743*, 2:729. In that adaptation, moreover, there is also an affirmation of silence as the highest level of Torah study, a state that is completely beyond comprehension and hence above the letters of speech (*otiyyot ha-dibbur*) revealed in both the exoteric text (*nigleh de-torah*) and in the letters of the esoteric in its two facets (*razin* and *razin de-razin*). This silent gnosis is linked as well to scent, which is associated with the Messiah (pp. 729–730). There is only a brief allusion to silence in the rendering printed in *Torat Menaḥem: Sefer ha-Ma'amarim Meluqaṭ*, 2:183.

66. Schneerson, *Torat Menaḥem: Hitwwa'aduyyot 5716*, 2:230. See Schneerson, *Iggerot Qodesh*, no. 1095, 4:376–377.

67. Schneerson, *Torat Menaḥem: Hitwwa'aduyyot 5716*, 2:237. On the elevation in status of languages other than Hebrew by their utilization in prayer and/or Torah study, see Shneur Zalman of Liadi, *Torah Or*, 77d.

68. Shneur Zalman of Liadi, *Liqquṭei Amarim: Tanya*, part 4, sec. 25, 141a.

69. Exod 37:2.

70. Schneerson, *Torat Menaḥem: Hitwwa'aduyyot 5716*, 3:95.

71. Concerning this kabbalistic idea and other scholarly discussions thereof, see Wolfson, *Language, Eros, Being*, p. 527, n. 216.

72. For an alternate schema, see the passage discussed in chapter 4, n. 126.

73. Schneerson, *Torat Menaḥem: Hitwwa'aduyyot 5716*, 2:230.

74. Schneerson, *Torat Menaḥem: Hitwwa'aduyyot 5743*, 2:929–930.

75. An allusion to the description of the image of the glory in Ezek 1:26.

76. Schneerson, *Torat Menaḥem: Hitwwa'aduyyot 5714*, 1:91–92.

77. Shneur Zalman of Liadi, *Liqquṭei Amarim: Tanya,* part 1, chapter 9, 13b–14b, chapter 19, 24a–25b, chapter 28, 35a–b; Jacobs in his introduction to Schneersohn, *Tract on Ecstasy,* pp. 16–20, and *Seeker of Unity,* pp. 67–68; Loewenthal, *Communicating the Infinite*, p. 54; Elior, *The Paradoxical Ascent to God*, pp. 115–124.

78. Shneur Zalman of Liadi, *Liqquṭei Amarim: Tanya*, part 3, chapter 6, 95b–96b. On occasion, the animal soul is described as being rooted in an aspect of the divine that is higher than the divine soul, the aspect of kingship (*melukhah*), a point related to the scriptural motif of the Edomite kings who reigned before there was an Israelite king (Gen 36:31). See Shneur Zalman of Liadi, *Torah Or*, 9a.

79. Schneerson, *Torat Menaḥem: Hitwwa'aduyyot 5714*, 1:92.

80. Shneur Zalman of Liadi, *Liqquṭei Amarim: Tanya*, part 1, chapter 4, 8a.

81. Elior, *The Paradoxical Ascent to God*, pp. 49–57. See also the comments of Jacobs in his introduction to Schneersohn, *Tract on Ecstasy,* pp. 7–8; Jacobs, *Seeker of Unity,* pp. 11, 15; and Foxbrunner, *Ḥabad*, pp. 63–93.

82. As far as I could detect, the expression becomes prominent in sixteenth- and seventeenth-century sources, and from there passes into the Ḥasidic glossary. See, for example, Cordovero, *Sefer Yeṣirah*, chapter 2, p. 122, chapter 5, p. 164, chapter 6, p. 169; Luzzatto, *Qelaḥ Pitḥei Ḥokhmah*, chapter 96, p. 289, chapter 109, pp. 311–312, chapter 110, p. 313; *Adir ba-Marom*, part 2, p. 50; *Sod ha-Merkavah*, pp. 266, 267. On the use of this expression in Luzzatto, see Pachter, *Roots of Faith and Devequt*, pp. 149–150. The particular

influence of Cordovero and Luzzatto on Ḥasidic masters has been documented. Regarding the influence of Cordovero, see Schatz-Uffenheimer, *Hasidism as Mysticism*, p. 263, n. 16; Sack, "An Investigation"; "The Influence of *Reshit Ḥokhmah,*" pp. 251–257, and reference to other scholars cited on p. 251, n. 3; Idel, *Hasidism*, pp. 65–81, 86–89, 109–111, 159–162, 165–168, 178–180, 191–203, 215–216. And for Luzzatto's influence, see Tishby, *Messianic Mysticism*, pp. 486–527.

83. A number of scholars have weighed in on this topic. For my own work, see Wolfson, "Negative Theology"; "*Via Negativa.*"

84. Schneerson, *Torat Menaḥem: Hitwwa'aduyyot 5714*, 1:93.

85. See the brief but incisive reflections of Tracy, "The Post-Modern Re-Naming."

86. See Schneersohn, *Sefer ha-Ma'amarim 5689*, p. 113.

87. Schneersohn, *Sefer ha-Ma'amarim 5679*, p. 268.

88. Schneerson, *Torat Menaḥem: Hitwwa'aduyyot 5711*, 1:265. For an alternative distinction between two types of *re'uta de-libba*, see Schneerson, *Torat Menaḥem: Sefer ha-Ma'amarim 5722*, p. 231. See also the formulation of Schneersohn in *We-Qibbel ha-Yehudim*, p. 195.

89. Schneerson, *Sefer ha-Ma'amarim 5720–5721*, p. 173.

90. Schneerson, *Torat Menaḥem: Hitwwa'aduyyot 5712*, 2:22. Regarding the locution *nequddah yehudit* and the zoharic tradition that identifies the letter *yod* as a point, see Liebes, "The Vilner Gaon School," pp. 271–277.

91. Shneur Zalman of Liadi, *Liqquṭei Amarim: Tanya*, p. 1, chapter 19, 24a–25b. On the divine root of the soul, see Hallamish, "Theoretical System," pp. 174–176.

92. *Zohar* 2:25b, 69a, 93b, 260b; 3:224b (*Ra'aya Meheimna*).

93. *Zohar* 2:93b.

94. Ibid., 260b.

95. Shneur Zalman of Liadi, *Liqquṭei Torah*, Shir ha-Shirim, 2:35a.

96. On the literary history of this composition, see Elior, *Theory of Divinity*, p. 123, n. 12.

97. Shneur Zalman of Liadi, *Torah Or*, 27a.

98. Shneur Zalman of Liadi, *Liqquṭei Amarim: Tanya*, part 1, chapter 39, 52a.

99. Shneur Zalman of Liadi, *Liqquṭei Torah*, Ki Teṣe, 2:35d.

100. Schneersohn, *Sha'arei Orah*, 93b.

101. Schneerson, *Torat Menaḥem: Sefer ha-Ma'amarim Meluqaṭ*, 3:10.

102. Ibid., p. 2.

103. Schneerson, *Reshimot*, sec. 125, 4:120.

104. Shneur Zalman of Liadi, *Liqquṭei Amarim: Tanya*, part 4, sec. 4, 105a–b.

105. Schneerson, *Torat Menaḥem: Hitwwa'aduyyot 5712*, 1:111–112. On the two types of redemption, the particular (*peraṭit*) and the universal (*kelalit*), see Schneerson, *Liqquṭei Siḥot*, 34:252; 38:101, 225; *Iggerot Qodesh*, no. 8496, 22:303; no. 9517, 25:184; *Torat Menaḥem: Hitwwa'aduyyot 5718*, 3:106; *Torat Menaḥem: Sefer ha-Ma'amarim Meluqaṭ*, 2:449; Loewenthal, "Contemporary Habad."

106. Schneerson, *Torat Menaḥem: Sefer ha-Ma'amarim 5729*, p. 62.

107. Ibid., pp. 62–63.

108. To my ear, this theme of Ḥabad thought resonates with Heidegger's insight regarding the identification of the mystery of being as concealment, which is unconcealment as such. See Wolfson, *Language, Eros, Being*, pp. 17–19. On the dialectic of revealing and concealing in Heidegger, see Vail, *Heidegger and Ontological Difference*, pp. 25–46.

109. Schneerson, *Torat Menaḥem: Hitwwa'aduyyot 5713*, 2:53.

110. Ibid., p. 54.

111. *Zohar* 1:11b; see Schatz-Uffenheimer, *Hasidism as Mysticism*, p. 263.

112. Schneerson, *Torat Menaḥem: Hitwwa'aduyyot 5712*, 2:179.

113. Shneur Zalman of Liadi, *Torah Or*, 13b.

114. Palestinian Talmud, Yoma 1:5, 39a.

115. *Midrash Shemot Rabbah* 38:8, in *Midrash Rabbah im Kol ha-Mefarshim*, 3:409.

116. *Midrash Bere'shit Rabba* 49:2, pp. 498–499.

117. Schneerson, *Torat Menaḥem: Sefer ha-Ma'amarim Meluqaṭ*, 1:74.

118. On the correlation of circumcision (*milah*) and the Tetragrammaton (YHWH), see Wolfson, "Circumcision and the Divine Name." The critical verse whence this correlation is derived is "who can ascend to heaven for us," *mi ya'aleh lanu ha-shamaimah* (Deut 30:12), the first letters spell *milah* and the last letters YHWH. See, however, the view of Shneur Zalman of Liadi cited in n. 124, this chapter.

119. Shneur Zalman of Liadi, *Liqquṭei Torah*, Tazri'a, 1:20d; Schneersohn, *Torat Ḥayyim: Bere'shit*, 66b; *Perush ha-Millot*, 54c; Schneersohn, *Sefer Tehillim*, p. 384; Schneersohn, *Liqquṭei Torah: Torat Shmu'el 5640*, 1:246; Schneersohn, *Be-Sha'ah she-Hiqdimu*, 1:438, 2:956.

120. On the identification of Hadar as *yesod de-adam qadmon*, see Viṭal, *Eṣ Ḥayyim*, 3:2, 17a; 9:8, 47a; 10:3, 48d. For elaboration of this Lurianic motif, see Luzzatto, *Adir ba-Marom*, part 1, p. 305; Ḥaver, *Pitḥei She'arim*, Netiv Olam ha-Tiqqun, chapter 8, 67a; *Beit Olamin al ha-Idra Rabba*, 5b, 10a, 227b, 238a; *Massekhet Aṣilut*, p. 45. On the myth of the Edomite kings, see postface, n. 156.

121. See n. 39, this chapter.

122. Shneur Zalman of Liadi, *Liqquṭei Torah*, Tazri'a, 1:21d. See Schneersohn, *Derekh Miṣwotekha*, 9a–b, 11b; Schneersohn, *Liqquṭei Torah: Torat Shmu'el 5640*, 1:244–246; Schneersohn, *Be-Sha'ah she-Hiqdimu*, 1:199.

123. Babylonian Talmud, Nedarim 31b.

124. Shneur Zalman of Liadi, *Torah Or*, 13c–d. For a more complete translation and analysis of this text, see Wolfson, *Alef, Mem, Tau*, pp. 113–114.

125. Mishnah, Yoma 5:3–4.

126. Schneerson, *Torat Menaḥem: Sefer ha-Ma'amarim Meluqaṭ*, 1:80.

127. Babylonian Talmud, Yoma 86a.

128. Babylonian Talmud, Megillah 17b.

129. I have utilized the word *hypernomian* in a number of my previous works, but in the most sustained manner in Wolfson, *Venturing Beyond*, pp. 186–285.

130. Schneerson, *Torat Menaḥem: Sefer ha-Ma'amarim Meluqaṭ*, 1:75.

131. Schneerson, *Liqquṭei Siḥot*, 14:321.

132. Visotzky, *Midrash Mishle*, chapter 9, p. 66.

133. Schneerson, *Torat Menaḥem: Hitwwa'aduyyot 5718*, 2:130. The festival of Purim, and especially the figure of Esther, served a similar symbolic role for other Jewish communities, for instance, the Sabbatians and conversos in the seventeenth century. See Scholem, *Sabbatai Ṣevi*, pp. 145–146, 803–804, 851; Roth, "The Religion of the Marranos," pp. 26–27; Yerushalmi, *From Spanish Court to Italian Ghetto*, p. 38, n. 56; Bodian, *Hebrew of the Portuguese Nation*, p. 10.

134. Babylonian Talmud, Yoma 86b.

135. Shneur Zalman of Liadi, *Torah Or*, 99a.

136. *Tiqqunei Zohar*, sec. 21, 57b. See Schneerson, *Liqquṭei Siḥot*, 4:1278–1279; 11:334; *Iggerot Qodesh*, no. 5220, 14:443, and no. 5260, 14:479.

137. Schneerson, *Torat Menaḥem: Hitwwa'aduyyot 5718*, 2:132.

138. Schneerson, *Torat Menaḥem: Hitwwa'aduyyot 5718*, 2:100. An affinity to the Rebbe's perspective can be found in the remark of the contemporary kabbalist, Itamar Shwartz, on the talmudic dictum that on Purim one must drink to the point of not knowing the difference between "cursed is Haman" and "blessed is Mordecai" in *Bilevavi Mishkan Evneh*, p. 209: "For the two of them are equal numerologically (502) . . . and from the perspective of the inner depth, the point that is above 'you have chosen us' is revealed. . . . When a person begins the worship, he starts it, as it were, during the course of Nisan, the course of Passover. It takes 12 months [in a leap year, 13 months] until he reaches the course of the disclosure of Purim. From this perspective, a person begins his worship from the standpoint that there is worship, until he reaches the end of the festivals, and the point that is above worship is revealed to him—the conjunction to him, blessed be he, the walking beyond the root." Purim is the culmination of the path of ritual, as it signifies union (*hitdabbequt*) with the divine that is the point above worship, the walking beyond the root (*halikhah aḥar ha-shoresh*). Not only does this walking (*halikhah*) supersede the ritual law (*halakhah*), but it dissolves the distinction between Jew and non-Jew and thus problematizes Israel's claim to being God's chosen people. The author tries to recoil from the implications of his own thinking by invoking the depiction of the ten *sefirot* in *Sefer Yeṣirah*, "their end is fixed in their beginning," to anchor the idea that after Purim the cycle stars all over again. While the strategy of this move is understandable, and indeed embraces a conception of time that is both linear and circular, a view that I have articulated as well (see introduction, n. 118), it does not deal adequately with the hypernomian dimension of Jewish messianic speculation. If, as the author unambiguously claims, the point of the ritual cycle is to move from the perspective of worship, and the implied chosenness of the Jewish people, to the point beyond worship, in which the ethnic boundaries are blurred, why should one have to undergo the process again? Why is there no allowance for a final liberation from the cycle? And, if there is no such allowance, how is the return to the cycle enhanced by imagining the possibility of extending beyond it?

139. Noam, *Megillat Ta'anit*, pp. 119–120, 303. Compare Palestinian Talmud, Megillah 1:4, 70d. In that context, the ostensible clash between the statement that no prophet instituted a new practice, since all the commandments were given by Moses and the addition of reading the scroll on Purim instituted by Mordecai and Esther, is explained by the assumption that there is a textual basis for all parts of Scripture in the verse "Then the Lord said to Moses, 'Inscribe this in a document as a reminder' [*ketov zo't zikkaron ba-sefer*]" (Exod

17:14), the word "this" (*zo't*) alludes to the Torah, "reminder" (*zikkaron*) to the Prophets, and "document" (*sefer*) to the Writings. Esther thus fulfilled the words revealed to Moses by writing down the events connected to Purim (Esther 9:29–32). This is further supported in the continuation of the talmudic passage by the explicit claim that the scroll of Esther was revealed to Moses at Sinai, but "there is no before or after in the Torah." Regarding this principle, see the primary and secondary sources cited in the introduction, n. 114.

140. Schneerson, *Torat Menaḥem: Hitwwa'aduyyot* 5720, 1:423.

141. Ibid.

142. Schneerson, *Liqquṭei Siḥot*, 11:334.

143. Schneerson, *Torat Menaḥem: Hitwwa'aduyyot 5718*, 2:131.

144. Schneerson, *Torat Menaḥem: Hitwwa'aduyyot* 5722, 2:194.

145. Moses ben Maimon, *Mishneh Torah*, Megillah 2:15.

146. Schneerson, *Torat Menaḥem: Hitwwa'aduyyot* 5720, 1:426.

147. The language is closest to *Zohar* 2:60a. See Tishby, *Wisdom of the Zohar*, pp. 1085–1086.

148. The reference is to a passage from the *Mishneh Torah* (see n. 145, this chapter), which Shneur Zalman cites and interprets in *Liqquṭei Amarim: Tanya*, part 1, chapter 2, 6a–7a.

149. Shneur Zalman of Liadi, *Liqquṭei Amarim: Tanya*, part 1, chapter 4, 8a–b.

150. *Tiqqunei Zohar*, introduction, 17a, and see also the editor's note, ibid., sec. 70, 121a. The zoharic slogan *leit maḥashavah tefisa beih kelal* was a favorite amongst Ḥasidic masters. Ideally, the use of this dictum in Ḥabad literature should be considered in relation to other sources, but that is a project that lies beyond the scope of this study.

151. See, for instance, Shneur Zalman of Liadi, *Liqquṭei Amarim: Tanya*, part 4, sec. 18, 127a.

152. Shneur Zalman of Liadi, *Liqquṭei Amarim: Tanya*, part 3, chapter 7, 84a.

153. Shneur Zalman of Liadi, *Torah Or*, 110b. See ibid., 71a.

154. Shneur Zalman of Liadi, *Liqquṭei Torah*, Bemidbar, 1:14b.

155. *Zohar* 1:15a.

156. Shneur Zalman of Liadi, *Ma'amerei Admor ha-Zaqen* 5567, p. 392; *Liqquṭei Torah*, Behar, 1:45a. See Loewenthal, *Communicating the Infinite*, p. 155. On the world being sustained through the letters, see Shneur Zalman of Liadi, *Liqquṭei Amarim: Tanya*, part 2, chapter 1, 76b–77a, which Idel, *Hasidism*, pp. 216–217, presents as an example of the "immanentist linguistic" orientation.

157. Shneur Zalman of Liadi, *Liqquṭei Torah*, Behar, 1:45a, Bemidbar, 1:8b.

158. Shneur Zalman of Liadi, *Liqquṭei Torah*, Hosafot, 1:53d.

159. Wolfson, "Imago Templi," p. 125: "In the cultural ambiance of medieval kabbalah, language performs this function by expressing the inexpressible, rendering the invisible visible. The symbol brings the unknown into relation with the known, but without reducing the difference that binds the two incongruities into a selfsame identity. In the kabbalistic mindset, accordingly, every signified becomes a signifier vis-à-vis another signified, which quickly turns into another signifier, and so on *ad infinitum*, in an endless string that winds its way finally to the in/significant, which may be viewed either as the signified to which no signifier can be affixed or the signifier to which no signified can be assigned."

160. Shneur Zalman of Liadi, *Liqquṭei Torah*, Behar, 1:43b–c.

161. Schneersohn, *Torat Ḥayyim: Shemot*, 370c.

162. The source for the image of the curtain that divides is Viṭal, *Eṣ Ḥayyim*, 8:2, 36a: "After he constricted himself [*ṣimṣem aṣmo*], he left a curtain in the middle of his body, in the place of the navel, in order to create a barrier in the middle, and this is the secret of 'Let there be a firmament in the midst of the waters, and it shall separate the water from the water' (Gen 1:6)." On the image of the curtain (*parsa*) and the process of constriction (*ṣimṣum*), see Schneerson, *Torat Menaḥem: Hitwwa'aduyyot 5713*, 3:78.

163. Schneersohn, *Torat Ḥayyim: Shemot*, 194d. For further discussion of the status of the primordial Torah and the essence of the Infinite, see ibid., 183a–d, 370b–c.

164. See ibid., 192a, where the aspect of the concealment of the curtain (*beḥinat hester zeh de-parsa*) is compared to the "matter of the garment of the parable [*levush ha-mashal*] in relation to the intellect specifically, for the parable speaks entirely through strange matters [*inyanim zarim*] but through it that which is rendered parabolically [*nimshal*] is comprehended." On the identification of the curtain (*parsa*) as the parable (*mashal*), see also Horowitz, *Sha'arei ha-Yiḥud*, part 2, 19b–20a. The metaphoric use of the image of the curtain to depict the nature of metaphor is related to the act of concealing (*hastarah*), which is connected to the former. See Elior, *Theory of Divinity*, pp. 31–32.

165. Shneur Zalman of Liadi, *Liqquṭei Amarim: Tanya*, part 1, chapter 35, 44b.

166. Schneersohn, *Be-Sha'ah she-Hiqdimu*, 3:1404.

167. Shneur Zalman of Liadi, *Torah Or*, 42b.

168. Schneersohn, *Sefer ha-Ma'amarim: Qunṭreisim*, 1:204. The text, which is a meditation on the central tenet of Jewish monotheism, the proclamation of God's unity (Deut 6:4), was a discourse delivered in conjunction with 12–13 Tammuz 5690 (July 8–9, 1930), the festival of redemption that commemorates his own release from imprisonment on 12–13 Tammuz 5687 (July 12–13, 1927). See introduction, n. 103. Coincidentally, the sixth Rebbe's date of birth was 12 Tammuz 5640 (June 21, 1880). On the depiction of the divine as being beyond time and place, see Schneersohn, *Liqquṭei Torah: Torat Shmu'el, 5627*, p. 224. According to that passage, the eradication of the temporal and spatial is implied in the notion of God's unity, which is signified by the word *eḥad*. On the application of the term *yaḥid u-meyuḥad* to the divine prior to and after the creation, see Shneur Zalman of Liadi, *Liqquṭei Amarim: Tanya*, part 3, chapter 6, 110a.

169. Shneur Zalman of Liadi, *Torah Or*, 98b.

170. Wolfson, *Language, Eros, Being*, pp. 190–260.

171. Wolfson, "Suffering Eros and Textual Incarnation," pp. 342–353.

172. Schneersohn, *Liqquṭei Torah: Torat Shmu'el 5626*, p. 300.

173. Schneerson, *Sefer ha-Ma'amarim: Ba'ti le-Ganni*, 1:195. On the image of the primordial parable (*meshal ha-qadmoni*) in the teaching of Schneerson, see Dahan, "'Dira Bataḥtonim,'" pp. 59–64.

174. It is worth noting here the distinction made by Naḥman of Bratslav, *Liqquṭei MoHaRaN*, I, 56:3, between two types of concealment applied to God: the first is one in which the divine is singly concealed and the second is one in which the divine is doubly

concealed, that is, the "concealment is itself concealed" (*ha-hastarah be-aṣmah nisteret*), and hence the person does not even know that God is hidden. The double concealment, in my judgment, underlies the disclosure of secrecy on the part of the Ḥabad-Lubavitch masters, especially conspicuous in the seventh Rebbe. The extent to which this hermeneutic of esotericism continues to inform the kabbalistic orientation can be seen, for example, from the following passage in Shwartz, *Qol Demamah Daqqah*, p. 100: "In the end, since the substance of the secret is the secret [*mahut ha-sod hu sod*], which is hidden [*ṣanu'a*], it is impossible that there will be a complete disclosure in actuality [*gilluy gamur mammash*]. Rather, every disclosure is from the perspective of the external aspect that is in it, but from the perspective of the essence of its substance, since its substance is the hidden secret, it is necessary that it remains a hidden secret." I thank Shaul Magid for calling this passage to my attention. An interesting formulation of the inherently esoteric nature of the secret is offered by Shwartz, ibid., p. 150, as an interpretation of the rabbinic dictum "When wine goes in, the secret comes out" (see n. 35, this chapter): "The intention is not that the secret is revealed externally and is thenceforth no longer a secret, for if this were so, then it would be an accidental and not an essential secret, for anything that changes is accidental and not essential. Rather, even though 'the secret comes out,' it nevertheless remains a complete secret. The meaning of 'the secret comes out' is that even though it is revealed on the outside, the disclosure is naught but concealment, a secret." On the dialectic unity of concealment and disclosure, see also ibid., pp. 284–285. Regarding this author, see n. 138, this chapter. On the paradox of concealment and disclosure in Shneur Zalman of Liadi, see Hallamish, "Theoretical System," pp. 97–101, and on the need to reveal the secret, see p. 394.

175. See Berger, "Miracles." See as well Ravitzky, "The Anthropological Theory"; and Halbertal, *By Way of Truth*, pp. 149–180. On the status of the miracle in Shneur Zalman of Liadi, which applies to all of nature as a disclosure of the infinite light, see Hallamish, "Theoretical System," pp.134–135.

176. Schneerson, *Torat Menaḥem: Sefer ha-Ma'amarim 5711–5712*, pp. 262–265. Compare Shneur Zalman, *Torah Or*, 93c–d, 100a.

177. Kraus, "'Living with the Times,'" pp. 97–105; *The Seventh*, pp. 36–40; Dahan, "'Dira Bataḥtonim,'" pp. 147–196; Kohanzad, "Messianic Doctrine," pp. 152–169.

178. Shneur Zalman of Liadi, *Ma'amerei Admor ha-Zaqen 5571*, p. 137.

179. Based on the formulation in *Tiqqunei Zohar*, introduction, 5b.

180. This expression of Shneur Zalman (see the following note) is based on the description of the *sefirot* of the world of emanation in *Tiqqunei Zohar*, introduction, 3b: *malka behon ihu we-garmeih ḥad behon ihu we-ḥayyoi ḥad behon* ("The king is in them, he and his self are one in them, he and his vitality are one in them"). It is likely, however, that Shneur Zalman was more directly influenced by the paraphrase of the zoharic passage in Viṭal, *Eṣ Ḥayyim*, 42:4, 91c. In that context, Viṭal states that wisdom is the life that infuses all of the worlds, a theme that is central to Shneur Zalman's orientation as well.

181. Shneur Zalman of Liadi, *Torah Or*, 43b.

182. For discussion of the role of *mashal* in Dov Baer's thought, see Loewenthal, *Communicating the Infinite*, pp. 154–157, 167–173.

2. A/voiding Place

1. Elior, "Lubavitch Messianic Resurgence," p. 387.

2. It is for this reason that I am also not persuaded by the sociological argument offered by Szubin, "Why Lubavitch Wants the Messiah Now," that the millenarian activism should be explained by the influx of new immigrants into the Ḥabad movement in the 1970s and 1980s. While it is reasonable to assume that this factor is an important part of the story, I think it is excessively reductionist to account for the belief in the imminent coming of the redemption solely on the basis of this criterion.

3. I owe the term *apophatic body* to the conference "Apophatic Bodies: Infinity, Ethics, and Incarnation" held at Drew University in October 2006. An earlier version of this chapter will appear in the proceedings of that conference, edited by Christopher Boesel and Catherine Keller, to be published by Fordham University Press.

4. In the 1916 essay "On Language as Such and on the Language of Man," in Benjamin, *Selected Writings,* vol. 1: *1913–1926*, p. 63. The literature on the role of language in Benjamin's thought is considerable. See the brief discussion in Wolfson, *Language, Eros, Being*, pp. 11–12, and reference to other scholars cited on pp. 405–406, n. 78. The conception of embodiment and language that I have elicited from Ḥabad philosophy accords conspicuously with the view of Merleau-Ponty, which has influenced my own thinking. See Wolfson, *Language, Eros, Being*, pp. xxii–xxiv, 24–25, 191–196. For a representative list of other scholarly treatments, see Kwant, *Phenomenology of Language*; Olson, "The Human Body"; Grosz, *Volatile Bodies*; Sato, "The Incarnation of Consciousness"; Dastur, "Word, Flesh, Vision"; Barbaras, *The Being of the Phenomenon*, pp. 41–78, 147–203; Steeves, *Imagining Bodies*. See chapter 3, n. 19.

5. This is not to say that there is no conflict between Ḥabad thought and contemporary science. See discussion and sources cited in the introduction, n. 1.

6. Heidegger, "Supplements," p. 85. The view expressed by Heidegger resonates with the position taken by Rosenzweig with respect to the new thinking as a hybrid of philosophy and theology. For a more extensive discussion, see Wolfson, "Light Does Not Talk."

7. Shneur Zalman of Liadi, *Liqquṭei Amarim: Tanya*, part 1, chapter 38, 50b.

8. The expression *intellectual enlightenment or illumination* is derived from Richard M. Bucke's characterization of cosmic consciousness. See Marshall, *Mystical Encounters*, pp. 50–52. Needless to say, my appropriation of this terminology to characterize Ḥabad mysticism is not meant to suggest that it is harmonious with the position of Bucke. A crucial difference is that, in the case of Ḥabad, intellectual consciousness of the whole is predicated on the experiential unity with the whole.

9. Hallamish, "Theoretical System," pp. 200–209; Elior, "ḤaBaD," pp. 160, 191–198; *The Paradoxical Ascent to God*, p. 138.

10. Schatz-Uffenheimer, *Hasidism*, pp. 256–260, and reference to other scholarly discussions cited on pp. 256–257, nn. 2–3; Elior, *The Paradoxical Ascent to God*, pp. 167–172; Loewenthal, *Communicating the Infinite*, pp. 77–86. Also relevant here is the discussion of two types of piety in Ḥasidism, the "mystical, contemplative piety" and the "piety of faith," the former represented by the Maggid of Międzyrzecz and the latter by

Naḥman of Bratslav, in Weiss, *Studies*, pp. 43–55. On the role of faith in early Ḥasidism, see Margolin, "On the Substance of Faith."

11. See Loewenthal, "'Reason' and 'Beyond Reason'"; and the innovative analysis by Rosenberg, "Faith and Language."

12. Shneur Zalman of Liadi, *Torah Or*, 6a. Compare the criticism of Gentile philosophers in Shneur Zalman of Liadi, *Ma'amerei Admor ha-Zaqen: Al Inyanim*, pp. 41–42. The belief (*emunah*) of the Jews is set in contrast to the opinion of the philosophers, which is based exclusively on rational inquiry (*ḥaqirat ha-sekhel*).

13. Schneersohn, *Quntres ha-Tefillah*, p. 11; *Tract on Prayer*, pp. 26–27.

14. In this chapter, I will not consistently qualify my use of the term *human* as denoting the Jew, but it should be understood that this qualification is in fact justified textually. I discuss the matter more extensively in chapter 6.

15. Shneur Zalman of Liadi, *Torah Or*, 6b.

16. Regarding this technical term, see chapter 1, n. 82.

17. The terms *mahut* (being) and *aṣmut* (essence) are used interchangeably to refer to that which we cannot know or name, the light that is all things in virtue of being none of those things, the concealment revealed in the concealment of its revelation. See Shneur Zalman, *Liqquṭei Amarim: Tanya*, part 2, chapter 7, 82a: "the aspect of place and time are actually annihilated in existence in relation to his being and his essence, blessed be he [*beḥinat ha-maqom we-ha-zeman beṭelim bi-meṣi'ut mammash legabbei mahuto we-aṣmuto yitbarakh*], like the light of the sun in the sun." Many other examples could be adduced, but this is sufficient to make the point and to justify my own language analyzing this material. For discussion of the concept of *aṣmut*, see Kohanzad, "Messianic Doctrine," pp. 123–151.

18. Schneersohn, *Perush ha-Millot*, 112c: "'He draws mysteries out of darkness' (Job 12:22) . . . and the aspect of darkness is the black that is also above the aspect of the essential light of the resplendent luminosity [*or ha-aṣmi de-or ṣaḥ*], for the aspect of the essence [*ha-aṣmut*] is greatly above the aspect of the essential light [*or ha-aṣmi*]. However, that the darkness shines against its nature is also precisely the aspect of the essential light, as it says 'Darkness is not dark for You' (Ps 139:12)."

19. Schneersohn, *Be-Sha'ah she-Hiqdimu*, 1:134.

20. Shneur Zalman of Liadi, *Liqquṭei Torah*, Wa'etḥanan, 2:8d. On the symbol of the supernal darkness, see ibid., 2:9a; Ha'azinu, 2:73a; Schneersohn, *Torat Ḥayyim: Bere'shit*, 60c, 60d, 61a, 125a, 125b, 157c, 161c, 161d, 162b, 162d, 185c; *Torat Ḥayyim: Shemot*, 16b, 343d; *Derushei Ḥatunah*, 2:547.

21. Schneersohn, *Ma'amerei Admor ha-Emṣa'i: Hanaḥot* , p. 344. The image of the supernal light appears frequently in Ḥabad teaching, often citing Viṭal, *Eṣ Ḥayyim*, 1:2, 11c. I delineate here only some of the relevant sources: Shneur Zalman of Liadi, *Liqquṭei Amarim: Tanya*, part 4, sec. 10, 115a–b; *Torah Or*, 11b, 33b; *Liqquṭei Torah*, Maṭot, 1:85c, 86d; *Liqquṭei Torah*, Re'eh, 2:27a, Neṣavim, 2:51c, Derushim le-Rosh ha-Shanah, 2:59a, 61b, 65d; Schneersohn, *Sha'arei Orah*, 68b, 71a, 80a, 132a; *Torat Ḥayyim: Bere'shit*, 87d; *Perush ha-Millot*, 33d; Schneersohn, *Or ha-Torah: Bemidbar*, 3:891–892; 4:1161, 1207; *Derekh Miṣwotekha*, 9b; Schneersohn, *Liqquṭei Torah: Torat Shmu'el 5629*, p. 409; Schneersohn, *Be-Sha'ah she-Hiqdimu*, 1:13, 19, 20, 50, 54, 129, 623, 2:790, 1003, 3:1323; Schneersohn, *Sefer ha-Ma'amarim 5689*, pp. 253, 255; *Sefer ha-Ma'amarim 5692–5693*,

pp. 66, 74, 229, 255; Schneerson, *Iggerot Qodesh*, no. 143, 1:268; *Torat Menaḥem: Hitwwa'aduyyot 5713*, 2:187; *Torat Menaḥem: Sefer ha-Ma'amarim Meluqaṭ*, 2:384.

22. Shneur Zalman of Liadi, *Torah Or*, 14a. On the distinction between the Infinite (*ein sof*) and the infinite light (*or ein sof*), see Hallamish, "Theoretical System," pp. 38–42.

23. Schneersohn, *Sefer ha-Ma'amarim 5678*, p. 99. See also Schneersohn, *Sefer ha-Ma'amarim 5692–5693*, pp. 165–166; Schneerson, *Torat Menaḥem: Sefer ha-Ma'amarim 5717*, p. 62.

24. Schneerson, *Torat Menaḥem: Sefer ha-Ma'amarim 5717*, p. 63. I note, parenthetically, that this discourse was delivered after the recitation of *qabbalat shabbat* at the commencement of Sabbath, 20 Kislev 5717, which corresponds to November 23, 1956, the date of my birth. In fact, as I was born shortly after the arrival of Sabbath, the Rebbe's talk, more or less, coincided with my entry into this world. On the custom to commemorate the festival of redemption on 19 and 20 Kislev, see Schneerson, *Torat Menaḥem: Hitwwa'aduyyot 5744*, 4:2204, 2206–2207.

25. Schneersohn, *Sha'arei Teshuvah*, 23c.

26. Schatz-Uffenheimer, *Hasidism as Mysticism*, p. 263, grasped this essential dimension of Ḥabad thinking from the writings of Shneur Zalman, though she does not use the precise language of incarnation. Thus, she noted that the Lurianic notion of withdrawal (*ṣimṣum*) is no longer set in opposition to divine immanence, but it is rather a "form of revelation." Paradoxically, "the act of divine revelation is more likely in the world through His hiddenness and concealment and being embodied therein . . . the external act of Creation is an aspect of His concealment and hiddenness; the hiddenness and absorption of God within the world is itself an act of creation." In using the term *incarnation* to depict Ḥabad philosophy, I am not insensitive to the question of the implicit Christological nuance, though, of course, that expression is not necessarily limited in this way. My deployment of the topos of incarnation here is consistent with my previous work on the history of Jewish mysticism. While one must be careful about making facile links between biographical data and intellectual history, it would be irresponsible not to make note of the well-known fact that the Alter Rebbe's son, Moshe, was famously converted to Christianity in 1820 by the Catholic priest Josaphat Siodlowski in the Belarusian town Beshenkovichi. For a detailed account, see Assaf, *Caught in the Thicket*, pp. 51–136. I am not suggesting that the son's apostasy can or should be linked reductively to his father's religious philosophy, and there does not seem to be any documentation to this effect, but it is not unreasonable to speculate whether the latter was not part of what was an undoubtedly complex mix of different factors, including the question of Moshe's mental state.

27. Shneur Zalman of Liadi, *Liqquṭei Torah*, Beḥuqotai, 1:48b.

28. Shneur Zalman of Liadi, *Torah Or*, 28c.

29. See discussion of this theme and citation of some relevant sources in Idel, *Hasidism*, pp. 123–124.

30. Elior, *The Paradoxical Ascent to God*, pp. 185–189. For the background of the quietistic ideal and the annihilation of the self, see Schatz-Uffenheimer, *Hasidism as Mysticism*, pp. 65–79. See also Piekarz, *Between Ideology and Reality*, pp. 55–81, 104–149; Margolin, *The Human Temple*, pp. 343–378.

31. The technical term that can be rendered as "incorporation" is *hitkallelut*. See Idel, "Universalization and Integration," pp. 41–45; Elior, *The Paradoxical Ascent to God*, pp. 44–45; Loewenthal, *Communicating the Infinite*, pp. 153, 170.

32. Shneur Zalman of Liadi, *Liqquṭei Amarim: Tanya*, part 1, chapter 19, 24a–b.

33. Ibid., 24b–25a. See also Shneur Zalman of Liadi, *Liqquṭei Torah*, Re'eh, 2:18b. The theme is repeatedly emphasized in Ḥabad literature. For example, see Schneerson, *Liqquṭei Siḥot*, 12:408, and the Hebrew translation in *Torat Menaḥem: Hitwwa'aduyyot 5712*, 3:187.

34. The point is made in numerous texts, but the source that is often mentioned in Ḥabad literature is *Zohar* 1:12a, where the fourth of fourteen commandments is "to know that the Lord [YHWH] is God [Elohim], as it is written 'Know this day, and consider in your hearts that the Lord is God' (Deut 4:39), to contain the name Elohim in the name YHWH, to know that they are one and there is no division in them."

35. This idiom appears recurrently in Ḥabad literature. Its *locus classicus* is Shneur Zalman of Liadi, *Liqquṭei Amarim: Tanya*, part 1, chapter 3, 7b. See Hallamish, "Theoretical System," pp. 506–560.

36. Schneerson, *Torat Menaḥem: Sefer ha-Ma'amarim 5716,* p. 79: "By means of contemplation of matters that are suitable to the animal soul, that is, corporeal matters, the understanding and comprehension of the divine soul also takes on the aspect of an actual sensible comprehension [*hassagah muḥashit mammash*], as it is written, 'Lift your eyes upward and see who created these' (Isa 40:26) . . . by way of sensible vision [*re'iyyah muḥashit*], and by means of this the contemplation of the divine soul is in corporeal matters." The disclosure of the essence (*gilluy ha-aṣmut*) connected to the Sinaitic theophany is also described as a physical vision, an idea linked exegetically to the verse "It has been shown to you to know that the Lord alone is God," *attah har'eta lada'at ki yhwh hu ha-elohim* (Deut 4:35). Reading these words esoterically, one gains gnosis (*da'at*) of the essence of the Infinite, signified by the second-person pronoun *attah*, by way of a vision (*har'eta*), which is akin to physical sight that penetrates to the interiority of the matter. See Schneerson, *Torat Menaḥem: Hitwwa'aduyyot 5743*, 1:290, 293. On the supremacy of the ocular to the auditory, and the specific connection made between Moses and the vision of God, see Schneerson, *Torat Menaḥem: Hitwwa'aduyyot 5715*, 2:239; see also *Liqquṭei Siḥot*, 39:10.

37. Shneur Zalman of Liadi, *Ma'amerei Admor ha-Zaqen 5565*, 2:728–738.

38. See chapter 1, n. 149.

39. Shneur Zalman of Liadi, *Liqquṭei Torah*, Balaq, 1:69c.

40. Schneersohn, *Qunṭres ha-Hitpa'alut*, in *Ma'amerei Admor ha-Emṣa'i: Qunṭresim,* p. 98.

41. Ibid., pp. 53, 57–58, 111; see also Shneur Zalman of Liadi, *Seder Tefillot*, 163a.

42. Schneersohn, *Sha'arei Orah*, 64a. See Schneersohn, *Qunṭres ha-Hitpa'alut*, p. 54: "Conjunction is the life and bond of the soul in the life of lives, the essence of the light of the Infinite, blessed be he, which is called the soul of the lives of all the souls."

43. The expressions "place that is above place" and "time that is above time" were used by the seventh Rebbe in a discourse delivered on 23 Elul 5712 (September 13, 1952). A transcribed version of the Yiddish is printed in Schneerson, *Liqquṭei Siḥot*, 2:407–408, and a Hebrew translation appears in *Torat Menaḥem: Hitwwa'aduyyot, 5712*, 3:186–188. The text is analyzed in detail in chapter 6 at n. 188.

44. Shneur Zalman of Liadi, *Ma'amerei Admor ha-Zaqen 5571*, p. 305.

45. Shneur Zalman of Liadi, *Liqquṭei Amarim: Tanya*, part 1, chapter 38, 50b. See reference to Idel cited in n. 31, this chapter.

46. On the role of the commandments and ritual, see Kraus, *The Seventh*, pp. 132–176.

47. Wolfson, *Language, Eros, Being*, pp. 190–260, and, for references to other scholars who have discussed this motif, see p. 422, n. 251.

48. Shneur Zalman of Liadi, *Torah Or*, 14a.

49. Schneerson, *Qunṭres Inyanah shel Torat ha-Ḥasidut*, p. 20. Compare the translation in *On the Essence of Chasidus*, pp. 94–97. It is interesting to note the partial attempt to cast the masculine orientation of the original in more neutral gender terms. Thus, in the passage that I have translated, the expression *aṣmuto yitbarakh* is rendered as "the Essence of G-d" and *or ein sof barukh hu* as "the *Or Ein Sof*." I have no problem understanding and even supporting the motivation here to soften the patriarchal tone of the original, but engaging Schneerson's thinking critically requires that one be cognizant of his exact language. This would be valid in any form of historical-textual scholarship, but especially so when studying a thinker for whom the nature of reality is linguistic in nature. I trust this minimal philological point will stand the test of time and the pressures of political correctness.

50. *Midrash Tanḥuma*, Naso, 17. See ibid., Beḥuqotai, 3; *Midrash Bemidbar Rabbah* 13:6, in *Midrash Rabbah im Kol ha-Mefarshim*, 5:306.

51. Shneur Zalman of Liadi, *Liqquṭei Amarim: Tanya*, part 1, chapter 36, 45b. For scholarly assessments of the importance of this motif, principally in the teaching of the seventh Rebbe, see Kraus, "'Living with the Times,'" pp. 38–72; and Dahan, "'Dira Bataḥtonim.'" For a coherent but uncritical attempt to render this concept as the focal point of a unified system of thought—a "down to earth weltanschauung"—elicited from the seventh Rebbe's talks and writings, see Levin, *Heaven on Earth*.

52. Shneur Zalman of Liadi, *Liqquṭei Torah*, Ha'azinu, 2:75d.

53. Schneerson, *Torat Menaḥem: Sefer ha-Ma'amarim 5711*, 1:196–197. See *Torat Menaḥem: Hitwwa'aduyyot 5716*, 3:87; *Torat Menaḥem: Hitwwa'aduyyot 5720*, 1:287.

54. Wolfson, *Venturing Beyond*, p. 22. The claim that ontology and ethics cannot be separated is predicated on using the latter term uncritically and, specifically, without exploring the underlying anthropological assumption, a point that I challenged in the aforementioned study. A recent example of such an oversight is Ornet, "*Ratso va-shov.*" In my judgment, the author's failure to raise the question of the status of the non-Jewish other in the Alter Rebbe's thought renders her use of the term *ethical* suspect.

55. My view should be seen as a critique of the characterization of Ḥasidism by Buber, adopted by Scholem as well, as "Kabbalism turned Ethos," which was meant to insinuate that the originality of Ḥasidic thought was in transforming "the exploration of the theosophical mysteries" into the "quest for the true substance of ethico-religious conceptions" and "their mystical glorification." See Scholem, *Major Trends*, pp. 342–343. The emphasis on the nexus between ontology and ethics challenges this portrayal of Ḥasidism. An even more useful paradigm to explain the convergence of the ontological and the ethical in Ḥabad is offered by Carey, "Cultivating Ethos," p. 24, in his claim that Merleau-Ponty presents an "ontology of the flesh that effectively overcomes the dualisms of traditional metaphysics (e.g., subject and object, mind and body), which have prevented the cultivation of a healthy

and holistically based *ethos*. By navigating between these dualisms, Merleau-Ponty opens the door to understanding our capacities of the body as ethical tasks. That is, understood ontologically, the body is a means for overcoming egoism and opening to the ontological depth of others." The problem of "the other" (*Autrui*) in Merleau-Ponty's phenomenological ontology has engaged numerous scholars. For a representative treatment, see Barbaras, *The Being of the Phenomenon*, pp. 19–40.

56. Schneersohn, *Sha'arei Orah*, 9a.

57. Schneersohn, *Torat Ḥayyim: Bere'shit*, 185a. See n. 188, this chapter.

58. Schneersohn, *Torat Ḥayyim: Shemot*, 292a. See Schneersohn, *Torat Ḥayyim: Bere'shit*, 49c, 219c. Compare Schneerson, *Iggerot Qodesh*, no. 220, 2:117–118: "The supernal unity is the nullification of the ray of sunlight in the sun, the nullification of the world of emanation, the nullification of existence [*biṭṭul bi-meṣi'ut*] . . . for he does not feel himself to be something at all. The lower unity, that is, the nullification of the worlds of creation, formation, and doing, the nullification of something [*biṭṭul ha-yesh*], that is, he feels as if he is something, but he comprehends with his intellect that he has been annihilated, since he is found in the source of his being, as the ray of sunlight in the sun (however, all this is in his understanding and not in his feeling). Thus, the nullification of the supernal unity is attained when he feels his source. And when does he feel his source? When the source, even though it proceeds to engender and to sustain, inasmuch as it emanates the world of emanation, nonetheless does not ensue in the garments that conceal [*bi-levushim ha-mastirim*]. . . . But the nullification of the lower unity is attained when he comprehends that he is found in his course but he does not feel it—this happens when the source proceeds, but in its procession it is garbed in the garment that hides [*bi-levush ha-ma'lim*], and therefore the created entity occurs as separate in his feeling." See chapter 5, n. 55.

59. Schneersohn, *Sha'arei Orah*, 39a. The concluding line is derived from the words *we-nafshi ke-afar la-kol tihyeh* from the meditation *yihyu le-raṣon imrei fi*, which is recited at the end of the standing prayer (*amidah*), the central part of the traditional liturgy.

60. Horowitz, *Sha'arei Avodah*, part 2, chapter 32, 46b. See Jacobs, *Seeker of Unity*, pp. 107–108, 130–131.

61. Shneur Zalman of Liadi, *Liqquṭei Amarim: Tanya*, part 1, chapter 42, 59a; *Liqquṭei Torah*, Maṭot, 1:83a, and Shir ha-Shirim, 2:37d; Schneersohn, *Torat Ḥayyim: Shemot*, 140b, 280c; Schneersohn, *Or ha-Torah: Bemidbar*, 3:822; Schneerson, *Torat Menaḥem: Hitwwa'aduyyot 5711*, 1:231. The "supernal knowledge" is also identified as the "foundation of the Father" (*yesod de-abba*), and hence the root of Mosaic prophecy is said to be in the "interiority of the Father" (*penimiyyut abba*). See Schneersohn, *Torat Ḥayyim: Shemot*, 115b; and compare *Sha'arei Teshuvah*, 98b–99a. On the image of *penimiyyut abba*, see Shneur Zalman of Liadi, *Liqquṭei Torah*, Pequdei, 1:8a, Ṣaw, 1:12d; Schneersohn, *Torat Ḥayyim: Bere'shit*, 27b; *Perush ha-Millot*, 3b; Schneersohn, *Or ha-Torah: Bemidbar*, 2:419; *Sefer Tehillim*, p. 335; Schneersohn, *Liqquṭei Torah: Torat Shmu'el 5631*, 1:373; *Liqquṭei Torah: Torat Shmu'el 5633*, 1:250; *Liqquṭei Torah: Torat Shmu'el 5633*, 2:523; Schneerson, *Torat Menaḥem: Hitwwa'aduyyot 5714*, 3:123. Also noteworthy is the identification of the interiority of the Father (*penimiyyut abba*) and the interiority of the Ancient One (*penimiyyut attiq*) affirmed repeatedly in the Ḥabad sources and frequently in the effort to demarcate the ontic source of the Torah in the Godhead. See, for example, Shneur

Zalman of Liadi, *Liqquṭei Torah*, Ṣaw, 1:10c; Schneersohn, *Or ha-Torah:Bemidbar*, 2:699; *Sefer Tehillim*, p. 353; Schneersohn, *Liqquṭei Torah: Torat Shmu'el 5631*, 1:68, 77; *Liqquṭei Torah: Torat Shmu'el 5632*, 1:68, 141; *Liqquṭei Torah: Torat Shmu'el 5632*, 2:461; *Liqquṭei Torah: Torat Shmu'el 5633*, 2:537 ; *Liqquṭei Torah: Torat Shmu'el 5640*, 2:582; Schneersohn, *Be-Sha'ah she-Hiqdimu*, 1:264, 433, 2:736, 1117; 3:1277, 1322, 1324, 1332, 1422; Schneerson, *Iggerot Qodesh*, no. 265, 2:198; no. 466, 3:88; no. 7586, 20:161; *Torat Menaḥem: Hitwwa'aduyyot 5711*, 2:11, 140; *Torat Menaḥem: Hitwwa'aduyyot 5713*, 1:149; *Torat Menaḥem: Hitwwa'aduyyot 5713*, 3:134, 137; *Torat Menaḥem: Hitwwa'aduyyot 5715*, 2:149; *Torat Menaḥem: Hitwwa'aduyyot 5716*, 1:250; *Torat Menaḥem: Hitwwa'aduyyot 5717*, 1:90; *Torat Menaḥem: Hitwwa'aduyyot 5717*, 2:272; *Torat Menaḥem: Hitwwa'aduyyot 5718*, 1:117, 173, 285; *Torat Menaḥem: Hitwwa'aduyyot 5720*, 1:22, 31; *Torat Menaḥem: Hitwwa'aduyyot 5720*, 2:35; *Liqquṭei Siḥot*, 34:269; *Torat Menaḥem: Sefer ha-Ma'amarim Meluqaṭ*, 1:117. On the identification of the Beshṭ as *penimiyyut attiq* and the Alter Rebbe as *penimiyyut abba*, see Schneerson, *Torat Menaḥem: Hitwwa'aduyyot 5720*, 1:31. Finally, mention should be made of the fact that above the identification of *penimiyyut abba* and *penimiyyut attiq* is the inherent aspect of *penimiyyut attiq*, the root of messianic consciousness; see chapter 4, n. 96.

62. Shneur Zalman of Liadi, *Ma'amerei Admor ha-Zaqen 5565*, 1:184–185.

63. Schneersohn, *Torat Ḥayyim: Shemot*, 115a.

64. Schneerson, *Torat Menaḥem: Sefer ha-Ma'amarim 5717*, pp. 238–239.

65. Schneersohn, *Torat Ḥayyim: Bere'shit*, 65c.

66. Heidegger, *Hölderlins Hymnen "Germanien" und "Der Rhein,"* p. 293: "Echte Wiederholung entspringt aus ursprünglicher Verwandlung."

67. Heidegger, *Elucidations of Hölderlin's Poetry*, p. 225; German original: *Erläuterungen zu Hölderlins Dichtung*, p. 196. Significantly, the notion of the juxtaposition of the unfamiliar is expressed in Heidegger's gloss on the nature of intimacy (*Innigkeit*). See Warnek, "Translating *Innigkeit*."

68. Shneur Zalman of Liadi, *Ma'amerei Admor ha-Zaqen 5569*, p. 206: "*Alef* is the master of the world [*alufo shel olam*] above all the worlds, and it is called the aspect of the supernal wonder [*pele elyon*] through the transposition of letters. It is the aspect of the interiority of *Keter* in which there is the light of the Infinite itself in the aspect of the concealment of the essence [*he'lem ha-aṣmut*]." These words are repeated verbatim in Schneersohn, *Or ha-Torah: Bemidbar*, 2:521. The paradox of incarnation is made even more explicitly by Schneersohn, *Imrei Binah*, introduction, 1b: "Seemingly these are two contradictory matters, for *pele* is the opposite of *alef*, and thus how could there be an emanation of *alef* from *pele*, one thing from its opposite? This is what is alluded to elsewhere [*Midrash Bere'shit Rabba* 68:9, p. 777] that 'he is the place of the world but the world is not his place.' The implication is the world is not his place because he is the aspect of *pele*, and he is the place of the world in the aspect of *alef*, the master of the world [*alufo shel olam*]. Thus everything is one in actuality, for the one is dependent on the other." See Schatz-Uffenheimer, *Hasidism as Mysticism*, pp. 75–76.

69. My language is indebted to Heidegger, *Hölderlins Hymnen "Germanien" und "Der Rhein,"* p. 250: "Wenn jedoch dieses Geheimnis als ein solches genannt und gesagt wird, dann ist es damit offenbar, aber die Enthüllung seiner Offenbarkeit ist gerade das

Nicht-erklären-wollen, vielmehr das Verstehen seiner als der sich verbergenden Verborgenheit." For an English rendering and analysis, see Warnek, "Translating *Innigkeit*," p. 63.

70. Schneersohn, *Liqquṭei Dibburim*, 1:390; Schneerson, *Qunṭres Inyanah shel Torat ha-Ḥasidut*, p. 28 (the passage is from the Rebbe's talk delivered on the last day of Passover, 22 Nisan 5730 [April 28, 1970], which was included in this publication); *Torat Menaḥem: Sefer ha-Ma'amarim Meluqaṭ*, 3:126.

71. Schneersohn, *Yom Ṭov shel Rosh ha-Shanah,* p. 3.

72. This principle is deployed in other Ḥasidic texts with a meaning quite similar to Ḥabad usage. See Hallamish, "The Teachings of R. Menahem Mendel," p. 280.

73. Schneersohn, *Yom Ṭov shel Rosh ha-Shanah,* p. 3. In that context, the human intellect (*sekhel enoshi*), which is said to derive from the Tree of Knowledge of Good and Evil, is contrasted with the Torah, which emanates from the supernal Wisdom (*ḥokhmah ila'ah*), the something (*yesh*) whence one can discern the nothing (*ayin*).

74. Schneersohn, *Ner Miṣwah we-Torah Or*, 9b.

75. Schneerson, *Sefer ha-Ma'amarim 5711–5712,* p. 136.

76. Schneersohn, *Be-Sha'ah she-Hiqdimu*, 1:134.

77. Shneur Zalman of Liadi, *Torah Or*, 123d. It should be noted that this passage is from the supplements (*hosafot*) to the text that were apparently redacted by the Mitteler Rebbe. See also Schneersohn, *Sha'arei Orah*, 33a.

78. Shneur Zalman of Liadi, *Liqquṭei Amarim: Tanya*, part 1, chapter 38, 50b. The expression *eḥad ha-shaweh* is based on *aḥdut ha-shaweh*, the technical term used in kabbalistic sources from the thirteenth century to denote the *coincidentia oppositorum*, that is, the indifferent one in which opposites are no longer distinguishable as opposites in their opposition. See introduction, n. 5.

79. See n. 21, this chapter.

80. Shneur Zalman of Liadi, *Torah Or*, 55b; Schneersohn, *Imrei Binah*, part 1, 20a; Schneersohn, *Derekh Miṣwotekha*, 124a; Schneerson, *Torat Menaḥem: Hitwwa'aduyyot 5712*, 2:200–201; *Torat Menaḥem: Hitwwa'aduyyot 5716*, 3:212; *Torat Menaḥem: Hitwwa'aduyyot 5717*, 1:174, 308; *Torat Menaḥem: Hitwwa'aduyyot 5717*, 2:229–230, 346; *Torat Menaḥem: Hitwwa'aduyyot 5720*, 1:10; *Sefer ha-Ma'amarim 5730–5731*, p. 135.

81. Schneerson, *Torat Menaḥem: Hitwwa'aduyyot 5745*, 3:1800.

82. Schneersohn, *Derekh Miṣwotekha*, 121b.

83. See introduction, n. 5.

84. Schneerson, *Torat Menaḥem: Hitwwa'aduyyot 5745*, 3:1800.

85. Schneersohn, *Derekh Miṣwotekha*, 121b.

86. Schneerson, *Qunṭres Inyanah shel Torat ha-Ḥasidut*, p. 20. For an alternative translation, see *On the Essence of Chasidus*, pp. 94–95.

87. Schneerson, *Torat Menaḥem: Hitwwa'aduyyot 5711*, 1:132–133.

88. Schneerson, *Torat Menaḥem: Sefer ha-Ma'amarim Meluqaṭ*, 1:159.

89. Schneerson, *Torat Menaḥem: Hitwwa'aduyyot 5711*, 1:234.

90. On the knowledge of God, the problem of attributes, and the *via negativa*, see Hallamish, "Theoretical System," pp. 44–50. On the tendency to synchronize Maimonidean philosophy and Ḥasidic mysticism, see Gotlieb, "Habad's Harmonistic Approach," pp.

34–48, 115–278; Kohanzad, "Messianic Doctrine," pp. 21, 75–84, 95–100, 154–159, 171–177. For discussion of this theme in the Ḥabad and Izbica/Radzin dynasties, see Nadler, "The 'Rambam Revival,'" pp. 251–255. For a more extensive discussion of the attempted synthesis of the *Guide of the Perplexed* and the *Zohar* in the reconstruction of esotericism in the school of Izbica and Radzin, see Magid, *Hasidism on the Margin*, pp. 40–71. On the inclusion of Maimonides in the list of medieval sages who promulgated kabbalistic views, which includes as well Rashi, Abraham Ibn Ezra, Naḥmanides, and Baḥya ben Asher, see Schneersohn, *Sefer ha-Siḥot 5701*, p. 132.

91. Many scholars have written on the apophatic elements of Maimonidean thought. For two recent treatments, see Wolfson, "*Via Negativa*" (a partial list of other scholarly contributions is given on pp. 365–366, n. 6); and the Wittgensteinian reading offered by McCallum, *Maimonides' Guide for the Perplexed.*

92. Shneur Zalman of Liadi, *Liqquṭei Amarim: Tanya*, part 5, 156b.

93. Shneur Zalman of Liadi, *Torah Or*, 111a. See ibid., 55a.

94. Ibid., 66b.

95. Shneur Zalman's interpretation of the Lurianic concept of the break (*shevirah*) as the metaphoric trope to mark the transition from the aspect of boundlessness (*bilti ba'al gevul*) of the Infinite to the aspect of boundary (*gevul*) is expressed lucidly by his student, Aaron Halevi Horowitz of Staroselye, *Sha'arei ha-Yiḥud we-ha-Emunah*, part 3, 20b–21a: "Thus, in order for there be a disclosure of the potency for boundary in the power of the Infinite, blessed be he [*gilluy koaḥ ha-gevul she-be-khoḥo ha-ein sof barukh hu*], it was necessary for there to be the aspect of the break [*beḥinat shevirah*], that is, the light is removed so that there will be a disclosure from the aspect of the Infinite, blessed be he, so that there will be a place for the disclosure of the potency for boundary, for if there was not a removal of his light, blessed be he, in the aspect of the Infinite, then the boundary that is in his power, blessed be he, would not have been revealed even though in the power of his essence, blessed be he, everything was in complete equanimity." See Jacobs, *Seeker of Unity,* pp. 90–112; Elior, *Theory of Divinity*, pp. 72–73.

96. Shneur Zalman of Liadi, *Torah Or*, 111a.

97. The expression *ayin mammash,* actual nothing, appears repeatedly in Ḥabad literature. For example, see Shneur Zalman of Liadi, *Torah Or*, 22d, 90a, 90b, 90c, 92b, 109a, 109d, 114d; *Liqquṭei Torah*, Behar, 1:42b, 42d, Bemidbar, 1:12a, 12d; Schneersohn, *Sha'arei Orah*, 35b, 39a, 54b, 55a, 56a, 79b, 124b; *Sha'arei Teshuvah*, 56d.

98. Shneur Zalman of Liadi, *Torah Or*, 111a.

99. Schneersohn, *Perush ha-Millot*, 79c.

100. Shneur Zalman of Liadi, *Liqquṭei Amarim: Tanya*, part 2, chapter 4, 79a. See also Schneerson, *Torat Menaḥem: Sefer ha-Ma'amarim Meluqaṭ*, 2:102.

101. Shneur Zalman of Liadi, *Torah Or*, 22c.

102. The conceptual point is bolstered by the numerological equivalence of the words *ha-ṭeva* (5 + 9 + 2 + 70 = 86) and *elohim* (1 + 30 + 5 + 10 + 40 = 86). Regarding the history of this numerology, see Idel, "*Deus sive Natura.*"

103. Shneur Zalman of Liadi, *Liqquṭei Amarim: Tanya*, part 2, chapter 4, 78b–79a.

104. Ibid., chapter 6, 80a–b.

105. Schneerson, *Torat Menaḥem: Sefer ha-Ma'amarim Meluqaṭ*, 4:114.

106. Ibid., 4:116.

107. Schneerson, *Sefer ha-Ma'amarim 5711–5712*, pp. 134–135.

108. Schneerson, *Torat Menaḥem: Hitwwa'aduyyot 5745*, 2:1245.

109. Schneersohn, *Be-Sha'ah she-Hiqdimu*, 2:750, 751, 3:1404; Schneerson, *Torat Menaḥem: Hitwwa'aduyyot 5744*, 1:343. On occasion the abbreviated version *mafli la'asot* is used. See Schneersohn, *Ma'amerei Admor ha-Ṣemaḥ Ṣedeq 5614–5615*, p. 214; Schneerson, *Torat Menaḥem: Hitwwa'aduyyot 5713*, 3:29.

110. Schneerson, *Sefer ha-Ma'amarim 5711–5712*, p. 138.

111. Schneersohn, *Derekh Miṣwotekha*, 62a.

112. Shneur Zalman of Liadi, *Liqquṭei Amarim: Tanya*, part 2, chapter 7, 83a–b. See ibid., part 1, chapter 21, 27a, chapter 49, 68b–69a; *Liqquṭei Torah*, Emor, 1:34b, Beḥuqotai, 1:46c–d, Shelaḥ, 1:47c, Ḥuqat, 1:59d; Hallamish, "Theoretical System," pp. 95–97; Jacobs, *Seeker of Unity*, pp. 49–63. See also the brief account of the Lurianic doctrine of *ṣimṣum* offered by Schneerson, *Iggerot Qodesh*, no. 11, 1:19–21.

113. See, for instance, Goodman, "Maimonidean Naturalism."

114. Shneur Zalman of Liadi, *Ma'amerei Admor ha-Zaqen ha-Qeṣarim*, p. 469.

115. The description of Maimonides is derived from the collection of studies by Blumenthal, *Philosophic Mysticism*.

116. Shneur Zalman of Liadi, *Liqquṭei Torah*, Shir ha-Shirim, 2:31b.

117. Schneersohn, *Derekh Miṣwotekha*, 71b. One should also bear in mind the two titles of another treatise by this author, *Sefer ha-Ḥaqirah* and *Derekh Emunah*. The implication of this dual title is that the exploration of creation, the central topic of the work, demands rational analysis (*ḥaqirah*) and belief (*emunah*). Not only are both necessary, but they are two sides of one coin or, utilizing a different metaphor, two byways on a single path that one must traverse. It is important to recall that, in spite of his philosophical inclinations, the Ṣemaḥ Ṣedeq was a strong opponent of the *haskalah*, the Jewish enlightenment movement. The historical recounting of this opposition is the subject of the pamphlet by Schneersohn, *Admor ha-Ṣemaḥ Ṣedeq u-Tenu'at ha-Haskalah*, reprinted in Schneersohn, *Sefer ha-Ḥaqirah*, pp. 427–479. Needless to say, the enlightenment is not rejected because of the value it placed on reason as an arbiter of truth, but because of the secularization of reason and the consequent elimination of any place for faith in the equation. The faith affirmed by the Ṣemaḥ Ṣedeq, however, is not antithetical to reason, at least not in the way that he construes the intellectual capacity of the human soul, and one can even conjecture that the Ḥabad emphasis on faith and reason more generally is, at least in part, a response to the separation between the two suggested by Haskalah philosophers. The charge of rationalism against Ḥabad by other Ḥasidic masters can also be seen in this light, as noted by Loewenthal, *Communicating the Infinite*, pp. 173–175.

118. For discussion of some of the relevant Ḥabad sources, see reference in the introduction, n. 118.

119. Schneersohn, *Derekh Miṣwotekha*, 72a.

120. See chapter 1, n. 150.

121. Schneersohn, *Derekh Miṣwotekha*, 71b.

122. See the letter written by Menaḥem Mendel Schneerson to Reuven Avinoam on 10 Tammuz 5722 (July 12, 1962), printed in *Iggerot Qodesh*, no. 8466, 22:272–273.

Schneerson remarked that in the times of persecution and the Crusades, the "simple people [*anashim peshuṭim*] gave their lives for the sake of our religion and our faith much more easily than the masters of intellect, understanding, and comprehension. Even though the ones and the others are 'believers who are sons of believers' [Babylonian Talmud, Shabbat 97a], and in both there is the essence of Judaism [*nequddat ha-yahadut*, literally, the "point of Judaism," a Hebrew rendering of the Yiddish idiom *dos pintele yid*, as noted in chapter 1], which is the source of their self-sacrifice, but from the perspective that the way of the masters of intellect is to orient all their matters in accord with the intellect, and habit becomes second nature, they had to find a reason and explanation [*ṭa'am wa-da'at*] in this as well, which is not the case with the simple people who approach the test through the matter of faith, as their essence of Judaism is aroused without any garments and without any boundaries." There is no way to verify Schneerson's observation historically, but from a psychological standpoint it is of course very understandable.

123. Schneerson, *Iggerot Qodesh*, no. 4126, 12:306–307. The recipient of the letter was Solomon Stenzel from Tel-Aviv. I should note that one area that proves an exception to the rule is the attempt to deal rationally with the horror of the Holocaust. I cannot give a full account of this matter here, but it is of interest to note that in several contexts Schneerson stressed that we must maintain belief in God even if the suffering of so many innocent people is beyond comprehension. For instance, see the letter to Elie Wiesel in *Liqquṭei Siḥot*, 33:256 (reprinted in *Iggerot Qodesh*, no. 8969, 23:370–371), and the discourse from 10 Ṭevet 5751 (December 27, 1990) in *Sefer ha-Siḥot 5751*, 1:233–234. It must also be noted, however, that occasionally Schneerson opted for the more customary theodicy, explaining the suffering seemingly caused by God as a means of spiritual enhancement for the victims. See, for instance, Schneerson, *Torat Menaḥem: Hitwwa'aduyyot 5720*, 1:428–429. In that context, which was a talk delivered on the festival of Purim, 14 Adar 5720 (March 13, 1960), the murder of so many innocent Jews is explained as a way "to abolish the concealments and obstructions that do not allow the divine soul to guide the body" (*levaṭṭel et kol ha-he'lemot we-ha-hesterim she-ein maniḥim le-nefesh ha-elohit lehanhig et ha-guf*). Schneerson connects the destruction of European Jewry to the scriptural rendering of the decree of Ahasuerus to carry out the desire of Haman to slaughter all the Jews on a single day (Esther 3:13), that is, even secular Jews were forced by the Nazi policies to confront their Judaism, as they suffered the same fate as observant Jews. The suffering is explained, therefore, as the means by which the community of Israel was reunited in fulfilling the will of God with an undivided heart. For discussion of Ḥabad's reactions to the Holocaust, see Greenberg, "Assimilation as Churban"; "Redemption After the Holocaust."

124. Moses ben Maimon, *Mishneh Torah*, Yesodei Torah, 1:1; *Zohar* 2:25a. On the amalgamation of faith and rationality in Schneerson's messianism, see Loewenthal, "Contemporary Habad," pp. 391–394.

125. Davidson, "The Study of Philosophy."

126. Shneur Zalman of Liadi, *Liqquṭei Amarim: Tanya*, part 4, sec. 19, 128a.

127. Shneur Zalman of Liadi, *Torah Or*, 11a. According to this passage, Abraham figuratively represents the aspect of intellect that is above rational comprehension.

128. Schneersohn, *Sha'arei Orah*, 63b.

129. Schneersohn, *Derekh Mişwotekha*, 27b.

130. Schneersohn, *Or ha-Torah: Bemidbar*, 3:1030. See also Schneersohn, *Liqquṭei Torah: Torat Shmu'el 5633*, 1:224, where mention is made of the "supernal knowledge before which everything is considered as naught" (*de'ah elyonah de-kholla qameih ke-lo ḥashiv*). The latter expression, which appears regularly in Ḥabad literature, is based on Daniel 4:32.

131. Moses ben Maimon, *Mishneh Torah*, Yesodei Torah 2:10, and compare Shneur Zalman of Liadi, *Liqquṭei Amarim: Tanya*, part 1, chapter 2, 6a, chapter 4, 8a–b.

132. Schneersohn, *Torat Ḥayyim: Shemot*, 279c.

133. Three studies that amply illustrate the point are Loewenthal, *Communicating the Infinite*; Elior, *The Paradoxical Ascent to God*; and Foxbrunner, *Ḥabad*.

134. For a cogent articulation, see Shneur Zalman of Liadi, *Torah Or*, 5d–6a; *Liqquṭei Torah*, Shelaḥ, 1:37b–c. Countless other sources could be cited.

135. Ravitzky, *Messianism*, p. 199; "The Messianism;" and, in much greater detail, Kraus, "'Living with the Times'" and *The Seventh*.

136. Scholem, *The Messianic Idea in Judaism*, pp. 223–227. On acosmism in Ḥabad, see Scholem, *Major Trends*, p. 341. Elior, "Ḥabad," pp. 163–164, delineated seven "basic axioms concerning the relationship between God and world" in Ḥabad: pantheism, acosmism, creation, immanence, panentheism, the world as manifestation of God, dialectical reciprocity between God and world such that the former has no separate existence without the latter. For discussion of the terms *acosmism, pantheism, and panentheism,* see also Hallamish, "Theoretical System," pp. 56–60, 127–132.

137. Shneur Zalman of Liadi, *Torah Or*, 55c, 98b.

138. Schneersohn, *Sefer ha-Ma'amarim: Qunṭreisim*, 1:204; Schneerson, *Torat Menaḥem: Hitwwa'aduyyot 5712*, 2:200. On the distinction between *yaḥid* and *eḥad*, see n. 80, this chapter.

139. On the numerology of *elohim* and *ha-ṭeva*, see n. 102, this chapter.

140. Schneersohn, *Sefer ha-Ma'amarim: Qunṭreisim*, 1:204.

141. Shneur Zalman of Liadi, *Liqquṭei Amarim: Tanya*, part 2, chapter 7, 82a–b.

142. Schneerson, *Iggerot Qodesh*, no. 405, 2:392. See n. 43, this chapter. On the "disclosure of the essence of the light of the Infinite in the Temple," see Schneersohn, *Be-Sha'ah she-Hiqdimu*, 2:769.

143. Schneersohn, *Or ha-Torah: Siddur Tefillah*, p. 364.

144. Schneerson, *Torat Menaḥem: Sefer ha-Ma'amarim Meluqaṭ*, 4:119.

145. Schneerson, *Torat Menaḥem: Hitwwa'aduyyot 5715*, 1:127–128.

146. Keller, *Face of the Deep*, p. 219. My gratitude to Virginia Burrus for calling my attention to Keller's evocative discussion, which has helped me sort out my understanding of the complex cosmological patterns found in Ḥabad. It is worth recalling here as well the expression "pan(a)theistic acosmism" used by Cunningham, *Genealogy of Nihilism*, pp. 59–73, to describe the monistic philosophy of Spinoza. Consider the following summation of the author's perspective: "Spinoza reduces all that is to naturalistic explanation, leaving no space for metaphysical mischief. Yet he goes further, and reduces Nature itself to 'naturalistic' explanation. Nature itself does not, as it were, exist. Spinoza manages this undeclared mental gymnastics by playing Nature against the idea of God, i.e., by reducing God to Nature he must perforce also reduce Nature to God. Thereby he ensures Nature does not

exist in any metaphysical sense. This Nature does not exist—its diversities, separations, finalities and pathos are all illusions. In this way, Spinoza manages to do away with God and Nature by simultaneous evocation, for each carries within it an infinitude that ensures its metaphysical dissolution. The category Substance is lost, because there is only one, and it exists purely in attributional modifications which are themselves nothing. So Substance has no more content than attribute and mode; the same goes for God and Nature. . . . This is the nihilistic logic that has the nothing be *as* something. Spinoza's God is vitalistic, and voluntarist, while Nature is transcendental (each being in the absence of the other), so allowing for a plenitudinal nihilism" (pp. 69-71). See chapter 3, n. 103.

147. The decoding of the word *ḥokhmah* as *koaḥ mah* to indicate the hylic nature of divine wisdom is attested already in kabbalistic sources from the thirteenth and fourteenth centuries. See, for example, Azriel of Gerona, *Commentary on Talmudic Aggadoth*, pp. 84 and 111; *Zohar* 3:28a (*Ra'aya Meheimna*), 220b, 235b (*Ra'aya Meheimna*); *Tiqqunei Zohar*, introduction, 4a; sec. 19, 40a; sec. 69, 99b, 102b, 112b. This *jeu de mots* appears often in Ḥabad literature, and here I offer only a small sampling from the writings of Shneur Zalman of Liadi: *Liqquṭei Amarim: Tanya*, part 1, chapter 3, 7b; *Torah Or*, 12d, 73d; *Liqquṭei Torah*, Pequdei, 1:6b, 8b, Aḥarei, 1:27c; Bemidbar, 1:14a; Qoraḥ, 1:55b; Ḥuqat, 1:61a; Maṭot, 1:87b; Mas'ei, 1:90a; Eqev, 2:16c, 17d; Re'eh, 2:29b; Ki Teṣe, 2:37b; Derushim le-Rosh ha-Shanah, 2:56b; Ha'azinu, 2:77c; Shir ha-Shirim, 2:26d.

148. Shneur Zalman of Liadi, *Torah Or*, 61b; *Liqquṭei Torah*, Shelaḥ, 1:46d; Re'eh, 2:19c.

149. Elior, *The Paradoxical Ascent to God*, p. 62, seems to be expressing a similar sentiment: "However, Hasidic thought is strained to the ultimate stage in a dialectical way, just as there is no separate reality and no discriminate essence in the world without God, so also God has no revealed and discriminate existence without the world. That is, just as one cannot speak of the existence of the world without God, so too one cannot speak of the existence of God without the world." Ḥabad, in particular, presents the greatest challenge to what Hartshorne, "Theism," p. 403, has described as the "basic paradox" of the theistic tradition, "the idea that the world and God are exclusively on opposite sides of categorical contrasts—as though one pole of a contrast could retain its meaning without the contrast, and hence the other pole, also applying." See the view of Kohanzad cited in n. 187, this chapter.

150. Shneur Zalman of Liadi, *Liqquṭei Torah*, Devarim, 2:42d, 43c.

151. Schneersohn, *Liqquṭei Torah: Torah Shmu'el 5633*, 1:284. See *Liqquṭei Torah: Torah Shmu'el 5631*, 1:132; *Liqquṭei Torah: Torah Shmu'el 5633*, 2:498–499.

152. The allusion is to the Lurianic doctrine of the trace or vestige (*reshimu*) of light that remains in the space from which the Infinite withdraws its light. From that residue, the aspect of the shell, which is the darkness that stands over and against the light, eventually comes forth from that trace, but in its root it is itself light. On the Lurianic conception of the *reshimu*, see Scholem, *Major Trends*, p. 264; Tishby, *Doctrine of Evil*, pp. 24–25; Fine, *Physician of the Soul*, pp. 130–131, 147–148. For a different emphasis, see Wolfson, "Suffering Eros," pp. 362–365.

153. Schneersohn, *Be-Sha'ah she-Hiqdimu*, 1:257. See ibid., 3:1346.

154. Schneerson, *Torat Menaḥem: Hitwwa'aduyyot 5711*, 1:155.

155. Ibid., 1:202.

156. Shneur Zalman of Liadi, *Torah Or*, 12a–b, 46b, 63a. On the concept of renewal (*hithaddeshut*) of the Infinite in created entities, compare also Schneersohn, *Liqquṭei Torah: Torat Shmu'el 5633*, 1:291; Schneersohn, *Be-Sha'ah she-Hiqdimu*, 2:820.

157. Shneur Zalman of Liadi, *Liqquṭei Amarim: Tanya*, part 1, chapter 33, 42a. On the status of creation and the question of concealment and negation, see Hallamish, "Theoretical System," pp. 112–126.

158. Shneur Zalman of Liadi, *Liqquṭei Torah*, Bemidbar, 1:18d.

159. The identification of nature as an expression of the divine is reinforced by the numerical equivalence of the name *elohim* and the word *ha-ṭeva*. See n. 102, this chapter.

160. Shneur Zalman of Liadi, *Liqquṭei Amarim: Tanya*, part 3, chapter 29, 149b; *Liqquṭei Torah*, Bemidbar, 1:19d . On the future disclosure of the "substance of the supernal delight" (*mahut ta'anug ha-elyon*), which is linked exegetically to the verse "Oh, give me of the kisses of your mouth" (Song of Songs 1:2), see Shneur Zalman of Liadi, *Torah Or*, 8c. On the role of eros in Ḥasidic lore, with special reference to the concept of delight (*ta'anug*), see Idel, *Hasidism*, pp. 133–140, 234–235; *Kabbalah and Eros*, pp. 228–229; "Ta'anug," pp. 131–145.

161. Wolfson, *Circle in the Square*, pp. 69–72, 189–192, nn. 174–180; *Language, Eros, Being*, pp. 273–287.

162. Shneur Zalman of Liadi, *Liqquṭei Torah*, Bemidbar, 1:18c. The expressions used more frequently to convey the erotic-noetic sport of the divine are the "bemusement of the king in his essence" (*sha'ashu'a ha-melekh be-aṣmuto*), the "bemusements of the king in his essence" (*sha'ashu'ei ha-melekh be-aṣmuto*), or the "bemusements of the king in himself" (*sha'ashu'ei ha-melekh be-aṣmo*). See Shneur Zalman of Liadi, *Liqquṭei Torah*, Beshallaḥ, 1:1b, Ṣaw, 1:9a; Re'eh, 2:29a; Derushim le-Shemini Aṣeret, 2:83d, Shir ha-Shirim, 2:1c, 12b, 27a; *Ma'amerei Admor ha-Zaqen 5566*, 1:364, 2:734–736, 740–743, 752, 758; *Ma'amerei Admor ha-Zaqen 5566*, 2:736, 738, 747-748, 768–770, 772; *Ma'amerei Admor ha-Zaqen 5569*, pp. 8, 10, 52, 227; Schneersohn, *Derushei Ḥatunah*, 2:414, 425, 450, 453, 456, 497, 500, 501, 503, 514, 518, 520, 524, 550, 558–560, 566, 603, 626, 628, 632, 643, 699; *Imrei Binah*, part 1, 44c; *Ma'amerei Admor ha-Emṣa'i: Hanaḥot*, pp. 94, 112, 164, 265, 271; *Ma'amerei Admor ha-Emṣa'i: Shemot*, 2:453; *Ma'amerei Admor ha-Emṣa'i: Qunṭresim*, pp. 345, 570, 571, 575; *Ner Miṣwah we-Torah Or*, 61b, 122a, 126b, 127a; *Perush ha-Millot*, 4d, 5c, 9d, 40b, 83b, 90c; *Sha'arei Orah*, 15a, 75a, 100a, 145a; *Sha'arei Teshuvah*, 104a; *Torat Ḥayyim: Bere'shit*, 18c, 45b, 55b, 62c, 78d, 96d, 131b, 135a, 136b, 137b, 152d, 159d, 172d, 182d, 215a, 225c, 226b–d, 228a; *Torat Ḥayyim: Shemot*, 23b, 61b, 92d, 135d, 155c, 168a, 189a, 204a, 220b, 221c, 224c, 239d, 237d, 291a, 301d, 318b, 330c, 331c, 336b, 342a, 404c, 408a, 412b, 413c, 429d, 430b, 432d, 453d; Schneersohn, *Derekh Miṣwotekha*, 39a, 41a, 42a, 73a; *Or ha-Torah: Bemidbar*, 1:12, 256, 3:889, 1007, 4:1128, 1140, 1143, 1144; *Sefer Tehillim*, p. 466; Schneersohn, *Liqquṭei Torah: Torat Shmu'el 5629*, pp. 11, 326, 406; *Liqquṭei Torah: Torat Shmu'el 5632*, 2:503, 568, 586; *Liqquṭei Torah: Torat Shmu'el 5633*, 2:555; *Liqquṭei Torah: Torat Shmu'el 5635*, 2 :327; *Liqquṭei Torah: Torat Shmu'el 5639*, 1:287; *Liqquṭei Torah: Torat Shmu'el 5640*, 1:287, 294; Schneersohn, *Be-Sha'ah she-Hiqdimu*, 1:351, 352, 353, 461, 2:1083; Schneerson, *Iggeret Qodesh*, no. 782, 4:18; *Torat Menaḥem:*

Hitwwa'aduyyot 5711, 1:13; *Torat Menaḥem: Hitwwa'aduyyot 5711*, 2:138, 140, 168; *Torat Menaḥem: Hitwwa'aduyyot 5712*, 1:73, 97; *Torat Menaḥem: Hitwwa'aduyyot 5718*, 3:39; *Torat Menaḥem: Hitwwa'aduyyot 5719*, 1:51; *Torat Menaḥem: Hitwwa'aduyyot 5720*, 1:110–113; *Torat Menaḥem: Sefer ha-Ma'amarim Meluqaṭ*, 1:48, 59.

163. Shneur Zalman of Liadi, *Torah Or*, 22c.

164. On the distinction between *ithapkha* and *itkafya*, see Hallamish, "Theoretical System," pp. 374–382; Goldberg, "Zaddik's Soul," pp. 176–177; Dahan, "'Dira Bataḥtonim,'" pp. 119–128; Levin, *Heaven on Earth*, pp. 65–71.

165. Schneersohn, *Sefer ha-Siḥot 5703*, p. 57.

166. On the distinction between origin and beginning in early kabbalistic symbolism, see Wolfson, *Alef, Mem, Tau,* pp. 119–126; and see Ciucu, "Neo-Platonism." I agree with much of Ciucu's analysis, though I would contest her attempt to contrast her view with my own, as she puts it, Heideggerian and Sufi interpretation. As I have communicated to the author, I believe she places too much emphasis on the distinction between "deferred" and "veiled." She contends that my reading of origin presumes that there is something that is being hidden behind the veil. This fails to take into account the full paradox of my thinking, which is indeed inspired by Heidegger's notion of the swaying-ground, the ground that grounds as absence of ground. Similarly, in my interpretation of the Sufi tradition about the veil, the face that is unmasked is itself naught but another veil to be unveiled. My sense of origin, therefore, is the very deferral she describes and thus I was somewhat perplexed that she presented her view as such a sharp alternative to my own.

167. Schneerson, *Qunṭres Inyanah shel Torat ha-Ḥasidut*, p. 20.

168. See Shneur Zalman of Liadi, *Liqquṭei Torah*, Shemini, 1:18b; Schneerson, *Torat Menaḥem: Hitwwa'aduyyot 5712*, 2:162.

169. Schneerson, *Torat Menaḥem: Hitwwa'aduyyot 5713*, 3:80.

170. Ibid. See also Schneerson, *Torat Menaḥem: Hitwwa'aduyyot 5715*, 1:126–127.

171. Scholem, *The Messianic Idea in Judaism*, p. 224, and the observation of Jacobs in Schneersohn, *Tract on Ecstasy,* p. 7, that the Ḥabad interpretation of the Lurianic conception of divine withdrawal (*ṣimṣum*) "receives a fresh and subtle interpretation remarkably reminiscent of Far-Eastern notions on the illusory nature of the universe." The view is repeated in Jacobs, *Seeker of Unity,* pp. 65–66. See also Garb, "Mystics' Critiques," pp. 316–317.

172. *Tiqqunei Zohar*, sec. 70, 122b: *leit atar panuy minneih*, "there is no place devoid of you." It is interesting to wonder if this oft-cited dictum is not based on a scribal error. The plausibility of this suggestion gains support from the parallel in *Zohar* 3:257b (*Ra'aya Meheimna*), *leit ever panuy minnah*, "there is no limb devoid of you." The difference between the words *atar* and *ever* is the second letter, in the former a *taw* and in the latter a *beit*. Although these letters are not typically confused, the possibility of a copyist making a mistake should not be ruled out categorically.

173. For a rich philosophical analysis of this theme, see Marshall, *Mystical Encounters*, pp. 111–144.

174. Schneerson, *Reshimot*, sec. 136, 4:235.

175. Marshall, *Mystical Encounters*, pp. 240–268.

176. Shneur Zalman of Liadi, *Torah Or*, 18d.

177. The expression to denote the indifference, *shaweh u-mashweh*, is derived from the description of God's judicial impartiality as *ha-shaweh u-mashweh qaṭon we-gadol*, "he renders the small and great as equal," in the liturgical poem *ha-oḥez be-yad middat mishpaṭ*, composed by the sixth-century Palestinian poet Yannai. See Yannai, *Piyyute Yannai*, p. 338.

178. This is the view of Lurianic kabbalah promulgated by Scholem, *Major Trends*, p. 274. For a critique of Scholem, see Dahan, "'Dira Bataḥtonim,'" p. 197, n. 1.

179. Schneerson, *Torat Menaḥem: Hitwwa'aduyyot 5712*, 2:201.

180. Schneerson, *Torat Menaḥem: Hitwwa'aduyyot 5750*, 3:21.

181. See Wolfson, *Language, Eros, Being*, pp. 26–31.

182. Schneersohn, *Sefer ha-Ma'amarim 5699–5700*, part 2, p. 26.

183. Schneersohn, *Torat Ḥayyim: Bere'shit*, 134a; Schneerson, *Torat Menaḥem: Hitwwa'aduyyot 5713*, 3:79.

184. On the portrayal of the revelation of God as one in which the visual and auditory modes are not differentiated, see Schneersohn, *Liqquṭei Torah: Torat Shmu'el 5627*, p. 118. The separation of vision and hearing is indicative of an exilic state.

185. Loewenthal, *Communicating the Infinite*, p. 137.

186. Schneersohn, *Sha'arei Orah*, 59b.

187. Schneerson, *Liqquṭei Siḥot*, 17:92–99, especially p. 93. These descriptions are taken from a literary account of talks given by the seventh Rebbe in 5731 (1971) and 5736 (1976) on the Sabbath when the section Shemini (Lev 9:1–11:47) was read liturgically. As one would expect from the fact that the narrative in the Torah portion is set on the eighth day after the dedication of the Tabernacle, the focus of the meditation is on the number eight, in particular its messianic valence, inspired by the rabbinic tradition that the harp of David had seven strings in contrast to the harp of the Messiah, which has eight strings. See Schneerson, *Torat Menaḥem: Hitwwa'aduyyot 5748,* 2:115–116. On the topos of the messianic harp, see Ginzberg, *The Legends of the Jews*, 6:262, n. 81. The eschatological significance of the number eight is not unique to Ḥabad Ḥasidism, or even to Ḥasidism more generally; it assumed that relevance in much earlier kabbalistic sources, reflected, for instance, in the identification of *Binah*, the eighth emanation counting from the bottom, as the world-to-come. The messianic import of this number is also enhanced by the identification of *Yesod*, the eighth emanation counting from *Ḥokhmah* downward, as the *ṣaddiq*, the righteous one, who is the foundation of the world (Prov 10:25). For an alternative illustration of this symbolism, see Wolfson, "The Cut That Binds." Finally, let me note that a similar conclusion to my view can be found in the observation of Kohanzad, "Messianic Doctrine," p. 136: "In the vision of the future, it is hard to see how the theistic ontological distinction between God and the world can any longer apply. Both God and the World will be one: there will be no divisions; the world that is experienced will become divine, without hierarchies, or inner-outer dichotomies." A crucial difference between our perspectives, however, consists of the fact that I have argued that the promise of seeing the essence without a veil is itself nothing but the final veil, and hence the distinction between divinity and nature is preserved even as it is abolished. Kohanzad's description of the unqualified identity of God and world suggests that he did not grasp the paradoxical nature of the ultimate paradox.

188. Schneersohn, *Torat Ḥayyim: Bere'shit*, 185a. In that context, the "essential nothing" (*ha-ayin ha-aṣmi*) is classified as one of two aspects of the "aspect of nothingness" (*beḥinat*

ha-ayin), the other being the "nothing of the something" (*ayin shel ha-yesh*). The latter is further delineated as the darkness that God places as his mystery (Ps 18:12) or the darkness that precedes the light of creation (Babylonian Talmud, Shabbat 77b), the aspect of the withdrawal (*beḥinat ha-ṣimṣum*), which is linked to the name Elohim or to the attribute of judgment. On the use of the term *ha-ayin ha-aṣmi,* see also ibid., 18c, 27b, 48b, 65c.

189. Schneersohn, *Sefer ha-Ma'amarim 5689*, p. 64. The expression *he'lem ha-aṣmi* is used frequently by exponents of Ḥabad philosophy. See, for instance, Schneersohn, *Sha'arei Orah*, 111a, 134a; *Torat Ḥayyim: Bere'shit*, 161b; Schneersohn, *Torat Ḥayyim: Shemot*, 96b, 229b, 298b; *Perush ha-Millot*, 26c, 69d, 103d; *Derushei Ḥatunah*, 2:476; Schneersohn, *Liqquṭei Torah: Torat Shmu'el 5627*, p. 412; *Liqquṭei Torah: Torat Shmu'el 5632*, 1:136–137; *Liqquṭei Torah: Torat Shmu'el 5633*, 2:510; Schneersohn, *Be-Sha'ah she-Hiqdimu*, 1:82, 404, 417, 420, 421, 460, 461, 474, 482, 586, 2:644, 663. 900, 905, 906, 3:1270, 1271, 1276, 1277, 1287, 1298, 1299; Schneerson, *Torat Menaḥem: Hitwwa'aduyyot 5712*, 1:129; *Torat Menaḥem: Hitwwa'aduyyot 5712*, 2:179; *Torat Menaḥem: Hitwwa'aduyyot 5713*, 2:113; *Torat Menaḥem: Sefer ha-Ma'amarim 5714*, pp. 9, 41–42.

190. Schneersohn, *Sha'arei Orah*, 21b.

191. See n. 147, this chapter.

192. Shneur Zalman of Liadi, *Torah Or*, 114c.

193. Schneersohn, *Sefer ha-Ma'amarim 5659*, p. 98; *Sefer ha-Ma'amarim 5669*, p. 137.

194. Schneersohn, *Sha'arei Orah*, 21b.

195. Ibid., 51a, 111a.

196. Shneur Zalman of Liadi, *Liqquṭei Torah*, Pequdei, 1:3d. The idea is linked exegetically to the verse *yashet ḥoshekh sitro* (Ps 18:12), which is rendered theopoetically as "He made darkness his mystery," and to the rabbinic dictum describing the creation, "at first darkness and afterwards light," *be-reisha ḥashokha we-hadar nehora* (Babylonian Talmud, Shabbat 77b).

197. Schneersohn, *Torat Ḥayyim: Bere'shit*, 161a.

198. Schelling's characterization of the original ground as the nonground had profound implications for Heidegger, who similarly described the ground as pulling-away or leaping from the ground. See Wolfson, *Language, Eros, Being*, pp. 13–14, and the appended notes.

199. Schelling, *Philosophical Investigations*, pp. 68–69.

200. Utilizing a more contemporary formulation, the essence spoken of by the Ḥabad masters could be described as the "matrixial borderspace," the "im-pure zone of *neither* day *nor* night, of *both* light *and* darkness." See Ettinger, *Matrixial Borderspace*, p. 109.

201. Shneur Zalman of Liadi, *Ma'amerei Admor ha-Zaqen 5566*, 1:165.

202. Wolfson, *Language, Eros, Being*, pp. 178–186.

203. Wolfson, *Through a Speculum That Shines*, pp. 358–359; "Woman," pp. 186–187; *Circle in the Square*, pp. 38–41, 88–89; *Language, Eros, Being,* pp. 140–141.

204. *Zohar* 2:129a; see Wolfson, *Language, Eros, Being*, pp. 179–180.

205. Shneur Zalman of Liadi, *Torah Or*, 72c; Schneerson, *Reshimot*, sec. 152, 4:425.

206. An interesting illustration of the point can be found in the famed Lithuanian interpreter of the kabbalah of the Gaon of Vilna, Solomon Eliashiv (1841–1924). For instance, consider Eliashiv, *Leshem Shevo we-Aḥlamah*, part 2, 4:15.3, p. 186.

207. This crucial point, it seems to me, has not been fully appreciated by scholars who have written about the dialectical nature of reality according to Ḥabad and the implied unity of opposites. See Elior, "Ḥabad," pp. 164–167; *The Paradoxical Ascent to God*, pp. 67–77; *Mystical Origins*, pp. 106–114.

208. Shneur Zalman of Liadi, *Torah Or*, 13c; Schneersohn, *Torat Ḥayyim: Shemot*, 180c.

209. Schneersohn, *Be-Sha'ah she-Hiqdimu*, 2:1003.

210. Schneersohn, *Sefer ha-Siḥot 5688–5691*, p. 153.

211. Schneerson, *Liqquṭei Siḥot*, 17:95.

212. Schneerson, *Torat Menaḥem: Sefer ha-Ma'amarim Meluqaṭ*, 2:102–103.

213. Ben-Shlomo, *The Mystical Theology of Moses Cordovero*, pp. 95–100, 268–269; Meroz, "Redemption," pp. 105–106, 139; Wolfson, "Divine Suffering," pp. 110–115; *Language, Eros, Being,* p. 27. For the impact of the dialectic of disclosure and concealment on Ḥabad, see Elior, *Theory of Divinity*, pp. 67–71; *The Paradoxical Ascent to God*, pp. 116–117, 121–122.

214. Schneerson, *Iggerot Qodesh*, no. 6776, 18:281.

215. Shneur Zalman of Liadi, *Liqquṭei Torah*, Derushim le-Rosh ha-Shanah, 2:62a.

216. As I have noted elsewhere, this way of thinking brings to mind the Heideggerian *Lichtung*, which similarly is imagined to be a clearing that manifests by concealing; this clearing is the mythopoeic equivalent to the scientific category of world. See Wolfson, "Divine Suffering," p. 154, n. 112; *Language, Eros, Being,* pp. 18–19, 412, n. 155.

217. Shneur Zalman of Liadi, *Liqquṭei Amarim: Tanya*, part 1, chapter 21, 27a. For a slightly better reading, see *Liqquṭei Amarim,* 1st ed., pp. 151–152.

218. *Zohar* 1:11b: "everything before him is considered as naught" (*kolla qameih ke-lo ḥashivin).* See also *Zohar* 2:170:b: "everything before him is considered as nothing" (*kolla qameih ke-ayin hu ḥashiv*).

219. Shneur Zalman of Liadi, *Torah Or*, 94b.

220. Schneersohn, *Sefer ha-Ma'amarim 5699–5700*, part 2, p. 24.

221. Schneersohn, *Sha'arei Orah*, 86b; *Sha'arei Teshuvah*, 12b; Schneerson, *Torat Menaḥem: Hitwwa'aduyyot 5712*, 1:6; *Torat Menaḥem: Hitwwa'aduyyot 5717*, 1:169.

222. The source for this expression in Ḥabad literature is Viṭal, *Eṣ Ḥayyim*, 42:1, 89c. See Shneur Zalman, *Liqquṭei Torah*, Shir ha-Shirim, 2:42b; Schneerson, *Torat Menaḥem: Hitwwa'aduyyot 5710*, p. 59; *Torat Menaḥem: Hitwwa'aduyyot 5713*, 1:107; *Torat Menaḥem: Hitwwa'aduyyot 5713*, 2:56; *Torat Menaḥem: Hitwwa'aduyyot 5717*, 1:7; *Torat Menaḥem: Hitwwa'aduyyot 5718*, 3:18; *Torat Menaḥem: Hitwwa'aduyyot 5720*, 1:237; *Torat Menaḥem: Hitwwa'aduyyot 5720*, 2:266.

223. Schneersohn, *Sefer ha-Ma'amarim 5699–5700*, part 2, p. 22.

224. On the thematic and linguistic link between the traditional expression *yoke of the kingdom of heaven* (*ol malkhut ha-shamayim*) and the kabbalistic symbol of the kingship of the Infinite (*malkhut de-ein sof*), see Schneersohn, *Liqquṭei Torah: Torat Shmu'el 5629*, p. 246.

225. Schneerson, *Torat Menaḥem: Hitwwa'aduyyot 5712*, 2:168.

226. Schneersohn, *Derekh Miṣwotekha*, 136a.

227. *Pirqei Rabbi Eli'ezer*, chapter 3, 5b. The aggadic dictum was interpreted in a similar way in older kabbalistic sources. See Meroz, "Redemption," pp. 185–186.

228. Schneerson, *Sefer ha-Ma'amarim 11 Nisan*, 2:398.

229. Schneerson, *Torat Menaḥem: Hitwwa'aduyyot 5712*, 2:165.

230. Schneersohn, *Sefer ha-Ma'amarim 5699–5700* , part 2, p. 23.

231. Ibid., p. 21.

232. On occasion the expression *he'lem de-he'lem*, "concealment of concealment," designates the Infinite in its essential hiddenness. See Schneersohn, *Perush ha-Millot*, 24a.

233. Horowitz, *Sha'ar ha-Tefillah*, 49a.

234. Horowitz, *Sha'arei Avodah*, part 1, chapter 32, 44a.

235. There are numerous studies of the Mādhyamika, the Mahāyāna Buddhist school of the middle. I will mention here only a few examples that have been useful to me as a nonspecialist: Stcherbatsky, *The Conception of Buddhist Nirvāna*, pp. 36–44; Kalupahana, *Nāgārjuna*; Huntington, *The Emptiness of Emptiness*; Musashi, "Mahāyāna Philosophies"; Wood, *Mind Only*; *Nāgārjunian Disputations*; Nāgārjuna, *Fundamental Wisdom*; Burton, *Emptiness Appraised*; Napper, *Dependent-Arising*. For a lucid discussion of the Mādhyamika logic, see Bagger, *The Uses of Paradox*.

236. Katsura, "Nāgārjuna and the Tetralemma"; Garfield, *Empty Words*, pp. 99–104.

237. My attempt to interpret the Ḥabad material through the prism of the *madhyamaka* shares the same methodological orientation of scholars of Mahāyāna Buddhism, who have compared the tetralemma logic to Derridean deconstruction, especially to his conception of the tetrapharmakon. For a representative list of relevant studies, see Magliola, *Derrida on the Mend*; Loy, *Nonduality*, pp. 248–260; "The Deconstruction of Buddhism"; Olson, *Zen*; *Indian Philosophers*; Wang, *Buddhism and Deconstruction*; and the essays in *Buddhisms and Deconstructions*, edited by Park. The reader should be apprised of the select bibliography prepared by William Edelglass, ibid., pp. 271–279. For a different approach, which is based on a comparison of the Buddhist Centrist philosophy, particularly as it is enunciated by Nāgārjuna and Chandrakīrti, to the thought of Wittgenstein, see Loizzo, "Introduction." On the use of Wittgenstein to illumine the implications of the *madhyamaka*, see also Garfield, *Empty Words*, pp. 88–90, 98–99.

238. Bagger, *The Uses of Paradox*, pp. 88–89, compares the Mādhyamika doctrine of emptiness to the Liar Paradox of Epimenides the Cretan, "All Cretans are [always] liars." Clearly, for this statement to be true, it must be false, but it can be false only if it is true. Other scholars have noted the relevance of this comparison. See, for instance, Garfield, *Empty Words*, pp. 89, 104–105. Also relevant and worthy of consultation is Slater, *Paradox and Nirvana*, pp. 65–111.

239. Garfield, *Empty Words*, pp. 96–99.

240. Nāgārjuna, *Fundamental Wisdom*, p. 282. Bagger cites the passage in *The Uses of Paradox*, p. 89.

241. Text cited in Döl-ḃo-ḃa, *Mountain Doctrine*, p. 328.

242. Ibid., pp. 328–329. Part of the passage is cited in Tāranātha, *The Essence of Other-Emptiness*, p. 83.

243. Viṭal, *Eṣ Ḥayyim*, 42:1, 89b: "That which precedes the void [*tohu*] is called *efes*, as [in the verse] 'they are considered by him to be from nothing and the void [*me-efes wa-tohu neḥshevu lo*] (Isa 40:17). And the matter is that the Infinite [*ein sof*] is called *efes*, for there is no comprehension of it, since there is no matter or form there at all, and after

it came forth the void [*tohu*], which is *Keter*, and afterwards came forth the chaos [*bohu*], which comprises the four elements, *Ḥokhmah*, *Binah*, *Tif'eret* and *Malkhut*." A parallel version appears in Viṭal, *Adam Yashar*, p. 46. The only notable variation is the inclusion of the remark "there is the negation of the material" (*sham afisat ha-ḥomer*) prior to "since there is no matter or form there at all."

244. Shneur Zalman of Liadi, *Torah Or*, 114c.

245. Schneersohn, *Or ha-Torah: Devarim*, 6:2204; Schneersohn, *Liqquṭei Torah: Torat Shmu'el 5627*, p. 413. The expression *afisat ha-ra'yon* as a designation of *Keter* is found in Cordovero, *Pardes Rimmonim*, 23:1, 7c, 23:8, 18c; *Or Ne'erav*, chapter 7, p. 57. But the source cited by both Menaḥem Mendel and his son Shmuel is Poppers, *Me'orot Natan*, 10b, no. 111: "*Efes* [is the name by which] the Infinite is called, for there is no comprehension of it [*ki ein bo tefisah*], and in it is the negation of thought [*u-vo afisat ha-ra'yon*]." The work of Poppers is referred to as *Me'orei Or*. On the title page of the *editio princeps*, the title *Me'orot Natan* is said to be numerically equivalent to the expression that names the two parts of the text, *me'orei or we-ya'ir nativ*, that is, both equal 1153. The passage is mentioned as well in the addenda to Shneur Zalman of Liadi, *Torah Or*, 114c (from the supplements edited by his son, Dov Baer).

246. Shneur Zalman of Liadi, *Torah Or*, 114c: "According to the words of the *Eṣ Ḥayyim* one can say that *efes* and *tohu* are two aspects in *Keter*, the lower aspect that is in the Emanator is the aspect of *Attiq*, which is called *efes*, and the aspect of *Arikh Anpin*, the source of all emanated beings, is called *tohu*." See chapter 4, n. 96.

247. Schneersohn, *Sefer ha-Ma'amarim 5652–5653*, p. 10.

248. Maitreya, *Middle Beyond Extremes*, p. 25.

249. Ibid., p. 37.

250. *Mountain Doctrine*, p. 329.

251. Schneersohn, *Or ha-Torah: Siddur Tefillah*, p. 352.

252. Schneersohn, *Derekh Miṣwotekha*, 62a.

253. Ibid., 136a.

254. Schneersohn, *Or ha-Torah: Siddur Tefillah*, p. 364.

255. Schneersohn, *Liqquṭei Torah: Torat Shmu'el 5633*, 2:493.

256. Schneersohn, *Be-Sha'ah she-Hiqdimu*, 1:569. See ibid., 2:1158.

257. Horowitz, *Sha'arei Avodah*, part 2, chapter 31, 45b. Compare Horowitz, *Sha'arei ha-Yiḥud we-ha-Emunah*, part 2, 47b: "in relation to him, blessed be he, the something and nothing are equal" (*ha-yesh we-ha-ayin shawin*).

258. Nāgārjuna, *Fundamental Wisdom*, p. 61.

259. Here I follow the view of Garfield in Nāgārjuna, *Fundamental Wisdom*, pp. 94–95, 176–177. See further references in the following note.

260. Wood, *Nāgārjunian Disputations*, pp. 124–125, 194–199. On the compatibility of emptiness and dependent-arising, see also Napper, *Dependent-Arising*, pp. 126–133, 149–150. For a conceptually nuanced analysis of *śūnyatā*, see Chang, *The Buddhist Teaching of Totality*, pp. 60–120.

261. Wood, *Mind Only*, p. 10.

262. Ibid., p. 11.

263. The words *mahut* and *tehom* are made up of the same letters.

264. For instance, see Shneur Zalman of Liadi, *Liqquṭei Amarim: Tanya*, part 1, chapter 36, 46a–b; *Seder Tefillot*, 132a; Schneersohn, *Sha'arei Teshuvah*, 142d; Schneerson, *Liqquṭei Siḥot*, 9:63–64.

265. For instance, see Gikatilla, *Sha'arei Orah*, 1:207: "In the future-to-come, however, when the *Shekhinah* returns to her place, God [*ha-shem*, literally, "the name," i.e., YHWH] will take off all those garments, epithets, and wings, and then Israel shall see God with the eye, and this is the secret 'Your master will no longer be covered and your eyes will see your master' (Isa 30:20), that is, 'will no longer be covered' [*lo yikkanef*]—he will no longer wear those epithets, which are called 'wings' [*kenafayim*], for God, blessed be he, was covered and hidden from Israel and they did not merit to see him. And this is the secret of 'Your master will no longer be covered.' What is written after it? 'Your eyes will see your master.' And this is the secret 'For every eye shall behold the Lord when he returns to Zion' (Isa 52:8)." The erotic implications of the divesting of the garments are made more overtly in a passage from his earlier treatise, *Sha'arei Ṣedeq*, 20b, where Gikatilla cites the verse from Isaiah to support the idea that the king is not afraid to disrobe in the presence of the members of his household, who are most dear to him, though he stands completely naked only before the queen. Similar parabolic language is used in *Sha'arei Orah*, 1:196, but without any reference to Isa 30:20. See also *Tiqqunei Zohar*, sec. 58, 92a, where the Sinaitic theophany is depicted as a moment in which the masculine and feminine aspects of the divine were conjoined "in the closeness of the flesh without any garment at all" (*be-qiruv bisra be-lo levusha kelal*), an idea that is supported by two verses, "The two of them were naked, the man and his wife" (Gen 2:25) and "Your master will no longer be covered and your eyes will see your master" (Isa 30:20), the former related to creation and the latter to redemption. Finally, it is worth noting a reversal of this imagery in the passage from Dov Baer Schneersohn cited in chapter 4 at n. 72.

266. Wolfson, *Luminal Darkness*, pp. 259–260, 283, n. 8.

267. Azulai, *Ḥesed le-Avraham*, part 2, sec. 5, 12b.

268. Wolfson, *Luminal Darkness*, p. 73; *Language, Eros, Being*, p. 222.

269. Schneersohn, *Sefer ha-Ma'amarim 5655–5656*, p. 319. For the continuation of this passage, see chapter 3 at n. 105.

270. Babylonian Talmud, Sanhedrin 100b.

271. Shneur Zalman of Liadi, *Liqquṭei Amarim: Tanya*, part 1, chapter 36, 45b–46a.

272. Ibid., part 1, chapter 38, 50b.

273. Ibid., part 1, chapter 49, 69a–70a.

274. Shneur Zalman of Liadi, *Liqquṭei Torah*, Derushim le-Shabbat Shuvah, 2:65d.

275. A possible source for the Ḥabad perspective may have been the depiction of the eschatological vision in *Zohar* 1:126a.

276. Schneersohn, *Sefer ha-Ma'amarim 5699–5700* , part 2, p. 26.

277. Shneur Zalman of Liadi, *Torah Or*, 114c.

278. Shneur Zalman of Liadi, *Seder Tefillot*, 132a.

279. Ibid., 131d.

280. Schneersohn, *Torat Ḥayyim: Shemot*, 437b: "But this illumination is from the delight of the essence of the essential repose of the world-to-come [*oneg ha-aṣmut di-menuḥah ha-aṣmiyyut de-olam ha-ba*], and this is the aspect of the hidden pleasure that

is in the concealment of the essence of the Infinite [*oneg ha-ne'lam she-be-he'lem ha-aṣmiyyut de-ein sof*], which is above every delight of the will, and this is the world-to-come." See ibid., 343d; Schneersohn, *Qunṭres ha-Hitpa'alut*, in *Ma'amerei Admor ha-Emṣa'i: Qunṭresim,* pp. 109–110; Schneersohn, *Derekh Miṣwotekha*, 92b.

281. Compare Schneersohn, *Qunṭres ha-Hitpa'alut*, in *Ma'amerei Admor ha-Emṣa'i: Qunṭresim,* p. 118: "The divine soul in its root receives from the essential divine light without concealment or garment." And see the description, ibid., p. 121, of the "comprehension of the understanding of the divine soul when it is sustained by the essential divine splendor in the Garden of Eden without partition or concealment at all." Also relevant here is Dov Baer's insistence, ibid., pp. 134–136, that the ecstasy of the divine soul, as opposed to the ecstasy of the natural soul, is devoid of all physical desires and divested of any materialization and thus attains the status of the angels. It is also of interest to note the contrast between the sage and the prophet made by Schneersohn, *Perush ha-Millot*, 25b. Both are portrayed as having a vision of the essence and substance of the divine, but the prophet always sees through a speculum (*aspaqlaryah*) or a looking glass (*maḥazeh*), whereas the sage sees directly without any intermediary at all. The distinction is linked to the teaching transmitted in the name of Ameimar in the Babylonian Talmud, Baba Batra 12a, that "a sage is preferable to a prophet" (*ḥakham adif mi-navi*). See also Schneersohn, *Sefer ha-Ma'amarim 5657*, p. 9, where the same talmudic dictum is cited to validate the point that the sage is granted a "vision of the substance through wisdom" (*re'iyyat ha-mahut be-ḥokhmah*), which is the "knowledge of reality" (*yedi'at ha-meṣi'ut*) without an intermediary, whereas the vision of the prophet is always mediated through an image (*demut*). See n. 288, this chapter.

282. Schneerson, *Sha'arei Teshuvah*, 142d.

283. Schneersohn, *Sefer ha-Ma'amarim: Qunṭreisim*, 2:826.

284. Schneersohn, *Liqquṭei Torah: Torat Shmu'el 5631*, 1:52.

285. Schneerson, *Torat Menaḥem: Hitwwa'aduyyot 5713*, 2:94.

286. Babylonian Talmud, Berakhot 17a.

287. Schneersohn, *Yom Ṭov shel Rosh ha-Shanah,* pp. 226–227.

288. Schneersohn, *Be-Sha'ah she-Hiqdimu*, 2:716: "The prophecy of Moses is from the essence of the emanation, which is not at all in the aspect of a source for being, for vis-à-vis this gradation, the spiritual and the physical are equal, and the manner of the prophetic disclosure is not by means of [an image] being engraved in the senses, but rather one sees the essence and substance of the matter."

289. Schneersohn, *Yom Ṭov shel Rosh ha-Shanah*, pp. 98–99. See n. 281, this chapter.

290. Ibid., p. 228.

291. Schneerson, *Sefer ha-Ma'amarim: Ba'ti le-Ganni*, 1:235, reprinted in Schneerson, *Sefer ha-Ma'amarim 5730–5731*, p. 119. See introduction, n. 100.

292. In the seventh Rebbe's words (see the following note for reference), there is an obvious wordplay: *qerashim*, "planks," has the same consonants as *mi-sheqer*, "from deceit," with an additional *yod*. From the lies of the world, which is to say, the lie that is the world (*sheqer de-olam*), the Jew, in particular, has the responsibility to construct the edifice that will house the divine glory and to create the bond (*qesher*) that conjoins the infinite light and finite matter. See Schneerson, *Torat Menaḥem: Hitwwa'aduyyot 5711*, 1:236: by means of the proper worship, the "deceit" (*sheqer*) and knot (*qesher*) of the

world are transformed into the "planks of the Tabernacle" (*qarshei ha-mishkan*). The passage is cited in the introduction at n. 101.

293. Schneerson, *Sefer ha-Ma'amarim: Ba'ti le-Ganni*, 1:243, reprinted in *Sefer ha-Ma'amarim 5730–5731*, p. 129.

294. Schneersohn, *Or ha-Torah: Siddur Tefillah*, p. 364.

295. Shneur Zalman of Liadi, *Liqquṭei Torah*, Derushim le-Rosh ha-Shanah, 2:62a.

296. Schneersohn, *Sefer ha-Ma'amarim 5654*, p. 40.

297. Schneersohn, *Sefer ha-Ma'amarim 5710–5711*, part 2, pp. 159–161. Compare Schneerson, *Liqquṭei Siḥot*, 30:158–159: "The complete truth is that there is no existence to anything in the world apart from him, may he be blessed (and if it does not appear so to the eyes it is only on account of the concealment of the face that covers the truth). . . . The entire reality of the adversary [*ha-menagged*] is merely due to the concealment that covers the truth, for 'there is none beside him' (Deut 4:35), and nothing in the world has existence apart from him, may he be blessed. Hence, if a man cleaves to God to the point that his true unity, may he be blessed, is revealed in him, the reality of the adversary is abolished, as the darkness that is pushed away before the light, for, in truth, it has no existence at all." On the distinction between two kinds of deceit, see Schneersohn, *Sefer ha-Ma'amarim 5692–5693*, pp. 237 and 489. In the first passage, the general claim is made that "the body hides and conceals the truth" (*ha-guf mekhasseh u-mastir al ha-emet*), but then a distinction is made between the corporeal (*ha-gashmi*) that "conceals the truth" and the material (*ha-ḥomri*) that "makes the lie into truth." In the second passage, the dream is identified as the type of deceit that dissimulates as truth as opposed to the deceit that covers the truth. For discussion of the dream as an admixture of truth and falsehood in Ḥabad sources, see Wolfson, "Oneiric Imagination," pp. 148–149.

298. The (a)temporal eternality of the present is attested, for example, in the explanation of the name *Judah* (*yehudah*) in Shneur Zalman of Liadi, *Torah Or*, 44a. On the one hand, the name is said to refer to the source of the souls of Israel that is "above time" (*lema'lah min ha-zeman*), but, on the other hand, the first letter, *yod*, "instructs about the present" (*morah al ha-howeh*). There is no contradiction, however, since the present in its perpetuity is precisely the characteristic of being beyond temporality. See also Schneerson, *Torat Menaḥem: Hitwwa'aduyyot 5723*, 2:102–105. In the context of explicating the talmudic tradition that Jacob did not die (see introduction, n. 53), the seventh Rebbe noted that the power of the Jew relates to the ability to control the past as well as the future, whence is derived the credo that the Jew is invested with the mission through ritual performance to actualize the element of eternality above time in the world constricted by temporal coordinates.

299. Schneerson, *Iggerot Qodesh*, no. 1527, 5:331.

300. *Midrash Shir ha-Shirim Rabbah* 2:22, p. 68.

301. Schneersohn, *Sefer ha-Siḥot 5696—Ḥoref 5700*, p. 316. See Schneersohn, *Arba'a Qol ha-Qore*, p. 6 (Hebrew text, p. 31), also printed in Schneersohn, *Iggerot Qodesh*, no. 1447, 5:367.

302. Schneerson, *Torat Menaḥem: Hitwwa'aduyyot 5712*, 1:101. See also Schneerson, *Torat Menaḥem: Hitwwa'aduyyot 5712*, 2:177; *Torat Menaḥem: Hitwwa'aduyot 5720*, 1:190.

303. Schneerson, *Torat Menaḥem: Hitwwa'aduyyot 5716*, 2:259.

304. Schneerson, *Torat Menaḥem: Hitwwa'aduyyot 5751*, 4:169.

305. As one finds, for instance, in Hegel's idealist thought. See the Heideggerian analysis of this theme in Carlson, *Indiscretion*, pp. 51–79.

306. Shneur Zalman of Liadi, *Ma'amerei Admor ha-Zaqen: Ma'arzal*, p. 474.

307. Schneersohn, *Or ha-Torah: Siddur Tefillah*, p. 364.

308. Schneersohn, *Sefer ha-Ma'amarim 5652–5653*, p. 10.

309. Horowitz, *Sha'arei Avodah*, part 2, chapter 32, 48b.

310. Schneerson, *Liqquṭei Siḥot*, 5:386.

311. Schneerson, *Torat Menaḥem: Hitwwa'aduyyot 5752*, 2:242. For the fuller context whence this passage is elicited, see the text cited in the introduction at n. 120.

312. Schneerson, *Torat Menaḥem: Hitwwa'aduyyot 5750*, 3:23.

313. Ibid., 3:23–24.

314. See n. 227, this chapter.

315. Schneerson, *Torat Menaḥem: Hitwwa'aduyyot 5712*, 2:169.

316. Ibid., 2:170.

317. Schneerson, *Torat Menaḥem: Hitwwa'aduyyot 5745*, 4:2494.

318. Babylonian Talmud, Sukkah 27b.

319. Schneerson, *Torat Menaḥem: Sefer ha-Ma'amarim Meluqaṭ*, 1:140.

320. Ibid., 1:140–141.

3. Semiotic Transubstantiation of the Somatic

1. Cited by Kripal, *Esalen*, p. 200. For a fuller discussion of the somatic practices of Esalen, see ibid., pp. 222–246, and for the assessment of the future possibilities of the utopian ideal of the "enlightenment of the body," pp. 456–463.

2. For a sophisticated and nuanced analysis of the role of healing, the attitude to experiential reality, and the relationship of mind and matter in New Age patterns of thinking and practice, see Hanegraff, *New Age Religion*. Consider as well the chapter on religious healing in Myers, *Kabbalah and the Spiritual Quest*, pp. 137–179. For an illuminating study that provides some of the conceptual background for more recent appropriations of the sexual and the somatic in contemporary spiritual practices, see Urban, *Magia Sexualis*.

3. Numerous works have appeared that reflect the shift in orientation and the reclaiming of the body inspired by the writings of thinkers as diverse as Nietzsche, Freud, Heidegger, Henry, Merleau-Ponty, Sartre, Foucault, Lacan, and Gendlin, just to name a handful of the better-known authors. Perhaps most influential in the field of feminist studies has been the work of Butler, *Bodies That Matter;* and see the collection of critical essays edited by Armour and St. Ville, *Bodily Citations*. For a selective list of some other relevant works, see Jaggar and Bordo, *Gender/Body/Knowledge*; Sheets-Johnstone, *Giving the Body Its Due*; Cooey, *Religious Imagination and the Body*; Raschke, *Fire and Roses*; Coakley, *Religion and the Body*; Sadoff, *Sciences of the Flesh*; Welton, *Body and Flesh*; Welton, *The Body*; Birke, *Feminism and the Biological Body*; Judovitz, *The Culture of the Body*; Vallega-Neu, *The Bodily Dimension in Thinking*.

4. A representative example of this trend is Michaelson, *God in Your Body*. See also Garb, *"The Chosen will Become Herds"*, pp. 49, 80–82, 204.

5. The text is published as the appendix in Schneerson, *Torat Menaḥem: Hitwwa'aduyyot 5721*, 1:317.

6. The allusion is to the statement in Babylonian Talmud, Berakhot 57a, to the effect that if one sees the name Ḥanina, Ḥananiah, or Yoḥanan in a dream, many miracles will be wrought for him. See Schneerson, *Reshimot*, sec. 3, 1:42.

7. Ibid., sec. 133, 4:209.

8. For elaboration of this point, see Schneersohn, *Sefer ha-Ma'amarim*: *Qunṭresim*, 3:139. Compare Schneerson, *Reshimot*, sec. 35, 2:332, and discussion in chapter 2.

9. Schneerson, *Reshimot*, sec. 133, 4:211. On the geographic expansion of the land of Israel in the future, see *Sifre on Deuteronomy*, sec. 1, p. 7; Schneerson, *Torat Menaḥem: Sefer ha-Ma'amarim Meluqaṭ*, 4:233. See chapter 6 at n. 10, and the discussion in Garb, *"The Chosen will Become Herds"*, pp. 91–93, 121–125.

10. The eschatological erasure of the difference between the land of Israel and the Diaspora is anticipated on each Sabbath when the light of emanation shines below by means of its being garbed in the creation. See Shneur Zalman of Liadi, *Torah Or*, 13a. In that context, the disclosure of light without any barrier is related to the ritual cutting of the foreskin in the act of circumcision, which is interpreted mystically as the transformation of "I" (*ani*) into "nothing" (*ayin*), the elevation of *Malkhut* to *Keter*.

11. Schneerson, *Reshimot*, sec. 9, 1:255. Compare Schneerson, *Torat Menaḥem: Hitwwa'aduyyot 5710*, p. 113: the task of the emissaries to purify the materiality of the world is marked as turning the place to which they are sent into the land of Israel. Clearly, the concept of the land here is not simply topographical.

12. The connection between the land of Israel and the interiority of the Torah is offered as the rationale for the sixth Rebbe establishing the Kefar Ḥabad within the boundaries of the land, even as it is acknowledged that the spreading forth of the wellsprings of Ḥasidic wisdom began in the Diaspora and from there influenced those living in the land. See Schneerson, *Torat Menaḥem: Hitwwa'aduyyot 5716*, 3:92. On the depiction of Kefar Ḥabad as the place in the land of Israel whence the wellsprings of the Beshṭ and the rest of the Ḥabad masters until the Friediker Rebbe spread outward, see Schneerson, *Torat Menaḥem: Hitwwa'aduyyot 5716*, 2:356. In spite of these passages, and others that could have been cited, in which the traditional privileging of Israel is affirmed as the center of the Jewish world—indeed, the center of the world more generally—it is also clear that under the leadership of the seventh Rebbe the world headquarters of the Lubavitch movement in the complex of buildings on Eastern Parkway in the Crown Heights section of Brooklyn became the center and, in some sense, attained the holiness usually reserved for Israel or, even more specifically, the Temple Mount in Jerusalem. See Goldschmidt, "Crown Heights."

13. Schneersohn, *Sefer ha-Siḥot 5703*, p. 58.

14. See Schneerson, *Torat Menaḥem: Hitwwa'aduyyot 5716*, 3:92: "From the perspective of the matter of 'your wellsprings will spread outward,' there must be a spreading of the wellsprings also in the land of Israel, since the land of Israel is also included in what is outside."

15. Schneerson, *Torat Menaḥem: Hitwwa'aduyyot 5712*, 2:153. See Schneerson, *Torat Menaḥem: Hitwwa'aduyyot 5715*, 1:202.

16. Schneerson, *Torat Menaḥem: Hitwwa'aduyyot 5752*, 1:422.

17. Ibid., 1:423–425.

18. Schneerson, *Torat Menaḥem: Hitwwa'aduyyot 5743*, 2:933.

19. My thinking here is indebted to Leder, *The Absent Body*. I have obviously applied Leder's insights to material that is beyond the scope of his own analysis, and the conclusions he reaches are not identical to my own, but I have nonetheless been influenced by his analysis of the ecstatic/recessive structure of embodiment. My interpretation of embodiment in Ḥabad also betrays the notion of the lived body proffered by Merleau-Ponty. Compare the characterization in Carey, "Cultivating Ethos," p. 24: "In his monumental work, *The Phenomenology of Perception*, Merleau-Ponty reveals that the body is a living center of intentionality upon which rational reflection depends. The body-subject cannot be understood solely from an idealistic or materialistic perspective because the body is simultaneously presence *and* absence, incarnation *and* transcendence, being *and* consciousness." See chapter 2, nn. 4 and 55.

20. Schneersohn, *Torat Ḥayyim: Bere'shit*, 68b. See also ibid., 100b; *Torat Ḥayyim: Shemot*, 313c, 438d; Schneersohn, *Be-Sha'ah she-Hiqdimu*, 3:1468; Schneerson, *Torat Menaḥem: Hitwwa'aduyyot 5716*, 1:139; *Torat Menaḥem: Hitwwa'aduyyot 5720*, 1:129. On the application of the principle of corporeality-within-spirituality (*gashmiyyut she-be-ruḥaniyyut*) to establishing institutions in the world to carry out the work of Ḥabad, see Schneerson, *Iggerot Qodesh*, no. 1911, 7:41. The seventh Rebbe's emphasis on the overcoming of the spiritual-material binary in the messianic disclosure of the infinite essence is duly analyzed by Kohanzad, "Messianic Doctrine," pp. 134–137. As the author correctly notes, "The spiritual will not exist as distinct from the physical, nor the physical from the spiritual, but rather the spiritual will be physical and the physical spiritual" (p. 136). I concur that the eschaton is marked by this fusion of opposites, but my interpretation differs insofar as it rests on the assumption that Schneerson affirmed the notion of a transfigured flesh—the semiotic body—that is more amenable to the ascetic renunciation of the sensual associated with traditional forms of mystical pietism. For instance, compare Schneerson, *Torat Menaḥem: Hitwwa'aduyyot 5717*, 3:56, where it is emphasized (based on Maimonides) that the essential pleasure (*ta'anug*) in the messianic era is spiritual or intellectual and not physical, even though material beneficence is not entirely denied.

21. Schneerson, *Torat Menaḥem: Hitwwa'aduyyot 5720*, 1:174–175.

22. Schneerson, *Iggerot Qodesh*, no. 200, 2:67–68.

23. See chapter 2, nn. 217–218.

24. Schneersohn, *Liqquṭei Torah: Torat Shmu'el 5629*, p. 157. The words of the fourth Rebbe are based on previous Ḥabad sources. For example, see Shneur Zalman of Liadi, *Ma'amerei Admor ha-Zaqen 5566*, 1:8-9, 22, 404; Schneersohn, *Imrei Binah*, introduction, 2d; *Torat Ḥayyim: Shemot*, 434b; Schneersohn, *Or ha-Torah: Bemidbar*, 4:1323. See also Schneerson, *Torat Menaḥem: Hitwwa'aduyyot 5715*, 2:73; *Torat Menaḥem: Hitwwa'aduyyot 5717*, 1:271, 308; *Torat Menaḥem: Hitwwa'aduyyot 5717*, 2:346; *Torat Menaḥem: Hitwwa'aduyyot 5718*, 3:174, 250; *Torat Menaḥem: Hitwwa'aduyyot 5719*, 3:91; *Torat Menaḥem: Sefer ha-Ma'amarim Meluqaṭ*, 1:141; *Torat Menaḥem: Sefer ha-Ma'amarim Meluqaṭ*, 2:11, 187, 258; *Torat Menaḥem: Sefer ha-Ma'amarim Meluqaṭ*, 4:278; and the passage cited in chapter 5, n. 55.The expression *alufo shel olam* is applied

to God in rabbinic and kabbalistic sources, but its exegetical link to the letter *alef* became more explicit and popular in Ḥasidic texts.

25. Schneersohn, *Sefer ha-Ma'amarim 5699–5700*, part 2, p. 30.

26. Derrida, *Given Time*, p. 160

27. The expression is based on the rabbinic depiction of the world-to-come as "a world that is entirely good," *olam she-kullo ṭov*. See Babylonian Talmud, Qiddushin 39b.

28. Ps 84:8.

29. Schneerson, *Iggerot Qodesh*, no. 5767, 15:443.

30. Schneerson, *Torat Menaḥem: Hitwwa'aduyyot 5711*, 1:266.

31. The expression "world of deceit" (*alma de-shiqra*) is used regularly in the eighteenth and nineteenth centuries by both Ḥasidic masters and Lithuanian kabbalists from the circle of the Vilna Gaon. Typically, the term communicates the fact that human beings are predominantly deceitful, but, according to the Ḥabad interpretation, the deceit consists of the fact that the world presents itself as a reality that appears to be independent of God. The deceitfulness, therefore, is an epistemological and not a moral calculation. See Shneur Zalman of Liadi, *Torah Or*, 86c: "All of the worlds are nullified in a complete nullification in relation to him . . . and even though the worlds appear to us as something, this is a complete lie [*sheqer gamur*]." See also Schneersohn, *Liqquṭei Torah: Torat Shmu'el 5627*, p. 101; *Liqquṭei Torah: Torat Shmu'el 5632*, 2:275, 349; *Liqquṭei Torah: Torat Shmu'el 5638*, p. 22; *Liqquṭei Torah: Torat Shmu'el 5640*, 1:226, 227, 2:724, 863.

32. Kahn, *Shi'urim be-Torat Ḥabad*, p. 39.

33. Ibid.

34. The degree of Kahn's ethnocentrism can be gauged from his comments (ibid., pp. 53–54) that, even with respect to the highest aspect of the divine, the nondifferentiated One, where Jews and non-Jews are equal (*ad she-yisra'el we-ha-ummot shawim*), we must still speak of God choosing Israel freely and being bound to them in a way that renders them distinct amongst the nations. For a fuller articulation, see Kahn, *Mahutam shel Yisra'el*.

35. See Rapoport-Albert, "God and the Zaddik," pp. 300–301, and the recent analysis of Kaufman, "Between Immanence and Religious Behavior." See also Hallamish, "Theoretical System," pp. 305–309.

36. Schneerson, *Iggerot Qodesh*, no. 323, 2:287.

37. Schneerson, *Torat Menaḥem: Hitwwa'aduyyot 5720*, 2:187. See chapter 2, n. 172.

38. For a typical articulation of this perspective, see Jacobs, "The Uplifting of Sparks," pp. 115–116.

39. My interpretation concurs with the analysis in Krassen, *Uniter of Heaven and Earth*, pp. 178–185. See Margolin, *The Human Temple*, pp. 145–287; Ornet, "*Ratso va-shov*," pp. 79–90.

40. Shneur Zalman of Liadi, *Tanya*, part 1, chapter 32, 41a. The point was well comprehended by Isaac Meir Morgenstern, who comments as follows in *Yam ha-Ḥokhmah 5769*, p. 455: "The entire way of the Besht was to reveal that all the aspects of the supernal worlds are in the soul of Israel, and know that the essence of the worship and the routine of creation relates to the male and female of the [world of] emanation. This is what the author of *Tanya* came to explain in his holy book, that there are two parts in man, the divine soul, which is the part of man that wants constantly to be conjoined to the Lord and to rectify

his ways, and the animal soul, which is drawn to materiality and to what is remote from the truth of worship. In every matter, the principles of worship are comprised, so that the divine soul will overpower the animal soul, and this is the foundation of the book of *Tanya*."

41. Shneur Zalman of Liadi, *Torah Or*, 67a. See Shneur Zalman of Liadi, *Liqquṭei Torah*, Shir ha-Shirim, 2:25b; Schneersohn, *Liqquṭei Torah: Torat Shmu'el 5632*, 1:84, 245; *Liqquṭei Torah: Torat Shmu'el 5633*, 1:190.

42. Shneur Zalman of Liadi, *Tanya*, part 1, chapter 9, 14a; and see the explication of this passage in Schneerson, *Torat Menaḥem: Hitwwa'aduyyot 5712*, 1:167–168. For discussion of the divine and animal souls, see Hallamish, "Theoretical System," pp. 163–173; Ornet, "Relationship Between the Divine Soul and the Animal Soul," pp. 79–125. See also Jacobson, "Animal Soul."

43. Shneur Zalman of Liadi, *Tanya*, part 1, chapter 39, 48b.

44. Schneersohn, *Be-Sha'ah she-Hiqdimu*, 3:1405. See ibid., 1:506. On the image of breaking the shell of the nut as a way to depict the control of the animal soul, see Shneur Zalman of Liadi, *Seder Tefillot*, 287d.

45. Shneur Zalman of Liadi, *Torah Or*, 94a.

46. See, for instance, Shneur Zalman of Liadi, *Torah Or*, 57b, 67a; *Liqquṭei Torah*, Bemidbar, 1:8d, 10c, 62b; Shir ha-Shirim, 2:21c, 28d; Schneersohn, *Torat Ḥayyim: Shemot*, 74c, 252a, 288d; Schneersohn, *Liqquṭei Torah: Torat Shmu'el 5632*, 2:415; *Liqquṭei Torah: Torat Shmu'el 5633*, 1:59.

47. Shneur Zalman of Liadi, *Torah Or*, 45b.

48. Ibid.

49. Schneersohn, *Sha'arei Teshuvah*, 94d.

50. From the excerpt of a letter of the RaShaB placed at the beginning of *Ha-Yom Yom*, p. 4.

51. Schneerson, *Torat Menaḥem: Hitwwa'aduyyot 5745*, 5:2797.

52. Schneersohn, *Qunṭres ha-Hitpa'alut*, in *Ma'amerei Admor ha-Emṣa'i: Qunṭresim*, pp. 134–135; Schneerson, *Torat Menaḥem: Sefer ha-Ma'amarim Meluqaṭ*, 2: 308 (explicating a passage from the tenth chapter of *Ba'ti le-Ganni* in Schneersohn, *Sefer ha-Ma'amarim 5710–5711*, part 1, p. 125), 405; *Torat Menaḥem: Hitwwa'aduyyot 5710*, p. 37; *Ha-Yom Yom*, p. 44 (12 Nisan).

53. Schneerson, *Torat Menaḥem: Hitwwa'aduyyot 5716*, 2:244, 246. On the instrumental role assigned to the body as the vessel to serve the soul, see the comments of Schneerson, *Torat Menaḥem: Hitwwa'aduyyot 5723*, 2:107–108.

54. Babylonian Talmud, Makkot 23b.

55. Schneerson, *Liqquṭei Siḥot*, 21:458.

56. Schneerson, *Liqquṭei Siḥot*, 5:434. See Schneerson, *Torat Menaḥem: Hitwwa'aduyyot 5713*, 2:235; *Torat Menaḥem: Hitwwa'aduyyot 5720*, 2:186.

57. Job 31:2.

58. Babylonian Talmud, Ḥagigah 5b.

59. Schneerson, *Liqquṭei Siḥot*, 5:434–435. See also Schneerson, *Torat Menaḥem: Hitwwa'aduyyot 5745*, 4:2522–2523.

60. Schneerson, *Liqquṭei Siḥot*, 5:436.

61. Ibid., 5:437. There are occasions, however, where the seventh Rebbe asserts that the intent of contemplation (*hitbonenut*) is to break the materiality of the animal soul and the existence of the body, which allows the soul to be conjoined with the light whence it emerged. See, for instance, Schneerson, *Torat Menaḥem: Hitwwa'aduyyot 5718*, 1:71.

62. Schneerson, *Torat Menaḥem: Sefer ha-Ma'amarim Meluqaṭ*, 2:307 (an explication of the discussion of sacrifices in the second chapter of the sixth Rebbe's *Ba'ti le-Ganni*; see Schneersohn, *Sefer ha-Ma'amarim 5710–5711*, part 1, pp. 112–114). Compare Schneerson, *Torat Menaḥem: Hitwwa'aduyyot 5745*, 2:1247–1248.

63. Schneerson, *Iggerot Qodesh*, no. 1413, 6:196; also no. 1834, 6:328–329; no. 876, 4:134. For additional references, see n. 61, this chapter. On *sheḥiṭah* as a metaphor for sacrificing the evil inclination, see Schneerson, *Iggerot Qodesh*, no. 104, 1:190 (where reference is made to Babylonian Talmud, Sanhedrin 43b). Also relevant here is the seventh Rebbe's view regarding the change in the status of sacrifices in the future Temple; see Schneerson, *Torat Menaḥem: Hitwwa'aduyyot 5717*, 1:241. In the final stages of editing this book, I came across the following passage in Schneerson, *Torat Menaḥem: Hitwwa'aduyyot 5718*, 2:69–70, which corroborates the perspective I adopted in the body of this chapter: "The sacrificial rite was given specifically to the human [*adam*], for he is called *human* on account of 'I will be likened to the most high' [*eddammeh le-elyon*] (Isa 14:14) . . . it is in his power to ascend above and the draw down from there. One must contemplate the matter of the human being likened to the most high [*adam eddammeh le-elyon*], for the created beings are worthless in relation to the Creator, and hence how is it possible to say of a creature that he is likened to the most high? The difficulty of the example can be understood if we begin by explicating the supernal anthropos [*adam ha-elyon*]. Concerning the blessed One it says 'for he is not human' [*ki lo adam hu*] (1 Sam 15:29), and if this is so, how can we ascribe a human attribute to him? But the matter is that the lower anthropos below has 248 limbs and 365 veins, and it is known that the 248 limbs correspond to the positive commandments and the 365 veins to the negative commandments. Therefore, by means of human worship [*avodat ha-adam*] through the fulfillment of the commandments . . . the form of the supernal anthropos [*ṣiyyur adam ha-elyon*] is made. That is, even though from the perspective of himself 'he is not human,' nevertheless by means of the fulfillment of the commandments there comes to be the aspect of 'upon the semblance of the throne, there was the semblance of the appearance of a human' (Ezek 1:26), and this is what is written 'and do them' [*wa-asitem otam*] (Lev 26:3), [*otam*] is written [orthographically] *attem* ['you'], I consider it as if you have made me. According to this you can understand how the lower anthropos is likened to the most high, for the image of the supernal anthropos is made by means of the fulfillment of the commandments of the lower anthropos." Rejecting a literal interpretation of the anthropomorphic imagery applied to God, the imaginal body of the divine anthropos is constructed on the basis of the ritual observance of Israel, the terrestrial anthropos, since the human anatomy is correlated with the edifice of the Torah, the linguistic body par excellence. For an alternative meaning of the image of the not-human (*lo adam*) in Schneerson's thought, see discussion in chapter 6, and other references cited in n. 91.

64. Meir Ibn Gabbai, *Tola'at Ya'aqov*, pp. 16–17; Menaḥem Azariah of Fano, *Sefer Asarah Ma'amarot*, p. 58; Horowitz, *Shenei Luḥot ha-Berit*, 1:8, and 3:17–18, 128, 135, 390, 435.

65. Given the numerous times that this exegesis occurs in Ḥabad sources, I can only offer a modest list of examples: Shneur Zalman of Liadi, *Torah Or*, 69b, 76b; *Liqquṭei Torah*, Wayyiqra, 1:2c, 8b; Bemidbar, 1:81c; Devarim, 2:4b; *Ma'amerei Admor ha-Zaqen 5566*, 1:201; Schneersohn, *Sha'arei Teshuvah*, 61d, 62b, 68b, 68d, 111d; Schneerson, *Iggerot Qodesh*, no. 7450, 20:6; no. 9170, 24:171; *Torat Menaḥem: Hitwwa'aduyyot 5714*, 3:174.

66. Wolfson, *Venturing Beyond*, pp. 42–57, 73–124.

67. Schneerson, *Sefer ha-Ma'amarim 5711–5712*, p. 137. It is of interest to recall the manner in which the messianic plea is phrased in Schneersohn, *Sefer ha-Siḥot 5702*, p. 109: "The hour has arrived when it is necessary to purify the air. . . . The purification of the air is by means of the letters of the Torah. When we are standing in the store, walking in the street, or travelling by carriage, and we utter letters of the Torah we thereby purify the air." The sixth Rebbe goes on to say that this purification of the air is the responsibility of the literate Jews—"those who know the book and those who know the Torah"—to commit texts to memory, so that they can contemplate and utter the holy letters "in every place and in every time." I presume that underlying this practice is the belief in the linguistic nature of corporeality.

68. Schneerson, *Torat Menaḥem: Hitwwa'aduyyot 5714*, 3:174; *Iggerot Qodesh*, no. 5429, 15:112.

69. Schneerson, *Torat Menaḥem: Hitwwa'aduyyot 5743*, 4:1733.

70. Shneur Zalman of Liadi, *Liqquṭei Torah*, Balaq, 1:71c.

71. Shneur Zalman of Liadi, *Torah Or*, 25b.

72. Ibid., 3b, 28c; Shneur Zalman of Liadi, *Liqquṭei Torah*, Ha'azinu, 2:75d.

73. Shneur Zalman of Liadi, *Torah Or*, 111a.

74. See chapter 2, n. 31.

75. Elior, "ḤaBaD," pp. 178–181. For a partial critique of Elior's dialectical approach and an alternate explanation based on positing two complimentary types of worship, see Idel, *Hasidism*, pp. 123–124. The position I have staked seeks the middle ground between Elior and Idel.

76. Shneur Zalman of Liadi, *Torah Or*, 28d. For an elaboration of this theme, and citation of many of the relevant texts, see Wolfson, "Oneiric Imagination."

77. Schneerson, *Torat Menaḥem: Hitwwa'aduyyot 5714*, 3:163–175; the text is also printed in *Torat Menaḥem: Sefer ha-Ma'amarim 5714*, pp. 216–225.

78. Babylonian Talmud, Berakhot 26a–b.

79. This theme is repeated frequently in Ḥabad sources, For instance, see Shneur Zalman of Liadi, *Liqquṭei Torah*, Devarim, 2:1a; *Torah Or*, 97a. A notably concise and lucid account is given in Schneersohn, *Liqquṭei Torah: Torat Shmu'el 5629*, p. 88: "The thanksgiving is only the aspect of nullification on account of the gratefulness, even though one does not comprehend how or what, for this is the aspect of darkness and concealment, as one does not understand the matter as it is."

80. Schneerson, *Torat Menaḥem: Hitwwa'aduyyot 5714*, 3:164. For an alternative explanation, see *Torat Menaḥem: Hitwwa'aduyyot 5747*, 3:256.

81. Schneerson, *Torat Menaḥem: Hitwwa'aduyyot 5714*, 3:169.

82. Ibid., pp. 169–170.

83. Schneersohn, *Torat Shalom: Sefer ha-Siḥot*, pp. 127–128; Schneersohn, *Sefer ha-Ma'amarim 5698*, p. 219; Schneerson, *Iggerot Qodesh*, no. 323, 2:287; no. 4013, 12:202, no. 4022, 12:209; no. 5041, 14:279; *Torat Menaḥem: Hitwwa'aduyyot 5714*, 2:56; *Torat Menaḥem: Hitwwa'aduyyot 5747*, 3:256; *Torat Menaḥem: Hitwwa'aduyyot 5751*, 1:143; *Torat Menaḥem: Hitwwa'aduyyot 5752*, 1:242, 295; *Torat Menaḥem: Sefer ha-Ma'amarim, 5711–5712*, p. 153; *Liqquṭei Siḥot*, 20:44; *Sefer ha-Siḥot 5751*, 2:685. For discussion of this theme and citation of other sources, see Dahan, "'Dira Bataḥtonim,'" pp. 267–270.

84. Schneerson, *Iggerot Qodesh*, no. 4022, 12:209.

85. Schneerson quotes this midrashic explanation in the name of the rabbis and also as a citation from the *Me'orei Or* of Meir Poppers, published as *Me'orot Natan*, 15a, no. 182. Regarding this work, see chapter 2, n. 245. The closest rabbinic source that I was able to discover is the dictum transmitted in the name of R. Yoḥanan in *Midrash Esther Rabbah* 3:10 (*Midrash Rabbah im Kol ha-Mefarshim*, part 2, 3:43): "Every place that it says in this scroll 'to the King Ahasuerus,' the verse is speaking about the King Ahasuerus, and every place that it simply says 'king,' the holy matter makes use of the profane." That is to say, the allusion to God is figuratively cast in the image of the mortal monarch. See the comments of Moses Ḥayyim Luzzatto on the book of Esther, which are printed in *Oṣerot RaMḤaL*, p. 206: "Ahasuerus is the blessed holy One, for he is a brother [*aḥ*] and the head [*we-rosh*], a brother to Israel . . . and also the head [*ro'sh*], for he was their leader and ruler." See also Koidonover, *Qaw ha-Yashar*, chapter 97, 2:511–512.

86. Babylonian Talmud, Megillah 13a.

87. Schneerson, *Iggerot Qodesh*, no. 6016, 16:242.

88. Schneerson, *Iggerot Qodesh*, no. 5041, 14:279; see also *Torat Menaḥem: Hitwwa'aduyyot 5715*, 1:279: "And the ultimate perfection of this matter will be in the future-to-come, for then there will be established the matter of the 'female encircling the male,' that is, the level of what is below will be felt, the level of the corporeal body of each and every Jew, for this is the truth of the matter of the 'essence of the Presence is in the beings below' . . . especially in the body of the Jew, for in it is the purpose of the intention." This passage attests to the fact that femaleness and maleness are not primarily an anatomical taxonomy, but they are rather gender categories determined by function. Thus there is a correlation of female and body, but this applies to *every* Jew and not just to women. As I will argue in chapter 5, I do not deny that Schneerson's utilization of the kabbalistic gender symbolism impacted his attitude to the role and status of Jewish women in a socio-anthropological sense, but those who fail to uphold the distinction between gender as a cultural marker and sex as biological facticity have not engaged his thought properly. The messianic shift of the female encircling the male bespeaks the ideal of embodied consciousness, which is relevant to Jewish men and women alike.

89. Schneersohn, *Yom Ṭov shel Rosh ha-Shanah*, p. 528. See in more detail the discussion in chapter 5.

90. Schneerson, *Iggerot Qodesh*, no. 266, 2:199. In a letter written on the first day of the month of Adar 5707, that is, 30 Shevaṭ (February 20, 1947), to the board of the girls' school Beit Rivkah in Paris, Schneerson drew a comparison between the Sinaitic revelation and Purim (see chapter 4 at n. 23), "for just as the giving of the Torah was dependent on women who were first to want to receive it, according to the saying of the rabbis, blessed

be their memory (*Shemot Rabbah* 28:2), similarly, the essence of the miracle of Purim was by means of the women." On the special connection of Jewish women and Purim, see also Schneerson, *Iggerot Qodesh*, no. 2037, 7:180; no. 9109, 24:93; no. 10,742, 28:171. In several of these passages, Schneerson noted the obvious fact that there are other time-bound positive commandments in which women are included for the same rationale, for example, the lighting of the Ḥanukah candles (Babylonian Talmud, Shabbat 23a) or the drinking of four cups of wine at the Passover seder (Babylonian Talmud, Pesaḥim 108a–b), but the reading of the scroll of Esther on Purim is upheld as distinctive on account of the fact that the essential agent for the miracle was Esther. See Schneerson, *Reshimot*, sec. 149, 4:379–380; *Torat Menaḥem: Hitwwa'aduyyot 5712*, 1:232; *Torat Menaḥem: Hitwwa'aduyyot 5713*, 2:36–39; *Torat Menaḥem: Hitwwa'aduyyot 5719*, 2:153.

91. Mishnah, Qiddushin 1:7.

92. Babylonian Talmud, Megillah 4a.

93. Schneerson, *Torat Menaḥem: Hitwwa'aduyyot 5717*, 2:193.

94. Shneur Zalman of Liadi, *Torah Or*, 93d.

95. Schneerson, *Torat Menaḥem: Hitwwa'aduyyot 5717*, 2:194. An earlier version was published in *Liqquṭei Siḥot*, 4:1279.

96. Schneerson, *Torat Menaḥem: Hitwwa'aduyyot 5717*, 2:195.

97. Schneerson, *Torat Menaḥem: Hitwwa'aduyyot 5715*, 1:333. In support of his view, the seventh Rebbe cited the Lurianic tradition that Jewish women in the last generation prior to the messianic era are the reincarnation of the ancient Israelite women, who refused to contribute their jewelry to be used in the construction of the golden calf, and therefore they rule over the men. See Viṭal, *Liqquṭei Torah*, p. 130; *Sefer ha-Liqquṭim*, p. 147 (in that context, women are said to dominate especially over male scholars, the *ba'alei torah*).

98. Esther 6:8. See Shneur Zalman of Liadi, *Torah Or*, 90a, 90c, 113d; *Liqquṭei Torah*, Bemidbar, 2:20d, Derushim le-Rosh ha-Shanah, 2:59b; Schneersohn, *Sha'arei Orah*, 54a, 56a.

99. Schneerson, *Torat Menaḥem: Hitwwa'aduyyot 5713*, 2:37.

100. Schneerson, *Torat Menaḥem: Hitwwa'aduyyot 5752*, 1:295.

101. Schatz-Uffenheimer, *Hasidism as Mysticism*, pp. 255–289.

102. Schneerson, *Torat Menaḥem: Sefer ha-Ma'amarim Meluqaṭ*, 2:100.

103. A proper analysis of the intent of Spinoza's maxim is obviously beyond the confines of this study. For a relatively recent attempt to narrow the alleged gap separating Spinozistic monism and a more philosophically oriented monotheism, see Fraenkel, "Maimonides' God." By contrast, consider the view of Cunnigham mentioned in chapter 2, n. 146. For a comparative discussion of the relationship of the divine and the world in Shneur Zalman of Liadi and the thought of Spinoza, see Teitelbaum, *Der Rabh Von Ladi,* pp. 99–120. On Spinoza and early Ḥasidism, see the impressionistic comments of Buber, *Hasidism*, pp. 97–104.

104. The passage is cited in chapter 2 at n. 269.

105. Schneersohn, *Sefer ha-Ma'amarim 5655–5656*, p. 319.

106. Schneerson, *Reshimot*, sec. 3, 1:43.

107. *Midrash Wayyiqra Rabbah* 27:10, pp. 643–644.

108. A partial Yiddish record of the talk, edited by the seventh Rebbe, was printed in Schneerson, *Liqquṭei Siḥot*, 3:916–923, and a far more expanded Hebrew version in *Torat Menaḥem: Hitwwa'aduyyot 5719*, 2:100–163. My translations are based on the former, but I have also consulted the latter.

109. Babylonian Talmud, Megillah 16b.

110. An expression based on the description of God in the traditional *havdalah* service said on Saturday night to mark the transition from Sabbath to the weekday, *ha-mavdil bein qodesh le-ḥol bein or le-ḥoshekh bein yisra'el la-ammim bein yom ha-shevi'i le-sheshet yemei ha-ma'aseh,* "the one who distinguishes between holiness and the profane, light and darkness, Israel and the nations, the seventh day and the six days of action." See *Seder Avodat Yisra'el*, p. 312.

111. Compare Schneerson, *Liqquṭei Siḥot*, 2:603–604; *Liqquṭei Siḥot*, 15:62, and the Hebrew version in *Sefer ha-Ma'amarim 5737*, p. 374.

112. See chapter 1, n. 77.

113. Schneerson, *Liqquṭei Siḥot*, 3:917–918; 34:106–109; *Torat Menaḥem: Hitwwa'aduyyot 5719*, 2:102–103; *Iggerot Qodesh*, no. 11,149, 29:170, no. 11,217, 29:236.

114. Schneerson, *Liqquṭei Siḥot*, 3:920; *Torat Menaḥem: Hitwwa'aduyyot 5719*, 2:106.

115. Moses ben Maimon, *Guide of the Perplexed,* 3:49, p. 609.

116. Schneerson, *Liqquṭei Siḥot*, 3:920-921; *Torat Menaḥem: Hitwwa'aduyyot 5719*, 2:106-107. On the ascetic tendencies in Maimonides and the seventh Rebbe, see Gotlieb, "Habad's Harmonistic Approach," pp. 191–198.

117. Schneerson, *Torat Menaḥem: Hitwwa'aduyyot 5710*, p. 111; *Ha-Yom Yom*, p. 23 (28 Shevaṭ); see, however, *Torat Menaḥem: Hitwwa'aduyyot 5720*, 2:107, where the ascent of the soul through purification of the animal soul is compared to breaking the shell of a nut. On this image, see n. 44, this chapter.

118. This section, which was not reviewed by Schneerson, is lacking in the Yiddish but included in the Hebrew.

119. Schneerson, *Torat Menaḥem: Hitwwa'aduyyot 5710*, p. 110. Citing the sixth Rebbe, Schneerson says explicitly that "in the future-to-come, the bodies of the nations will be like animals [*ba'alei ḥayyim*] . . . they are not at all in the level of the human [*adam*], and Israel particularly are in the level of the human, as it written 'you are called adam' (Ezek 34:31)." The semblance of non-Jews in the present as humans (specifically the erect posture) is explained in terms of the need for them to have free will. This explanation is neither coherent nor inoffensive, but my task as scholar is to present the facts without censorship or apology.

120. The passages referred to by the seventh Rebbe (see the following note) are from *Liqquṭei Amarim: Tanya*, part 1, chapter 2, 6a and chapter 32, 41a.

121. Schneerson, *Torat Menaḥem: Hitwwa'aduyyot 5750*, 2:117.

122. Schneerson, *Iggerot Qodesh*, no. 10,370, 27:379. On the contrast between the two etymologies of the word *adam*, which correspond respectively to the somatic (*afar min ha-adamah*) and the pneumatic (*eddammeh le-elyon*), see Horowitz, *Shenei Luḥot ha-Berit*, 3:18 and 135.

123. Shneur Zalman of Liadi, *Liqquṭei Torah*, Devarim, 2:4b.

124. Shneur Zalman of Liadi, *Tanya*, part 1, chapter 49, 69b–70a.

125. Schneerson, *Torat Menaḥem: Hitwwa'aduyyot 5750*, 2:119.

126. Schneersohn, *Sefer ha-Ma'amarim 5710–5711*, part 2, p. 288.

127. Schneerson, *Torat Menaḥem: Hitwwa'aduyyot 5721*, 2:25.

128. Babylonian Talmud, Shabbat 56a.

129. Babylonian Talmud, Yevamot 20a.

130. Schneerson, *Torat Menaḥem: Hitwwa'aduyyot 5721*, 2:27.

131. Ibid., p. 28.

132. Based on the rabbinic dictum (Babylonian Talmud, Yevamot 61a) that Israel, as opposed the nations of the world, are called *adam*. For discussion of this theme, see reference to my work cited in n. 66, this chapter.

133. Schneerson, *Liqquṭei Siḥot*, 10:103.

134. Ibid., 10:104.

135. Ibid., 10:105.

136. Ibid., 10:106.

137. Schneerson, *Torat Menaḥem: Hitwwa'aduyyot 5711*, 1:180. Compare Schneerson, *Iggerot Qodesh*, no. 11,015, 29:45–48.

138. Dodd, *Idealism and Corporeity*, p. 123.

139. Ibid., pp. 61–81.

140. Levin, *Heaven on Earth*, p. 13; see also p. 23, where the author extols the virtue of ritual performance that involves the body and the physical world on grounds that one does not commune with God by "releasing some hidden meaning and significance latent in the physical" or by "sublimating the physical," but rather in relating to God "as found in the physical itself—precisely in the absence of spiritual meaning and significance, specifically because it is physical and not sublime." In this passage as well, or so it seems to me, there is not enough attention paid to the hyperlinguistic character of the corporeal as understood in the complex dialectic of what I have called the acosmic naturalism of Ḥabad. A similar critique can be leveled against the discussion of matter as the primary locus of the disclosure of the essence in Kohanzad, "Messianic Doctrine," pp. 137–142. I agree with Kohanzad that a corollary to the notion of a revelation of the essentially concealed essence is that "*reality*, or *things as they are*, paradoxically become the greatest revelation of God," and hence "the mundane world itself becomes the substance of the essential divinity" (p. 141). What I find lacking in this analysis is proper attentiveness to the insight regarding the linguistic nature of reality, a crucial point in assessing the claim that the world is the disclosure of the divine essence. By contrast, Dahan, "'Dira Bataḥtonim,'" pp. 42–81, begins his analysis of the messianic posture of Schneerson by discussing the power of language. In my judgment, this is correct, as the ontology, cosmology, epistemology, and psychology enunciated by Ḥabad masters all rest on the assumption that reality is made up of letters and, since all of the letters are contained in the ineffable name, everything is an articulation of the latter. Without taking this into consideration, the presumed positive valorization of the body promoted by Schneerson is grossly overstated. Thus, consider the observation of Kohanzad, "Messianic Doctrine," pp. 227-228, with respect to the tradition of ascetic practices: "The Rebbe's teaching ultimately rejects this tradition and massively reaffirms

the goodness of the physical world. This affirmation of the physical is arguably even more unusual within Hasidic thought, which in some of its manifestations has been deeply influenced by asceticism. . . . This process of reorientation is what the Rebbe means by *devekut*, which is, therefore, world-affirming rather than world-negating. It does not involve a flight from this world to another, nor the annihilation of self, but rather a joyful engagement with this material world and a quickening of the sense of self." I do not quibble with the assertion that Schneerson rejected extreme forms of ascetic denial, but the statement that he "massively" reaffirmed the "goodness of the physical world" is not entirely accurate, nor is it accurate to ignore the vestiges of asceticism that are found in his teachings. The matter is more complex, both in terms of his understanding of the linguistic nature of body and also because of his acceptance that the life of ritual is meant to transform the somatic, to elevate the animal instincts and carnal desires to a level of divinity. Moreover, while I concur that Schneerson's application of the pietistic ideal of conjunction is world affirming rather than world negating, I cannot accept Kohanzad's diminishing of the importance of the annihilation of self. In my judgment, the seventh Rebbe's stance is more paradoxical: the self that is affirmed is the self that is negated. To speak simply of a "joyful engagement with this material world" flattens the intricacy and tension of his religious philosophy. On the possible adoption of ascetic renunciation on the part of Schneerson, see Dahan, "The Last Redeemer," pp. 304–309. For a critique of celibacy, personified in the life of Ben Azzai, see Schneerson, *Torat Menaḥem: Hitwwa'aduyyot 5714*, 1:203.

141. Schneersohn, *Be-Sha'ah she-Hiqdimu*, 1:179; see also 175, 273, 583, 2:654; Schneersohn, *Sefer ha-Ma'amarim 5700*, p. 25; Schneerson, *Torat Menaḥem: Hitwwa'aduyyot 5711*, 1:263.

142. Schneersohn, *Sefer ha-Ma'amarim 5700*, p. 26.

143. Shneur Zalman of Liadi, *Liqquṭei Amarim: Tanya*, part 3, chapter 6, 110a.

144. Ibid., part 1, chapter 36, 45b.

4. Messianic Torah

1. Shneur Zalman of Liadi, *Liqquṭei Torah*, Ki Teṣe, 36a.

2. Schneerson, *Sefer ha-Ma'amarim 5720–5721*, pp. 176–177.

3. See chapter 2, n. 164.

4. Shneur Zalman of Liadi, *Torah Or*, 17d–18a. In that context, the "transmutation of darkness to light" (*ithapkha ḥashokha li-nehora*) is said to come about through the "nullification of something to nothing" (*biṭṭul ha-yesh le-ayin*), which is attained by self-sacrifice (*mesirat nefesh*) in prayer and by fulfillment of the Torah and the commandments.

5. Schneerson, *Iggerot Qodesh*, no. 3396, 11:20. Compare Shneur Zalman of Liadi, *Liqquṭei Amarim: Tanya*, part 5, 162a–b.

6. The coincidence of opposites within the Torah can be expressed as well in terms of the fact that it is an intermediary between the light of the Infinite and the worlds or between that light and the souls of Israel. See Schneerson, *Torat Menaḥem: Hitwwa'aduyyot 5716*, 2:310.

7. Babylonian Talmud, Baba Batra 16a; Qiddushin 30b.

8. Schneerson, *Qunṭres Inyanah shel Torat ha-Ḥasidut*, p. 20.

9. See Schneerson, *Torat Menaḥem: Hitwwa'aduyyot 5711*, 1:24.

10. Shneur Zalman of Liadi, *Liqquṭei Amarim: Tanya*, part 4, sec. 8, 113b.

11. Schneerson, *Torat Menaḥem: Hitwwa'aduyyot 5744*, 2:794.

12. Schneerson, *Liqquṭei Siḥot*, 31:24.

13. Palestinian Talmud, Sanhedrin 1:1, 18a; Babylonian Talmud, Shabbat 55a; *Midrash Bere'shit Rabba* 81:2, p. 971; *Midrash Devarim Rabbah* 1:10, in *Midrash Rabbah im Kol ha-Mefarshim*, 6:7–8; *Midrash Shir ha-Shirim Rabbah* 1:45, p. 38.

14. Schneerson, *Liqquṭei Siḥot*, 31:26. In the continuation, the seventh Rebbe connects his depiction of the final redemption as knowledge of the name with the Maimonidean account of the messianic era offered at the end of the *Mishneh Torah* and his description of the knowledge of the name of God given at the beginning of that composition.

15. Schneerson, *Torat Menaḥem: Sefer ha-Ma'amarim Meluqaṭ*, 1:207. Compare Schneerson, *Liqquṭei Siḥot*, 12:36.

16. For analysis and reference to some of the relevant sources, see Wolfson, *Venturing Beyond*, pp. 239–240, 265. See also Schneerson, *Liqquṭei Siḥot*, 12:175–176; Kimelman, *The Mystical Meaning*, pp. 100, 123, 176. For an alternative presumed etymology that links *ḥazir* with the expression *meḥazzeret aṭarah*, "she restores the crown," see Schneersohn, *Liqquṭei Torah: Torat Shmu'el 5627*, p. 496.

17. Shneur Zalman of Liadi, *Torah Or*, 25a.

18. Shneur Zalman of Liadi, *Ma'amerei Admor ha-Zaqen 5572*, p. 91. For an earlier source that is likely to have influence the Ḥabad-Lubavitch masters, see Cordovero, *Pardes Rimmonim*, 18:6, 84d.

19. Shneur Zalman of Liadi, *Liqquṭei Torah*, Re'eh, 2:30b. Much of this passage is copied without attribution in the first text of the Mitteler Rebbe cited in the following note.

20. Schneersohn, *Ner Miṣwah we-Torah Or*, 74a; *Imrei Binah*, part 1, 17c; *Torat Ḥayyim: Bere'shit*, 196a, 216a, 216d, 248d; *Perush ha-Millot*, 95b; Schneersohn, *Or ha-Torah: Bemidbar*, 4:1392; *Derekh Miṣwotekha*, 70b; Schneersohn, *Liqquṭei Torah: Torat Shmu'el 5631*, 1:360, 361; *Liqquṭei Torah: Torat Shmu'el 5632*, 1:270, 2:545; *Liqquṭei Torah: Torat Shmu'el 5633*, 1:156, 157; *Liqquṭei Torah: Torat Shmu'el 5640*, 1:29.

21. Schneersohn, *Torat Ḥayyim: Bere'shit*, 195d–196a.

22. Schneerson, *Liqquṭei Siḥot*, 35:118. See also *Iggerot Qodesh*, no. 507, 3:153. In that context, a letter from 24 Tammuz 5709 (July 21, 1949), the seventh Rebbe distinguished two stages to the eschaton, the first one in which the pig is rendered pure and the second in which all impure animals become permissible, since the spirit of impurity will be obliterated entirely from the world.

23. Schneerson, *Torat Menaḥem: Hitwwa'aduyyot 5713*, 2:24.

24. Shneur Zalman of Liadi, *Torah Or*, 97a. On the thematic link between Purim and the ideals of self-sacrifice and sanctification of the divine name in Shneur Zalman of Liadi, see Loewenthal, *Communicating the Infinite*, pp. 90–97. See also Schneersohn, *Liqquṭei Torah: Torat Shmu'el 5639*, 1:338.

25. Schneerson, *Torat Menaḥem: Hitwwa'aduyyot 5713*, 2:24–25; see also p. 13.

26. Babylonian Talmud, Shabbat 88b.

27. Esther 3:13.

28. This discourse occupies a special place for Lubavitchers, since it was the last one that Schneerson personally distributed prior to his stroke on 27 Adar I 5752 (March 2, 1992). Just as the *Ba'ti le-Ganni* discourse from 10 Shevaṭ 5711 (January 17, 1951) is considered to be the first address of Schneerson's appearance as the seventh Rebbe, so this one, *We-Attah Teṣawweh*, has the status of the final address. The discourse is printed in Schneerson, *Torat Menaḥem: Sefer ha-Ma'amarim Meluqaṭ*, 3:34–43. See as well Schneerson, *We-Attah Teṣawweh*.

29. Schneersohn, *Sefer ha-Ma'amarim 5687–5688*, pp. 110–125.

30. See introduction, nn. 38–47.

31. Schneerson, *Torat Menaḥem: Sefer ha-Ma'amarim Meluqaṭ*, 3:35–38.

32. Schneerson, *Torat Menaḥem: Sefer ha-Ma'amarim 5722*, p. 46.

33. Compare, however, Schneerson, *Qunṭres Inyanah shel Torat ha-Ḥasidut*, p. 15, where the Rebbe asserts that, according to the teaching of Ḥasidism, all of the commandments, including those commandments for which an ostensible reason is given, have their root in "the supernal Will that is above reason" (*raṣon ha-elyon she-lema'lah me-ha-ṭa'am*). Comments like this one lend credence to my surmise regarding the hypernomian exceeding, in contrast to the antinomian elimination, of the law. In that respect, my approach should be contrasted with the unqualified characterization of Schneerson's orientation as antinomian in Kohanzad, "Messianic Doctrine," pp. 109, 134, 153, 157–158, 161, 173–175, 217–218, 221–222, 229.

34. Schneerson, *Torat Menaḥem: Hitwwa'aduyyot 5719*, 1:245; *Torat Menaḥem: Hitwwa'aduyyot 5721*, 2:27.

35. Babylonian Talmud, Soṭah 3a. On the use of this rabbinic dictum to substantiate the claim that the spirit of folly covers the truth, see Schneersohn, *Liqquṭei Torah: Torat Shmu'el 5632*, 1:115; Schneersohn, *Sefer ha-Ma'amarim 5689*, pp. 251, 261; *Sefer ha-Ma'amarim 5692–5693*, p. 503; Schneerson, *Torat Menaḥem: Hitwwa'aduyyot 5714*, 2:5.

36. Schneersohn, *Be-Sha'ah she-Hiqdimu*, 1:634; see ibid., 2:1040. The matter of folly in Ḥabad can be fruitfully compared to similar expressions of madness in Ḥasidic literature. See Green, *Tormented Master*, pp. 172–174; Mark, "*Dibbuk* and *Devekut*." On the RaShaB's own struggle with mental illness, see Schneider and Berke, "Sigmund Freud and the Lubavitcher Rebbe."

37. Schneersohn, *Qunṭres u-Ma'yan*, 26:1, pp. 131–132, 27:2, p. 135.

38. Schneersohn, *Sefer ha-Ma'amarim 5710–5711*, part 1, pp. 114–115.

39. Schneerson, *Torat Menaḥem: Hitwwa'aduyyot 5711*, 1:201; see also 1:213; *Torat Menaḥem: Hitwwa'aduyyot 5714*, 2:5; *Torat Menaḥem: Hitwwa'aduyyot 5715*, 1:216; *Torat Menaḥem: Hitwwa'aduyyot 5716*, 2:26; *Torat Menaḥem: Hitwwa'aduyyot 5717*, 2:6; *Torat Menaḥem: Hitwwa'aduyyot 5723*, 2:177; *Torat Menaḥem: Sefer ha-Ma'amarim Meluqaṭ*, 2:397, 487.

40. Schneerson, *Torat Menaḥem: Hitwwa'aduyyot 5711*, 1:223.

41. Ibid., 1:224.

42. On the claim that the exoteric explanation (*perush al derekh ha-peshaṭ*), which corresponds to the world of doing (*olam ha-asiyyah*), and the esoteric explanation (*perush al derekh ha-sod*),which corresponds to the world of emanation (*olam ha-aṣilut*), are not exclusive, see the discourse on Lag Ba-Omer 1988, in Schneerson, *Sefer ha-Siḥot 5748*,

2:447. In this matter as well, the seventh Rebbe followed his predecessors very closely. To cite one of numerous examples, Schneersohn, *Ner Miṣwah we-Torah Or*, 89a: "Just as through Moses the revealed Torah was given and proceeded to us, so through the Messiah the inner Torah and its secrets will proceed to us . . . and hence the distinction between the externality of the Torah revealed to us and the internality of the Torah, even though the internal is within the external, for it consists precisely of the reasons and secrets of every law and regulation in the revealed Torah."

43. Schneerson, *Torat Menaḥem: Hitwwa'aduyyot 5717*, 2:87.

44. *Midrash Wayyiqra Rabbah* 13:3, p. 278. The version attested in that edition is *ḥiddush torah*, but the reading *torah ḥadashah* does appear in the Vilna and Warsaw editions of the text. See Davies, *The Torah in the Messianic Age*, pp. 60–61, n. 19a. On the notion of the "new Torah," see the passages of Elijah Kohen Ittamari and Levi Yiṣḥaq of Berditchev cited respectively by Scholem, *On the Kabbalah*, pp. 74–75, 82. For discussions of this motif in Schneerson, see references cited in chapter 1, n. 177.

45. Schneersohn, *Liqquṭei Torah: Torat Shmu'el 5631*, 1:375.

46. Schneerson, *Torat Menaḥem: Sefer ha-Ma'amarim Meluqaṭ*, 1:299.

47. Schneerson, *Sha'arei Ge'ullah*, 2:62, n. 32, 125–127. Consider the formulation of Luzzatto, *Tiqqunim Ḥadashim*, pp. 51–52: "The Faithful Shepherd came and began to expound: Master, master, surely the five books of the Torah are from the perspective of the supernal *he*, the six orders of the Mishnah are from the perspective of the *waw*, the Gemara is from the perspective of the lower *he*, *yod* is the new Torah, concerning which it says 'for the new Torah issues from me,' and this is the Torah of emanation, which exists through the permutation of the highest secrets, and this is new—for it is constantly renewed [*mitḥaddeshet tamid*], from the one about whom it says [in the hymn *yoṣer or* included in the traditional morning prayer] 'he renews through his goodness every day [the act of creation],' for the lights are constantly renewed, and on account of it, it is said [Rashi on Exod 19:1], 'words of Torah should always be new in your eyes.' However, below [it is written] 'what was is what shall be etc. and there is nothing new underneath the sun' (Eccles 1:9), for what was made [above] revolves in its permutations and goes forth below."

48. Shneur Zalman of Liadi, *Liqquṭei Torah*, Shir ha-Shirim, 2:48a; Schneersohn, *Liqquṭei Torah: Torat Shmu'el 5633*, 1:90; Schneerson, *Torat Menaḥem: Hitwwa'aduyyot 5718*, 1:88; *Liqquṭei Siḥot*, 38:227; *Sefer ha-Siḥot 5752*, p. 318. See also *Keter Shem Ṭov*, sec. 242, pp. 139–140. In that context, the "new Torah" is explained as an awareness that in the future the Torah, which presently assumes the seemingly banal form of narratives about this world, issues forth from the divine essence. See Heller, *Liqquṭim Yeqarim*, sec. 250, 76b–77a.

49. Schneerson, *Liqquṭei Siḥot*, 32:269.

50. Schneerson, *Torat Menaḥem: Hitwwa'aduyyot 5711*, 1:122. On occasion, the didactic point of a discourse or homily required the Rebbe to deploy a rhetoric of difference, and thus he emphasized that the external and the internal meanings were radically distinct, the former linked to the Tree of Knowledge and the latter to the Tree of Life. For instance, see Schneerson, *Torat Menaḥem: Hitwwa'aduyyot 5719*, 3:119. In that context, the distinction is also expressed in terms of the contrast between Torah study in this world by an embodied soul and Torah study in the heavenly academy or in Paradise after the soul

departs from the body at death: the former comprises the exoteric and the esoteric, the latter only the esoteric.

51. Schneerson, *Torat Menaḥem: Sefer ha-Ma'amarim Meluqaṭ*, 3:312–313.

52. For instance, see Shneur Zalman of Liadi, *Torah Or*, 10b; *Liqquṭei Torah*, Shir ha-Shirim, 2:35c; *Ma'amerei Admor ha-Zaqen 5566*, 2:639; Schneersohn, *Sha'arei Teshuvah*, 133b; *Ner Miṣwah we-Torah Or*, 101b; *Ma'amerei Admor ha- Emṣa'i: Hanaḥot*, pp. 37, 39, 311; Schneersohn, *Or ha-Torah: Bemidbar*, 1:128 (see introduction, n. 1), 2:478, 545, and 22 of the supplemental section, 3:764 and 770, 4:1123 and 1368; *Sefer Tehillim*, pp. 207, 240, 241, 508, 539, 546; *Derekh Miṣwotekha*, 39a; *Derekh Ḥaqirah*, 55b; Schneersohn, *Liqquṭei Torah: Torat Shmu'el 5627*, pp. 98, 235, 243, 422; *Liqquṭei Torah: Torat Shmu'el 5629*, pp. 214, 224; *Liqquṭei Torah: Torat Shmu'el 5631*, 1:328; *Liqquṭei Torah: Torat Shmu'el 5632*, 2:544. An earlier source for the symbolic identification of *anokhi* and *Keter* is *Zohar* 3:256b (*Ra'aya Meheimna*).

53. Schneersohn, *Ma'amerei Admor ha-Emṣa'i: Hanaḥot*, pp. 37–39.

54. Schneerson, *Liqquṭei Siḥot*, 14:222, 311, 317, 321.

55. Ibid., p. 321.

56. Ibid., p. 324.

57. Schneerson, *Torat Menaḥem: Hitwwa'aduyyot 5711*, 1:341.

58. Schneerson, *Torat Menaḥem: Sefer ha-Ma'amarim Meluqaṭ*, 3:287. See also *Reshimat ha-Menorah*, pp. 112–114: "Engagement in the exoteric [*nigleh*] and esoteric [*nistar*] of the Torah is the life and actions of a man. The Torah is the wisdom of the holy One . . . and the one who studies Torah and comprehends some deduction or law of the Torah, his intellect is united at that moment with the wisdom of the holy One, for just as the Torah is above, it descends below."

59. Schneerson, *Qunṭres Inyanah shel Torat ha-Ḥasidut*, p. 3.

60. Schneerson, *Torat Menaḥem: Hitwwa'aduyyot 5719*, 1:179. The use of the images of engagement and marriage to depict the contrast between the present and the messianic future is found in older rabbinic sources. For instance, see *Midrash Shemot Rabbah* 15:31, in *Midrash Rabbah im Kol ha-Mefarshim*, 3:192.

61. Schneerson, *Torat Menaḥem: Hitwwa'aduyyot 5711*, 2:142.

62. Compare Shneur Zalman of Liadi, *Seder Tefillot*, 132a, and see n. 48, this chapter.

63. Ibid., 138c. Shneur Zalman's text has also been analyzed by Magid, "Ritual," p. 207.

64. Shneur Zalman of Liadi, *Torah Or*, 74a; cf. Schneersohn, *Sefer Tehillim*, pp. 434, 652.

65. Schneersohn, *Ma'amerei Admur ha-Ṣemaḥ Ṣedeq 5614–5615*, p. 58.

66. Shneur Zalman of Liadi, *Liqquṭei Amarim: Tanya*, part 1, chapter 37, 46b.

67. Shneur Zalman of Liadi, *Ma'amerei Admor ha-Zaqen 5572*, p. 188.

68. Mishnah, Sanhedrin 10:1.

69. Schneersohn, *Imrei Binah*, part 1, 25d.

70. Ibid. See Schneersohn, *Ma'amerei Admor ha-Emṣa'i: Qunṭresim*, p. 324.

71. The influence of Ḥabad is discernible in Shwartz, *Qol Demamah Daqqah*, pp. 98–99: the aspect of *aṭeret ba'lah*, the "crown of her husband," is identified as the "aspect that is above the Torah," the gradation of *Keter*, which is the "complete perfection" (*tiqqun ha-shalem*).

72. Schneersohn, *Ma'amerei Admor ha-Emṣa'i: Quntresim*, p. 325.

73. See the passages cited in chapter 2, n. 265.

74. Schneersohn, *Imrei Binah*, part 2, 25d.

75. Schneersohn, *Sha'arei Teshuvah*, 143a. On the symbolic interpretation of the distinction between the weekday prayer and the Sabbath prayer, see Schneersohn, *Torat Ḥayyim: Shemot*, 437c–d; see also Shneur Zalman of Liadi, *Torah Or*, 70b; Schneersohn, *Torat Ḥayyim: Bere'shit*, 241b; *Torat Ḥayyim: Shemot*, 107a, 322c, 330b.

76. Shneur Zalman of Liadi, *Liqquṭei Torah*, Balaq, 1:72a–b; Schneerson, *Torat Menaḥem: Hitwwa'aduyyot 5723*, 1:152. The labor of the six weekdays and the Torah study and prayer of the Sabbath are contrasted in Schneerson, *Reshimot*, sec. 12, 1:340–341. On the connection between Sabbath and the silence above speech, see Shneur Zalman of Liadi, *Liqquṭei Torah*, Ṣaw, 1:11d; *Torah Or*, 113a; Schneerson, *Reshimot*, sec. 165, 5:147.

77. Schneersohn, *Imrei Binah*, part 2, 25d.

78. Shneur Zalman of Liadi, *Ma'amerei Admor ha-Zaqen ha-Qeṣarim*, p. 144.

79. Moses ben Maimon, *Guide of the Perplexed*, I:1, pp. 24–25.

80. Babylonian Talmud, Pesaḥim 50b.

81. Schneerson, *Torat Menaḥem: Hitwwa'aduyyot 5720*, 1:351–353.

82. Shapira, *Megalleh Amuqot*, 1:88d.

83. Babylonian Talmud, Shabbat 87a.

84. Palestinian Talmud, Ta'anit 4:8, 68c.

85. Schneerson, *Torat Menaḥem: Hitwwa'aduyyot 5714*, 3:180–181.

86. Shneur Zalman of Liadi, *Torah Or*, 45b.

87. Shneur Zalman of Liadi, *Liqquṭei Torah*, Hosafot, 1:51a–b.

88. Babylonian Talmud, Yoma 86b. See Schneerson, *Torat Menaḥem: Hitwwa'aduyyot 5717*, 1:132–133. In that context, the Rebbe emphasized that the one who repents is greater than one who has always been righteous, for the former has both merits and demerits whereas the latter only has the merits.

89. Schneerson, *Liqquṭei Siḥot*, 29:108.

90. Schneersohn, *Torat Ḥayyim: Bere'shit*, 162d.

91. Schneerson, *Torat Menaḥem: Hitwwa'aduyyot 5717*, 1:209.

92. Schneerson, *Torat Menaḥem: Hitwwa'aduyyot 5720*, 1:422.

93. For the distinction between study of the Torah, which is without limit, and observance of the commandments, which are limited, see Schneerson, *Liqquṭei Siḥot*, 14:179–182 (and the Yiddish version in *Liqquṭei Siḥot*, 15:137–141). In that context, the Rebbe made a further distinction: each commandment is limited, but the totality of the commandments—that is, ritual obligation as such—is without limit, and thus practice is as infinite as study. On the limitlessness of the commandments in the future, which is related to their serving as the means by which one is openly bound to the boundlessness of the divine, see Schneerson, *Torat Menaḥem: Hitwwa'aduyyot 5715*, 1:43.

94. *Midrash Bere'shit Rabba* 1:4, p. 6.

95. Schneerson, *Torat Menaḥem: Hitwwa'aduyyot 5716*, 2:252. See *Torat Menaḥem: Hitwwa'aduyyot 5714*, 2:55. Compare Schneersohn, *Yom Ṭov shel Rosh ha-Shanah*, p. 105: "The souls of Israel are rooted in the aspect of the essence in actuality, which is above

the aspect of the wisdom of the Torah . . . and thus, in the future, they will ascend to this aspect and to this gradation."

96. On the identification of *Attiq* as the highest aspect of *Keter* or the lowest aspect of *Ein Sof*, as opposed to *Arikh*, which is the lowest aspect of *Keter* or the aspect of the exteriority (*ḥiṣoniyyut*) of the light in relation to all the emanations that issue from it, see Schneersohn, *Sefer ha-Ma'amarim 5659*, p. 194, and compare Schneerson, *Torat Menaḥem: Hitwwa'aduyyot 5719*, 1:244. See chapter 2, n. 246. On the supremacy of the Messiah vis-à-vis Moses, see Schneerson, *Torat Menaḥem: Hitwwa'aduyyot 5717*, 2:272: "The future redemption, which will come about through the messianic king, is in the aspect of wonders vis-à-vis the redemption of the exodus from Egypt, which came about through Moses our master. Moses is the first redeemer and the last redeemer, but the future redemption in actuality will be by means of the messianic king, for he specifically will reveal the future wonders. This can be understood according to what is explained elsewhere with respect to the matter of the interiority of the Ancient One [*penimiyyut attiq*] being above the interiority of the Father [*penimiyyut abba*], for even though the interiority of the Father is the interiority of the Ancient One, it is not comparable to the interiority of the Ancient One as it is in its place, that is, the interiority of the Ancient One when it is in its place is above the interiority of the Ancient One when it is found in the interiority of the Father. According to this the superiority of the messianic king to Moses can be understood. Moses received the Torah, and the Torah is the interiority of Wisdom [*penimiyyut ha-ḥokhmah*], that is, Moses is the interiority of the Father, and the interiority of the Father is the interiority of the Ancient One, and thus Moses is the first redeemer and the final redeemer, but nevertheless the messianic king is even higher, since he is in the aspect of the interiority of the Ancient One as it is in its place, which is above the interiority of the Father that is the interiority of the Ancient One." The messianic moment is marked, therefore, by the disclosure of the higher aspect, *yeḥidah* or *penimiyyut attiq*, the suprarational element that exceeds the nomian constrictions of the Torah, which derive from *penimiyyut abba*. See Schneerson, *Torat Menaḥem: Hitwwa'aduyyot 5717*, 2:279, 281; *Torat Menaḥem: Hitwwa'aduyyot 5718*, 2:281; *Torat Menaḥem: Hitwwa'aduyyot 5719*, 2:252; *Torat Menaḥem: Hitwwa'aduyyot 5719*, 3:227; *Torat Menaḥem: Hitwwa'aduyyot 5720*, 2:35. The caution against an antinomian rejection of the Torah based on the ontic distinction between Moses and the Messiah is dealt with directly by Schneerson, *Torat Menaḥem: Hitwwa'aduyyot 5718*, 2:284. The higher status is assigned to the Messiah, but the seventh Rebbe insists that by means of the study of the revealed Torah and the performance of the rituals one can reach "the essence in actuality." Compare the discussion in Garb, *"The Chosen will Become Herds,"* pp. 150–152. Regarding the technical terms *penimiyyut abba* and *penimiyyut attiq*, see chapter 2, n. 61.

97. The text is printed in Schneersohn, *Be-Sha'ah she-Hiqdimu*, 3:766–768.

98. Schneerson, *Quntres Inyanah shel Torat ha-Ḥasidut*, p. 2.

99. Ibid., pp. 12–13. Following a long-standing tradition, Schneerson justifies this ethnocentric orientation by citing the rabbinic claim (Babylonian Talmud, Yevamot 61a) that the Jews, as opposed to the idolatrous nations, are called *adam*, a contention that on occasion led to the symbolic dehumanization of the non-Jew. Regarding this viewpoint and its

impact on kabbalistic sources, see Wolfson, *Venturing Beyond*, pp. 42–44, 73–124. For discussion of this matter in Ḥabad sources, see the section "Israel's Humanity: Jewish Particularity as Idiomatic of Self-Nullification" in chapter 6.

100. Schneerson, *Quntres Inyanah shel Torat ha-Ḥasidut*, p. 5; *Liqquṭei Siḥot*, 21:351.

101. Schneerson, *Quntres Inyanah shel Torat ha-Ḥasidut*, pp. 5–6.

102. Ibid., p. 16.

103. Ibid., p. 17.

104. Shneur Zalman of Liadi, *Liqquṭei Amarim: Tanya*, part 1, chapter 36, 46b. The end of days (*qeṣ ha-yamin*) is described as the time "when the corporeality of the body and of the world will be purified, and they will be able to receive the disclosure of the light of the Lord that he will shine upon Israel by means of the Torah . . . and from the surplus of light to Israel the darkness of the nations will be illumined as well."

105. Schneerson, *Torat Menaḥem: Sefer ha-Ma'amarim Meluqaṭ*, 2:64.

106. Cited in Schneerson, *Haggadah shel Pesaḥ*, p. 5. On the presence of the souls of converts at the Sinaitic epiphany, see *Torat Menaḥem: Hitwwa'aduyyot 5714*, 2:135; see chapter 6, n. 176.

107. Wolfson, *Luminal Darkness*, pp. 264–271; *Venturing Beyond*, pp. 165–185.

108. *Midrash Bere'shit Rabba* 63:10, p. 693.

109. Regarding this kabbalistic principle, see Idel, "The Evil Thought of the Deity"; Farber-Ginat, "'The Shell Precedes the Fruit.'"

110. Schneerson, *Reshimot*, sec. 19, 2:118–121.

111. Schneerson, *Torat Menaḥem: Hitwwa'aduyyot 5722*, 3:238–240.

112. Mishnah, Avot 1:17: *we-lo ha-midrash hu ha-iqqar ella ha-ma'aseh,* "It is not study but action that is the essence." See, for instance, the letter of the seventh Rebbe to Louis Finkelstein in Schneerson, *Iggerot Qodesh*, no. 7438, 19:442; *Torat Menaḥem: Hitwwa'aduyyot 5750*, 2:172; *Torat Menaḥem: Hitwwa'aduyyot 5750*, 4:241.

113. Schneerson, *Torat Menaḥem: Hitwwa'aduyyot 5744*, 2:1015.

114. Based on the summary of Yosef Yiṣḥaq Schneersohn to section 9 of Schneersohn, *Quntres ha-Tefillah*, p. 22; *Tract on Prayer*, pp. 94–95.

115. For a more extensive discussion, see Wolfson, *Venturing Beyond*, pp. 186–285. On the clash between the "mystical" and "ethical," see also Ornet, "*Ratso va-shov,*" pp. 242–284.

116. Schneerson, *Torat Menaḥem: Hitwwa'aduyyot 5714*, 1:280.

117. Shneur Zalman of Liadi, *Ma'amerei Admor ha-Zaqen 5572*, p. 196; Schneersohn, *Derushei Ḥatunah*, 2:417–418, 426, 450, 491; Schneersohn, *Be-Sha'ah she-Hiqdimu*, 3:1263, 1272. And see the entry for a wedding on 13 Sivan 5706 (June 12, 1946) in Schneerson, *Reshimot*, sec. 149, 4:383.

118. Schneersohn, *Derushei Ḥatunah*, 2:439. See ibid., pp. 443, 493.

119. Schneerson, *Torat Menaḥem: Hitwwa'aduyyot 5714*, 1:186. See *Sefer ha-Siḥot 5752*, p. 164, where the messianic name Pereṣ is linked to the spreading forth of the wellsprings of Torah from the "house of Joseph," which is identified as the place where the sixth Rebbe settled the last years of his life. The point is substantiated by the numerical equivalence of the expression *paraṣta*, "you will spread out," which equals 770, an obvious allusion to the world headquarters of Lubavitch in 770 Eastern Parkway, Brooklyn, New York. On the image of squandering as a higher form of bestowal rooted in the interiority of

Keter, see Schneersohn, *Torat Ḥayyim: Shemot*, 227a, 228a, 228d, 231d–232c, 235a, 235c; Schneersohn, *Sefer ha-Ma'amarim 5710–5711*, part 1, pp. 131–132; Schneerson, *Torat Menaḥem: Sefer ha-Ma'amarim Meluqaṭ*, 2:309, 317, 322, 339; *Torat Menaḥem: Sefer ha-Ma'amarim Meluqaṭ*, 3:151. On the correlation of *bizbuz* and the dissemination of the secrets of the Torah, see Schneerson, *Torat Menaḥem: Hitwwa'aduyyot 5714*, 1:271, 273.

120. Schneerson, *Torat Menaḥem: Sefer ha-Ma'amarim Meluqaṭ*, 1:46, 284. See *Torat Menaḥem: Hitwwa'aduyyot 5712*, 1:113.

121. Schneerson, *Torat Menaḥem: Hitwwa'aduyyot 5715*, 1:279.

122. Also relevant to understand this motif in Ḥabad literature is the rabbinic dictum that the king is an individual who breaches the boundary. See Babylonian Talmud, Pesaḥim 110a, Baba Batra 100b; Schneersohn, *Or ha-Torah: Bemidbar*, 3:1080.

123. Schneerson, *Torat Menaḥem: Hitwwa'aduyyot 5713*, 2:179. Compare *Liqquṭei Siḥot*, 16:199: the biblical description of the divine glory descending upon the mount (Exod 19:20) is explained in terms of the drawing down (*hamshakhat*) and disclosure (*hitgallut*) of the secret that is within the Torah (*sod she-ba-torah*), also identified as the soul of Torah (*nishmata de-orayyta*) and as the account of the chariot (*ma'aseh merkavah*). The secret of the Torah is described further as the "disclosure of the unity of the Creator" (*gilluy beḥinat aḥdut ha-bore*).

124. Schneerson, *Torat Menaḥem: Hitwwa'aduyyot 5713*, 1:44.

125. Schneerson, *Torat Menaḥem: Hitwwa'aduyyot 5712*, 1:193. The Rebbe's comments are offered as an exegesis of the zoharic passage "Three gradations are bound one to another, the blessed holy One, Torah, and Israel, and each one is a gradation upon gradation, hidden and revealed" (3:73a). See chapter 6, n. 35.

126. Schneerson, *Quntres Inyanah shel Torat ha-Ḥasidut*, p. 7. See ibid., pp. 8–9, where the seventh Rebbe emphasized that Ḥasidic doctrine contributes to all four kinds of meaning that may be elicited from the scriptural text, *peshaṭ*, *remez*, *derash*, and *sod*—the analogy to which he appeals is that the four levels, encoded in the acrostic *pardes*, correspond to the four levels of soul, *nefesh*, *ruaḥ*, *neshamah*, and *ḥayyah*, and the Ḥasidic meaning corresponds to *yeḥidah*, the fifth level of soul, which comprises all the others. This hermeneutical understanding "negates the supposition that Ḥasidism comes only to explicate the portion of secrecy that is in the Torah." I surmise that Schneerson is tacitly reacting to the scholarly presentation of Ḥasidism exclusively as one of the major trends of Jewish mysticism.

127. Schneerson, *Iggerot Qodesh*, no. 3388, 11:11.

128. See chapter 2, n. 47.

129. *Zohar* 3:75a, 159a. See Scholem, *On the Kabbalah*, p. 51.

130. Schneerson, *Torat Menaḥem: Hitwwa'aduyyot 5713*, 1:44; *Torat Menaḥem: Sefer ha-Ma'amarim, 5722*, p. 251.

131. Schneerson, *Iggerot Qodesh*, no. 3497, 11:112.

132. For an earlier source, which likely influenced the formulation of the Ḥabad masters, see Shapira, *Megalleh Amuqot*, 1:79c: "The world is fourfold, and their secret is *aṣilut*, *beri'ah*, *yeṣirah*, and *asiyyah*, and thus there are four garments to the Torah, for in each world the Torah is garbed in a different garment." See ibid., 1:25b and 2:9d. In Lurianic sources, the four worlds are correlated with the four major categories of Torah study: the

world of emanation corresponds to kabbalah, the world of creation to Talmud, the world of formation to Mishnah, and the world of doing to Scripture. See Fine, *Physician of the Soul*, pp. 210–211.

133. Schneerson, *Torat Menaḥem: Hitwwa'aduyyot* 5720, 1:192. This passage is from a talk the seventh Rebbe gave on 19 Kislev 5720 (December 20, 1959).

134. Babylonian Talmud, Qiddushin 40b.

135. Schneerson, *Ha-Yom Yom*, p. 9 (5 Ṭevet).

136. Schneerson, *Torat Menaḥem: Hitwwa'aduyyot* 5720, 1:192.

137. Various scholars have commented on the theurgical element of the theosophic kabbalah. Let me cite one representative passage that accords well with the view upheld by Schneerson and the other Ḥabad masters. Viṭal, *Eṣ ha-Da'at Ṭov*, 233c: "Just as a man is composed of body [*guf*], soul [*nefesh*], spirit [*ruaḥ*], and pneuma [*neshamah*], so he must comprise the four aspects of Torah, the body, which is the literal [*peshaṭ*], the soul, which is the homiletical [*derash*], the spirit, which is the allegorical [*remez*], and the pneuma, which is the secret [*sod*], and all of them are established together, and a man is worthy of them by means of the performance of the commandments [*ma'aseh ha-miṣwot*], for they are the literal sense in the image of the body that sustains and establishes all of them. And this is why it is written 'to observe it' (Deut 30:14) at the end, for when a man observes the commandments in a literal manner, he should intend all four matters that are in it, which are the acrostic *pardes*." According to another statement of Viṭal, *Sha'ar ha-Gilgulim*, introduction, sec. 11, 14a, it is incumbent upon each male Jew to study the Torah in accord with the four levels of meaning, and until this objective is realized, one is subject to return in the cycle of reincarnation. By contrast, see Viṭal, *Liqquṭei Torah*, p. 281, where a sharp distinction is made between the external (*nigleh*) or literal (*peshaṭ*) and the hidden (*nistar*) or mystical (*sod*), the former bestowed upon the "populace" (*hamon am*), also troped as "men who are like women" (*anashim ha-domim la-nashim*), and the latter revealed to the "holy, righteous men" (*anashim ṣaddiqim ha-qedoshim*), who are compared to angels (*asher hem ke-mal'akhim*). In Viṭal, *Sefer ha-Liqquṭim*, pp. 311–312, the task of comprehending *pardes ha-torah*, i.e., the text in its four levels, is presented as the means to be conjoined to the "mystery of emanation" (*sod ha-aṣilut*) and to rectify the sin of Adam. Regarding the latter, see ibid., p. 210, and the more extended and technical discussion in Viṭal, *Liqquṭei Torah*, pp. 17–20.

138. Schneerson, *Torat Menaḥem: Hitwwa'aduyyot,* 5720, 1:194.

139. Ibid., p. 281.

140. Palestinian Talmud, Ḥagigah 2:1, 77b; Babylonian Talmud, Qiddushin 39b, Ḥullin 142a.

141. See chapter 1, n. 134.

142. Scholem, *On the Kabbalah*, pp. 68–69; Tishby, *Wisdom of the Zohar*, pp. 1101–1108; Giller, *Enlightened Will Shine*, p. 60; Wolfson, *Venturing Beyond*, pp. 268–273.

143. Schneerson, *Torat Menaḥem: Hitwwa'aduyyot,* 5751, 3:286–287.

144. Ibid., p. 287. The Rebbe's orientation is based on earlier Ḥabad sources. See, for instance, Schneersohn, *Torat Ḥayyim: Bere'shit*, 160c: "This is what it says in the midrash, 'for the teaching will issue from me' (Isa 51:4), a new Torah will issue from me [*torah ḥadashah me-itti teṣe*], and the halakhah will be renewed. That is, the new Torah is the

aspect of the Torah that is above, which is the aspect of the Tree of Life in actuality, and this is above our Torah, which is garbed in the Tree of Knowledge of Good and Evil, to purify and to separate . . . and in the future-to-come, in the completion of the purification of the 288 [sparks] in their entirety, there will be no more sustenance for evil at all." See also Schneersohn, *Derekh Miṣwotekha*, 177a; Schneersohn, *Liqquṭei Torah: Torat Shmu'el 5633*, 2:587–588. Compare Schneerson, *Liqquṭei Siḥot*, 30:171. Interpreting the description of the messianic era in the end of Maimonides's *Mishneh Torah* (see chapter 6, n. 106), the seventh Rebbe remarked that engagement with the Torah in the eschaton will not involve study of the laws but knowledge of the Creator.

145. On the distinction between the status of the Tree of Knowledge of Good and Evil prior to and after the transgression, see Schneersohn, *Torat Ḥayyim: Bere'shit*, 216b.

146. Schneerson, *Torat Menaḥem: Hitwwa'aduyyot 5751*, 3:288.

147. Babylonian Talmud, Makkot 10a.

148. See n. 44, this chapter.

149. Schneerson, *Torat Menaḥem: Hitwwa'aduyyot 5751*, 3:288–290.

150. See also Schneerson, *Torat Menaḥem: Hitwwa'aduyyot 5713*, 2:116; *Torat Menaḥem: Hitwwa'aduyyot 5713*, 3:160; *Torat Menaḥem: Hitwwa'aduyyot 5715*, 1:43. A strong antimonian interpretation of Schneerson's conception of the messianic Torah can be found in the dissertation of Kohanzad; see reference in n. 33, this chapter.

151. Babylonian Talmud, Niddah 61b.

152. Shneur Zalman of Liadi, *Liqquṭei Torah*, Derushim le-Rosh ha-Shanah, 2:54d; Schneerson, *Torat Menaḥem: Sefer ha-Ma'amarim Meluqaṭ*, 1:12.

153. Schneerson, *Sefer ha-Siḥot 5751*, 2:694.

154. Babylonian Talmud, Rosh ha-Shanah 31a, Sanhedrin 97a, Tamid 33b.

155. Babylonian Talmud, Avodah Zarah 3a.

156. Schneerson, *Torat Menaḥem: Hitwwa'aduyyot 5717*, 1:201.

157. Shneur Zalman of Liadi, *Torah Or*, 10a; see *Liqquṭei Torah*, Bemidbar, 1:4c (the text is translated and analyzed in Wolfson, *Alef, Mem, Tau*, pp. 115–116). For other passages where this image appears, see chapter 5, nn. 43 and 75, to which many more examples could have been added.

158. *Zohar* 3:124b–125a, a critical passage cited by Shneur Zalman of Liadi in his *Iggeret ha-Qodesh* (see n. 171, this chapter).

159. Schneersohn, *Sha'arei Teshuvah*, 97b–d.

160. An amalgamation of the rabbinic idiom, *alah be-maḥashavah*, "it arose in thought," which denotes an act of divine volition, and the words in the *lekha dodi* hymn of Solomon Alqabeṣ, *sof ma'aseh be-maḥashavah teḥillah*, "the end of action is first in thought." For an analysis of this poetic dictum in light of earlier kabbalistic sources, see Kimelman, *The Mystical Meaning*, pp. 47–48; Wolfson, *Language, Eros, Being*, pp. 173, 506, n. 207. On the background of the saying, see Stern, "'The First in Thought'"; see chapter 6, n. 164.

161. The sentence is drawn from the prayer *tikkanta shabbat* in the *musaf* service on Sabbath, according to the Ashkenazi rite. See *Seder Avodat Yisra'el*, pp. 238–239.

162. Schneersohn, *Ner Miṣwah we-Torah Or*, 65a.

163. Schneersohn, *Torat Ḥayyim: Bere'shit*, 236a. The two possibilities are presented and explained in Schneersohn, *Ma'amerei Admor ha-Emṣa'i: Shemot*, 1:226.

164. Shneur Zalman of Liadi, *Ma'amerei Admor ha-Zaqen 5565*, 1:261, 293–294.

165. Babylonian Talmud, Rosh ha-Shanah 31a, Sanhedrin 97a.

166. Schneersohn, *Torat Ḥayyim: Shemot*, 292d. Compare Schneerson, *Ma'amerei Admor ha-Emṣa'i: Bemidbar*, 5:1624.

167. Compare Schneersohn, *Liqquṭei Torah: Torat Shmu'el 5633*, 1:291.

168. Schneersohn, *Ma'amerei Admor ha-Emṣa'i: Shemot*, 1:226; *Ma'amerei Admor ha-Emṣa'i: Bemidbar*, 5:1624; *Derushei Ḥatunah*, 2:581.

169. Schneerson, *Torat Menaḥem: Hitwwa'aduyyot 5713*, 2:234. It is noteworthy that the locution used for the time of the rewards for the commandments is the "future-to-come" (*atid lavo*) and not the more typical "world-to-come" (*olam ha-ba*).

170. Schneersohn, *Perush ha-Millot*, 93b.

171. Shneur Zalman of Liadi, *Liqquṭei Amarim: Tanya*, part 4, 145a–b. See Foxbrunner, *Ḥabad*, pp. 86–88.

172. See n. 158, this chapter.

173. Shneur Zalman of Liadi, *Liqquṭei Amarim: Tanya*, part 4, 142a–b.

174. In kabbalistic symbolism, markedly pronounced in Lurianic sources but already expressed in the zoharic corpus, the world of the demonic is structured around four shells, whose names are derived from Ezek 1:4, *anan*, *ruaḥ se'arah*, *esh mitlaqqaḥat*, and *nogah*. The fourth shell is the one in closest proximity to the inner core, and thus it is a mixture of good and evil and assumes a liminal status between the divine and the mundane. See Shneur Zalman of Liadi, *Liqquṭei Amarim: Tanya*, part 1, chapter 37, 47b–48a; and scholarly analyses in Scholem, *On the Mystical Shape of the Godhead*, p. 78; Tishby, *Wisdom of the Zohar*, p. 463; *Doctrine of Evil*, pp. 69–72; Giller, *Reading the Zohar*, pp. 48–50. See also Hallamish, "Theoretical System," pp. 163, 241.

175. Shneur Zalman of Liadi, *Liqquṭei Amarim: Tanya*, part 4, 145a–b.

176. *Iggeret ha-Qodesh* was first published in the Königsberg edition of the *Tanya*, printed in 1811, and then under this title in Shklov 1814. The parentheses appear in both editions, but this does not prove conclusively that they are the responsibility of the author as opposed to a later scribal interpolation. The matter requires further investigation.

177. Shneur Zalman of Liadi, *Liqquṭei Amarim: Tanya*, part 1, chapter 37, 47b–48a.

178. For instance, see Schneerson, *Torat Menaḥem: Hitwwa'aduyyot 5749*, 4:134, and see n. 169, this chapter. For a clearer delineation of the three temporal periods, this world (*olam ha-zeh*), the days of the Messiah (*yemot ha-mashiaḥ*), and the resurrection of the dead (*teḥiyyat ha-metim*), see the letter to Elḥanan Cohen from the summer of 5705 (1945) in Schneerson, *Iggerot Qodesh*, no. 200, 2:67–71. The time of this world is characterized by the struggle between good and evil, the material and the spiritual; the time of the messianic era is marked by the completion of the process of the purification of the physical and the separation of good from evil, and the consequent restoration to the Edenic state; the time of the resurrection signals the absolute obliteration of the force of impurity from existence and the disclosure of the essence of the Infinite. Both eschatological phases are for the sake of providing a habitation for the divine in the world, but the final perfection occurs only in the resurrection.

179. In some contexts, a further distinction is made between two phases in the world-to-come or the state of resurrection, the former in which the commandments are still viable

and the second in which they are nullified. See Schneerson, *Liqquṭei Siḥot*, 14:182–183 (and the Yiddish version in *Liqquṭei Siḥot*, 15:141–142).

5. Female Encircles Male

1. Schneerson, *Sefer ha-Siḥot 5700*, p. 78. The sixth Rebbe reports that his father, Shalom Dovber, the fifth Rebbe, told him that he heard from his father, Shmuel, the fourth Rebbe, that "the Ba'al Shem Ṭov called the meal of the last day of Passover by the name 'feast of the Messiah' [*se'udat mashiaḥ*]." See ibid., p. 83; Schneerson, *Sefer ha-Siḥot 5702*, p. 194; *Sefer ha-Siḥot 5703*, p. 121; Schneerson, *Liqquṭei Siḥot*, 4:1298; *Ha-Yom Yom*, p. 47 (22 Nisan); *Torat Menaḥem: Hitwwa'aduyyot 5714*, 2:174–175, 209; *Torat Menaḥem: Hitwwa'aduyyot 5715*, 2:26.

2. Schneersohn, *Sefer ha-Siḥot 5700*, pp. 75–76; *Sefer ha-Ma'amarim 5699–5700*, part 2, pp. 28–29; Schneerson, *Iggerot Qodesh*, no. 2617, 8:358; no. 8406, 22:211; *Liqquṭei Siḥot*, 4:1298–1299.

3. Babylonian Talmud, Rosh ha-Shanah 11a; *Zohar* 2:120a (*Ra'aya Meheimna*), 3:249a (*Ra'aya Meheimna*).

4. Schneersohn, *Sefer ha-Siḥot 5702*, p. 109.

5. Schneersohn, *Sefer ha-Siḥot 5704*, p. 107; Schneerson, *Iggerot Qodesh*, no. 242, 2:161. The subject of this letter, written on 22 Tammuz 5706 (July 21, 1946), is the traditional ceremony of redeeming the firstborn male child, but Schneerson offers a figurative interpretation related to the liberation from exile that extends the matter to both genders.

6. For instance, see Schneerson, *Reshimot*, sec. 12, 1:343. In the context of explaining that the biological process of menstruation was part of Eve's punishment, the young Schneerson wrote: "And after the sin, impurity and evil come to be predominantly in the woman, for she alludes to the body and the animal soul."

7. Schneerson, *Sefer ha-Ma'amarim 5720–5721*, pp. 171–172.

8. Schneerson, *Torat Menaḥem Hitwwa'aduyyot 5713*, 2:54.

9. Schneerson, *Qunṭres Inyanah shel Torat ha-Ḥasidut*, p. 5.

10. Many sources could have been cited, but I offer here one example from Epstein, *Ma'or wa-Shemesh*, p. 85 (ad Gen 31:49) that illustrates the more standard Ḥasidic perspective: "What emerges from our words is that there is nothing in the world, from the lowest point in this lowly world, that does not have within it the holiness of his divinity, blessed be his name, which sustains it, and this is the interiority that is within it. Similarly, in the supernal worlds, each world is like a garment to the inner light from the world that is above it, which shines within it to sustain it. And this is the essence of the worship of the Jewish man [*ish ha-yisra'eli*] in his worship through Torah, prayer, and the fulfillment of the commandments, to purify the materiality as well, and to know that in every corporeal thing there is found a spiritual matter that sustains it, and he must elevate everything to its source, the light of his holiness, blessed be his name, who creates and sustains everything." See, however, the text from *Ma'or wa-Shemesh* cited at n. 40, this chapter.

11. Schneerson, *Torat Menaḥem: Sefer ha-Ma'amarim Meluqaṭ*, 3:202.

12. Schneerson, *Reshimot*, sec. 136, 4:235.

13. Schneerson, *Torat Menaḥem: Hitwwa'aduyyot 5751*, 2:93.

14. Schneerson, *Sefer ha-Ma'amarim 5732–5733*, p. 463.

15. See the daring formulation of this principle in Shneur Zalman of Liadi, *Seder Tefillot*, 132a: "and the aspect of the chaos [*beḥinat ha-tohu*] is much higher than the aspect of the rectification [*beḥinat ha-tiqqun*]." See also Shneur Zalman of Liadi, *Liqquṭei Torah*, Shir ha-Shirim, 2:48b (cited in n. 41, this chapter), and the analysis in Foxbrunner, *Ḥabad*, pp. 76–77. The view expressed by Shneur Zalman reflects a position affirmed in earlier kabbalistic sources. For instance, see Viṭal, *Eṣ Ḥayyim*, 42:1, 89b: "This aspect is *Keter*, which is called *tohu*, for there is no element in it, and therefore it is not hinted at all in the name YHWH but only in the tip of the *yod* . . . for *Keter* is in the image of the primary matter that is called *hyle*, as there is in it the source of all the four elements in potentiality and not in actuality, and hence it is called *tohu*, for it confounds the thoughts of men when they say 'we see that there is no form in it at all, but we nevertheless see that it emanates and in it is the potency of all four forms.' It follows that it is possible to call it *Ein Sof* and the Emanator . . . and it is possible to call it by the name of the emanated."

16. Schneerson, *Torat Menaḥem: Hitwwa'aduyyot 5714*, 3:197–198; *Torat Menaḥem: Hitwwa'aduyyot 5715*, 1:262. On the enrootedness of *Malkhut* in the essence of the Infinite, see Schneerson, *Torat Menaḥem: Hitwwa'aduyyot 5713*, 2:38; *Torat Menaḥem: Sefer ha-Ma'amarim Meluqaṭ*, 1:47; and the passage cited at n. 46, this chapter.

17. *Sefer Yeṣirah* 1:7. Compare Schneerson, *Qunṭres Inyanah shel Torat ha-Ḥasidut*, p. 19. See also the passage from Dov Baer Schneersohn cited in n. 70, this chapter.

18. Schneerson, *Torat Menaḥem: Hitwwa'aduyyot 5714*, 3:198–199; *Sefer ha-Ma'amarim 5732–5733*, pp. 389, 462–463. Compare the discourse celebrating the *hillula* of the fourth Rebbe, Shmuel Schneersohn, on 13 Tishrei 5735 (September 29, 1974) in Schneerson, *Sefer ha-Ma'amarim 5734–5735*, p. 253: "On the first day [of Sukkot], *Keter* and *Malkhut* receive the illumination of *Attiqa Qaddisha* through *Binah*, and this is the superiority of the citron [*etrog*] to the palm-branch [*lulav*] and its species, for the citron is the aspect of *Malkhut*. . . . It is superior, for the root of *Malkhut* is in the interiority of *Keter*, as it is known that the root of all the *sefirot* is in *Arikh*, which is not the case with respect to the root of *Malkhut* in *Attiq*, the aspect of the head-that-is-not known [*reisha de-lo ityeda*]."

19. *Zohar* 3:292a.

20. On the motif of walking as a trope for sexual pairing, see Wolfson, *Along the Path*, pp. 89–109, and see discussion of some of the relevant Ḥabad sources cited on pp. 226–227, n. 6.

21. Schneerson, *Torat Menaḥem: Hitwwa'aduyyot 5714*, 3:197–199, also printed in *Torat Menaḥem: Derushei Ḥatunah*, pp. 105–107.

22. Wolfson, "Coronation of the Sabbath Bride."

23. Shneur Zalman of Liadi, *Torah Or*, 94a.

24. For an analysis of the messianic transformation of the recipient into that which overflows, see Liwer, "Oral Torah," pp. 31–35.

25. Compare the Rebbe's discourse for Shabbat Beshallaḥ 5715 (1955) in Schneerson, *Torat Menaḥem: Hitwwa'aduyyot 5715*, 1:262–263. See also Schneerson, *Reshimot*, sec. 7, 1:177.

26. Linguistically, it is somewhat deficient to speak of an "itself" in relation to *Ein Sof*, the one whose ipseity it is (or is not) to be nothing.

27. For instance, see the passages translated in Wolfson, *Language, Eros, Being*, pp. 71–72, 185-186, 375, and other references cited on p. 591, n. 11.

28. Schneersohn, *Liqquṭei Torah: Torat Shmu'el 5626*, p. 81.

29. I have expanded on this theme in a number of scholarly writings. Especially noteworthy are the extended analyses in *Language, Eros, Being*, pp. 177–189, 333–371.

30. Schneersohn, *Quntres Derushei Ḥatunah*, p. 9.

31. Ibid., p. 11.

32. Previous discussions include Magid, "Ritual," pp. 206–210, and Liwer, "Oral Torah," p. 33, n. 80.

33. Compare Schneersohn, *Liqquṭei Torah: Torat Shmu'el 5632*, 2:544.

34. Babylonian Talmud, Ḥullin 60b.

35. Shneur Zalman of Liadi, *Ma'amerei Admor ha-Zaqen 5572*, p. 188. On the application of the term *aṭarah* to *Keter* and to *Malkhut*, see Hallamish, "Theoretical System," pp. 88–89.

36. Shneur Zalman of Liadi, *Seder Tefillot*, 132b; *Liqquṭei Torah*, Shir ha-Shirim, 2:43d.

37. See chapter 4, n. 160 and chapter 6, n. 164.

38. Babylonian Talmud, Baba Batra 75b.

39. Shneur Zalman of Liadi, *Seder Tefillot*, 138d–139a. See ibid., 286a, 287b.

40. Epstein, *Ma'or wa-Shemesh*, p. 199 (ad Exod 15:3). Regarding this text, see Polen, "Miriam's Dance." A portion of the passage is translated independently, with the appropriate title "The End of Hierarchy," in Lamm, *Religious Thought*, pp. 602–603. It should be noted, however, that elsewhere in *Ma'or wa-Shemesh*, the supernal level of the Godhead is described as a containment of the left in the right, the female in the male, rather than as an overcoming of the dimorphic structure. See, for instance, pp. 80–81 (ad Gen 29:32).

41. Shneur Zalman of Liadi, *Seder Tefillot*, 139a–b. Compare Shneur Zalman of Liadi, *Liqquṭei Torah*, Shir ha-Shirim, 2:48b: "And this is the matter of 'a woman of valor is a crown of her husband' (Prov 12:4), for in her shines the light of the 'good sense and knowledge' (Ps 119:66) that was stored away and hidden, that is, the aspect of the concealed brain [*moaḥ setima'ah*] . . . and the light then will be disclosed, and the chaos [*tohu*] will be in a level higher than the rectification [*tiqqun*] . . . for the light will be higher after the purification [*berur*]. . . . This is [alluded to] in the final two matrimonial blessings: initially, one says 'to gladden the bridegroom and the bride' [*mesammeaḥ ḥatan we-khallah*] and, finally, one says 'to gladden the bridegroom with the bride' [*mesammeaḥ ḥatan im ha-kallah*], for now the bride receives from the bridegroom, and this is 'to gladden the bridegroom and the bride,' but in the future they will be equal in stature, one crown for the two of them, as it was prior to the diminution, and this is 'to gladden the bridegroom with the bride.' . . . Then there will be the disclosure of the concealed brain, the supernal delight [*ta'anug elyon*], the ultimate perfection [*takhlit ha-sheleimut*], and then there will be a revelation of the interiority of the reasons of the law [*hitgallut penimit ṭa'amei ha-torah*]." For an abbreviated account, see Shneur Zalman of Liadi, *Torah Or*, 44b–45a.

42. Shneur Zalman of Liadi, *Torah Or*, 94b.

43. Schneersohn, *Derushei Ḥatunah*, 1:24–25.

44. Ibid., 2: 461. Loewenthal, "Women and the Dialectic of Spirituality," p. 65, n. 192, noted these passages from Dov Baer as well as some other relevant sources. See also Loewenthal, *Communicating the Infinite*, pp. 200–205. I do not think Loewenthal's attempt to contrast the views of Shneur Zalman and Dov Baer on the question of the identity versus the privileging of the female vis-à-vis the male can be substantiated textually. An adequate analysis lies beyond the scope of this study, but I may return to this matter in the future.

45. Schneersohn, *Sha'arei Teshuvah*, 15d. See ibid., 109c, where the words *lo adam* are applied to *malkhut de-ein sof*, which is said to be above the aspect of the human that is marked by the three dimensions of left, right, and center.

46. Schneersohn, *Sefer ha-Ma'amarim 5659*, p. 97.

47. Ibid., p. 98.

48. Ibid.

49. In passing, it is worthy to note the inversion of the correlation that one finds typically in kabbalistic symbolism, whereby concealment, the internal, is gendered as masculine, and disclosure, the external, as female, though the trope of the interior of the female is not unknown or unimportant in some of the older sources. See Wolfson, "Occultation of the Feminine."

50. Schneersohn, *Sefer ha-Ma'amarim 5659*, p. 99.

51. See introduction, nn. 67, 74; and Goldberg, "Zaddik's Soul," pp. 179–181.

52. Schneerson, *Torat Menaḥem: Hitwwa'aduyyot 5713*, 1:106–107. For a different formulation, see Schneerson, *Qunṭres Inyanah shel Torat ha-Ḥasidut*, p. 17: "The potency of *Malkhut* to create something from nothing [*leḥaddesh yesh me-ayin*] is precisely from the essence of the light of the Infinite [*aṣmut or ein sof*], which is above the classification that is appropriate to the worlds."

53. On the depiction of *Malkhut* as the point situated beneath *Yesod*, see Schneersohn, *Ner Miṣwah we-Torah Or*, 24b; Schneerson, *Torat Menaḥem: Hitwwa'aduyyot 5752*, 1:309.

54. Schneerson, *Torat Menaḥem: Hitwwa'aduyyot 5713*, 1:108–109.

55. Ibid., p. 109. An interesting and succinct formulation of the relationship between *Keter* and *Malkhut*, the beginning and the end circumscribed within an apophatic circle, is offered by Schneerson, *Iggerot Qodesh*, no. 220, 2:117. In the context of contrasting the nullification of existence and the nullification of something, associated respectively with the supernal unity and the lower unity (see chapter 2, n. 58), he offers the following exegesis of the word *eḥad* in Deut 6:4 (see chapter 3, n. 24) to elucidate the former type of unification: "All this is alluded in the letter *alef*—the master of the world [*alufo shel olam*], which proceeds by means of the *ḥeit*, the supernal Wisdom [*ḥokhmah illa'ah*], the beginning of the concatenation, until it emanates the world by means of the *dalet*—Speech [*dibbur*]. However, the Speech is bound to its source in Thought [*maḥashavah*], and even higher: the Speech that is in its source, that is, the Speech that is in Thought, and therefore the *dalet* is enlarged." For a similar explication, see Schneerson, *Torat Menaḥem: Hitwwa'aduyyot 5716*, 1:27–28; *Torat Menaḥem: Sefer ha-Ma'amarim Meluqaṭ*, 4:326.

56. See chapter 2, n. 213.

57. Numerous texts could be cited in support of this claim, but one that I will mention that is exceptionally clear is the statement of Schneersohn, *Be-Sha'ah she-Hiqdimu*, 1:41: "The ten *sefirot* that are revealed issue from the ten *sefirot* that are hidden in their Emanator, that is, the roots of the lights contained in the light of the Infinite prior to the withdrawal [*shorshei ha-orot ha-kelulim be-or ein sof she-lifnei ha-ṣimṣum*], for their emanation is by means of this withdrawal [*hamshakhatam hu al yedei ha-ṣimṣum*]. The matter of this withdrawal can be explained by the fact that in the light of the Infinite prior to the withdrawal, all of the ten *sefirot* were in the aspect of unity and admixture [*hit'aḥadut we-hit'arvut*], and they were then essentially in a higher and superior level, for they were not in an aspect of being and existence discernible in and of themselves [*beḥinat mahut u-meṣi'ut nikkeret le'aṣman*], and in their unity the supreme light, which is above the lights themselves, shone in them." See ibid., pp. 676–677: "By means of the withdrawal the interiority is concealed and the exteriority is revealed, for through this an aspect of interiority and exteriority came to be in the light. And the matter is that prior to the withdrawal there was no division at all between interiority and exteriority, and this is the matter of the light and darkness were intermingled [*mishtammeshin be-irbuvya*], as the darkness is the light . . . and they were mixed together [*me'uravim yaḥad*]. . . . In this light are two gradations, the one that is in the characteristic of that which bestows and the other that is in the characteristic of that which receives. And all of this is in the exteriority of the light, for appropriate to this are the two gradations, the characteristic of that which bestows and the characteristic of that which receives, which are the aspects of interiority and exteriority, but in the actual interiority of the light, that is, vis-à-vis that which bestows itself this is not appropriate. All of this came about by means of the withdrawal of that which bestows, for it withdrew its light so that there would be an aspect of the light appropriate to that which receives, for by means of this there is general division and particular divisions within the light." The expression *mishtammeshin be-irbuvya* is derived from the commentary of Rashi to Gen 1:4.

58. As far as I can tell, the locution "point of the trace" (*nequddat ha-reshimu*) was coined by Shalom Dovber Schneersohn. See, for instance, *Be-Sha'ah she-Hiqdimu*, 1:161: "Also above this *yod* is the aspect of the point of the trace, for this point comprises everything that will be revealed in the totality of the concatenation." And ibid., 2:736: "Just as there is something of the essence in the point of the trace, so it is in the point of Wisdom (and this is the point that remains after the withdrawal), but the trace is concealed and the Wisdom revealed." See ibid., 2:867–868.

59. For references to scholarly discussions of this Lurianic symbol, see chapter 2, n. 152.

60. My language is indebted to, but also subversive of, the descriptions of the trace in Derrida, *Speech and Phenomena*, pp. 127–128, n. 14, 156; *Of Grammatology*, p. 61; and *Margins of Philosophy*, pp. 66–67. See Wolfson, "Assaulting the Border," pp. 506–507; and "Structure, Innovation," pp. 149–150, 162–163, n. 38.

61. Schneersohn, *Be-Sha'ah she-Hiqdimu*, 1:14–15. In that context, the lights that have no existence are said to derive from the aspect of the line that extends from the Infinite before the withdrawal, whereas the vessels come to be from the point of the trace, which is also demarcated as the aspect of place (*maqom*). See ibid., 1:181, 2:677, 944.

62. Schneerson, *Sefer ha-Ma'amarim 5732–5733*, p. 309. On the supremacy of the body in the world-to-come, see the discourse from Shabbat Aḥarei Mot 5733 (1973), in ibid., pp. 388–391.

63. Ibid., p. 310.

64. *Pirqei Rabbi Eli'ezer,* chapter 3, 5b. Compare Shneur Zalman of Liadi, *Liqquṭei Torah,* Shir ha-Shirim, 2:5a. The potentiality of the divine to emanate its light is identified as "the aspect of his name that is contained in his essence" (*shemo ha-kalul be-aṣmuto*). See also Schneersohn, *Be-Sha'ah she-Hiqdimu,* 1:138, 139, 417, 569; 3:1270, 1287, 1346, 1407, 1408, 1415, 1421, 1422, 1423.

65. Schneerson, *Sefer ha-Ma'amarim 11 Nisan*, 2:398.

66. Schneerson, *Liqquṭei Siḥot,* 9:63–64.

67. Similar language was used already by Shneur Zalman of Liadi, *Seder Tefillot,* 132a: "When the purification will be complete in the future and the ultimate perfection will be in creation, then his light will be revealed without any garment concealing at all." For other references to this motif, see chapter 2, n. 264.

68. Schneerson, *Sefer ha-Ma'amarim 11 Nisan,* 2:422–424.

69. Schneerson, *Torat Menaḥem: Hitwwa'aduyyot 5713,* 1:4.

70. *Tiqqunei Zohar,* introduction, 17a. Compare Schneersohn, *Ner Miṣwah we-Torah Or,* 51a: "This is [the import of] 'their beginning is fixed in their end and their end in their beginning,' for the beginning is the aspect of the nothing of Wisdom [*ayin de-ḥokhmah*] . . . and this potency is fixed in the end especially, which is the action [*ha-ma'aseh*], for she has within herself the capacity to create the nothing into something [*koaḥ ha-meḥaddesh me-ayin le-yesh*], which is above the aspect of Wisdom that is in the beginning . . . and this is the something from nothing [*we-hu yesh me-ayin*] . . . but the action creates the nothing into something [*meḥaddesh me-ayin le-yesh*] like the potency of *Keter*, for from the nothing of *Keter* there emanates the Wisdom that becomes a something . . . (and this is what is said that the crown of kingship is the supernal crown [*keter malkhut de-ihu keter elyon*], and in the formation of the lines *Malkhut* stands beneath the median line of *Tif'eret Yisra'el,* which ascends to the inwardness of *Keter* . . . for their beginning is fixed in their end, that is, the light of *Keter* in *Malkhut,* and similarly their end is fixed [in their beginning]). . . . Hence, in *Malkhut* of the emanation, which is called the 'end of everything' [*sof ha-kol*], the aspect of the action [*beḥinat ha-ma'aseh*], there is the potency of the beginning of the essence of the Infinite that is in the light of *Keter* of the emanation [*yesh bah koaḥ hatḥalah de-aṣmut ein sof she-be-or ha-keter de-aṣilut*] to create something from nothing in actuality [*leḥaddesh yesh me-ayin mammash*], as it was in the primordial of all the primordial beings [*qadmon le-khol ha-qedumim*] to create the Wisdom from nothing to something [*she-meḥaddesh et ha-ḥokhmah me-ayin le-yesh*]."

71. Schneerson, *Torat Menaḥem: Hitwwa'aduyyot 5751,* 3:163.

72. See chapter 2, n. 222.

73. Schneerson, *Torat Menaḥem: Hitwwa'aduyyot 5713,* 2:56. Compare Shneur Zalman of Liadi, *Ma'amerei Admor ha-Zaqen 5566,* 1:54.

74. Shneur Zalman of Liadi, *Liqquṭei Torah*, Derushim le-Shabbat Shuvah, 2:67b.

75. Schneerson, *Siḥot Qodesh 5752,* 1:73. See chapter 3, n. 88.

76. Schneerson, *Torat Menaḥem: Hitwwa'aduyyot 5752,* 1:309.

77. On the decoding of the word Kislev as a compound of *kes* and *lo,* respectively the masculine and the feminine, see the letter to Schneerson written by his father on 6 Kislev 5689 (19 November 1928) in Schneersohn, *Liqquṭei Levi Yiṣḥaq,* p. 205.

78. Schneerson, *Sefer ha-Siḥot* 5752, p. 159.

79. Schneerson, *Torat Menaḥem: Hitwwa'aduyyot* 5752, 2:260–266. On the special role accorded to Jewish women in bringing the redemption, see Ochs, "Waiting for the Messiah."

80. For example, Schneerson, *Torat Menaḥem: Hitwwa'aduyyot* 5713, 2:38; and see nn. 16 and 46, this chapter.

81. Handelman, "Putting Women in the Picture," pp. 3–5. On the role of women in Ḥabad under the leadership of the seventh Rebbe, see also Goldberg, "Imagining the Feminine"; Ehrlich, *The Messiah of Brooklyn,* pp. 197–211; Loewenthal, "Religious Development and Experience"; Davidman, *Tradition in a Rootless World*, pp. 165–172; Loewenthal, "Women and the Dialectic of Spirituality," pp. 58–62; "'Daughter/Wife of Hasid'"; Fishkoff, *The Rebbe's Army,* pp. 244–245; Feldman, *Lubavitchers as Citizens,* pp. 7–8, 135–167; Werczberger, "Feminine Messianism and Messianic Femininity"; Levine, *Mystics, Mavericks, and Merrymakers.*

82. Loewenthal, "Women and the Dialectic of Spirituality," p. 25, n. 59, cites a comment of Yosef Yiṣḥaq Schneersohn to the effect that the fourth Rebbe of the Lubavitch dynasty, Shmuel, had already publicly called for women to study Ḥasidic teachings. On the innovations of the sixth Rebbe, see Loewenthal, "Communicating Jewish Spirituality"; and "Spiritual Experience."

83. Loewenthal, "Women and the Dialectic of Spirituality," pp. 19–26.

84. Schneerson, *Iggerot Qodesh,* no. 6044, 16:268–269; Rapoport-Albert, "On Women in Hasidism," pp. 523–525, nn. 82–83; Loewenthal, "Women and the Dialectic of Spirituality," pp. 42–52; Handelman, "Women and the Study of Torah"; Dahan, "'Dira Bataḥtonim,'" pp. 188–196.

85. Schneerson, *Iggerot Qodesh,* no. 2375, 8:133–134, and see also the fragment from a letter written on 29 Ṭevet 5721 (January 17, 1961) in Schneerson, *Liqquṭei Siḥot,* 34:265; and compare Loewenthal, "Women and the Dialectic of Spirituality," p. 52.

86. Schneerson, *Sefer ha-Siḥot* 5750, 1:426. On the role of women in promoting a messianic activism surrounding the seventh Rebbe, see Davidman, *Tradition in a Rootless World,* pp. 152–153; Feldman, *Lubavitchers as Citizens,* p. 167; and Ravitzky, *Messianism,* p. 201.

87. On the educational initiatives and contributions of Ḥabad women, see Ehrlich, *The Messiah of Brooklyn,* pp. 205–207.

88. The idiom I have translated as "schoolchildren" is the rabbinic *tinoqot shel beit rabban.* See Babylonian Talmud, Berakhot 5a, 53b, 62b; Shabbat 33b, 119b; Soṭah 35a; Giṭṭin 29a, 57b, 58a; Avodah Zarah 3b; Ḥullin 81b.

89. Schneerson, *Torat Menaḥem: Hitwwa'aduyyot* 5713, 2:38.

90. The seventh Rebbe's exegesis seems to be in conversation with Dov Baer Schneersohn's commentary on Gen 24:13 in *Torat Ḥayyim: Bere'shit,* 128a: "It is known that the aspect of the 'spring of water' [*ein ha-mayim*] is the aspect of the spring of wisdom [*ma'yan ha-ḥokhmah*] . . . which issues from the source of the supernal Wisdom."

91. The biblical idiom *el olam* is usually translated as "everlasting God," but I have rendered it in a way that conforms to Schneerson's interpretation.

92. See chapter 2, nn. 150–151, 153–155.

93. Schneerson, *Reshimot,* sec. 67, 3:218–219.

94. Schneerson, *Quntres Inyanah shel Torat ha-Ḥasidut,* p. 18.

95. See chapter 1, n. 17.

96. Schneerson, *Quntres Inyanah shel Torat ha-Ḥasidut,* p. 23.

97. Schneerson, *Torat Menaḥem: Hitwwa'aduyyot 5751,* 3:163.

6. Apocalyptic Crossing

1. Schneersohn, *Sefer ha-Siḥot 5702*, p. 110; see also the introduction to Schneersohn, *Sefer ha-Siḥot 5688–5691*, pp. 68, 71.

2. Schneersohn, *Iggerot Qodesh*, no. 3828, 11:109; see also Schneerson, *Iggerot Qodesh*, no. 6428, 17:279.

3. Schneersohn, *Arba'a Qol ha-Qore*, p. 3 (Hebrew text, p. 28). See also the pessimistic evaluation of American Jewry in Schneersohn, *Iggerot Qodesh*, no. 2238, 8:118–119.

4. Schneersohn, *Sefer ha-Siḥot 5703*, p. 132.

5. Ibid., p. 134.

6. Ibid., p. 142.

7. Ibid., p. 140, where the quality of innocence (*temimut*) is associated with the American experience.

8. Schneerson, *Iggerot Qodesh*, no. 8593, 22:410; *Liqquṭei Siḥot* 6:364. See also the description of the sixth Rebbe's intention of coming to America in Schneerson, *Torat Menaḥem: Hitwwa'aduyyot 5720*, 1:468.

9. Schneerson, *Torat Menaḥem: Hitwwa'aduyyot 5712*, 1:155. Compare the remark in a letter from 1 Adar 5715 (February 23, 1955), in Schneerson, *Iggerot Qodesh*, no. 3323, 10:365: "The blessed holy One is the master of the world, literally, and the United States is also in this category." On the affirmation of God's complete presence in America, see *Torat Menaḥem: Hitwwa'aduyyot 5715*, 1:238. On the special role accorded the Jews in America, particularly in terms of supporting Jews in the Soviet Union, see Schneerson, *Iggerot Qodesh*, no. 6398, 17:249. The analogy used there is that all of Israel is a single body, and one limb has the ability to strengthen another limb. On the quality of Americans to give charity, which is related to their presumed propensity to accumulate things in a center-point whence they spread forth like branches, see Schneerson, *Torat Menaḥem: Hitwwa'aduyyot 5715*, 1:147. On the generous quality of Americans, see also *Torat Menaḥem: Hitwwa'aduyyot 5717*, 2:48. For a more negative assessment regarding the lack of knowledge on the part of American Jewry, see the letter of 3 Tammuz 5715 (June 23, 1955) in Schneerson, *Iggerot Qodesh*, no. 3616, 11:229.

10. Schneerson, *Torat Menaḥem: Hitwwa'aduyyot 5717*, 2:364.

11. From a discourse on 19 Kislev 5747 (December 21, 1986), in Schneerson, *Torat Menaḥem: Hitwwa'aduyyot 5747*, 2:54–55.

12. Babylonian Talmud, Shabbat 21b.

13. Schneerson, *Torat Menaḥem: Hitwwaʿaduyyot 5750*, 2:66–67.

14. Babylonian Talmud, Giṭṭin 10b.

15. For an historical account of this narrative, see Rigg, *Rescued From the Reich.*

16. Schneerson, *Torat Menaḥem: Hitwwaʿaduyyot 5743*, 2:1734.

17. Ibid., 2:1735–1736.

18. Schneerson, *Torat Menaḥem: Hitwwaʿaduyyot 5744*, 2:894.

19. Ibid., 2:895. On the spiritual import of the slogan "In God we trust," see also Schneerson, *Torat Menaḥem: Hitwwaʿaduyyot 5744*, 3:1435; *Torat Menaḥem: Hitwwaʿaduyyot 5746*, 2:203; *Torat Menaḥem: Hitwwaʿaduyyot 5750*, 2:67; *Torat Menaḥem: Hitwwaʿaduyyot 5751*, 4:49. It is of interest to note that the Web site http://www.otzar770.com, which includes a picture of the Rebbe with the messianic slogan *yeḥi adonenu morenu we-rabbenu melekh ha-mashiaḥ leʿolam waʿed*, features a replication of an American coin with the words "Liberty In God We Trust" and the date 1986.

20. See Ravitzky, *Messianism*, pp. 188–193; Ehrlich, *The Messiah of Brooklyn*, pp. 107–108; Kraus, "'Living with the Times,'" pp. 280–290; *The Seventh*, pp. 80–83, 224–249. For a recent constructive, but not critical, presentation of the seven Noahide laws that in the main follows, but to some extent also deviates from, the path of the Rebbe, see Ginsburgh, *Kabbalah and Meditation for the Nations.*

21. Transcriptions and facsimiles of the letter exchange between Reagan and Schneerson, as well as the proclamation of the "National Day of Reflection" itself, are available at http://www.chabad.org/therebbe/article_cdo/aid/142535/jewish/The-Rebbe-and-President.

22. The matter of the seven Noahide laws is repeated in the proclamation issued by Reagan declaring April 2, 1985, as "Education Day, U.S.A., 1985," in honor of the seventh Rebbe's eighty-third birthday, and again in the proclamation issued by Reagan declaring April 20, 1986, as "Education Day, U.S.A., 1986," in honor of his eighty-fourth birthday. Reference to these laws is found as well in Schneerson's letters to Regan from May 17, 1987, and September 6, 1987. Transcripts of all of these documents are available in the Web site mentioned in the previous note. Reference to the "Noahide Law—and standards of conduct duly derived from them—promulgated around the globe" by Schneerson is made in the proclamation issued on April 14, 1989, declaring "Education Day, U.S.A" on April 16, 1989, and April 6, 1990, in honor of the Rebbe's eighty-seventh birthday. The text is available at http://www.presidency.ucsb.edu/ws/?pid=23514.

23. Schneerson, *Torat Menaḥem: Hitwwaʿaduyyot 5744*, 1:893; *Torat Menaḥem: Hitwwaʿaduyyot 5745*, 3:1839–1840; *Liqquṭei Siḥot*, 35:97–98.

24. Moses ben Maimon, *Mishneh Torah*, Melakhim 8:10.

25. Schneerson, *Torat Menaḥem: Hitwwaʿaduyyot 5747*, 2:57.

26. Schneerson, *Torat Menaḥem: Hitwwaʿaduyyot 5743*, 2:1733.

27. Schneerson, *Torat Menaḥem: Hitwwaʿaduyyot 5745*, 2:900.

28. Schneerson, *Torat Menaḥem: Hitwwaʿaduyyot 5745*, 5:2797.

29. Schneerson, *Torat Menaḥem: Hitwwaʿaduyyot 5743*, 1:924.

30. Ibid., 1:933.

31. Moses ben Maimon, *Mishneh Torah*, Melakhim 8:10. See the extended analysis in Schneerson, *Liqquṭei Siḥot*, 26:132–144.

32. Schneerson, *Torat Menaḥem: Hitwwa'aduyyot 5751*, 3:269.

33. See chapter 2, n. 54.

34. Schneerson, *Torat Menaḥem: Hitwwa'aduyyot 5711*, 1:125, 266. See passage cited in chapter 1, n. 99, and Hallamish, "Theoretical System," pp. 184, 190.

35. Schneerson, *Liqquṭei Siḥot*, 2:604, 23:181, 30:153, 31:51, 35:51, 36:122, 186; 37:105, 39:332, 359, 361, 363, 370, 371, 426; *Iggerot Qodesh*, no. 1635, 6:115; *Torat Menaḥem: Hitwwa'aduyyot 5712*, 1:305; *Torat Menaḥem: Hitwwa'aduyyot 5715*, 1:278; *Torat Menaḥem: Hitwwa'aduyyot 5716*, 2:44, 147; *Torat Menaḥem: Hitwwa'aduyyot 5717*, 2:57; *Torat Menaḥem: Hitwwa'aduyyot 5719*, 3:68; *Torat Menaḥem: Sefer ha-Ma'amarim Meluqaṭ*, 1:120, 2:150, 415; 3:20, 95, 125, 253, 276. The more typical formulation, based on *Zohar* 3:73a, affirms the unity of God, Torah, and Israel (see chapter 4, n. 125), though the precise language, *yisra'el orayyta we-qudsha berikh hu kolla ḥad*, is closer to the expression *qudsha berikh hu orayyta we-yisra'el kolla ḥad*. Regarding this saying, see Tishby, *Messianic Mysticism*, pp. 454–485. This is repeated on numerous occasions in the seventh Rebbe's discourses and letters. See, for instance, Schneerson, *Iggerot Qodesh*, no. 799, 4:39, no. 1009, 4:282, no. 1095, 4:376, 378, no. 1215, 4:500; no. 1319, 5:111; no. 2157, 7:302, no. 2211, 7:351; no. 4173, 12:358; no. 5151, 14:387; no. 7384, 19:386; no. 8331, 22:127; no. 10,655, 28:95; *Torat Menaḥem: Hitwwa'aduyyot 5711*, 1:55; *Torat Menaḥem: Hitwwa'aduyyot 5711*, 2:330; *Torat Menaḥem: Hitwwa'aduyyot 5712*, 1:200; *Torat Menaḥem: Hitwwa'aduyyot 5712*, 3:182; *Torat Menaḥem: Hitwwa'aduyyot 5713*, 1:259; *Torat Menaḥem: Hitwwa'aduyyot 5714*, 1:19, 210; *Torat Menaḥem: Hitwwa'aduyyot 5714*, 3:147; *Torat Menaḥem: Hitwwa'aduyyot 5716*, 2:307, 316, 318; *Torat Menaḥem: Hitwwa'aduyyot 5717*, 1:121; *Torat Menaḥem: Hitwwa'aduyyot 5717*, 2:167; *Torat Menaḥem: Hitwwa'aduyyot 5718*, 1:145; *Torat Menaḥem: Hitwwa'aduyyot 5718*, 3:33, 260; *Torat Menaḥem: Hitwwa'aduyyot 5719*, 3:196; *Torat Menaḥem: Sefer ha-Ma'amarim Meluqaṭ*, 1:201; 2:221, 414; 3:60, 64, 99, 137, 289; *Liqquṭei Siḥot*, 39:365.

36. Schneersohn, *Liqquṭei Torah: Torat Shmu'el 5626*, p. 242; Schneerson, *Torat Menaḥem: Hitwwa'aduyyot 5716*, 2:216.

37. Shneur Zalman of Liadi, *Seder Tefillot*, 287b–c. On the distinction between substance (*mahut*) and reality (*meṣi'ut*), see Hallamish, "Theoretical System," pp. 41–42. See also Shneur Zalman of Liadi, *Ma'amerei Admor ha-Zaqen: Al Inyanim*, p. 127. After discussing the mandate of Israel to love God with an all-encompassing yearning, the Alter Rebbe noted: "The nations, however, are from the shells from the aspect of the back, and thus even the ones who believe in the divinity follow themselves and they do not desire to be conjoined to him, blessed be he." In the continuation, the "aspect of the back" is identified as physical lust, whereas the "aspect of the face," which is assigned exclusively to Israel, is identified as the element of divinity.

38. Schneersohn, *Derekh Miṣwotekha*, 27b.

39. Schneerson, *Torat Menaḥem: Hitwwa'aduyyot 5713*, 3:9; *Torat Menaḥem: Hitwwa'aduyyot 5714*, 2:15; *Torat Menaḥem: Hitwwa'aduyyot 5714*, 3:222, 228; *Torat Menaḥem: Hitwwa'aduyyot 5717*, 1:77, 118, 119; *Torat Menaḥem: Hitwwa'aduyyot 5718*, 3:200, 260; *Torat Menaḥem: Hitwwa'aduyyot 5719*, 2:95. The experience is also referred to as the "discernment of the essence by the essence" (*hakkarat eṣem ba-eṣem*); see Schneerson, *Torat Menaḥem: Hitwwa'aduyyot 5719*, 2:96, 97, 172.

40. Schneersohn, *Torat Ḥayyim: Bere'shit*, 161d.

41. See chapter 3, n. 79.

42. Shneur Zalman of Liadi, *Torah Or*, 99a. See Schneerson, *Torat Menaḥem: Hitwwa'aduyyot 5747*, 3:258.

43. Shneur Zalman of Liadi, *Torah Or*, 25a (in that context, the source beyond the river is identified as *Keter*), 75d, 76c; *Liqquṭei Torah*, Beḥuqotai, 1:46d–47a, Mas'ei, 1:93d; *Liqquṭei Torah*, Shir ha-Shirim, 2:37c; *Ma'amerei Admor ha-Zaqen 5565*, 1:290; Schneersohn, *Torat Ḥayyim: Shemot*, 279a, 281b; Schneersohn, *Derekh Miṣwotekha*, 82b; Schneersohn, *Be-Sha'ah she-Hiqdimu*, 1:124; Schneerson, *Torat Menaḥem: Hitwwa'aduyyot 5711*, 1:233; *Torat Menaḥem: Hitwwa'aduyyot 5720*, 2:3–4, 8–9; *Torat Menaḥem: Sefer ha-Ma'amarim Meluqaṭ*, 1:253.

44. Schneersohn, *Sefer ha-Ma'amarim 5689*, p. 112.

45. Schneerson, *Torat Menaḥem: Sefer ha-Ma'amarim Meluqaṭ*, 1:298. See *Liqquṭei Siḥot*, 22:163.

46. Schneerson, *Iggerot Qodesh*, no. 6714, 18:211.

47. Schneerson, *Ha-Yom Yom*, p. 104 (14 Ḥeshvan).

48. Schneerson, *Torat Menaḥem: Hitwwa'aduyyot 5717*, 2:137.

49. See chapter 3, nn. 65–66. It should be noted that on occasion there is an attempt to follow a distinction enunciated in the Tosafot, the medieval commentary on the Talmud, between the expressions *adam* and *ha-adam*, that is, the former is exclusive to Israel and the latter encompasses the nations of the world as well. See, for example, Schneerson, *Sefer ha-Ma'amarim 5737*, p. 273. I am of the opinion that this distinction does not truly attenuate the ethnocentric implications of Ḥabad anthropology.

50. Shneur Zalman of Liadi, *Liqquṭei Amarim: Tanya*, part 1, chapter 19, 24a–b; *Liqquṭei Torah*, Wayyiqra, 1:2d, Bemidbar, 1:8b; *Torah Or*, 39b. Numerous other sources could have been cited, including many passages in the oeuvre of the seventh Rebbe. For instance, see Schneerson, *Iggerot Qodesh*, no. 6644, 18:143, no. 6902, 18:420, no. 6606, 18:425, no. 6972, 18:497; no. 8948, 23:338; no. 9156, 24:153; no. 9509, 25:167; no. 1122, 27:121, no. 1399, 27:412; *Torat Menaḥem: Hitwwa'aduyyot 5713*, 1:238, 251, 303; *Torat Menaḥem: Hitwwa'aduyyot 5714*, 3:223; *Torat Menaḥem: Hitwwa'aduyyot 5715*, 2:92, 291; *Torat Menaḥem: Hitwwa'aduyyot 5717*, 1:83; *Torat ha-Menaḥem: Sefer ha-Ma'amarim Meluqaṭ*, 3:368.

51. Babylonian Talmud, Yevamot 61a.

52. Schneerson, *Torat Menaḥem: Sefer ha-Ma'amarim Meluqaṭ*, 1:31–33. See chapter 3, n. 87.

53. See chapter 3, n. 65.

54. Shneur Zalman of Liadi, *Ma'amerei Admor ha-Zaqen 5566*, 1:201.

55. Schneerson, *Iggerot Qodesh*, no. 876, 4:134; no. 8626, 22:450–451.

56. Schneerson, *Reshimot*, sec. 132, 4:193.

57. Shneur Zalman of Liadi, *Liqquṭei Amarim: Tanya*, part 1, chapter 1, 6a.

58. See chapter 4, n. 16.

59. *Midrash Wayyiqra Rabbah* 13:5, p. 293. On the depiction of Esau as the pig, see Schneersohn, *Liqquṭei Torah: Torat Shmu'el 5639*, 1:338; Schneerson, *Torat Menaḥem: Hitwwa'aduyyot 5716*, 2:243, 250.

60. Schneerson, *Liqquṭei Siḥot*, 35:118.

61. Schneerson, *Iggerot Qodesh*, no. 2871, 9:247.

62. Schneerson, *Torat Menaḥem: Hitwwa'aduyyot 5713*, 3:79.

63. Schneerson, *Torat Menaḥem: Hitwwa'aduyyot 5720*, 1:397.

64. Schneerson, *Liqquṭei Siḥot*, 4:1147.

65. Schneerson, *Iggerot Qodesh*, no. 1039, 4:316; *Torat Menaḥem: Hitwwa'aduyyot 5711*, 1:290–291; *Torat Menaḥem: Sefer ha-Ma'amarim Meluqaṭ*, 3:59–60.

66. Loizzo, "Introduction," p. 116.

67. See chapter 4, n. 112.

68. Schneerson, *Torat Menaḥem: Hitwwa'aduyyot 5711*, 2:303.

69. Schneerson, *Iggerot Qodesh*, no. 2393, 8:151. See also Schneerson, *Iggerot Qodesh*, no. 6329, 17:181; *Torat Menaḥem: Hitwwa'aduyyot 5715*, 1:70 and 328. The saying is cited in the name of the Mitteler Rebbe by the sixth Rebbe in a talk from the night of 10 Kislev 5697 (November 23, 1936); see Schneersohn, *Sefer ha-Siḥot 5696—Ḥoref 5700*, p. 210, from which it was copied into *Ha-Yom Yom*, p. 13 (20 Ṭevet). See the talk from Shemini Aṣeret–Simḥat Torah of that year in *Sefer ha-Siḥot 5696—Ḥoref 5700*, p. 186; and the letter from 24 Iyyar 5688 (May 14, 1928), in Schneersohn, *Iggerot Qodesh*, no. 383, 2:73.

70. Schneerson, *Torat Menaḥem: Hitwwa'aduyyot 5714*, 1:268.

71. Schneerson, *Torat Menaḥem: Hitwwa'aduyyot 5720*, 1:277.

72. Schneerson, *Torat Menaḥem: Hitwwa'aduyyot 5717*, 1:269.

73. Schneerson, *Liqquṭei Siḥot*, 23:178–181. The point is not acknowledged by Kohanzad, "Messianic Doctrine," who emphasized in an unqualified way the positive attitude of the seventh Rebbe to Gentiles, even to the point of suggesting that the gap between Jew and non-Jew is effectively obliterated in his eschatological vision of the new Torah (pp. 16, 154, and 161).

74. For discussion of the Maharal's view regarding the divine image, see Wolfson, *Venturing Beyond*, pp. 116–120, and reference to other scholars cited on p. 117, n. 423. For a sustained discussion of the influence of this figure on East European pietism, see Safran, "Maharal and Early Hasidism"; and reference to other scholars cited on p. 91, nn. 1–4.

75. Schneersohn, *Or ha-Torah: Bemidbar*, pp. 171–174; Schneersohn, *Sefer ha-Ma'amarim 5702*, pp. 104–109.

76. Mishnah, Avot 3:14.

77. Schneerson, *Sefer ha-Ma'amarim 5737*, pp. 273–274, and the Yiddish version in *Liqquṭei Siḥot*, 15:60–61. On the depiction of Israel as the sons of God and the idea of consubstantiality in Schneerson's teaching, see Idel, *Ben*, pp. 563–565.

78. Schneerson, *Sefer ha-Ma'amarim 5737*, pp. 274–276. The depiction of the Torah as the "cherished vessel" is from the continuation of Aqiva's dictum transmitted in Mishnah, Avot 3:14.

79. Shneur Zalman of Liadi, *Ma'amerei Admor ha-Zaqen 5566*, 2:464.

80. Shneur Zalman of Liadi, *Torah Or*, 71b. See ibid., 76d-77a.

81. Shneur Zalman of Liadi, *Ma'amerei Admor ha-Zaqen 5569*, p. 173. See also Schneersohn, *Or ha-Torah: Bemidbar*, 1:49, 2:954.

82. *Zohar* 3:129a (Idra Rabba). On occasion, the zoharic image of the one eye (ibid., 129b), is also used to convey the same idea of transcending binaries. See, for example, Shneur Zalman of Liadi, *Liqquṭei Torah*, Re'eh, 2:24c; Schneerson, *Torat Menaḥem: Sefer*

ha-Ma'amarim Meluqaṭ, 2:407. For discussion of these themes, see Wolfson, *Venturing Beyond*, pp. 218–224.

83. Shneur Zalman of Liadi, *Torah Or*, 72c. Compare Shneur Zalman of Liadi, *Liqquṭei Torah*, Bemidbar, 1:9c; *Ma'amerei Admor ha-Zaqen 5569*, p. 173. A critical passage that informed the Ḥabad speculation on the supernal anthropos that is above anthropomorphic representation is *Zohar* 3:136b (Idra Rabba). In that context, 1 Sam 9:29 is interpreted in the following way: the highest aspect of the Godhead, the "eternality of Israel," is portrayed as a forehead without a full face, and hence the term *adam* is not ascribed to it. See Shneur Zalman, *Liqquṭei Torah*, Shir ha-Shirim, 2:23c.

84. Compare Schneerson, *Iggerot Qodesh*, no. 449, 3:64–65.

85. Shneur Zalman of Liadi, *Torah Or*, 71d. See passage from Dov Baer Schneersohn mentioned in chapter 5, at n. 45.

86. Shneur Zalman of Liadi, *Torah Or*, 71d, 72c, 77a; *Liqquṭei Torah*, Tazri'a, 1:21b, Bemidbar, 1:9c, Megillat Esther, 1:122a; Schneersohn, *Sha'arei Teshuvah*, 92b; *Imrei Binah*, part 1, 83a; *Sha'arei Orah*, 95b.

87. Schneersohn, *Ner Miṣwah we-Torah Or*, 106b. See ibid., 89a.

88. Schneersohn, *Sha'arei Teshuvah*, 42a; *Ner Miṣwah we-Torah Or*, 122b.

89. Schneersohn, *Sha'arei Teshuvah*, 104d.

90. Schneerson, *Torat Menaḥem: Sefer ha-Ma'amarim Meluqaṭ*, 2:212–213. For an alternative transcription, see Schneerson, *Liqquṭei Siḥot*, 30:218–219; see also *Liqquṭei Siḥot*, 4:1140–1143. The description of the unity of the body politic of Israel as having no head or end, and thus comparable to a circle, is found in earlier Ḥabad sources. For example, see Shneur Zalman, *Liqquṭei Torah*, Neṣavim, 2:44a.

91. Schneerson, *Torat Menaḥem: Sefer ha-Ma'amarim Meluqaṭ*, 2:310, 317–318. On the image of the not-human, the anthropos beyond limitation and measurement and hence beyond anthropomorphization, see also Schneerson, *Torat Menaḥem: Hitwwa'aduyyot 5715*, 2:98, 148, 172–179, 219; *Torat Menaḥem: Hitwwa'aduyyot 5716*, 1:6-10, and compare the passage cited in chapter 3, n. 63.

92. Schneersohn, *Sefer ha-Ma'amarim 5710–5711*, part 1, pp. 153–154.

93. Schneerson, *Torat Menaḥem: Sefer ha-Ma'amarim Meluqaṭ*, 2:407.

94. Schneerson, *Torat Menaḥem: Hitwwa'aduyyot 5713*, 2:203.

95. Ibid. See Schneerson, *Torat Menaḥem: Hitwwa'aduyyot 5715*, 2:173–174.

96. See the view of Shalom Dovber discussed in chapter 2, n. 281. It is also of interest here to note the contrast made between the revelation at Sinai and that of Purim in Schneersohn, *Liqquṭei Torah: Torat Shmu'el 5639*, 1:338: in the case of the former, the epiphany was (in language derived from Ezek 1:26) from the perspective of the "human appearance" (*ke-mar'eh adam*), whereas in the case of the latter the increase in the degree of self-denial occasioned an emanation above the anthropomorphic mold, which is the metaphorical depiction of the divine in the image of the gazelle (based on Song of Songs 2:9). The intent of this observation can be elicited from the concluding statement in which the talmudic dictum "Be swift as the gazelle, and be courageous as a lion, to fulfill the will of your Father in heaven" (Babylonian Talmud, Pesaḥim 112a) is cited, that is, the imaginary representation of the divine as a gazelle is proportionate to the one who acts like a gazelle in being swift to carry out God's will.

97. See chapter 2, n. 288.

98. Schneerson, *Liqquṭei Siḥot*, 4:1143. On the symbol of the supernal light, see chapter 2, n. 21.

99. Schneerson, *Torat Menaḥem: Hitwwa'aduyyot 5714*, 1:152. See *Torat Menaḥem: Hitwwa'aduyyot 5711*, 1:24. On the symbol of the supernal darkness (*ḥoshekh elyon*), see chapter 2, n. 20.

100. *Tiqqunei Zohar*, sec. 70, 135b. I have translated the text as it appears in the work of Shneur Zalman (see the following note), even though some words from the original were left out.

101. Shneur Zalman of Liadi, *Liqquṭei Torah*, Shir ha-Shirim, 2:4c–d.

102. Schneerson, *Torat Menaḥem: Hitwwa'aduyyot 5718*, 1:163. See *Torat Menaḥem: Sefer ha-Ma'amarim Meluqaṭ*, 1:191.

103. Schneersohn, *Liqquṭei Torah: Torat Shmu'el 5632*, 2:395, 402; Schneerson, *Torat Menaḥem: Hitwwa'aduyyot 5715*, 2:176–177.

104. Schneerson, *Torat Menaḥem: Hitwwa'aduyyot 5720*, 1:195.

105. Moses ben Maimon, *Mishneh Torah*, Melakhim 12:4. As one might imagine, Maimonidean eschatology has been analyzed by a plethora of scholars. Here I note only a select number of studies that are useful in assessing the impact of the concept of the individual and universal redemption in the medieval sage on Schneerson. See Kraemer, "On Maimonides' Messianic Posture"; Ravitzky, "'To the Utmost of Human Capacity'"; Schwartz, *Messianism in Medieval Jewish Thought*, pp. 49–53, 69–89, 92–111, 133–154. For the historical and sociological background against which the Maimonidean perspective should be evaluated, see Friedman, *Maimonides*, pp. 9–49.

106. Moses ben Maimon, *Mishneh Torah*, Melakhim, 12:5. See Schneerson, *Liqquṭei Siḥot*, 23:174–175. The language of Maimonides is cited routinely in the seventh Rebbe's writings and discourses. See, for instance, Schneerson, *Qunṭres Inyanah shel Torat ha-Ḥasidut*, p. 4; *Iggerot Qodesh*, no. 6211, 17:66; *Torat Menaḥem: Hitwwa'aduyyot 5713*, 1:180; *Torat Menaḥem: Hitwwa'aduyyot 5717*, 3:56–57; *Torat Menaḥem: Hitwwa'aduyyot 5711*, 1:341; *Liqquṭei Siḥot*, 30:171–172; *Liqquṭei Siḥot*, 31:26; 32:35; 34:178, 216; 35:30, 98, 208, 289; 37:79.

107. Moses ben Maimon, *Mishneh Torah*, Yesodei Torah 1:1; Schneerson, *Torat Menaḥem: Hadranim al ha-Rambam we-Shas*, pp. 96–97. The text is based on talks delivered by the seventh Rebbe on 11 and 22 of Nisan 5745 (April 2 and 13, 1985). For a different Hebrew transcription of these talks, see *Torat Menaḥem: Hitwwa'aduyyot 5745*, 3:1715–1716, 1833–1836. See Gotlieb, "Habad's Harmonistic Approach," pp. 275–276.

108. Schneerson, *Torat Menaḥem: Hadranim al ha-Rambam we-Shas*, pp. 145–146, 149–150. The text is printed as well in *Torat Menaḥem: Hitwwa'aduyyot 5748*, 2:243, 246.

109. Wolfson, "*Via Negativa*," pp. 371–373.

110. Moses ben Maimon, *Mishneh Torah*, Melakhim, 12:1. See also *Guide of the Perplexed*, II.28, p. 335, 29, p. 345. Note as well I.32, p. 70, where Maimonides (citing Isa 5:20) considers the confusion of opposites to be a "deficiency" in the law. As I have argued in this book, such a confusion is precisely what the Ḥabad masters envision as indicative of the final redemption. See also ibid., I.52, p. 114, where Maimonides writes of the

imagination's faulty desire to establish a means to connect contraries, which should remain separate. On the delineation of the nature of governance as the division of light and darkness, see ibid., II.6, p. 261.

111. See chapter 4, n. 140.

112. Moses ben Maimon, *Mishneh Torah*, Teshuvah 9:2; Schneerson, *Sha'arei Ge'ullah*, 2:60–63, 123–133; *Torat Menaḥem: Hadranim al ha-Rambam we-Shas*, p. 156 (*Torat Menaḥem: Hitwwa'aduyyot 5748*, 2:251); Gotlieb, "Habad's Harmonistic Approach," pp. 239–240.

113. Schneerson, *Torat Menaḥem: Reshimat ha-Yoman*, p. 243.

114. Babylonian Talmud, Megillah 7b.

115. Schneersohn, *Sha'arei Orah*, 144b.

116. Schneersohn, *Torat Ḥayyim: Bere'shit*, 76b–c.

117. Levinas, *Difficult Freedom*, p. 136.

118. From a conceptual standpoint, there are many affinities between the Ḥabad teaching initiated by Shneur Zalman of Liadi and the speculative kabbalah that can be traced to Elijah ben Solomon, the Gaon of Vilna. Obviously, I cannot engage this topic here, but consider, for example, the discussion of the passage in Ḥayyim of Volozhyn's *Nefesh ha-Ḥayyim* in Wolfson, "Secrecy, Modesty, and the Feminine," pp. 213–216. A careful glance at that discussion leads us to conclude that the characteristic doctrine of Ḥabad, which I have termed apophatic embodiment, is affirmed by Ḥayyim of Volozhyn. I hope to dedicate a separate study of this phenomenon in the kabbalistic ruminations attributed to the Vilna Gaon and his school. An interesting later repercussion of this intellectual crisscrossing is the reference to Shneur Zalman's notion of infinity and the contraction of the divine in the essay *Halakhic Man* by Joseph B. Soloveitchik, a descendant of Ḥayyim of Volozhyn. See Schwartz, *Religion or Halakha*, pp. 168, 178–183. It should also be noted that Soloveitchik studied as a child with the Ḥabad teacher Baruch Rizberg. See ibid., p. 182, n. 89. On the controversial question of Soloveitchik's relationship to Schneerson in Berlin and later in New York, see Deutsch, *Larger Than Life*, 2: 71–73, 113–119, 279, 282, 289.

119. Levinas, *Difficult Freedom*, p. 225. For translation and analysis of some other relevant texts, see Wolfson, "Secrecy, Modesty, and the Feminine," pp. 198–200.

120. Butler, *Giving an Account of Oneself*, p. 94.

121. Ibid., p. 96. For an alternative and far more sympathetic, I would even say apologetic, reading of the relationship between the ethical and the political in Levinas, or more specifically, his conception of Judaism as alterity and the role assigned to the state of Israel, see Meir, *Levinas's Jewish Thought*, pp. 216–235.

122. See chapter 4, n. 19.

123. Shneur Zalman of Liadi, *Liqquṭei Torah*, Devarim, 2:30b–31a; Schneersohn, *Sha'arei Teshuvah*, 74a; *Imrei Binah*, part 1, 17c; *Torat Ḥayyim: Bere'shit*, 196a; *Perush ha-Millot*, 95b; Schneersohn, *Or ha-Torah: Bemidbar*, 1:20, 2:393; Schneersohn, *Liqquṭei Torah: Torat Shmu'el 5632*, 1:263, 2:545; *Liqquṭei Torah: Torat Shmu'el 5639*, 1:259, 307, 310; Schneersohn, *Be-Sha'ah she-Hiqdimu*, 1:376; Schneerson, *Torat Menaḥem: Hitwwa'aduyyot 5716*, 2:243, 250.

124. Babylonian Talmud, Qiddushin 30a.

125. Schneerson, *Sha'arei Teshuvah*, 74a.

126. Ibid., 142d.

127. Shneur Zalman of Liadi, *Torah Or*, 95a; *Liqquṭei Torah*, Ṣaw, 1:16a, Mas'ei, 1:92a; Schneersohn, *Liqquṭei Torah: Torat Shmu'el 5627*, p. 156; *Liqquṭei Torah: Torat Shmu'el 5631*, 1:192.

128. Schneerson, *Reshimot*, sec. 7, 1:194–201; sec. 15, 2:6; sec. 100, 3:309-310; *Torat Menaḥem: Hitwwa'aduyyot 5712*, 2:36; *Torat Menaḥem: Hitwwa'aduyyot 5715*, 1:285; *Torat Menaḥem: Hitwwa'aduyyot 5718*, 2:87.

129. Shneur Zalman of Liadi, *Ma'amerei Admor ha-Zaqen 5565*, 1:393–394; *Ma'amerei Admor ha-Zaqen 5669*, p. 75; Schneersohn, *Sha'arei Orah*, 61b, 87b; Schneersohn, *Ma'amerei Admor ha-Ṣemaḥ Ṣedeq 5614–5615*, p. 227; Schneersohn, *Liqquṭei Torah: Torat Shmu'el 5631*, 1:192–193; Schneersohn, *Sefer ha-Ma'amarim: Qunṭreisim*, 2:572-573. See also Shneur Zalman of Liadi, *Ma'amerei Admor ha-Zaqen 5563*, 1:200, where Amaleq is described as the "will above the intellect" on the side of the demonic shell, which corresponds to *Keter*, the "will of the heart that is above the intellect" on the side of holiness.

130. The depiction of indolence as royalty without a crown is transmitted as a tradition of R. Sheshet in Babylonian Talmud, Sanhedrin 99b. See Shneur Zalman of Liadi, *Torah Or*, 95a; *Ma'amerei Admor ha-Zaqen 5563*, 1:200; *Ma'amerei Admor ha-Zaqen 5572*, p. 206; Schneersohn, *Sha'arei Orah*, 87b.

131. Schneersohn, *Sefer ha-Ma'amarim 5655–5656*, pp. 20–21. Compare Schneerson, *Reshimat ha-Menorah*, p. 118.

132. Shneur Zalman of Liadi, *Torah Or*, 95a; *Ma'amerei Admor ha-Zaqen 5563*, 1:200–201. See also Schneersohn, *Or Torah: Bemidbar*, 3:1053–1054; *Sefer Tehillim*, p. 232.

133. Shneur Zalman of Liadi, *Ma'amerei Admor ha-Zaqen 5572*, p. 169.

134. On the biblical command to eradicate Amaleq, see Feldman, "*Remember Amalek!*" and on the persistence of Haman and Amaleq as the paradigm of the enemy of the Jewish people, see Horowitz, *Reckless Rites*, pp. 81–146.

135. *Midrash Tanḥuma*, Ki Teṣe, 11; Solomon ben Isaac, *Perushei Rashi al ha-Torah*, p. 233 (ad Exod 17:16); Moses ben Naḥman, *Perushei ha-Torah le-R. Mosheh ben Naḥman*, 1:354 (ad Exod 15:2), 1:373 (ad Exod 17:16).

136. Pedaya, *Name and Sanctuary*, pp. 103–147.

137. Shneur Zalman, *Torah Or*, 121b. The aspect of Haman that is transformed is marked as the "eighth that is within the eighth." See discussion of this symbolism in the concluding part of the postface and other references cited there, n. 152. On the attempt to narrow the gap between the unholiness of Amaleq and the holiness of Israel, see Schneerson, *Reshimot*, sec. 7, 1:201, where the name *Amaleq* is decoded as an acrostic for Amram, Moshe, Levi, and Qehat. Drawing out the implications of this acrostic, whose source, as Schneerson noted, is Shapira, *Megalleh Amuqot*, 1:64d, he wrote: "The sustenance of the shell and the other side is through attachment to the side of holiness. The sustenance of Esau and the members of his household is through Isaac from whom Esau came forth (Pesaḥim 56a, *Wayyiqra Rabbah* 36). Therefore in order to subdue him, a level higher than him, and closer to the source, is necessary" (ibid., pp. 201–202).

138. Schneersohn, *Sha'arei Orah*, 62b, 73b, 74a, 134a. See Schneersohn, *Torat Ḥayyim: Shemot*, 366d; *Ma'amerei Admur ha-Emṣa'i: Wayyiqra*, 2:447; Schneerson, *Liqquṭei Siḥot*, 22:162.

139. The link between Amaleq and knowledge is supported by the comment in Babylonian Talmud, Ḥullin 139b, "Whence do we know of Haman from the Torah? [It says] 'Did you eat from the Tree?' (Gen 3:11)." That is, the preposition *from, ha-min*, has the same consonants as the proper name *haman*, and on this basis a connection is established between Haman and the Tree of Knowledge.

140. Schneersohn, *Ma'amerei Admor ha-Emṣa'i: Qunṭresim*, p. 241.

141. Tishby, *Wisdom of the Zohar*, pp. 447–474; Scholem, *On the Mystical Shape of the Godhead*, pp. 56–87; Wolfson, "Left Contained in the Right"; "Light Through Darkness." Revised versions of these two essays appear in Wolfson, *Luminal Darkness*, pp. 1–55.

142. Schneersohn, *Liqquṭei Torah: Torat Shmu'el 5627*, p. 156. On the inability of Amaleq to be redeemed, see ibid., pp. 179, 183; Schneersohn, *Liqquṭei Torah: Torat Shmu'el 5631*, 1:192, 197, 273–274.

143. This seems to be implied by Schneersohn, *Ma'amerei Admor ha-Ṣemaḥ Ṣedeq, 5614–5615*, p. 227.

144. See Shneur Zalman of Liadi, *Torah Or*, 119d: "the seven evil attributes are nullified, since before him in actuality everything is considered as naught and there is no separate thing."

145. See, however, Schneersohn, *Liqquṭei Torah: Torat Shmu'el 5627*, p. 54, where Zeph 3:9 is cited to support the view that Jacob, who is the aspect of rectification (*tiqqun*), bestows a gift-offering (*minḥah*) to Esau (Gen 32:19), whose root is in the world of chaos (*olam ha-tohu*), in order to annihilate his potency in the world.

146. Schneersohn, *Be-Sha'ah she-Hiqdimu*, 2:769–770. See ibid., 1:210.

147. See chapter 2, n. 222.

148. Shneur Zalman of Liadi, *Ma'amerei Admor ha-Zaqen 5566*, 1:54.

149. Schneersohn, *Be-Sha'ah she-Hiqdimu*, 2:770.

150. The terms *po'el* and *nif'al*, which respectively denote the subject that acts and the object acted upon, are well-attested in the medieval Hebrew philosophical lexicon. For an earlier appearance of the exact phrase *ha-po'el ba-nif'al*, see Abraham Abulafia, *Oṣar Eden Ganuz*, p. 280; *Or ha-Sekhel*, p. 44. For Abulafia, the terms *po'el* and *nif'al* are attributed respectively to the Creator and to matter. See *Sefer ha-Ḥesheq*, p. 29. A possible source for this expression may have been Judah Halevi, *Sefer ha-Kuzari*, 5:20, as noted by Schatz-Uffenheimer in her edition of Dov Baer of Międzyrzecz, *Maggid Devaraw le-Ya'aqov*, p. 19. For an alternative explanation, see Jacobson, "Exile and Redemption in Ger Hasidism," p. 177, n. 10.

151. On the use of the expression *koaḥ ha-po'el ba-nif'al* to denote the presence of the divine efflux in the material universe, see Shneur Zalman of Liadi, *Liqquṭei Amarim: Tanya*, part 2, chapter 2, 77b; part 4, sec. 25, 139a. Although the terminology is much older (see the previous note), it became popular in Ḥasidic sources as a way of marking either the immanence of the divine in every aspect of the material creation or the presence of the Infinite in the Torah. See, for instance, Menaḥem Mendel of Vitebsk, *Peri ha-Areṣ*, p. 36: "In truth, 'You made everything in wisdom' (Ps 104:22), it is necessary that all of them are contained in him, for the potency of the agent is in that which is acted upon." Ibid., p. 116: "The human being is the microcosm that is comprised of all the worlds that emanate from him, blessed be he, for the power of the agent is in that which is acted upon." See

also Jacob Joseph of Polonnoye, *Ben Porat Yosef*, 112d (the source cited there is the commentary to *Sefer Yeṣirah* attributed to Abraham ben David of Posquières but actually written by Joseph ben Shalom Ashkenazi; I have not found this precise language in that work, although the idea is well attested; for example, see Joseph ben Shalom Ashkenazi, *Perush Sefer Yeṣirah*, in *Sefer Yeṣirah*, 3a, 28b–29a); Heller, *Liqquṭim Yeqarim*, sec. 250, 76b; Zev Wolf of Zhitomir, *Or ha-Me'ir*, 1:73, 107, 121, 184, 2:138, 147, 312; Menaḥem Naḥum of Chernobyl, *Me'or Einayim*, 1:1, 31, 133, 138, 228, 230, 285, 294, 368, 2:491.

152. Isa 29:14.

153. Shneur Zalman of Liadi, *Liqquṭei Amarim: Tanya*, part 2, chapter 2, 77b; part 4, sec. 25, 139a.

154. The line appears in the second stanza of the traditional *Aleinu* prayer; see *Seder Avodat Yisra'el*, p. 132.

155. Schneerson, *Iggeret Qodesh*, no. 5093, 14:323; *Iggeret Qodesh*, no. 8816, 23:75; *Torat Menaḥem: Hitwwa'aduyyot 5717*, 1:51, 251–252.

156. Schneerson, *Torat Menaḥem: Hitwwa'aduyyot 5715*, 1:136; *Torat Menaḥem: Hitwwa'aduyyot 5716*, 3:105.

157. Schneerson, *Torat Menaḥem: Hitwwa'aduyyot 5712*, 1:163.

158. Schneerson, *Torat Menaḥem: Hitwwa'aduyyot 5711*, 1:155.

159. The text of Maimonides is from the uncensored version of the *Mishneh Torah*, Melakhim, 11:4.

160. Schneerson, *Torat Menaḥem: Hitwwa'aduyyot 5712*, 1:170, 208; *Torat Menaḥem: Hitwwa'aduyyot 5714*, 1:148. I do not think that Schneerson's perspective accords with the more radical interpretation of Zeph 3:9, attributed to R. Joseph (explicating the position of R. Eliezer) in Babylonian Talmud, Avodah Zarah 24a, to the effect that all the nations will become proselytes in the future-to-come. On balance, Schneerson, following Maimonides, accords with the position of Abbaye that the verse only implies that the nations will turn away from idolatry. See, however, the reference to R. Nissim of Gerona's interpretation added to Schneerson, *Liqquṭei Siḥot*, 23:179, n. 76, and the explication in Ginsburgh, *Kabbalah and Meditation for the Nations*, pp. 86–87, 95–96, n. 80. I thank Jody Myers for reminding me of the reference in Ginsburgh. For a more strident presentation regarding the relationship of Jew and non-Jew, see Ginsburgh, *Rectifying the State*. In that work as well Ginsburgh advocates for the reunification of Jew and non-Jew to serve God together in the messianic era; prior to that time, however, the two must be separated as light and darkness were divided in creation (pp. 25–26). The redemptive task, therefore, is to transform darkness into light (pp. 26–36), but this can only be achieved by preserving the difference between them (p. 143, n. 12). An even stronger stance against non-Jews can be found in other writings of Ginsburgh, including the tirade against Amaleq in *Qunṭres Barukh ha-Gever*, written in response to the massacre of Palestinian worshippers in Hebron by Barukh Goldstein on February 25, 1994, and in the condemnation of Egypt and Babylonia in the pamphlet *Ma'amar Mappelet Bavel*, inspired by the Gulf War of 1991 but published in 1997. I cannot elaborate further here on this important topic in Ginsburgh's thought, although I note that an adequate account would require delving into the Hebrew texts based on his teaching, as these present a more complex and, in my judgment, more negative view concerning the non-Jew. For an extended discussion of the

apocalyptic implications of Ginsburgh's teachings, see Harari, "Mysticism as a Messianic Rhetoric." On the Zionist-nationalistic orientation of Ginsburgh, see Garb, *"The Chosen will Become Herds,"* pp. 93–95, 125–127.

161. Schneersohn, *Derushei Ḥatunah*, 2:547.

162. Schneerson, *Torat Menaḥem: Hitwwa'aduyyot 5751*, 3:405.

163. Schneerson, *Torat Menaḥem: Hitwwa'aduyyot 5713*, 3:56. The Rebbe's comments are an explication of a distinction made by the RaShaB (*Sefer ha-Ma'amarim 5669*, p. 39; see introduction, n. 41) between Moses and the Messiah: in the case of the former, the encompassing light (*or maqqif*) shines within the internal light (*or penimi*) by constricting its essence, whereas in the case of the latter there is a conjunction (*hitḥabberut*) of the two lights to the point that they are completely identical, and thus the encompassing light is revealed in the internal light in its essence without any constriction (*ṣimṣum*) or attire (*hitlabbeshut*).

164. *Midrash Bere'shit Rabba* 1:4, p. 6. Compare Shneur Zalman of Liadi, *Liqquṭei Amarim: Tanya*, part 1, chapter 2, 6a: "The souls of Israel arose in thought, as it is written 'My firstborn son is Israel' (Exod 4:22), 'You are children unto the Lord your God' (Deut 14:1), that is, just as the child derives from the brain of the father, so, as it were, does the soul of each and every Jew derive from his thought and his wisdom, may he be blessed." See chapter 4, n. 160 and chapter 5 at n. 37.

165. *Zohar* 3:253a (*Ra'aya Meheimna*).

166. See Schneersohn, *Derekh Miṣwotekha*, 58b; *Or ha-Torah: Ma'amerei Razal we-Inyanim*, p. 84.

167. See, however, Schneerson, *Torat Menaḥem: Hitwwa'aduyyot 5711*, 1:231–233, where the aspect of transcendence, the shore beyond the river, is described as the source of the different types of the Jewish souls, the souls of the world of emanation and the souls of the worlds of creation, formation, and doing. On the basis of Jer 31:26, the former are called the "seed of the human" (*zera adam*), and the latter the "seed of the beast" (*zera behemah*). Moses, who is in the aspect of the supernal knowledge (*da'at elyon*), is entrusted with the task of imparting knowledge to the latter so that they may be transformed into the former. Compare Schneerson, *Torat Menaḥem: Hitwwa'aduyyot 5714*, 2:82; and, on the symbol of the supernal knowledge, see chapter 2, n. 61.

168. *Zohar* 1:15a. See chapter 1, nn. 157–158.

169. Schneerson, *Torat Menaḥem: Hitwwa'aduyyot 5720*, 2:3–4.

170. Schneerson, *Torat Menaḥem: Sefer ha-Ma'amarim Meluqaṭ*, 1:253.

171. Schneerson, *Torat Menaḥem: Hitwwa'aduyyot 5720*, 2:9.

172. See chapter 1, n. 158.

173. Steinbock, *Phenomenology and Mysticism*, p.263, n. 31. The author asserts that the claim of Dov Baer, and other "mystics within the Jewish tradition," that the "divine soul is specific to Israel . . . cannot be rooted in a biological or vitalistic orientation since one can convert to Judaism. . . . Rather, it concerns a spiritual vocation (which in principle must be open to all), one in which the Jewish person takes on the given, awe-filled responsibility, expressed by the covenant, for the return of all God's people to him and establishing God's exiled presence in human history." The claim that the spiritual vocation assigned to Israel is open to all is an apologetic statement that is contradicted by countless texts, and the

appeal to conversion to substantiate the point reflects a failure to understand the dynamics of this phenomenon according to the kabbalistic interpretation adopted by the Mitteler Rebbe and other Lubavitch masters. I will cite one passage from *Quntres ha-Hitpa'alut*, in *Ma'amerei Admor ha-Emṣa'i: Quntresim,* pp. 139–140, which demonstrates the inaccuracy of Steinbock's surmise: "However, there is something akin to an actual nature in everyone from Israel also in his [task to fulfill] 'Shun evil and do good' (Ps 34:15) in actuality, precisely from the perspective of the root of his divine soul, which is the natural and essential aspect, and not from the perspective of his choice or his worship at all." From this we may conclude that the distinctiveness of the Jew's calling is determined primarily on the basis of ontology and not on behavior or functionality.

174. Babylonian Talmud, Yevamot 48b, 62a, 97b; Bekhorot 47a.

175. Azulai, *Midbar Qedemot*, 3:3, 10b.

176. Tosefta, Soṭah 7:5; Babylonian Talmud, Shevu'ot 39a; Porton, *The Stranger Within Your Gates*, pp. 32, 42, 120, 177, 217, 242, n. 71, 311, n. 250, 354, n. 22.

177. Schneerson, *Torat Menaḥem: Hitwwa'aduyyot 5718*, 2:61–62.

178. See chapter 4, n. 107. On the status of the convert's soul and the body, see Schneerson, *Iggerot Qodesh*, no. 2666, 9:53.

179. Schneerson, *Torat Menaḥem: Hitwwa'aduyyot 5743*, 2:925. On the depiction of conversion as a "new arousal" (*hit'orerut ḥadashah*) of a soul that already exists in the body of the convert, see Shneur Zalman of Liadi, *Ma'amerei Admor ha-Zaqen: Al Inyanim*, p. 205. Also relevant to this understanding of temporality implied by the phenomenon of conversion is the rabbinic belief that the souls of converts were present at Sinai (see n. 176, this chapter). This presence suggests that when the conversion takes place, it is a reversion to an original condition. See Schneerson, *Torat Menaḥem: Hitwwa'aduyyot 5714*, 1:248.

180. Schneersohn, *Sha'arei Teshuvah*, 142d; *Imrei Binah*, part 1, 86d–87a; *Torat Ḥayyim: Bere'shit*, 121b–c, 124c, 125a–b. The source for the souls of the righteous Gentiles is similarly identified as the shell of *nogah*, which is also the source of the natural soul in the Jew, whereas the soul of all other Gentiles is from the three shells of impurity. See Hillel ben Meir of Paritch, *Liqquṭei Be'urim,* on *Quntres ha-Hitpa'alut*, in Schneersohn, *Ma'amerei Admor ha-Emṣa'i: Quntresim,* p. 144; Schneerson, *Iggerot Qodesh*, no. 2666, 9:53. These passages are mentioned by Loewenthal, *Communicating the Infinite*, p. 297, n. 128. While the positive remark concerning the righteous of the Gentiles is emphasized, no mention is made about the corresponding negative remark regarding the rest of the Gentiles. It is said of them that whatever good they do is motivated by egocentric desires and not for the sake of fulfilling the will of God or out of a sense of compassion for fellow human beings.

181. The expression is rabbinic in origin, but the key text that influenced the Ḥabad material is *Zohar* 1:13a–b.

182. Schneersohn, *Ma'amerei Admor ha-Emṣa'i: Hanaḥot*, p. 10. See Shneur Zalman of Liadi, *Ma'amerei Admor ha-Zaqen 5565*, 1:372–373.

183. Schneersohn, *Ner Miṣwah we-Torah Or*, 141a.

184. Schneerson, *Torat Menaḥem: Hitwwa'aduyyot 5720*, 2:107–108.

185. Schneerson, *Torat Menaḥem: Hitwwa'aduyyot 5750*, 4:242.

186. See n. 60, this chapter.

187. Schneerson, *Torat Menaḥem: Hitwwa'aduyyot 5717*, 3:242.

188. A transcribed version of the Yiddish is printed in Schneerson, *Liqquṭei Siḥot,* 2:407–408, and a Hebrew translation appears in *Torat Menaḥem: Hitwwa'aduyyot 5712,* 3:186–188.

189. The disclosure in the Temple of the Tetragrammaton, which is above time and place, is upheld as the messianic revelation in Schneerson, *Qunṭres Inyanah shel Torat ha-Ḥasidut,* p. 5.

190. A similar explanation is given for the rabbinic explanation of the miracle of Ḥanukah as the light of the menorah going out from the Temple to benefit all the inhabitants of the world. See Schneerson, *Torat Menaḥem: Hitwwa'aduyyot 5750,* 2:17.

191. Schneerson, *Torat Menaḥem: Hitwwa'aduyyot 5716,* 2:357.

192. Schneerson, *Liqquṭei Siḥot,* 6:317–318.

193. Moses ben Maimon, *Mishneh Torah,* Melakhim 8:11.

194. *Zohar* 3:221b.

195. Judah Halevi, *Sefer ha-Kuzari,* 2:36, 44.

Postface

1. Babylonian Talmud, Berakhot 8a. Ely Stillman kindly reminded me of the following dictum transmitted in the name of R. Ḥunah in the Palestinian Talmud, Berakhot 5:1, 8d: "Whoever does not enter a synagogue in this world will not enter a synagogue in the future-to-come." It is plausible that Simḥah Bunim of Przysucha had this passage in mind as well.

2. Yehuda Aryeh Leib of Gur, *Sefat Emet*: *Devarim*, p. 210.

3. Galli, *Franz Rosenzweig*, p. 259.

4. Rosenzweig, *The Star of Redemption*, pp. 314–315.

5. Hollander, "On the Significance," pp. 562–563; *Exemplarity and Chosenness*, pp. 189–191.

6. Schwarzschild, "Franz Rosenzweig's Anecdotes,", pp. 210–211. I am grateful to Robert Gibbs for drawing my attention to Schwarzschild's study.

7. Galli, *Franz Rosenzweig*, pp. 259–260. The brief exchange between Rosenzweig and Cohen reflects their divergence regarding the nature of history, myth, time, and the messianic future. See Kluback, "Time and History."

8. Scholem, *The Messianic Idea in Judaism*, p. 35, and compare the analysis in Mosès, *The Angel of History*, pp. 129–144, especially 131–133. For discussion of Rosenzweig's apocalyptic temporality, see Mosès, *System and Revelation*, pp. 174–217; *The Angel of History*, pp. 49–61; Wolfson, "Facing the Effaced," pp. 55–57; Dagan, "Hatramah," pp. 392–396, 405–406. While I accept much of Dagan's presentation—indeed, in many respects, it parallels my own analysis, though he seems unaware of my study published in 1997—I am not certain of his claim that Rosenzweig's eschatology negates the apocalyptic propensity, since the future can be drawn into the present at any and each moment (ibid., pp. 398–400). I would argue, to the contrary, that this potential is itself apocalyptic in nature, related to the possibility of hastening the end, a theme that Dagan himself discusses (ibid., pp. 401–403). In a manner similar to my own, Dagan also notes that Rosenzweig

operates with two types of temporality, the linear-historical and the cyclic-ritualistic (ibid., pp. 406–407). However, there is a crucial difference between our approaches. According to Dagan, there is an apparent contradiction: for the one that draws the future into the present, there would seemingly be no need for the cycle of ritual, whereas for the one that lives this cyclical time, and hence turns the end into the beginning, why is there need for the intrusion of the future perpetually in the present? Dagan's response is that the individual's drawing of the future into the present is dependent on the sense of community, which establishes love of the other, and thus there is a need for both forms of temporality. In my view, Rosenzweig's conception of time embraces what I have called a linear circularity or a circular linearity (see introduction, n. 118), according to which there is no contradiction, since the eternity of time in the present is made possible by the return of the future to the past that has been. I have elaborated on the hermeneutics of Rosenzweig's diremptive temporality in "Light Does Not Talk."

9. Wolfson, "The Cut That Binds," p. 121.

10. Kafka, *Parables and Paradoxes*, p. 81.

11. Wolfson, "The Cut That Binds," pp. 106, 109–111.

12. Derrida, *Psyche*, p. 24. For a comparative analysis of the messianic temporality in Rosenzweig and Derrida, see Hollander, *Exemplarity and Chosenness*, pp. 184–201. The Derridean conception of the unpredictability of the event as the inessential essence of time has been confirmed by other philosophers. For instance, see Romano, "Le possible et l'événement"; and Dastur, "Phenomenology of the Event." See n. 68, this chapter.

13. Derrida, *Psyche*, p. 39.

14. Ibid., pp. 45, 47.

15. Ibid., p. 46.

16. Ibid., p. 30.

17. Hodge, *Derrida on Time*, p. 7.

18. See Wolfson, "Assaulting the Border," pp. 480–482. Some of the texts cited and analyzed in that study are repeated here.

19. Derrida, *Specters of Marx*, p. 59. See the analysis in Hamacher, "Lingua Amissa."

20. Derrida and Vattimo, *Religion*, p. 17.

21. Ibid., p. 51.

22. Ibid., p. 31.

23. Irigaray, *Sexes and Genealogies*, p. 53.

24. Keller, *God and Power*, p. 63.

25. Ettinger, *Matrixial Borderspace*, p. 85.

26. Keller, *God and Power*, p. 64.

27. Derrida, *Specters of Marx*, p. 37.

28. Ibid.

29. Derrida, *Adieu to Emmanuel Levinas*, p. 67.

30. See chapter 1, n. 174.

31. Schneerson, *Iggerot Qodesh*, no. 2316, 8:71.

32. Schneersohn, *Quntres ha-Tefillah*, p. 12; *Tract on Prayer*, pp. 32–35. See introduction, n. 7.

33. The interpretative stance that I have adopted is informed by the technical use of the term *indifference* in Schelling's thought. For a more elaborate discussion, see Wolfson, *Language. Eros, Being*, pp. 99–105, and the brief review in chapter 2, at n. 199.

34. Shneur Zalman of Liadi, *Ma'amerei Admor ha-Zaqen 5566*, 1:165.

35. Schneerson, *Torat Menaḥem: Hitwwa'aduyyot 5721*, 2:27.

36. Schneerson, *Sefer ha-Ma'amarim 5730–5731*, p. 129.

37. For references, see chapter 5, n. 1.

38. Schneerson, *Torat Menaḥem: Hitwwa'aduyyot 5747*, 3:111.

39. See chapter 4, nn. 142–143.

40. Schneerson, *Torat Menaḥem: Hitwwa'aduyyot 5716*, 2:310.

41. Menaḥem Mendel Schneerson, *Sefer ha-Siḥot 5752*, p. 40.

42. Kravel-Tovi and Bilu, "Work of the Present," pp. 69–75.

43. Schneerson, *Sefer ha-Siḥot 5752*, p. 173; *Torat Menaḥem: Hitwwa'aduyyot 5752*, 1:277; *Torat Menaḥem: Hitwwa'aduyyot 5752*, 2:252.

44. Moses ben Maimon, *Mishneh Torah*, Melakhim 11:1.

45. Schneerson, *Liqquṭei Siḥot*, 20:234; *Torat Menaḥem: Hitwwa'aduyyot 5717*, 1:299 (in that context, the comment is connected to the renowned saying of the sixth Rebbe, *le'altar li-teshuvah le'altar li-ge'ullah*); *Torat Menaḥem: Hitwwa'aduyyot 5717*, 2:40.

46. Schneerson, *Liqquṭei Siḥot*, 20:23; 37:126; *Sefer ha-Ma'amarim Meluqaṭ*, 2:198. See also ibid., p. 262; *Torat Menaḥem: Hitwwa'aduyyot 5745*, 5:2618–2619.

47. For a more extensive discussion, see Wolfson, *Alef, Mem, Tau*, pp. 107–117.

48. Shneur Zalman of Liadi, *Liqquṭei Amarim: Tanya*, part 2, chapter 7, pp. 162–163.

49. Based on the liturgical formulation *yhwh melekh, yhwh malakh, yhwh yimlokh le'olam wa'ed.*

50. Isa 54:7.

51. Schneersohn, *Derekh Miṣwotekha*, 151a–b.

52. On the connotation of *rega qaṭan*, see also Shneur Zalman of Liadi, *Liqquṭei Torah*, Derushim le-Rosh ha-Shanah, 2:61a, Shir ha-Shirim, 2:3d; Schneersohn, *Torat Shmu'el: Sefer ha-Ma'amarim 5633*, 1: 65; Schneerson, *Torat Menaḥem: Hitwwa'aduyyot 5716*, 3:83. For the use of the term to specify the ephemerality of human existence, see Schneerson, *Iggerot Qodesh*, no. 10,252, 27:254, and *Torat Menaḥem: Hitwwa'aduyyot 5720*, 2:186.

53. Schneerson, *Iggerot Qodesh*, no. 9109, 24:93.

54. Schneerson, *Torat Menaḥem: Hitwwa'aduyyot 5712*, 3:130; see also *Torat Menaḥem: Hitwwa'aduyyot 5714*, 1:326. On the use of the expression *tekhef u-mi-yad* to denote an immediate response without hesitation, see Shneur Zalman of Liadi, *Liqquṭei Amarim: Tanya*, part 3, chapter, 11, 100a.

55. This expression was used by the previous Ḥabad masters, including the sixth Rebbe. See Schneersohn, *Sefer ha-Siḥot 5680–5687*, p. 169; *Sefer ha-Siḥot 5688–5691*, p. 163; *Sefer ha-Siḥot 5706–5710*, pp. 304, 387. The seventh Rebbe employed this phrase in conjunction with the hope for the immediate arrival of the messianic redemption hundreds of times in his oral discourses and written documents.

56. See introduction, n. 17.

57. See introduction, n. 18.

58. Shneur Zalman of Liadi, *Liqquṭei Amarim: Tanya*, part 1, chapter 23, 28a–b.

59. Compare Schneersohn, *Qunṭres u-Ma'yan*, 9:1, p. 84: "When it arises in his will to move his feet, he moves them immediately and without delay, with no deferral of time at all [*tekhef u-mi-yad beli shum shehiyyat zeman kelal*]."

60. That this motif was not unique to Ḥabad can be seen, for instance, in the following passage in Menaḥem Naḥum of Chernobyl, *Me'or Einayim*, 2:430, "This world is in time, but prior to the world there was no aspect of time at all. Therefore, there is no time in the rectification of repentance but for the moment [*ein zeman be-tiqqun ha-teshuvah ella ke-rega*], since it comes to be beyond temporality. Hence, he rectifies everything as if in the blink of the eye and there is no need for a delay of time. He who imagines in his mind that repentance is dependent on time, this is not complete repentance, for one must believe that everything will be rectified without time. . . . For it is not repentance at all when one does not believe that repentance is above time, and that everything will be rectified in a moment."

61. See chapter 4, nn. 51–52.

62. Shneur Zalman of Liadi, *Ma'amerei Admor ha-Zaqen 5566*, 2:755.

63. Shneur Zalman of Liadi, *Liqquṭei Amarim: Tanya*, part 3, chapter 11, 100a–b.

64. Ibid., part 1, chapter 25, 31b.

65. Shneur Zalman of Liadi, *Torah Or*, 94b. See *Liqquṭei Torah*, Derushim le-Shemini Aṣeret, 1:91a: "This is the matter of the drawing down in the aforementioned aspect of betrothal [*qiddushin*], which is above the aspect of encompassing all worlds, the aspect of the betrothal ring, in which everything is equal in relation to him, he was, he is, and he will be, in one moment, and there is no change in him."

66. Shneur Zalman of Liadi, *Ma'amerei Admur ha-Zaqen 5572*, p. 255. Technically speaking, according to the teaching of the Alter Rebbe, the notion of eternality (*niṣḥiyyut*) is itself an aspect of temporality, the limitless extension of the flux of time (*hemshekh ha-zeman*), and hence it should not be applied to the infinite essence that completely transcends the category of time (*geder ha-zeman*). The compresence of the three temporal modes signified by the Tetragrammaton, and the messianic redemption linked to this gnosis, is neither temporal nor eternal. Compare Shneur Zalman of Liadi, *Liqquṭei Torah*, Derushim le-Shabbat Shuvah, 2:67c.

67. See introduction, n. 14.

68. Schneerson, *Torat Menaḥem: Hitwwa'aduyyot 5716*, 2:239. Influenced by many of the same philosophers, who have shaped my own thinking, particularly Husserl, Heidegger, and Merleau-Ponty, Dastur, "Phenomenology of the Event," similarly characterizes the "transitional character" of time by "its non-being or non-essence." The "structural eventuality of time," accordingly, implies that "time is in itself what brings contingency, unpredictability, and chance into the world" (p. 179). Building on the Heideggerian notion of time as "ekstasis" and the Levinasian conception of "dia-chrony," Dastur conjectures: "The event in the strong sense of the word is therefore always a surprise, something which takes possession of us in an unforeseen manner, without warning, and which brings us toward an unanticipated future. The *eventum*, which arises in the becoming, constitutes something which is irremediably excessive in comparison to the usual representation of

time as flow. It appears as something that dislocates time and gives a new form to it, something that puts the flow of time out of joint and changes its direction. . . . For the event, as such, is upsetting. It does not integrate itself as a specific moment in the flow of time. . . . It does not happen in a world—it is, on the contrary, as if a new world opens up through its happening, The event constitutes the critical moment of temporality—a critical moment which nevertheless allows the continuity of time. . . . Against all expectation, even if it has been partially expected and anticipated, such is in fact the 'essence' of the event. Based on this we could say without paradox that it is an 'impossible possible.' The event, in its internal contradiction, is the impossible which happens, in spite of everything, in a terrifying or marvelous manner. It always comes to us by surprise, or from that side whence, precisely, it was not expected" (pp. 182–183). For an elaboration of the author's "phenomenological chrono-logy," see Dastur, *Telling Time*. I have cited Dastur at length because her depiction of the inherent eventuality of time bears a striking affinity to my analysis of the diremptive nature of time and messianic expectation in the seventh Rebbe of Lubavitch. The coming of the Messiah is the "impossible possible," the event that cannot occur in the temporal flow of the world but which nonetheless is the very condition that accounts for the continuity of time in the world.

69. Schneersohn, *Sefer ha-Siḥot 5702*, p. 110.

70. The formulation *de-lo ikkevan afillu ke-heref ayin* is derived from the explanation of Exod 12:41 in the *Mekhilta de-Rabbi Ishmael*, p. 51. The source for Schneerson likely would have been the eleventh-century biblical commentary of Rashi to that verse, where the words of the older rabbinic midrash are cited. See Solomon ben Isaac, *Perushei Rashi al ha-Torah*, p. 211 (ad Exod 12:41).

71. Schneerson, *Torat Menaḥem: Hitwwa'aduyyot 5747*, 3:111, 260; *Torat Menaḥem: Hitwwa'aduyyot 5750*, 2:249; *Torat Menaḥem: Hitwwa'aduyyot 5751*, 4:30.

72. Schneerson, *Torat Menaḥem: Hitwwa'aduyyot 5712*, 2:242. Here it is pertinent to recall the substance of Schneerson's critique of Einstein's relativity theory in *Iggerot Qodesh*, no. 283, 2:224–225: the scientific conception relates only to one aspect of time, the time that is measurable (*zeman ha-meshu'ar*), but not to the essence of the flux of time (*eṣem hemshekh ha-zeman*), the root of time (*shoresh ha-zeman*), which is designated *seder ha-zemannim*. On this rabbinic terminology and its reverberation in kabbalistic sources, see Wolfson, *Alef, Mem, Tau,* pp. 62, 73, 77–79, 84–88, 94. For the use of the expression in Ḥabad sources, see ibid., pp. 109–111, 115. On the distinction between the two aspects of temporality, see Schneerson, *Iggerot Qodesh*, no. 156, 1:294, and on the locution *hemshekh ha-zeman*, see Shneur Zalman of Liadi, *Liqquṭei Torah*, Derushim le-Shabbat Shuvah, 2:67c; Schneerson, *Torat Menaḥem: Hitwwa'aduyyot 5712*, 1:244; *Torat Menaḥem: Ma'amarim Meluqaṭ*, 2:422; and the introduction, n. 31.

73. Schneerson, *Torat Menaḥem: Hitwwa'aduyyot 5745*, 5:2615.

74. Palestinian Talmud, Berakhot 2:3, 5a. Compare Schneerson, *Torat Menaḥem: Ma'amarim Meluqaṭ*, 4:319.

75. Schneerson, *Torat Menaḥem: Hitwwa'aduyyot 5745*, 5:2622.

76. *Zohar* 1:179a.

77. Ibid., 1:129a.

78. Babylonian Talmud, Avodah Zarah 4b.

79. Schneerson, *Torat Menaḥem: Hitwwa'aduyyot 5745*, 5:2622–2623.

80. Schneerson, *Torat Menaḥem: Hitwwa'aduyyot 5747*, 3:111.

81. Schneerson, *Torat Menaḥem: Hitwwa'aduyyot 5713*, 2:85.

82. The metaphor of crossing the river symbolizes the disclosure of the transcendental essence that is beyond the emanation. See Shneur Zalman of Liadi, *Liqquṭei Torah*, Ṣaw, 1:15d, 17c. The image is related exegetically to the positioning of the forefathers of the Jews "beyond the river" (Josh 24:2); see chapter 6, n. 43.

83. Shneur Zalman of Liadi, *Seder Tefillot*, 285d–286a.

84. Schneerson, *Torat Menaḥem: Hitwwa'aduyyot 5750*, 2:241.

85. Babylonian Talmud, Sanhedrin 97b.

86. *Zohar* 1:129a–b: "Praiseworthy are those who repent, for in one moment, in one day, in one second, they draw close to the blessed holy One, something that is not possible even for the completely righteous, who draw close to the blessed holy One over several years."

87. Schneerson, *Torat Menaḥem: Hitwwa'aduyyot 5714*, 2:210–211.

88. The imminent possibility of the advent of the eschaton underlies the seventh Rebbe's conviction regarding the inestimable value of each moment of the final generation of the exile, the footsteps of the Messiah. See Schneerson, *Iggerot Qodesh*, no. 1542, 6:17; no. 4701, 13:444.

89. *Mekhilta de-Rabbi Ishmael*, p. 73; *Midrash Tanḥuma*, Bo, 13.

90. Solomon ben Isaac, *Perushei Rashi al ha-Torah*, p. 214 (ad Exod 13:14).

91. Schneerson, *Liqquṭei Siḥot*, 31:61–68; for an abbreviated Yiddish version of the talk, see *Liqquṭei Siḥot*, 6:268–270.

92. Schneerson, *Torat Menaḥem: Hitwwa'aduyyot 5744*, 1:65.

93. Schneerson, *Sefer ha-Siḥot 5751*, 2:595; see ibid., 2:692.

94. A remark that Schneerson made to a reporter from the *New York Post,* cited in Lipkin, *Ḥeshbono shel Olam*, p. 149.

95. A view expressed by Avraham Alashvili, cited ibid., p. 167. See also Kohanzad, "Messianic Doctrine," pp. 147–148.

96. Babylonian Talmud, Ta'anit 31a., and see the comment of Rashi, *ad locum*, which matches Schneerson's formulation more precisely. The source for Rashi apparently was *Midrash Shemot Rabbah* 23:15, in *Midrash Rabbah im Kol ha-Mefarshim*, 3:267.

97. Schneerson, *Torat Menaḥem: Hitwwa'aduyyot 5752*, 1:241–242.

98. Galli, *Franz Rosenzweig*, p. 259. German original in Rosenzweig, *Der Mensch und sein Werk*, p. 201.

99. Benjamin, *Selected Writings,* vol. 4: *1938–1940*, p. 397. It should be noted that Benjamin appropriates the traditional Jewish messianic belief in order to depict the task of the historian as forging a constellation of the past and the present, as constructing a continuum out of the inherently discontinuous nature of time. As a consequence, the historian "establishes a conception of the present as now-time shot through with splinters of messianic time" (ibid.). See Weber, "Elijah's Futures"; Hamacher, "'Now.'"

100. *Midrash Tehillim* 90:19, 198a; commentary of Rashi to Babylonian Talmud, Sukkah 41a; *Zohar* 1:28a; 2:59a, 108a; 3:221a; Schneerson, *Torat Menaḥem: Hitwwa'aduyyot 5714*, 1:82. On the third Temple, see *Iggerot Qodesh*, no. 1112, 4:394;

no. 4485, 13:217; *Torat Menaḥem: Hitwwa'aduyyot 5712*, 2:77; *Torat Menaḥem: Hitwwa'aduyyot 5715*, 1:283; *Torat Menaḥem: Hitwwa'aduyyot 5715*, 2:240; *Torat Menaḥem: Hitwwa'aduyyot 5716*, 2:357; *Torat Menaḥem: Hitwwa'aduyyot 5717*, 3:198; *Torat Menaḥem: Hitwwa'aduyyot 5718*, 1:242; *Liqquṭei Siḥot*, 36:130; 39:10–11. In some of these passages, Schneerson follows the opinion expressed by Maimonides (*Mishneh Torah*, Melakhim 11:1) that the future Temple will be built by the human hands of the Messiah. On the synthesis between the "miraculous" and the "naturalistic" perspectives in the seventh Rebbe's messianic teaching, see Gotlieb, "Habad's Harmonistic Approach," pp. 253–254.

101. See, for example, Schneerson, *Iggerot Qodesh*, no. 89, 1:162; no. 1112, 4:394; no. 1849, 6:345; no. 2323, 8:80; no. 5629, 15:311; no. 7074, 19:45, no. 7398, 19:399; no. 8495, 22:302; no. 9012, 23:431, no. 9015, 23:434; no. 10,070, 27:77; no. 10,167, 27:173; no. 10,618, 28:58; *Liqquṭei Siḥot*, 31:147, 225, 241, 244; 32:190, 195; 34:252; 36:130, 255, 37:60, 106, 117, 136, 173, 177–179 (see n. 150, this chapter); 39:290, 338, 352, 374, 391, 449, 453, 468; *Torat Menaḥem: Hitwwa'aduyyot 5711*, 2:89; *Torat Menaḥem: Hitwwa'aduyyot 5715*, 1:283, 334; *Torat Menaḥem: Hitwwa'aduyyot 5717*, 3:198; *Torat Menaḥem: Hitwwa'aduyyot 5718*, 1:242; *Torat Menaḥem: Hitwwa'aduyyot 5718*, 3:217; *Torat Menaḥem: Ma'amarim Meluqaṭ*, 1:245, 342, 377; 2:168, 177, 185, 192, 405; 3:43, 121, 418; 4:111.

102. Schneerson, *Torat Menaḥem: Hitwwa'aduyyot 5714*, 2:24–25; *Torat Menaḥem: Hitwwa'aduyyot 5718*, 2:60; *Torat Menaḥem: Hitwwa'aduyyot 5718*, 3:238; *Torat Menaḥem: Ma'amarim Meluqaṭ*, 1:9; *Liqquṭei Siḥot*, 30:42, 124; 38:233.

103. Palestinian Talmud, Yoma 1:1, 38c; Schneerson, *Iggeret Qodesh*, no. 5629, 15:311; no. 10,618, 28:57; *Torat Menaḥem: Hitwwa'aduyyot 5714*, 2:25; *Liqquṭei Siḥot*, 36:130.

104. Schneerson, *Torat Menaḥem: Hitwwa'aduyyot 5714*, 2:49. See Schneerson, *Torat Menaḥem: Hitwwa'aduyyot 5720*, 1:475; *Torat Menaḥem: Hitwwa'aduyyot 5720*, 2:11; *Liqquṭei Siḥot*, 31:77. And see Schneerson, *Torat Menaḥem: Hitwwa'aduyyot 5716*, 2:353, where the agency for drawing down the already existing third Temple is ascribed to Jewish women—the larger point made in that context is that the women of the generation of the Messiah are comparable to the righteous women of the generation of the desert. See Schneerson, *Torat Menaḥem: Hitwwa'aduyyot 5720*, 1:475.

105. See chapter 2, n. 301.

106. Schneerson, *Iggerot Qodesh*, no. 4497, 13:230; *Liqquṭei Siḥot*, 7:104, 22:79.

107. Schneersohn, *Sefer ha-Siḥot 5688–5691*, p. 42; Schneerson, *Torat Menaḥem: Hitwwa'aduyyot 5714*, 1:326; *Torat Menaḥem: Hitwwa'aduyyot 5716*, 1:283; *Torat Menaḥem: Hitwwa'aduyyot 5747*, 2:173, 236; *Torat Menaḥem: Sefer ha-Ma'amarim Meluqaṭ*, 1:298; *Liqquṭei Siḥot*, 25:481, 29:286; *Sefer ha-Siḥot 5748*, 1:279; *Sefer ha-Siḥot 5750*, 2:538. In the last years of his life, the seventh Rebbe emphasized that even the task of polishing the buttons had been completed. See Schneerson, *Torat Menaḥem: Hitwwa'aduyyot 5747*, 2:301; *Sefer ha-Siḥot 5748*, 1:355; *Sefer ha-Siḥot 5751*, 1:138; *Sefer ha-Siḥot 5751*, 2:595; *Sefer ha-Siḥot 5752*, pp. 163, 351.

108. Babylonian Talmud, Ḥagigah 12b.

109. *Keter Shem Ṭov*, pp. 45–46. The interpretation of the rabbinic aggadah is reported in the name of the Maggid of Międzyrzecz by his student Gershon Lutzker in Heller,

Yosher Divrei Emet, sec. 3, 111a. For discussion of this passage, see Krassen, *Uniter of Heaven and Earth*, pp. 174–175. The same tradition is reported, however, in the name of the Beshṭ by his grandson, Moses Ḥayyim Ephraim of Sudlikov, *Degel Maḥaneh Efrayim*, pp. 3 and 118. A similar explanation of the primordial light being hidden for the righteous in the Torah is combined with the capacity of the Beshṭ to discern matters by gazing into the text of the *Zohar* in the tale of the Beshṭ and Jonah of Kamenka concerning the oxen of his brother Barukh included in *Shivḥei ha-Beshṭ*, pp. 136–138; for an English rendition, see *In Praise of the Baal Shem Tov*, pp. 89–90. The tale is cited and analyzed by Schneerson, *Sefer ha-Ma'amarim 5732–5733*, p. 484. The same combination of the practice of opening the *Zohar* and the belief that God hid the primordial light in the Torah is found in another tale from *Shivḥei ha-Beshṭ*, pp. 84–85; *In Praise of the Baal Shem Tov*, p. 49. See also Zev Wolf of Zhitomir, *Or ha-Me'ir*, 1:189. See, however, Menaḥem Naḥum of Chernobyl, *Me'or Einayim*, 1:145, where the notion that God secreted the light in the Torah is followed by the tradition that the Beshṭ would look into the Torah to discover information about mundane matters. These and some other sources were cited by Mondshine, *Shivhei ha-Baal Shem Tov*, pp. 262–263.

110. The view attributed to the Beshṭ is anticipated in a passage in the zoharic section of *Midrash ha-Ne'lam* on Ruth. See *Zohar Ḥadash*, 85a–b.

111. Schneerson, *Torat Menaḥem: Hitwwa'aduyyot 5711*, 1:55.

112. Babylonian Talmud, Berakhot 6b.

113. Schneerson, *Torat Menaḥem: Hitwwa'aduyyot 5751*, 4:30.

114. The first word of the Hebrew *bekha* is composed of the consonants *beit* and *kaf*, whose numerical value is twenty-two, which relates to the date of Ḥaya Mushqa's passing from the world, 22 Shevaṭ 5748 (February 10, 1988).

115. Schneerson, *Torat Menaḥem: Hitwwa'aduyyot 5752*, 2:266.

116. The words are a direct citation from Schneerson's response to the request of him by Gary Tochman, a correspondent from CNN, to sum up his message about the Messiah. The exchange, which took place as the seventh Rebbe was handing out dollars on 12 Ḥeshvan 5752 (October 20, 1991), is available on YouTube with the title "The Rebbe's message to the world about Moshiach." It also can be accessed at http://www.chabad.org/multimedia/media_cdo/aid132931/jewish/CNN-With-the-Rebbe.htm. Initially, Schneerson replied to Tochman's query, "It was printed in all the press of the countries: Moshiach is ready to come now, it is only on our part to do something additional in the realm of goodness and kindness." Extrapolating what he thought to be the gist of Schneerson's comments, Tochman reflected back to him, "So people should be doing goodness and kindness for him to come?" To which Schneerson retorted, "At least a little more, then Moshiach will come immediately."

117. Schneerson, *Torat Menaḥem: Hitwwa'aduyyot 5752*, 2:250–251. The expectation (ibid., 2:266) that his father-in-law and wife will rise from the grave should be contextualized in terms of the coupling of two eschatological beliefs, the coming of the Messiah and the resurrection of the dead. It is not, as some enthusiastic followers maintain, proof that the seventh Rebbe subscribed to the view that the redeemer, in particular, is to be resurrected. See also Schneerson, *Iggerot Qodesh*, no. 5083, 14:315; *Torat Menaḥem: Hitwwa'aduyyot 5710*, p. 114 (the hope expressed there is explicitly that the sixth Rebbe

should come back and lead us to greet the Messiah). Regarding the promise of the third Temple, see n. 100, this chapter.

118. For reference, see chapter 1, n. 49.

119. Schneerson, *Torat Menaḥem: Hitwwa'aduyyot 5718*, 2:132. An earlier version of this talk, which was delivered on Purim 5718 (1958), is printed in Schneerson, *Liqquṭei Siḥot*, 11:334.

120. Babylonian Talmud, Sanhedrin 97a.

121. Schneerson, *Torat Menaḥem: Hitwwa'aduyyot 5750*, 2:174. See Schneerson, *Sefer ha-Siḥot 5751*, 2:692.

122. See chapter 1, n. 136.

123. This is not to deny some interesting changes that have occurred in Ḥabad communities, in great measure inspired by the seventh Rebbe's teaching, that empower women in some respect. See further analysis in chapter 5 and references to other scholars cited in the relevant notes.

124. See chapter 1, n. 133.

125. Schneersohn, *Qunṭres ha-Tefillah*, the fourth page of the unnumbered facsimile of the handwritten introduction by Yosef Yiṣḥaq Schneersohn (*Tract on Prayer*, p. 21).

126. Schneerson, *Sefer ha-Siḥot 5704*, pp. 114–115.

127. For references, see chapter 4, n. 13.

128. Schneerson, *Torat Menaḥem: Hitwwa'aduyyot 5713*, 2:88.

129. Schneerson, *Sefer ha-Ma'amarim 5710–5711*, part 2, pp. 289–290. Compare the explication of this passage in Schneerson, *Torat Menaḥem: Hitwwa'aduyyot 5711*, 2:213–214.

130. Shneur Zalman of Liadi, *Liqquṭei Amarim: Tanya*, part 5, 161b. On the expression *kelot ha-nefesh*, see chapter 1, n. 50.

131. For references to this motif in primary and secondary sources, see Wolfson, *Circle in the Square*, pp. 110–112, 227–228, nn. 158–160 and 228, n. 168. See also Fine, *Physician of the Soul,* pp. 137, 242–243, 245, 256, 396, nn. 41–42.

132. Shneur Zalman of Liadi, *Ma'amerei Admor ha-Zaqen 5566*, 1:9. In his *Qunṭres ha-Tefillah*, pp. 11–12 (*Tract on Prayer*, pp. 32–33), the RaShaB argues that, even with respect to the "aspect of realization that is entirely without limit" (*hitpa'alut bilti mugbelet legamrei*), one can still speak of different levels (*ḥilluqei madregot*), for example, the distinction between the "running of the rectification" (*raṣo de-tiqqun*) and the "running that is from the aspect of chaos" (*raṣo she-mi-beḥinat ha-tohu*).

133. See chapter 1, n. 22.

134. Schneerson, *Torat Menaḥem: Hitwwa'aduyyot 5713*, 3:56.

135. On this expression, see the introduction, nn. 106–107.

136. Schneerson, *Torat Menaḥem: Hitwwa'aduyyot 5718*, 3:54–55. On the depiction of the ḥasid as a "part" of the Rebbe, see Schneersohn, *Sefer ha-Siḥot 5701*, p. 37, and on the bond between disciple and master, see Schneerson, *Reshimot*, sec. 9, 1:255–256; *Iggerot Qodesh*, no. 809, 4:52–53. My claim that the seventh Rebbe's eschatological mission sought to undermine the distinction between savior and saved dovetails with the portrayal of Schneerson as a "Gnostic redeemer" intent on maximizing personal redemption through a change in consciousness with respect to the nature of God and the world

presented by Kohanzad, "Messianic Doctrine," pp. 21–23, 123, 148, 176, 228–229. The philosophical argument that I have offered also complements the sociological analysis of Ḥabad offered by Wexler, *Mystical Interactions*, pp. 130-139. More specifically, Wexler argues that the "social, contextual and theoretical frameworks for understanding Habad may more fruitfully be initiated from perspectives arising from post-modern social conditions and from post-modern social theorizing." Wexler surmises, moreover, that Ḥabad should be viewed as a prophetic movement, but its prophecy is found less in its "messianic and apocalyptic ideas" and more in its "embodied social, educative practices" (p. 131). I am not convinced that the importance of the messianic and apocalyptic ideas should be minimized, but I do concur with Wexler's emphasis on the need to view the embodied social and educational practices "in terms of a post-modern sense of a multi-dimensional, even multi-planal, field of sometimes contradictory, disparate, yet interrelated processes. . . . Habad can thus be taken as an ideal type case . . . of an anticipatory, 'projective' harbinger of a more de-centered reconstitution of sacredness by different means under significantly altered social conditions" (pp. 131–132). I thank the author for drawing my attention to his work, which was prompted by my relating to him the crux of my own hypothesis that at the core of the seventh Rebbe's messianic teaching is an effort to destabilize the master-disciple hierarchy.

137. Mishnah, Soṭah 9:15.

138. Schneerson, *Iggerot Qodesh*, no. 1958, 7:90.

139. Schneerson, *Torat Menaḥem: Hitwwa'aduyyot 5713*, 1:212: "It states in the Gemara that 'in the footsteps of the Messiah insolence will be augmented.' However, all of these unwanted matters, which are mentioned in the Gemara concerning the time of the footsteps of the Messiah, are like the curses of the rebuke [Deut 28:15–69], for 'according to the truth they are only blessings' [Shneur Zalman of Liadi, *Liqquṭei Torah*, Wayyiqra, 1:48a]." See also Schneerson, *Iggerot Qodesh*, no. 6933, 18:452, also printed in *Liqquṭei Siḥot*, 32:240.

140. Schneerson, *Iggerot Qodesh*, no. 7438, 19:443. It is of interest to note that the word *menaḥem*, which means the comforter, is interpreted by the seventh Rebbe as signifying the transformation of adversity into fortune. The supreme solace consists, therefore, of the coincidence of opposites such that it is no longer possible to speak of evil in contradistinction to good. See Schneerson, *Torat Menaḥem: Hitwwa'aduyyot 5712*, 3:125. One wonders if this does not contain an allusion to the messianic significance of his own name. On the identification of Menaḥem as one of the names of the Messiah (based on Lam 1:16), see Babylonian Talmud, Sanhedrin 98b; Schneerson, *Liqquṭei Siḥot*, 39:331. Compare Schneerson, *Torat Menaḥem: Hitwwa'aduyyot 5712*, 2:8, where the word *mashiaḥ* is decoded as an acrostic for the various names of the Messiah delineated in the talmudic passage, to wit, Menaḥem, Shilah, Yinnon, and Ḥaninah. Significantly, the Rebbe glosses this tradition by noting that "in the time of exile as well there is the Messiah." See also Schneersohn, *Liqquṭei Levi Yiṣḥaq*, p. 106; Schneerson, *Torat Menaḥem: Hitwwa'aduyyot 5715*, 2:63.

141. Schneerson, *Torat Menaḥem: Hitwwa'aduyyot 5750*, 2:172.

142. Ibid, 2:174. Another crucial dimension of the messianic teaching is related here to the fact that Ṭevet is the tenth month, and the number ten, which is correlated with holiness

based on Lev 27:32, signifies the absolute perfection of the "true and complete redemption through our righteous Messiah."

143. Schneerson, *Torat Menaḥem: Hitwwa'aduyyot 5713*, 2:88. On the empowering of the donor by the agency of the recipient, see Schneerson, *Torat Menaḥem: Hitwwa'aduyyot 5714*, 3:199.

144. Schneerson, *Torat Menaḥem: Sefer ha-Ma'amarim Meluqaṭ*, 2:212–213; *Liqquṭei Siḥot*, 30:218–219.

145. Schneerson, *Torat Menaḥem: Sefer ha-Ma'amarim Meluqaṭ*, 3:42–43.

146. See Schneersohn, *Iggerot Qodesh*, no. 5114, 14:124: "What emerges from this is that faith shall overpower the intellect, not only in its essential substance but also in its activity over the intellect. . . . And this will be comprehended only when they can prevail from their own power [*be-khoaḥ aṣmam*], and notably when all of their interest is to draw down the intellect to themselves and to materialize it, and then they will comprehend it in accord with what they can comprehend." On the use of the term *be-khoaḥ aṣmam*, see also Shneur Zalman of Liadi, *Ma'amerei Admor ha-Zaqen 5572*, p. 168; Schneersohn, *Ner Miṣwah we-Torah Or*, 30b; *Torat Ḥayyim: Bere'shit*, 6b, 7a, 11a; *Torat Ḥayyim: Shemot*, 402b; Schneersohn, *Liqquṭei Torah: Torat Shmu'el 5633*, 1:385; Schneersohn, *Sefer ha-Ma'amarim 5692–5693*, p. 429.

147. Schneerson, *Torat Menaḥem: Sefer ha-Ma'amarim Meluqaṭ*, 3:42.

148. See Schneersohn, *Liqquṭei Torah: Torat Shmu'el 5633*, 1:385: "the Patriarchs fulfilled the Torah from their own power [*be-khoaḥ aṣmam*], that is, by sacrifice of the self [*bi-mesirat nefesh*]."

149. Schneerson, *Torat Menaḥem: Hitwwa'aduyyot 5751*, 3:119.

150. Ibid., p. 117. See also the Passover message of the seventh Rebbe delivered on 11 Nisan 5751 (March 26, 1991) in *Liqquṭei Siḥot*, 37:174–179. Schneerson underscored that the Torah section of Shemini (Lev 9) was to be read three consecutive weeks that year, a special omen that signifies the miraculous and messianic potential, since the number eight instructs about the "divine disclosure that is above creation," as opposed to the number seven, which symbolizes the "divine illumination constricted within creation." Just as the dwelling of the Presence in the Tabernacle was linked to the "eighth day" (*ba-yom ha-shemini*), so the "third" time this section of Leviticus was to be read (*shemini ha-shelishi*) refers to the third Temple, "in which there will be the harp of the eight strings" (p. 179). See, however, Schneerson, *Torat Menaḥem: Ma'amarim Meluqaṭ*, 2:185, where the ten-string harp of the world-to-come (as opposed to the eight-string harp of the messianic epoch) is said to reside in the third and eternal Temple. On the third Temple, see nn. 100–103, this chapter, and on the eight-string harp, see n. 152, this chapter.

151. The connection between the number eight and the aspect of the divine that transcends time and space is frequently affirmed in Ḥabad teaching, as I discussed in chapter 1, but the Sabbath, which relates to the number seven, is described in similar terms. For instance, see Schneerson, *Torat Menaḥem: Hitwwa'aduyyot 5751*, 3:268. See also the discussion of the thematic nexus between Sabbath and the commandment of *haqhel*, the assembling of all Israel during the Sukkot festival following the sabbatical year, which is the beginning of the eighth (Deut 31:9–13; Mishnah, Soṭah 7:8), in Schneerson, *Reshimot*, sec. 165, 5:140–152, especially 147–148.

152. This is obviously underscored by the traditional rabbinic notion that the messianic harp consists of eight strings. See chapter 1, n. 39. It is also relevant to recall here the explanation of the two names of his father-in-law that Schneerson offered in a letter from 21 Shevaṭ 5715 (February 13, 1955): the name Yosef (whose numerical value equals 6 x 26 = 156) denotes that he was the sixth generation from the Alter Rebbe and the name Yiṣḥaq (whose numerical value is 8 x 26 = 208) that he was the eighth generation from the Beshṭ. See Schneerson, *Iggerot Qodesh*, no. 3291, 10:333, also printed in *Liqquṭei Siḥot*, 38:213. On the use of the expression *eighth generation,* see also Schneersohn, *Sefer ha-Siḥot 5680–5687*, p. 32, and see Schneersohn, *Sefer ha-Siḥot 5688–5691*, p. 69. See n. 162, this chapter.

153. Shneur Zalman of Liadi, *Torah Or*, 119c, 121b; *Ma'amerei Admor ha-Zaqen 5566*, 1:332, 334; *Ma'amerei Admor ha-Zaqen* 5572, p. 206; Schneersohn, *Sha'arei Orah*, 62b, 73b, 128a; *Torat Ḥayyim: Shemot*, 303a, 366b; *Perush ha-Millot*, 98a; *Ma'amerei Admor ha-Emṣa'i: Qunṭresim*, pp. 388–389; Schneersohn, *Or ha-Torah: Bemidbar*, 2:153; *Or ha-Torah: Bemidbar*, 3:1041; Schneersohn, *Liqquṭei Torah: Torat Shmu'el 5631*, 1:274; *Liqquṭei Torah: Torat Shmu'el 5638*, p. 135; *Liqquṭei Torah: Torat Shmu'el 5641*, p. 201.

154. Babylonian Talmud, Soṭah 5a.

155. Schneerson, *Torat Menaḥem: Hitwwa'aduyyot 5711*, 2:151.

156. Tishby, *Wisdom of the Zohar*, pp. 276–277, 289; *Doctrine of Evil*, pp. 28–34; Liebes, *Studies in the Zohar*, pp. 66–67; Meroz, "Redemption," pp. 114–115, 128–151, 203–208, 239–245; Wolfson, *Language, Eros, Being*, pp. 311, 386–387; Fine, *Physician of the Soul*, pp. 135–136. The source often cited in Ḥabad literature is *Zohar* 3:142a (Idra Rabba).

157. See chapter 1, n. 120.

158. On occasion, *yesod de-adam qadmon* is designated explicitly as the "upper phallus" or, literally, the "supernal covenant" (*berit elyon*). See Schneersohn, *Liqquṭei Torah: Torat Shmu'el 5638*, 2:461. The phallic implications of this symbol are also attested in the theurgical explanation of circumcision as a means to stimulate the overflow of light from this aspect of the Godhead. See chapter 1, n. 122.

159. Schneersohn, *Or ha-Torah: Bemidbar*, 2:499–500; *Or ha-Torah: Bemidbar*, 3:849; *Sefer Tehillim*, pp. 334, 336, 384; Schneersohn, *Liqquṭei Torah: Torat Shmu'el 5639*, 1:209; *Liqquṭei Torah: Torat Shmu'el 5640*, 1:244; Schneersohn, *Be-Sha'ah she-Hiqdimu*, 1:438.

160. Shneur Zalman of Liadi, *Torah Or*, 103b. Compare Schneersohn, *Liqquṭei Torah: Torat Shmu'el 5639* 1:5: "The seven kings of chaos are the seven attributes, and the rectification issues from a higher aspect, as it is known that the eighth king, Hadar (the root of the world of rectification) is higher than the seven primordial kings, for they are the seven lower [aspects] of the kingship of the primordial anthropos [*malkhut de-adam qadmon*], and Hadar the king is the foundation of the primordial anthropos [*yesod de-adam qadmon*], and this is the essence of the rectification." See Schneersohn, *Liqquṭei Torah: Torat Shmu'el 5640*, 1:244: "The disclosure of the foundation of the primordial anthropos is above the aspect of chaos, for this is the matter of the eighth king Hadar, the root of the rectification."

161. Schneersohn, *Sefer Tehillim*, p. 384.

162. Schneersohn, *Liqquṭei Torah: Torat Shmu'el 5633*, 2:606–607. In that context, the messianic gesture of separating the sparks from the chaos so that they will be comprised in the aspect of rectification is attributed to Joseph, whose source is branded as the phallic potency of the primordial anthropos (*yesod de-adam qadmon*). In other sources, Joseph is identified himself as the upper phallic potency. See Shneur Zalman of Liadi, *Torah Or*, 103b, 103d, 104a, 104c; *Liqquṭei Torah*, Ṣaw, 1:10c, Qedoshim, 1:30d, Derushim le-Yom Kippur, 1:71b; Schneersohn, *Derushei Ḥatunah*, p. 578; Schneersohn, *Liqquṭei Torah: Torat Shmu'el 5627*, p. 70; *Liqquṭei Torah: Torat Shmu'el 5631*, 1:350; *Liqquṭei Torah: Torat Shmu'el 5632*, 1:196–197. On the possibility of the aspect of *yesod*, which corresponds to Joseph, reaching the highest facet of the Godhead, the "interiority of the Ancient One as it is in its place" (*penimiyyut attiq kemo she-hu bi-meqomo*), the locus of the messianic redeemer in the divine edifice, see Schneerson, *Torat Menaḥem: Hitwwa'aduyyot 5718*, 1:285. See chapter 4, n. 96.

163. The messianic implications of this symbol are also evident in Schneersohn, *Liqquṭei Torah: Torat Shmu'el 5627*, p. 70, where Joseph, who is designated the *yesod de-adam qadmon*, is also described (on the basis of Jer 11:16) as the "source of the oil" that overflows to the beard (Ps 133:2), that is, the thirteen attributes of mercy, which are the wellspring of forgiveness. For the background of the zoharic image of the beard and the thirteen attributes of mercy, see Wolfson, *Venturing Beyond*, pp. 207–208, 226–228. On the messianic future, Hadar, the eighth day, the essence, and the foundation of the primordial anthropos, see Shneur Zalman of Liadi, *Liqquṭei Torah*, Ṣaw, 1:11a.

164. Schneerson, *Iggerot Qodesh*, no. 180, 2:27; *Torat ha-Menaḥem: Sefer ha-Ma'amarim Meluqaṭ*, 2:167. On circumcision, the eight days of Ḥanukah, the eight-stringed harp of the messianic epoch, and the disclosure of concealment related to the name YHWH, see Shneur Zalman of Liadi, *Liqquṭei Torah*, Tazri'a, 1:21d; see also the introduction, n. 112.

165. Schneerson, *Torat Menaḥem: Hitwwa'aduyyot 5742*, 2:592 (from a letter of the Rebbe on the first day of Ḥanukah 5742, December 21, 1981). See Schneerson, *Reshimat ha-Menorah*, p. 135; *Torat Menaḥem: Hitwwa'aduyyot 5714*, 1:302; *Iggerot Qodesh*, no. 4968, 14:209, no. 4969, 14:210, no. 4971, 14:212; no. 9421, 25:53; *Liqquṭei Siḥot*, 35:209; *Torat Menaḥem: Sefer ha-Ma'amarim Meluqaṭ*, 2:168. The symbolic identification of the redeemer is based on the delineation of the eight princes (Mic 5:4) in Babylonian Talmud, Sukkah 52b. According to what I presume is the correct order, preserved, for example, in *Midrash Shir ha-Shirim Rabbah* 8:11, pp. 175–176, the Messiah is the eighth name on the list. On Hadar, the eighth of the Edomite kings, and the eight human princes, see Shneur Zalman of Liadi, *Liqquṭei Torah*, Tazri'a, 1:22a.

166. See introduction, n. 73.

167. See introduction, n. 41.

168. Schneerson, *Torat Menaḥem: Hitwwa'aduyyot 5718*, 1:278–279.

169. The point is enhanced by the connection of *yesod de-adam qadmon* and circumcision, which occurs on the eighth day and thus exceeds the sevenfold of the temporal week. See Schneersohn, *Liqquṭei Torah: Torat Shmu'el 5640*, 1:246: "The aspect of circumcision is to remove the covering so that the foundation of the primordial anthropos will be revealed, for this is above the repose of Sabbath."

170. Schneerson, *Torat ha-Menaḥem: Sefer ha-Ma'amarim Meluqaṭ*, 2:167.

171. It should be noted that the eschatological world-to-come is occasionally linked by the Ḥabad masters to the number seven rather than eight, following the tradition transmitted in the name of R. Qaṭina, which posits a cosmic Sabbath, or a millennium of desolation, after the historical cycle of six millennia (see references cited in chapter 4, n. 165), a tradition enhanced by the rabbinic designation of the eschaton as the "day that is entirely Sabbath" (chapter 4, n. 154). See, for instance, Shneur Zalman of Liadi, *Torah Or*, 8c, 9b, 10a, 21c, 25c, 73c; *Liqquṭei Torah*, Bemidbar, 1:4c, Beḥuqotai, 1:50d; Re'eh, 2:24a; *Ma'amerei Admor ha-Zaqen 5566*, 1:315; *Ma'amerei Admor ha-Zaqen 5569*, pp. 13, 45, 195, 223; *Ma'amerei Admor ha-Zaqen* 5572, p. 29; Schneersohn, *Sha'arei Teshuvah*, 13c, 66a, 67b, 67c, 67d, 68b, 97b.

BIBLIOGRAPHY

Primary Sources

Abraham Abulafia, *Or ha-Sekhel*. Jerusalem, 2001.

——*Oṣar Eden Ganuz*. Jerusalem, 2000.

——*Sefer ha-Ḥesheq*. Jerusalem, 2002.

Azriel of Gerona. *Commentary on Talmudic Aggadoth*. Ed. Isaiah Tishby. Jerusalem: Magnes, 1983 (Hebrew).

Azulai, Abraham. *Ḥesed le-Avraham*. Amsterdam, 1685.

Azulai, Ḥayyim Joseph David. *Midbar Qedemot*. Ed. Yischar Baer Rottenberg. Jerusalem: Horeb, 1962.

Cordovero, Moses. *Or Ne'erav*. Jerusalem, 1974.

——*Pardes Rimmonim*. Jerusalem, 1962.

——*Sefer Yeṣirah im Perush Or Yaqar*. Jerusalem, 1989.

Dov Baer of Międzyrzecz. *Maggid Devaraw le-Ya'aqov*. Ed. Rivka Schatz-Uffenheimer. Jerusalem: Magnes, 1976.

Eliashiv, Solomon. *Leshem Shevo we-Aḥlamah: Derushei Olam ha-Tohu*. Pietrekow, 1911.

Epstein, Qalonymus Qalman. *Ma'or wa-Shemesh*. Jerusalem, 1992.

Epstein, Yiṣḥaq Aizaq. *Ma'amar ha-Shiflut we-ha-Simḥah*. Jerusalem, 1996.

——*Ma'amar Yeṣi'at Miṣrayim*. Vilna, 1877.

Gikatilla, Joseph. *Sha'arei Orah*. Ed. Joseph Ben-Shlomo. 2 vols. Jerusalem: Mosad Bialik, 1981.

——*Sha'arei Ṣedeq*. Cracow, 1881.

Halevi, Judah. *Sefer ha-Kuzari*. Trans. Yehudah Even Shmuel. Tel Aviv: Dvir, 1972.

Ḥaver, Yiṣḥaq Aiziq. *Beit Olamin al ha-Idra Rabba*. Warsaw, 1889.

——*Massekhet Aṣilut im Perush Ginzei Meromim le-Rav Yiṣḥaq Aiziq Ḥaver*. Jerusalem, 2000.

——*Pitḥei She'arim*. Warsaw, 1888.

Heller, Meshullam Feibush, of Zbarazh. *Yosher Divrei Emet*. In *Liqquṭim Yeqarim*. Jerusalem: Yeshivat Toledot Aharon, 1974.

Horowitz, Aaron Halevi, of Staroselye. *Sha'ar ha-Tefillah*. Jerusalem: Maqor, 1972.

——*Sha'arei Avodah*. Shklov, 1821.

——*Sha'arei ha-Yiḥud we-ha-Emunah*. Shklov, 1820.

Horowitz, Isaiah. *Shenei Luḥot ha-Berit ha-Shalem*. Ed. Meyer Katz. Vols. 1 and 3. Haifa: Yad Ramah Institute, 1997–2006.

Ibn Gabbai, Meir. *Tola'at Ya'aqov*. Jerusalem: Shevilei Orḥot ha-Ḥayyim, 1996.

Ibn Paquda, Baḥya ben Joseph. *Sefer Torat Ḥovot ha-Levavot*. Ed. and trans. Joseph Kafiḥ. Jerusalem, 1973.

Jacob Joseph of Polonnoye. *Ben Porat Yosef*. Brooklyn, 1976.

Joseph ben Shalom Ashkenazi. *Perush Sefer Yeṣirah*. In *Sefer Yeṣirah*. Jerusalem: Yeshivat Qol Yehudah, 1990.

Keter Shem Ṭov. Ed. Jacob Immanuel Schochet. Brooklyn: Kehot, 2004.

Koidonover, Zevi Hirsch. *Qaw ha-Yashar*. 2 vols. Jerusalem, 1993–1999.

Levi Yiṣḥaq of Berditchev. *Qedushat Levi*. Jerusalem, 1993.

Luzzatto, Moses Ḥayyim. *Adir ba-Marom*. Part 1. Jerusalem, 1990.

——*Adir ba-Marom*. Part 2. Jerusalem, 1988.

——*Oṣerot RaMḤaL*. Ed. Ḥayyim Friedlander. Benei-Beraq, 1986.

——*Qelaḥ Pitḥei Ḥokhmah*. Ed. Ḥayyim Friedlander. Benei-Beraq, 1992.

——*Sod ha-Merkavah*. In *Sefer Ginzei Ramḥal*. Ed. Ḥayyim Friedlander. 2d ed. Benei-Beraq, 1984.

——*Tiqqunim Ḥadashim*. Jerusalem, 1997.

Mekhilta de-Rabbi Ishmael. Ed. Hayyim S. Horovitz and Israel A. Rabin. Jerusalem: Wahrmann, 1970.

Menaḥem Azariah of Fano. *Sefer Asarah Ma'amarot im Perush Yad Yehudah*. Jerusalem: Beit Oved, 1988.

Menaḥem Mendel of Vitebsk, *Peri ha-Areṣ*. Jerusalem: Hamesorah, 1989.

Menaḥem Naḥum of Chernobyl. *Me'or Einayim im Yismaḥ Lev*. 2 vols. New Square: Me'or ha-Torah, 1997.

Midrash Bere'shit Rabba: Critical Edition with Notes and Commentary. Ed. Julius Theodor and Chanoch Albeck. Jerusalem: Wahrmann, 1965.

Midrash Rabbah im Kol ha-Mefarshim. 6 vols. Jerusalem: Vagshal, 2001.

Midrash Shir ha-Shirim Rabbah. Ed. Shimshon Dunaski. Jerusalem: Dvir, 1980.

Midrash Tanḥuma. Jerusalem: Eshkol. 1972.

Midrash Tehillim. Ed. Solomon Buber. Vilna: Rom, 1891.

Midrash Wayyiqra Rabbah: A Critical Edition Based on Manuscripts and Genizah Fragments with Variants and Notes. Ed. Mordecai Margulies. New York: Jewish Theological Seminary of America, 1993.

Mondshine, Yehoshua. *Shivhei ha-Baal Shem Tov: A Facsimile of a Unique Manuscript, Variant Versions, and Appendices*. Jerusalem, 1982 (Hebrew).

Morgenstern, Isaac Meir. *Yam ha-Ḥokhmah 5769*. Jerusalem: Makhon Yam ha-Ḥokhmah, 2008.

Moses ben Maimon (Maimonides). *The Guide of the Perplexed*. Ed. and trans. Shlomo Pines. Chicago: University of Chicago Press, 1963.

——*Mishneh Torah*. New York: Schlusinger, 1947.

Moses ben Naḥman (Naḥmanides). *Perushei ha-Torah le-R. Mosheh ben Naḥman*. Ed. Ḥayyim D. Chavel. 2 vols. Jerusalem: Mosad ha-Rav Kook, 1959–1960.

Moses Ḥayyim Ephraim of Sudlikov, *Degel Maḥaneh Efrayim*. Jerusalem: Mir, 1995.

Moses of Kiev. *Shoshan Sodot*. Korets, 1784.
Naḥman of Bratslav. *Liqquṭei MoHaRaN*. Benei-Beraq: Yeshivat Breslov, 1972.
Noam, Vered. *Megillat Ta'anit: Versions, Interpretation, History, with a Critical Edition*. Jerusalem: Yad ben-Zvi, 2003 (Hebrew).
Pirqei Rabbi Eli'ezer. Warsaw, 1852.
Poppers, Meir. *Me'orot Natan*. Frankfurt, 1709.
Schneersohn, Dov Baer. *Derushei Ḥatunah*. 2 vols. Brooklyn: Kehot, 1988–1991.
——*Imrei Binah*. Brooklyn: Kehot, 1975.
——*Ma'amerei Admor ha-Emṣa'i: Bemidbar*, vol. 5. Brooklyn: Kehot, 1990.
——*Ma'amerei Admor ha-Emṣa'i: Hanaḥot*. Brooklyn: Kehot, 1994.
——*Ma'amerei Admor ha-Emṣa'i: Qunṭresim*. Brooklyn: Kehot, 1991.
——*Ma'amerei Admor ha-Emṣa'i: Shemot*, vol. 1. Brooklyn: Kehot, 1989.
——*Ma'amerei Admor ha-Emṣa'i: Shemot*, vol. 2. Brooklyn: Kehot, 1989.
——*Ma'amerei Admor ha-Emṣa'i: Wayyiqra*, vol. 2. Brooklyn: Kehot, 1985.
——*Ner Miṣwah we-Torah Or*. Brooklyn: Kehot, 1995.
——*Perush ha-Millot*. Brooklyn: Kehot, 1993.
——*Sha'arei Orah*. Brooklyn: Kehot, 1979.
——*Sha'arei Teshuvah*. Brooklyn: Kehot, 1995.
——*Torat Ḥayyim: Bere'shit*. Brooklyn: Kehot, 1993.
——*Torat Ḥayyim: Shemot*. Brooklyn: Kehot, 2003.
——*Tract on Ecstasy*. Ed. and trans., with introduction, Louis Jacobs. London: Vallentine Mitchell, 1963.
Schneersohn, Levi Yiṣḥaq. *Liqquṭei Levi Yiṣḥaq: Liqquṭim al Pesuqei Tanakh u-Ma'amerei Ḥazal, Iggerot Qodesh*. 3d ed. Brooklyn: Kehot, 1985.
Schneersohn, Menaḥem Mendel. *Derekh Miṣwotekha*. Brooklyn: Kehot, 1993.
——*Ma'amerei Admor ha-Ṣemaḥ Ṣedeq 5614–5615*. Brooklyn: Kehot, 1997.
——*Or ha-Torah: Bemidbar*. Vols. 1–4. Brooklyn: Kehot, 1995–2000.
——*Or ha-Torah: Devarim*. Vol. 6. Brooklyn: Kehot, 1984.
——*Or ha-Torah: Ma'amerei Razal we-Inyanim*. Brooklyn: Kehot, 1983.
——*Or ha-Torah: Siddur Tefillah*. Brooklyn: Kehot, 1984.
——*Sefer ha-Ḥaqirah*. Brooklyn: Kehot, 1993.
——*Sefer Tehillim: Ohel Yosef Yiṣḥaq im Perush Yahel Or*, 3d ed. Brooklyn: Kehot, 2002.
Schneersohn, Shalom Dovber. *Be-Sha'ah she-Hiqdimu 5672*. 3 vols. Brooklyn: Kehot, 1991.
——*Qunṭres ha-Tefillah*. Brooklyn: Kehot, 2002.
——*Qunṭres u-Ma'yan mi-Beit ha-Shem*. Ed., with introduction, Yosef Yiṣḥaq Schneersohn. Rev. ed. Brooklyn: Kehot, 2002.
——*Sefer ha-Ma'amarim 5652–5653*. Brooklyn: Kehot, 1987.
——*Sefer ha-Ma'amarim 5655–5656*. 2d ed. Brooklyn: Kehot, 1991.
——*Sefer ha-Ma'amarim 5659*. Brooklyn: Kehot, 1991.
——*Sefer ha-Ma'amarim 5669*. Brooklyn: Kehot, 2006.
——*Sefer ha-Ma'amarim 5678*. Brooklyn: Kehot, 1984.
——*Sefer ha-Ma'amarim 5679*. Brooklyn: Kehot, 1988.
——*Torat Shalom: Sefer ha-Siḥot*. Brooklyn: Kehot, 2003.

——*Tract on Prayer: A Chasidic Treatise by Rabbi Shalom Dovber Schneersohn of Lubavitch*. Ed. Avraham D. Vaisfiche, trans. Y. Eliezer Danzinger. Rev. ed. Brooklyn: Kehot, 2007.

——*Yom Ṭov shel Rosh ha-Shanah 5666*. Brooklyn: Kehot, 1999.

Schneersohn, Shmuel. *Liqquṭei Torah: Torat Shmu'el 5626*. Brooklyn: Kehot, 1989.

——*Liqquṭei Torah: Torat Shmu'el 5627*. Brooklyn: Kehot, 2000.

——*Liqquṭei Torah: Torat Shmu'el 5629*. Brooklyn: Kehot, 1992.

——*Liqquṭei Torah: Torat Shmu'el 5631*. Vol. 1. Brooklyn: Kehot, 2004.

——*Liqquṭei Torah: Torat Shmu'el 5632*. Vol. 1. Brooklyn: Kehot, 1999.

——*Liqquṭei Torah: Torat Shmu'el 5632*. Vol. 2. Brooklyn: Kehot, 1999.

——*Liqquṭei Torah: Torat Shmu'el 5633*. Vol. 1. Brooklyn: Kehot, 1994.

——*Liqquṭei Torah: Torat Shmu'el 5633*. Vol. 2. Brooklyn: Kehot, 1994.

——*Liqquṭei Torah: Torat Shmu'el 5635*. Vol. 1. Brooklyn: Kehot, 1991.

——*Liqquṭei Torah: Torat Shmu'el 5635*. Vol. 2. Brooklyn: Kehot, 1991.

——*Liqquṭei Torah: Torat Shmu'el 5638*. Brooklyn: Kehot, 2001.

——*Liqquṭei Torah: Torat Shmu'el 5639*. Vol. 1. Brooklyn: Kehot, 2004.

——*Liqquṭei Torah: Torat Shmu'el 5640*. Vol. 1. Brooklyn: Kehot, 2004.

——*Liqquṭei Torah: Torat Shmu'el 5640*. Vol. 2. Brooklyn: Kehot, 2004.

Schneersohn, Yosef Yiṣḥaq. *Arba'a Qol ha-Qore me-ha-Admor Sheliṭa mi-Lubavitch*. Jerusalem: Salomon, 1942–1943.

——*Iggerot Qodesh*. 14 vols. Brooklyn: Kehot, 1982–1998.

——*Liqquṭei Dibburim*. 3 vols. Brooklyn: Kehot, 1990.

——*Quntres Derushei Ḥatunah*. Brooklyn: Kehot, 1992.

——*Sefer ha-Ma'amarim 5687–5688*. Brooklyn: Kehot, 1986.

——*Sefer ha-Ma'amarim 5689*. Brooklyn: Kehot, 1990.

——*Sefer ha-Ma'amarim 5692–5693*. Brooklyn: Kehot, 2004.

——*Sefer ha-Ma'amarim 5698*. Brooklyn: Kehot, 1988.

——*Sefer ha-Ma'amarim 5699–5700*. Brooklyn: Kehot, 1986.

——*Sefer ha-Ma'amarim 5701*. Brooklyn: Kehot, 1986.

——*Sefer ha-Ma'amarim 5702*. Brooklyn: Kehot, 1986.

——*Sefer ha-Ma'amarim 5708–5709*. Brooklyn: Kehot, 1986.

——*Sefer ha-Ma'amarim 5710–5711*. Brooklyn: Kehot, 1986.

——*Sefer ha-Ma'amarim: Quntreisim*. Vol. 1. Brooklyn: Kehot, 1962.

——*Sefer ha-Ma'amarim: Quntreisim*. Vol. 2. Brooklyn: Kehot, 1986.

——*Sefer ha-Siḥot 5680–5687*. 2d ed. Brooklyn: Kehot, 2004.

——*Sefer ha-Siḥot 5688–5691*. Brooklyn: Kehot, 2002.

——*Sefer ha-Siḥot 5696—Ḥoref 5700*. Brooklyn: Kehot, 1989.

——*Sefer ha-Siḥot 5700*. Brooklyn: Kehot, 1992.

——*Sefer ha-Siḥot 5701*. Brooklyn: Kehot, 1992.

——*Sefer ha-Siḥot 5702*. Brooklyn: Kehot, 1992.

——*Sefer ha-Siḥot 5703*. Brooklyn: Kehot, 1992.

——*Sefer ha-Siḥot 5705*. Brooklyn: Kehot, 1992.

——*Sefer ha-Siḥot 5706–5710*. Brooklyn: Kehot, 2001.

——*We-Qibbel ha-Yehudim*. In *We-Attah Teṣawweh: Haḥdarat ha-Emunah be-Yisra'el*. Ed. Yekutiel Green. Kefar Ḥabad, 1999.

Schneerson, Menaḥem Mendel. *Diedushka: The Lubavitcher Rebbe and Russian Jewry*. Ed. Zusha Wolf. Kefar Habad: Yad ha-Ḥamishah, 2006 (Hebrew).

——*Haggadah shel Pesaḥ im Liqquṭei Ṭe'amim u-Minhagim*. Brooklyn: Kehot, 2002.

——*Ha-Yom Yom*. Brooklyn: Kehot, 1995.

——*Iggerot Qodesh*. 29 vols. Brooklyn: Kehot, 1987–2008.

——*Liqquṭei Siḥot*. 39 vols. Brooklyn: Kehot, 1962–2001.

——*On the Essence of Chasidus: A Chasidic Discourse by the Lubavitcher Rebbe, Rabbi Menachem Mendel Schneerson*. Brooklyn: Kehot, 2003.

——*Qiṣṣurim we-He'arot le-Sefer Amarim Tanya*. Brooklyn: Kehot, 1989.

——*Qunṭres Inyanah shel Torat ha-Ḥasidut*. Brooklyn: Kehot, 2004.

——*Reshimat ha-Menorah: Seder Hadlaqat ha-Nerot be-Veit ha-Miqdash*. Brooklyn: Kehot, 1998.

——*Reshimot*. 5 vols. Brooklyn: Kehot, 2003.

——*Sefer ha-Ma'amarim 11 Nisan*. 2 vols. Brooklyn: Kehot, 1998–1999.

——*Sefer ha-Ma'amarim 5711–5712*. Brooklyn: Vaad Hanochos BLahak, 2006.

——*Sefer ha-Ma'amarim 5720–5721*. Brooklyn: Kehot, 1994.

——*Sefer ha-Ma'amarim 5730–5731*. Brooklyn: Vaad Kitvei Qodesh, 1989.

——*Sefer ha-Ma'amarim 5732–5733*. Brooklyn: Vaad Kitvei Qodesh, 1989.

——*Sefer ha-Ma'amarim 5734–5735*. Brooklyn: Vaad Kitvei Qodesh, 1989.

——*Sefer ha-Ma'amarim 5737*. Brooklyn: Vaad Kitvei Qodesh, 1994.

——*Sefer ha-Ma'amarim: Ba'ti le-Ganni*. Vol. 1. Brooklyn: Kehot, 1988.

——*Sefer ha-Siḥot 5748*. 2 vols. Brooklyn: Kehot, 1989.

——*Sefer ha-Siḥot 5750*. 2 vols. Brooklyn: Kehot, 1992.

——*Sefer ha-Siḥot 5751*. 2 vols. Brooklyn: Kehot, 1992.

——*Sefer ha-Siḥot 5752*. Brooklyn: Kehot, 1992.

——*Sha'arei Ge'ullah*. 2 vols. Jerusalem: Heikhal Menaḥem, 1992.

——*Siḥot Qodesh 5752*. 2 vols. Brooklyn: Vaad Kitvei Qodesh, 1992.

——*Torat Menaḥem: Derushei Ḥatunah*. Brooklyn: Lahak Hanochos, 2000.

——*Torat Menaḥem: Hadranim al ha-Rambam we-Shas*. 2d ed. Brooklyn: Vaad Hanochos BLahak, 2000.

——*Torat Menaḥem: Hitwwa'aduyyot 5710–5723*. 36 vols. Brooklyn: Vaad Hanochos BLahak, 1992–2007.

——*Torat Menaḥem: Hitwwa'aduyyot 5742–5752*. 43 vols. Brooklyn: Lahak Hanochos, 1990–1994.

——*Torat Menaḥem: Reshimat ha-Yoman*. Brooklyn: Kehot, 2006.

——*Torat Menaḥem: Sefer ha-Ma'amarim 5711–5712*. Brooklyn: Vaad Hanochos BLahak, 2006.

——*Torat Menaḥem: Sefer ha-Ma'amarim 5716*. Brooklyn: Lahak Hanochos, 2006.

——*Torat Menaḥem: Sefer ha-Ma'amarim 5717*. Brooklyn: Lahak Hanochos, 2006.

——*Torat Menaḥem: Sefer ha-Ma'amarim 5722*. Brooklyn: Lahak Hanochos, 2001.

——*Torat Menaḥem: Sefer ha-Ma'amarim 5729*. Brooklyn: Lahak Hanochos, 2003.

——*Torat Menaḥem: Sefer ha-Ma'amarim Meluqaṭ al Seder Ḥodshei ha-Shanah.* 4 vols. Brooklyn: Vaad Hanochos BLahak, 2002.

——*We-Attah Teṣawweh: Haḥdarat ha-Emunah be-Yisra'el.* Ed. Yequtiel Green. Kefar Ḥabad: Ḥasidut le-Am, 1999.

Seder Avodat Yisra'el. Ed. Seligman Baer. A corrected edition based on a facsimile of the Rödelheim edition of 1868. Berlin: Schocken, 1937.

Sefer ha-Zohar. Ed. Reuven Margaliot. 3 vols. Jerusalem: Mosad ha-Rav Kook, 1984.

Sefer Yeṣirah. Jerusalem: Yeshivat Qol Yehudah, 1990.

Shapira, Natan Neṭa. *Megalleh Amuqot.* 2 vols. Lemberg, 1795.

——*Megalleh Amuqot: RN"B Ofanim al Wa-Etḥanan.* Benei-Beraq: Shomrei Emunim, 1992.

Shivḥei ha-Besht. Ed., with introduction, Avraham Rubinstein. Jerusalem: Rubin Mass, 1991. *In Praise of the Baal Shem Tov [Shivḥei ha-Besht]: The Earliest Collection of Legends About the Founder of Hasidism.* Ed. and trans. Dan Ben-Amos and Jerome R. Mintz. Bloomington: Indiana University Press, 1970.

Shneur Zalman of Liadi. *Liqquṭei Amarim: Tanya.* Brooklyn: New York, 1984.

——*Liqquṭei Amarim.* 1st ed. Brooklyn: Kehot, 1981.

——*Liqquṭei Torah.* 2 vols. Brooklyn: Kehot, 1996–1998.

——*Ma'amerei Admor ha-Zaqen 5563.* Vol. 1. Brooklyn: Kehot, 1981.

——*Ma'amerei Admor ha-Zaqen 5565.* Vol. 1. Brooklyn: Kehot, 1980.

——*Ma'amerei Admor ha-Zaqen 5566.* Vol. 1. Brooklyn: Kehot, 2004.

——*Ma'amerei Admor ha-Zaqen 5566.* Vol. 2. Brooklyn: Kehot, 2005.

——*Ma'amerei Admor ha-Zaqen 5567.* Brooklyn: Kehot, 1979.

——*Ma'amerei Admor ha-Zaqen 5569.* Brooklyn: Kehot, 1981.

——*Ma'amerei Admor ha-Zaqen 5571.* Brooklyn: Kehot, 1995.

——*Ma'amerei Admor ha-Zaqen 5572.* Brooklyn: Kehot, 2006.

——*Ma'amerei Admor ha-Zaqen: Al Inyanim.* Rev. ed. Brooklyn: Kehot, 2008.

——*Ma'amerei Admor ha-Zaqen: Ma'arzal.* Brooklyn: Kehot, 1984.

——*Ma'amerei Admor ha-Zaqen ha-Qeṣarim.* 2d ed. Brooklyn: Kehot, 1986.

——*Seder Tefillot mi-kol ha-Shanah.* Brooklyn: Kehot, 1986.

——*Torah Or.* Brooklyn: Kehot, 1991.

Shwartz, Itamar. *Bilevavi Mishkan Evneh: Mo'adim.* Jerusalem, n.d.

——*Qol Demamah Daqqah* [*Bilevavi Mishkan Evneh*, vol. 10]. Jerusalem, n.d.

Sifre on Deuteronomy. Ed. Louis Finkelstein. New York: Jewish Theological Seminary of America, 1969.

Solomon ben Isaac. *Perushei Rashi al ha-Torah.* Ed. Ḥayyim D. Chavel. Jerusalem: Mosad ha-Rav Kook, 1983.

Tiqqunei Zohar. Ed. Reuven Margaliot. Jerusalem: Mosad ha-Rav Kook, 1978.

Visotzky, Burton L. *Midrash Mishle: A Critical Edition Based on Vatican MS. Ebr. 44.* New York: Jewish Theological Seminary of America, 1990 (Hebrew).

Viṭal, Ḥayyim. *Adam Yashar.* Jerusalem, 1994.

——*Eṣ ha-Da'at Ṭov: Derashot al Kol ha-Torah be-Derekh Pardes.* Jerusalem: Wagshell, 1985.

——*Eṣ Ḥayyim*. Jerusalem, 1963.
——*Liqquṭei Torah*. Jerusalem: Yeshivat Qol Yehudah, 1995.
——*Sefer ha-Liqquṭim*. Jerusalem: Yeshivat Qol Yehudah, 1995.
——*Sha'ar ha-Gilgulim*. Jerusalem, 1903.
——*Sha'ar ha-Pesuqim*. Jerusalem: Yeshivat Qol Yehudah, 1995.
Yalles, Ya'aqov Ṣevi. *Qehillat Ya'aqov*. Lemberg, 1870.
Yannai. *Piyyute Yannai: Liturgical Poems of Yannai*. Ed. Menahem Zulay. Berlin: Schocken, 1938 (Hebrew).
Yehuda Aryeh Leib of Gur. *Sefat Emet*: *Devarim*. Merkaz Shapira: Yeshivat Or Etzion, 2000.
Zev Wolf of Zhitomir. *Or ha-Me'ir*. 2 vols. Jerusalem: Even Israel, 2000.
Zohar Ḥadash. Edited Reuven Margaliot. Jerusalem: Mosad ha-Rav Kook, 1978.

Secondary Sources

Altshuler, Mor. *The Messianic Secret of Hasidism*. Leiden: Brill, 2006.
Armour, Ellen T., and Susan M. St. Ville, eds. *Bodily Citations: Religion and Judith Butler*. New York: Columbia University Press, 2006.
Assaf, David. *Caught in the Thicket: Chapters of Crisis and Discontent in the History of Hasidism*. Jerusalem: Zalman Shazar Center for Jewish History, 2006 (Hebrew).
Badiou, Alain. *Being and Event*. Trans. Oliver Feltham. London: Continuum, 2005.
Bagger, Matthew. *The Uses of Paradox* (*Religion, Self-Transformation, and the Absurd*). New York: Columbia University Press, 2007.
Barbaras, Renaud. *The Being of the Phenomenon: Merleau-Ponty's Ontology*. Trans. Ted Toadvine and Leonard Lawlor. Bloomington: Indiana University Press, 2004.
Bauminger, Mordecai. "Letters of Our Rabbi Israel Ba'al Shem Ṭov and His Son-in-Law Rabbi Yeḥiel Mikhl to Rabbi Abraham Gershon of Kuṭov," *Sinai* 71 (1971): 248–269 (Hebrew).
Benjamin, Walter. *Selected Writings,* vol. 1: *1913–1926*. Ed. Marcus Bullock and Michael W. Jennings. Cambridge: Harvard University Press, 1996.
——*Selected Writings,* vol. 4: *1938–1940*. Ed. Howard Eiland and Michael W. Jennings. Cambridge: Harvard University Press, 2003.
Ben-Shlomo, Joseph. *The Mystical Theology of Moses Cordovero*. Jerusalem: Mosad Bialik, 1965 (Hebrew).
Berger, David. "Miracles and the Natural Order in Naḥmanides." In Isadore Twersky, ed., *Rabbi Moses Naḥmanides (Ramban): Explorations in His Religious and Literary Virtuosity,* 107–128. Cambridge: Harvard University Press, 1983.
——*The Rebbe, the Messiah, and the Scandal of Orthodox Indifference*. London: Littman Library of Jewish Civilization, 2001.
Birke, Lynda. *Feminism and the Biological Body*. New Brunswick: Rutgers University Press, 2000.
Blumenthal, David R. *Philosophic Mysticism: Studies in Rational Religion*. Ramat Gan: Bar-Ilan University Press, 2006.

Bodian, Miriam. *Hebrew of the Portuguese Nation: Conversos and Community in Early Modern Amsterdam*. Bloomington: Indiana University Press, 1997.

Buber, Martin. *Hasidism*. New York: Philosophical Library, 1948.

Burton, David. *Emptiness Appraised: A Critical Study of Nāgārjuna's Philosophy*. London: RoutledgeCurzon, 1999.

Butler, Judith. *Bodies That Matter: On the Discursive Limits of "Sex."* New York: Routledge, 1993.

——*Giving an Account of Oneself*. New York: Fordham University Press, 2005.

Butman, Shmuel. *Countdown to Moshiach: Can the Rebbe Still Be Moshiach?* Brooklyn: International Campaign to Bring Moshiach, 1995.

Branover, Herman. *A Prophet from the Midst of Thee: A Biography of the Lubavitcher Rebbe*. Kefar Ḥabad: CHISH Hafatsat Maaynot, 2007 (Hebrew).

——"The Lubavitcher Rebbe on Science and Technology." *B'or ha-Torah* 9 (1995): 13–32.

Carey, Seamus. "Cultivating Ethos Through the Body." *Human Studies* 23 (2000): 23–42.

Carlson, Thomas A. *Indiscretion: Finitude and the Naming of God*. Chicago: University of Chicago Press, 1999.

Chang, Garma C. C. *The Buddhist Teaching of Totality: The Philosophy of Hwa Yen Buddhism*. London: Allen and Unwin, 1972.

Ciucu, Cristina. "Neo-Platonism and the Cabalistic Structure of the Divine Emanation." *Echinox Notebooks* 12 (2007): 184–193.

Coakley, Sarah, ed. *Religion and the Body*. Cambridge: Cambridge University Press, 1997.

Cooey, Paula M. *Religious Imagination and the Body: A Feminist Analysis*. New York: Oxford University Press, 1994.

Cunningham, Conor. *Genealogy of Nihilism: Philosophies of Nothing and the Difference of Theology*. London: Routledge, 2002.

Dagan, Hagai. "Hatramah and Dehikat ha-Kez in F. Rosenzweig's Concept of Redemption," *Da'at* 50–52 (2003): 391–407 (Hebrew).

Dahan, Alon. "'Dira Bataḥtonim': The Messianic Doctrine of Rabbi Menachem Mendel Schneersohn (the Lubavitcher Rebbe)." Ph.D. thesis, Hebrew University, 2006 (Hebrew).

——"The Last Redeemer Without a Successor: Did R. Menahem Mendel Schneerson Choose Not to Appoint an Heir for Messianic Reasons?" *Kabbalah: Journal for the Study of Jewish Mystical Texts* 17 (2008): 289–309 (Hebrew).

Dalfin, Chaim. *The Seven Chabad Lubavitch Rebbes*. Northvale: Aronson, 1998.

Dan, Joseph. "The Duality of Hasidic Messianism." In Immanuel Etkes, David Assaf, Israel Bartal, and Elchanan Reiner, eds., *Within Hasidic Circles: Studies in Hasidism in Memory of Mordecai Wilensky*, 99–315. Jerusalem: Mosad Bialik, 1999 (Hebrew).

——*The Modern Jewish Messianism*. Israel: Ministry of Defense, 1999 (Hebrew).

Dastur, Françoise. "Phenomenology of the Event: Waiting and Surprise." *Hypatia* 15 (2000): 178–189.

——*Telling Time: Sketch of a Phenomenological Chrono-Logy*. Trans. Edward Bullard. London: Athlone Press, 2000.

——"Word, Flesh, Vision." In Fred Evans and Leonard Lawlor, eds. *Chiasms: Merleau-Ponty's Notion of Flesh*, 23–49. Albany: State University of New York Press, 2000.

Davidman, Lynn. *Tradition in a Rootless World: Women Turn to Orthodox Judaism*. Berkeley: University of California Press, 1991.

Davidson, Herbert A. "The Study of Philosophy as a Religious Obligation." In Sholmo D. Goiten,, ed., *Religion in a Religious Age: Proceedings of Regional Conferences Held at the University of California, Los Angeles and Brandeis University in April, 1973*, 53–68. Cambridge: Association for Jewish Studies, 1974.

Davies, William D. *The Torah in the Messianic Age*. Philadelphia: Society of Biblical Literature, 1952.

Deleuze, Gilles. *Difference and Repetition*. Trans. Paul Patton. New York: Columbia University Press, 1994.

Derrida, Jacques. *Adieu to Emmanuel Levinas*. Trans. Pascale-Anne Brault and Michael Naas. Stanford: Stanford University Press, 1999.

—— *Given Time: I. Counterfeit Money*. Trans. Peggy Kamuf. Chicago: University of Chicago Press, 1992.

—— *Margins of Philosophy*. Trans. Alan Bass. Chicago: University of Chicago Press, 1982.

—— *Of Grammatology*. Trans. Gayatri Spivak. Baltimore: Johns Hopkins University Press, 1976.

——*Psyche: Inventions of the Other*. Vol. 1. Ed. Peggy Kamuf and Elizabeth Rottenberg. Stanford: Stanford University Press, 2007.

——*Specters of Marx: The State of the Debt, the Work of Mourning, and the New International*. Trans. Peggy Kamuf. New York: Routledge, 1994.

——*Speech and Phenomena and Other Essays on Husserl's Theory of Signs*. Trans., with introduction, David B. Allison. Evanston: Northwestern University Press, 1973.

Derrida, Jacques, and Gianni Vattimo, *Religion*. Stanford: Stanford University Press, 1998.

Deutsch, Shaul S. *Larger Than Life: The Life and Times of the Lubavitcher Rebbe Rabbi Menachem Mendel Schneerson*. 2 vols. New York: Chasidic Historical, 1995–1997.

Dinur, Benzion. "The Origins of Hasidism and Its Social and Messianic Foundations." In Gershon David Hundert, ed., *Essential Papers on Hasidism: Origins to Present*, 86–208. New York: New York University Press, 1991.

Dodd, James. *Idealism and Corporeity: An Essay on the Problem of the Body in Husserl's Phenomenology*. Dordrecht: Kluwer Academic, 1997.

Döl-ḃo-ḃa Ṡhay-rap-gyel-tsen. *Mountain Doctrine: Tibet's Fundamental Treatise on Other-Emptiness and the Buddha Matrix*. Ed. Kevin Vose, trans., with introduction, Jeffrey Hopkins. Ithaca: Snow Lion, 2006.

Drob, Sanford. "A Rational Mystical Ascent: The Coincidence of Opposites in Kabbalistic and Hasidic Thought." www.newkabbalah.com.

—— *Kabbalistic Metaphors: Jewish Mystical Themes in Ancient and Modern Thought*. Northvale: Aronson, 2000.

——"The Doctrine of *Coincidentia Oppositorum* in Jewish Mysticism." www.newkabbalah.com.

Dubnow, Simon. "The Beginnings: The Baal Shem Tov (Besht) and the Center in Podolia." In Gershon David Hundert, ed., *Essential Papers on Hasidism: Origins to Present*, 25–85. New York: New York University Press, 1991.

Ehrlich, Avrum M. *Leadership in the HaBaD Movement: A Critical Evaluation of HaBaD Leadership, History, and Succession*. Northvale: Aronson, 2000.

——*The Messiah of Brooklyn: Understanding Lubavitch Hasidism Past and Present*. Jersey City: Ktav, 2004.

Elior, Rachel. "Ḥ aBaD: The Contemplative Ascent to God." In Arthur Green, ed., *Jewish Spirituality from the Sixteenth Century Revival to the Present*, 157–205. New York: Crossroad, 1987.

——"The Lubavitch Messianic Resurgence: The Historical and Mystical Background, 1939–1996." In Peter Schäfer and Mark R. Cohen, eds., *Toward the Millennium: Messianic Expectations From the Bible to Waco*, 383–408. Leiden: Brill, 1998.

——*The Mystical Origins of Hasidism*. Oxford: Litman Library of Jewish Civilization, 2006.

——*The Paradoxical Ascent to God: The Kabbalistic Theosophy of Habad Hasidism*. Albany: State University of New York Press, 1993.

——*The Theory of Divinity of Hasidut Habad: Second Generation*. Jerusalem: Magnes, 1982 (Hebrew).

Etkes, Immanuel. *The Besht: Magician, Mystic, and Leader*. Trans. Saadya Sternberg. Waltham: Brandeis University Press, 2005.

Ettinger, Bracha L. *The Matrixial Borderspace*. Ed., with afterword, Brian Massumi. Minneapolis: University of Minnesota Press, 2006.

Farber-Ginat, Asi. "'The Shell Precedes the Fruit'—On the Question of the Origin of Metaphysical Evil in Early Kabbalistic Thought." In Haviva Pedaya, ed., *Myth and Judaism*, 118–142. Jerusalem: Mosad Bialik, 1996 (Hebrew).

Feldman, Jan. *Lubavitchers as Citizens: A Paradox of Liberal Democracy*. Ithaca: Cornell University Press, 2003.

Feldman, Louis H. *"Remember Amalek!" Vengeance, Zealotry, and Group Destruction in the Bible According to Philo, Pseudo-Philo, and Josephus*. Cincinnati: Hebrew Union College Press, 2004.

Fine, Lawrence. *Physician of the Soul, Healer of the Cosmos: Isaac Luria and His Kabbalistic Fellowship*. Stanford: Stanford University Press, 2003.

Fishkoff, Sue. *The Rebbe's Army: Inside the World of Chabad-Lubavitch*. New York: Schocken, 2003.

Foxbrunner, Roman A. *Ḥabad: The Hasidism of R. Shneur Zalman of Lyady*. Northvale: Aronson, 1993.

Fraenkel, Carlos. "Maimonides' God and Spinoza's *Deus sive Natura*." *Journal of the History of Philosophy* 44 (2006): 169–215.

Frankel, David. *Letters from the Besht of Blessed Memory and His Disciples*. Lvov, 1923 (Hebrew).

Friedman, Menachem. "Habad as Messianic Fundamentalism: From Local Particularism to Universal Mission." In Martin E. Marty and R. Scott Appleby, eds., *The Fundamentalism Project,* 4:328–357. Chicago: University of Chicago Press, 1994.

—— "Messiah and Messianism in Habad-Lubavitch Hasidism." In David Ariel-Joel, ed., *The War of Gog and Magog: Messianism and Apocalypticism in Judaism in the Past and in the Present,* 174–229. Tel Aviv: Yedi'ot Aḥaronot–Sifrei Ḥemed, 2001 (Hebrew).

Friedman, Mordechai Akiva. *Maimonides: The Yemenite Messiah and Apostasy*. Jerusalem: Yad ben-Zvi, 2002 (Hebrew).

From Exile to Redemption: Chassidic Teachings of the Lubavitcher Rebbe, Rabbi Menachem M. Schneerson, and the Preceding Rebbeim of Chabad on the Future Redemption and the Coming of Mashiach. 2 vols. Brooklyn: Kehot, 1992–1996.

Galli, Barbara E. *Franz Rosenzweig and Jehuda Halevi: Translating, Translations, and Translators*. Montreal: McGill-Queen's University Press, 1995.

Garb, Jonathan. "Mystics' Critiques of Mystical Experience." *Revue de l'histoire des religions* 221 (2004): 293–325.

—— *"The Chosen will Become Herds": Studies in Twentieth-Century Kabbalah*. Jerusalem: Carmel, 2005 (Hebrew).

Garfield, Jay L. *Empty Words: Buddhist Philosophy and Cross-Cultural Interpretation.* Oxford: Oxford University Press, 2002.

Giller, Pinchas. *Reading the Zohar: The Sacred Text of the Kabbalah*. Oxford: Oxford University Press. 2001.

——*The Enlightened Will Shine: Symbolization and Theurgy in the Later Strata of the Zohar*. Albany: State University of New York Press, 1993.

Ginsburgh, Yitzchak. *Kabbalah and Meditation for the Nations*. Ed. Moshe Genuty. Jerusalem: Gal Einai, 2007.

——*Rectifying the State of Israel: A Political Platform Based on Kabbalah*. Jerusalem: Gal Einai, 2002.

Ginzberg, Louis. *The Legends of the Jews*. 7 vols. Philadelphia: Jewish Publication Society of America, 1968.

Goldberg, Robin Claire. "Imaging the Feminine: Storying and Re-storying Womanhood Among Lubavitch Hasidic Women." Ph.D. thesis, Northwestern University, 1991.

Goldberg, Shelly. "The Zaddik's Soul After His 'Histalkut' (Death): Continuity and Change in the Writings of 'Nesiey' (Presidents of) Habad." Ph.D. thesis, Bar-Ilan University, 2003 (Hebrew).

Goldreich, Amos. "Clarifications in the Self-Perception of the Author of *Tiqqunei Zohar*." In Michal Oron and Amos Goldreich, eds., *Massu'ot: Studies in Kabbalistic Literature and Jewish Philosophy in Memory of Prof. Ephraim Gottlieb*, 459–496. Jerusalem: Mosad Bialik, 1994 (Hebrew).

Goldschmidt, Henry. "Crown Heights Is the Center of the World: Reterritorializing a Jewish Diaspora." *Diaspora* 9 (2000): 83–106.

Goodman, Lenn E. "Maimonidean Naturalism." In Robert S. Cohen and Hillel Levine, eds., *Maimonides and the Sciences*, 57–85. Dordrecht: Kluwer Academic, 2000.

Gotlieb, Jacob. "Habad's Harmonistic Approach to Maimonides." Ph.d. thesis, Bar-Ilan University, 2003 (Hebrew).

Green, Arthur. *Tormented Master: A Life of Rabbi Nahman of Bratslav*. University: University of Alabama Press, 1979.

Greenberg, Gershon. "Assimilation as Churban According to Wartime American Orthodoxy (Chabad Chassidism)." *Studies in Jewish Civilization* 2 (1992): 161–177.

——"Redemption After the Holocaust According to Mahane Israel—Lubavitch, 1940–1945." *Modern Judaism* 12 (1992): 61–84.

Grosz, Elizabeth. *Volatile Bodies: Toward a Corporeal Feminism.* Bloomington: Indiana University Press, 1994.

Halbertal, Moshe. *By Way of Truth: Nahmanides and the Creation of Tradition.* Jerusalem: Shalom Hartman Institute, 2006 (Hebrew).

Hallamish, Moshe. "The Teachings of R. Menahem Mendel of Vitebsk." In Ada Rapoport-Albert, ed., *Hasidism Reappraised*, 268–287. London: Litman Library of Jewish Civilization, 1996.

——"The Theoretical System of R. Shneur Zalman of Liady (Its Sources in Kabbalah and Hasidism)." Ph.D. thesis, Hebrew University, 1976 (Hebrew).

Hamacher, Werner. "Lingua Amissa: The Messianism of Commodity-Language and Derrida's *Specters of Marx*." In Richard Rand, ed., *Futures of Jacques Derrida*, 130–178. Stanford: Stanford University Press, 2001.

——"'Now': Walter Benjamin on Historical Time," in Andrew Benjamin, ed., *Walter Benjamin and History*, 38–68. London: Continuum, 2005.

Handelman, Susan. "Putting Women in the Picture." www.chabad.org/theJewishWoman/article_cdo/aid/16`694/jewish/Putting-Women-in-the-Picture.htm.

——"Women and the Study of Torah in the Thought of the Lubavitcher Rebbe." In Micah D. Halperin and Chana Safrai, eds., *Jewish Legal Writings by Women*, 143–178. Jerusalem: Urim, 1998.

Hanegraff, Wouter J. *New Age Religion and Western Culture: Esotericism in the Mirror of Secular Thought.* Albany: State University of New York Press, 1998.

Harari, Yehiel. "Mysticism as a Messianic Rhetoric in the Works of Rabbi Yitzchak Ginsburgh." Ph.D. thesis, Tel-Aviv University, 2005 (Hebrew).

Hartshorne, Charles. "Theism in Asian and Western Thought." *Philosophy East and West* 28 (1978): 401–411.

Heidegger, Martin. *Elucidations of Hölderlin's Poetry.* Trans. Keith Hoeller. Amherst: Humanity, 2000.

——*Erläuterungen zu Hölderlins Dichtung*. Frankfurt: Klostermann, 1981.

——*Hölderlins Hymnen "Germanien" und "Der Rhein"*. Frankfurt: Klostermann, 1980.

——"Supplements to *The Doctrine of Categories and Meaning in Duns Scotus*." In Theodore Kisiel and Thomas Sheehan, eds., *Becoming Heidegger: On the Trail of His Early Occasional Writings, 1910–1927*, 73–85. Evanston: Northwestern University Press, 2007.

Heschel, Abraham J. *Heavenly Torah as Refracted Through the Generations*. Ed. and trans. Gordon Tucker and Leonard Levin. New York: Continuum, 2005.

Hodge, Joanna. *Derrida on Time*. London: Routledge, 2007.

Hollander, Dana. *Exemplarity and Chosenness: Rosenzweig and Derrida on the Nation of Philosophy*. Stanford: Stanford University Press, 2008.

——"On the Significance of the Messianic Idea in Rosenzweig," *Cross Currents* 53 (2004): 555–565.

Horowitz, Elliott. *Reckless Rites: Purim and the Legacy of Jewish Violence*. Princeton: Princeton University Press, 2006.

Huntington, Jr., C. W., with Geshé Namgyal Wangchen. *The Emptiness of Emptiness: An Introduction to Early Indian Mādhyamika*. Honolulu: University of Hawaii Press, 1989.

Idel, Moshe. *Ascensions on High in Jewish Mysticism: Pillars, Lines, Ladders*. Budapest: Central European University Press, 2005.

——*Ben: Sonship and Jewish Mysticism*. London: Continuum, 2007.

——"*Deus sive Natura*—the Metamorphosis of a Dictum from Maimonides to Spinoza." In Robert S. Cohen and Hillel Levine, eds., *Maimonides and the Sciences*, 87–110. Dordrecht: Kluwer Academic, 2000.

——*Hasidism: Between Ecstasy and Magic*. Albany: State University of New York Press, 1995.

——*Kabbalah and Eros*. New Haven: Yale University Press, 2005.

——*Kabbalah: New Perspectives*. New Haven: Yale University Press, 1988.

——*Messianic Mystics*. New Haven: Yale University Press, 1998.

——"Ta'anug: Erotic Delights From Kabbalah to Hasidism." In Wouter J. Hanegraaff and Jeffrey J. Kripal, eds., *Hidden Intercourse: Eros and Sexuality in the History of Western Esotericism*, 111–151. Leiden: Brill, 2008.

——"The Evil Thought of the Deity," *Tarbiṣ* 49 (1980) 356–364 (Hebrew).

——"Universalization and Integration: Two Conceptions of Mystical Union in Jewish Mysticism." In Moshe Idel and Bernard McGinn, eds., *Mystical Union and Monotheistic Faith: An Ecumenical Dialogue*, 27–57. New York: Macmillan, 1989.

Irigaray, Luce. *Sexes and Genealogies*. Trans. Gillian C. Gill. New York: Columbia University Press, 1993.

Jacobs, Louis. "The Uplifting of Sparks in Later Jewish Mysticism." In Arthur Green, ed., *Jewish Spirituality from the Sixteenth-Century Revival to the Present*, 99–126. New York: Crossroad, 1987.

——*Seeker of Unity: The Life and Works of Aaron of Starosselje*. London: Vallentine Mitchell, 1966.

Jacobson, Yoram. "Exile and Redemption in Ger Hasidism." *Da'at* 2 (1978/79): 175–215 (Hebrew).

——"The Animal Soul in the Teaching of R. Shneur Zalman of Liadi." In Michal Oron and Amos Goldreich, eds., *Massu'ot Studies in Kabbalistic Literature and Jewish Philosophy in Memory of Prof. Ephraim Gottlieb*, 224–242. Jerusalem: Mosad Bialik, 1994 (Hebrew).

Jaggar, Alison M., and Susan R. Bordo, eds. *Gender/Body/Knowledge: Feminist Reconstructions of Being and Knowing*. New Brunswick: Rutgers University Press, 1989.

Judovitz, Dalia. *The Culture of the Body: Genealogies of Modernity*. Ann Arbor: University of Michigan Press, 2001.

Jung, Carl G. *The Archetypes and the Collective Unconscious*. 2d ed. Princeton: Princeton University Press, 1968.

——*Dream Analysis: Notes on the Seminar Given in 1928–1930*. Ed. William McGuire. Princeton: Princeton University Press, 1984.

Kafka, Franz. *Parables and Paradoxes*. New York: Schocken, 1971.

Kahn, Yoel. *Mahutam shel Yisra'el be-Mishnat ha-Ḥasidut*. Brooklyn: Heichal Menachem, 2001.

——*Shi'urim be-Torat Ḥabad*. Netanya: Ma'yenotekha, 2006.

Kalupahana, David J. *Nāgārjuna: The Philosophy of the Middle Way*. Albany: State University of New York Press, 1986.

Katsura, Shōryū. "Nāgārjuna and the Tetralemma (*Catuṣkoṭi*)." In Jonathan A. Silk, ed., *Wisdom, Compassion, and the Search for Understanding: The Buddhist Studies Legacy of Gadjin M. Nagao*, 201–220. Honolulu: University of Hawai'i Press, 2000.

Katz, Maya Balakirsky. "On the Master-Disciple Relationship in Hasidic Visual Culture: The Life and Afterlife of Rebbe Portraits in Habad, 1798–2006," *Images: A Journal of Jewish Art and Visual Culture* 1 (2007): 55–79.

Kaufman, Tzifi. "Between Immanence and Religious Behavior: *Avodah be-Gashmiyut* in Early Stages of Hasidism." Ph.D. thesis, Hebrew University, 2004 (Hebrew).

Keller, Catherine. *Face of the Deep: A Theology of Becoming*. London: Routledge, 2003.

——*God and Power: Counter-Apocalyptic Journeys*. Minneapolis: Fortress, 2005.

Kimelman, Reuven. *The Mystical Meaning of Lekhah Dodi and Kabbalat Shabbat*. Jerusalem: Magnes, 2003 (Hebrew).

Kluback, William. "Time and History: The Conflict Between Hermann Cohen and Franz Rosenzweig." In Wolfdietrich Schmied-Kowarzik, ed., *Der Philosoph Franz Rosenzweig (1886–1929): Internationaler Kongreß-Kassel 1986*, 2:801–813. 2 vols. Freiburg: Alber, 1988.

Kohanzad, Max Ariel. "The Messianic Doctrine of the Lubavitcher Rebbe, Rabbi Menachem Mendel Schneerson (1902–1994)." Ph.D. thesis, University of Manchester, 2006.

Koren, Israel. *The Mystery of the Earth: Mysticism and Hasidism in Buber's Thought*. Haifa: University of Haifa Press, 2005 (Hebrew).

Kraemer, Joel L. "On Maimonides' Messianic Posture." In Isadore Twersky, ed., *Studies in Medieval Jewish History and Literature*, 2:109–142. Cambridge: Harvard University Press, 1984.

Krassen, Miles. *Uniter of Heaven and Earth: Rabbi Meshullam Feibush Heller of Zbarazh and the Rise of Hasidism in Eastern Galicia*. Albany: State University of New York Press, 1998.

Kraus, Yitzchak. "'Living with the Times': Reflection and Leadership, Theory, and Practice in the World of the Rebbe of Lubavitch, Rabbi Menachem Mendel Schneerson." Ph.D. thesis, Bar-Ilan University, 2001 (Hebrew).

—— *The Seventh: Messianism in the Last Generation of Habad*. Tel Aviv: Yedi'ot Aḥaronot, 2007 (Hebrew).

Kravel-Tovi, Michal, and Yoram Bilu. "The Work of the Present: Constructing Messianic Temporality in the Wake of Failed Prophecy Among Chabad Hasidim." *American Ethnologist* 35 (2008): 64–80.

Kripal, Jeffrey J. *Esalen: America and the Religion of No Religion*. Chicago: University of Chicago Press, 2007.

Kwant, Remy C. *Phenomenology of Language*. Pittsburgh: Duquesne University Press, 1965.

Lamm, Norman. *The Religious Thought of Hasidism: Text and Commentary*. With contributions by Alan Brill and Shalom Carmy. Hoboken: Ktav, 1999.

Leder, Drew. *The Absent Body*. Chicago: University of Chicago Press, 1990.

Lederberg, Netanel. *Sod ha-Da'at: Rabbi Israel Ba'al Shem Tov, His Spiritual Character and Social Leadership*. Jerusalem: Rubin Mass, 2007 (Hebrew).

Lenowitz, Harris. *The Jewish Messiahs: From the Galilee to Crown Heights*. Oxford: Oxford University Press, 1998.

Levin, Faitel. *Heaven on Earth: Reflections on the Theology of the Lubavitcher Rebbe, Rabbi Menachem M. Schneerson*. Brooklyn: Kehot, 2002.

Levinas, Emmanuel. *Difficult Freedom: Essays on Judaism*. Trans. Seán Hand. Baltimore: Johns Hopkins University Press, 1990.

Levine, Stephanie Wellen. *Mystics, Mavericks, and Merrymakers: An Intimate Journey Among Hasidic Girls*. New York: New York University Press, 2003.

Lieberman, Haim. *Ohel Raḥel*. Vol. 1. Brooklyn: Empire, 1980.

Liebes, Yehuda. *On Sabbateanism and Its Kabbalah: Collected Essays*. Jerusalem: Mosad Bialik, 1995 (Hebrew).

——*Studies in the Zohar*. Trans. Arnold Schwartz, Stephanie Nakache, and Penina Peli. Albany: State University of New York Press, 1993.

——"The Vilner Gaon School, Sabbateanism, and Dos Pintele Yid." *Da'at* 50–52 (2003): 255–290 (Hebrew).

Lipkin, Benjamin. *Ḥeshbono shel Olam*. 2d ed. Lod: Makhon ha-Sefer, 2000.

Liwer, Amira. "Oral Torah in the Writings of R. Zadok ha-Kohen of Lublin." Ph.D. thesis, Hebrew University, 2006 (Hebrew).

Loewenthal, Kate M. "Religious Development and Experience in Habad-Hasidic Women." *Journal of Psychology and Judaism* 12 (1988): 5–20.

Loewenthal, Naftali. "Communicating Jewish Spirituality to Women and Girls in Riga, 1937–1941: A Model for Today?" In Herman Branover and Ruvin Ferner, eds., *Jews in A Changing World: Materials of the First International Conference, Riga, August 28–29, 1995*, 188–196. Riga: M. Dubin Foundation "Shamir," 1997.

——*Communicating the Infinite: The Emergence of the Habad School*. Chicago: University of Chicago Press, 1990.

——"Contemporary Habad and the Paradox of Redemption." In Alfred L. Ivry, Elliot R. Wolfson, and Allan Arkush, eds., *Perspectives on Jewish Thought and Mysticism*, 381–402. Australia: Harwood Academic, 1998.

——"'Daughter/Wife of Hasid' or 'Hasidic Woman'?" *Jewish History* 40 (2000): 21–28.

——"'Reason' and 'Beyond Reason' in Ḥabad Ḥasidism." In Moshe Hallamish, ed., *'Alei Shefer: Studies in the Literature of Jewish Thought Presented to Rabbi Dr. Alexandre Safran*, 109–126 (English section). Ramat Gan: Bar-Ilan University Press, 1990.

——"Spiritual Experience for Hasidic Youths and Girls in Pre-Holocaust Europe: A Confluence of Tradition and Modernity." In Adam Mintz and Lawrence Schiffman, eds., *Jewish Spirituality and Divine Law*, 407–454. Jersey City: Ktav, 2005.

——"The Neutralisation of Messianism and the Apocalypse." *Jerusalem Studies in Jewish Thought* 13 (1996): 59–73 (English section).

——"Women and the Dialectic of Spirituality in Hasidism." In Immanuel Etkes, David Assaf, Israel Bartal, and Elchanan Reiner, eds., *Within Hasidic Circles: Studies in Hasidism in Memory of Mordecai Wilensky*, 7–65. Jerusalem: Mosad Bialik, 1999 (English section).

Loy, David. *Nonduality: A Study in Comparative Philosophy*. New Haven: Yale University Press, 1988.

——"The Deconstruction of Buddhism." In Harold Coward and Toby Foshay, eds., *Derrida and Negative Theology*, 227–253. Albany: State University of New York Press, 1992.

McCallum, Donald. *Maimonides' Guide for the Perplexed: Silence and Salvation*. London: Routledge, 2007.

Magid, Shaul. *Hasidism on the Margin: Reconciliation, Antinomianism, and Messianism in Izbica/Radzin Hasidism*. Madison: University of Wisconsin Press, 2003.

——"The Ritual Is Not the Hunt: The Seven Wedding Blessings, Redemption, and Jewish Ritual as Fantasy." In Randi Rashkover and C. C. Pecknold, eds., *Liturgy, Time, and the Politics of Redemption*, 188–211. Grand Rapids: Eerdmans, 2006.

Magliola, Robert. *Derrida on the Mend*. West Lafayette: Purdue University Press, 1984.

Maitreya. *Middle Beyond Extremes: Maitreya's Madhyãntavibhãga, with Commentaries by Khenpo Shenga and Ju Mipham*. Trans. Dharmachakra Translation Committee. Ithaca: Snow Lion, 2006.

Marcus, Joel. "The Once and Future Messiah in Early Christianity and Chabad." *New Testament Studies* 47 (2001): 381–401.

Margolin, Ron. *The Human Temple: Religious Interiorization and the Structuring of Inner Life in Early Hasidism*. Jerusalem: Magnes, 2005 (Hebrew).

——"On the Substance of Faith in Hasidism: A Historical-Conceptual Perspective." In Moshe Halbertal, David Kurzweil, and Avi Sagi, eds., *On Faith: Studies in the Concept of Faith and its History in the Jewish Tradition*, 328–362. Jerusalem: Keter, 2005 (Hebrew).

Mark, Zvi. "*Dibbuk* and *Devekut* in *In Praise of the Baal Shem Tov*: Notes on the Phenomenology of Madness in Early Hasidism." In Immanuel Etkes, David Assaf, Israel Bartal, and Elchanan Reiner, eds., *Within Hasidic Circles: Studies in Hasidism in Memory of Mordecai Wilensky*, 247–286. Jerusalem: Mosad Bialik, 1999 (Hebrew).

——*Mysticism and Madness in the Work of R. Nahman of Bratslav*. Tel Aviv: Am Oved, 2003 (Hebrew).

——*Scroll of Secrets: The Hidden Messianic Vision of R. Nahman of Bratslav*. Ramat Gan: Bar-Ilan University Press, 2006 (Hebrew).

Marshall, Paul. *Mystical Encounters with the Natural World: Experiences and Explanations*. Oxford: Oxford University Press, 2005.

Meir, Ephraim. *Levinas's Jewish Thought: Between Jerusalem and Athens*. Jerusalem: Magnes, 2008.

Meroz, Ronit. "Redemption in the Lurianic Teaching." Ph.D. thesis, Hebrew University, 1988 (Hebrew).

Michaelson, Jay. *God in Your Body: Kabbalah, Mindfulness, and Embodied Spiritual Practice*. Woodstock: Jewish Lights, 2007.

Mindel, Nissan. *The Letter and the Spirit*. Brooklyn: Kehot, 1998.

Morgenstern, Arie. *Mysticism and Messianism from Luzzatto to the Vilna Gaon*. Jerusalem: Ma'or, 1999 (Hebrew).

Mosès, Stéphane. *The Angel of History: Rosenzweig, Benjamin, Scholem*. Trans. Barbara Harshav. Stanford: Stanford University Press, 2009.

——*System and Revelation: The Philosophy of Franz Rosenzweig*. Trans. Catherine Tihanyi. Detroit: Wayne State University Press, 1992.

Musashi, Tachikawa. "Mahāyāna Philosophies: The Mādhyamika Tradition." In Takeuchi Yoshinori, ed., in association with Jan Van Bragt, James W. Heisig, Joseph S. O'Leary, and Paul L. Swanson, *Buddhist Spirituality: Indian, Southeast Asian, Tibetan, Early Chinese*, 188–202. New York: Crossroad, 1993.

Myers, Jody. *Kabbalah and the Spiritual Quest: The Kabbalah Centre in America*. Westport: Praeger, 2007.

Nadler, Allan. "The 'Rambam Revival' in Early Modern Jewish Thought: Maskilim, Mitnagdim, and Hasidim on Maimonides' *Guide of the Perplexed*." In Jay M. Harris, ed., *Maimonides After 800 Years: Essays on Maimonides and His Influence*, 231–256. Cambridge: Harvard University Press, 2007.

Nāgārjuna. *The Fundamental Wisdom of the Middle Way: Nāgārjuna's Mūlamadhyamakakārikā*. Trans. Jay L. Garfield. Oxford: Oxford University Press, 1995.

——*Nāgārjuna's Reason Sixty with Chandrakīrti's Commentary*. Trans., with introduction, Joseph John Loizzo. New York: American Institute of Buddhist Studies, 2007.

Napper, Elizabeth. *Dependent-Arising: A Tibetan Buddhist Interpretation of Mādhyamika Philosophy Emphasizing the Compatibility of Emptiness and Conventional Phenomena*. Boston: Wisdom, 2003.

Ochs, Vanessa L. "Waiting for the Messiah, a Tambourine in Her Hand." *Nashim: A Journal of Jewish Women's Studies and Gender Issues* 9 (2005): 144–169.

Olson, Carl. "The Human Body as a Boundary Symbol: A Comparison of Merleau-Ponty and Dōgen." *Philosophy East and West* 36 (1986): 107–120.

——*Indian Philosophers and Postmodern Thinkers: Dialogues on the Margins of Culture*. Oxford: Oxford University Press, 2002.

——*Zen and the Art of Postmodern Philosophy: Two Paths of Liberation from the Representational Mode of Thinking*. Albany: State University of New York Press, 2000.

Ornet, Leah. "*Ratso va-shov, Running and Returning*": *Ethical and Mystical Perspectives in the Teaching of R. Shneur Zalman of Liadi—A Comparative Study*. Tel-Aviv: Hakibbutz Hameuchad, 2007 (Hebrew).

——"The Relationship Between the Divine Soul and the Animal Soul in the Ethical Teaching of R. Shneur Zalman of Liadi." MA thesis, Hebrew University, 1991 (Hebrew).

Pachter, Mordecai. *Roots of Faith and Devequt: Studies in the History of Kabbalistic Ideas*. Los Angeles: Cherub, 2004.

Park, Jin Y, ed. *Buddhisms and Deconstructions*. Lanham: Rowman and Littlefield, 2006.

Pedaya, Haviva. *Name and Sanctuary in the Teaching of R. Isaac the Blind: A Comparative Study in the Writings of the Earliest Kabbalists*. Jerusalem: Magnes, 2001 (Hebrew).

——"The Baal Shem Tov's Iggeret Hakodesh Toward a Critique of the Textual Versions and an Exploration of Its Convergence with the World-Picture: Messianism, Revelation, Ecstasy, and the Sabbatean Background." *Zion* 70 (2005): 311–354 (Hebrew).

Piekarz, Mendel. *Between Ideology and Reality: Humility, Ayin, Self-Negation, and Devekut in the Hasidic Thought*. Jerusalem: Mosad Bialik, 1994 (Hebrew).

——"The Messianic Idea in the Beginnings of Ḥasidism as Reflected in the Homiletical and Ethical Literature." In *The Messianic Idea in Jewish Thought: A Study Conference in Honour of the Eightieth Birthday of Gershom Scholem Held 4–5 December 1977*, 237–253. Jerusalem: Israel Academy of Sciences and Humanities, 1982 (Hebrew).

Polen, Nehemia. "Miriam's Dance: Radical Egalitarianism in Hasidic Thought." *Modern Judaism* 12 (1992): 1–12.

Porton, Gary G. *The Stranger Within Your Gates: Converts and Conversion in Rabbinic Literature*. Chicago: University of Chicago Press, 1994.

Rapoport-Albert, Ada. "God and the Zaddik as the Two Focal Points of Hasidic Worship." In Gershon D. Hundert, ed., *Essential Papers on Hasidism: Origins to Present*, 299–329. New York: New York University Press, 1993.

——"On Women in Hasidism: S. A. Hordecky and The Maid of Ludmir Tradition." In Ada Rapoport-Albert and Steven Zipperstein, eds., *Jewish History: Essays in Honour of Chimen Abramsky*, 495–525. London: Halban, 1988.

Rapoport, Chaim. *The Messiah Problem: Berger, the Angel, and the Scandal of Reckless Indiscrimination*. Ilford: Chaim Rapoport, 2002.

Raschke, Carl A. *Fire and Roses: Postmodernity and the Thought of the Body*. Albany: State University of New York Press, 1996.

Ravitzky, Aviezer. "The Anthropological Theory of Miracles in Medieval Jewish Philosophy." In Isadore Twersky, ed., *Studies in Medieval Jewish History and Literature*, 2:231–272. Cambridge: Harvard University Press, 1984.

——*Messianism, Zionism, and Jewish Religious Radicalism*. Trans. Michael Swirsky and Jonathan Chipman. Chicago: University of Chicago Press, 1996.

——"The Messianism of Success in Contemporary Judaism." In Stephen J. Stein, ed., *The Encyclopedia of Apocalypticism*, vol. 3: *Apocalypticism in the Modern Period and the Contemporary Age*, 204–229. New York: Continuum, 1998.

——"'To the Utmost of Human Capacity': Maimonides on the Days of Messiah." In Joel L. Kraemer, ed., *Perspectives on Maimonides: Philosophical and Historical Studies*, 221–256. London: Littman Library of Jewish Civilization, 1996.

Rigg, Bryan M. *Rescued from the Reich: How One of Hitler's Soldiers Saved the Lubavitcher Rebbe*. New Haven: Yale University Press, 2004.

Romano, Claude. "Le possible et l'événement." *Philosophie* 40 (1993): 68–95, *Philosophie* 41 (1994): 60–86.

Rosenberg, Simeon Gershon. "Faith and Language According the Admor ha-Zaqen of Habad from the Philosophical Perspective on Language of Wittgenstein." In Moshe Halbertal, David Kurzweil, and Avi Sagi, eds., *On Faith: Studies in the Concept of Faith and Its History in the Jewish Tradition*, 365–387. Jerusalem: Keter, 2005 (Hebrew).

Rosenzweig, Franz. *Der Mensch und sein Werk: Gesammelte Schriften IV. Sprachdenken im Übersetzen, 1: Band Hymnen und Gedichte des Jehuda Halevi*. Ed. Reinhold and Annemarie Mayer. Dordrecht: Nijhoff, 1984.

——*The Star of Redemption*. Trans. Barbara E. Galli. Madison: University of Wisconsin Press, 2005.

Rosman, Moshe. *Founder of Hasidism: A Quest for the Historical Ba'al Shem Tov*. Berkeley: University of California Press, 1996.

——*Stories That Changed History: The Unique Career of Shivhei ha-Besht*. Syracuse: Syracuse University Press, 2007.

Roth, Cecil. "The Religion of the Marranos," *Jewish Quarterly Review* 22 (1931–1932): 1–33.

Sack, Bracha. "An Investigation of the Influence of R. Moses Cordovero on Hasidism." *Eshel Beer Sheva* 3 (1986): 229–246.

——The Influence of *Reshit Ḥokhmah* on the Teachings of the Maggid of Mezhirech." In Ada Rapoport-Albert, ed., *Hasidism Reappraised*, 251–257. London: Litman Library of Jewish Civilization, 1996.

Sadoff, Dianne F. *Sciences of the Flesh: Representing Body and Subject in Psychoanalysis*. Stanford: Stanford University Press, 1998.

Safran, Bezalel. "Maharal and Early Hasidism." In Bezalel Safran, ed., *Hasidism: Continuity or Innovation?* 47–144. Cambridge: Harvard University Press, 1988.

Sato, Mariot. "The Incarnation of Consciousness and the Carnalization of the World in Merleau-Ponty's Philosophy." *Analecta Husserliana* 58 (1998): 3–15.

Schatz-Uffenheimer, Rivka. *Hasidism as Mysticism: Quietistic Elements in Eighteenth-Century Hasidic Thought*. Trans. Jonathan Chipman. Princeton: Princeton University Press, 1993.

——"Self-Redemption in Hasidic Thought." In R. J. Zwi Werblowsky and C. Jouco Bleeker, eds., *Types of Redemption: Contributions to the Theme of the Study-Conference Held at Jerusalem 14 to 19 July 1968*, 207–212. Leiden: Brill, 1970.

——"The Messianic Element in Ḥasidic Thought," *Molad* 1 (1967): 105–111 (Hebrew).

Schelling, Friedrich W. J. *Philosophical Investigations Into the Essence of Human Freedom*. Ed. and trans., with introduction, Jeff Love and Johannes Schmidt. Albany: State of New York University Press, 2006.

Schlüter, Margarte. "The Creative Force of a Hermeneutic Rule: The Principle 'There Is No Earlier and Later in the Torah' in Midrashic and Talmudic Literature." In Rachel Elior and Peter Schäfer, eds., *Creation and Re-Creation in Jewish Thought: Festschrift in Honor of Joseph Dan on the Occasion of His Seventieth Birthday*, 59–84. Tübingen: Mohr Siebeck, 2005.

Schneider, Stanley, and Joseph H. Berke. "Sigmund Freud and the Lubavitcher Rebbe." *Psychoanalytic Review* 87 (2000): 39–59.

Scholem, Gershom. *Major Trends in Jewish Mysticism*. New York: Schocken, 1954.

——*On the Kabbalah and Its Symbolism*. Trans. Ralph Manheim. New York: Schocken, 1965.

——*On the Mystical Shape of the Godhead: Basic Concepts in the Kabbalah*. Ed. Jonathan Chipman., trans. Joachim Neugroschel. New York: Schocken, 1991.

——*Origins of the Kabbalah*. Ed. R. J. W. Werblowsky, trans. Allan Arkush. Princeton: Princeton University Press, 1987.

—— *Sabbatai Ṣevi: The Mystical Messiah*. Trans. R. J. Zwi Werblowsky. Princeton: Princeton University Press, 1973.

——*The Messianic Idea in Judaism and Other Essays on Jewish Spirituality*. New York: Schocken, 1971.

Schwartz, Dov. *Messianism in Medieval Jewish Thought*. Ramat Gan: Bar-Ilan University Press, 1997 (Hebrew).

——*Religion or Halakha: The Philosophy of Rabbi Joseph B. Soloveitchik*. Trans. Batya Stein. Vol. 1. Leiden: Brill, 2007.

Schwarzschild, Steven S. "Franz Rosenzweig's Anecdotes About Hermann Cohen." In Herbert A. Strauss and Kurt R. Grossman, eds., *Gegenwart im Rückblick: Festgabe für die Jüdische Gemeinde zu Berlin 25 Jahre nach dem Neubeginn*, 209–218. Heidelberg: Lothar Stiehm, 1970.

Selya, Rena. "Torah and Madda? Evolution in the Jewish Educational Context." In Geoffrey Cantor and Marc Swetlitz, eds., *Jewish Tradition and the Challenge of Darwinism*, 188–207. Chicago: University of Chicago Press, 2006.

Shandler, Jeffrey. "The Virtual Rebbe." In Jim Hoberman and Jeffrey Shandler, eds., *Entertaining America: Jews, Movies, and Broadcasting*, 264–267. Princeton: Princeton University Press, 2003.

Sharot, Stephen. *Messianism, Mysticism, and Magic: A Sociological Analysis of Jewish Religious Movements*. Chapel Hill: University of North Carolina Press, 1982.

Sheets-Johnstone, Maxine. *Giving the Body Its Due*. Albany: State University of New York Press, 1992.

Slater, Robert Lawson. *Paradox and Nirvana: A Study of Religious Ultimates with Special Reference to Burmese Buddhism*. Chicago: University of Chicago Press, 1951.

Stcherbatsky, Theodore. *The Conception of Buddhist Nirvāna*. New York: Weiser, 1968.

Steeves, James B. *Imagining Bodies: Merleau-Ponty's Philosophy of Imagination*. Pittsburgh: Duquesne University Press, 2004.

Steinbock, Anthony J. *Phenomenology and Mysticism: The Verticality of Religious Experience*. Bloomington: Indiana University Press, 2007.

Stern, Samuel M. "'The First in Thought Is the Last in Action': The History of a Saying Attributed to Aristotle." *Journal of Semitic Studies* 7 (1962): 234–252.

Student, Gil. *Can the Rebbe Be Moshiach? Proofs From Gemara, Midrash, and Rambam That the Rebbe zt"l Cannot Be Moshiach*. Boca Raton: Universal, 2002.

Szubin, Adam Jacob. "Why Lubavitch Wants the Messiah Now: Religious Immigration as a Cause of Millenarianism." In Albert I. Baumgarten, ed., *Apocalyptic Time*, 215–240. Leiden: Brill, 2000.

Tāranātha. *The Essence of Other-Emptiness*. Ed. and trans. Jeffrey Hopkins, with Lama Lodrö Namgyel. Ithaca: Snow Lion, 2007.

Teitelbaum, Mordecai. *Der Rabh Von Ladi: Sein Lebeu, Werke und System sowie die Geschichte der Sekte Chabad*. Warsaw: Tushiyah, 1914 (Hebrew).

Tishby, Isaiah. *Messianic Mysticism: Moses Hayim Luzzatto and the Padua School*. Trans. Morris Hoffman. Oxford: Littman Library of Jewish Civilization, 2008.

——*The Doctrine of Evil and the "Kelippah" in Lurianic Kabbalism*. Jerusalem: Magnes, 1984 (Hebrew).

——"The Messianic Idea and the Messianic Tendencies in the Beginnings of Hasidism." *Zion* 32 (1967): 1–45 (Hebrew).

——*The Wisdom of the Zohar: An Anthology of Texts*. Trans. David Goldstein. Oxford: Oxford University Press, 1989.

Tracy, David. "The Post-Modern Re-Naming of God as Incomprehensible and Hidden." *Cross Currents* 50 (2000): 240–247.

Urban, Hugh B. *Magia Sexualis: Sex, Magic, and Liberation in Modern Western Esotericism*. Berkeley: University of California Press, 2006.

Vail, Loy M. *Heidegger and Ontological Difference*. University Park: Pennsylvania State University Press, 1972.

Vallega-Neu, Daniela. *The Bodily Dimension in Thinking*. Albany: State University of New York Press, 2005.

Wang, Youxuan. *Buddhism and Deconstruction: Towards a Comparative Semiotics*. Richmond: Curzon, 2001.

Warnek, Peter. "Translating *Innigkeit*: The Belonging Together of the Strange." In Drew A. Hyland and John Panteleimon Manoussakis, eds., *Heidegger and the Greeks: Interpretive Essays*, 57–82. Bloomington: Indiana University Press, 2006.

Weber, Elisabeth. "Elijah's Futures. In Richard Rand, ed., *Futures of Jacques Derrida*, 201–218. Stanford: Stanford University Press, 2001.

Weiss, Joseph. *Studies in Eastern European Jewish Mysticism*. Ed. David Goldstein. Oxford: Oxford University Press, 1985.

Welton, Donn, ed. *Body and Flesh: A Philosophical Reader*. Oxford: Blackwell, 1998.

——*The Body: Classic and Contemporary Readings*. With introduction. Oxford: Blackwell, 1999.

Werblowsky, R. J. Zwi. "Mysticism and Messianism: The Case of Hasidism." In Eric J. Sharpe and John R. Hinnells, eds., *Man and His Salvation: Essays in Memory of S. G. F. Brandon*, 305–314. Manchester: Manchester University Press, 1973.

Werczberger, Rachel. "Feminine Messianism and Messianic Femininity: An Ethnography of Women's *Shiur* in Habad." M.A. thesis, Hebrew University, 2003 (Hebrew).

Wexler, Philip. *Mystical Interactions: Sociology, Jewish Mysticism and Education*. Los Angeles: Cherub Press, 2007.

Wolfson, Elliot R. *Abraham Abulafia—Kabbalist and Prophet: Hermeneutics, Theosophy, and Theurgy*. Los Angeles: Cherub, 2000.

——*Alef, Mem, Tau: Kabbalistic Musings on Time, Truth, and Death*. Berkeley: University of California Press, 2006.

——*Along the Path: Studies in Kabbalistic Myth, Symbolism, and Hermeneutics*. Albany: State University of New York Press, 1995.

——"Assaulting the Border: Kabbalistic Traces in the Margins of Derrida." *Journal of the American Academy of Religion* 70 (2002): 475–514.

——*Circle in the Square: Studies in the Use of Gender in Kabbalistic Symbolism*. Albany: State University of New York Press, 1995.

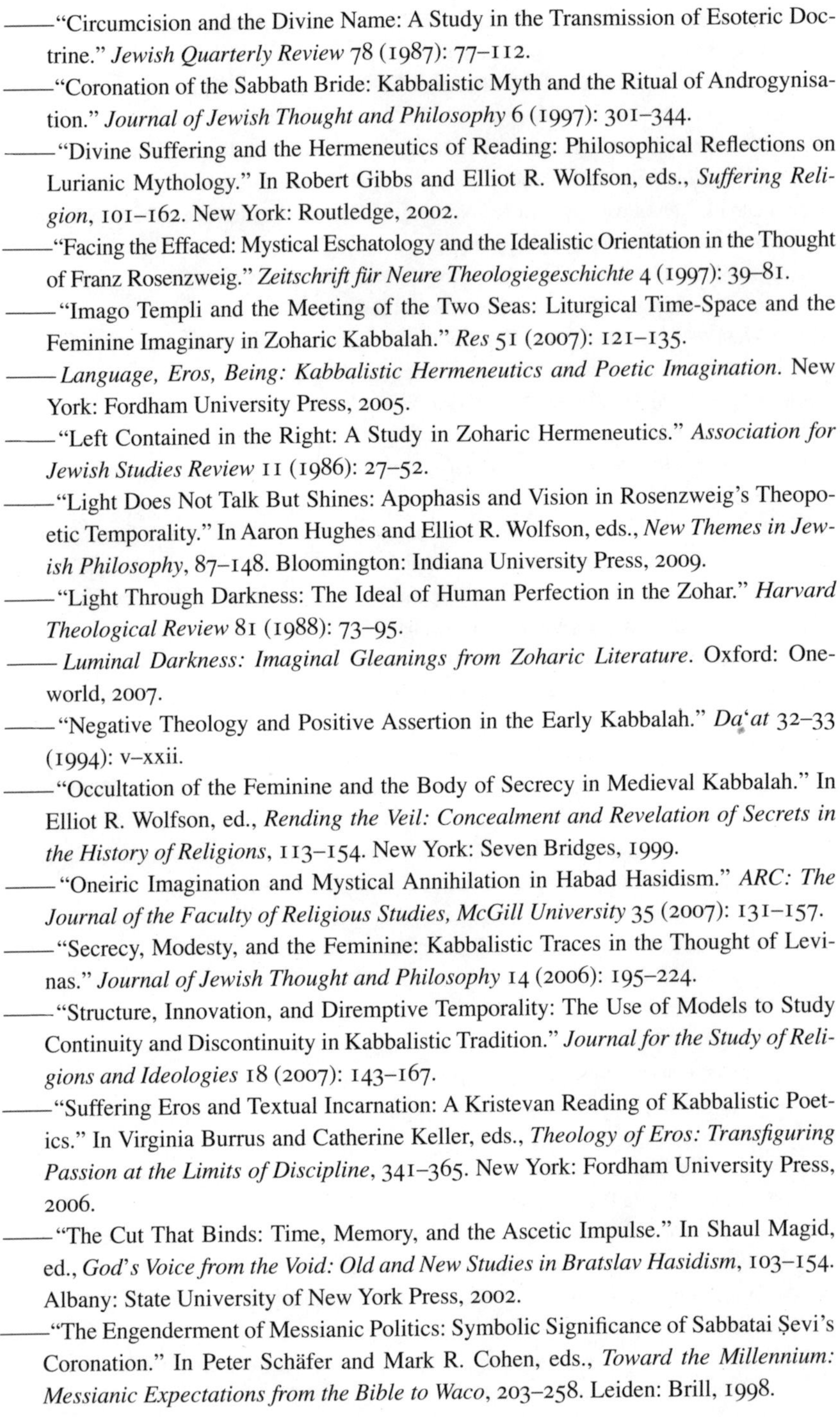

——"Circumcision and the Divine Name: A Study in the Transmission of Esoteric Doctrine." *Jewish Quarterly Review* 78 (1987): 77–112.

——"Coronation of the Sabbath Bride: Kabbalistic Myth and the Ritual of Androgynisation." *Journal of Jewish Thought and Philosophy* 6 (1997): 301–344.

——"Divine Suffering and the Hermeneutics of Reading: Philosophical Reflections on Lurianic Mythology." In Robert Gibbs and Elliot R. Wolfson, eds., *Suffering Religion*, 101–162. New York: Routledge, 2002.

——"Facing the Effaced: Mystical Eschatology and the Idealistic Orientation in the Thought of Franz Rosenzweig." *Zeitschrift für Neure Theologiegeschichte* 4 (1997): 39–81.

——"Imago Templi and the Meeting of the Two Seas: Liturgical Time-Space and the Feminine Imaginary in Zoharic Kabbalah." *Res* 51 (2007): 121–135.

——*Language, Eros, Being: Kabbalistic Hermeneutics and Poetic Imagination.* New York: Fordham University Press, 2005.

——"Left Contained in the Right: A Study in Zoharic Hermeneutics." *Association for Jewish Studies Review* 11 (1986): 27–52.

——"Light Does Not Talk But Shines: Apophasis and Vision in Rosenzweig's Theopoetic Temporality." In Aaron Hughes and Elliot R. Wolfson, eds., *New Themes in Jewish Philosophy*, 87–148. Bloomington: Indiana University Press, 2009.

——"Light Through Darkness: The Ideal of Human Perfection in the Zohar." *Harvard Theological Review* 81 (1988): 73–95.

——*Luminal Darkness: Imaginal Gleanings from Zoharic Literature.* Oxford: Oneworld, 2007.

——"Negative Theology and Positive Assertion in the Early Kabbalah." *Daʿat* 32–33 (1994): v–xxii.

——"Occultation of the Feminine and the Body of Secrecy in Medieval Kabbalah." In Elliot R. Wolfson, ed., *Rending the Veil: Concealment and Revelation of Secrets in the History of Religions*, 113–154. New York: Seven Bridges, 1999.

——"Oneiric Imagination and Mystical Annihilation in Habad Hasidism." *ARC: The Journal of the Faculty of Religious Studies, McGill University* 35 (2007): 131–157.

——"Secrecy, Modesty, and the Feminine: Kabbalistic Traces in the Thought of Levinas." *Journal of Jewish Thought and Philosophy* 14 (2006): 195–224.

——"Structure, Innovation, and Diremptive Temporality: The Use of Models to Study Continuity and Discontinuity in Kabbalistic Tradition." *Journal for the Study of Religions and Ideologies* 18 (2007): 143–167.

——"Suffering Eros and Textual Incarnation: A Kristevan Reading of Kabbalistic Poetics." In Virginia Burrus and Catherine Keller, eds., *Theology of Eros: Transfiguring Passion at the Limits of Discipline*, 341–365. New York: Fordham University Press, 2006.

——"The Cut That Binds: Time, Memory, and the Ascetic Impulse." In Shaul Magid, ed., *God's Voice from the Void: Old and New Studies in Bratslav Hasidism*, 103–154. Albany: State University of New York Press, 2002.

——"The Engenderment of Messianic Politics: Symbolic Significance of Sabbatai Ṣevi's Coronation." In Peter Schäfer and Mark R. Cohen, eds., *Toward the Millennium: Messianic Expectations from the Bible to Waco*, 203–258. Leiden: Brill, 1998.

——*Through a Speculum That Shines: Vision and Imagination in Medieval Jewish Mysticism*. Princeton: Princeton University Press,1994.

——*Venturing Beyond: Law and Morality in Jewish Mysticism*. Oxford: Oxford University Press, 2006.

——"*Via Negativa* in Maimonides and Its Impact on Thirteenth-Century Kabbalah." *Maimonidean Studies* 5 (2008): 363–412.

——"Woman—the Feminine as Other in Theosophic Kabbalah: Some Philosophical Observations on the Divine Androgyne." In Laurence L. Silberstein and Robert L. Cohn, eds., *The Other in Jewish Thought and History: Constructions of Jewish Culture and Identity*, 166–204. New York: New York University Press, 1994.

Wood, Thomas E. *Mind Only: A Philosophical and Doctrinal Analysis of the Vijñānavāda*. Honolulu: University of Hawaii Press, 1991.

——*Nāgārjunian Disputations: A Philosophical Journey through an Indian Looking-Glass*. Honolulu: University of Hawaii Press, 1994.

Yerushalmi, Yosef Hayim. *From Spanish Court to Italian Ghetto: Isaac Cardoso—A Study in Seventeenth-Century Marranism and Jewish Apologetics*. Seattle: University of Washington Press, 1981.

INDEX

Carleton College Library
One North College Street
Northfield, MN 55057

WITHDRAWN